STATE OF WASHINGTON

2016 Washington State Adult Sentencing Guidelines Manual

Washington State Caseload Forecast Council

The Caseload Forecast Council is not liable for errors or omissions in the manual, for sentences that may be inappropriately calculated as a result of a practitioner's or court's reliance on the manual, or for any other written or verbal information related to adult or juvenile sentencing. The scoring sheets are intended to provide assistance in most cases but do not cover all permutations of the scoring rules. If you find any errors or omissions, we encourage you to report them to the Caseload Forecast Council.

State of Washington

Caseload Forecast Council

Derek Stanford, Chair
Washington State Representative

David Schumacher, Vice Chair
Director, Office of Financial Management

Bruce Chandler
Washington State Representative

Jeannie Darneille
Washington State Senator

Andy Hill
Washington State Senator

Patricia Lashway
Acting Secretary
Department of Social and Health Services

Council Staff

Elaine Deschamps
Executive Director

Erik Cornellier
Deputy Director

Kathleen Turnbow
Confidential Secretary

Gongwei Chen
Senior Caseload Forecaster

Jennifer Jones
Research Analyst

Thuy Le
Research Analyst

Duc Luu
Database and Sentencing
Administration Manager

Ed Vukich
Senior Caseload Forecaster

Shidong Zhang
Senior Caseload Forecaster

The Caseload Forecast Council is not liable for errors or omissions in the manual, for sentences that may be inappropriately calculated as a result of a practitioner's or court's reliance on the manual, or for any other written or verbal information related to adult or juvenile sentencing. The scoring sheets are intended to provide assistance in most cases but do not cover all permutations of the scoring rules. If you find any errors or omissions, we encourage you to report them to the Caseload Forecast Council.

ACKNOWLEDGMENTS

The Caseload Forecast Council acknowledges the work of Ed Vukich and Jennifer Jones in updating, reviewing, proofing, and offering language and formatting suggestions for revisions in the current manual.

We also acknowledge Judge Ronald Kessler, of the King County Superior Court, for providing the update for the Sentencing Reform Act portion of the *Criminal Caselaw Notebook©*.

The Council also appreciates the suggestions for improvements and additions to the manual received from users.

We always welcome suggestions for making the manual easier to use.

© Copyright 2016 State of Washington
Caseload Forecast Council

All rights reserved. Portions of this document may be reproduced without permission for non-commercial purposes.

The Caseload Forecast Council is not liable for errors or omissions in the manual, for sentences that may be inappropriately calculated as a result of a practitioner's or court's reliance on the manual, or for any other written or verbal information related to adult or juvenile sentencing. The scoring sheets are intended to provide assistance in most cases but do not cover all permutations of the scoring rules. If you find any errors or omissions, we encourage you to report them to the Caseload Forecast Council.

TABLE OF CONTENTS

ACKNOWLEDGMENTS iii
USE OF THIS MANUAL 1
INTRODUCTION 3
SECTION 1 - FELONY OFFENSES AFFECTED BY 2016 SESSION LAW 5
SECTION 2 - CASE LAW RELATED TO THE SENTENCING REFORM ACT 13
   Caselaw Review – 2016 Update 13
      SRA: Exceptional Sentences 13
      SRA: Procedure 13
      SRA: Same Criminal Conduct 14
SECTION 3 - SENTENCING GUIDELINES 15
   Determining Felony Class 15
      Felonies Defined in Title 9A RCW 15
      Felonies Defined Outside Title 9A 15
   Determining The Offense Seriousness Level 16
      General Felony Crimes 16
      Drug Crimes 16
      Unranked Felony Crimes 16
   Determining The Offender Score 16
   Criminal History Collection 17
      Adult Criminal History 17
      Juvenile Criminal History 18
      "Wash Out" of Certain Prior Felonies 18
      Federal, Out-of-State or Foreign Convictions 19
   Scoring Criminal History 19
   Scoring Multiple Current Convictions 20
      Multiple Offense Scoring Steps: 20
   Scoring Offender Status While on Community Custody 22
   Determining the Standard Range Using the Sentencing Grid 22
      Anticipatory Offenses (Non-VUCSA Attempts, Conspiracies, and Solicitations) 23
      Anticipatory Offenses (VUCSA Attempts, Conspiracies, and Solicitations) 25
   Second or Subsequent Offense (RCW 69.50.408) 27
   Terms of Confinement 27

The Caseload Forecast Council is not liable for errors or omissions in the manual, for sentences that may be inappropriately calculated as a result of a practitioner's or court's reliance on the manual, or for any other written or verbal information related to adult or juvenile sentencing. The scoring sheets are intended to provide assistance in most cases but do not cover all permutations of the scoring rules. If you find any errors or omissions, we encourage you to report them to the Caseload Forecast Council.

- Standard Range Sentence 27
- "Unranked" Offenses 27
- Persistent Offenders 28
- "Two Strikes" 28
- Non-Persistent Sex Offenders (Determinate-Plus) 28
- Exceptional Sentences 29
  - Mitigating Circumstances for Exceptional Sentences 30
  - Aggravating Circumstances for Exceptional Sentences 30
- Consecutive and Concurrent Sentences 30
  - Offenses that Constitute Same Criminal Conduct 30
  - Multiple Serious Violent Offenses 31
  - Certain Firearm-Related Offenses 31
  - Felony DUI/Felony APC 31
  - Weapon Enhancements 31
  - Felony Committed While Offender was Under Sentence for Another Felony 31
  - Felonies Committed While Offender was not Under Sentence for Another Felony 32
  - Probation Revocation 32
  - Serving Total Confinement with Consecutive Sentences 32
- Limits on Earned Release 32
- Review of Sentences 33
- Violation of Community Custody Conditions 34
  - Arrest and Confinement (RCW 9.94A.631) 34
  - Sanctions and Procedures (RCW 9.94A.633) 35
  - Sanctions – Where Served (RCW 9.94A.6331) 36
  - Sanctions – Which Entity Imposes (RCW 9.94A.6332) 37
  - Sanctions – Modification of Sentence (RCW 9.94A.6333) 37
  - DOC Structured Violation Process (RCW 9.94A.737) 38
- Discharge and Vacation of Conviction Record 40
  - Discharge 40
  - Vacation of Conviction Record 41
- Alternatives to Confinement 42
  - Alternative Conversions 42
  - Work Crew 43
  - Home Detention 43

The Caseload Forecast Council is not liable for errors or omissions in the manual, for sentences that may be inappropriately calculated as a result of a practitioner's or court's reliance on the manual, or for any other written or verbal information related to adult or juvenile sentencing. The scoring sheets are intended to provide assistance in most cases but do not cover all permutations of the scoring rules. If you find any errors or omissions, we encourage you to report them to the Caseload Forecast Council.

  Restitution 45

  Restitution in Cases involving Fraud or Deceptive Practice 46

  Restitution in Cases involving a Fraudulent Filing of a Vehicle Report of Sale 46

 Fines 46

  Other Legal Financial Obligations 47

  Contact With Individuals 48

SECTION 4 - SENTENCING GRIDS AND FELONY OFFENSES 49

 Sentencing Grid D: For Crimes Committed After July 24, 1999 49

 Sentencing Grid D – Anticipatories – For Crimes Committed After July 24, 1999 50

 Offense Seriousness Levels For Standard Grid (RCW 9.94A.515) 51

 Drug Sentencing Grid B For Sentences Imposed On or After July 1, 2013 60

 Drug Sentencing Grid B For Sentences Imposed On or After July 1, 2013 (Solicitations for Offenses Under Chapter 69.50 RCW, Anticipatories for Offenses Not Under Chapter 69.50 RCW) 60

 Offense Seriousness Levels For Drug Sentencing Grid (RCW 9.94A.518) 61

 Sentencing Grid C – For Crimes Committed July 27, 1997, through July 24, 1999* 63

 Sentencing Grid B - For Crimes Committed July 1, 1990 through July 26, 1997* 64

 Sentencing Grid A - For Crimes Committed Before July 1,1990* 65

 Drug Sentencing Grid A For Offenses Committed On or After July 1, 2003 and Sentenced Before July 1, 2013 66

 Serious Violent Offenses 67

 Violent Offenses 68

 Sex Offenses 70

 Drug Offenses 72

 Most Serious Offenses (Persistent Offender or "Three Strikes") 73

 Persistent Offender Offenses ("Two Strikes") 76

 Crime Against Persons Offenses 77

 Offenses Requiring Sex Offender Registration 82

 Sex Offender Registration (9A.44.140) 82

 Nonviolent Offenses 86

 Unranked Offenses 104

 Mandatory Remand Offenses 115

 Felony Index By Offense 117

 Felony Index By Classification 137

 Felony Index By RCW 157

The Caseload Forecast Council is not liable for errors or omissions in the manual, for sentences that may be inappropriately calculated as a result of a practitioner's or court's reliance on the manual, or for any other written or verbal information related to adult or juvenile sentencing. The scoring sheets are intended to provide assistance in most cases but do not cover all permutations of the scoring rules. If you find any errors or omissions, we encourage you to report them to the Caseload Forecast Council.

SECTION 5 - QUICK REFERENCE SHEETS 177
    Sentencing Alternatives 177
    First-Time Offender Waiver (FTOW) (RCW 9.94A.650) 177
    Parenting Sentencing Alternative (RCW 9.94A.655) 177
    Drug Offender Sentencing Alternative (DOSA) (RCW 9.94A.660) 180
    Special Sex Offender Sentencing Alternative (SSOSA) (RCW 9.94A.670) 181
    Sentencing Enhancements 183
        Felony Traffic Enhancements 183
        Firearm and Deadly Weapon Enhancements 184
        Drug-Related Enhancements 184
        Sex Offense Enhancements 185
        Law Enforcement Enhancement 186
        Criminal Street Gang-Related Enhancement 186
        Robbery of a Pharmacy Enhancement 186
    Community Custody 187

SECTION 6 – GENERAL FELONY SCORING FORMS 189
    Deadly Weapon Enhancement 190
    General Nonviolent Offense Where Domestic Violence Has Been Plead And Proven 191
    General Nonviolent/Sex Offense Where Domestic Violence Has Been Plead And Proven 192
    General Nonviolent Offense With A Sexual Motivation Finding 193
    General Drug Offense Where Domestic Violence Has Been Plead And Proven 194
    General Drug Offense With A Sexual Motivation Finding 195
    General Serious Violent Offense Where Domestic Violence Has Been Plead And Proven 196
    General Serious Violent/Sex Offense Where Domestic Violence Has Been Plead And Proven 197
    General Serious Violent Offense With A Sexual Motivation Finding 198
    General Violent Offense Where Domestic Violence Has Been Plead And Proven 199
    General Violent/Sex Offense Where Domestic Violence Has Been Plead And Proven 200
    General Violent Offense With A Sexual Motivation Finding 201
    General Burglary First Degree Offense Where Domestic Violence Has Been Plead And Proven 202
    General Burglary Second Degree Or Residential Burglary Offense Where Domestic Violence Has Been Plead and Proven 203
    General Unranked Offense With A Sexual Motivation Finding 204

SECTION 7 – ALPHABETIZED FELONY SCORING FORMS 205
    Abandonment Of Dependent Persons First Degree 207

The Caseload Forecast Council is not liable for errors or omissions in the manual, for sentences that may be inappropriately calculated as a result of a practitioner's or court's reliance on the manual, or for any other written or verbal information related to adult or juvenile sentencing. The scoring sheets are intended to provide assistance in most cases but do not cover all permutations of the scoring rules. If you find any errors or omissions, we encourage you to report them to the Caseload Forecast Council.

Offense	Page
Abandonment Of Dependent Persons Second Degree	208
Advancing Money Or Property For Extortionate Extension Of Credit	209
Aggravated Murder First Degree	210
Animal Cruelty First Degree Sexual Contact Or Conduct	211
Arson First Degree	212
Arson Second Degree	213
Assault First Degree	214
Assault First Degree With A Finding Of Sexual Motivation	215
Assault Second Degree	216
Assault Second Degree With A Finding Of Sexual Motivation	217
Assault Third Degree Excluding Assault 3 Of A Peace Officer With A Projectile Stun Gun (RCW 9a.36.031(1)(H))	218
Assault Third Degree Of A Peace Officer With A Projectile Stun Gun	219
Assault By Watercraft	220
Assault Of A Child First Degree	221
Assault Of A Child First Degree With A Finding Of Sexual Motivation	222
Assault Of A Child Second Degree	223
Assault Of A Child Second Degree With A Finding Of Sexual Motivation	224
Assault Of A Child Third Degree	225
Attempting To Elude Pursuing Police Vehicle	226
Bail Jumping With Class A Felony	227
Bail Jumping With Class B Or C Felony	228
Bail Jumping With Murder 1	229
Bribe Received By Witness Bribing A Witness	230
Bribery	231
Burglary First Degree	232
Burglary First Degree With A Finding Of Sexual Motivation	233
Burglary Second Degree	234
Burglary Second Degree With A Finding Of Sexual Motivation	235
Cheating First Degree	236
Child Molestation First Degree	237
Child Molestation Second Degree	238
Child Molestation Third Degree	239

The Caseload Forecast Council is not liable for errors or omissions in the manual, for sentences that may be inappropriately calculated as a result of a practitioner's or court's reliance on the manual, or for any other written or verbal information related to adult or juvenile sentencing. The scoring sheets are intended to provide assistance in most cases but do not cover all permutations of the scoring rules. If you find any errors or omissions, we encourage you to report them to the Caseload Forecast Council.

Civil Disorder Training ... 240

Commercial Bribery ... 241

Commercial Sexual Abuse Of A Minor Known As Patronizing A Juvenile Prostitute Prior To 7/22/2007 ... 242

Communication With A Minor For Immoral Purposes Subsequent Violation Or Prior Sex Offense Conviction ... 243

Computer Trespass First Degree ... 244

Controlled Substance Homicide ... 245

Counterfeiting Third Conviction And Value $10,000 Or More ... 246

Counterfeiting - Endanger Public Health Or Safety ... 247

Create, Deliver Or Possess A Counterfeit Controlled Substance Schedule I Or II Narcotic Or Flunitrazepam Or Methamphetamine ... 248

Create, Deliver Or Possess A Counterfeit Controlled Substance Schedule I-II Nonnarcotic, Schedule III-V Except Flunitrazepam Or Methamphetamine ... 249

Criminal Gang Intimidation ... 250

Criminal Mistreatment First Degree ... 251

Criminal Mistreatment Second Degree ... 252

Custodial Assault ... 253

Custodial Sexual Misconduct First Degree ... 254

Cyberstalking With Prior Harassment Conviction Or Threat Of Death ... 255

Dealing In Depictions Of A Minor Engaged In Sexually Explicit Conduct First Degree ... 256

Dealing In Depictions Of A Minor Engaged In Sexually Explicit Conduct Second Degree ... 257

Deliver Or Possess With Intent To Deliver Methamphetamine ... 258

Delivery Of Imitation Controlled Substance By Person 18 Or Over To Person Under 18 ... 259

Delivery Of A Material In Lieu Of A Controlled Substance ... 260

Domestic Violence Court Order Violation ... 261

Drive-By Shooting ... 262

Driving While Under The Influence Of Intoxicating Liquor Or Any Drug ... 263

Endangerment With A Controlled Substance ... 264

Escape First Degree ... 265

Escape Second Degree ... 266

Escape From Community Custody ... 267

Explosive Devices Prohibited ... 268

Extortion First Degree ... 269

The Caseload Forecast Council is not liable for errors or omissions in the manual, for sentences that may be inappropriately calculated as a result of a practitioner's or court's reliance on the manual, or for any other written or verbal information related to adult or juvenile sentencing. The scoring sheets are intended to provide assistance in most cases but do not cover all permutations of the scoring rules. If you find any errors or omissions, we encourage you to report them to the Caseload Forecast Council.

Extortion Second Degree 270

Extortionate Extension Of Credit/Use of Extortionate Means To Collect Extensions Of Credit 271

Failure To Register As A Sex Offender Second Or Subsequent Violation Committed On Or After 6/7/2006 But Before 6/10/2010.. 272

Failure To Register As A Sex Offender Second Violation Committed On Or After 6/10/2010 273

Failure To Register As A Sex Offender Third Or Subsequent Violation Committed On Or After 6/10/2010 274

False Verification For Welfare 275

Forged Prescription Legend Drug.. 276

Forged Prescription For A Controlled Substance 277

Forgery... 278

Harassment Subsequent Conviction Or Threat Of Death 279

Health Care False Claims 280

Hit And Run - Death... 281

Hit And Run - Injury.. 282

Hit And Run With A Vessel – Injury Accident 283

Homicide By Abuse 284

Homicide By Abuse With A Finding Of Sexual Motivation 285

Homicide By Watercraft While Under The Influence Of Intoxicating Liquor Or Any Drug 286

Homicide By Watercraft Disregard For The Safety Of Others 287

Homicide By Watercraft In A Reckless Manner 288

Identity Theft First Degree... 289

Identity Theft Second Degree 290

Improperly Obtaining Financial Information 291

Incest First Degree 292

Incest Second Degree... 293

Indecent Exposure To A Person Under Age 14 Subsequent Conviction Or Has Prior Sex Offense Conviction 294

Indecent Liberties With Forcible Compulsion 295

Indecent Liberties With Forcible Compulsion 296

Indecent Liberties Without Forcible Compulsion 297

Influencing Outcome Of Sporting Event 298

Intimidating A Judge, Intimidating A Juror, Intimidating A Witness... 299

Intimidating A Public Servant 300

The Caseload Forecast Council is not liable for errors or omissions in the manual, for sentences that may be inappropriately calculated as a result of a practitioner's or court's reliance on the manual, or for any other written or verbal information related to adult or juvenile sentencing. The scoring sheets are intended to provide assistance in most cases but do not cover all permutations of the scoring rules. If you find any errors or omissions, we encourage you to report them to the Caseload Forecast Council.

Title	Page
Introducing Contraband First Degree	301
Introducing Contraband Second Degree	302
Involving A Minor In Drug Dealing	303
Kidnapping First Degree	304
Kidnapping First Degree With A Finding Of Sexual Motivation	305
Kidnapping First Degree With A Finding Of Sexual Motivation	306
Kidnapping Second Degree	307
Kidnapping Second Degree With A Finding Of Sexual Motivation	308
Kidnapping Second Degree With A Finding Of Sexual Motivation	309
Leading Organized Crime Inciting Criminal Profiteering	310
Leading Organized Crime Organizing Criminal Profiteering	311
Maintaining A Dwelling Or Place For Controlled Substances	312
Maintaining A Dwelling Or Place For Controlled Substances (Subsequent)	313
Malicious Explosion Of A Substance First Degree	314
Malicious Explosion Of A Substance Second Degree	315
Malicious Explosion Of A Substance Third Degree	316
Malicious Harassment	317
Malicious Injury To Railroad Property	318
Malicious Mischief First Degree	319
Malicious Mischief Second Degree	320
Malicious Placement Of An Explosive First Degree	321
Malicious Placement Of An Explosive Second Degree	322
Malicious Placement Of An Explosive Third Degree	323
Malicious Placement Of An Imitation Device First Degree	324
Malicious Placement Of An Imitation Device Second Degree	325
Manslaughter First Degree	326
Manslaughter Second Degree	327
Manufacture, Deliver Or Possess With Intent To Deliver Amphetamine	328
Manufacture, Deliver Or Possess With Intent To Deliver Marijuana	329
Manufacture, Deliver Or Possess With Intent To Deliver Narcotics From Schedule I Or II Or Flunitrazepam From Schedule IV	330
Manufacture, Deliver Or Possess With Intent To Deliver Narcotics From Schedule III, IV Or V Or Nonnarcotics From Schedule I-V Except Marijuana, Amphetamine, Methamphetamine Or Flunitrazepam	331

The Caseload Forecast Council is not liable for errors or omissions in the manual, for sentences that may be inappropriately calculated as a result of a practitioner's or court's reliance on the manual, or for any other written or verbal information related to adult or juvenile sentencing. The scoring sheets are intended to provide assistance in most cases but do not cover all permutations of the scoring rules. If you find any errors or omissions, we encourage you to report them to the Caseload Forecast Council.

Manufacture, Distribute Or Possess With Intent To Distribute An Imitation Controlled Substance 332

Manufacture, Distribute Or Possess With Intent To Distribute An Imitation Controlled Substance By A Person 18 Or Older To A Person Under 18 333

Manufacture Methamphetamine 334

Mortgage Fraud 335

Murder First Degree... 336

Murder First Degree With A Finding Of Sexual Motivation 337

Murder First Degree With A Finding Of Sexual Motivation 338

Murder Second Degree 339

Murder Second Degree With A Finding Of Sexual Motivation.. 340

Murder Second Degree With A Finding Of Sexual Motivation.. 341

Organized Retail Theft First Degree 342

Organized Retail Theft Second Degree 343

Over 18 And Deliver Heroin, Methamphetamine, A Narcotic From Schedule I Or II Or Flunitrazepam From Schedule IV To Someone Under 18... 344

Over 18 And Deliver Narcotic From Schedule III, IV, Or V Or A Nonnarcotic, Except Flunitrazepam Or Methamphetamine, From Schedule IV To Someone Under 18 And 3 Years Junior 345

Perjury First Degree... 346

Perjury Second Degree 347

Persistent Prison Misbehavior.. 348

Physical Control Of A Vehicle While Under The Influence Of Intoxicating Liquor Or Any Drug 349

Possession Of Controlled Substance That Is Either Heroin Or Narcotics From Schedule I Or II............. 350

Possession Of Controlled Substance That Is A Narcotic From Schedule III, IV Or V Or Nonnarcotic From Schedule I-V 351

Possession Of Depictions Of Minor Engaged In Sexually Explicit Conduct First Degree 352

Possession Of Depictions Of Minor Engaged In Sexually Explicit Conduct Second Degree.................. 353

Possession Of Ephedrine, Pseudoephedrine Or Anhydrous Ammonia With Intent To Manufacture Methamphetamine 354

Possession Of An Incendiary Device.. 355

Possession Of A Machine Gun, Short-Barreled Shotgun Or Short-Barreled Rifle 356

Possession Of A Stolen Firearm 357

Possession Of Stolen Property First Degree Other Than A Firearm Or Motor Vehicle............................ 358

Possession Of Stolen Property Second Degree Other Than A Firearm Or Motor Vehicle 359

Possession Of A Stolen Vehicle 360

The Caseload Forecast Council is not liable for errors or omissions in the manual, for sentences that may be inappropriately calculated as a result of a practitioner's or court's reliance on the manual, or for any other written or verbal information related to adult or juvenile sentencing. The scoring sheets are intended to provide assistance in most cases but do not cover all permutations of the scoring rules. If you find any errors or omissions, we encourage you to report them to the Caseload Forecast Council.

Promoting Commercial Sexual Abuse Of A Minor	361
Promoting Prostitution First Degree	362
Promoting Prostitution Second Degree	363
Rape First Degree	364
Rape First Degree	365
Rape Second Degree	366
Rape Second Degree	367
Rape Third Degree	368
Rape Of A Child First Degree	369
Rape Of A Child First Degree	370
Rape Of A Child Second Degree	371
Rape Of A Child Second Degree	372
Rape Of A Child Third Degree	373
Reckless Burning First Degree	374
Rendering Criminal Assistance First Degree	375
Residential Burglary	376
Residential Burglary With A Finding Of Sexual Motivation	377
Retail Theft With Special Circumstances First Degree	378
Retail Theft With Special Circumstances Second Degree	379
Robbery First Degree	380
Robbery Second Degree	381
Securities Act Violation	382
Selling For Profit (Controlled Or Counterfeit) Any Controlled Substance In Schedule I	383
Sending, Bringing Into The State Depictions Of Minor Engaged In Sexually Explicit Conduct First Degree	384
Sending, Bringing Into The State Depictions Of Minor Engaged In Sexually Explicit Conduct Second Degree	385
Sexual Exploitation Of A Minor	386
Sexual Misconduct With A Minor First Degree	387
Sexually Violating Human Remains	388
Sexually Violent Predator Escape	389
Stalking	390
Taking Motor Vehicle Without Permission First Degree	391
Taking Motor Vehicle Without Permission Second Degree	392

The Caseload Forecast Council is not liable for errors or omissions in the manual, for sentences that may be inappropriately calculated as a result of a practitioner's or court's reliance on the manual, or for any other written or verbal information related to adult or juvenile sentencing. The scoring sheets are intended to provide assistance in most cases but do not cover all permutations of the scoring rules. If you find any errors or omissions, we encourage you to report them to the Caseload Forecast Council.

Tampering With A Witness 393

Telephone Harassment With Prior Harassment Conviction Or Threat Of Death 394

Theft First Degree Excluding Firearm And Motor Vehicle 395

Theft Second Degree Excluding Firearm And Motor Vehicle 396

Theft Of Ammonia 397

Theft Of A Firearm 398

Theft Of Livestock First Degree 399

Theft Of Livestock Second Degree 400

Theft Of A Motor Vehicle 401

Theft Of Rental, Leased, Lease-Purchased Or Loaned Property Valued At $5,000 Or More 402

Theft Of Rental, Leased, Lease-Purchased Or Loaned Property Valued At $750 Or More But Less Than $5,000 403

Theft With Intent To Resell First Degree 404

Theft With Intent To Resell Second Degree 405

Threats To Bomb 406

Trafficking In Insurance Claims Subsequent Violation 407

Trafficking In Stolen Property First Degree 408

Trafficking In Stolen Property Second Degree 409

Unlawful Factoring Of A Credit Or Payment Card Transaction 410

Unlawful Factoring Of A Credit Or Payment Card Transaction Subsequent Violation 411

Unlawful Imprisonment 412

Unlawful Issuance Of Checks Or Drafts Value Greater Than $750 413

Unlawful Possession Of Fictitious Identification 414

Unlawful Possession Of Instruments Of Financial Fraud 414

Unlawful Possession Of Payment Instruments 414

Unlawful Possession Of A Personal Identification Device 414

Unlawful Production Of Payment Instruments 414

Unlawful Possession Of A Firearm First Degree 415

Unlawful Possession Of A Firearm Second Degree 416

Unlawful Practice Of Law Subsequent Violation 417

Unlawful Storage Of Ammonia 418

Unlawful Use Of Building For Drug Purposes 419

Unlawful Trafficking Of Food Stamps 420

Unlawful Redemption Of Food Stamps 420

The Caseload Forecast Council is not liable for errors or omissions in the manual, for sentences that may be inappropriately calculated as a result of a practitioner's or court's reliance on the manual, or for any other written or verbal information related to adult or juvenile sentencing. The scoring sheets are intended to provide assistance in most cases but do not cover all permutations of the scoring rules. If you find any errors or omissions, we encourage you to report them to the Caseload Forecast Council.

Unlicensed Practice Of A Profession Or Business Subsequent Violation 421
Use Of Proceeds Of Criminal Profiteering 422
Use Of Machine Gun In Commission Of A Felony 423
Vehicle Prowl First Degree 424
Vehicle Prowling Second Degree (Third or Subsequent Offense) 425
Vehicular Assault Disregard For The Safety Of Others 426
Vehicular Assault In A Reckless Manner Or While Under The Influence Of Intoxicating Liquor Or Any Drug 427
Vehicular Homicide Disregard For The Safety Of Others 428
Vehicular Homicide In A Reckless Manner 429
Vehicular Homicide While Under The Influence Of Intoxicating Liquor Or Any Drug 430
Viewing Depictions Of Minor Engaged In Sexually Explicit Conduct First Degree 431
Voyeurism 432

The Caseload Forecast Council is not liable for errors or omissions in the manual, for sentences that may be inappropriately calculated as a result of a practitioner's or court's reliance on the manual, or for any other written or verbal information related to adult or juvenile sentencing. The scoring sheets are intended to provide assistance in most cases but do not cover all permutations of the scoring rules. If you find any errors or omissions, we encourage you to report them to the Caseload Forecast Council.

USE OF THIS MANUAL

The Adult Sentencing Guidelines Manual provides comprehensive information for criminal justice practitioners, public officials and citizens on adult felony sentencing in the state of Washington. This manual offers specific guidance on how to determine the appropriate standard sentence range for an offense by identifying the seriousness level of the offense and by "scoring" the offender's criminal history. This manual also addresses: reviews, modifications and discharges of sentences, as well as vacating conviction records. As an aid to judges, prosecutors, defense attorneys and other criminal justice professionals, this manual also includes forms for use in "scoring" an offender's criminal history.

Adult felony sentencing in Washington is governed by the Sentencing Reform Act (SRA) of 1981, Chapter 9.94A RCW, as amended. This manual includes a digest of recent appellate and Supreme Court decisions interpreting and affecting the SRA, and is excerpted from the *Criminal Caselaw Notebook©* courtesy of Judge Ronald Kessler, King County Superior Court.

Persons interested in a comprehensive legal analysis of the SRA are advised to read *Sentencing in Washington*, by David Boerner (Butterworth Legal Publishers) and the 2011-2012 supplement to *Washington Practice Volume 13A: Criminal Law*, by Seth Aaron Fine (West Publishing Co.).

This edition of the manual has been updated to reflect amendments to the SRA enacted during the 2016 Legislative session. Earlier editions of this manual should be retained for reference on offenses committed prior to the effective dates of the recently enacted legislation.

Copies of the 1987 through 2016 Adult Sentencing Guidelines Manuals and supplements are available electronically on the Council's website.

> http://www.cfc.wa.gov

Bound copies of the 2011 through 2016 Adult Sentencing Guidelines Manuals are available for purchase through the web site as well.

Comments or suggestions related to this manual should be directed to:

Ed Vukich
Senior Caseload Forecaster
Washington State Caseload Forecast Council
P.O. Box 40962
Olympia, WA 98504-0962

Telephone: (360) 664-9374
E-mail: Ed.Vukich@cfc.wa.gov

The Caseload Forecast Council is not liable for errors or omissions in the manual, for sentences that may be inappropriately calculated as a result of a practitioner's or court's reliance on the manual, or for any other written or verbal information related to adult or juvenile sentencing. The scoring sheets are intended to provide assistance in most cases but do not cover all permutations of the scoring rules. If you find any errors or omissions, we encourage you to report them to the Caseload Forecast Council.

The Caseload Forecast Council is not liable for errors or omissions in the manual, for sentences that may be inappropriately calculated as a result of a practitioner's or court's reliance on the manual, or for any other written or verbal information related to adult or juvenile sentencing. The scoring sheets are intended to provide assistance in most cases but do not cover all permutations of the scoring rules. If you find any errors or omissions, we encourage you to report them to the Caseload Forecast Council.

INTRODUCTION

Adult offenders who committed felonies on or after July 1, 1984, are subject to the provisions of the Sentencing Reform Act of 1981, as amended (SRA). The goal of Washington's sentencing system, which is based on a determinate sentencing model and eliminates parole and probation, is to ensure that offenders who commit similar crimes and have similar criminal histories receive equivalent sentences. The enabling legislation, RCW Section 9.94A *et seq.*, contains guidelines and procedures used by courts to impose sentences that apply equally to offenders in all parts of the state, without discrimination as to any element that does not relate to the crime or to a defendant's previous criminal record. The SRA guides judicial discretion by providing presumptive sentencing ranges for the courts to follow. The ranges are structured so that offenses involving greater harm to a victim and to society result in greater punishment. Sentences that depart from the standard presumptive ranges must be based upon substantial and compelling reasons and may be appealed by either the prosecutor or the defendant.

The Sentencing Guidelines Commission (Commission) developed the initial guidelines and continues to advise the Legislature on necessary adjustments. The Commission is composed of twenty voting members; sixteen appointed by the Governor. Those sixteen appointed members include: four Superior Court judges; two defense attorneys; two elected county prosecutors; four citizens (one of whom is a victim of crime or a crime victims' advocate); one juvenile court administrator; one elected city official; one elected county official; and the chief of a local law enforcement agency. Four voting members serve in an *ex-officio* capacity to their state positions: the Secretary of the Department of Corrections; the Director of the Office of Financial Management; the Assistant Secretary of the Department of Social and Health Services' Juvenile Rehabilitation Administration; and the Chair of the Indeterminate Sentence Review Board. The Speaker of the House of Representatives and the President of the Senate each appoint two nonvoting members from their respective chamber, one from each of the two largest caucuses in each body.

The SRA mandated that the Sentencing Guidelines Commission develop and maintain computerized databases of adult felony and juvenile dispositions, produce annual updates to adult and juvenile sentencing manuals, and conduct research related to adult and juvenile sentencing. In addition, the Commission has traditionally assessed the prison and jail impacts of proposed sentencing policy changes as part of the state's "fiscal note" process.

The state legislature, in ESSB 5891 passed during the 2011 legislative session, transferred responsibility for the sentencing databases, sentencing manuals, research on sentencing and analysis of policy impacts from the Commission to the Caseload Forecast Council (Council), effective August 24, 2011.

In order to carry out its mandate, the Council will continue to rely upon the cooperation and assistance of the superior court clerks of all thirty-nine counties in the state. The clerks transmit copies of Judgment and Sentence forms issued in all adult felony convictions to the Caseload Forecast Council. The Council staff extracts data from the forms relating to the crime, the offender, the sentencing judge, the sentence, and alternatives to incarceration, where applicable, and enters the information into a computerized database. Using this database the Council produces and distributes descriptive reports on actual sentences and analyzes the effects of changes in the law on prison and jail populations.

The Caseload Forecast Council is not liable for errors or omissions in the manual, for sentences that may be inappropriately calculated as a result of a practitioner's or court's reliance on the manual, or for any other written or verbal information related to adult or juvenile sentencing. The scoring sheets are intended to provide assistance in most cases but do not cover all permutations of the scoring rules. If you find any errors or omissions, we encourage you to report them to the Caseload Forecast Council.

The Council database is also the source of information used in preparation of annual statistical summaries of sentencing practices and other reports and studies related to felony sentencing in the state. Please direct questions about the sentencing manuals, databases and sentencing research to the Council office.

The Caseload Forecast Council is not liable for errors or omissions in the manual, for sentences that may be inappropriately calculated as a result of a practitioner's or court's reliance on the manual, or for any other written or verbal information related to adult or juvenile sentencing. The scoring sheets are intended to provide assistance in most cases but do not cover all permutations of the scoring rules. If you find any errors or omissions, we encourage you to report them to the Caseload Forecast Council.

SECTION 1 - FELONY OFFENSES AFFECTED BY 2016 SESSION LAW

RCW	RCW Title	Effective Date	Summary	Session Law	Section	Bill Number
RCW 9.94A.030	Definitions.	6/9/2016	Expands the definition of criminal history.	Ch. 81	§16	2ESHB 1553
RCW 9.94A.660	Drug offender sentencing alternative—Prison-based or residential alternative.	4/1/2016	Makes two technical corrections.	Ch. 29	§524	E3SHB 1713
RCW 9.94A.753	Restitution—Application dates.	6/9/2016	Expands provisions regarding restitution by adding fraudulent or unknown vehicle reports of sale. Defines loss.	Ch. 86	§5	ESHB 2274
RCW 46.61.502	Driving under the influence.	6/9/2016	Raises the felony class for felony DUI from Class C to Class B.	Ch. 87	§1	HB 2280
RCW 9A.90.030	Definitions.	6/9/2016	Establishes definitions for a new chapter (Chapter 9A.90 RCW) in Title 9A RCW.	Ch. 164	§3	E2SHB 2375
RCW 9A.90.040	Computer trespass in the first degree.	6/9/2016	Establishes the ranked Class C felony offense of computer trespass in the first degree.	Ch. 164	§4	E2SHB 2375
RCW 9A.90.060	Electronic data service interference.	6/9/2016	Establishes the ranked Class C felony offense of electronic data service interference.	Ch. 164	§6	E2SHB 2375
RCW 9A.90.080	Electronic data tampering in the first degree.	6/9/2016	Establishes the ranked Class C felony offense of electronic data tampering in the first degree.	Ch. 164	§8	E2SHB 2375
RCW 9A.90.100	Electronic data theft.	6/9/2016	Establishes the ranked Class C felony offense of electronic data theft.	Ch. 164	§10	E2SHB 2375
RCW 9A.90.100	Commission of other crime.	6/9/2016	Establishes provisions concerning the commission of any other crime while committing a crime under Chapter 9A.90 RCW.	Ch. 164	§11	E2SHB 2375
RCW 9A.52.010	Definitions.	6/9/2016	Removes several definitions concerning burglary and trespass.	Ch. 164	§12	E2SHB 2375
RCW 9.94A.515	Table 2—Crimes included within each seriousness level.	6/9/2016	Makes several technical corrections to offenses ranked on the adult felony sentencing grid.	Ch. 164	§13	E2SHB 2375

The Caseload Forecast Council is not liable for errors or omissions in the manual, for sentences that may be inappropriately calculated as a result of a practitioner's or court's reliance on the manual, or for any other written or verbal information related to adult or juvenile sentencing. The scoring sheets are intended to provide assistance in most cases but do not cover all permutations of the scoring rules. If you find any errors or omissions, we encourage you to report them to the Caseload Forecast Council.

SECTION 1 – Felony Offenses Affected by 2016 Session Law

RCW	RCW Title	Effective Date	Summary	Session Law	Section	Bill Number
			Ranks the Class C felony of electronic data service interference at Seriousness Level II on the adult felony sentencing grid.			
			Ranks the Class C felony of data tampering in the first degree at Seriousness Level II on the adult felony sentencing grid.			
			Ranks the Class C felony of electronic data theft at Seriousness Level II on the adult felony sentencing grid.			
RCW 9A.52.110	Computer trespass in the first degree.	6/9/2016	Repeals the ranked Class C felony offense of computer trespass in the first degree to reflect that it is now RCW 9A.90.040.	Ch. 164	§14	E2SHB 2375
RCW 9A.52.130	Computer trespass—Commission of other crime.	6/9/2016	Repeals the section "Computer trespass—Commission of other crime." to reflect that it is now RCW 9A.90.100.	Ch. 164	§14	E2SHB 2375
Ch. 9A.90 RCW	Washington cybercrime act.	6/9/2016	Mandates that Sections 3 through 11 of the bill constitute a new chapter (Chapter 9A.90 RCW) in Title 9A RCW.	Ch. 164	§15	E2SHB 2375
RCW 9A.86.010	Disclosing intimate images.	6/9/2016	Makes a technical correction to the unranked Class C felony offense of disclosing intimate images.	Ch. 91	§1	HB 2384
RCW 9.41.330	Felony firearm offenders—Determination of registration.	6/9/2019	Establishes provisions under which an offender must be required to register as a felony firearm offender.	Ch. 94	§1	SSB 2410
RCW 9.94A.860	Sentencing guidelines commission—Membership—Appointments—Terms of office—Expenses and compensation.	6/9/2016	Makes a technical correction.	Ch. 179	§3	HB 2587
RCW 9.94A.533	Adjustments to standard sentences.	6/9/2016	Makes three technical corrections. Amends the sentence enhancement for vehicular	Ch. 203	§7	ESHB 2700

The Caseload Forecast Council is not liable for errors or omissions in the manual, for sentences that may be inappropriately calculated as a result of a practitioner's or court's reliance on the manual, or for any other written or verbal information related to adult or juvenile sentencing. The scoring sheets are intended to provide assistance in most cases but do not cover all permutations of the scoring rules. If you find any errors or omissions, we encourage you to report them to the Caseload Forecast Council.

SECTION 1 – Felony Offenses Affected by 2016 Session Law

RCW	RCW Title	Effective Date	Summary	Session Law	Section	Bill Number
			homicide – under the influence.			
			Allows for extraordinary medical placement for offenders serving a sentence for vehicular homicide – under the influence.			
RCW 9.94A.704	Community custody—Supervision by the department—Conditions.	6/9/2016	Specifies that subsection 5 is not intended to reduce the authority of DOC to impose no-contact conditions regardless of the offense.	Ch. 108	§1	HB 2838
RCW 9.94.041	Narcotic drugs, controlled substances, alcohol, marijuana, other intoxicant, cell phone, or other form of electronic telecommunications device—Possession, etc., by prisoners—Penalty.	6/9/2016	Expands the definition of the unranked Class C felony offense of possession of a controlled substance by a prisoner (state facility) to include alcohol, marijuana, other intoxicant, a cell phone or other form of an electronic telecommunications device. Expands the definition of the unranked Class C felony offense of possession of a controlled substance by a prisoner (county or local facility) to include alcohol, marijuana, other intoxicant, a cell phone or other form of an electronic telecommunications device.	Ch. 199	§1	SHB 2900
RCW 46.37.640	Air bags—Definitions.	6/9/2016	Amends the definition of air bag. Amends the definition of non-deployed salvage air bag. Establishes a definition for counterfeit air bag. Establishes a definition for nonfunctional air bag.	Ch. 213	§1	SSB 6160
RCW 46.37.650	Air bags—Manufacture, importation, sale, or installation of counterfeit, nonfunctional, damaged, or previously deployed—Penalties.	6/9/2016	Removes an existing gross misdemeanor offense. Establishes the ranked Class C felony offense of manufacture or import counterfeit, nonfunctional, damaged, or	Ch. 213	§2	SSB 6160

The Caseload Forecast Council is not liable for errors or omissions in the manual, for sentences that may be inappropriately calculated as a result of a practitioner's or court's reliance on the manual, or for any other written or verbal information related to adult or juvenile sentencing. The scoring sheets are intended to provide assistance in most cases but do not cover all permutations of the scoring rules. If you find any errors or omissions, we encourage you to report them to the Caseload Forecast Council.

SECTION 1 – Felony Offenses Affected by 2016 Session Law

RCW	RCW Title	Effective Date	Summary	Session Law	Section	Bill Number
			previously deployed air bag (causing bodily injury or death).			
			Establishes the ranked Class C felony offense of manufacture or import counterfeit, nonfunctional, damaged, or previously deployed air bag.			
			Establishes the ranked Class C felony offense of sale, install, [or] reinstall counterfeit, nonfunctional, damaged, or previously deployed airbag.			
			Establishes the ranked Class C felony offense of sale, install, [or] reinstall counterfeit, nonfunctional, damaged, or previously deployed airbag.			
RCW 46.37.660	Air bags—Replacement requirements, diagnostic system—Penalties.	6/9/2016	Establishes the ranked Class C felony offense of air bag replacement requirements (causing bodily injury or death).	Ch. 213	§3	SSB 6160
			Establishes the ranked Class C felony offense of air bag replacement requirements.			
			Establishes the ranked Class C felony offense of air bag diagnostic systems (causing bodily injury or death).			
			Establishes the ranked Class C felony offense of air bag diagnostic systems.			
RCW 9.94A.515	Table 2—Crimes included within each seriousness level.	6/9/2016	Ranks the Class C felony offense of air bag diagnostic systems (causing bodily injury or death) at Seriousness Level VII on the adult felony sentencing grid.	Ch. 213	§5	SSB 6160
			Ranks the Class C felony offense of air bag replacement requirements (causing bodily injury or death) at Seriousness Level VII on the adult felony			

The Caseload Forecast Council is not liable for errors or omissions in the manual, for sentences that may be inappropriately calculated as a result of a practitioner's or court's reliance on the manual, or for any other written or verbal information related to adult or juvenile sentencing. The scoring sheets are intended to provide assistance in most cases but do not cover all permutations of the scoring rules. If you find any errors or omissions, we encourage you to report them to the Caseload Forecast Council.

SECTION 1 – Felony Offenses Affected by 2016 Session Law

RCW	RCW Title	Effective Date	Summary	Session Law	Section	Bill Number
			sentencing grid.			
			Ranks the Class C felony offense of manufacture or import counterfeit, nonfunctional, damaged, or previously deployed air bag (causing bodily injury or death) at Seriousness Level VII on the adult felony sentencing grid.			
			Ranks the Class C felony offense of sale, install, [or] reinstall counterfeit, nonfunctional, damaged, or previously deployed airbag at Seriousness Level VII on the adult felony sentencing grid.			
			Ranks the Class C felony offense of air bag diagnostic systems at Seriousness Level V on the adult felony sentencing grid.			
			Ranks the Class C felony offense of air bag replacement requirements at Seriousness Level V on the adult felony sentencing grid.			
			Ranks the Class C felony offense of manufacture or import counterfeit, nonfunctional, damaged, or previously deployed air bag at Seriousness Level V on the adult felony sentencing grid.			
			Ranks the Class C felony offense of sale, install, [or] reinstall counterfeit, nonfunctional, damaged, or previously deployed airbag at Seriousness Level V on the adult felony sentencing grid.			
RCW 9.41.190	Unlawful firearms—Exceptions.	6/9/2016	Amends provisions concerning short-barreled rifles.	Ch. 214	§1	SSB 6165
RCW 69.41.030	Sale, delivery, or possession of legend drug without prescription or order prohibited—	6/9/2016	Makes a technical correction to the unraked Class B felony offense of sale, delivery or possession with intent to sell	Ch. 148	§11	ESSB 6203

The Caseload Forecast Council is not liable for errors or omissions in the manual, for sentences that may be inappropriately calculated as a result of a practitioner's or court's reliance on the manual, or for any other written or verbal information related to adult or juvenile sentencing. The scoring sheets are intended to provide assistance in most cases but do not cover all permutations of the scoring rules. If you find any errors or omissions, we encourage you to report them to the Caseload Forecast Council.

SECTION 1 – Felony Offenses Affected by 2016 Session Law

RCW	RCW Title	Effective Date	Summary	Session Law	Section	Bill Number
	Exceptions—Penalty.		legend drug without prescription.			
RCW 9.94A.515	Table 2—Crimes included within each seriousness level.	6/9/2016	Raises the Seriousness Level of vehicular homicide, by the operation of any vehicle in a reckless manner from Seriousness Level VIII to Seriousness Level XI on the adult felony sentencing grid.	Ch. 6	§1	SSB 6219
RCW 9.94A.535	Departures from the guidelines.	6/9/2016	Establishes a new mitigated exceptional sentence reason concerning vehicular homicide, by the operation of any vehicle in a reckless manner.	Ch. 6	§2	SSB 6219
RCW 69.50.402	Prohibited acts: B—Penalties.	6/9/2016	Amends the definition of the unranked Class C felony offense of dispensing violation (VUCSA).	Ch. 150	§1	SSB 6238
Ch. 21.20 RCW	Securities act of Washington.	6/9/2016	Makes numerous technical corrections to sections related to the ranked Class B felony offense of securities act violation.	Ch. 61	§§1-16	SSB 6283
RCW 70.345.010	Definitions.	6/28/2016	Establishes definitions for a new chapter (Chapter 70.345 RCW) in Title 70 RCW.	Ch. 38 1st sp.s.	§4	ESSB 6328
RCW 70.345.030	License required—Must allow inspections—Sale of certain substances prohibited—Penalties.	8/1/2016	Establishes the unranked Class C felony offense of retail sales, distribution or delivery sales of vapor products without a license.	Ch. 38 1st sp.s.	§6	ESSB 6328
RCW 70.345.090	Mail and internet sales—License required—Age and identity verification—Penalties—Enforcement—Application of consumer protection act—Rules.	6/28/2016	Establishes the unranked Class C felony offense of engaging in delivery sales of vapor products without a license, or without proper shipping documentation.	Ch. 38 1st sp.s.	§17	ESSB 6328
Ch. 70.345 RCW	Vapor products.	6/28/2016	Mandates that Sections 3 through 8, 10-22 and 24 through 26 of the bill constitute a new chapter (Chapter 70.345 RCW) in Title 70 RCW.	Ch. 38 1st sp.s.	§31	ESSB 6328
RCW 9.94A.718	Supervision of offenders—Peace officers have authority to assist.	6/9/2016	Establishes provisions pertaining to law enforcement officers assisting DOC with the supervision of offenders.	Ch. 234	§1	SB 6459
RCW 9A.40.090	Luring.	6/9/2016	Amends the definition of the	Ch. 11	§1	SSB 6463

The Caseload Forecast Council is not liable for errors or omissions in the manual, for sentences that may be inappropriately calculated as a result of a practitioner's or court's reliance on the manual, or for any other written or verbal information related to adult or juvenile sentencing. The scoring sheets are intended to provide assistance in most cases but do not cover all permutations of the scoring rules. If you find any errors or omissions, we encourage you to report them to the Caseload Forecast Council.

SECTION 1 – Felony Offenses Affected by 2016 Session Law

RCW	RCW Title	Effective Date	Summary	Session Law	Section	Bill Number
			unranked Class C felony offense of luring.			
RCW 9.94A.501	Department must supervise specified offenders—Risk assessment of felony offenders.	6/28/2016	Makes five technical corrections. Establishes a provision specifying the period of time DOC is authorized to supervise offenders.	Ch. 28 1st sp.s.	§1	SSB 6531

The Caseload Forecast Council is not liable for errors or omissions in the manual, for sentences that may be inappropriately calculated as a result of a practitioner's or court's reliance on the manual, or for any other written or verbal information related to adult or juvenile sentencing. The scoring sheets are intended to provide assistance in most cases but do not cover all permutations of the scoring rules. If you find any errors or omissions, we encourage you to report them to the Caseload Forecast Council.

The Caseload Forecast Council is not liable for errors or omissions in the manual, for sentences that may be inappropriately calculated as a result of a practitioner's or court's reliance on the manual, or for any other written or verbal information related to adult or juvenile sentencing. The scoring sheets are intended to provide assistance in most cases but do not cover all permutations of the scoring rules. If you find any errors or omissions, we encourage you to report them to the Caseload Forecast Council.

SECTION 2 - CASE LAW RELATED TO THE SENTENCING REFORM ACT

CASELAW REVIEW – 2016 UPDATE

Excerpted from the *Criminal Caselaw Notebook©*, with permission, by Judge Ronald Kessler, King County Superior Court.

SRA: Exceptional Sentences

State v. Gipson, 191 Wn.App. 780 (2015)
    Public official aggravator, RCW 9.94A.535(3)(x) (2013), does not include a law enforcement officer as an element of assault 3° as charged, RCW 9A.36.031(1)(g) (2013), is that victim is a police officer; II.

State v. Solis-Diaz, 194 Wn.App. 129 (2016)
    For an auto-declined juvenile sentencing court must take into account observations that generally show a reduced sense of responsibility, increased impetuousness, increased susceptibility to outside pressures including peer pressure and a great claim to forgiveness and time of amendment of live, *Miller v. Alabama*, ___ U.S. ___, 183 L.Ed.2d 407 (2012), *Graham v. Florida*, 560 U.S. 48 (2010), *Roper v. Simmons*, 543 U.S. 551, 161 L.Ed.2d 1 (2005), *State v. O'Dell*, 183 Wn.2d 680 (2015); II.

SRA: Procedure

State v. Sandholm, 184 Wn.2d 726, 736-39 (2015)
    In determining offender score for felony DUI all prior convictions that have not washed count, *State v. Hernandez*, 185 Wn.App. 680 (2015), *State v. McAninch*, 189 wn.App. 619 (2015), overruling *State v. Martinez-Morales*, 168 Wn.App. 489 (2012) and *State v. Jacob*, 176 Wn.App. 351 (2013); 9-0.

State v. Miller, 185 Wn.2d 111 (2016)
    Defendant is sentenced to consecutive sentences for two counts of murder, RCW 9.94A.589(1)(b) (2002), defendant files untimely collateral attack seeking resentencing because *Pers. Restraint of Mulholland*, 161 Wn.2d 322 (2007) authorized court to impose concurrent exceptional sentences, trial court agrees it was unaware it had the authority and imposes concurrent sentences, state appeals; held: *Mulholland* did not qualify as a significant change in the law, *Pers. Restraint of Gentry*, 179 Wn.2d 614, 625 (2014), RCW 10.73.100(6) (1989), could have argued at original sentencing for concurrent sentences thus concurrent sentences vacated; 8-1.

State v. Weatherwax, 193 Wn.App. 667, 673-76 (2016)

SECTION 2- Case Law As Related to the Sentencing Reform – 2016 Update

Where defendant is convicted of two or more serious violent offenses and of an attempt to commit a serious violent offense, RCW 9.94A.589(1)(b) requires that the full offender score applies to the a completed offense and not the the anticipatory offense, *but see: State v. Breaux,* 167 Wn.App. 166 (2012); 2-1, III.

State v. Baker, 194 Wn.App. 678 (2016)
Offender score for **escape** is limited to prior escape convictions, RCW 9.94A.525(14) (2013); III.

SRA: Same Criminal Conduct

State v. Chenoweth, 185 Wn.2d 218 (2016)
Rape of a child and incest based upon the same act is not the same criminal conduct, *State v. Calle,* 125 Wn.2d 769 (1995), *State v. Smith,* 177 Wn.2d 533, 545-50 (2013); 5-4.

SECTION 3 - SENTENCING GUIDELINES

This section explains the rules for applying the sentencing guidelines to **felony crimes committed after June 30, 1984,** including changes enacted by the 2015 legislative session.

DETERMINING FELONY CLASS

Felonies defined in Title 9A and Title 9 of the Revised Code of Washington (RCW) fall into one of three classes: Class A, Class B or Class C. The class of these felonies is either defined explicitly as part of the definition of the offense, or implicitly, based on the statutory maximum period of incarceration. A felony washout period (RCW 9.94A.525(2)), vacation of conviction record (RCW 9.94A.640), status as a violent offense (RCW 9.94A.030(55)) and statutory maximum period of incarceration are functions of offense class.

Felonies Defined in Title 9A RCW

Felonies defined by Title 9A RCW have an A, B or C class designation explicitly stated. These felonies carry the following maximum penalties (RCW 9A.20.021):

Class A	Life in prison, $50,000 fine
Class B	Ten years in prison, $20,000 fine
Class C	Five years in prison, $10,000 fine

Felonies Defined Outside Title 9A

Some felonies are defined outside Title 9A RCW without an explicit felony class. The 1996 Legislature[1] enacted RCW 9.94A.035, establishing the classes of such offenses for SRA purposes. The class is based on the maximum period of incarceration provided for the first conviction of violating the statute creating the offense:

Class A	20 years or more
Class B	Eight or more, less than 20 years
Class C	Less than eight years

Therefore, statutes increasing the maximum sentence for subsequent convictions do not affect the classification of the offense for SRA purposes, even though they increase the maximum sentence that may be imposed.

---

[1] Historically, RCW 9A.20.040 was used to determine the class of these "unclassed" offenses for SRA sentencing purposes, based on the same relationship between the offense and the maximum sentence as shown. A 1995 decision of the Court of Appeals, Division II (*State v. Kelley*, 77 Wn. App. 66) held that RCW 9A.20.040 should not be used to determine the class of crimes defined outside Title 9A, or where the statutory maximum has been doubled as a result of sentencing enhancements. The 1996 legislation was intended to be consistent with the *Kelley* decision.

The Caseload Forecast Council is not liable for errors or omissions in the manual, for sentences that may be inappropriately calculated as a result of a practitioner's or court's reliance on the manual, or for any other written or verbal information related to adult or juvenile sentencing. The scoring sheets are intended to provide assistance in most cases but do not cover all permutations of the scoring rules. If you find any errors or omissions, we encourage you to report them to the Caseload Forecast Council.

SECTION 3 – Sentencing Guidelines

Felonies for which no maximum punishment is specifically prescribed are punished by confinement for not more than ten years and a fine not to exceed $20,000 or both, and are classified as Class B felonies (See RCW 9.92.010, as amended in 1996).

DETERMINING THE OFFENSE SERIOUSNESS LEVEL

The offense of *conviction* determines the offense seriousness level.

General Felony Crimes

The seriousness level is measured on the vertical axis of the sentencing guidelines grid (Section 4, page 49). Offenses are divided into 16 seriousness levels ranging from low (Level I) to high (Level XVI). RCW 9.94A.515 lists the crimes within each seriousness level (Section 4, page 51).

This edition of the Manual includes the grids applicable to offenses committed after July 24, 1999, as well as the 2012 changes to the list of offenses ranked on the adult felony sentencing grid. Previous versions of the grid can be found in Section 4.

On the grid, numbers in the first horizontal row of each seriousness category represent sentencing midpoints in months (m). Numbers in the second and third rows represent standard sentencing ranges in months, or in days if so designated. 12+ equals one year and one day.

Drug Crimes

Drug offenses committed on or after July 1, 2003, are divided into three seriousness levels and sentenced according to the drug grid (Section 4, page 60). RCW 9.94A.518 lists the crimes within each seriousness level (Section 4, page 61).

Unranked Felony Crimes

Some felonies are not included in the Seriousness Level table and are referred to as "unranked." Sentences for unranked felonies are entered without reference to a standard sentence range and do not require sentence calculations. The sentencing options for unranked felonies are described in Section 3, page 27.

DETERMINING THE OFFENDER SCORE

The offender score, one factor affecting a felony sentence, is measured on the horizontal axis of the sentencing guidelines grid. An offender may receive from 0 to 9+ points on that axis. In general, the number of points an offender receives depends on five factors: (1) the number of prior criminal convictions or

SECTION 3 – Sentencing Guidelines

juvenile dispositions; (2) the relationship between any prior offense(s) and the current offense of conviction; (3) the presence of other current convictions; (4) the offender's community custody status at the time the crime was committed; and (5) the length of the offender's crime-free behavior between offenses.

CRIMINAL HISTORY COLLECTION

Pursuant to RCW 9.94A.030(11), criminal history includes the defendant's prior adult convictions and juvenile court dispositions, whether in this state, in federal court, or elsewhere, and any issued certificates of restoration of opportunity. Although an offender's criminal history consists almost exclusively of *felony* convictions, in some instances, it also includes misdemeanors. The effect of criminal history also relates to the felony class of the crime (Class A, Class B or Class C), and the type of offense (i.e. serious violent, violent, nonviolent, sex, etc.). Lists of such felony offenses can be found in Section 5.

Adult Criminal History

The Criminal Justice Information Act (Chapter 10.98 RCW) established the Washington State Patrol Identification and Criminal History Section (the Section) as the primary source of information on state felony conviction histories. The Act directs judges to ensure that felony defendants are fingerprinted and that arrest and fingerprint forms are transmitted to the Washington State Patrol (RCW 10.98.050(2)). After filing charges, prosecutors contact the Section for an offender's Washington criminal history. Prosecutors also obtain out-of-state or federal criminal history information from the Federal Bureau of Investigation or other appropriate sources.

A conviction is defined as a verdict of guilty, a finding of guilty, or an acceptance of a plea of guilty. RCW 9.94A.525(1) defines a prior conviction as one existing before the date of the sentencing for the offense for which the offender score is being computed. Convictions entered or sentenced on the same date as the conviction for which the offender score is being computed are deemed "other current offenses" within the meaning of RCW 9.94A.589.

Prior adult convictions should be counted as criminal history unless:

- "Wash out" provisions apply; or
- A court has previously determined that they constituted "same criminal conduct" as defined by RCW 9.94A.589; or
- They were not previously deemed "same criminal conduct" but their sentences were served concurrently and a court now determines that they were committed at the same time, in the same place, and involved the same victim; or
- The sentences were served concurrently and they were committed before July 1, 1986.

RCW 9.94A.030(11) provides that, when the information is available, criminal history should include the length and terms of any probation and/or incarceration. This information is often collected as part of the Pre-sentence Investigation Report.

The Caseload Forecast Council is not liable for errors or omissions in the manual, for sentences that may be inappropriately calculated as a result of a practitioner's or court's reliance on the manual, or for any other written or verbal information related to adult or juvenile sentencing. The scoring sheets are intended to provide assistance in most cases but do not cover all permutations of the scoring rules. If you find any errors or omissions, we encourage you to report them to the Caseload Forecast Council.

SECTION 3 – Sentencing Guidelines

Juvenile Criminal History

All felony dispositions in juvenile court must be counted as criminal history for purposes of adult sentencing, except under the general "wash-out" provisions that apply to adult offenses. Juvenile offenses sentenced on the same day must be counted separately unless they constitute the "same criminal conduct" as defined in RCW 9.94A.589(1)(a) or unless the date(s) of the offenses were prior to July 1, 1986.

Although juvenile records generally are sealed, RCW 13.50.050(10) provides that after a charge has been filed, juvenile offense records of an adult criminal defendant or witness in an adult criminal proceeding shall be released upon request to the prosecution and defense counsel, subject to the rules of discovery. Any charging of an adult felony subsequent to the sealing has the effect of nullifying the sealing order of a juvenile record.

"Wash Out" of Certain Prior Felonies

The rules governing which prior convictions are included in the offender score can be found in RCW 9.94A.525 and are summarized as follows:
- Prior Class A and felony sex convictions are always included in the offender score.
- Prior Class B (juvenile or adult) felony convictions, other than sex offenses, are *not* included in the offender score if, since the last date of release from confinement (including full-time residential treatment) pursuant to a felony conviction, if any, or since the entry of judgment and sentence, the offender had spent ten consecutive years in the community without having been convicted of any crime.
- Prior Class C (juvenile or adult) felony convictions, other than sex offenses, are *not* included in the offender score if, since the last date of release from confinement (including full-time residential treatment) pursuant to a felony conviction, if any, or since the entry of judgment and sentence, the offender had spent five consecutive years in the community without having been convicted of any crime.
- Prior (juvenile or adult) serious traffic convictions are *not* included in the offender score if, since the last date of release from confinement (including full-time residential treatment) pursuant to a felony conviction, if any, or since the entry of judgment and sentence, the offender had spent five years in the community without having been convicted of any crime.
- Prior convictions for repetitive domestic violence offense, as defined in RCW 9.94A.030(42), are *not* included in the offender score if the offender has spent ten consecutive years in the community without committing any crime resulting in a conviction since the last date of release.

The Sentencing Reform Act permits vacating records of conviction under certain conditions and provides that vacated convictions "shall not be included in the offender's criminal history for purposes of determining a sentence in any subsequent conviction." RCW 9.94A.640. Vacation of the conviction record does not affect or prevent the use of an offender's prior conviction in a later criminal prosecution.

The eligibility rules for vacation of conviction record are similar to the "wash-out" rules. Because the "wash-out" rules are automatic and do not require court action, an offense will "wash out" before formal

SECTION 3 – Sentencing Guidelines

record vacation occurs. (The main distinction between vacation of record of conviction and "wash-out" is that, after vacation, an offender may indicate on employment forms that he or she was not convicted of that crime.)

Federal, Out-of-State or Foreign Convictions

In order for a prior federal, out-of-state, or foreign conviction to be included in an offender's history, and thereby affect the offender score, the elements of the offense in other jurisdictions must be compared with Washington State laws. (RCW 9.94A.525(3)). In instances where the foreign conviction is not clearly comparable to an offense under Washington State law, or where the offense is usually considered a felony subject to exclusive federal jurisdiction, the offense is scored as a Class C felony equivalent.

SCORING CRIMINAL HISTORY

Once relevant prior convictions are identified, the criminal history portion of the offender score may be calculated. The rules for scoring prior convictions are contained in RCW 9.94A.525. It should be noted that the scoring rules for some offenses are calculated differently, depending upon the category of the offense. Offense scoring forms can be found in Section 7 of this manual and specify the correct number of points for prior convictions depending on the current offense. The forms are intended to provide assistance in most cases but do not cover all permutations of the scoring rules or are provided for all offenses. A thorough understanding of the criminal history rules is important in order to use these forms correctly and to perform calculations not covered by the forms.

General consideration should also be given to often-applicable exceptions to general scoring rules. For instance, misdemeanors generally are not included in offender score calculations. An exception exists where the current conviction is for a felony traffic offense. In such cases, serious traffic offenses are included in the offender score.[2] Additionally, with present convictions of anticipatory offenses (criminal attempt, solicitation, or conspiracy) prior convictions of felony anticipatory offenses count the same and are scored as if they were convictions for completed offenses.[3] Exceptions to the general scoring rules also exist for Burglary 1°[4], Burglary 2° and Residential Burglary,[5] for Manufacturing Methamphetamine and other drug offenses,[6] for Escape offenses,[7] for Failure to Register as a Sex Offender,[8] for crimes involving the taking, theft, or possession of a stolen motor vehicle,[9] or for felony domestic violence where domestic violence was plead and proven.[10]

---

[2] See RCW 9.94A.525(2)(e), (11) and (12)
[3] See RCW 9.94A.525(4)-(6)
[4] See RCW 9.94A.525(10)
[5] See RCW 9.94A.525 (16)
[6] See RCW 9.94A.525(13)
[7] See RCW 9.94A.525 (14) and (15)
[8] See RCW 9.94A.525(18)
[9] See RCW 9.94A.525 (20)
[10] See RCW 9.94A.525(21)

The Caseload Forecast Council is not liable for errors or omissions in the manual, for sentences that may be inappropriately calculated as a result of a practitioner's or court's reliance on the manual, or for any other written or verbal information related to adult or juvenile sentencing. The scoring sheets are intended to provide assistance in most cases but do not cover all permutations of the scoring rules. If you find any errors or omissions, we encourage you to report them to the Caseload Forecast Council.

SECTION 3 – Sentencing Guidelines

Prior convictions for felony anticipatory offenses (attempts, solicitations, and conspiracies) are scored as if they were convictions for completed offenses. RCW 9.94A.525(4).

Finally, an exception should also be noted for convictions with a finding of sexual motivation. A finding of sexual motivation changes the underlying offense to a sex offense as defined in RCW 9.94A.030(47), changing the scoring rules and impacting the sentence options. This scoring rule only applies to crimes committed on or after July 1, 1990 (See RCW 9.94A.525 (17)).

SCORING MULTIPLE CURRENT CONVICTIONS

Multiple convictions may also affect the offender score. For multiple current offenses, separate sentence calculations are necessary for *each* offense because the law requires that each receive a separate sentence unless the offenses are ruled the same criminal conduct (See RCW 9.94A.589).

Multiple Offense Scoring Steps:

1. If the current offenses do *not* include two or more serious violent offenses arising from separate and distinct criminal conduct, apply RCW 9.94A.589(1)(a):
   a. Calculate the score for *each* offense.
   b. For each offense, score the prior adult and juvenile convictions.
   c. For each offense, score the other current offenses on the scoring form line entitled "Other Current Offenses."
   d. The court may find that some or all of the current offenses encompass the same criminal conduct and are to be counted as one crime.
   e. In cases of Vehicular Homicide or Vehicular Assault with multiple victims, offenses against each victim may be charged as separate offenses, even if the victims occupied the same vehicle. The resulting multiple convictions need not be scored as constituting the same criminal conduct.
   f. Convictions entered or sentenced on the same date as the conviction for which the offender score is being computed are scored as "Other Current Offenses."

   Example: Assume that an offender is convicted of one count of Theft in the First Degree and one count of Forgery, with both offenses arising from separate and distinct criminal conduct, and that the offender's criminal history consisted of one conviction for Burglary in the Second Degree. In this case, the rules in RCW 9.94A.589(1)(a) apply, and the theft and forgery must be separately scored. The prior burglary and the current forgery are included in the offender score for the theft, resulting in an offender score of two and a sentence range of 3 to 9 months. The prior burglary and the current theft are included in the offender score for the forgery, resulting in an offender score of two and a sentence range of 2 to 5 months. The sentence for each offense will run concurrently.

   Example: Assume that an offender is convicted of one count of Theft in the Second Degree and one count of Possession of Stolen Property in the Second Degree in a circumstance where

SECTION 3 – Sentencing Guidelines

both counts encompassed the same criminal conduct, and that the offender had no criminal history. In this case, the other current offense is not counted in the offender score because under RCW 9.94A.589(1)(a) where current offenses are found to encompass the same criminal conduct, those current offenses shall be counted as one crime. Therefore, the theft and possession would both be scored with offender scores of zero, with a sentence range for each crime of 0 to 60 days. The sentence for each offense will run concurrently.

Example: Assume an offender is convicted on one count of Assault in the Third Degree, with a criminal history consisting of adult convictions for Theft in the Second Degree and Forgery and a single adjudication of Assault in the Second Degree as a juvenile. Pursuant to RCW 9.94A.589(1)(a), the prior Theft in the Second Degree and Forgery are included in the offender score as one point each, and the juvenile Assault in the Second Degree also scores as one point, resulting in an offender score of three points. The sentence range is 9 to 12 months.

2. If the current offenses include two or more serious violent offenses arising from separate and distinct conduct, apply RCW 9.94A.589(1)(b):
    a. Calculate the score for *each* offense.
    b. Identify the serious violent offense with the *highest* seriousness level. Calculate the sentence for that crime using the offender's prior adult and juvenile convictions. Do not include any other current serious violent offenses as part of the offender score, but do include other current offenses that are not serious violent offenses.
    c. Score all remaining serious violent current offenses, calculating the sentence for the crime using an offender score of *zero*.
    d. For any current offenses that are not serious violent offenses, score according to the rules in (A) above.

    Example: Assume that an offender is convicted of two counts of Kidnapping in the First Degree and one count of Assault in the First Degree. These offenses constitute serious violent offenses. Assume further that these offenses arose from separate and distinct criminal conduct and that the offender's criminal history consists of one Assault in the Third Degree conviction. The scoring for this offender follows the rules in RCW 9.94A.589(1)(b). First, the crime with the highest seriousness level must be identified and scored. Since Assault in the First Degree is more serious (Level XII) than Kidnapping in the First Degree (Level X), that offense is scored by counting the prior Assault in the Third Degree as part of the adult criminal history. This calculation results in an offender score of one and a sentence range of 102 to 136 months. Next, the Kidnapping in the First Degree convictions are scored using a criminal history of zero. These calculations result in two sentence ranges of 51 to 68 months. The three sentences will run *consecutively*.

3. If the current offenses include Unlawful Possession of a Firearm in the First or Second Degree and one, or both, of the felony crimes of Theft of a Firearm or Possession of a Stolen Firearm, score according to the rules in RCW 9.94A.589(1)(c).

The Caseload Forecast Council is not liable for errors or omissions in the manual, for sentences that may be inappropriately calculated as a result of a practitioner's or court's reliance on the manual, or for any other written or verbal information related to adult or juvenile sentencing. The scoring sheets are intended to provide assistance in most cases but do not cover all permutations of the scoring rules. If you find any errors or omissions, we encourage you to report them to the Caseload Forecast Council.

SECTION 3 – Sentencing Guidelines

SCORING OFFENDER STATUS WHILE ON COMMUNITY CUSTODY

The offender score also reflects whether the offense was committed while the offender was under community custody. An additional point is added to the offender score for crimes committed on or after July 1, 1988, while the offender was on community custody. RCW 9.94A.525(19). Community custody includes community placement and post-release supervision as defined in RCW 9.94A.030.

DETERMINING THE STANDARD RANGE USING THE SENTENCING GRID

Once the offense seriousness level has been determined and the offender score has been calculated, the presumptive standard sentence range may be identified on the appropriate sentencing grid.

The standard sentence range for any offense *not* covered under Chapter 69.50 RCW (controlled substances) is established by referring to the standard sentencing grid (RCW 9.94A.510). For each current offense, the intersection of the column defined by the offender score and the row defined by the offense seriousness level determines the standard sentence range. Alternatively, the same range is identified on the individual offense scoring forms provided in this manual. In those cases where the presumptive sentence duration exceeds the statutory maximum sentence for the offense, the statutory maximum sentence is the presumptive sentence unless the offender is a persistent offender. If the addition of a firearm enhancement increases the sentence so that it would exceed the statutory maximum for the offense, the portion of the sentence representing the enhancement may not be reduced. RCW 9.94A.599.

SENTENCES IMPOSED for aggravated first degree murder on or after June 1, 2014, **REGARDLESS OF THE DATE OF THE OFFENSE**, should be calculated and entered in accordance with the sentencing grid in Section 4, page 49 of this manual and as set forth in RCW 9.94A.510.

SENTENCES IMPOSED on or after July 1, 2013 for drug crimes, **REGARDLESS OF THE DATE OF THE OFFENSE**, should be calculated and entered in accordance with the drug sentencing grid in Section 4, page 60 of this manual and as set forth in RCW 9.94A.517.

SENTENCES IMPOSED before July 1, 2013 for drug crimes committed on or after July 1, 2003 should be calculated and entered in accordance with the drug sentencing grid in Section 4, page 66 of this manual.

Sentences for crimes committed on or after July 25, 1999, and not affected by the 2002 amendments to the SRA, should be determined according to the sentencing grid in Section 4, page 49.

Sentences for crimes committed on or after July 27, 1997, and before July 25, 1999, should be determined according to the sentencing grid in Section 4, page 63.

Sentences for crimes committed on or after July 1, 1990, and before July 27, 1997, should be determined according to the sentencing grid in Section 4, page 64.

The Caseload Forecast Council is not liable for errors or omissions in the manual, for sentences that may be inappropriately calculated as a result of a practitioner's or court's reliance on the manual, or for any other written or verbal information related to adult or juvenile sentencing. The scoring sheets are intended to provide assistance in most cases but do not cover all permutations of the scoring rules. If you find any errors or omissions, we encourage you to report them to the Caseload Forecast Council.

SECTION 3 – Sentencing Guidelines

Sentences for crimes committed prior to July 1, 1990, should be determined according to the sentencing grid in Section 4, page 65.

Anticipatory Offenses (Non-VUCSA Attempts, Conspiracies, and Solicitations)

The standard sentence range for persons convicted of an anticipatory offense (criminal attempt, solicitation, or conspiracy) is 75 percent of the standard sentence range of the completed offense, determined by using the offender score and offense seriousness level (RCW 9.94A.595). For aid in calculating the range, refer to the anticipatory offense grids in Section 4.

Relevant Statutes – Non VUCSA Offenses

Criminal Attempt (RCW 9A.28.020)

1. A person is guilty of an attempt to commit a crime if, with intent to commit a specific crime, he or she does any act which is a substantial step toward the commission of that crime.

2. If the conduct in which a person engages otherwise constitutes an attempt to commit a crime, it is no defense to a prosecution of such attempt that the crime charged to have been attempted was, under the attendant circumstances, factually or legally impossible of commission.

3. An attempt to commit a crime is a:
   a. Class A felony when the crime attempted is Murder in the First Degree, Murder in the Second Degree, Arson in the First Degree, Child Molestation in the First Degree, Indecent Liberties by Forcible Compulsion, Rape in the First Degree, Rape in the Second Degree, Rape of a Child in the First Degree, or Rape of a Child in the Second Degree;
   b. Class B felony when the crime attempted is a Class A felony other than an offense listed in (a) of this subsection;
   c. Class C felony when the crime attempted is a Class B felony;
   d. Gross misdemeanor when the crime attempted is a Class C felony;
   e. Misdemeanor when the crime attempted is a gross misdemeanor or misdemeanor.

Criminal Solicitation (RCW 9A.28.030)

1. A person is guilty of criminal solicitation when, with intent to promote or facilitate the commission of a crime, he or she offers to give or gives money or other thing of value to another to engage in specific conduct which would constitute such crime or which would establish complicity of such

SECTION 3 – Sentencing Guidelines

other person in its commission or attempted commission had such crime been attempted or committed.

2. Criminal solicitation shall be punished in the same manner as criminal attempt under RCW 9A.28.020.

Criminal Conspiracy (RCW 9A.28.040)

1. A person is guilty of criminal conspiracy when, with intent that conduct constituting a crime be performed, he or she agrees with one or more persons to engage in or cause the performance of such conduct, and any one of them takes a substantial step in pursuance of such agreement.

2. It shall not be a defense to criminal conspiracy that the person or persons with whom the accused is alleged to have conspired:
    a. Has not been prosecuted or convicted; or
    b. Has been convicted of a different offense; or
    c. Is not amenable to justice; or
    d. Has been acquitted; or
    e. Lacked the capacity to commit an offense; or
    f. Is a law enforcement officer or other government agent who did not intend that a crime be committed.

3. Criminal conspiracy is a:
    a. Class A felony when an object of the conspiratorial agreement is Murder in the First Degree;
    b. Class B felony when an object of the conspiratorial agreement is a Class A felony other than Murder in the First Degree;
    c. Class C felony when an object of the conspiratorial agreement is a Class B felony;
    d. Gross misdemeanor when an object of the conspiratorial agreement is a Class C felony;
    e. Misdemeanor when an object of the conspiratorial agreement is a gross misdemeanor or misdemeanor.

Anticipatory Offenses (RCW 9.94A.595)

For persons convicted of the anticipatory offenses of criminal attempt, solicitation, or conspiracy under Chapter 9A.28 RCW, the presumptive sentence is determined by locating the sentencing grid sentence range defined by the appropriate offender score and the seriousness level of the crime, and multiplying the range by 75 percent.

In calculating an offender score, count each prior conviction as if the present conviction were for the completed offense. When these convictions are used as criminal history, score them the same as a completed offense.

SECTION 3 – Sentencing Guidelines

Anticipatory Offenses (VUCSA Attempts, Conspiracies, and Solicitations)

The calculation of sentences stemming from anticipatory VUCSA offenses (Chapter 69.50 RCW) presents different challenges than calculating sentences for anticipatory offenses arising under the criminal code.

An attempt or conspiracy to commit a VUCSA offense is specifically addressed in RCW 69.50.407, which provides that such offenses are punishable by "...imprisonment or fine or both which may not exceed the maximum punishment prescribed for the offense..." The appellate courts have consistently held that for VUCSA offenses, RCW 69.50.407 takes precedence over Chapter 9A.28 RCW. Although current statute and case law should be reviewed for definitive guidance in this area, the following summarizes current sentencing practices.

An attempt or conspiracy to commit a VUCSA offense is typically sentenced as an "unranked" offense (0-12 months). In State v. Mendoza, the Court of Appeals held that since "a conspiracy conviction under RCW 69.50.407 has no sentencing directions from the Legislature, it is punished under the unspecified crimes provisions of RCW 9.94A.505(2)(b)." 63 Wn. App. 373 (1991).

A *solicitation* to commit a VUCSA offense is not specifically addressed in Chapter 69.50 RCW. It is usually charged under Chapter 9A.28 RCW and sentenced under RCW 9.94A.510 at 75 percent of the standard range. Solicitations to commit VUCSA offenses are not considered "drug offenses", but do score as such and are subject to the multiple "scoring" requirement. See RCW 9.94A.525(4), (6) and State v. Howell, 102 Wn. App. 288, 6 P. 3d 1201 (2000).

Table 1 presents the current status of statute and case law on appropriate sentence ranges for anticipatory VUCSA offenses.

Table 1. Sentence Ranges for Anticipatory VUCSA Offenses

Offense Type	Sentence Range	Statute
Attempt**	Unranked (0 to 12)	RCW 69.50.407
Conspiracy**	Unranked (0 to 12)	RCW 69.50.407
Solicitation*	75% of Standard Range	RCW 9A.28.030

Relevant Statutes for VUCSA Offenses

Delivery Definition (RCW 69.50.101(g))

"Deliver" or "delivery" means the actual or constructive transfer from one person to another of a substance, whether or not there is an agency relationship.

The Caseload Forecast Council is not liable for errors or omissions in the manual, for sentences that may be inappropriately calculated as a result of a practitioner's or court's reliance on the manual, or for any other written or verbal information related to adult or juvenile sentencing. The scoring sheets are intended to provide assistance in most cases but do not cover all permutations of the scoring rules. If you find any errors or omissions, we encourage you to report them to the Caseload Forecast Council.

SECTION 3 – Sentencing Guidelines

Criminal Conspiracy (RCW 69.50.407)

Any person who attempts or conspires to commit any offense defined in this chapter is punishable by imprisonment or fine or both which may not exceed the maximum punishment prescribed for the offense, the commission of which was the object of the attempt or conspiracy.
[1971 ex.s. c 308 § 69.50.407.]

**Sentences (RCW 9.94A.505(2)(b))

If a standard sentence range has not been established for the offender's crime, the court shall impose a determinate sentence which may include not more than one year of confinement; community restitution work; a term of community custody under RCW 9.94A.702 not to exceed one year; and/or other legal financial obligations. The court may impose a sentence which provides more than one year of confinement and a community custody term under 9.94A.701 if the court finds reasons justifying an exceptional sentence as provided in RCW 9.94A.535.

Criminal Solicitation (RCW 9A.28.030)

1. A person is guilty of criminal solicitation when, with intent to promote or facilitate the commission of a crime, he offers to give or gives money or other thing of value to another to engage in specific conduct which would constitute such crime or which would establish complicity of such other person in its commission or attempted commission had such crime been attempted or committed.

2. Criminal solicitation shall be punished in the same manner as criminal attempt under RCW 9A.28.020.

*Solicitations drop one class from the underlying offense (e.g., a solicitation to commit a Class B felony is a Class C felony). Solicitations to commit Class C felonies are gross misdemeanors.

The Washington State Court of Appeals ruled that although solicitations to commit violations of Chapter 69.50 RCW are not considered drug offenses as defined in 9.94A.030, they do score as a drug offense. See State v. Howell, 102 Wn. App. 288, 6 P.3d 1201 (2000).

The Supreme Court clarified that solicitations to commit violations of the Uniform Controlled Substances Act (Chapter 69.50 RCW) are not "drug offenses" and are not subject to the community custody requirement for drug offenses, under RCW 9.94A.701 and 9.94A.702. See In re Hopkins, 137 Wn.2d 897 (1999).

The Caseload Forecast Council is not liable for errors or omissions in the manual, for sentences that may be inappropriately calculated as a result of a practitioner's or court's reliance on the manual, or for any other written or verbal information related to adult or juvenile sentencing. The scoring sheets are intended to provide assistance in most cases but do not cover all permutations of the scoring rules. If you find any errors or omissions, we encourage you to report them to the Caseload Forecast Council.

SECTION 3 – Sentencing Guidelines

SECOND OR SUBSEQUENT OFFENSE (RCW 69.50.408)

1. Any person convicted of a second or subsequent offense under this chapter may be imprisoned for a term up to twice the term otherwise authorized, fined an amount up to twice that otherwise authorized, or both.

2. For purposes of this section, an offense is considered a second or subsequent offense, if, prior to his or her conviction of the offense, the offender has at any time been convicted under this chapter or under any statute of the United States or of any state relating to narcotic drugs, marijuana, depressant, stimulant, or hallucinogenic drugs.

3. This section does not apply to offenses under RCW 69.50.4013.
[2003 c 53 § 341; 1989 c 8 § 3; 1971 ex.s. c 308 §69.50.408 .]

TERMS OF CONFINEMENT

Standard Range Sentence

The sentencing grid prescribes the standard sentence range for most of the commonly charged felonies. RCW 9.94A.599 provides that if the presumptive sentence duration given in the sentencing grid exceeds the statutory maximum sentence for the offense, the statutory maximum sentence shall be the presumptive sentence.

The ranges in the sentencing grid are expressed in terms of total confinement. A term of confinement of one year and one day (12+), or a sentence under the Drug Offender Sentencing Alternative or Family Offender Sentencing Alternative, is to be served in a state facility or institution. In addition, any sex offense sentenced under RCW 9.94A.507 of one year or less will be served in a state facility or institution. A term of one year or less (other than those described above) is to be served in a county facility unless, when combined with other felony terms, the total time to be served exceeds one year (RCW 9.94A.190). A court may convert total confinement sentences to partial confinement or community service for some offenders. Offenders who have received a sentence greater than one year, and who also have received another sentence less than one year are required to serve the entire period of time in a state facility or institution.

"Unranked" Offenses

Offenders convicted of "unranked crimes," crimes without an established seriousness level, are not subject to standard sentence ranges. In such cases, courts are required to impose a determinate sentence which may include zero to 365 days of confinement and may also include community service, legal financial

SECTION 3 – Sentencing Guidelines

obligations, a term of community custody not to exceed one year and/or a fine. Orders of confinement longer than one year constitute exceptional sentences, which must be justified in writing. RCW 9.94A.505(2)(b); RCW 9.94A.535.

Persistent Offenders

Voters approved Initiative 593 ("Three Strikes and You're Out") in 1993. The law, which became effective on December 2, 1993, established the penalty of life in prison without the possibility of release for "persistent offenders." The life sentence applies to both "Three Strike" and "Two Strike" offenders.

"Three Strikes"

The original "Three Strikes" legislation defined a "persistent offender" as an offender who is convicted of a "most serious offense" and who has at least two prior convictions for most serious offenses that would be included in the offender score under 9.94A.525. In order to be applicable to the three strikes statute, the first prior conviction must have occurred before the second prior conviction offense was committed. See Section 5, page 73 for a list of the "most serious offenses" as defined by RCW 9.94A.030(33).

"Two Strikes"

The definition of persistent offender also includes "Two Strike" sex offenders. To qualify as a persistent sex offender, an offender must have two separate convictions of specified sex offenses. The 1997 Legislature broadened the list of offenses that qualify as strikes under the "Two Strikes" law. The specific offenses qualifying as "Two Strikes" are enumerated in the "persistent offender" definition in RCW 9.94A.030(38)(b) and can be found in Section 5, page 76.

An offender convicted of one of these offenses, who has at least one previous conviction for one of these offenses, must be sentenced to life in prison without the possibility of release.

Non-Persistent Sex Offenders (Determinate-Plus)

During the 2001 Second Special Session, the Legislature enacted 3ESSB 6151 – The Management of Sex Offenders in the Civil Commitment and Criminal Justice Systems. The resulting "non-persistent offender" system is also called "determinate-plus", but it is an indeterminate sentence. An offender must be sentenced to an indeterminate term if he or she is not a persistent offender but:

- is sentenced for any of the "two strike" offenses listed in Section 5, page 76; or
- is sentenced for any sex offense, except failure to register, and has a prior conviction for a "two-strike" offense.

The Caseload Forecast Council is not liable for errors or omissions in the manual, for sentences that may be inappropriately calculated as a result of a practitioner's or court's reliance on the manual, or for any other written or verbal information related to adult or juvenile sentencing. The scoring sheets are intended to provide assistance in most cases but do not cover all permutations of the scoring rules. If you find any errors or omissions, we encourage you to report them to the Caseload Forecast Council.

SECTION 3 – Sentencing Guidelines

This sentencing rule does not apply to offenders seventeen years old or younger at the time of the offense and who have been convicted of Rape of a Child in the First Degree, Rape of a Child in the Second Degree or Child Molestation in the First Degree.

A "determinate-plus" sentence must contain a minimum term of confinement that falls within the standard range, according to the seriousness level of the offense and the offender score, and a maximum term equaling the statutory maximum sentence for the offense. The minimum term may also constitute an exceptional sentence as provided by RCW 9.94A.535. A "determinate-plus" offender is eligible for earned release pursuant to RCW 9.94A.728 and is given the opportunity to receive sex offender treatment while incarcerated. Some "determinate-plus" offenders are eligible for the Special Sex Offender Sentencing Alternative as provided in RCW 9.94A.670, unless they have committed Rape in the First Degree, Rape in the Second Degree or any of the following offenses with sexual motivation: Murder in the First Degree, Murder in the Second Degree, Homicide by Abuse, Kidnapping in the First Degree, Kidnapping in the Second Degree, Assault in the First Degree, Assault in the Second Degree, Assault of a Child in the First Degree, Assault of a Child in the Second Degree or Burglary in the First Degree. Additionally, all sentences under this provision must be served in prison, regardless of the sentence length.

Offenders given "determinate plus" sentences fall under the purview of the Indeterminate Sentence Review Board through the maximum term of the sentence. Those released from prison will be supervised by the Department of Corrections and will remain on community custody through the maximum term of the sentence.

EXCEPTIONAL SENTENCES

The standard sentence range is presumed to be appropriate for the *typical* felony case. The SRA, per RCW 9.94A.535, however, provides that the court "may impose a sentence outside the standard sentence range for that offense if it finds, considering the purpose of this chapter, that there are substantial and compelling reasons justifying an exceptional sentence."

An exceptional sentence must be for a determinate term and cannot exceed the statutory maximum for the crime. An exceptional sentence cannot include a term less than a mandatory minimum term of confinement if one exists. RCW 9.94A.540 sets a mandatory minimum term of confinement for certain offenses. RCW 10.95.030 sets a lifetime imprisonment term for Aggravated Murder in the First Degree. Per RCW 9.94A.570's terms, persistent offenders sentenced to life in prison are not eligible for exceptional sentences.

Pursuant to the United States Supreme Court, before a court is permitted to impose sentences above the standard range, "[o]ther than the fact of a prior conviction, any fact that increases the penalty for a crime beyond the prescribed statutory maximum must be submitted to a jury, and proved beyond a reasonable doubt." Blakely v. Washington, 542 U.S. 296, 124 S.Ct. 2531, 159 L.Ed.2d 403 (2004).

If an exceptional sentence is given, the sentencing court is required to set forth the reasons for the departure from the standard range (RCW 9.94A.535) or from the consecutive/concurrent policy (RCW 9.94A.589(1)

The Caseload Forecast Council is not liable for errors or omissions in the manual, for sentences that may be inappropriately calculated as a result of a practitioner's or court's reliance on the manual, or for any other written or verbal information related to adult or juvenile sentencing. The scoring sheets are intended to provide assistance in most cases but do not cover all permutations of the scoring rules. If you find any errors or omissions, we encourage you to report them to the Caseload Forecast Council.

SECTION 3 – Sentencing Guidelines

and (2)) in written Findings of Fact and Conclusions of Law. Exceptional sentences may be appealed by the offender or by the state.

RCW 9.94A.535 provides a list of factors that the court may consider in deciding whether to impose an exceptional sentence.

Mitigating Circumstances for Exceptional Sentences

Mitigating circumstances justifying a sentence below the standard range can found in RCW 9.94A.535(1). The circumstances on this list are provided as examples only. It is not intended to be an exclusive list of reasons for a departure below the standard range.

Aggravating Circumstances for Exceptional Sentences

Unlike mitigating circumstances, an exceptional sentence that is aggravated must be based on one or more of the circumstances listed in the statute. The list is not illustrative.

The court may impose an aggravated exceptional sentence *without* a finding of fact by a jury if the defendant and state both stipulate that justice is best served by an exceptional sentence and the court agrees that the stipulation is in the interest of justice and consistent with the Sentencing Reform Act under RCW 9.94A.535(2).

The court may also impose an exceptional sentence above the standard range if the procedures specified in RCW 9.94A.537 are followed and a jury makes findings of fact supporting any of the aggravating circumstances found in RCW 9.94A.535(3).

CONSECUTIVE AND CONCURRENT SENTENCES

RCW 9.94A.589 sets forth the rules regarding consecutive and concurrent sentences. Generally, sentences for multiple offenses set at one sentencing hearing are served concurrently unless there are two or more separate serious violent offenses or weapon offenses. In those cases, the sentences are served consecutively, unless an exceptional sentence is entered. (RCW 9.94A.589(1)(a)). The exceptions to this general rule are as follows:

Offenses that Constitute Same Criminal Conduct

If the court enters a finding that some or all of the current offenses required the same criminal intent, were committed at the same time and place, and involved the same victim, the offenses are treated as one offense. RCW 9.94A.589(1)(a). A departure from this rule requires an exceptional sentence. (RCW 9.94A.535).

The Caseload Forecast Council is not liable for errors or omissions in the manual, for sentences that may be inappropriately calculated as a result of a practitioner's or court's reliance on the manual, or for any other written or verbal information related to adult or juvenile sentencing. The scoring sheets are intended to provide assistance in most cases but do not cover all permutations of the scoring rules. If you find any errors or omissions, we encourage you to report them to the Caseload Forecast Council.

SECTION 3 – Sentencing Guidelines

Multiple Serious Violent Offenses

In the case of two or more serious violent offenses arising from separate and distinct criminal conduct, the sentences for these serious violent offenses are served consecutively to each other and concurrently with any other sentences imposed for current offenses (RCW 9.94A.589(1)(b)). A departure from this rule requires an exceptional sentence. (RCW 9.94A.535).

Certain Firearm-Related Offenses

In the case of an offender convicted of Unlawful Possession of a Firearm in the First or Second Degree *and* for one or both of the crimes of Theft of a Firearm or Possession of a Stolen Firearm, the sentences for these crimes are served consecutively for each conviction of the felony crimes listed and for each firearm unlawfully possessed[11]. (RCW 9.94A.589(1)(c)). A departure from this rule requires an exceptional sentence. (RCW 9.94A.535).

Felony DUI/Felony APC

All sentences imposed under RCW 46.61.502(6), RCW 46.61.504(6) and RCW 46.61.5055(4) shall be served consecutively to any sentences imposed under RCW 46.20.740 and RCW 46.20.750. (RCW 9.94A.589(1)(d)). Additionally, under RCW 46.20.740 and RCW 46.20.750, any sentences imposed under RCW 46.20.740 and RCW 46.20.750 shall be served consecutively to each other, as well as consecutively to RCW 46.61.502(6), RCW 46.61.504(6) or RCW 46.61.5055(4).

Under RCW 46.20.750, any sentences imposed under RCW 46.20.750 shall be served consecutively with any sentence imposed under RCW 46.61.520(1)(a) or RCW 46.61.522(1)(b). However, this is not codified under RCW 9.94A.589.

Weapon Enhancements

In the case of an offender receiving a deadly weapon enhancement for offenses committed after July 23, 1995, the deadly weapon enhancement portion of the standard range is served consecutively to all other sentencing provisions, including other firearm or deadly weapon enhancements (RCW 9.94A.533). A departure from this rule requires an exceptional sentence (RCW 9.94A.535).

Felony Committed While Offender was Under Sentence for Another Felony

Whenever a current offense is committed while the offender is under sentence for a previous felony and the offender was also sentenced for another term of imprisonment, the latter term may not begin until expiration

---

[11] Part of Initiative 159. Effective for offenses committed after July 23, 1995 (RCW 9.41.040(6))

The Caseload Forecast Council is not liable for errors or omissions in the manual, for sentences that may be inappropriately calculated as a result of a practitioner's or court's reliance on the manual, or for any other written or verbal information related to adult or juvenile sentencing. The scoring sheets are intended to provide assistance in most cases but do not cover all permutations of the scoring rules. If you find any errors or omissions, we encourage you to report them to the Caseload Forecast Council.

SECTION 3 – Sentencing Guidelines

of all prior terms (RCW 9.94A.589(2)). A departure from this rule requires an exceptional sentence (RCW 9.94A.535).

Felonies Committed While Offender was not Under Sentence for Another Felony

This rule applies when offenders face multiple charges or have multiple convictions from different jurisdictions. Subject to the above policies, whenever a person is sentenced under a felony that was committed while the person was *not* under sentence for a felony, the sentence runs concurrently with felony sentences previously imposed by any court in this or another state or by a federal court, unless the court pronouncing the subsequent sentence expressly orders that they be served consecutively (RCW 9.94A.589(3)).

Probation Revocation

Whenever any person granted probation under RCW 9.95.210 or RCW 9.92.060, or both, has a probationary sentence revoked and a prison sentence imposed, this sentence runs consecutively to any sentence imposed, unless the court pronouncing the subsequent sentence expressly orders that they be served concurrently (RCW 9.94A.589(4)). This rule applies when an offender's pre-Sentencing Reform Act case probation is revoked and he or she is also sentenced on a conviction for a crime committed after June 30, 1984, the inception date of the SRA.

Serving Total Confinement with Consecutive Sentences

In the case of consecutive sentences, all periods of total confinement must be served before any periods of partial confinement, community service, community supervision or any other requirement or condition of a sentence (RCW 9.94A.589(5)). This rule applies to offenders who have not completed their sentence requirements from a previous conviction and are sentenced to total confinement on a new offense. A departure from this rule requires an exceptional sentence (RCW 9.94A.535).

LIMITS ON EARNED RELEASE

RCW 9.94A.728 provides that an offender's sentence may be reduced by "earned release time." This time is earned through good behavior and good performance, as determined by the correctional agency that has jurisdiction over the offender. An offender can accumulate "earned release time" while serving a sentence and during pre-sentence incarceration.

The state Legislature passed ESSB 5990 during the 2003 Legislative Session. The legislation amended RCW 9.94A.728, in part, to increase earned release time for good behavior up to fifty (50) percent of a sentence. The increase became effective July 1, 2003. The right to earn early release time at the rate of 50 percent does not apply to offenders convicted after July 1, 2010.

The Caseload Forecast Council is not liable for errors or omissions in the manual, for sentences that may be inappropriately calculated as a result of a practitioner's or court's reliance on the manual, or for any other written or verbal information related to adult or juvenile sentencing. The scoring sheets are intended to provide assistance in most cases but do not cover all permutations of the scoring rules. If you find any errors or omissions, we encourage you to report them to the Caseload Forecast Council.

SECTION 3 – Sentencing Guidelines

Offenders convicted of a serious violent offense or a sex offense that is a Class A felony committed between July 1, 1990, and July 1, 2003, are prohibited from earning release time in excess of fifteen (15) percent. Offenders committing these offenses on or after July 1, 2003, will not earn release time credit in excess of ten (10) percent.

In the case of an offender sentenced pursuant to RCW 10.95.030(3) or RCW 10.95.035, the offender may not receive any earned release time during the minimum term of confinement imposed by the court; for any remaining portion of the sentence served by the offender, the aggregate earned release time may not exceed 10% of the sentence.

Offenders sentenced under the Special Sex Offender Sentencing Alternative are not eligible to accrue any earned release time while serving a suspended sentence.

An offender may not receive any earned release time for that portion of a sentence that results from any firearm and/or deadly weapon enhancements.

Finally, no matter how much release time has been earned under RCW 9.94A.728, an offender sentenced for a crime that has a mandatory minimum sentence shall not be released from total confinement before the completion of the mandatory minimum for that crime unless allowable under RCW 9.94A.540.

REVIEW OF SENTENCES

Sentences within the standard range cannot be appealed. (RCW 9.94A.585). These include sentences imposed pursuant to the First-Time Offender provisions found in RCW 9.94A.650. Sentences outside the standard range may be appealed by the defendant or by the prosecutor.

Review is limited to the record made before the sentencing court. Pending review, the sentencing court or the Court of Appeals may order the defendant confined or placed on condition release, including bond.

Before reversing a sentence that is outside the sentence range, the Court of Appeals must find that:

- the reasons supplied by the sentencing judge were not supported by the record; or
- they do not justify a sentence outside the range; or
- the sentence imposed was clearly excessive or clearly too lenient.

The Department of Corrections may request a review of a sentence committing an offender to the custody or jurisdiction of the department. This review must be limited to errors of law and must be filed with the court of Appeals no later than 90 days after the department has actual knowledge of the term of the sentence. The department must certify that all reasonable efforts to resolve the dispute at the Superior Court level have been exhausted.

The Caseload Forecast Council is not liable for errors or omissions in the manual, for sentences that may be inappropriately calculated as a result of a practitioner's or court's reliance on the manual, or for any other written or verbal information related to adult or juvenile sentencing. The scoring sheets are intended to provide assistance in most cases but do not cover all permutations of the scoring rules. If you find any errors or omissions, we encourage you to report them to the Caseload Forecast Council.

SECTION 3 – Sentencing Guidelines

A person convicted of one or more crimes committed prior to the person's eighteenth birthday may petition the ISRB for early release after serving no less than 20 years of total confinement (RCW 9.94A.730(1)), provided the person has not been convicted for any crime committed subsequent to the person's eighteenth birthday, the person has not committed a major violation in the twelve months prior to filing the petition for early release, and the current sentence was not imposed under RCW 10.95.030 or RCW 9.94A.507.

RCW 10.95.030 mandates that any person who was sentenced prior to June 1, 2014, to a term of life without the possibility of parole for an offense committed prior to their eighteenth birthday, shall be returned to the sentencing court or the sentencing court's successor for sentencing consistent with RCW 10.95.030.

VIOLATION OF COMMUNITY CUSTODY CONDITIONS

An offender who violates any condition or requirement of a sentence **may be sanctioned by the court with up to sixty days'** confinement for each violation or **by the department with up to thirty days'** confinement as provided in RCW 9.94A.737.

Any time served in confinement awaiting the violation hearing must be credited against any confinement order. If a court finds that a violation was not willful, the court may dismiss the violation and regarding payment of legal financial obligations and community service obligations or modify its previous order. In all cases of community custody escape, escape charges may also be filed, if appropriate.

These rules and procedures apply retroactively and prospectively regardless of the date of an offender's underlying offense.

Arrest and Confinement (RCW 9.94A.631)

If an offender violates any condition or requirement of a sentence, a community corrections officer may arrest or cause the arrest of the offender without a warrant, pending a determination by the court or by the department. If there is reasonable cause to believe that an offender has violated a condition or requirement of the sentence, a community corrections officer may require an offender to submit to a search and seizure of the offender's person, residence, automobile, or other personal property.

For the safety and security of department staff, an offender may be required to submit to pat searches, or other limited security searches, by community corrections officers, correctional officers, and other agency approved staff, without reasonable cause, when in or on department premises, grounds, or facilities, or while preparing to enter department premises, grounds, facilities, or vehicles. Pat searches of offenders shall be conducted only by staff who are the same gender as the offender, except in emergency situations.

A community corrections officer may also arrest an offender for any crime committed in his or her presence. The facts and circumstances of the conduct of the offender shall be reported by the community corrections officer, with recommendations, to the court, local law enforcement, or local prosecution for consideration of

SECTION 3 – Sentencing Guidelines

new charges. The community corrections officer's report shall serve as the notice that the department will hold the offender for not more than three days from the time of such notice for the new crime, except if the offender's underlying offense is a felony offense listed in RCW 9.94A.737(5), in which case the department will hold the offender for thirty days from the time of arrest or until a prosecuting attorney charges the offender with a crime, whichever occurs first. This does not affect the department's authority under RCW 9.94A.737.

If a community corrections officer arrests or causes the arrest of an offender under this section, the offender shall be confined and detained in the county jail of the county in which the offender was taken into custody, and the sheriff of that county shall receive and keep in the county jail, where room is available, all prisoners delivered to the jail by the community corrections officer, and such offenders shall not be released from custody on bail or personal recognizance, except upon approval of the court or authorized department staff, pursuant to a written order.

Sanctions and Procedures (RCW 9.94A.633)

An offender who violates any condition or requirement of a sentence may be sanctioned by the court with up to sixty days' confinement for each violation or by the department with up to thirty days' confinement as provided in RCW 9.94A.737.

In lieu of confinement, an offender may be sanctioned with work release, home detention with electronic monitoring, work crew, community restitution, inpatient treatment, daily reporting, curfew, educational or counseling sessions, supervision enhanced through electronic monitoring, or any other community-based sanctions.

1. If an offender was under community custody pursuant to one of the following statutes, the offender may be sanctioned as follows:
    a. If the offender was transferred to community custody in lieu of earned early release in accordance with RCW 9.94A.728, the offender may be transferred to a more restrictive confinement status to serve up to the remaining portion of the sentence, less credit for any period actually spent in community custody or in detention awaiting disposition of an alleged violation.
    b. If the offender was sentenced under the drug offender sentencing alternative set out in RCW 9.94A.660, the offender may be sanctioned in accordance with that section.
    c. If the offender was sentenced under the parenting sentencing alternative set out in RCW 9.94A.655, the offender may be sanctioned in accordance with that section.
    d. If the offender was sentenced under the special sex offender sentencing alternative set out in RCW 9.94A.670, the suspended sentence may be revoked and the offender committed to serve the original sentence of confinement.
    e. If the offender was sentenced to a work ethic camp pursuant to RCW 9.94A.690, the offender may be reclassified to serve the unexpired term of his or her sentence in total confinement.
    f. If a sex offender was sentenced pursuant to RCW 9.94A.507, the offender may be transferred to a more restrictive confinement status to serve up to the remaining portion of the sentence,

SECTION 3 – Sentencing Guidelines

less credit for any period actually spent in community custody or in detention awaiting disposition of an alleged violation.

If a probationer is being supervised by the department pursuant to RCW 9.92.060, 9.95.204, or 9.95.210, the probationer may be sanctioned pursuant to subsection (1) of this section. The department shall have authority to issue a warrant for the arrest of an offender who violates a condition of community custody, as provided in RCW 9.94A.716. Any sanctions shall be imposed by the department pursuant to RCW 9.94A.737. Nothing in this subsection is intended to limit the power of the sentencing court to respond to a probationer's violation of conditions.

2. The parole or probation of an offender who is charged with a new felony offense may be suspended and the offender placed in total confinement pending disposition of the new criminal charges if:

    a. The offender is on parole pursuant to RCW 9.95.110(1); or
    b. The offender is being supervised pursuant to RCW 9.94A.745 and is on parole or probation pursuant to the laws of another state.

Sanctions – Where Served (RCW 9.94A.6331)

1. If a sanction of confinement is imposed by the court, the following applies:
    a. If the sanction was imposed pursuant to RCW 9.94A.633(1), the sanction shall be served in a county facility.
    b. If the sanction was imposed pursuant to RCW 9.94A.633(2), the sanction shall be served in a state facility.
    c. If a sanction of confinement is imposed by the department, and if the offender is an inmate as defined by RCW 72.09.015, no more than eight days of the sanction, including any credit for time served, may be served in a county facility. The balance of the sanction shall be served in a state facility. In computing the eight-day period, weekends and holidays shall be excluded. The department may negotiate with local correctional authorities for an additional period of detention.
    d. If a sanction of confinement is imposed by the board, it shall be served in a state facility.
    e. Sanctions imposed pursuant to RCW 9.94A.670(3) shall be served in a county facility.

    As used in this section, "county facility" means a facility operated, licensed, or utilized under contract by the county, and "state facility" means a facility operated, licensed, or utilized under contract by the state.

SECTION 3 – Sentencing Guidelines

Sanctions – Which Entity Imposes (RCW 9.94A.6332)

1. The procedure for imposing sanctions for violations of sentence conditions or requirements is as follows:
   a. If the offender was sentenced under the drug offender sentencing alternative, any sanctions shall be imposed by the department or the court pursuant to RCW *9.94A.660*.
   b. If the offender was sentenced under the special sex offender sentencing alternative, any sanctions shall be imposed by the department or the court pursuant to RCW *9.94A.670*.
   c. If the offender was sentenced under the parenting sentencing alternative, any sanctions shall be imposed by the department or by the court pursuant to RCW 9.94A.655.
   d. If a sex offender was sentenced pursuant to RCW 9.94A.507, any sanctions shall be imposed by the board pursuant to RCW 9.95.435.
   e. If the offender was released pursuant to RCW 9.94A.730, any sanctions shall be imposed by the board pursuant to RCW 9.95.435.
   f. If the offender was sentenced pursuant to RCW 10.95.030(3) or 10.95.035, any sanctions shall be imposed by the board pursuant to RCW 9.95.435.
   g. In any other case, if the offender is being supervised by the department, any sanctions shall be imposed by the department pursuant to RCW 9.94A.737. If a probationer is being supervised by the department pursuant to RCW 9.92.060, 9.95.204, or 9.95.210, upon receipt of a violation hearing report from the department, the court retains any authority that those statutes provide to respond to a probationer's violation of conditions.
   h. If the offender is not being supervised by the department, any sanctions shall be imposed by the court pursuant to RCW 9.94A.6333.

Sanctions – Modification of Sentence (RCW 9.94A.6333)

If an offender violates any condition or requirement of a sentence, and the offender is not being supervised by the department, the court may modify its order of judgment and sentence and impose further punishment in accordance with this section.

1. If an offender fails to comply with any of the conditions or requirements of a sentence the following provisions apply:
   a. The court, upon the motion of the state, or upon its own motion, shall require the offender to show cause why the offender should not be punished for the noncompliance. The court may issue a summons or a warrant of arrest for the offender's appearance;
   b. The state has the burden of showing noncompliance by a preponderance of the evidence;
   c. If the court finds that a violation has been proved,
      i. it may impose the sanctions specified in RCW *9.94A.633*(1).
      ii. Alternatively, the court may:
         a. Convert a term of partial confinement to total confinement;
         b. Convert community restitution obligation to total or partial confinement; or

SECTION 3 – Sentencing Guidelines

      c. Convert monetary obligations, except restitution and the crime victim penalty assessment, to community restitution hours at the rate of the state minimum wage as established in RCW 49.46.020 for each hour of community restitution;
2. If the court finds that the violation was not willful, the court may modify its previous order regarding payment of legal financial obligations and regarding community restitution obligations; and
3. If the violation involves a failure to undergo or comply with a mental health status evaluation and/or outpatient mental health treatment, the court shall seek a recommendation from the treatment provider or proposed treatment provider.

Enforcement of orders concerning outpatient mental health treatment must reflect the availability of treatment and must pursue the least restrictive means of promoting participation in treatment. If the offender's failure to receive care essential for health and safety presents a risk of serious physical harm or probable harmful consequences, the civil detention and commitment procedures of chapter 71.05 RCW shall be considered in preference to incarceration in a local or state correctional facility.

Any time served in confinement awaiting a hearing on noncompliance shall be credited against any confinement ordered by the court.

Nothing in this section prohibits the filing of escape charges if appropriate.

DOC Structured Violation Process (RCW 9.94A.737)

If an offender is accused of violating any condition or requirement of community custody, the Department of Corrections (DOC) shall address the violation behavior. The department may hold offender disciplinary proceedings not subject to chapter 34.05 RCW. The department shall notify the offender in writing of the violation process.

1. The offender's violation behavior shall determine the sanction the department imposes.

    a. The department shall adopt rules creating a structured violation process that includes presumptive sanctions, aggravating and mitigating factors, and definitions for low level violations and high level violations.
    b. After an offender has committed and been sanctioned for five low level violations, all subsequent violations committed by that offender shall automatically be considered high level violations.
    c. The department must define aggravating factors that indicate the offender may present a current and ongoing foreseeable risk, which elevates an offender's behavior to a high level violation process.
    d. The state and its officers, agents, and employees may not be held criminally or civilly liable for a decision to elevate or not to elevate an offender's behavior to a high level violation process under this subsection unless the state or its officers, agents, and employees acted with reckless disregard.

The Caseload Forecast Council is not liable for errors or omissions in the manual, for sentences that may be inappropriately calculated as a result of a practitioner's or court's reliance on the manual, or for any other written or verbal information related to adult or juvenile sentencing. The scoring sheets are intended to provide assistance in most cases but do not cover all permutations of the scoring rules. If you find any errors or omissions, we encourage you to report them to the Caseload Forecast Council.

SECTION 3 – Sentencing Guidelines

The department may intervene when an offender commits a low level violation as follows.

1. For a first low-level violation, the department may sanction the offender to one or more non-confinement sanctions.
2. For a second or subsequent low-level violation, the department may sanction the offender to not more than three days in total confinement.
3. The department shall develop rules to ensure that each offender subject to a short-term confinement sanction is provided the opportunity to respond to the alleged violation prior to imposition of total confinement.
4. The offender may appeal the short-term confinement sanction to a panel of three reviewing officers designated by the secretary or by the secretary's designee. The offender's appeal must be in writing and hand-delivered to department staff, or postmarked within seven days after the sanction is imposed.

If an offender is accused of committing a high-level violation, the department may sanction the offender to not more than thirty days in total confinement per hearing.

1. The offender is entitled to a hearing prior to the imposition of sanctions; and
2. The offender may be held in total confinement pending a sanction hearing. Prehearing time served must be credited to the offender's sanction time.
3. If the offender's underlying offense is one of the following felonies and the violation behavior constitutes a new misdemeanor, gross misdemeanor, or felony, the offender shall be held in total confinement, pending a sanction hearing, until the sanction expires, or a prosecuting attorney files new charges against the offender, whichever occurs first:

    (a) Assault in the first degree, as defined in RCW 9A.36.011;
    (b) Assault of a child in the first degree, as defined in RCW 9A.36.120;
    (c) Assault of a child in the second degree, as defined in RCW 9A.36.130;
    (d) Burglary in the first degree, as defined in RCW 9A.52.020;
    (e) Child molestation in the first degree, as defined in RCW 9A.44.083;
    (f) Commercial sexual abuse of a minor, as defined in RCW 9.68A.100;
    (g) Dealing in depictions of a minor engaged in sexually explicit conduct, as defined in RCW 9.68A.050;
    (h) Homicide by abuse, as defined in RCW 9A.32.055;
    (i) Indecent liberties with forcible compulsion, as defined in RCW 9A.44.100(1)(a);
    (j) Indecent liberties with a person capable of consent, as defined in RCW 9A.44.100(1)(b);
    (k) Kidnapping in the first degree, as defined in RCW 9A.40.020;
    (l) Murder in the first degree, as defined in RCW 9A.32.030;
    (m) Murder in the second degree, as defined in RCW 9A.32.050;
    (n) Promoting commercial sexual abuse of a minor, as defined in RCW 9.68A.101;
    (o) Rape in the first degree, as defined in RCW 9A.44.040;
    (p) Rape in the second degree, as defined in RCW 9A.44.050;
    (q) Rape of a child in the first degree, as defined in RCW 9A.44.073;
    (r) Rape of a child in the second degree, as defined in RCW 9A.44.076;
    (s) Robbery in the first degree, as defined in RCW 9A.56.200;

The Caseload Forecast Council is not liable for errors or omissions in the manual, for sentences that may be inappropriately calculated as a result of a practitioner's or court's reliance on the manual, or for any other written or verbal information related to adult or juvenile sentencing. The scoring sheets are intended to provide assistance in most cases but do not cover all permutations of the scoring rules. If you find any errors or omissions, we encourage you to report them to the Caseload Forecast Council.

SECTION 3 – Sentencing Guidelines

    (t) Sexual exploitation of a minor, as defined in RCW 9.68A.040; or
    (u) Vehicular homicide while under the influence of intoxicating liquor or any drug, as defined in RCW 46.61.520(1)(a).

The department shall adopt rules creating hearing procedures for high-level violations. The hearings are offender disciplinary proceedings and are not subject to chapter 34.05 RCW.

1. The procedures shall include the following:
   a. The department shall provide the offender with written notice of the alleged violation and the evidence supporting it. The notice must include a statement of the rights specified in this subsection, and the offender's right to file a personal restraint petition under court rules after the final decision.
   b. Unless the offender waives the right to a hearing, the department shall hold a hearing, and shall record it electronically. For offenders not in total confinement, the department shall hold a hearing within fifteen business days, but not less than twenty-four hours, after written notice of the alleged violation. For offenders in total confinement, the department shall hold a hearing within five business days, but not less than twenty-four hours, after written notice of the alleged violation;
   c. The offender shall have the right to:
      i. Be present at the hearing;
      ii. Have the assistance of a person qualified to assist the offender in the hearing; appointed by the hearing officer if the offender has a language or communications barrier;
      iii. Testify or remain silent;
      iv. Call witnesses and present documentary evidence;
      v. Question witnesses who appear and testify; and
      vi. Receive a written summary of the reasons for the hearing officer's decision.

The hearings officer may not rely on unconfirmed or unconfirmable allegations to find that the offender violated a condition.

DISCHARGE AND VACATION OF CONVICTION RECORD

Discharge

When an offender reaches the end of supervision with the Department of Corrections, and has completed all of the requirements of sentence except payment of legal financial obligations, the department shall notify the county clerk who will then supervise payment of legal financial obligations.

When an offender completes all of his or her sentence requirements, the department (or the county clerk, if the clerk has been supervising payment of legal financial obligations) must notify the sentencing court in accordance with RCW 9.94A.637.

The Caseload Forecast Council is not liable for errors or omissions in the manual, for sentences that may be inappropriately calculated as a result of a practitioner's or court's reliance on the manual, or for any other written or verbal information related to adult or juvenile sentencing. The scoring sheets are intended to provide assistance in most cases but do not cover all permutations of the scoring rules. If you find any errors or omissions, we encourage you to report them to the Caseload Forecast Council.

SECTION 3 – Sentencing Guidelines

If an offender is not subject to supervision by the department or does not complete all of his sentence requirements while under department supervision, it is the offender's responsibility to provide the court with verification of the completion of sentence conditions other than the payment of legal financial obligations.

When the court has adequate notice from the department, the court clerk, and/or the offender, the court then discharges the offender and provides him or her with a certificate of discharge. This certificate restores all civil rights lost upon conviction. It is not, however, based on a finding of rehabilitation.

Every signed certificate and order of discharge shall be filed with the county clerk of the sentencing county. The court shall also send a copy of the certificate and order to the department. The county clerk shall also enter the offender's name, date of discharge and date of conviction and offense, into the database maintained by the Administrative Office of the Courts.

Following discharge, the offender's prior record may be used to determine the sentence for any later convictions and may also be used in later criminal prosecution as an element of an offense or for impeachment purposes. Unless specifically ordered by the sentencing court, the certificate of discharge will not terminate the offender's obligation to comply with an order issued under Chapter 10.99 RCW that excludes or prohibits the offender from having contact with a specified person or coming within a set distance of any specified location that was contained in the judgment and sentence. Offenders may still be prosecuted for violating any such provisions.

An offender who is not convicted of a violent offense or a sex offense and is sentenced to a term of community supervision may be considered for a discharge of sentence by the sentencing court prior to the completion of community supervision, provided that the offender has completed at least one-half of the term of community supervision and has met all other sentence requirements.

Upon release from custody, the offender may apply to the department for counseling and help in adjusting to the community. The voluntary help may be provided for up to one year following the release from custody.

Vacation of Conviction Record

Every offender discharged under the above provision may apply to the sentencing court for a vacation of the conviction record as provided in RCW 9.94A.640. The offender's record cannot be cleared if:

- Any criminal charges are pending against the offender in any court in this state, another state, or federal court;
- The offense was a violent offense (as defined in RCW 9.94A.030);
- The offense was a crime against children or other persons (as defined in RCW 43.43.830);
- The offender has been convicted of a new crime in this state, another state, or federal court since the date of the offender's discharge;
- The offense was a Class B felony, and less than ten years have passed since the date the applicant was discharged;

The Caseload Forecast Council is not liable for errors or omissions in the manual, for sentences that may be inappropriately calculated as a result of a practitioner's or court's reliance on the manual, or for any other written or verbal information related to adult or juvenile sentencing. The scoring sheets are intended to provide assistance in most cases but do not cover all permutations of the scoring rules. If you find any errors or omissions, we encourage you to report them to the Caseload Forecast Council.

SECTION 3 – Sentencing Guidelines

- The offense was a Class C felony, other than felony Driving Under the Influence of Intoxicating Liquor or any Drug or felony Physical Control While Under the Influence of Intoxicating Liquor or any Drug and less than five years have passed since the date the applicant was discharged; or
- The offense was felony Driving Under the Influence of Intoxicating Liquor or any Drug or felony Physical Control While Under the Influence of Intoxicating Liquor or any Drug.

If the offender meets these tests, the court may clear the record of conviction by:

- Permitting the offender to withdraw his/her guilty plea and to enter a plea of not guilty; or
- Setting aside the guilty verdict, if the offender was convicted after a plea of not guilty; and
- Dismissing the information or indictment against the offender.

Once the court vacates a record of conviction, the offender's conviction may not be included in the offender's criminal history for purposes of determining a sentence in any subsequent conviction, and the offender must be released from all penalties and disabilities resulting from the offenses. For all purposes, including responding to questions on employment applications, an offender whose record of conviction has been vacated may state that he or she has never been convicted of that crime. However, a vacated conviction record may be used as an element of a crime in a later criminal prosecution.

The sentencing guidelines allow automatic "wash-out" of prior convictions that meet the requirements of vacation of conviction. This policy allows offenders who do not formally apply to the court to have eligible offenses excluded from their criminal history in subsequent convictions. (See Determining Offender Score, Criminal History Collection in this section for further discussion of this policy.)

ALTERNATIVES TO CONFINEMENT

Alternative Conversions

The sentencing grid ranges are expressed in terms of total confinement (RCW 9.94A.530). For certain offenders, a court may convert terms of total confinement to partial confinement or to community service. This provision allows courts to take advantage of available alternatives to confinement in cases where it is deemed appropriate. *If the court does not use an alternative conversion for a nonviolent offense with a sentence range of one year or less, the reason why must be stated on the Judgment and Sentence form (RCW 9.94A.680).*

The 1999 Legislature modified the requirements for offenders convicted of **non-violent or non-sex** offenses with a sentence of one year or less. Where a court finds that a chemical dependency contributed to the crime, the court may authorize the county jail to convert jail confinement to an available county-supervised community option. The court may require the offender to perform affirmative conditions, such as rehabilitative treatment, which are reasonably related to the circumstances of the crime and are reasonably necessary or beneficial to the offender and to the community.

The Caseload Forecast Council is not liable for errors or omissions in the manual, for sentences that may be inappropriately calculated as a result of a practitioner's or court's reliance on the manual, or for any other written or verbal information related to adult or juvenile sentencing. The scoring sheets are intended to provide assistance in most cases but do not cover all permutations of the scoring rules. If you find any errors or omissions, we encourage you to report them to the Caseload Forecast Council.

SECTION 3 – Sentencing Guidelines

For all offenders with sentences of one year or less, one day of total confinement may be converted to one day of partial confinement. Non-violent offenders with sentences of one year or less are also eligible for conversion of total confinement to community service (one day of confinement equals eight hours of service). This community service conversion, however, is limited to 30 days or 240 hours. If a community service conversion is ordered and the determinate sentence is greater than 30 days, the balance of the term is to be served in total or partial confinement.

Partial confinement sentences may allow the offender to serve the sentence in work release, home detention, work crew, or a combination of work crew and home detention. If the offender violates the rules of the work release facility, work crew, or home detention program, or fails to remain employed or enrolled in school, the facility director may transfer the offender to the county detention facility. The offender may then request an administrative hearing. Pending the hearing, or in the absence of a request for such a hearing, the offender shall serve the remainder of the term of confinement in total confinement (RCW 9.94A.731).

Work Crew

Work crew is a partial confinement option created by the 1991 Legislature. Offenders who qualify must have committed the offense on or after July 28, 1991. The offense may not be a sex offense. For offenses committed before July 25, 1993, the offender must be sentenced to a facility operated or utilized under contract by a county (*i.e.*, the sentence must be one year or less in length); this restriction does not apply to offenses committed after that date. If the sentence is 9 months or more, at least 30 days of total confinement must be served before the offender becomes eligible for work crew. Work crew may be simultaneously imposed with electronic home detention. Work crew hours served may include work on civic improvement tasks, substance abuse counseling, job skills training or a maximum of 24 hours per week at approved, verified work.

To be eligible to receive credit for approved, verified work, offenders must first successfully complete 4 weeks of work crew, each week comprised of 35 hours of service. Work crew projects specified by the work crew supervisor must be completed in coordination with approved, verified work. Unless exempted by the court, offenders using approved, verified employment as part of their work crew hours must pay a monthly supervision assessment. RCW 9.94A.725.

Home Detention

Home detention is a subset of electronic monitoring and means a program of partial confinement available o offenders wherein the offender is confined in a private residence twenty-four hours a day, unless an absence from the residence is approved, authorized, or otherwise permitted in the order by the court or other supervising agency that ordered home detention. The option was created by the 1988 Legislature and is available for offenders convicted of nonviolent or non-sex offenses committed on or after June 9, 1988. Because partial confinement programs are limited to sentences of one year or less, home detention is not an option for offenders with prison sentences.

The Caseload Forecast Council is not liable for errors or omissions in the manual, for sentences that may be inappropriately calculated as a result of a practitioner's or court's reliance on the manual, or for any other written or verbal information related to adult or juvenile sentencing. The scoring sheets are intended to provide assistance in most cases but do not cover all permutations of the scoring rules. If you find any errors or omissions, we encourage you to report them to the Caseload Forecast Council.

SECTION 3 – Sentencing Guidelines

Eligibility for home detention is generally conditioned upon (a) employment or school attendance, (b) program rules adherence, and (c) compliance with court-ordered legal financial obligations (RCW 9.94A.734(4)).

Convictions for any of the following offenses make the offender **ineligible** for home detention unless imposed as partial confinement in the parenting program under RCW 9.94A.6551:

- A violent offense;
- Any sex offense;
- A drug offense;
- Reckless Burning in the First or Second Degree;
- Assault in the Third Degree;
- Assault of a Child in the Third Degree; or
- Unlawful Imprisonment or Harassment.

Home detention may be imposed for offenders convicted of Possession of a Controlled Substance (RCW 69.50.4013) or of Forged Prescription for a Controlled Substance (RCW 69.50.403), providing the offender fulfills the participation conditions set forth in this section and is monitored for drug use.

Offenders convicted of Burglary in the Second Degree or Residential Burglary must meet the following eligibility conditions for home detention: (a) successful completion of a twenty-one day work release program; (b) no convictions for Burglary in the Second Degree or Residential Burglary during the preceding two years and not more than two prior convictions for Burglary or Residential Burglary; (c) no convictions for a violent felony offense during the preceding two years and not more than two prior convictions for a violent felony offense; (d) no prior charges of escape; and (e) fulfillment of the other conditions of the home detention program.

Offenders convicted of Theft of a Motor Vehicle Without Permission in the Second Degree, Theft of a Motor Vehicle, or Possession of a Stolen Motor Vehicle must meet the following eligibility conditions for home detention: (a) no convictions for any of these crimes during the preceding five years and not more than two prior convictions for any of these offenses; (b) no prior convictions of a violent felony offense during the preceding two years and not more than two prior convictions for a violent felony offense; (c) no prior charges of escape; and (d) fulfillment of the other conditions of the home detention program.

Home detention may also be ordered for an offender whose medical or health-related conditions, concerns, or treatment would be better addressed under the home detention program, or where the health and welfare of the offender, other inmates, or staff would be jeopardized by the offender's incarceration. Participation in the home detention program for medical or health-related reasons is conditioned on the offender abiding by the rules of the home detention program and complying with court-ordered legal financial obligations.

A sentencing court shall deny the imposition of home detention if the court finds that (1) the offender has previously and knowingly violated the terms of a home detention program and (2) the previous violation is not a technical, minor, or nonsubstantive violation.

The Caseload Forecast Council is not liable for errors or omissions in the manual, for sentences that may be inappropriately calculated as a result of a practitioner's or court's reliance on the manual, or for any other written or verbal information related to adult or juvenile sentencing. The scoring sheets are intended to provide assistance in most cases but do not cover all permutations of the scoring rules. If you find any errors or omissions, we encourage you to report them to the Caseload Forecast Council.

SECTION 3 – Sentencing Guidelines

A sentencing court may deny the imposition of home detention if the court finds that (1) the offender has previously and knowingly violated the terms of a home detention program and (2) the previous violation or violations were technical, minor, or nonsubstantive violation.

A home detention program must be administered by a monitoring agency that meets the conditions described in RCW 9.94A.736.

RESTITUTION

Restitution is generally governed by RCW 9.94A.750 and 9.94A.753, but RCW 9.94A.505(8) requires a court to order restitution whenever a felony results in injury to a person or damage or property loss. If restitution is not ordered, the court must indicate the extraordinary reasons on the record.

Restitution may also be ordered to pay for an injury, loss, or damage if the offender pleads guilty to a lesser offense or fewer offenses and agrees with the prosecutor's recommendation that he or she pay restitution for any offenses not prosecuted pursuant to a plea agreement.

Restitution is based on three factors:

- Easily ascertainable damages for injury to or loss of property;
- Actual expenses incurred in treatment for injury to persons; and
- Lost wages resulting from injury.

Restitution for the crimes of Rape of a Child in the First, Second, or Third Degree, in which the victim becomes pregnant, must include:

- Victim's medical expenses associated with the rape and resulting pregnancy; and
- Support for any child born as a result of the rape, if child support is ordered.

Restitution shall *not* include reimbursement for damages for mental anguish, pain and suffering and other intangible losses, but may include reimbursement for counseling reasonably related to the offense. The amount of restitution may not exceed double the amount of the offender's gain or the victim's loss from the commission of the crime.

Restitution is to be determined at the sentencing hearing or within 180 days. As part of the sentence, the court must set the terms and conditions under which the defendant makes restitution. It is required that the court be specific about the payment schedule for restitution, so that these sentence conditions may be appropriately monitored by the community corrections officer. The court may not reduce the total amount of restitution ordered because of the offender's lack of ability to pay the total amount.

For offenses committed prior to July 1, 2000, an offender's compliance with the restitution requirement may be supervised for ten years after the date of sentence or release from confinement. The restitution portion of

SECTION 3 – Sentencing Guidelines

a sentence may be modified as to amount, terms, and conditions during this period regardless of the community supervision term and the statutory maximum of the crime. A court may extend the restitution requirement for a second ten-year period.

For offenses committed on or after July 1, 2000, RCW 9.94A.760(4) reads: *"For an offense committed on or after July 1, 2000, the Court shall retain jurisdiction over the offender, for purposes of the offender's compliance with payment of the legal financial obligations, until the obligation is completely satisfied, regardless of the statutory maximum for the crime. The department may only supervise the offender's compliance with payment of the legal financial obligations during any period in which the department is authorized to supervise the offender in the community under RCW 9.4A.728, 9.94A.501, or in which the offender is confined in a state correctional institution or a correctional facility pursuant to a transfer agreement with the department, and the department shall supervise the offender's compliance during any such period. The department is not responsible for supervision of the offender during any subsequent period of time the offender remains under the court's jurisdiction. The county clerk is authorized to collect unpaid legal financial obligations at any time the offender remains under the jurisdiction of the court for purposes of his or her legal financial obligations."*

Restitution for victims is the first priority for payment by an offender.

Restitution in Cases involving Fraud or Deceptive Practice

If an offender or organization is found guilty of an offense involving fraud or other deceptive practice, a court may require that notice be given to the class of persons or sector of the public affected by the conviction or financially interested in the subject matter of the offense. The notice may be accomplished by mail, by advertising through designated media, or by other appropriate means (RCW 9.94A.753(8), RCW 9.94A.750(7)).

Restitution in Cases involving a Fraudulent Filing of a Vehicle Report of Sale

If a person has caused a victim to lose money or property through the filing of a vehicle report of sale in which the designated buyer had no knowledge of the vehicle transfer or the fraudulent filing of the report of sale, upon conviction or when the offender pleads guilty and agrees with the prosecutor's recommendation that the offender be required to pay restitution to a victim, the court may order the defendant to pay an amount, fixed by the court, not to exceed double the amount of the defendant's gain or victim's loss from the filing of the vehicle report of sale in which the designated buyer had no knowledge of the vehicle transfer or the fraudulent filing of the report of sale (RCW 9.94A.753(10)).

FINES

Unless otherwise provided by a statute of this state, on all adult sentences under this chapter the court may impose fines on offenders according to the following ranges (RCW 9.94A.550):

The Caseload Forecast Council is not liable for errors or omissions in the manual, for sentences that may be inappropriately calculated as a result of a practitioner's or court's reliance on the manual, or for any other written or verbal information related to adult or juvenile sentencing. The scoring sheets are intended to provide assistance in most cases but do not cover all permutations of the scoring rules. If you find any errors or omissions, we encourage you to report them to the Caseload Forecast Council.

SECTION 3 – Sentencing Guidelines

  Class A felonies $0 - $50,000
  Class B felonies $0 - $20,000
  Class C felonies $0 - $10,000

Unless the court finds the offender to be indigent, every person convicted of certain VUCSA violations (RCW 69.50.401 through 69.50.4013, 69.50.4015, 69.50.402, 69.50.403, 69.50.406, 69.50.407, 69.50.410, 69.50.415) shall be fined $1,000 in addition to any other fine or penalty imposed. The fine increases to $2,000 if the violation is a second or subsequent violation of one of the laws specified. RCW 69.50.430.

When a fine is imposed for Manufacture, Delivery or Possession with Intent to Manufacture or Deliver Methamphetamine, or for Possession of Ephedrine or Pseudo Ephedrine with Intent to Manufacture Methamphetamine, the first $3,000 may not be suspended and must be provided to the law enforcement entity responsible for cleaning up the methamphetamine lab site. RCW 69.50.401.

Other Legal Financial Obligations

The Sentencing Reform Act allows a court to impose several additional monetary obligations. These include:

- Court costs. (RCW 9.94A.030(31));
- Defense attorney's fees and defense costs. (RCW 9.94A.030(31));
- Contributions to a county or local drug fund. (RCW 9.94A.030(31));
- Crime victims' compensation assessment. (RCW 9.94A.030(31) and (RCW 7.68.035));
- Recoupments to the victim for the cost of counseling as a result of the offender's crime, in cases where the Special Sex Offender Sentencing Alternative is exercised. (RCW 9.94A.670(6)(g));
- Payment for the cost of incarceration, at the rate of $50 per day. (RCW 9.94A.760(2));
- Payment of up to $2,500 in costs incurred by public agencies in an emergency response to the incident that resulted in conviction for Vehicular Assault or Vehicular Homicide While Under the Influence of Intoxicating Liquor or Any Drug. (RCW 9.94A.030(31) and (RCW 38.52.430)) and/or
- A fine of $15, in addition to any penalty or fine imposed, for a violation of a domestic violence protection order issued under this chapter (RCW 26.50.110(1)(b)(ii)).

All other legal financial obligations for an offense committed prior to July 1, 2000, may be enforced at any time during the ten-year period following the offender's release from total confinement or within ten years of entry of the judgment and sentence, whichever period ends later. Prior to the expiration of the initial ten-year period, the superior court may extend the criminal judgment an additional ten years for payment of legal financial obligations including crime victims' assessments. All other legal financial obligations for an offense committed on or after July 1, 2000, may be enforced at any time the offender remains under the court's jurisdiction. For an offense committed on or after July 1, 2000, the court shall retain jurisdiction over the offender, for purposes of the offender's compliance with payment of the legal financial obligations, until the obligation is completely satisfied, regardless of the statutory maximum for the crime.

The Caseload Forecast Council is not liable for errors or omissions in the manual, for sentences that may be inappropriately calculated as a result of a practitioner's or court's reliance on the manual, or for any other written or verbal information related to adult or juvenile sentencing. The scoring sheets are intended to provide assistance in most cases but do not cover all permutations of the scoring rules. If you find any errors or omissions, we encourage you to report them to the Caseload Forecast Council.

SECTION 3 – Sentencing Guidelines

The department may only supervise the offender's compliance with payment of the legal financial obligations during any period in which the department is authorized to supervise the offender in the community under RCW 9.94A.728, 9.94A.501, or in which the offender is confined in a state correctional institution or a correctional facility pursuant to a transfer agreement with the department, and the department shall supervise the offender's compliance during any such period. The department is not responsible for supervision of the offender during any subsequent period of time the offender remains under the court's jurisdiction. The county clerk is authorized to collect unpaid legal financial obligations at any time the offender remains under the jurisdiction of the court for purposes of his or her legal financial obligations.

In order to assist the court in setting the monthly payment sum, the offender must truthfully report to DOC regarding earnings, property, and assets, and must supply requested documentation.

The DOC may recommend to the court modifications in the payment schedule if the offender's financial circumstances change during the period of supervision. In cases where the DOC sets the monthly assessment amount, the DOC may modify the monthly assessment without consulting the court.

Independent of the department or the county clerk, the party or entity to whom the legal financial obligation is owed shall have the authority to use any other remedies available to the party or entity to collect the legal financial obligation. These remedies include enforcement in the same manner as a judgment in a civil action by the party or entity to whom the legal financial obligation is owed.

Contact With Individuals

A court may prohibit an offender from contacting specified individuals or a specific class of individuals for a period not to exceed the maximum allowable sentence for the crime, regardless of the expiration of the community supervision or community placement term. The order prohibiting contact must relate directly to the circumstances of the crime of conviction.

The Caseload Forecast Council is not liable for errors or omissions in the manual, for sentences that may be inappropriately calculated as a result of a practitioner's or court's reliance on the manual, or for any other written or verbal information related to adult or juvenile sentencing. The scoring sheets are intended to provide assistance in most cases but do not cover all permutations of the scoring rules. If you find any errors or omissions, we encourage you to report them to the Caseload Forecast Council.

SECTION 4 - SENTENCING GRIDS AND FELONY OFFENSES

SENTENCING GRID D: FOR CRIMES COMMITTED AFTER JULY 24, 1999

"CURRENT"
RCW 9.94A.510

Seriousness Level	Offender Score 0	1	2	3	4	5	6	7	8	9+
LEVEL XVI	Life sentence without parole/death penalty for offenders at or over the age of eighteen. For offenders under the age of eighteen, a term of twenty-five years to life.*									
LEVEL XV	280m 240 - 320	291.5m 250 - 333	304m 261 - 347	316m 271 - 361	327.5m 281 - 374	339.5m 291 - 388	364m 312 - 416	394m 338 - 450	431.5m 370 - 493	479.5m 411 - 548
LEVEL XIV	171.5m 123 - 220	184m 134 - 234	194m 144 - 244	204m 154 - 254	215m 165 - 265	225m 175 - 275	245m 195 - 295	266m 216 - 316	307m 257 - 357	347.5m 298 - 397
LEVEL XIII	143.5m 123 - 164	156m 134 - 178	168m 144 - 192	179.5m 154 - 205	192m 165 - 219	204m 175 - 233	227.5m 195 - 260	252m 216 - 288	299.5m 257 - 342	347.5m 298 - 397
LEVEL XII	108m 93 - 123	119m 102 - 136	129m 111 - 147	140m 120 - 160	150m 129 - 171	161m 138 - 184	189m 162 - 216	207m 178 - 236	243m 209 - 277	279m 240 - 318
LEVEL XI	90m 78 - 102	100m 86 - 114	110m 95 - 125	119m 102 - 136	129m 111 - 147	139m 120 - 158	170m 146 - 194	185m 159 - 211	215m 185 - 245	245m 210 - 280
LEVEL X	59.5m 51 - 68	66m 57 - 75	72m 62 - 82	78m 67 - 89	84m 72 - 96	89.5m 77 - 102	114m 98 - 130	126m 108 - 144	150m 129 - 171	230.5m 149 - 198
LEVEL IX	36m 31 - 41	42m 36 - 48	47.5m 41 - 54	53.5m 46 - 61	59.5m 51 - 68	66m 57 - 75	89.5m 77 - 102	101.5m 87 - 116	126m 108 - 144	150m 129 - 171
LEVEL VIII	24m 21 - 27	30m 26 - 34	36m 31 - 41	42m 36 - 48	47.5m 41 - 54	53.5m 46 - 61	78m 67 - 89	89.5m 77 - 102	101.5m 87 - 116	126m 108 - 144
LEVEL VII	17.5m 15 - 20	24m 21 - 27	30m 26 - 34	36m 31 - 41	42m 36 - 48	47.5m 41 - 54	66m 57 - 75	78m 67 - 89	89.5m 77 - 102	101.5m 87 - 116
LEVEL VI	13m 12+ - 14	17.5m 15 - 20	24m 21 - 27	30m 26 - 34	36m 31 - 41	42m 36 - 48	53.5m 46 - 61	66m 57 - 75	78m 67 - 89	89.5m 77 - 102
LEVEL V	9m 6 - 12	13m 12+ - 14	15m 13 - 17	17.5m 15 - 20	25.5m 22 - 29	38m 33 - 43	47.5m 41 - 54	59.5m 51 - 68	72m 62 - 82	84m 72 - 96
LEVEL IV	6m 3 - 9	9m 6 - 12	13m 12+ - 14	15m 13 - 17	17.5m 15 - 20	25.5m 22 - 29	38m 33 - 43	50m 43 - 57	61.5m 53 - 70	73.5m 63 - 84
LEVEL III	2m 1 - 3	5m 3 - 8	8m 4 - 12	11m 9 - 12	14m 12+ - 16	19.5m 17 - 22	25.5m 22 - 29	38m 33 - 43	50m 43 - 57	59.5m 51 - 68
LEVEL II	0-90 days	4m 2 - 6	6m 3 - 9	8m 4 - 12	13m 12+ - 14	16m 14 - 18	19.5m 17 - 22	25.5m 22 - 29	38m 33 - 43	50m 43 - 57
LEVEL I	0-60 days	0-90 days	3m 2 - 5	4m 2 - 6	5.5m 3 - 8	8m 4 - 12	13m 12+ - 14	16m 14 - 18	19.5m 17 - 22	25.5m 22 - 29

*NOTE: 2SSB 5064, passed during the 2014 legislative session, amended the mandatory minimum term for aggravated first degree murder committed before the offender's 18th birthday. The changes were made retroactive and, therefore, apply regardless of the date of offense. Refer to RCW 9.94A.510, RCW 9.94A540, RCW 9.94A.729, RCW 10.95.030, and RCW 10.95.035.

The Caseload Forecast Council is not liable for errors or omissions in the manual, for sentences that may be inappropriately calculated as a result of a practitioner's or court's reliance on the manual, or for any other written or verbal information related to adult or juvenile sentencing. The scoring sheets are intended to provide assistance in most cases but do not cover all permutations of the scoring rules. If you find any errors or omissions, we encourage you to report them to the Caseload Forecast Council.

SECTION 4 – STANDARD SENTENCING GRIDS FOR ANTICIPATORY OFFENSES

SENTENCING GRID D – ANTICIPATORIES – FOR CRIMES COMMITTED AFTER JULY 24, 1999

"CURRENT"*

Seriousness Level / **Offender Score**

Level	0	1	2	3	4	5	6	7	8	9+
LEVEL XVI	Life sentence without parole/death penalty for offenders at or over the age of eighteen. For offenders under the age of eighteen, a term of twenty-five years to life.*									
LEVEL XV	180 - 240	187.5 - 249.75	195.75 - 260.25	203.25 - 270.75	210.75 - 280.5	218.25 - 291	234 - 312	253.5 - 337.5	277.5 - 369.75	308.25 - 411
LEVEL XIV	92.25 - 165	100.5 - 175.5	108 - 183	115.5 - 190.5	123.75 - 198.75	131.25 - 206.25	146.25 - 221.25	162 - 237	192.75 - 267.75	223.5 - 297.75
LEVEL XIII	92.25 - 123	100.5 - 133.5	108 - 144	115.5 - 153.75	123.75 - 164.25	131.25 - 174.75	146.25 - 195	162 - 216	192.75 - 256.5	223.5 - 297.75
LEVEL XII	69.75 - 92.25	76.5 - 102	83.25 - 110.25	90 - 120	96.75 - 128.25	103.5 - 138	121.5 - 162	133.5 - 177	156.75 - 207.75	180 - 238.5
LEVEL XI	58.5 - 76.5	64.5 - 85.5	71.25 - 93.75	76.5 - 102	83.25 - 110.25	90 - 118.5	109.5 - 145.5	119.25 - 158.25	138.75 - 183.75	157.5 - 210
LEVEL X	38.25 - 51	42.75 - 56.25	46.5 - 61.5	50.25 - 66.75	54 - 72	57.75 - 76.5	73.5 - 97.5	81 - 108	96.75 - 128.25	111.75 - 148.5
LEVEL IX	23.25 - 30.75	27 - 36	30.75 - 40.5	34.5 - 45.75	38.25 - 51	42.75 - 56.25	57.75 - 76.5	65.25 - 87	81 - 108	96.75 - 128.25
LEVEL VIII	15.75 - 20.25	19.5 - 25.5	23.25 - 30.75	27 - 36	30.75 - 40.5	34.5 - 45.75	50.25 - 66.75	57.75 - 76.5	65.25 - 87	81 - 108
LEVEL VII	11.25 - 15	15.75 - 20.25	19.5 - 25.5	23.25 - 30.75	27 - 36	30.75 - 40.5	42.75 - 56.25	50.25 - 66.75	57.75 - 76.5	65.25 - 87
LEVEL VI	9 - 10.5	11.25 - 15	15.75 - 20.25	19.5 - 25.5	23.25 - 30.75	27 - 36	34.5 - 45.75	42.75 - 56.25	50.25 - 66.75	57.75 - 76.5
LEVEL V	4.5 - 9	9 - 10.5	9.75 - 12.75	11.25 - 15	16.5 - 21.75	24.75 - 32.25	30.75 - 40.5	38.25 - 51	46.5 - 61.5	54 - 72
LEVEL IV	2.25 - 6.75	4.5 - 9	9 - 10.5	9.75 - 12.75	11.25 - 15	16.5 - 21.75	24.75 - 32.25	32.25 - 42.75	39.75 - 52.5	47.25 - 63
LEVEL III	0.75 - 2.25	2.25 - 6	3 - 9	6.75 - 9	9 - 12	12.75 - 16.5	16.5 - 21.75	24.75 - 32.25	32.25 - 42.75	38.25 - 51
LEVEL II	0 - 67.5 days	1.5 - 4.5	2.25 - 6.75	3 - 9	9 - 10.5	10.5 - 13.5	12.75 - 16.5	16.5 - 21.75	24.75 - 32.25	32.25 - 42.75
LEVEL I	0 - 45 days	0 - 67.5 days	1.5 - 3.75	1.5 - 4.5	2.25 - 6	3 - 9	9 - 10.5	10.5 - 13.5	12.75 - 16.5	16.5 - 21.75

*NOTE: 2SSB 5064, passed during the 2014 legislative session, amended the mandatory minimum term for aggravated first degree murder committed before the offender's 18th birthday. The changes were made retroactive and, therefore, apply regardless of the date of offense. Refer to RCW 9.94A.510, RCW 9.94A540, RCW 9.94A.729, RCW 10.95.030, and RCW 10.95.035.

The Caseload Forecast Council is not liable for errors or omissions in the manual, for sentences that may be inappropriately calculated as a result of a practitioner's or court's reliance on the manual, or for any other written or verbal information related to adult or juvenile sentencing. The scoring sheets are intended to provide assistance in most cases but do not cover all permutations of the scoring rules. If you find any errors or omissions, we encourage you to report them to the Caseload Forecast Council.

SECTION 4 - OFFENSE SERIOUSNESS LEVELS FOR STANDARD GRID (RCW 9.94A.515)

OFFENSE SERIOUSNESS LEVELS FOR STANDARD GRID (RCW 9.94A.515)

Seriousness Level	Statute (RCW)	Offense	Class
XVI	10.95.020	Aggravated Murder 1	A
XV	9A.32.055	Homicide by Abuse	A
	70.74.280(1)	Malicious Explosion of a Substance 1	A
	9A.32.030	Murder 1	A
	9A.28.020(3)(a)	Murder 1 – Criminal Attempt	A
	9A.28.040(3)(a)	Murder 1 - Criminal Conspiracy	A
	9A.28.030(2)	Murder 1 – Criminal Solicitation	A
XIV	9A.32.050	Murder 2	A
	9A.28.020(3)(a)	Murder 2 – Criminal Attempt	A
	9A.28.030(2)	Murder 2 – Criminal Solicitation	A
	9A.40.100(1)	Trafficking 1	A
XIII	70.74.280(2)	Malicious Explosion of a Substance 2	A
	70.74.270(1)	Malicious Placement of an Explosive 1	A
XII	9A.36.011	Assault 1	A
	9A.36.120	Assault of a Child 1	A
	70.74.272(1)(a)	Malicious Placement of an Imitation Device 1	B
	9.68A.101	Promoting Commercial Sexual Abuse of a Minor	A
	9A.44.040	Rape 1	A
	9A.28.020(3)(a)	Rape 1 – Criminal Attempt	A
	9A.28.030(2)	Rape 1 – Criminal Solicitation	A
	9A.44.073	Rape of a Child 1	A
	9A.28.020(3)(a)	Rape of a Child 1 – Criminal Attempt	A
	9A.28.030(2)	Rape of a Child 1 – Criminal Solicitation	A
	9A.40.100(3)	Trafficking 2	A
XI	9A.32.060	Manslaughter 1	A
	9A.44.050	Rape 2	A
	9A.28.020(3)(a)	Rape 2 – Criminal Attempt	A

The Caseload Forecast Council is not liable for errors or omissions in the manual, for sentences that may be inappropriately calculated as a result of a practitioner's or court's reliance on the manual, or for any other written or verbal information related to adult or juvenile sentencing. The scoring sheets are intended to provide assistance in most cases but do not cover all permutations of the scoring rules. If you find any errors or omissions, we encourage you to report them to the Caseload Forecast Council.

SECTION 4 - OFFENSE SERIOUSNESS LEVELS FOR STANDARD GRID (RCW 9.94A.515)

Seriousness Level	Statute (RCW)	Offense	Class
	9A.28.030(2)	Rape 2 – Criminal Solicitation	A
	9A.44.076	Rape of a Child 2	A
	9A.28.020(3)(a)	Rape of a Child 2 – Criminal Attempt	A
	9A.28.030(2)	Rape of a Child 2 – Criminal Solicitation	A
	46.61.520(1)(b)	Vehicular Homicide – In a Reckless Manner	A
	46.61.520(1)(a)	Vehicular Homicide – While Under the Influence of Intoxicating Liquor or any Drug	A
X	9A.44.083	Child Molestation 1	A
	9A.28.020(3)(a)	Child Molestation 1 – Criminal Attempt	A
	9A.28.030(2)	Child Molestation 1 – Criminal Solicitation	A
	9A.42.020	Criminal Mistreatment 1	B
	9A.44.100(1)(a)	Indecent Liberties - With Forcible Compulsion	A
	9A.28.020(3)(a)	Indecent Liberties - With Forcible Compulsion – Criminal Attempt	A
	9A.28.030(2)	Indecent Liberties - With Forcible Compulsion – Criminal Solicitation	A
	9A.40.020	Kidnapping 1	A
	9A.82.060(1)(a)	Leading Organized Crime – Organizing Criminal Profiteering	A
	70.74.280(3)	Malicious Explosion of a Substance 3	B
	9A.76.115	Sexually Violent Predator Escape	A
IX	9A.42.060	Abandonment of Dependent Persons 1	B
	9A.36.130	Assault of a Child 2	B
	70.74.180	Explosive Devices Prohibited	A
	46.52.020(4)(a)	Hit and Run - Death	B
	79A.60.050(1)(a)	Homicide by Watercraft – While Under the Influence of Intoxicating Liquor or any Drug	A
	9A.82.060(1)(b)	Leading Organized Crime - Inciting Criminal Profiteering	B
	70.74.270(2)	Malicious Placement of an Explosive 2	B
	9A.56.200	Robbery 1	A
	9.68A.040	Sexual Exploitation of a Minor	B
VIII	9A.48.020	Arson 1	A
	9A.28.020(3)(a)	Arson 1 – Criminal Attempt	A
	9A.28.030(2)	Arson 1 – Criminal Solicitation	A
	9.68A.100	Commercial Sexual Abuse of a Minor	B
	79A.60.050(1)(b)	Homicide by Watercraft – In a Reckless Manner	A
	9A.32.070	Manslaughter 2	B

The Caseload Forecast Council is not liable for errors or omissions in the manual, for sentences that may be inappropriately calculated as a result of a practitioner's or court's reliance on the manual, or for any other written or verbal information related to adult or juvenile sentencing. The scoring sheets are intended to provide assistance in most cases but do not cover all permutations of the scoring rules. If you find any errors or omissions, we encourage you to report them to the Caseload Forecast Council.

SECTION 4 - OFFENSE SERIOUSNESS LEVELS FOR STANDARD GRID (RCW 9.94A.515)

Seriousness Level	Statute (RCW)	Offense	Class
	9A.88.070	Promoting Prostitution 1	B
	69.55.010	Theft of Ammonia	C
VII	46.37.660(2)(b)	Air Bag Diagnostic Systems (Causing Bodily Injury or Death)	C
	46.37.660(1)(b)	Air Bag Replacement Requirements (Causing Bodily Injury or Death)	C
	9A.52.020	Burglary 1	A
	9A.44.086	Child Molestation 2	B
	9A.48.120	Civil Disorder Training	B
	9.68A.050(1)	Dealing in Depictions of Minor Engaged in Sexually Explicit Conduct 1	B
	9A.36.045	Drive-by Shooting	B
	79A.60.050(1)(c)	Homicide by Watercraft - Disregard for the Safety of Others	A
	9A.44.100(1)(b-c)	Indecent Liberties - Without Forcible Compulsion	B
	9A.76.140	Introducing Contraband 1	B
	70.74.270(3)	Malicious Placement of an Explosive 3	B
	46.37.650(1)(b)	Manufacture or Import Counterfeit, Nonfunctional, Damaged, or Previously Deployed Air Bag (Causing Bodily Injury or Death)	C
	46.37.675	Negligently Causing Death By Use of a Signal Preemption Device	B
	46.37.650(2)(b)	Sale, Install, [or] Reinstall Counterfeit, Nonfunctional, Damaged, or Previously Deployed Airbag	C
	9.68A.060(1)	Sending, Bringing into the State Depictions of Minor Engaged in Sexually Explicit Conduct 1	B
	9.41.040(1)	Unlawful Possession of a Firearm 1	B
	9.41.225	Use of Machine Gun in Commission of a Felony	A
	46.61.520(1)(c)	Vehicular Homicide - Disregard for the Safety of Others	A
VI	9A.76.170(3)(a)	Bail Jumping with Murder 1	A
	9A.68.010	Bribery	B
	9A.64.020(1)	Incest 1	B
	9A.72.160	Intimidating a Judge	B
	9A.72.130	Intimidating a Juror	B
	9A.72.110	Intimidating a Witness	B
	70.74.272(1)(b)	Malicious Placement of an Imitation Device 2	C
	9.68A.070(1)	Possession of Depictions of Minor Engaged in Sexually Explicit Conduct 1	B
	9A.44.079	Rape of a Child 3	C
	9A.56.300	Theft of a Firearm	B
	69.55.020	Unlawful Storage of Ammonia	C

The Caseload Forecast Council is not liable for errors or omissions in the manual, for sentences that may be inappropriately calculated as a result of a practitioner's or court's reliance on the manual, or for any other written or verbal information related to adult or juvenile sentencing. The scoring sheets are intended to provide assistance in most cases but do not cover all permutations of the scoring rules. If you find any errors or omissions, we encourage you to report them to the Caseload Forecast Council.

SECTION 4 - OFFENSE SERIOUSNESS LEVELS FOR STANDARD GRID (RCW 9.94A.515)

Seriousness Level	Statute (RCW)	Offense	Class
V	9A.42.070	Abandonment of Dependent Persons 2	C
	9A.82.030	Advancing Money or Property for Extortionate Extension of Credit	B
	46.37.660(2)(c)	Air Bag Diagnostic Systems	C
	46.37.660(1)(c)	Air Bag Replacement Requirements	C
	9A.76.170(3)(b)	Bail Jumping with Class A Felony	B
	9A.44.089	Child Molestation 3	C
	9A.42.030	Criminal Mistreatment 2	C
	9A.44.160	Custodial Sexual Misconduct 1	C
	9.68A.050(2)	Dealing in Depictions of Minor Engaged in Sexually Explicit Conduct 2	C
	26.50.110	Domestic Violence Court Order Violation	C
	46.61.502(6)	Driving While Under the Influence of Intoxicating Liquor or any Drug	B
	9A.56.120	Extortion 1	B
	9A.82.020	Extortionate Extension of Credit	B
	9A.82.040	Extortionate Means to Collect Extensions of Credit	B
	9A.64.020(2)	Incest 2	C
	9A.40.030(3)(a)	Kidnapping 2	B
	9A.40.030(3)(b)	Kidnapping 2 With a Finding of Sexual Motivation	A
	46.37.650(1)(c)	Manufacture or Import Counterfeit, Nonfunctional, Damaged, or Previously Deployed Air Bag	C
	9A.72.020	Perjury 1	B
	9.94.070	Persistent Prison Misbehavior	C
	46.61.504(6)	Physical Control of a Vehicle While Under the Influence of Intoxicating Liquor or any Drug	C
	9A.56.310	Possession of a Stolen Firearm	B
	9A.44.060	Rape 3	C
	9A.76.070(2)(a)	Rendering Criminal Assistance 1	B
	46.37.650(2)(c)	Sale, Install, [or] Reinstall Counterfeit, Nonfunctional, Damaged, or Previously Deployed Airbag	C
	9.68A.060(2)	Sending, Bringing into the State Depictions of Minor Engaged in Sexually Explicit Conduct 2	C
	9A.44.093	Sexual Misconduct with a Minor 1	C
	9A.44.105	Sexually Violating Human Remains	C
	9A.46.110	Stalking	B
	9A.56.070	Taking Motor Vehicle Without Permission 1	B
IV	9A.48.030	Arson 2	B

The Caseload Forecast Council is not liable for errors or omissions in the manual, for sentences that may be inappropriately calculated as a result of a practitioner's or court's reliance on the manual, or for any other written or verbal information related to adult or juvenile sentencing. The scoring sheets are intended to provide assistance in most cases but do not cover all permutations of the scoring rules. If you find any errors or omissions, we encourage you to report them to the Caseload Forecast Council.

SECTION 4 - OFFENSE SERIOUSNESS LEVELS FOR STANDARD GRID (RCW 9.94A.515)

Seriousness Level	Statute (RCW)	Offense	Class
	9A.36.021(2)(a)	Assault 2	B
	9A.36.021(2)(b)	Assault 2 With a Finding of Sexual Motivation	A
	9A.36.031(1)(h)	Assault 3 - Of a Peace Officer with a Projectile Stun Gun	C
	79A.60.060	Assault by Watercraft	B
	9A.72.100	Bribe Received by Witness	B
	9A.72.090	Bribing a Witness	B
	9.46.1961	Cheating 1	C
	9A.68.060	Commercial Bribery	B
	9.16.035(4)	Counterfeiting - Endanger Public Health or Safety	C
	9A.42.100	Endangerment With a Controlled Substance	B
	9A.76.110	Escape 1	B
	46.52.020(4)(b)	Hit and Run - Injury	C
	79A.60.200(3)	Hit and Run with Vessel - Injury Accident	C
	9.35.020(2)	Identity Theft 1	B
	9A.88.010(2)(c)	Indecent Exposure to a Person Under Age 14 (Subsequent Conviction or Has Prior Sex Offense Conviction)	C
	9A.82.070	Influencing Outcome of Sporting Event	C
	9A.36.080	Malicious Harassment	C
	9.68A.070(2)	Possession of Depictions of Minor Engaged in Sexually Explicit Conduct 2	C
	9A.52.025	Residential Burglary	B
	9A.56.210	Robbery 2	B
	9A.56.080	Theft of Livestock 1	B
	9.61.160	Threats to Bomb	B
	9A.82.050	Trafficking in Stolen Property 1	B
	9A.56.290(4)(b)	Unlawful Factoring of a Credit or Payment Card Transaction (Subsequent Violation)	B
	48.44.016(3)	Unlawful Transaction of Health Coverage as Health Care Service Contractor	B
	48.46.033(3)	Unlawful Transaction of Health Coverage as Health Maintenance Organization	B
	48.15.023(3)	Unlawful Transaction of Insurance Business	B
	48.17.063(2)	Unlicensed Practice as an Insurance Professional	B
	9A.82.080(1-2)	Use of Proceeds of Criminal Profiteering	B
	46.61.522(1)(a-b)	Vehicular Assault – In a Reckless Manner or While Under the Influence of Intoxicating Liquor or any Drug	B
	9A.52.100(3)	Vehicle Prowling 2 (third or subsequent offense)	C

The Caseload Forecast Council is not liable for errors or omissions in the manual, for sentences that may be inappropriately calculated as a result of a practitioner's or court's reliance on the manual, or for any other written or verbal information related to adult or juvenile sentencing. The scoring sheets are intended to provide assistance in most cases but do not cover all permutations of the scoring rules. If you find any errors or omissions, we encourage you to report them to the Caseload Forecast Council.

SECTION 4 - OFFENSE SERIOUSNESS LEVELS FOR STANDARD GRID (RCW 9.94A.515)

Seriousness Level	Statute (RCW)	Offense	Class
	9.68A.075(1)	Viewing Depictions of Minor Engaged in Sexually Explicit Conduct 1	B
	72.66.060	Willful Failure to Return from Furlough (*Repealed July 1, 2001*)	*
III	16.52.205(3)	Animal Cruelty 1 - Sexual Contact or Conduct	C
	9A.36.031(1)(a-g) & (i-j)	Assault 3 – Excluding Assault 3 of a Peace Officer with a Projectile Stun Gun	C
	9A.36.140	Assault of a Child 3	C
	9A.76.170(3)(c)	Bail Jumping with Class B or C Felony	C
	9A.52.030	Burglary 2	B
	9.68A.090(2)	Communication with Minor for Immoral Purposes (Subsequent Violation or Prior Sex Offense Conviction)	C
	9A.46.120	Criminal Gang Intimidation	C
	9A.36.100	Custodial Assault	C
	9.61.260(3)	Cyberstalking (With Prior Harassment Conviction or Threat of Death)	C
	9A.76.120	Escape 2	C
	9A.56.130	Extortion 2	C
	9A.46.020(2)(b)	Harassment (Subsequent Conviction or Threat of Death)	C
	9A.76.180	Intimidating a Public Servant	B
	9A.76.150	Introducing Contraband 2	C
	81.60.070	Malicious Injury to Railroad Property	B
	19.144.080	Mortgage Fraud	B
	46.37.674	Negligently Causing Substantial Bodily Harm By Use of a Signal Preemption Device	B
	9A.56.350(2)	Organized Retail Theft 1	B
	9A.72.030	Perjury 2	C
	9.40.120	Possession of Incendiary Device	B
	9.41.190	Possession of Machine Gun, Short-barreled Shotgun or Short-barreled Rifle	C
	9A.88.080	Promoting Prostitution 2	C
	9A.56.360(2)	Retail Theft with Special Circumstances 1	B
	21.20.400	Securities Act Violation	B
	9A.72.120	Tampering with a Witness	C
	9.61.230(2)	Telephone Harassment (With Prior Harassment Conviction or Threat of Death)	C
	9A.56.083	Theft of Livestock 2	C
	9A.56.340(2)	Theft with Intent to Resell 1	B
	9A.82.055	Trafficking in Stolen Property 2	C

The Caseload Forecast Council is not liable for errors or omissions in the manual, for sentences that may be inappropriately calculated as a result of a practitioner's or court's reliance on the manual, or for any other written or verbal information related to adult or juvenile sentencing. The scoring sheets are intended to provide assistance in most cases but do not cover all permutations of the scoring rules. If you find any errors or omissions, we encourage you to report them to the Caseload Forecast Council.

SECTION 4 - OFFENSE SERIOUSNESS LEVELS FOR STANDARD GRID (RCW 9.94A.515)

Seriousness Level	Statute (RCW)	Offense	Class
	77.15.410(3)(b)	Unlawful Hunting of Big Game 1	C
	9A.40.040	Unlawful Imprisonment	C
	69.04.938(3)	Unlawful Misbranding of Food Fish or Shellfish 1	C
	9.41.040(2)	Unlawful Possession of a Firearm 2	C
	77.15.120(3)(b)	Unlawful Taking of Endangered Fish or Wildlife 1	C
	77.15.260(3)(b)	Unlawful Trafficking in Fish, Shellfish or Wildlife 1	B
	77.15.530(4)	Unlawful Use of a Nondesignated Vessel	C
	46.61.522(1)(c)	Vehicular Assault - Disregard for the Safety of Others	B
	72.65.070	Willful Failure to Return from Work Release (*Repealed July 1, 2001*)	*
II	77.15.500(3)(b)	Commercial Fishing Without a License 1	C
	9A.90.040	Computer Trespass 1	C
	9.16.035(3)	Counterfeiting – Third Conviction and Value $10,000 or More	C
	9A.90.060	Electronic Data Service Interference	C
	9A.90.080	Electronic Data Tampering 1	C
	9A.90.100	Electronic Data Theft	C
	77.15.620(3)(b)	Engaging in Fish Dealing Activity Unlicensed 1	C
	72.09.310	Escape from Community Custody	C
	61.34.030	Equity Skimming*	B
	9A.44.132(1)(a)	Failure to Register as a Sex Offender (Second Violation Committed on or After 6/10/2010)	C
	9A.44.132(1)(a)	Failure to Register as a Sex Offender (Subsequent Violation Committed on or After 6/7/2006 but Before 6/10/2010)	C
	9A.44.132(1)(b)	Failure to Register as a Sex Offender (Third or Subsequent Violation Committed on or After 6/10/2010)	B
	48.80.030	Health Care False Claims	C
	9.35.020(3)	Identity Theft 2	C
	9.35.010	Improperly Obtaining Financial Information	C
	9A.48.070	Malicious Mischief 1	B
	9A.56.350(3)	Organized Retail Theft 2	C
	9A.56.068	Possession of a Stolen Vehicle	B
	9A.56.150	Possession of Stolen Property 1 (Other Than Firearm or Motor Vehicle)	B
	9A.56.360(3)	Retail Theft with Special Circumstances 2	C
	19.290.100	Scrap Processing, Recycling, or Supplying Without a License (Second or Subsequent Offense)	C
	9A.56.030	Theft 1 (Excluding Firearm and Motor Vehicle)	B

The Caseload Forecast Council is not liable for errors or omissions in the manual, for sentences that may be inappropriately calculated as a result of a practitioner's or court's reliance on the manual, or for any other written or verbal information related to adult or juvenile sentencing. The scoring sheets are intended to provide assistance in most cases but do not cover all permutations of the scoring rules. If you find any errors or omissions, we encourage you to report them to the Caseload Forecast Council.

SECTION 4 - OFFENSE SERIOUSNESS LEVELS FOR STANDARD GRID (RCW 9.94A.515)

Seriousness Level	Statute (RCW)	Offense	Class
	9A.56.065	Theft of a Motor Vehicle	B
	9A.56.096(5)(a)	Theft of Rental, Leased, Lease-purchased or Loaned Property (Valued at $5,000 or More)	B
	9A.56.340(3)	Theft with Intent to Resell 2	C
	48.30A.015	Trafficking in Insurance Claims (Subsequent Violation)	C
	9A.56.290(4)(a)	Unlawful Factoring of a Credit or Payment Card Transaction	C
	77.15.570(2)	Unlawful Participation of Non-Indians in Indian Fishery	C
	2.48.180	Unlawful Practice of Law (Subsequent Violation)	C
	18.130.190(7)(b)	Unlicensed Practice of a Profession or Business (Subsequent Violation)	C
	77.15.650(3)(b)	Unlawful Purchase or Use of a License 1	C
	77.15.260(3)(a)	Unlawful Trafficking in Fish, Shellfish or Wildlife 2	C
	9A.44.115	Voyeurism	C
I	46.61.024	Attempting to Elude Pursuing Police Vehicle	C
	74.08.055(2)	False Verification for Welfare	B
	9A.60.020	Forgery	C
	9A.60.060	Fraudulent Creation or Revocation of Mental Health Advance Directive	C
	9A.48.080	Malicious Mischief 2	C
	78.44.330	Mineral Trespass	C
	9A.56.160	Possession of Stolen Property 2 (Other Than Firearm or Motor Vehicle)	C
	9A.48.040	Reckless Burning 1	C
	77.15.450(3)(b)	Spotlighting Big Game 1	C
	77.15.670(3)(b)	Suspension of Department Privileges 1	C
	9A.56.075	Taking Motor Vehicle Without Permission 2	C
	9A.56.040	Theft 2 (Excluding Firearm and Motor Vehicle)	C
	9A.56.096(5)(b)	Theft of Rental, Leased, Lease-purchased or Loaned Property (Valued at $750 or More but Less Than $5,000)	C
	48.17.063(4)	Transaction of Insurance Business Beyond the Scope of Licensure (Violation of RCW 48.17.060)	B
	77.15.630(3)(b)	Unlawful Fish and Shellfish Catch Accounting 1	C
	9A.56.060(4)	Unlawful Issuance of Checks or Drafts (Value Greater Than $750)	C
	9A.56.320(3)	Unlawful Possession of a Personal Identification Device	C
	9A.56.320(4)	Unlawful Possession of Fictitious Identification	C
	9A.56.320(5)	Unlawful Possession of Instruments of Financial Fraud	C
	9A.56.320(2)	Unlawful Possession of Payment Instruments	C
	9A.56.320(1)	Unlawful Production of Payment Instruments	C

The Caseload Forecast Council is not liable for errors or omissions in the manual, for sentences that may be inappropriately calculated as a result of a practitioner's or court's reliance on the manual, or for any other written or verbal information related to adult or juvenile sentencing. The scoring sheets are intended to provide assistance in most cases but do not cover all permutations of the scoring rules. If you find any errors or omissions, we encourage you to report them to the Caseload Forecast Council.

SECTION 4 - OFFENSE SERIOUSNESS LEVELS FOR STANDARD GRID (RCW 9.94A.515)

Seriousness Level	Statute (RCW)	Offense	Class
	9.91.144	Unlawful Redemption of Food Stamps	C
	77.15.250(2)(b)	Unlawful Releasing, Planting, Possessing or Placing Deleterious Exotic Wildlife	C
	9.91.142(1)	Unlawful Trafficking in Food Stamps	C
	77.15.580(3)(b)	Unlawful Use of Net to Take Fish 1	C
	77.15.253(3)	Unlawful Use of Prohibited Aquatic Animal Species (Subsequent Violation)**	C
	9A.52.095	Vehicle Prowl 1	C
	77.15.550(3)(b)	Violating Commercial Fishing Area or Time 1	C

Notes:

*Equity Skimming is not found on the offense list under RCW 9.94A.518. RCW 61.34.030 language states "Equity skimming shall be classified as a level II offense under chapter 9.94A RCW, . . ." so it was included in this list.

**RCW 77.15.253 was repealed by 2014 c 202 § 310.

The Caseload Forecast Council is not liable for errors or omissions in the manual, for sentences that may be inappropriately calculated as a result of a practitioner's or court's reliance on the manual, or for any other written or verbal information related to adult or juvenile sentencing. The scoring sheets are intended to provide assistance in most cases but do not cover all permutations of the scoring rules. If you find any errors or omissions, we encourage you to report them to the Caseload Forecast Council.

SECTION 4 – Sentencing Grids (Levels I – III) For Sentences After July 1, 2013

DRUG SENTENCING GRID B FOR SENTENCES IMPOSED ON OR AFTER JULY 1, 2013
"CURRENT GRID"
RCW 9.94A.517

Seriousness Level	Offender Score		
	0 to 2	3 to 5	6 to 9+
LEVEL III	59.5m 51 - 68	84m 68+ - 100	110m 100+ - 120
LEVEL II	16m 12+ - 20	40m 20+ - 60	90m 60+ - 120
LEVEL I	3m 0 - 6	9m 6+ - 12	18m 12+ - 24

DRUG SENTENCING GRID B FOR SENTENCES IMPOSED ON OR AFTER JULY 1, 2013 (SOLICITATIONS FOR OFFENSES UNDER CHAPTER 69.50 RCW, ANTICIPATORIES FOR OFFENSES NOT UNDER CHAPTER 69.50 RCW)

"CURRENT GRID"
RCW 9.94A.517

Seriousness Level	Offender Score		
	0 to 2	3 to 5	6 to 9+
LEVEL III	38.25 - 51	51.02 - 75	75.02 - 90
LEVEL II	9.02 - 15	15.02 - 45	45.02 - 90
LEVEL I	0 - 4.5	4.52 - 9	9.02 - 18

The Caseload Forecast Council is not liable for errors or omissions in the manual, for sentences that may be inappropriately calculated as a result of a practitioner's or court's reliance on the manual, or for any other written or verbal information related to adult or juvenile sentencing. The scoring sheets are intended to provide assistance in most cases but do not cover all permutations of the scoring rules. If you find any errors or omissions, we encourage you to report them to the Caseload Forecast Council.

SECTION 4 - Offense Seriousness Levels For Drug Sentencing Grid (RCW 9.94A.518)

OFFENSE SERIOUSNESS LEVELS FOR DRUG SENTENCING GRID (RCW 9.94A.518)

This list includes most statutory drug offenses as well as drug-related offenses not defined as drug offenses under RCW 9.94A.030(22).

Seriousness Level	Statute (RCW)	Offense	Class
III	9.94A.602	Any felony offense under Chapter 69.50 RCW with a Deadly Weapon Special Verdict under RCW 9.94A.602	*
	69.50.415	Controlled Substance Homicide	B
	69.52.030(2)	Delivery of Imitation Controlled Substance by Person 18 or Over to Person Under 18	B
	69.50.4015	Involving a Minor in Drug Dealing	C
	69.50.401(2)(b)	Manufacture Methamphetamine	B
	69.50.406(1)	Over 18 and Deliver Heroin, Methamphetamine, a Narcotic from Schedule I or II, or Flunitrazepam from Schedule IV to Someone Under 18	A
	69.50.406(2)	Over 18 and Deliver Narcotic from Schedule III, IV or V, or a Nonnarcotic, Except Flunitrazepam or Methamphetamine, from Schedule I-V to Someone Under 18 and 3 Years Junior	B
	69.50.440	Possession of Ephedrine, Pseudoephedrine or Anhydrous Ammonia with Intent to Manufacture Methamphetamine	B
	69.50.410	Selling for Profit (Controlled or Counterfeit) any Controlled Substance in Schedule I	C
II	69.50.4011(2)(a-b)	Create, Deliver or Possess a Counterfeit Controlled Substance – Schedule I or II Narcotic or Flunitrazepam or Methamphetamine	B
	69.50.4011(2)(c-e)	Create, Deliver or Possess a Counterfeit Controlled Substance – Schedule I-II Nonnarcotic, Schedule III-V Except Flunitrazepam or Methamphetamine	C
	69.50.401(2)(b)	Deliver or Possess with Intent to Deliver - Methamphetamine	B
	69.50.4012	Delivery of a Material in Lieu of a Controlled Substance	C
	69.50.402	Maintaining a Dwelling or Place for Controlled Substances	C
	69.50.401(2)(a)	Manufacture, Deliver or Possess with Intent to Deliver - Narcotics from Schedule I or II or Flunitrazepam from Schedule IV	B
	69.50.401(2)(b)	Manufacture, Deliver or Possess with Intent to Deliver - Amphetamine	B
	69.50.401(2)(c-e)	Manufacture, Deliver or Possess with Intent to Deliver - Narcotics from Schedule III, IV, or V or Nonnarcotics from Schedule I-V (except Marijuana, Amphetamine, Methamphetamine, or Flunitrazepam)	C

The Caseload Forecast Council is not liable for errors or omissions in the manual, for sentences that may be inappropriately calculated as a result of a practitioner's or court's reliance on the manual, or for any other written or verbal information related to adult or juvenile sentencing. The scoring sheets are intended to provide assistance in most cases but do not cover all permutations of the scoring rules. If you find any errors or omissions, we encourage you to report them to the Caseload Forecast Council.

SECTION 4 - Offense Seriousness Levels For Drug Sentencing Grid (RCW 9.94A.518)

Seriousness Level	Statute (RCW)	Offense	Class
I	69.52.030(1)	Manufacture, Distribute or Possess with Intent to Distribute an Imitation Controlled Substance	C
	69.41.020	Forged Prescription - Legend Drug	B
	69.50.403	Forged Prescription for a Controlled Substance	C
	69.50.401(2)(c)	Manufacture, Deliver or Possess with Intent to Deliver - Marijuana	C
	69.50.4013	Possession of Controlled Substance That is a Narcotic from Schedule III, IV or V or Nonnarcotic from Schedule I-V	C
	69.50.4013	Possession of Controlled Substance That is Either Heroin or Narcotics from Schedule I or II	C
	69.53.010	Unlawful Use of Building for Drug Purposes	C

The Caseload Forecast Council is not liable for errors or omissions in the manual, for sentences that may be inappropriately calculated as a result of a practitioner's or court's reliance on the manual, or for any other written or verbal information related to adult or juvenile sentencing. The scoring sheets are intended to provide assistance in most cases but do not cover all permutations of the scoring rules. If you find any errors or omissions, we encourage you to report them to the Caseload Forecast Council.

SECTION 4 - Sentencing Grids For Crimes Committed July 27, 1997, through July 24, 1999

SENTENCING GRID C – FOR CRIMES COMMITTED JULY 27, 1997, THROUGH JULY 24, 1999*

Seriousness Level

	Offender Score									
	0	1	2	3	4	5	6	7	8	9+
LEVEL XV	LIFE SENTENCE WITHOUT PAROLE/DEATH PENALTY									
LEVEL XIV	280m 240 - 320	291.5m 250 - 333	304m 261 - 347	316m 271 - 361	327.5m 281 - 374	339.5m 291 - 388	364m 312 - 416	394m 338 - 450	431.5m 370 - 493	479.5m 411 - 548
LEVEL XIII	171.5m 123 - 220	184m 134 - 234	194m 144 - 244	204m 154 - 254	215m 165 - 265	225m 175 - 275	245m 195 - 295	266m 216 - 316	307m 257 - 357	347.5m 298 - 397
LEVEL XII	108m 93 - 123	119m 102 - 136	129m 111 - 147	140m 120 - 160	150m 129 - 171	161m 138 - 184	189m 162 - 216	207m 178 - 236	243m 209 - 277	279m 240 - 318
LEVEL XI	90m 78 - 102	100m 86 - 114	110m 95 - 125	119m 102 - 136	129m 111 - 147	139m 120 - 158	170m 146 - 194	185m 159 - 211	215m 185 - 245	245m 210 - 280
LEVEL X	59.5m 51 - 68	66m 57 - 75	72m 62 - 82	78m 67 - 89	84m 72 - 96	89.5m 77 - 102	114m 98 - 130	126m 108 - 144	150m 129 - 171	230.5m 149 - 198
LEVEL IX	36m 31 - 41	42m 36 - 48	47.5m 41 - 54	53.5m 46 - 61	59.5m 51 - 68	66m 57 - 75	89.5m 77 - 102	101.5m 87 - 116	126m 108 - 144	150m 129 - 171
LEVEL VIII	24m 21 - 27	30m 26 - 34	36m 31 - 41	42m 36 - 48	47.5m 41 - 54	53.5m 46 - 61	78m 67 - 89	89.5m 77 - 102	101.5m 87 - 116	126m 108 - 144
LEVEL VII	17.5m 15 - 20	24m 21 - 27	30m 26 - 34	36m 31 - 41	42m 36 - 48	47.5m 41 - 54	66m 57 - 75	78m 67 - 89	89.5m 77 - 102	101.5m 87 - 116
LEVEL VI	13m 12+ - 14	17.5m 15 - 20	24m 21 - 27	30m 26 - 34	36m 31 - 41	42m 36 - 48	53.5m 46 - 61	66m 57 - 75	78m 67 - 89	89.5m 77 - 102
LEVEL V	9m 6 - 12	13m 12+ - 14	15m 13 - 17	17.5m 15 - 20	25.5m 22 - 29	38m 33 - 43	47.5m 41 - 54	59.5m 51 - 68	72m 62 - 82	84m 72 - 96
LEVEL IV	6m 3 - 9	9m 6 - 12	13m 12+ - 14	15m 13 - 17	17.5m 15 - 20	25.5m 22 - 29	38m 33 - 43	50m 43 - 57	61.5m 53 - 70	73.5m 63 - 84
LEVEL III	2m 1 - 3	5m 3 - 8	8m 4 - 12	11m 9 - 12	14m 12+ - 16	19.5m 17 - 22	25.5m 22 - 29	38m 33 - 43	50m 43 - 57	59.5m 51 - 68
LEVEL II	0-90 days	4m 2 - 6	6m 3 - 9	8m 4 - 12	13m 12+ - 14	16m 14 - 18	19.5m 17 - 22	25.5m 22 - 29	38m 33 - 43	50m 43 - 57
LEVEL I	0-60 days	0-90 days	3m 2 - 5	4m 2 - 6	5.5m 3 - 8	8m 4 - 12	13m 12+ - 14	16m 14 - 18	19.5m 17 - 22	25.5m 22 - 29

*NOTE: 2SSB 5064, passed during the 2014 legislative session, amended the standard range of "Life Sentence Without Parole/Death Penalty" (i.e., the mandatory minimum term for aggravated first degree murder), where the offense was committed before the offender's 18th birthday to a minimum term of "25 years to life." The changes were made retroactive and, therefore, apply regardless of the date of offense. Refer to RCW 9.94A.510, RCW 9.94A540, RCW 9.94A.729, RCW 10.95.030, and RCW 10.95.035.

The Caseload Forecast Council is not liable for errors or omissions in the manual, for sentences that may be inappropriately calculated as a result of a practitioner's or court's reliance on the manual, or for any other written or verbal information related to adult or juvenile sentencing. The scoring sheets are intended to provide assistance in most cases but do not cover all permutations of the scoring rules. If you find any errors or omissions, we encourage you to report them to the Caseload Forecast Council.

SECTION 4 - Sentencing Grids For Crimes Committed July 1, 1990, through July 26, 1997

SENTENCING GRID B - FOR CRIMES COMMITTED JULY 1, 1990 THROUGH JULY 26, 1997*

Seriousness Level

	Offender Score									
	0	1	2	3	4	5	6	7	8	9+
LEVEL XV	LIFE SENTENCE WITHOUT PAROLE/DEATH PENALTY									
LEVEL XIV	280m 240 - 320	291.5m 250 - 333	304m 261 - 347	316m 271 - 361	327.5m 281 - 374	339.5m 291 - 388	364m 312 - 416	394m 338 - 450	431.5m 370 - 493	479.5m 411 - 548
LEVEL XIII	143.5m 123 - 164	156m 134 - 178	168m 144 - 192	179.5m 154 - 205	192m 165 - 219	204m 175 - 233	227.5m 195 - 260	252m 216 - 288	299.5m 257 - 342	347.5m 298 - 397
LEVEL XII	108m 93 - 123	119m 102 - 136	129m 111 - 147	140m 120 - 160	150m 129 - 171	161m 138 - 184	189m 162 - 216	207m 178 - 236	243m 209 - 277	279m 240 - 318
LEVEL XI	90m 78 - 102	100m 86 - 114	110m 95 - 125	119m 102 - 136	129m 111 - 147	139m 120 - 158	170m 146 - 194	185m 159 - 211	215m 185 - 245	245m 210 - 280
LEVEL X	59.5m 51 - 68	66m 57 - 75	72m 62 - 82	78m 67 - 89	84m 72 - 96	89.5m 77 - 102	114m 98 - 130	126m 108 - 144	150m 129 - 171	230.5m 149 - 198
LEVEL IX	36m 31 - 41	42m 36 - 48	47.5m 41 - 54	53.5m 46 - 61	59.5m 51 - 68	66m 57 - 75	89.5m 77 - 102	101.5m 87 - 116	126m 108 - 144	150m 129 - 171
LEVEL VIII	24m 21 - 27	30m 26 - 34	36m 31 - 41	42m 36 - 48	47.5m 41 - 54	53.5m 46 - 61	78m 67 - 89	89.5m 77 - 102	101.5m 87 - 116	126m 108 - 144
LEVEL VII	17.5m 15 - 20	24m 21 - 27	30m 26 - 34	36m 31 - 41	42m 36 - 48	47.5m 41 - 54	66m 57 - 75	78m 67 - 89	89.5m 77 - 102	101.5m 87 - 116
LEVEL VI	13m 12+ - 14	17.5m 15 - 20	24m 21 - 27	30m 26 - 34	36m 31 - 41	42m 36 - 48	53.5m 46 - 61	66m 57 - 75	78m 67 - 89	89.5m 77 - 102
LEVEL V	9m 6 - 12	13m 12+ - 14	15m 13 - 17	17.5m 15 - 20	25.5m 22 - 29	38m 33 - 43	47.5m 41 - 54	59.5m 51 - 68	72m 62 - 82	84m 72 - 96
LEVEL IV	6m 3 - 9	9m 6 - 12	13m 12+ - 14	15m 13 - 17	17.5m 15 - 20	25.5m 22 - 29	38m 33 - 43	50m 43 - 57	61.5m 53 - 70	73.5m 63 - 84
LEVEL III	2m 1 - 3	5m 3 - 8	8m 4 - 12	11m 9 - 12	14m 12+ - 16	19.5m 17 - 22	25.5m 22 - 29	38m 33 - 43	50m 43 - 57	59.5m 51 - 68
LEVEL II	0-90 days	4m 2 - 6	6m 3 - 9	8m 4 - 12	13m 12+ - 14	16m 14 - 18	19.5m 17 - 22	25.5m 22 - 29	38m 33 - 43	50m 43 - 57
LEVEL I	0-60 days	0-90 days	3m 2 - 5	4m 2 - 6	5.5m 3 - 8	8m 4 - 12	13m 12+ - 14	16m 14 - 18	19.5m 17 - 22	25.5m 22 - 29

*NOTE: 2SSB 5064, passed during the 2014 legislative session, amended the standard range of "Life Sentence Without Parole/Death Penalty" (i.e., the mandatory minimum term for aggravated first degree murder), where the offense was committed before the offender's 18th birthday to a minimum term of "25 years to life." The changes were made retroactive and, therefore, apply regardless of the date of offense. Refer to RCW 9.94A.510, RCW 9.94A540, RCW 9.94A.729, RCW 10.95.030, and RCW 10.95.035.

The Caseload Forecast Council is not liable for errors or omissions in the manual, for sentences that may be inappropriately calculated as a result of a practitioner's or court's reliance on the manual, or for any other written or verbal information related to adult or juvenile sentencing. The scoring sheets are intended to provide assistance in most cases but do not cover all permutations of the scoring rules. If you find any errors or omissions, we encourage you to report them to the Caseload Forecast Council.

SECTION 4 - Sentencing Grids For Crimes Committed Before July 1, 1990

SENTENCING GRID A - FOR CRIMES COMMITTED BEFORE JULY 1, 1990*

Seriousness Level		Offender Score									
		0	1	2	3	4	5	6	7	8	9+
	LEVEL XIV	LIFE SENTENCE WITHOUT PAROLE/DEATH PENALTY									
	LEVEL XIII	280m 240 - 320	291.5m 250 - 333	304m 261 - 347	316m 271 - 361	327.5m 281 - 374	339.5m 291 - 388	364m 312 - 416	394m 338 - 450	431.5m 370 - 493	479.5m 411 - 548
	LEVEL XII	143.5m 123 - 164	156m 134 - 178	168m 144 - 192	179.5m 154 - 205	192m 165 - 219	204m 175 - 233	227.5m 195 - 260	252m 216 - 288	299.5m 257 - 342	347.5m 298 - 397
	LEVEL XI	72m 62 - 82	80.5m 69 - 92	89.5m 77 - 102	99m 85 - 113	108m 93 - 123	116.5m 110 - 133	150m 129 - 171	162m 139 - 185	185.5m 159 - 212	210m 180 - 240
	LEVEL X	59.5m 51 - 68	66m 57 - 75	72m 62 - 82	78m 67 - 89	84m 72 - 96	89.5m 77 - 102	114m 98 - 130	126m 108 - 144	150m 129 - 171	230.5m 149 - 198
	LEVEL IX	36m 31 - 41	42m 36 - 48	47.5m 41 - 54	53.5m 46 - 61	59.5m 51 - 68	66m 57 - 75	89.5m 77 - 102	101.5m 87 - 116	126m 108 - 144	150m 129 - 171
	LEVEL VIII	24m 21 - 27	30m 26 - 34	36m 31 - 41	42m 36 - 48	47.5m 41 - 54	53.5m 46 - 61	78m 67 - 89	89.5m 77 - 102	101.5m 87 - 116	126m 108 - 144
	LEVEL VII	17.5m 15 - 20	24m 21 - 27	30m 26 - 34	36m 31 - 41	42m 36 - 48	47.5m 41 - 54	66m 57 - 75	78m 67 - 89	89.5m 77 - 102	101.5m 87 - 116
	LEVEL VI	13m 12+ - 14	17.5m 15 - 20	24m 21 - 27	30m 26 - 34	36m 31 - 41	42m 36 - 48	53.5m 46 - 61	66m 57 - 75	78m 67 - 89	89.5m 77 - 102
	LEVEL V	9m 6 - 12	13m 12+ - 14	15m 13 - 17	17.5m 15 - 20	25.5m 22 - 29	38m 33 - 43	47.5m 41 - 54	59.5m 51 - 68	72m 62 - 82	84m 72 - 96
	LEVEL IV	6m 3 - 9	9m 6 - 12	13m 12+ - 14	15m 13 - 17	17.5m 15 - 20	25.5m 22 - 29	38m 33 - 43	50m 43 - 57	61.5m 53 - 70	73.5m 63 - 84
	LEVEL III	2m 1 - 3	5m 3 - 8	8m 4 - 12	11m 9 - 12	14m 12+ - 16	19.5m 17 - 22	25.5m 22 - 29	38m 33 - 43	50m 43 - 57	59.5m 51 - 68
	LEVEL II	0-90 days	4m 2 - 6	6m 3 - 9	8m 4 - 12	13m 12+ - 14	16m 14 - 18	19.5m 17 - 22	25.5m 22 - 29	38m 33 - 43	50m 43 - 57
	LEVEL I	0-60 days	0-90 days	3m 2 - 5	4m 2 - 6	5.5m 3 - 8	8m 4 - 12	13m 12+ - 14	16m 14 - 18	19.5m 17 - 22	25.5m 22 - 29

*NOTE: 2SSB 5064, passed during the 2014 legislative session, amended the standard range of "Life Sentence Without Parole/Death Penalty" (i.e., the mandatory minimum term for aggravated first degree murder), where the offense was committed before the offender's 18th birthday to a minimum term of "25 years to life." The changes were made retroactive and, therefore, apply regardless of the date of offense. Refer to RCW 9.94A.510, RCW 9.94A540, RCW 9.94A.729, RCW 10.95.030, and RCW 10.95.035.

The Caseload Forecast Council is not liable for errors or omissions in the manual, for sentences that may be inappropriately calculated as a result of a practitioner's or court's reliance on the manual, or for any other written or verbal information related to adult or juvenile sentencing. The scoring sheets are intended to provide assistance in most cases but do not cover all permutations of the scoring rules. If you find any errors or omissions, we encourage you to report them to the Caseload Forecast Council.

SECTION 4 - Drug Sentencing Grid A For <u>Offenses Committed</u> On or After July 1, 2003 and Sentenced Before July 1, 2013

Drug Sentencing Grid A For <u>Offenses Committed</u> On or After July 1, 2003 and Sentenced Before July 1, 2013

Seriousness Level	Offender Score		
	0 to 2	3 to 5	6 to 9+
LEVEL III	59.5m 51 - 68	84m 68+ - 100	110m 100+ - 120
LEVEL II	16m 12+ - 20	40m 20+ - 60	90m 60+ - 120
LEVEL I	3m 0 - 6	12m 6+ - 18	18m 12+ - 24

The Caseload Forecast Council is not liable for errors or omissions in the manual, for sentences that may be inappropriately calculated as a result of a practitioner's or court's reliance on the manual, or for any other written or verbal information related to adult or juvenile sentencing. The scoring sheets are intended to provide assistance in most cases but do not cover all permutations of the scoring rules. If you find any errors or omissions, we encourage you to report them to the Caseload Forecast Council.

SECTION 4 – SERIOUS VIOLENT OFFENSES

Serious Violent Offenses

RCW 9.94A.030(46)

Statute (RCW)	Offense	Class	Seriousness Level
10.95.020	Aggravated Murder 1	A	XVI
9A.36.011	Assault 1	A	XII
9A.36.120	Assault of a Child 1	A	XII
9A.32.055	Homicide by Abuse	A	XV
9A.40.020	Kidnapping 1	A	X
9A.32.060	Manslaughter 1	A	XI
9A.32.030	Murder 1	A	XV
9A.32.050	Murder 2	A	XIV
9A.44.040	Rape 1	A	XII

Attempt, Solicitation or Conspiracy to commit one of these felonies

Any federal or out-of-state conviction for an offense that, under the laws of this state, would be a felony classified as a serious violent offense

SECTION 4 – VIOLENT OFFENSES

VIOLENT OFFENSES

RCW 9.94A.030(55)

Statute (RCW)	Offense	Class	Seriousness Level
9A.48.020	Arson 1	A	VIII
9A.48.030	Arson 2	B	IV
9A.36.021(2)(a)	Assault 2	B	IV
9A.36.021(2)(b)	Assault 2 With a Finding of Sexual Motivation	A	IV
9A.36.130	Assault of a Child 2	B	IX
9A.76.170(3)(a)	Bail Jumping with Murder 1	A	VI
9A.52.020	Burglary 1	A	VII
9A.44.083	Child Molestation 1	A	X
70.245.200(2)	Coerce Patient to Request Life-ending Medication	A	Unranked
9A.36.045	Drive-by Shooting	B	VII
70.74.180	Explosive Devices Prohibited	A	IX
9A.56.120	Extortion 1	B	V
70.245.200(1)	Forging Request for Medication	A	Unranked
79A.60.050(1)(c)	Homicide by Watercraft - Disregard for the Safety of Others	A	VII
79A.60.050(1)(b)	Homicide by Watercraft – In a Reckless Manner	A	VIII
79A.60.050(1)(a)	Homicide by Watercraft – While Under the Influence of Intoxicating Liquor or any Drug	A	IX
9A.44.100(1)(a)	Indecent Liberties - With Forcible Compulsion	A	X
9A.40.030(3)(a)	Kidnapping 2	B	V
9A.40.030(3)(b)	Kidnapping 2 With a Finding of Sexual Motivation	A	V
9A.82.060(1)(a)	Leading Organized Crime – Organizing Criminal Profiteering	A	X
70.74.280(1)	Malicious Explosion of a Substance 1	A	XV
70.74.280(2)	Malicious Explosion of a Substance 2	A	XIII
70.74.270(1)	Malicious Placement of an Explosive 1	A	XIII
9A.32.070	Manslaughter 2	B	VIII
69.50.406(1)	Over 18 and Deliver Heroin, Methamphetamine, a Narcotic from Schedule I or II, or Flunitrazepam from Schedule IV to Someone Under 18	A	DG-III
9.68A.101	Promoting Commercial Sexual Abuse of a Minor	A	XII
9A.44.050	Rape 2	A	XI
9A.44.073	Rape of a Child 1	A	XII

The Caseload Forecast Council is not liable for errors or omissions in the manual, for sentences that may be inappropriately calculated as a result of a practitioner's or court's reliance on the manual, or for any other written or verbal information related to adult or juvenile sentencing. The scoring sheets are intended to provide assistance in most cases but do not cover all permutations of the scoring rules. If you find any errors or omissions, we encourage you to report them to the Caseload Forecast Council.

SECTION 4 – VIOLENT OFFENSES

Statute (RCW)	Offense	Class	Seriousness Level
9A.44.076	Rape of a Child 2	A	XI
9A.56.200	Robbery 1	A	IX
9A.56.210	Robbery 2	B	IV
9A.76.115	Sexually Violent Predator Escape	A	X
9A.40.100(1)	Trafficking 1	A	XIV
9A.40.100(3)	Trafficking 2	A	XII
9.82.010	Treason	A	Unranked
9.41.225	Use of Machine Gun in Commission of a Felony	A	VII
46.61.522(1)(a-b)	Vehicular Assault – In a Reckless Manner or While Under the Influence of Intoxicating Liquor or any Drug	B	IV
46.61.520(1)(c)	Vehicular Homicide - Disregard for the Safety of Others	A	VII
46.61.520(1)(b)	Vehicular Homicide – In a Reckless Manner	A	XI
46.61.520(1)(a)	Vehicular Homicide – While Under the Influence of Intoxicating Liquor or any Drug	A	XI
Any offense currently listed as a Serious Violent offense			
Attempt, Solicitation or Conspiracy to commit a class A felony			
Any conviction for a felony offense in effect at any time prior to July 1, 1976, that is comparable to a felony classified as a violent.			
Any federal or out-of-state conviction for an offense that, under the laws of this state, would be a felony classified as a violent offense			

The Caseload Forecast Council is not liable for errors or omissions in the manual, for sentences that may be inappropriately calculated as a result of a practitioner's or court's reliance on the manual, or for any other written or verbal information related to adult or juvenile sentencing. The scoring sheets are intended to provide assistance in most cases but do not cover all permutations of the scoring rules. If you find any errors or omissions, we encourage you to report them to the Caseload Forecast Council.

SECTION 4 - SEX OFFENSES

SEX OFFENSES

RCW 9.94A.030(47)

Statute (RCW)	Offense	Class	Seriousness Level
9A.36.021(2)(b)	Assault 2 With a Finding of Sexual Motivation	A	IV
9A.44.083	Child Molestation 1	A	X
9A.44.086	Child Molestation 2	B	VII
9A.44.089	Child Molestation 3	C	V
9.68A.100	Commercial Sexual Abuse of a Minor	B	VIII
9.68A.090(2)	Communication with Minor for Immoral Purposes (Subsequent Violation or Prior Sex Offense Conviction)	C	III
9A.44.196	Criminal Trespass Against Children	C	Unranked
9A.44.160	Custodial Sexual Misconduct 1	C	V
9.68A.050(1)	Dealing in Depictions of Minor Engaged in Sexually Explicit Conduct 1	B	VII
9.68A.050(2)	Dealing in Depictions of Minor Engaged in Sexually Explicit Conduct 2	C	V
9A.44.132(1)(a)	Failure to Register as a Sex Offender (Second Violation Committed on or After 6/10/2010)	C	II
9A.44.132(1)(b)	Failure to Register as a Sex Offender (Third or Subsequent Violation Committed on or After 6/10/2010)	B	II
9A.64.020(1)	Incest 1	B	VI
9A.64.020(2)	Incest 2	C	V
9A.44.100(1)(a)	Indecent Liberties - With Forcible Compulsion	A	X
9A.44.100(1)(b-c)	Indecent Liberties - Without Forcible Compulsion	B	VII
9A.44.100(1)(d-f)	Indecent Liberties - Without Forcible Compulsion	B	Unranked
9A.40.030(3)(b)	Kidnapping 2 With a Finding of Sexual Motivation	A	V
9.68A.070(1)	Possession of Depictions of Minor Engaged in Sexually Explicit Conduct 1	B	VI
9.68A.070(2)	Possession of Depictions of Minor Engaged in Sexually Explicit Conduct 2	C	IV
9.68A.101	Promoting Commercial Sexual Abuse of a Minor	A	XII
9.68A.102	Promoting Travel for Commercial Sexual Abuse of a Minor	C	Unranked
9A.44.040	Rape 1	A	XII
9A.44.050	Rape 2	A	XI
9A.44.060	Rape 3	C	V
9A.44.073	Rape of a Child 1	A	XII

The Caseload Forecast Council is not liable for errors or omissions in the manual, for sentences that may be inappropriately calculated as a result of a practitioner's or court's reliance on the manual, or for any other written or verbal information related to adult or juvenile sentencing. The scoring sheets are intended to provide assistance in most cases but do not cover all permutations of the scoring rules. If you find any errors or omissions, we encourage you to report them to the Caseload Forecast Council.

SECTION 4 - SEX OFFENSES

Statute (RCW)	Offense	Class	Seriousness Level
9A.44.076	Rape of a Child 2	A	XI
9A.44.079	Rape of a Child 3	C	VI
9.68A.060(1)	Sending, Bringing into the State Depictions of Minor Engaged in Sexually Explicit Conduct 1	B	VII
9.68A.060(2)	Sending, Bringing into the State Depictions of Minor Engaged in Sexually Explicit Conduct 2	C	V
9.68A.040	Sexual Exploitation of a Minor	B	IX
9A.44.093	Sexual Misconduct with a Minor 1	C	V
9A.44.105	Sexually Violating Human Remains	C	V
9.68A.075(1)	Viewing Depictions of Minor Engaged in Sexually Explicit Conduct 1	B	IV
9.68A.075(2)	Viewing Depictions of Minor Engaged in Sexually Explicit Conduct 2	C	Unranked
9A.44.115	Voyeurism	C	II

Attempt, solicitation or conspiracy to commit any Class A or B felony listed above. An attempt, solicitation or conspiracy to commit a Class C felony above is a gross misdemeanor (RCW 9A.28-020-040) and, therefore, not a sex offense [RCW 9.94A.030(47) requires a crime to be a felony in order to be a sex offense].

Any felony with a finding of sexual motivation under RCW 9.94A.835 or 13.40.135

Any conviction for a felony offense in effect at any time prior to July 1, 1976, that is comparable to a felony classified as a sex offense in RCW 9.94A.030(47)(a)

Any federal or out-of-state conviction for an offense that, under the laws of this state, would be a felony classified as a sex offense under 9A.44 other than 9A.44.132.

The Caseload Forecast Council is not liable for errors or omissions in the manual, for sentences that may be inappropriately calculated as a result of a practitioner's or court's reliance on the manual, or for any other written or verbal information related to adult or juvenile sentencing. The scoring sheets are intended to provide assistance in most cases but do not cover all permutations of the scoring rules. If you find any errors or omissions, we encourage you to report them to the Caseload Forecast Council.

SECTION 4 – DRUG OFFENSES

DRUG OFFENSES

RCW 9.94A.030(22)

The offenses contained in this list are based on the statutory definition of a 'drug' offense per RCW 9.94A.030(22). It may not include all "drug-related" offenses

Statute (RCW)	Offense	Class	Seriousness Level
69.50.415	Controlled Substance Homicide	B	DG-III
69.50.416	Controlled Substance Label Violation	C	Unranked
69.50.4011(2)(a-b)	Create, Deliver or Possess a Counterfeit Controlled Substance – Schedule I or II Narcotic or Flunitrazepam or Methamphetamine	B	DG-II
69.50.4011(2)(c-e)	Create, Deliver or Possess a Counterfeit Controlled Substance – Schedule I-II Nonnarcotic, Schedule III-V Except Flunitrazepam or Methamphetamine	C	DG-II
69.50.401(2)(b)	Deliver or Possess with Intent to Deliver - Methamphetamine	B	DG-II
69.50.4012	Delivery of a Material in Lieu of a Controlled Substance	C	DG-II
69.50.402	Dispensing Violation (VUCSA)	C	Unranked
69.50.4015	Involving a Minor in Drug Dealing	C	DG-III
69.50.402	Maintaining a Dwelling or Place for Controlled Substances	C	DG-II
69.50.401(2)(b)	Manufacture Methamphetamine	B	DG-III
69.50.401(2)(b)	Manufacture, Deliver or Possess with Intent to Deliver - Amphetamine	B	DG-II
69.50.401(2)(c)	Manufacture, Deliver or Possess with Intent to Deliver - Marijuana	C	DG-I
69.50.401(2)(a)	Manufacture, Deliver or Possess with Intent to Deliver - Narcotics from Schedule I or II or Flunitrazepam from Schedule IV	B	DG-II
69.50.401(2)(c-e)	Manufacture, Deliver or Possess with Intent to Deliver - Narcotics from Schedule III, IV, or V or Nonnarcotics from Schedule I-V (except Marijuana, Amphetamine, Methamphetamine, or Flunitrazepam)	C	DG-II
69.50.406(1)	Over 18 and Deliver Heroin, Methamphetamine, a Narcotic from Schedule I or II, or Flunitrazepam from Schedule IV to Someone Under 18	A	DG-III
69.50.406(2)	Over 18 and Deliver Narcotic from Schedule III, IV or V, or a Nonnarcotic, Except Flunitrazepam or Methamphetamine, from Schedule I-V to Someone Under 18 and 3 Years Junior	B	DG-III
69.50.440	Possession of Ephedrine, Pseudoephedrine or Anhydrous Ammonia with Intent to Manufacture Methamphetamine	B	DG-III
69.50.410	Selling for Profit (Controlled or Counterfeit) any Controlled Substance in Schedule I	C	DG-III

The Caseload Forecast Council is not liable for errors or omissions in the manual, for sentences that may be inappropriately calculated as a result of a practitioner's or court's reliance on the manual, or for any other written or verbal information related to adult or juvenile sentencing. The scoring sheets are intended to provide assistance in most cases but do not cover all permutations of the scoring rules. If you find any errors or omissions, we encourage you to report them to the Caseload Forecast Council.

SECTION 4 – MOST SERIOUS OFFENSES (PERSISTENT OFFENDER OR "THREE STRIKES")

MOST SERIOUS OFFENSES (PERSISTENT OFFENDER OR "THREE STRIKES")

RCW 9.94A.030(33)

Statute (RCW)	Offense	Class	Seriousness Level
10.95.020	Aggravated Murder 1	A	XVI
9A.48.020	Arson 1	A	VIII
9A.36.011	Assault 1	A	XII
9A.36.021(2)(a)	Assault 2	B	IV
9A.36.021(2)(b)	Assault 2 With a Finding of Sexual Motivation	A	IV
9A.36.120	Assault of a Child 1	A	XII
9A.36.130	Assault of a Child 2	B	IX
9A.76.170(3)(a)	Bail Jumping with Murder 1	A	VI
9A.52.020	Burglary 1	A	VII
9A.44.083	Child Molestation 1	A	X
9A.44.086	Child Molestation 2	B	VII
70.245.200(2)	Coerce Patient to Request Life-ending Medication	A	Unranked
69.50.415	Controlled Substance Homicide	B	DG-III
70.74.180	Explosive Devices Prohibited	A	IX
9A.56.120	Extortion 1	B	V
70.245.200(1)	Forging Request for Medication	A	Unranked
9A.32.055	Homicide by Abuse	A	XV
79A.60.050(1)(c)	Homicide by Watercraft - Disregard for the Safety of Others	A	VII
79A.60.050(1)(b)	Homicide by Watercraft – In a Reckless Manner	A	VIII
79A.60.050(1)(a)	Homicide by Watercraft – While Under the Influence of Intoxicating Liquor or any Drug	A	IX
9A.64.020(1)	Incest 1 (When Committed Against a Child Under 14)	B	VI
9A.64.020(2)	Incest 2 (When Committed Against a Child Under 14)	C	V
9A.44.100(1)(a)	Indecent Liberties - With Forcible Compulsion	A	X
9A.44.100(1)(b-c)	Indecent Liberties - Without Forcible Compulsion	B	VII
9A.44.100(1)(d-f)	Indecent Liberties - Without Forcible Compulsion	B	Unranked
9A.40.020	Kidnapping 1	A	X
9A.40.030(3)(a)	Kidnapping 2	B	V

The Caseload Forecast Council is not liable for errors or omissions in the manual, for sentences that may be inappropriately calculated as a result of a practitioner's or court's reliance on the manual, or for any other written or verbal information related to adult or juvenile sentencing. The scoring sheets are intended to provide assistance in most cases but do not cover all permutations of the scoring rules. If you find any errors or omissions, we encourage you to report them to the Caseload Forecast Council.

SECTION 4 – MOST SERIOUS OFFENSES (PERSISTENT OFFENDER OR "THREE STRIKES")

Statute (RCW)	Offense	Class	Seriousness Level
9A.40.030(3)(b)	Kidnapping 2 With a Finding of Sexual Motivation	A	V
9A.82.060(2)(b)	Leading Organized Crime - Inciting Criminal Profiteering	B	IX
9A.82.060(1)(a)	Leading Organized Crime – Organizing Criminal Profiteering	A	X
70.74.280(1)	Malicious Explosion of a Substance 1	A	XV
70.74.280(2)	Malicious Explosion of a Substance 2	A	XIII
70.74.270(1)	Malicious Placement of an Explosive 1	A	XIII
9A.32.060	Manslaughter 1	A	XI
9A.32.070	Manslaughter 2	B	VIII
9A.32.030	Murder 1	A	XV
9A.32.050	Murder 2	A	XIV
69.50.406(1)	Over 18 and Deliver Heroin, Methamphetamine, a Narcotic from Schedule I or II, or Flunitrazepam from Schedule IV to Someone Under 18	A	DG-III
9.68A.101	Promoting Commercial Sexual Abuse of a Minor	A	XII
9A.88.070	Promoting Prostitution 1	B	VIII
9A.44.040	Rape 1	A	XII
9A.44.050	Rape 2	A	XI
9A.44.060	Rape 3	C	V
9A.44.073	Rape of a Child 1	A	XII
9A.44.076	Rape of a Child 2	A	XI
9A.56.200	Robbery 1	A	IX
9A.56.210	Robbery 2	B	IV
9.68A.040	Sexual Exploitation of a Minor	B	IX
9A.76.115	Sexually Violent Predator Escape	A	X
9A.40.100(1)	Trafficking 1	A	XIV
9A.40.100(3)	Trafficking 2	A	XII
9.82.010	Treason	A	Unranked
9.41.225	Use of Machine Gun in Commission of a Felony	A	VII
46.61.522(1)(a-b)	Vehicular Assault – In a Reckless Manner or While Under the Influence of Intoxicating Liquor or any Drug	B	IV
46.61.520(1)(c)	Vehicular Homicide - Disregard for the Safety of Others	A	VII
46.61.520(1)(b)	Vehicular Homicide – In a Reckless Manner	A	XI
46.61.520(1)(a)	Vehicular Homicide – While Under the Influence of Intoxicating Liquor or any Drug	A	XI
Any class A felony or criminal solicitation of or criminal conspiracy to commit a class A felony			

The Caseload Forecast Council is not liable for errors or omissions in the manual, for sentences that may be inappropriately calculated as a result of a practitioner's or court's reliance on the manual, or for any other written or verbal information related to adult or juvenile sentencing. The scoring sheets are intended to provide assistance in most cases but do not cover all permutations of the scoring rules. If you find any errors or omissions, we encourage you to report them to the Caseload Forecast Council.

SECTION 4 – MOST SERIOUS OFFENSES (PERSISTENT OFFENDER OR "THREE STRIKES")

Statute (RCW)	Offense	Class	Seriousness Level
	Attempt to commit one of these felonies		
	Any other class B felony offense with a finding of sexual motivation		
	Any other felony with a deadly weapon verdict under RCW 9.94A.825		
	Any felony offense in effect at any time prior to December 2, 1993, that is comparable to a most serious offense under this subsection, or any federal or out-of-state conviction for an offense that under the laws of this state would be a felony classified as a most serious offense under this subsection		
	A prior conviction for indecent liberties under **RCW 9A.88.100(1) (a), (b), and (c), chapter 260, Laws of 1975 1st ex. sess. as it existed until July 1, 1979, RCW 9A.44.100(1) (a), (b), and (c) as it existed from July 1, 1979, until June 11, 1986, and RCW 9A.44.100(1) (a), (b), and (d) as it existed from June 11, 1986, until July 1, 1988		
	A prior conviction for indecent liberties under RCW 9A.44.100(1)(c) as it existed from June 11, 1986, until July 1, 1988, if: (A) The crime was committed against a child under the age of fourteen; or (B) the relationship between the victim and perpetrator is included in the definition of indecent liberties under RCW 9A.44.100(1)(c) as it existed from July 1, 1988, through July 27, 1997, or RCW 9A.44.100(1) (d) or (e) as it existed from July 25, 1993, through July 27, 1997		
	Any out-of-state conviction for a felony offense with a finding of sexual motivation if the minimum sentence imposed was ten years or more; provided that the out-of-state felony offense must be comparable to a felony offense under Title 9 or 9A RCW and the out-of-state definition of sexual motivation must be comparable to the definition of sexual motivation contained in this section		

The Caseload Forecast Council is not liable for errors or omissions in the manual, for sentences that may be inappropriately calculated as a result of a practitioner's or court's reliance on the manual, or for any other written or verbal information related to adult or juvenile sentencing. The scoring sheets are intended to provide assistance in most cases but do not cover all permutations of the scoring rules. If you find any errors or omissions, we encourage you to report them to the Caseload Forecast Council.

SECTION 4 - PERSISTENT OFFENDER OFFENSES ("TWO STRIKES")

PERSISTENT OFFENDER OFFENSES ("TWO STRIKES")

RCW 9.94A.030(38)(b)

Statute (RCW)	Offense	Class	Seriousness Level
9A.36.011	Assault 1 With a Finding of Sexual Motivation	A	XII
9A.36.021(2)(b)	Assault 2 With a Finding of Sexual Motivation	A	IV
9A.36.120	Assault of a Child 1 With a Finding of Sexual Motivation	A	XII
9A.36.130	Assault of a Child 2 With a Finding of Sexual Motivation	B	IX
9A.52.020	Burglary 1 With a Finding of Sexual Motivation	A	VII
9A.44.083	Child Molestation 1 (where the offender was age 18 or older at the time of the offense)	A	X
9A.32.055	Homicide by Abuse With a Finding of Sexual Motivation	A	XV
9A.44.100(1)(a)	Indecent Liberties - With Forcible Compulsion	A	X
9A.40.020	Kidnapping 1 With a Finding of Sexual Motivation	A	X
9A.40.030(3)(b)	Kidnapping 2 With a Finding of Sexual Motivation	A	V
9A.32.030	Murder 1 With a Finding of Sexual Motivation	A	XV
9A.32.050	Murder 2 With a Finding of Sexual Motivation	A	XIV
9A.44.040	Rape 1	A	XII
9A.44.050	Rape 2	A	XI
9A.44.073	Rape of a Child 1 (where the offender was age 18 or older at the time of the offense)	A	XII
9A.44.076	Rape of a Child 2 (where the offender was age 18 or older at the time of the offense)	A	XI
Attempt to commit one of these felonies			

The Caseload Forecast Council is not liable for errors or omissions in the manual, for sentences that may be inappropriately calculated as a result of a practitioner's or court's reliance on the manual, or for any other written or verbal information related to adult or juvenile sentencing. The scoring sheets are intended to provide assistance in most cases but do not cover all permutations of the scoring rules. If you find any errors or omissions, we encourage you to report them to the Caseload Forecast Council.

SECTION 4 – CRIMES AGAINST PERSONS

CRIME AGAINST PERSONS OFFENSES

RCW 9.94A.411(2)

Statute (RCW)	Offense	Class	Seriousness Level
10.95.020	Aggravated Murder 1	A	XVI
9A.48.020	Arson 1	A	VIII
9A.36.011	Assault 1	A	XII
9A.36.021(2)(a)	Assault 2	B	IV
9A.36.031(1)(a-g) & (i-j)	Assault 3 – Excluding Assault 3 of a Peace Officer with a Projectile Stun Gun	C	III
9A.36.031(1)(h)	Assault 3 - Of a Peace Officer with a Projectile Stun Gun	C	IV
9A.36.120	Assault of a Child 1	A	XII
9A.36.130	Assault of a Child 2	B	IX
9A.36.140	Assault of a Child 3	C	III
9A.52.020	Burglary 1	A	VII
9A.44.083	Child Molestation 1	A	X
9A.44.086	Child Molestation 2	B	VII
9A.44.089	Child Molestation 3	C	V
9.68A.090(2)	Communication with Minor for Immoral Purposes (Subsequent Violation or Prior Sex Offense Conviction)	C	III
9.16.035(4)	Counterfeiting – Endanger Public Health or Safety	C	IV
9A.84.010(2)(b)	Criminal Mischief (If Against Person)	C	Unranked
9A.36.100	Custodial Assault	C	III
26.50.110	Domestic Violence Court Order Violation	C	V
46.61.502(6)	Driving While Under the Influence of Intoxicating Liquor or any Drug	B	V
9A.56.120	Extortion 1	B	V
9A.56.130	Extortion 2	C	III
9.35.020(2)	Identity Theft 1	B	IV
9.35.020(3)	Identity Theft 2	C	II
9A.64.020(1)	Incest 1	B	VI
9A.64.020(2)	Incest 2	C	V
9A.44.100(1)(a)	Indecent Liberties - With Forcible Compulsion	A	X

The Caseload Forecast Council is not liable for errors or omissions in the manual, for sentences that may be inappropriately calculated as a result of a practitioner's or court's reliance on the manual, or for any other written or verbal information related to adult or juvenile sentencing. The scoring sheets are intended to provide assistance in most cases but do not cover all permutations of the scoring rules. If you find any errors or omissions, we encourage you to report them to the Caseload Forecast Council.

SECTION 4 – CRIMES AGAINST PERSONS

Statute (RCW)	Offense	Class	Seriousness Level
9A.44.100(1)(b-c)	Indecent Liberties - Without Forcible Compulsion	B	VII
9A.44.100(1)(d-f)	Indecent Liberties - Without Forcible Compulsion	B	Unranked
9A.72.130	Intimidating a Juror	B	VI
9A.76.180	Intimidating a Public Servant	B	III
9A.72.110	Intimidating a Witness	B	VI
9A.40.020	Kidnapping 1	A	X
9A.40.030(3)(a)	Kidnapping 2	B	V
9A.32.060	Manslaughter 1	A	XI
9A.32.070	Manslaughter 2	B	VIII
9A.32.030	Murder 1	A	XV
9A.32.050	Murder 2	A	XIV
46.61.504(6)	Physical Control of a Vehicle While Under the Influence of Intoxicating Liquor or any Drug	C	V
9A.36.060	Promoting a Suicide Attempt	C	Unranked
9A.88.070	Promoting Prostitution 1	B	VIII
9A.44.040	Rape 1	A	XII
9A.44.050	Rape 2	A	XI
9A.44.060	Rape 3	C	V
9A.44.073	Rape of a Child 1	A	XII
9A.44.076	Rape of a Child 2	A	XI
9A.44.079	Rape of a Child 3	C	VI
9A.56.200	Robbery 1	A	IX
9A.56.210	Robbery 2	B	IV
9A.46.110	Stalking	B	V
9.61.160	Threats to Bomb (If Against Person)	B	IV
9A.40.040	Unlawful Imprisonment	C	III
46.61.522(1)(c)	Vehicular Assault - Disregard for the Safety of Others	B	III
46.61.522(1)(a-b)	Vehicular Assault – In a Reckless Manner or While Under the Influence of Intoxicating Liquor or any Drug	B	IV
46.61.520(1)(c)	Vehicular Homicide - Disregard for the Safety of Others	A	VII
46.61.520(1)(b)	Vehicular Homicide – In a Reckless Manner	A	XI
46.61.520(1)(a)	Vehicular Homicide – While Under the Influence of Intoxicating Liquor or any Drug	A	XI

The Caseload Forecast Council is not liable for errors or omissions in the manual, for sentences that may be inappropriately calculated as a result of a practitioner's or court's reliance on the manual, or for any other written or verbal information related to adult or juvenile sentencing. The scoring sheets are intended to provide assistance in most cases but do not cover all permutations of the scoring rules. If you find any errors or omissions, we encourage you to report them to the Caseload Forecast Council.

SECTION 4 - PATTERN OF STREET GANG ACTIVITY OFFENSES

Pattern Of Criminal Street Gang Activity Offenses

RCW 9.94A.030(37)

Defined as:
→ The commission, attempt, conspiracy, or solicitation of, or any prior juvenile adjudication of or adult conviction of, <u>two or more</u> of the following criminal street gang-related offenses;

→ That at least one of the offenses listed shall have occurred after July 1, 2008;

→ That the most recent committed offense listed occurred within three years of a prior offense listed; and

→ Of the offenses that were committed in this list, the offenses occurred on separate occasions or were committed by two or more persons.

Statute (RCW)	Offense	Class	Seriousness Level
10.95.020	Aggravated Murder 1	A	XVI
9.41.171	Alien Possession of a Firearm	C	Unranked
9A.48.020	Arson 1	A	VIII
9A.48.030	Arson 2	B	IV
9A.36.011	Assault 1	A	XII
9A.36.021(2)(a)	Assault 2	B	IV
9A.36.021(2)(b)	Assault 2 With a Finding of Sexual Motivation	A	IV
9A.76.170(3)(a)	Bail Jumping with Murder 1	A	VI
9A.52.020	Burglary 1	A	VII
9A.52.030	Burglary 2	B	III
9A.44.083	Child Molestation 1	A	X
70.245.200(2)	Coerce Patient to Request Life-ending Medication	A	Unranked
9A.46.120	Criminal Gang Intimidation	C	III
Chapter 69.50 RCW	Deliver or Possess with Intent to Deliver a Controlled Substance	*	*
9.41.110(8)	Delivery of Firearm by Dealer to Ineligible Person	C	Unranked
9.41.080	Delivery of Firearms to Ineligible Person	C	Unranked
9A.36.045	Drive-by Shooting	B	VII
70.74.180	Explosive Devices Prohibited	A	IX
9A.56.120	Extortion 1	B	V
9A.56.130	Extortion 2	C	III

The Caseload Forecast Council is not liable for errors or omissions in the manual, for sentences that may be inappropriately calculated as a result of a practitioner's or court's reliance on the manual, or for any other written or verbal information related to adult or juvenile sentencing. The scoring sheets are intended to provide assistance in most cases but do not cover all permutations of the scoring rules. If you find any errors or omissions, we encourage you to report them to the Caseload Forecast Council.

SECTION 4 - PATTERN OF STREET GANG ACTIVITY OFFENSES

Statute (RCW)	Offense	Class	Seriousness Level
70.245.200(1)	Forging Request for Medication	A	Unranked
9A.46.020(2)(b)	Harassment (Subsequent Conviction or Threat of Death)	C	III
79A.60.050(1)(c)	Homicide by Watercraft - Disregard for the Safety of Others	A	VII
79A.60.050(1)(b)	Homicide by Watercraft – In a Reckless Manner	A	VIII
79A.60.050(1)(a)	Homicide by Watercraft – While Under the Influence of Intoxicating Liquor or any Drug	A	IX
9A.44.100(1)(a)	Indecent Liberties - With Forcible Compulsion	A	X
9A.72.110	Intimidating a Witness	B	VI
9A.40.020	Kidnapping 1	A	X
9A.40.030(3)(a)	Kidnapping 2	B	V
9A.40.030(3)(b)	Kidnapping 2 With a Finding of Sexual Motivation	A	V
9A.82.060(1)(a)	Leading Organized Crime – Organizing Criminal Profiteering	A	X
70.74.280(1)	Malicious Explosion of a Substance 1	A	XV
70.74.280(2)	Malicious Explosion of a Substance 2	A	XIII
9A.36.080	Malicious Harassment	C	IV
9A.48.070	Malicious Mischief 1	B	II
9A.48.080	Malicious Mischief 2	C	I
70.74.270(1)	Malicious Placement of an Explosive 1	A	XIII
9A.32.060	Manslaughter 1	A	XI
9A.32.070	Manslaughter 2	B	VIII
9A.32.030	Murder 1	A	XV
9A.32.050	Murder 2	A	XIV
69.50.406(1)	Over 18 and Deliver Heroin, Methamphetamine, a Narcotic from Schedule I or II, or Flunitrazepam from Schedule IV to Someone Under 18	A	DG-III
9A.56.310	Possession of a Stolen Firearm	B	V
9A.56.068	Possession of a Stolen Vehicle	B	II
9.41.190	Possession of Machine Gun, Short-barreled Shotgun or Short-barreled Rifle	C	III
9.68A.101	Promoting Commercial Sexual Abuse of a Minor	A	XII
9A.44.040	Rape 1	A	XII
9A.44.050	Rape 2	A	XI
9A.44.073	Rape of a Child 1	A	XII
9A.44.076	Rape of a Child 2	A	XI
9A.52.025	Residential Burglary	B	IV
9A.56.200	Robbery 1	A	IX

The Caseload Forecast Council is not liable for errors or omissions in the manual, for sentences that may be inappropriately calculated as a result of a practitioner's or court's reliance on the manual, or for any other written or verbal information related to adult or juvenile sentencing. The scoring sheets are intended to provide assistance in most cases but do not cover all permutations of the scoring rules. If you find any errors or omissions, we encourage you to report them to the Caseload Forecast Council.

SECTION 4 - PATTERN OF STREET GANG ACTIVITY OFFENSES

Statute (RCW)	Offense	Class	Seriousness Level
9A.56.210	Robbery 2	B	IV
9A.76.115	Sexually Violent Predator Escape	A	X
9A.56.070	Taking Motor Vehicle Without Permission 1	B	V
9A.56.075	Taking Motor Vehicle Without Permission 2	C	I
9A.72.120	Tampering with a Witness	C	III
9A.56.300	Theft of a Firearm	B	VI
9A.56.065	Theft of a Motor Vehicle	B	II
9A.40.100(1)	Trafficking 1	A	XIV
9A.40.100(3)	Trafficking 2	A	XII
9.82.010	Treason	A	Unranked
9.41.040(1)	Unlawful Possession of a Firearm 1	B	VII
9.41.040(2)	Unlawful Possession of a Firearm 2	C	III
9.41.225	Use of Machine Gun in Commission of a Felony	A	VII
46.61.522(1)(a-b)	Vehicular Assault – In a Reckless Manner or While Under the Influence of Intoxicating Liquor or any Drug	B	IV
46.61.520(1)(c)	Vehicular Homicide - Disregard for the Safety of Others	A	VII
46.61.520(1)(b)	Vehicular Homicide – In a Reckless Manner	A	XI
46.61.520(1)(a)	Vehicular Homicide – While Under the Influence of Intoxicating Liquor or any Drug	A	XI

Any felony conviction by a person 18 years of age or older with a special finding involving a juvenile in a felony offense under RCW 9.94A.833

The Caseload Forecast Council is not liable for errors or omissions in the manual, for sentences that may be inappropriately calculated as a result of a practitioner's or court's reliance on the manual, or for any other written or verbal information related to adult or juvenile sentencing. The scoring sheets are intended to provide assistance in most cases but do not cover all permutations of the scoring rules. If you find any errors or omissions, we encourage you to report them to the Caseload Forecast Council.

SECTION 4 – OFFENSES REQUIRING SEX OFFENDER REGISTRATION

OFFENSES REQUIRING SEX OFFENDER REGISTRATION

SEX OFFENDER REGISTRATION (9A.44.140)

For further information on duration of registration and relief from registration, refer to RCW 9A.44.140 through RCW 9A.44.143. If the offender is required to register for a <u>federal, tribal or out-of-state conviction,</u> when the offender has spent 15 consecutive years in the community without being convicted of a disqualifying offense during that time, the offender may petition the court for relief from registration.

LIFETIME REGISTRATION

Statute (RCW)	Offense	Class	Seriousness Level
Chapter 71.09 RCW	Determined to be a Sexually Violent Predator	NA	NA
9A.44.100(1)(a)	Indecent Liberties - With Forcible Compulsion (If convicted as an adult for an offense committed on or after 6/8/2000.)	A	X
9A.28.020(3)(a)	Indecent Liberties - With Forcible Compulsion – Criminal Attempt (If convicted as an adult for an offense committed on or after 6/8/2000.)	A	X
9A.28.030(2)	Indecent Liberties - With Forcible Compulsion – Criminal Solicitation (If convicted as an adult for an offense committed on or after 6/8/2000.)	A	X
9A.44.040	Rape 1 (If convicted as an adult for an offense committed on or after 6/8/2000.)	A	XII
9A.28.020(3)(a)	Rape 1 – Criminal Attempt (If convicted as an adult for an offense committed on or after 6/8/2000.)	A	XII
9A.28.030(2)	Rape 1 – Criminal Solicitation (If convicted as an adult for an offense committed on or after 6/8/2000.)	A	XII
9A.44.050	Rape 2 (With Forcible Compulsion) (If convicted as an adult for an offense committed on or after 6/8/2000.)	A	XI
9A.28.020(3)(a)	Rape 2 (With Forcible Compulsion) – Criminal Attempt (If convicted as an adult for an offense committed on or after 6/8/2000.)	A	XI
9A.28.030(2)	Rape 2 (With Forcible Compulsion) – Criminal Solicitation (If convicted as an adult for an offense committed on or after 6/8/2000.)	A	XI

The Caseload Forecast Council is not liable for errors or omissions in the manual, for sentences that may be inappropriately calculated as a result of a practitioner's or court's reliance on the manual, or for any other written or verbal information related to adult or juvenile sentencing. The scoring sheets are intended to provide assistance in most cases but do not cover all permutations of the scoring rules. If you find any errors or omissions, we encourage you to report them to the Caseload Forecast Council.

SECTION 4 – OFFENSES REQUIRING SEX OFFENDER REGISTRATION

INDEFINITE REGISTRATION

Statute (RCW)	Offense	Class	Seriousness Level
9A.36.021(2)(b)	Assault 2 With a Finding of Sexual Motivation	A	IV
9A.44.083	Child Molestation 1	A	X
9A.28.020(3)(a)	Child Molestation 1 – Criminal Attempt	A	X
9A.28.030(2)	Child Molestation 1 – Criminal Solicitation	A	X
9A.40.030(3)(b)	Kidnapping 2 With a Finding of Sexual Motivation	A	V
9.68A.101	Promoting Commercial Sexual Abuse of a Minor	A	XII
9A.44.040	Rape 1 (For an offense committed prior to 6/8/2000.)	A	XII
9A.28.020(3)(a)	Rape 1 – Criminal Attempt (For an offense committed prior to 6/8/2000.)	A	XII
9A.28.030(2)	Rape 1 – Criminal Solicitation (For an offense committed prior to 6/8/2000.)	A	XII
9A.44.050	Rape 2 (With Forcible Compulsion) (For an offense committed prior to 6/8/2000.)	A	XI
9A.28.020(3)(a)	Rape 2 (With Forcible Compulsion) – Criminal Attempt (For an offense committed prior to 6/8/2000.)	A	XI
9A.28.030(2)	Rape 2 (With Forcible Compulsion) – Criminal Solicitation (For an offense committed prior to 6/8/2000.)	A	XI
9A.44.050	Rape 2 (Without Forcible Compulsion)	A	XI
9A.28.020(3)(a)	Rape 2 (Without Forcible Compulsion) – Criminal Attempt	A	XI
9A.28.030(2)	Rape 2 (Without Forcible Compulsion) – Criminal Solicitation	A	XI
9A.44.073	Rape of a Child 1	A	XII
9A.28.020(3)(a)	Rape of a Child 1 – Criminal Attempt	A	XII
9A.28.030(2)	Rape of a Child 1 – Criminal Solicitation	A	XII
9A.44.076	Rape of a Child 2	A	XI
9A.28.020(3)(a)	Rape of a Child 2 – Criminal Attempt	A	XI
9A.28.030(2)	Rape of a Child 2 – Criminal Solicitation	A	XI

Any Offense Listed Under RCW 9A.44.142(5)

Any Sex or Kidnapping Offense When the Defendant Already Has One or More Prior Convictions for a Sex or Kidnapping Offense

---

The Caseload Forecast Council is not liable for errors or omissions in the manual, for sentences that may be inappropriately calculated as a result of a practitioner's or court's reliance on the manual, or for any other written or verbal information related to adult or juvenile sentencing. The scoring sheets are intended to provide assistance in most cases but do not cover all permutations of the scoring rules. If you find any errors or omissions, we encourage you to report them to the Caseload Forecast Council.

SECTION 4 – OFFENSES REQUIRING SEX OFFENDER REGISTRATION

15 YEAR REGISTRATION

Duty to register shall end fifteen years after the last date of release from confinement, if any, (including full-time residential treatment) pursuant to the conviction, or entry of the judgment and sentence, if the person has spent fifteen consecutive years in the community without being convicted of a disqualifying offense during that time period.

Statute (RCW)	Offense	Class	Seriousness Level
9A.44.086	Child Molestation 2	B	VII
9.68A.100	Commercial Sexual Abuse of a Minor	B	VIII
9.68A.050(1)	Dealing in Depictions of Minor Engaged in Sexually Explicit Conduct 1	B	VII
9A.44.132(1)(b)	Failure to Register as a Sex Offender (Third or Subsequent Violation Committed on or After 6/10/2010)	B	II
9A.64.020(1)	Incest 1	B	VI
9A.44.100(1)(a)	Indecent Liberties - With Forcible Compulsion (For an offense committed prior to 6/8/2000.)	B	X
9A.28.020(3)(a)	Indecent Liberties - With Forcible Compulsion – Criminal Attempt (For an offense committed prior to 6/8/2000.)	B	X
9A.28.030(2)	Indecent Liberties - With Forcible Compulsion – Criminal Solicitation (For an offense committed prior to 6/8/2000.)	B	X
9A.44.100(1)(b-c)	Indecent Liberties - Without Forcible Compulsion	B	VII
9A.44.100(1)(d-f)	Indecent Liberties - Without Forcible Compulsion	B	Unranked
9.68A.070(1)	Possession of Depictions of Minor Engaged in Sexually Explicit Conduct 1	B	VI
9A.88.070	Promoting Prostitution 1*	B	VIII
9.68A.060(1)	Sending, Bringing into the State Depictions of Minor Engaged in Sexually Explicit Conduct 1	B	VII
9.68A.040	Sexual Exploitation of a Minor	B	IX
9.68A.075(1)	Viewing Depictions of Minor Engaged in Sexually Explicit Conduct 1	B	IV

No prior convictions for a sex or kidnapping offense
Current offense is not listed in RCW 9A.44.142(5)

The Caseload Forecast Council is not liable for errors or omissions in the manual, for sentences that may be inappropriately calculated as a result of a practitioner's or court's reliance on the manual, or for any other written or verbal information related to adult or juvenile sentencing. The scoring sheets are intended to provide assistance in most cases but do not cover all permutations of the scoring rules. If you find any errors or omissions, we encourage you to report them to the Caseload Forecast Council.

SECTION 4 – OFFENSES REQUIRING SEX OFFENDER REGISTRATION

10 YEAR REGISTRATION

Duty to register shall end ten years after the last date of release from confinement, if any, (including full-time residential treatment) pursuant to the conviction, or entry of the judgment and sentence, if the person has spent fifteen consecutive years in the community without being convicted of a disqualifying offense during that time period.

Statute (RCW)	Offense	Class	Seriousness Level
9A.44.089	Child Molestation 3	C	V
9.68A.090(2)	Communication with Minor for Immoral Purposes (Subsequent Violation or Prior Sex Offense Conviction)	C	III
9A.44.196	Criminal Trespass Against Children	C	Unranked
9A.44.160	Custodial Sexual Misconduct 1	C	V
9.68A.050(2)	Dealing in Depictions of Minor Engaged in Sexually Explicit Conduct 2	C	V
9A.44.132(1)(a)	Failure to Register as a Sex Offender (Second Violation Committed on or After 6/10/2010)	C	II
9A.64.020(2)	Incest 2	C	V
9.68A.070(2)	Possession of Depictions of Minor Engaged in Sexually Explicit Conduct 2	C	IV
9A.88.080	Promoting Prostitution 2*	C	III
9.68A.102	Promoting Travel for Commercial Sexual Abuse of a Minor	C	Unranked
9A.44.060	Rape 3	C	V
9A.44.079	Rape of a Child 3	C	VI
9.68A.060(2)	Sending, Bringing into the State Depictions of Minor Engaged in Sexually Explicit Conduct 2	C	V
9A.44.093	Sexual Misconduct with a Minor 1	C	V
9A.44.105	Sexually Violating Human Remains	C	V
9.68A.075(2)	Viewing Depictions of Minor Engaged in Sexually Explicit Conduct 2	C	Unranked
9A.44.115	Voyeurism	C	II
Violation of RCW 9.68A.090			
Violation of RCW 9A.44.096			
Attempt, solicitation or conspiracy to commit a class C sex offense			
Current offense is not listed in RCW 9A.44.142(5)			

The Caseload Forecast Council is not liable for errors or omissions in the manual, for sentences that may be inappropriately calculated as a result of a practitioner's or court's reliance on the manual, or for any other written or verbal information related to adult or juvenile sentencing. The scoring sheets are intended to provide assistance in most cases but do not cover all permutations of the scoring rules. If you find any errors or omissions, we encourage you to report them to the Caseload Forecast Council.

SECTION 4 – NONVIOLENT OFFENSES

NONVIOLENT OFFENSES

Statute (RCW)	Offense	Class	Seriousness Level
9A.42.060	Abandonment of Dependent Persons 1	B	IX
9A.42.070	Abandonment of Dependent Persons 2	C	V
29A.84.680(1)	Absentee Voting Violation	C	Unranked
46.52.130(5)(b)	Abstracts of Driving Records – Intentional Misuse	C	Unranked
20.01.460(2)	Acting as Commission Merchant, Dealer, Cash Buyer Without License	C	Unranked
9A.82.030(3)	Advancing Money or Property for Extortionate Extension of Credit	B	V
69.52.030	Advertising Imitation Controlled Substances	C	Unranked
46.37.660(2)(c)	Air Bag Diagnostic Systems	C	V
46.37.660(2)(b)	Air Bag Diagnostic Systems (Causing Bodily Injury or Death)	C	VII
46.37.660(1)(c)	Air Bag Replacement Requirements	C	V
46.37.660(1)(b)	Air Bag Replacement Requirements (Causing Bodily Injury or Death)	C	VII
30A.42.290(3)	Alien Bank or Bureau – Destroy or Secrete Records	B	Unranked
30A.42.290(2)	Alien Bank or Bureau – False Entry, Statements, etc.	B	Unranked
9.41.171	Alien Possession of a Firearm	C	Unranked
9.45.210	Altering Sample or Certificate of Assay	C	Unranked
9A.76.177	Amber Alert – Making False Statements to a Public Servant	C	Unranked
68.64.160	Anatomical Gift - Illegal Financial Gain	C	Unranked
68.64.150	Anatomical Gifts - Illegal Purchase or Sale	C	Unranked
16.52.205(2)	Animal Cruelty 1	C	Unranked
16.52.205(3)	Animal Cruelty 1 - Sexual Contact or Conduct	C	III
16.52.117	Animal Fighting	C	Unranked
9A.36.031(1)(a-g) & (i-j)	Assault 3 – Excluding Assault 3 of a Peace Officer with a Projectile Stun Gun	C	III
9A.36.031(1)(h)	Assault 3 - Of a Peace Officer with a Projectile Stun Gun	C	IV
79A.60.060	Assault by Watercraft	B	IV
9A.36.140	Assault of a Child 3	C	III
9.05.030	Assembly of Saboteurs	B	Unranked
72.23.170	Assist Escape of Mental Patient	C	Unranked
9A.82.080(3)	Attempt or Conspiracy to Violation 9A.82.080(1) or (2)	C	Unranked
46.61.024	Attempting to Elude Pursuing Police Vehicle	C	I

The Caseload Forecast Council is not liable for errors or omissions in the manual, for sentences that may be inappropriately calculated as a result of a practitioner's or court's reliance on the manual, or for any other written or verbal information related to adult or juvenile sentencing. The scoring sheets are intended to provide assistance in most cases but do not cover all permutations of the scoring rules. If you find any errors or omissions, we encourage you to report them to the Caseload Forecast Council.

SECTION 4 – NONVIOLENT OFFENSES

Statute (RCW)	Offense	Class	Seriousness Level
9A.76.170(3)(b)	Bail Jumping with Class A Felony	B	V
9A.76.170(3)(c)	Bail Jumping with Class B or C Felony	C	III
30A.12.100	Bank or Trust Company - Destroy or Secrete Records	B	Unranked
30A.12.090	Bank or Trust Company - False Entry, Statements, etc.	B	Unranked
30A.44.120	Bank or Trust Company - Receiving Deposits When Insolvent	B	Unranked
30A.44.110	Bank or Trust Company - Transfer of Assets Prior to Insolvency	B	Unranked
9A.64.010	Bigamy	C	Unranked
9A.72.100	Bribe Received by Witness	B	IV
9A.68.010	Bribery	B	VI
9A.72.090	Bribing a Witness	B	IV
9.46.155	Bribing to Obtain a License From Public Officials, Employees, Agents	C	Unranked
72.23.300	Bringing Narcotics, Liquor, or Weapons into State Institution or Grounds	B	Unranked
9.47.120	Bunco Steering	B	Unranked
9A.52.030	Burglary 2	B	III
46.87.260	Cab Card Forgery (Effective Until 7/1/2016)	B	Unranked
9.46.180	Causing Person to Violate Gambling Laws	B	Unranked
9.46.1961	Cheating 1	C	IV
9A.64.030(3)(b)	Child Buying	C	Unranked
49.12.410(2)	Child Labor Law Violation – Death/Disability	C	Unranked
9A.44.086	Child Molestation 2	B	VII
9A.44.089	Child Molestation 3	C	V
9A.64.030(3)(a)	Child Selling	C	Unranked
9A.48.120	Civil Disorder Training	B	VII
9A.40.110	Coercion of Involuntary Servitude	C	Unranked
9A.82.045	Collection of Unlawful Debt	C	Unranked
9A.68.060	Commercial Bribery	B	IV
77.15.500(3)(b)	Commercial Fishing Without a License 1	C	II
9.68A.100	Commercial Sexual Abuse of a Minor	B	VIII
19.158.160	Commercial Telephone Solicitor Deception (Value of $250 or More)	C	Unranked
30A.04.240	Commingling of Funds or Securities	B	Unranked
21.30.140	Commodity Transaction Violation	B	Unranked
9.68A.090(2)	Communication with Minor for Immoral Purposes (Subsequent Violation or Prior Sex Offense Conviction)	C	III

The Caseload Forecast Council is not liable for errors or omissions in the manual, for sentences that may be inappropriately calculated as a result of a practitioner's or court's reliance on the manual, or for any other written or verbal information related to adult or juvenile sentencing. The scoring sheets are intended to provide assistance in most cases but do not cover all permutations of the scoring rules. If you find any errors or omissions, we encourage you to report them to the Caseload Forecast Council.

SECTION 4 – NONVIOLENT OFFENSES

Statute (RCW)	Offense	Class	Seriousness Level
9A.90.040	Computer Trespass 1	C	II
69.50.465	Conducting or Maintaining a Marijuana Club	C	Unranked
19.144.100(2)	Control of Real Property Resulting from Mortgage Fraud Activities	B	Unranked
69.50.415	Controlled Substance Homicide	B	DG-III
69.50.416	Controlled Substance Label Violation	C	Unranked
9.16.035(4)	Counterfeiting - Endanger Public Health or Safety	C	IV
9.16.035(3)	Counterfeiting – Third Conviction and Value $10,000 or More	C	II
69.50.4011(2)(a-b)	Create, Deliver or Possess a Counterfeit Controlled Substance – Schedule I or II Narcotic or Flunitrazepam or Methamphetamine	B	DG-II
69.50.4011(2)(c-e)	Create, Deliver or Possess a Counterfeit Controlled Substance – Schedule I-II Nonnarcotic, Schedule III-V except Flunitrazepam or Methamphetamine	C	DG-II
46.87.260	Credential Forgery (Effective 7/1/2016)	B	Unranked
31.12.724(3)	Credit Union - Fraudulent Receipt of Credit Union Deposit	B	Unranked
31.12.724(2)	Credit Union - Transfer of Credit Union Assets Prior to Insolvency	B	Unranked
9.08.090	Crimes Against Animal Facilities	C	Unranked
9A.46.120	Criminal Gang Intimidation	C	III
9A.60.040	Criminal Impersonation 1	C	Unranked
9A.84.010(2)(b)	Criminal Mischief	C	Unranked
9A.42.020	Criminal Mistreatment 1	B	X
9A.42.030	Criminal Mistreatment 2	C	V
9A.82.160	Criminal Profiteering Lien After Service of Notice	C	Unranked
9.05.060(2)	Criminal Sabotage	B	Unranked
9A.44.196	Criminal Trespass Against Children	C	Unranked
9A.36.100	Custodial Assault	C	III
9A.40.060	Custodial Interference 1	C	Unranked
9A.40.070	Custodial Interference 2 (Subsequent Offense)	C	Unranked
9A.44.160	Custodial Sexual Misconduct 1	C	V
9.61.260(3)	Cyberstalking (With Prior Harassment Conviction or Threat of Death)	C	III
43.06.230	Damage Property or Cause Personal Injury after State of Emergency Proclaimed	B	Unranked
16.08.100(2)	Dangerous Dog Attack (Subsequent Offense)	C	Unranked
16.08.100(3)	Dangerous Dog Attack Resulting in Severe Injury or Death	C	Unranked
9.68A.050(1)	Dealing in Depictions of Minor Engaged in Sexually Explicit Conduct 1	B	VII
9.68A.050(2)	Dealing in Depictions of Minor Engaged in Sexually Explicit Conduct 2	C	V

The Caseload Forecast Council is not liable for errors or omissions in the manual, for sentences that may be inappropriately calculated as a result of a practitioner's or court's reliance on the manual, or for any other written or verbal information related to adult or juvenile sentencing. The scoring sheets are intended to provide assistance in most cases but do not cover all permutations of the scoring rules. If you find any errors or omissions, we encourage you to report them to the Caseload Forecast Council.

SECTION 4 – NONVIOLENT OFFENSES

Statute (RCW)	Offense	Class	Seriousness Level
22.09.310	Dealing in Unauthorized Warehouse Receipts for Agricultural Commodities	C	Unranked
39.44.101	Defraud a Facsimile Signature on Bonds and Coupons	B	Unranked
87.03.200	Defraud Facsimile Signatures on Bonds and Coupons – Irrigation Districts	B	Unranked
19.110.120	Defraud or Provide Misleading or Untrue Documents Related to a Business Opportunity Sale	B	Unranked
9A.61.030	Defrauding a Public Utility 1	B	Unranked
9A.61.040	Defrauding a Public Utility 2	C	Unranked
19.48.110(1)(b)	Defrauding an Innkeeper (Value of $75.00 or More)	B	Unranked
69.50.401(2)(b)	Deliver or Possess with Intent to Deliver - Methamphetamine	B	DG-II
69.50.4012	Delivery of a Material in Lieu of a Controlled Substance	C	DG-II
9.41.110(8)	Delivery of Firearm by Dealer to Ineligible Person	C	Unranked
9.41.080	Delivery of Firearms to Ineligible Person	C	Unranked
69.52.030(2)	Delivery of Imitation Controlled Substance by Person 18 or Over to Person Under 18	B	DG-III
35A.36.040	Designation of Bonds – Violation (Code Cities)	B	Unranked
35.36.040	Designation of Bonds – Violation (First Class Cities)	B	Unranked
27.44.040(1)	Destroying, Removing or Defacing Indian Graves	C	Unranked
68.60.040(1)	Destruction of Tomb, Plot, Marker, or Cemetery Property	C	Unranked
9.38.060	Digital Signatures Fraud	C	Unranked
9A.76.023(2)(a)	Disarming a Law Enforcement or Corrections Officer	C	Unranked
9A.76.023(2)(b)	Disarming a Law Enforcement or Corrections Officer and Firearm is Discharged	B	Unranked
9A.86.010	Disclosing Intimate Images	C	Unranked
19.110.075(2)	Disclosures Knowingly Not Provided at Sale of Business Opportunity (Violation of RCW 19.110.070)	B	Unranked
69.50.402	Dispensing Violation (VUCSA)	C	Unranked
82.26.190	Distributors and Retailer of Tobacco Products License Violation	C	Unranked
27.53.060	Disturbing Archaeological Resources or Site	C	Unranked
43.43.856	Divulging Confidential Investigative Information Pertaining to Organized Crime	B	Unranked
26.50.110	Domestic Violence Court Order Violation	C	V
46.61.502(6)	Driving While Under the Influence of Intoxicating Liquor or any Drug	B	V
29A.84.270	Duplication of Name – Conspiracy to Mislead	B	Unranked
29A.84.320	Duplication of Names on Declaration of Candidacy	B	Unranked
29A.84.655	Election Officer Permits Repeat Vote	C	Unranked

The Caseload Forecast Council is not liable for errors or omissions in the manual, for sentences that may be inappropriately calculated as a result of a practitioner's or court's reliance on the manual, or for any other written or verbal information related to adult or juvenile sentencing. The scoring sheets are intended to provide assistance in most cases but do not cover all permutations of the scoring rules. If you find any errors or omissions, we encourage you to report them to the Caseload Forecast Council.

SECTION 4 – NONVIOLENT OFFENSES

Statute (RCW)	Offense	Class	Seriousness Level
29A.84.720	Election Officers – Violation	C	Unranked
29A.84.030	Election or Mail Ballot Violation	C	Unranked
19.300.020	Electronic Communication Devices – Illegal Scanning	C	Unranked
9A.90.060	Electronic Data Service Interference	C	II
9A.90.080	Electronic Data Tampering 1	C	II
9A.90.100	Electronic Data Theft	C	II
79A.60.090	Eluding a Law Enforcement Vessel	C	Unranked
18.39.350	Embalmers/Funeral Directors Violation	C	Unranked
43.08.140	Embezzlement by State Treasurer	B	Unranked
9A.42.100	Endangerment With a Controlled Substance	B	IV
46.80.020(b)	Engage in Business of Wrecking Vehicles Without a License (Subsequent Offense)	C	Unranked
51.48.103(2)	Engaging in Business After Certificate of Coverage Revocation	C	Unranked
70.345.090	Engaging in Delivery Sales of Vapor Products Without a License, or Without Proper Shipping Documentation	C	Unranked
77.15.620(3)(b)	Engaging in Fish Dealing Activity Unlicensed 1	C	II
16.08.100(4)	Entering Dog in a Dog Fight	C	Unranked
61.34.030	Equity Skimming	B	II
9.68.060	Erotic Material (Third or Subsequent Offense)	B	Unranked
9A.76.110	Escape 1	B	IV
9A.76.120	Escape 2	C	III
9A.76.130(3)(b)	Escape 3 (Third or Subsequent Offense)	C	Unranked
72.09.310	Escape from Community Custody	C	II
51.48.020(1)	Evading Industrial Insurance Premiums	C	Unranked
82.42.085	Evading the Collection of Aircraft Fuel Tax	C	Unranked
74.09.260	Excessive Charges, Payments	C	Unranked
48.06.190	Exhibiting False Accounts of Insurer	B	Unranked
9A.56.130	Extortion 2	C	III
9A.82.020	Extortionate Extension of Credit	B	V
9A.82.040	Extortionate Means to Collect Extensions of Credit	B	V
19.25.040(2)(a)	Failure to Disclose Origin of Certain Recordings (At Least 100 Recordings or Subsequent Conviction)	B	Unranked
19.25.040(2)(b)	Failure to Disclose Origin of Certain Recordings (More than 10 but Less Than 100 Recordings)	C	Unranked

The Caseload Forecast Council is not liable for errors or omissions in the manual, for sentences that may be inappropriately calculated as a result of a practitioner's or court's reliance on the manual, or for any other written or verbal information related to adult or juvenile sentencing. The scoring sheets are intended to provide assistance in most cases but do not cover all permutations of the scoring rules. If you find any errors or omissions, we encourage you to report them to the Caseload Forecast Council.

SECTION 4 – NONVIOLENT OFFENSES

Statute (RCW)	Offense	Class	Seriousness Level
36.18.170	Failure to Pay Over Fees to County Treasurer	C	Unranked
9A.44.132(3)	Failure to Register as a Kidnapping Offender	C	Unranked
9A.44.132(1)(a)	Failure to Register as a Sex Offender (First Violation)	C	Unranked
9A.44.132(1)(a)	Failure to Register as a Sex Offender (Second Violation Committed on or After 6/10/2010)	C	II
9A.44.132(1)(a)	Failure to Register as a Sex Offender (Subsequent Violation Committed on or After 6/7/2006 but Before 6/10/2010)	C	II
9A.44.132(1)(b)	Failure to Register as a Sex Offender (Third or Subsequent Violation Committed on or After 6/10/2010)	B	II
19.146.050	Failure to Use a Trust Account	C	Unranked
19.142.080	Failure to Use a Trust Account or Furnish Bond for Health Studio	C	Unranked
38.42.050	False Affidavit Under Service Member Civil Relief Act	C	Unranked
74.08.100	False Age and Residency Public Assistance Verification	B	Unranked
42.24.100	False Claim from Municipal Corporation (Charged as Perjury 2)	C	Unranked
42.17A.750	False Documents Registered with Public Disclosure Commission	C	Unranked
51.48.020(2)	False Information in Industrial Insurance Claim (Charged as Theft)	*	*
48.30.230	False Insurance Claims (Value in Excess of $1,500)	C	Unranked
9.24.050	False Report of Corporation	B	Unranked
74.09.230	False Statement for Medical Assistance	C	Unranked
69.43.080	False Statement in Report of Precursor Drugs	C	Unranked
82.32.290(2)	False Statement to Department of Revenue	C	Unranked
19.230.300	False Statement, Misrepresentation or False Certification of Uniform Money services Record	C	Unranked
41.26.062	False Statements or Records to Defraud Law Enforcement Officers and Firefighters Retirement System	B	Unranked
41.32.055(1)	False Statements or Records to Defraud Teachers Retirement System	B	Unranked
74.09.250	False Statements Regarding Institutions, Facilities	C	Unranked
46.12.750(1)	False Statements, Illegal Transfers, Alterations or Forgeries of Vehicle Title	B	Unranked
65.12.740	False Swearing - Registration of Land Title (Charged as Perjury)	*	*
74.08.055(2)	False Verification for Welfare	B	I
26.20.030	Family Abandonment	C	Unranked
69.41.020	Forged Prescription - Legend Drug	B	DG-I
69.50.403	Forged Prescription for a Controlled Substance	C	DG-I
9A.60.020	Forgery	C	I
76.36.120	Forgery of Forest Product Mark	B	Unranked

The Caseload Forecast Council is not liable for errors or omissions in the manual, for sentences that may be inappropriately calculated as a result of a practitioner's or court's reliance on the manual, or for any other written or verbal information related to adult or juvenile sentencing. The scoring sheets are intended to provide assistance in most cases but do not cover all permutations of the scoring rules. If you find any errors or omissions, we encourage you to report them to the Caseload Forecast Council.

SECTION 4 – NONVIOLENT OFFENSES

Statute (RCW)	Offense	Class	Seriousness Level
65.12.760	Forgery of Registrar's Signature or Seal	B	Unranked
82.24.100	Forgery or Counterfeit Cigarette Tax Stamp	B	Unranked
19.100.210	Franchise Investment Protection Violation	B	Unranked
29A.84.711	Fraud in Certification of Nomination or Ballot	C	Unranked
9.45.170	Fraud in Liquor Warehouse Receipts	C	Unranked
9.45.124	Fraud in Measurement of Goods	B	Unranked
9.26A.110(3)	Fraud in Obtaining Telecommunications Services (Value Exceeds $250)	C	Unranked
67.24.010	Fraud in Sporting Contest	B	Unranked
9A.60.060	Fraudulent Creation or Revocation of Mental Health Advance Directive	C	I
76.48.141(1)(a)	Fraudulent Document as Specialized Forest Products Permit, Sales Invoice, Bill of Lading, etc.	C	Unranked
76.48.141(2)	Fraudulent Document for Specialized Forest Products Buyer	C	Unranked
9.45.270(3)	Fraudulent Filing of Vehicle Report of Sale (Value Exceeds $1,500)	B	Unranked
9.45.270(2)	Fraudulent Filing of Vehicle Report of Sale (Value Exceeds $250)	C	Unranked
9.24.020	Fraudulent Issue of Stock, Scrip, etc.	B	Unranked
48.102.160(3)	Fraudulent Life Insurance Settlement	B	Unranked
65.12.750	Fraudulent Procurement or False Entry on Land Title Registration	C	Unranked
76.48.141(1)(b)	Fraudulent Representation of Authority to Harvest Specialized Forest Products	C	Unranked
82.36.380	Fuel Tax Evasion	C	Unranked
9.46.160	Gambling Without License	B	Unranked
9.46.039	Greyhound Racing	B	Unranked
9A.46.020(2)(b)	Harassment (Subsequent Conviction or Threat of Death)	C	III
9A.76.200	Harming a Police Dog/Horse or an Accelerate Detection Dog	C	Unranked
48.80.030	Health Care False Claims	C	II
46.52.020(4)(a)	Hit and Run - Death	B	IX
46.52.020(4)(b)	Hit and Run - Injury	C	IV
79A.60.200(3)	Hit and Run with Vessel - Injury Accident	C	IV
9.94.030	Holding Hostages or Interfering with Officer's Duty	B	Unranked
9.35.020(2)	Identity Theft 1	B	IV
9.35.020(3)	Identity Theft 2	C	II
69.41.040	Illegal Issuance of Legend Drug Prescription	B	Unranked
9.16.020	Imitating Lawful Brands With Intent	C	Unranked
19.146.235(9)	Impairing Mortgage Broker Investigation	B	Unranked

The Caseload Forecast Council is not liable for errors or omissions in the manual, for sentences that may be inappropriately calculated as a result of a practitioner's or court's reliance on the manual, or for any other written or verbal information related to adult or juvenile sentencing. The scoring sheets are intended to provide assistance in most cases but do not cover all permutations of the scoring rules. If you find any errors or omissions, we encourage you to report them to the Caseload Forecast Council.

SECTION 4 – NONVIOLENT OFFENSES

Statute (RCW)	Offense	Class	Seriousness Level
9.35.010	Improperly Obtaining Financial Information	C	II
9A.64.020(1)	Incest 1	B	VI
9A.64.020(2)	Incest 2	C	V
9A.88.010(2)(c)	Indecent Exposure to a Person Under Age 14 (Subsequent Conviction or Has Prior Sex Offense Conviction)	C	IV
9A.44.100(1)(b-c)	Indecent Liberties - Without Forcible Compulsion	B	VII
9A.44.100(d-f)	Indecent Liberties - Without Forcible Compulsion	B	Unranked
9.45.126	Inducing Fraud in Measurement of Goods	B	Unranked
9A.82.070	Influencing Outcome of Sporting Event	C	IV
40.16.010	Injury to a Public Record	C	Unranked
40.16.020	Injury to and Misappropriation of Public Record by Officer	B	Unranked
88.08.050(1)	Injury to Lighthouses or United States Light	B	Unranked
9.24.030	Insolvent Bank Receiving Deposit	B	Unranked
48.06.030	Insurance Solicitation Permit Violation	B	Unranked
9.91.170(5)	Intentional Infliction, Injury or Death to a Guide Dog or Service Animal	C	Unranked
9.91.175(3)	Intentionally Injures, Disables or Causes Death of an On-Duty Search and Rescue Dog	C	Unranked
9.73.230	Intercepting, Transmitting or Recording Conversations Concerning Controlled Substances	C	Unranked
69.25.155(1)	Interference with Person Performing Official Duties	C	Unranked
69.25.155(2)	Interference with Person Performing Official Duties With a Deadly Weapon	B	Unranked
9A.72.160	Intimidating a Judge	B	VI
9A.72.130	Intimidating a Juror	B	VI
9A.76.180	Intimidating a Public Servant	B	III
9A.72.110	Intimidating a Witness	B	VI
70.74.275	Intimidation or Harassment With an Explosive	C	Unranked
9A.76.140	Introducing Contraband 1	B	VII
9A.76.150	Introducing Contraband 2	C	III
69.50.4015	Involving a Minor in Drug Dealing	C	DG-III
9A.60.070	Issuing a False Academic Credential	C	Unranked
16.52.320	Kill or Cause Substantial Harm With Malice to Livestock	C	Unranked
9A.82.060(1)(b)	Leading Organized Crime - Inciting Criminal Profiteering	B	IX
46.70.021	Licensing Violation for Car Dealers or Manufacturers (Subsequent Violation)	C	Unranked

The Caseload Forecast Council is not liable for errors or omissions in the manual, for sentences that may be inappropriately calculated as a result of a practitioner's or court's reliance on the manual, or for any other written or verbal information related to adult or juvenile sentencing. The scoring sheets are intended to provide assistance in most cases but do not cover all permutations of the scoring rules. If you find any errors or omissions, we encourage you to report them to the Caseload Forecast Council.

SECTION 4 – NONVIOLENT OFFENSES

Statute (RCW)	Offense	Class	Seriousness Level
30A.12.120	Loan to Officer or Employee from Trust Fund	B	Unranked
67.70.130	Lottery Fraud	B	Unranked
9A.40.090	Luring of a Child or Developmentally Disabled Person	C	Unranked
9A.56.370	Mail Theft	C	Unranked
9.47.090	Maintaining a Bucket Shop	C	Unranked
69.50.402	Maintaining a Dwelling or Place for Controlled Substances	C	DG-II
9.45.220	Making False Sample or Assay of Ore	C	Unranked
70.74.280(3)	Malicious Explosion of a Substance 3	B	X
9A.36.080	Malicious Harassment	C	IV
81.60.070	Malicious Injury to Railroad Property	B	III
9A.48.070	Malicious Mischief 1	B	II
9A.48.080	Malicious Mischief 2	C	I
70.74.270(2)	Malicious Placement of an Explosive 2	B	IX
70.74.270(3)	Malicious Placement of an Explosive 3	B	VII
70.74.272(1)(a)	Malicious Placement of an Imitation Device 1	B	XII
70.74.272(1)(b)	Malicious Placement of an Imitation Device 2	C	VI
9.62.010(1)	Malicious Prosecution	C	Unranked
9.45.260	Malicious Sprinkler Contractor Work	C	Unranked
69.50.401(2)(b)	Manufacture Methamphetamine	B	DG-III
46.37.650(1)(c)	Manufacture or Import Counterfeit, Nonfunctional, Damaged, or Previously Deployed Air Bag	C	V
46.37.650(1)(b)	Manufacture or Import Counterfeit, Nonfunctional, Damaged, or Previously Deployed Air Bag (Causing Bodily Injury or Death)	C	VII
69.50.401(2)(b)	Manufacture, Deliver or Possess with Intent to Deliver - Amphetamine	B	DG-II
69.50.401(2)(c)	Manufacture, Deliver or Possess with Intent to Deliver - Marijuana	C	DG-I
69.50.401(2)(a)	Manufacture, Deliver or Possess with Intent to Deliver - Narcotics from Schedule I or II or Flunitrazepam from Schedule IV	B	DG-II
69.50.401(2)(c-e)	Manufacture, Deliver or Possess with Intent to Deliver - Narcotics from Schedule III, IV, or V or Nonnarcotics from Schedule I-V (except Marijuana, Amphetamine, Methamphetamine, or Flunitrazepam)	C	DG-II
69.52.030(1)	Manufacture, Distribute or Possess with Intent to Distribute an Imitation Controlled Substance	C	DG-II
70.74.022(1)	Manufacture, Purchase, Sell or Store Explosive Device Without License	C	Unranked
46.20.0921(3)(a)	Manufacture, Sell or Deliver Forged Driver's License or Identicard	C	Unranked
82.24.570(2)	Manufacture, Sell or Possess Counterfeit Cigarettes	C	Unranked

The Caseload Forecast Council is not liable for errors or omissions in the manual, for sentences that may be inappropriately calculated as a result of a practitioner's or court's reliance on the manual, or for any other written or verbal information related to adult or juvenile sentencing. The scoring sheets are intended to provide assistance in most cases but do not cover all permutations of the scoring rules. If you find any errors or omissions, we encourage you to report them to the Caseload Forecast Council.

SECTION 4 – NONVIOLENT OFFENSES

Statute (RCW)	Offense	Class	Seriousness Level
82.24.570(3)	Manufacture, Sell or Possess Counterfeit Cigarettes (Subsequent Violation)	B	Unranked
69.51A.060	Medical Marijuana Fraudulent Records (Effective Until 7/1/2016)	C	Unranked
69.51A.240	Medical Marijuana – Unlawful Actions	C	Unranked
9.81.030	Member of Subversive Organization	C	Unranked
78.44.330	Mineral Trespass	C	I
42.20.070	Misappropriating and Falsifying Accounts by Public Officer	B	Unranked
42.20.090	Misappropriating and Falsifying Accounts by Treasurer	C	Unranked
9.82.030	Misprision of Treason	C	Unranked
29A.08.740	Misuse of Registered Voter Data	C	Unranked
29A.84.150	Misuse or Alteration of Registration Database	C	Unranked
9.45.070	Mock Auction	C	Unranked
9A.83.020	Money Laundering	B	Unranked
19.144.080	Mortgage Fraud	B	III
32.04.110	Mutual Savings Bank - Conceal or Destroy Evidence	B	Unranked
32.04.100	Mutual Savings Bank - Falsify Savings Book, Document or Statement	B	Unranked
32.24.080	Mutual Savings Bank - Transfer Bank Assets After Insolvency	B	Unranked
46.37.675	Negligently Causing Death By Use of a Signal Preemption Device	B	VII
46.37.674	Negligently Causing Substantial Bodily Harm By Use of a Signal Preemption Device	B	III
9A.60.030	Obtaining Signature by Deception or Duress	C	Unranked
46.70.180(5)	Odometer Offense	C	Unranked
40.16.030	Offering False Instrument for Filing or Record	C	Unranked
68.50.140(3)	Opening Graves With Intent to Sell or Remove Personal Effects or Human Remains	C	Unranked
90.56.540	Operation of a Vessel While Under the Influence of Intoxicating Liquor or Drugs	C	Unranked
9A.56.350(2)	Organized Retail Theft 1	B	III
9A.56.350(3)	Organized Retail Theft 2	C	II
69.50.406(2)	Over 18 and Deliver Narcotic from Schedule III, IV or V, or a Nonnarcotic, Except Flunitrazepam or Methamphetamine, from Schedule I-V to Someone Under 18 and 3 Years Junior	B	DG-III
9.46.215	Ownership or Interest in Gambling Device	C	Unranked
69.30.085	Participation in Shellfish Operation or Activities While License is Denied, Revoked or Suspended	C	Unranked
74.09.240(2)	Paying or Offering Bribes, Kickbacks or Rebates	C	Unranked

The Caseload Forecast Council is not liable for errors or omissions in the manual, for sentences that may be inappropriately calculated as a result of a practitioner's or court's reliance on the manual, or for any other written or verbal information related to adult or juvenile sentencing. The scoring sheets are intended to provide assistance in most cases but do not cover all permutations of the scoring rules. If you find any errors or omissions, we encourage you to report them to the Caseload Forecast Council.

SECTION 4 – NONVIOLENT OFFENSES

Statute (RCW)	Offense	Class	Seriousness Level
9A.72.020	Perjury 1	B	V
9A.72.030	Perjury 2	C	III
9.94.070	Persistent Prison Misbehavior	C	V
82.32.290(4)	Phantomware Violation	C	Unranked
46.61.504(6)	Physical Control of a Vehicle While Under the Influence of Intoxicating Liquor or any Drug	C	V
69.40.030	Placing Poison or Other Harmful Object or Substance in Food, Drinks, Medicine or Water	B	Unranked
69.40.020	Poison in Milk or Food Product	C	Unranked
9A.58.020	Possessing or Capturing Personal Identification Document	C	Unranked
9A.56.310	Possession of a Stolen Firearm	B	V
9A.56.068	Possession of a Stolen Vehicle	B	II
9.94.041(2)	Possession of Controlled Substance by Prisoner (County or Local Facility)	C	Unranked
9.94.041(1)	Possession of Controlled Substance by Prisoner (State Facility)	C	Unranked
9.94.045	Possession of Controlled Substance in Prison by Non-prisoner	C	Unranked
69.50.4013	Possession of Controlled Substance That is a Narcotic from Schedule III, IV or V or Nonnarcotic from Schedule I-V	C	DG-I
69.50.4013	Possession of Controlled Substance That is Either Heroin or Narcotics from Schedule I or II	C	DG-I
9.68A.070(1)	Possession of Depictions of Minor Engaged in Sexually Explicit Conduct 1	B	VI
9.68A.070(2)	Possession of Depictions of Minor Engaged in Sexually Explicit Conduct 2	C	IV
69.50.440	Possession of Ephedrine, Pseudoephedrine or Anhydrous Ammonia with Intent to Manufacture Methamphetamine	B	DG-III
9.40.120	Possession of Incendiary Device	B	III
9.41.190	Possession of Machine Gun, Short-barreled Shotgun or Short-barreled Rifle	C	III
69.41.350	Possession of Steroids in Excess of 200 tablets or (8) 2cc Bottles Without a Valid Prescription	C	Unranked
9A.56.380	Possession of Stolen Mail	C	Unranked
9A.56.150	Possession of Stolen Property 1 (Other Than Firearm or Motor Vehicle)	B	II
9A.56.160	Possession of Stolen Property 2 (Other Than Firearm or Motor Vehicle)	C	I
9.94.040(2)	Possession of Weapons by Prisoners (County or Local Facility)	C	Unranked
9.94.040(1)	Possession of Weapons by Prisoners (State Facility)	B	Unranked
9.94.043	Possession of Weapons in Prison by Non-prisoner	B	Unranked
9.94.010	Prison Riot	B	Unranked
9.46.220	Professional Gambling 1	B	Unranked

The Caseload Forecast Council is not liable for errors or omissions in the manual, for sentences that may be inappropriately calculated as a result of a practitioner's or court's reliance on the manual, or for any other written or verbal information related to adult or juvenile sentencing. The scoring sheets are intended to provide assistance in most cases but do not cover all permutations of the scoring rules. If you find any errors or omissions, we encourage you to report them to the Caseload Forecast Council.

SECTION 4 – NONVIOLENT OFFENSES

Statute (RCW)	Offense	Class	Seriousness Level
9.46.221	Professional Gambling 2	C	Unranked
9A.36.060	Promoting a Suicide Attempt	C	Unranked
67.08.015	Promoting Illegal Boxing, Martial Arts and Wrestling	C	Unranked
9.68.140	Promoting Pornography	C	Unranked
9A.88.070	Promoting Prostitution 1	B	VIII
9A.88.080	Promoting Prostitution 2	C	III
9.68A.102	Promoting Travel for Commercial Sexual Abuse of a Minor	C	Unranked
9A.88.085	Promoting Travel for Prostitution	C	Unranked
29A.84.311	Provides False Information or Conceals or Destroys Candidacy Declaration or Nominating Petition	C	Unranked
26.04.210	Providing False Statements in Affidavits for Marriage	C	Unranked
68.50.140(2)	Purchasing or Receiving Human Remains	C	Unranked
9A.44.060	Rape 3	C	V
9A.44.079	Rape of a Child 3	C	VI
74.09.240(1)	Receiving or Asking for Bribes, Kickbacks or Rebates	C	Unranked
9A.68.030	Receiving or Granting Unlawful Compensation	C	Unranked
81.60.080(2)	Receiving Stolen Railroad Property	C	Unranked
9A.48.040	Reckless Burning 1	C	I
90.56.530	Reckless Operation of a Tank Vessel	C	Unranked
19.110.075(2)	Registration Knowingly Not Obtained Prior to Sale of Business Opportunity (Violation of RCW 19.110.050)	B	Unranked
70.94.430(3)	Releasing Into Ambient Air Hazardous Air Pollutant	C	Unranked
46.12.560	Removal of Sticker on Vehicle Stating Previously Destroyed or Title 1 Loss	C	Unranked
68.50.140(4)	Removal, Disinterment or Mutilation of Human Remains	C	Unranked
68.60.050	Removes, Defaces or Destroys any Historic Grave	C	Unranked
68.50.140(1)	Removing Human Remains	C	Unranked
9.16.010	Removing Lawful Brands	C	Unranked
9A.76.070(2)(a)	Rendering Criminal Assistance 1	B	V
19.25.020(2)(a)	Reproduction of Sound Recording Without Consent of Owner - Recording Fixed Before 2/15/1972 (At Least 1,000 Recordings or Subsequent Conviction)	B	Unranked
19.25.020(2)(b)	Reproduction of Sound Recording Without Consent of Owner - Recording Fixed Before 2/15/1972 (More Than 100 but Less Than 1,000 Recordings)	C	Unranked
9A.68.020	Requesting Unlawful Compensation	C	Unranked
9A.52.025	Residential Burglary	B	IV

The Caseload Forecast Council is not liable for errors or omissions in the manual, for sentences that may be inappropriately calculated as a result of a practitioner's or court's reliance on the manual, or for any other written or verbal information related to adult or juvenile sentencing. The scoring sheets are intended to provide assistance in most cases but do not cover all permutations of the scoring rules. If you find any errors or omissions, we encourage you to report them to the Caseload Forecast Council.

SECTION 4 – NONVIOLENT OFFENSES

Statute (RCW)	Offense	Class	Seriousness Level
70.345.030	Retail Sales, Distribution or Delivery Sales of Vapor Products Without a License	C	Unranked
9A.56.360(2)	Retail Theft with Special Circumstances 1	B	III
9A.56.360(3)	Retail Theft with Special Circumstances 2	C	II
9A.56.360(4)	Retail Theft with Special Circumstances 3	C	Unranked
81.60.080(1)	Sabotaging Rolling Stock	C	Unranked
69.41.030(2)(a)	Sale, Delivery or Possession With Intent to Sell Legend Drug Without Prescription	B	Unranked
46.37.650(2)(b)	Sale, Install, [or] Reinstall Counterfeit, Nonfunctional, Damaged, or Previously Deployed Airbag	C	VII
46.37.650(2)(c)	Sale, Install, [or] Reinstall Counterfeit, Nonfunctional, Damaged, or Previously Deployed Airbag	C	V
33.36.040	Savings and Loan Association - Making False Statement of Assets or Liabilities	C	Unranked
33.36.030	Savings and Loan Association - Preference in Case of Insolvency	C	Unranked
33.36.060	Savings and Loan Association - Suppressing, Secreting or Destroying Evidence or Records	C	Unranked
19.290.100	Scrap Processing, Recycling, or Supplying Without a License (Second or Subsequent Offense)	C	II
19.60.067(2)	Second-hand Precious Metal Dealer Violations (Subsequent Violation)	C	Unranked
21.20.400	Securities Act Violation	B	III
46.20.0921(2)	Sell or Deliver a Stolen Driver's License or Identicard	C	Unranked
27.44.040(2)	Selling Artifacts or Human Remains from Indian Graves	C	Unranked
69.50.410	Selling for Profit (Controlled or Counterfeit) any Controlled Substance in Schedule I	C	DG-III
48.160.080	Sells Guaranteed Asset Protection Waivers Without Registration	B	Unranked
9.68A.060(1)	Sending, Bringing into the State Depictions of Minor Engaged in Sexually Explicit Conduct 1	B	VII
9.68A.060(2)	Sending, Bringing into the State Depictions of Minor Engaged in Sexually Explicit Conduct 2	C	V
9.68A.040	Sexual Exploitation of a Minor	B	IX
9A.44.093	Sexual Misconduct with a Minor 1	C	V
9A.44.105	Sexually Violating Human Remains	C	V
70.155.140	Shipping or Transporting Tobacco Products Ordered Through Mail or Internet	C	Unranked
82.38.270	Special Fuel Violations	C	Unranked
77.15.450(3)(b)	Spotlighting Big Game 1	C	I

The Caseload Forecast Council is not liable for errors or omissions in the manual, for sentences that may be inappropriately calculated as a result of a practitioner's or court's reliance on the manual, or for any other written or verbal information related to adult or juvenile sentencing. The scoring sheets are intended to provide assistance in most cases but do not cover all permutations of the scoring rules. If you find any errors or omissions, we encourage you to report them to the Caseload Forecast Council.

SECTION 4 – NONVIOLENT OFFENSES

Statute (RCW)	Offense	Class	Seriousness Level
9A.46.110	Stalking	B	V
67.70.160	State Lottery Violations Except Lottery Fraud and Unlicensed Lottery Activity	C	Unranked
30B.12.050	State Trust Company – False Entry, Conceal or Destroy Records	B	Unranked
9.45.020	Substitution of Child	B	Unranked
9.81.020	Subversive Acts	B	Unranked
77.15.670(3)(b)	Suspension of Department Privileges 1	C	I
9A.56.070	Taking Motor Vehicle Without Permission 1	B	V
9A.56.075	Taking Motor Vehicle Without Permission 2	C	I
9A.72.120	Tampering with a Witness	C	III
29A.84.550	Tampering with Election Materials	C	Unranked
9.40.105	Tampering with Fire Alarm, Emergency Signal, or Fire-fighting Equipment with Intent to Commit Arson	B	Unranked
88.08.020	Tampering with Lights or Signals	B	Unranked
29A.84.560	Tampering with Voting Machine	C	Unranked
9.61.230(2)	Telephone Harassment (With Prior Harassment Conviction or Threat of Death)	C	III
9A.56.030	Theft 1 (Excluding Firearm and Motor Vehicle)	B	II
9A.56.040	Theft 2 (Excluding Firearm and Motor Vehicle)	C	I
9A.56.300	Theft of a Firearm	B	VI
9A.56.065	Theft of a Motor Vehicle	B	II
69.55.010	Theft of Ammonia	C	VIII
9A.56.080	Theft of Livestock 1	B	IV
9A.56.083	Theft of Livestock 2	C	III
9A.56.096(5)(a)	Theft of Rental, Leased, Lease-purchased or Loaned Property (Valued at $5,000 or More)	B	II
9A.56.096(5)(b)	Theft of Rental, Leased, Lease-purchased or Loaned Property (Valued at $750 or More but Less Than $5,000)	C	I
9A.56.262	Theft of Telecommunication Service	C	Unranked
9A.56.340(2)	Theft with Intent to Resell 1	B	III
9A.56.340(3)	Theft with Intent to Resell 2	C	II
9A.36.090	Threats Against Governor or Family	C	Unranked
9.61.160	Threats to Bomb	B	IV
64.36.210	Timeshare Fraud	C	Unranked
64.36.020(5)(b)	Timeshare Registration Requirement Violation	C	Unranked

The Caseload Forecast Council is not liable for errors or omissions in the manual, for sentences that may be inappropriately calculated as a result of a practitioner's or court's reliance on the manual, or for any other written or verbal information related to adult or juvenile sentencing. The scoring sheets are intended to provide assistance in most cases but do not cover all permutations of the scoring rules. If you find any errors or omissions, we encourage you to report them to the Caseload Forecast Council.

SECTION 4 – NONVIOLENT OFFENSES

Statute (RCW)	Offense	Class	Seriousness Level
9A.68.040	Trading in Public Office	C	Unranked
9A.68.050	Trading in Special Influence	C	Unranked
48.30A.015	Trafficking in Insurance Claims (Subsequent Violation)	C	II
9A.82.050	Trafficking in Stolen Property 1	B	IV
9A.82.055	Trafficking in Stolen Property 2	C	III
48.17.063(4)	Transaction of Insurance Business Beyond the Scope of Licensure (Violation of RCW 48.17.060)	B	I
9.46.240	Transmission or Receiving Gambling Information by Internet	C	Unranked
70.105.085(1)(a)	Transport, Disposal or Export of Hazardous Waste That Places Another Person in Danger of Injury or Death	B	Unranked
70.105.085(1)(b)	Transport, Disposal or Export of Hazardous Waste That Places Another Person's Property in Danger of Harm	C	Unranked
82.24.110(2)	Transportation of More Than 10,000 Cigarettes Without Proper Stamps	C	Unranked
68.60.040(3)	Transports Removed Human Remains, Opens a Grave or Removes Personal Effects from Grave	C	Unranked
9.91.150(1)	Tree Spiking	C	Unranked
9.02.120	Unauthorized Abortion	C	Unranked
68.44.060	Unauthorized Loans to Cemetery Authority	C	Unranked
29A.84.545	Unauthorized Removal of Paper Record from Electronic Voting Device	C	Unranked
39.62.040	Unauthorized Use of Public Official Facsimile Signature or Seal	B	Unranked
68.05.330	Unfair Practice of Funeral or Cemetery Board	C	Unranked
19.225.110	Uniform Athlete Agent Act Violation	C	Unranked
69.43.070(1)	Unlawful Delivery of Precursor Drug with Intent to Use	B	Unranked
9A.49.020	Unlawful Discharge of a Laser 1	C	Unranked
74.09.290	Unlawful Disclosure of Patient Records or DSHS Information	C	Unranked
9A.56.290(4)(a)	Unlawful Factoring of a Credit or Payment Card Transaction	C	II
9A.56.290(4)(b)	Unlawful Factoring of a Credit or Payment Card Transaction (Subsequent Violation)	B	IV
69.53.020	Unlawful Fortification of Building for Drug Purposes	C	Unranked
77.15.410(3)(b)	Unlawful Hunting of Big Game 1	C	III
9A.40.040	Unlawful Imprisonment	C	III
9A.56.060(4)	Unlawful Issuance of Checks or Drafts (Value Greater Than $750)	C	I
9A.56.264	Unlawful Manufacture of a Telecommunication Device	C	Unranked
69.04.938(3)	Unlawful Misbranding of Food Fish or Shellfish 1	C	III
88.46.080(2)(b)	Unlawful Operation of a Covered Vessel (Subsequent Violation)	C	Unranked

The Caseload Forecast Council is not liable for errors or omissions in the manual, for sentences that may be inappropriately calculated as a result of a practitioner's or court's reliance on the manual, or for any other written or verbal information related to adult or juvenile sentencing. The scoring sheets are intended to provide assistance in most cases but do not cover all permutations of the scoring rules. If you find any errors or omissions, we encourage you to report them to the Caseload Forecast Council.

SECTION 4 – NONVIOLENT OFFENSES

Statute (RCW)	Offense	Class	Seriousness Level
90.56.300(2)(b)	Unlawful Operation of Onshore or Offshore Facility (Subsequent Conviction)	C	Unranked
77.15.570(2)	Unlawful Participation on Non-Indians in Indian Fishery	C	II
9.41.040(1)	Unlawful Possession of a Firearm 1	B	VII
9.41.040(2)	Unlawful Possession of a Firearm 2	C	III
9A.56.320(3)	Unlawful Possession of a Personal Identification Device	C	I
9A.56.320(4)	Unlawful Possession of Fictitious Identification	C	I
9A.56.320(5)	Unlawful Possession of Instruments of Financial Fraud	C	I
9A.56.320(2)	Unlawful Possession of Payment Instruments	C	I
2.48.180	Unlawful Practice of Law (Subsequent Violation)	C	II
9.41.115	Unlawful Private Transfer of a Firearm (Subsequent Offense)	C	Unranked
9A.56.320(1)	Unlawful Production of Payment Instruments	C	I
77.15.650(3)(b)	Unlawful Purchase or Use of a License 1	C	II
69.43.070(2)	Unlawful Receipt of Precursor Drug with Intent to Use	B	Unranked
9.91.144	Unlawful Redemption of Food Stamps	C	I
77.15.250(2)(b)	Unlawful Releasing, Planting, Possessing or Placing Deleterious Exotic Wildlife	C	I
9A.56.266	Unlawful Sale of a Telecommunication Device	C	Unranked
9A.56.230	Unlawful Sale of Subscription Television Services	C	Unranked
46.12.750(3)	Unlawful Sale of Vehicle Certificate of Ownership	C	Unranked
18.64.046(7)	Unlawful Selling of Ephedrine, Pseudoephedrine or Phenylpropanolamine by a Wholesaler	C	Unranked
65.12.730	Unlawful Stealing or Carrying Away Certification of Land Registration (Charged as Theft)	*	*
69.55.020	Unlawful Storage of Ammonia	C	VI
19.116.080(1)	Unlawful Subleasing of Motor Vehicle	C	Unranked
77.15.120(3)(b)	Unlawful Taking of Endangered Fish or Wildlife 1	C	III
77.15.770(2)	Unlawful Trade in Shark Fins 1	C	Unranked
77.15.260(3)(b)	Unlawful Trafficking in Fish, Shellfish or Wildlife 1	B	III
77.15.260(3)(a)	Unlawful Trafficking in Fish, Shellfish or Wildlife 2	C	II
9.91.142(1)	Unlawful Trafficking in Food Stamps	C	I
77.15.135(4)(d)	Unlawful Trafficking in Species With Extinction 1	C	Unranked
48.44.016(3)	Unlawful Transaction of Health Coverage as Health Care Service Contractor	B	IV
48.46.033(3)	Unlawful Transaction of Health Coverage as Health Maintenance	B	IV

The Caseload Forecast Council is not liable for errors or omissions in the manual, for sentences that may be inappropriately calculated as a result of a practitioner's or court's reliance on the manual, or for any other written or verbal information related to adult or juvenile sentencing. The scoring sheets are intended to provide assistance in most cases but do not cover all permutations of the scoring rules. If you find any errors or omissions, we encourage you to report them to the Caseload Forecast Council.

SECTION 4 – NONVIOLENT OFFENSES

Statute (RCW)	Offense	Class	Seriousness Level
	Organization		
48.15.023(3)	Unlawful Transaction of Insurance Business	B	IV
19.116.080(2)	Unlawful Transfer of Ownership of Motor Vehicle	C	Unranked
77.15.530(4)	Unlawful Use of a Nondesignated Vessel	C	III
18.04.370(1)(b)	Unlawful Use of a Professional Title	C	Unranked
69.53.010	Unlawful Use of Building for Drug Purposes	C	DG-I
18.04.370(1)(c)	Unlawful Use of CPA Title After Suspension	C	Unranked
77.15.630	Unlawful Use of Fish Buying and Dealing License 1	C	Unranked
69.53.030	Unlawful Use of Fortified Building	C	Unranked
77.15.811	Unlawful Use of Invasive Species 1	C	Unranked
66.44.120(2)(b)	Unlawful Use of Liquor Board Seal (Third or Subsequent Offense)	C	Unranked
77.15.580(3)(b)	Unlawful Use of Net to Take Fish	C	I
19.310.120	Unlawfully Engaging in Business as an Exchange Facilitator (RCW 19.310.100(1)-(9))	B	Unranked
82.24.500	Unlawfully Purchase, Sell, Consign or Distribute Cigarettes	C	Unranked
48.102.160(4)	Unlicensed Life Insurance Provider	B	Unranked
67.70.140	Unlicensed Lottery Activity	B	Unranked
48.17.063(2)	Unlicensed Practice as an Insurance Professional	B	IV
18.130.190(7)(b)	Unlicensed Practice of a Profession or Business (Subsequent Violation)	C	II
48.102.160(5)	Unlicensed Settlement Broker	B	Unranked
29A.84.660	Unqualified Person Voting	C	Unranked
29A.84.140	Unqualified Voting Registration	C	Unranked
19.210.040	Unused Property, Merchants –Prohibited Sales (Third or Subsequent Offense Within 5 Years)	C	Unranked
46.37.673	Use of a Signal Preemption Device Resulting in Property Damage or Less Substantial Bodily Harm	C	Unranked
9A.82.080(1-2)	Use of Proceeds of Criminal Profiteering	B	IV
19.25.030(2)(a)	Use of Recording of Live Performance Without Consent of Owner (At Least 1,000 Recordings or at Least 100 Unauthorized Audiovisual Recordings or Subsequent Offense)	B	Unranked
19.25.030(2)(b)	Use of Recording of Live Performance Without Consent of Owner (At Least 100 but Less Than 1,000 Recordings or More than 10 but Less Than 100 Unauthorized Audiovisual Recording or Subsequent Offense)	C	Unranked
19.144.100(1)	Use or Investment of Proceeds from Mortgage Fraud Activities	B	Unranked
9A.52.095	Vehicle Prowl 1	C	I

The Caseload Forecast Council is not liable for errors or omissions in the manual, for sentences that may be inappropriately calculated as a result of a practitioner's or court's reliance on the manual, or for any other written or verbal information related to adult or juvenile sentencing. The scoring sheets are intended to provide assistance in most cases but do not cover all permutations of the scoring rules. If you find any errors or omissions, we encourage you to report them to the Caseload Forecast Council.

SECTION 4 – NONVIOLENT OFFENSES

Statute (RCW)	Offense	Class	Seriousness Level
9A.52.100(3)	Vehicle Prowling 2 (Third or Subsequent Offense)	C	IV
46.61.522(1)(c)	Vehicular Assault - Disregard for the Safety of Others	B	III
9.68A.075(1)	Viewing Depictions of Minor Engaged in Sexually Explicit Conduct 1	B	IV
9.68A.075(2)	Viewing Depictions of Minor Engaged in Sexually Explicit Conduct 2	C	Unranked
77.15.550(3)(b)	Violating Commercial Fishing Area or Time 1	C	I
29A.84.230(1)	Violation by Signer – Initiative or Referendum with False Name	C	Unranked
26.50.110(5)	Violation of a Foreign Protection Order (Third or Subsequent Violation)	C	Unranked
29A.84.240(1)	Violations By Signers – Recall Petition With False Name	B	Unranked
29A.84.130	Voter Violation of Registration Law	C	Unranked
29A.84.650(1)	Voting Repeater – More Than One Vote at Any Election	C	Unranked
9A.44.115	Voyeurism	C	II
48.30.220	Willful Destruction, Injury, Secretion of Insured Property	C	Unranked
10.66.090	Willfully Disobeys an Off-limits Order (Subsequent Violation or Enters Protected Against Drug Trafficking Area)	C	Unranked

The Caseload Forecast Council is not liable for errors or omissions in the manual, for sentences that may be inappropriately calculated as a result of a practitioner's or court's reliance on the manual, or for any other written or verbal information related to adult or juvenile sentencing. The scoring sheets are intended to provide assistance in most cases but do not cover all permutations of the scoring rules. If you find any errors or omissions, we encourage you to report them to the Caseload Forecast Council.

SECTION 4 - UNRANKED OFFENSES

UNRANKED OFFENSES

Statute (RCW)	Offense	Class	Seriousness Level
29A.84.680(1)	Absentee Voting Violation	C	Unranked
46.52.130(5)(b)	Abstracts of Driving Records – Intentional Misuse	C	Unranked
20.01.460(2)	Acting as Commission Merchant, Dealer, Cash Buyer Without License	C	Unranked
69.52.030(3)	Advertising Imitation Controlled Substances	C	Unranked
30A.42.290(3)	Alien Bank or Bureau – Destroy or Secrete Records	B	Unranked
30A.42.290(2)	Alien Bank or Bureau – False Entry, Statements, etc.	B	Unranked
9.41.171	Alien Possession of a Firearm	C	Unranked
9.45.210	Altering Sample or Certificate of Assay	C	Unranked
9A.76.177	Amber Alert – Making False Statements to a Public Servant	C	Unranked
68.64.160	Anatomical Gift - Illegal Financial Gain	C	Unranked
68.64.150	Anatomical Gifts - Illegal Purchase or Sale	C	Unranked
16.52.205(2)	Animal Cruelty 1	C	Unranked
16.52.117	Animal Fighting	C	Unranked
9.05.030	Assembly of Saboteurs	B	Unranked
72.23.170	Assist Escape of Mental Patient	C	Unranked
9A.82.080(3)	Attempt or Conspiracy to Violate RCW 9A.82.080(1) or (2)	C	Unranked
30A.12.100	Bank or Trust Company - Destroy or Secrete Records	B	Unranked
30A.12.090	Bank or Trust Company - False Entry, Statements, etc.	B	Unranked
30A.44.120	Bank or Trust Company - Receiving Deposits When Insolvent	B	Unranked
30A.44.110	Bank or Trust Company - Transfer of Assets Prior to Insolvency	B	Unranked
9A.64.010	Bigamy	C	Unranked
9.46.155	Bribing to Obtain a License From Public Officials, Employees, Agents	C	Unranked
72.23.300	Bringing Narcotics, Liquor, or Weapons into State Institution or Grounds	B	Unranked
9.47.120	Bunco Steering	B	Unranked
46.87.260	Cab Card Forgery (Effective Until 7/1/2016)	B	Unranked
9.46.180	Causing Person to Violate Gambling Laws	B	Unranked
9A.64.030(3)(b)	Child Buying	C	Unranked
49.12.410(2)	Child Labor Law Violation – Death/Disability	C	Unranked
9A.64.030(3)(a)	Child Selling	C	Unranked

The Caseload Forecast Council is not liable for errors or omissions in the manual, for sentences that may be inappropriately calculated as a result of a practitioner's or court's reliance on the manual, or for any other written or verbal information related to adult or juvenile sentencing. The scoring sheets are intended to provide assistance in most cases but do not cover all permutations of the scoring rules. If you find any errors or omissions, we encourage you to report them to the Caseload Forecast Council.

SECTION 4 - Unranked Offenses

Statute (RCW)	Offense	Class	Seriousness Level
70.245.200(2)	Coerce Patient to Request Life-ending Medication	A	Unranked
9A.40.110	Coercion of Involuntary Servitude	C	Unranked
9A.82.045	Collection of Unlawful Debt	C	Unranked
19.158.160	Commercial Telephone Solicitor Deception (Value of $250 or More)	C	Unranked
30A.04.240	Commingling of Funds or Securities	B	Unranked
21.30.140	Commodity Transaction Violation	B	Unranked
69.50.465	Conducting or Maintaining a Marijuana Club	C	Unranked
19.144.100(2)	Control of Real Property Resulting from Mortgage Fraud Activities	B	Unranked
69.50.416	Controlled Substance Label Violation	C	Unranked
46.87.260	Credential Forgery (Effective 7/1/2016)	B	Unranked
31.12.724(3)	Credit Union – Fraudulent Receipt of Credit Union Deposit	B	Unranked
31.12.724(2)	Credit Union – Transfer of Credit Union Assets Prior to Insolvency	B	Unranked
9.08.090	Crimes Against Animal Facilities	C	Unranked
9A.60.040	Criminal Impersonation 1	C	Unranked
9A.84.010(2)(b)	Criminal Mischief	C	Unranked
9A.82.160	Criminal Profiteering Lien After Service of Notice	C	Unranked
9.05.060(2)	Criminal Sabotage	B	Unranked
9A.44.196	Criminal Trespass Against Children	C	Unranked
9A.40.060	Custodial Interference 1	C	Unranked
9A.40.070	Custodial Interference 2 (Subsequent Offense)	C	Unranked
43.06.230	Damage Property or Cause Personal Injury after State of Emergency Proclaimed	B	Unranked
16.08.100(2)	Dangerous Dog Attack (Subsequent Offense)	C	Unranked
16.08.100(3)	Dangerous Dog Attack Resulting in Severe Injury or Death	C	Unranked
22.09.310	Dealing in Unauthorized Warehouse Receipts for Agricultural Commodities	C	Unranked
39.44.101	Defraud a Facsimile Signature on Bonds and Coupons	B	Unranked
87.03.200	Defraud Facsimile Signatures on Bonds and Coupons – Irrigation Districts	B	Unranked
19.110.120	Defraud or Provide Misleading or Untrue Documents Related to a Business Opportunity Sale	B	Unranked
9A.61.030	Defrauding a Public Utility 1	B	Unranked
9A.61.040	Defrauding a Public Utility 2	C	Unranked
19.48.110(1)(b)	Defrauding an Innkeeper (Value of $75.00 or More)	B	Unranked
9.41.110(8)	Delivery of Firearm by Dealer to Ineligible Person	C	Unranked
9.41.080	Delivery of Firearms to Ineligible Person	C	Unranked

The Caseload Forecast Council is not liable for errors or omissions in the manual, for sentences that may be inappropriately calculated as a result of a practitioner's or court's reliance on the manual, or for any other written or verbal information related to adult or juvenile sentencing. The scoring sheets are intended to provide assistance in most cases but do not cover all permutations of the scoring rules. If you find any errors or omissions, we encourage you to report them to the Caseload Forecast Council.

SECTION 4 - Unranked Offenses

Statute (RCW)	Offense	Class	Seriousness Level
35A.36.040	Designation of Bonds – Violation (Code Cities)	B	Unranked
35.36.040	Designation of Bonds – Violation (First Class Cities)	B	Unranked
27.44.040(1)	Destroying, Removing or Defacing Indian Graves	C	Unranked
68.60.040(1)	Destruction of Tomb, Plot, Marker, or Cemetery Property	C	Unranked
9.38.060	Digital Signatures Fraud	C	Unranked
9A.76.023(2)(a)	Disarming a Law Enforcement or Corrections Officer	C	Unranked
9A.76.023(2)(b)	Disarming a Law Enforcement or Corrections Officer and Firearm is Discharged	B	Unranked
9A.86.010	Disclosing Intimate Images	C	Unranked
19.110.075(2)	Disclosures Knowingly Not Provided at Sale of Business Opportunity (Violation of RCW 19.110.070)	B	Unranked
69.50.402	Dispensing Violation (VUCSA)	C	Unranked
82.26.190	Distributors and Retailer of Tobacco Products License Violation	C	Unranked
27.53.060	Disturbing Archaeological Resources or Site	C	Unranked
43.43.856	Divulging Confidential Investigative Information Pertaining to Organized Crime	B	Unranked
29A.84.270	Duplication of Name – Conspiracy to Mislead	B	Unranked
29A.84.320	Duplication of Names on Declaration of Candidacy	B	Unranked
29A.84.655	Election Officer Permits Repeat Vote	C	Unranked
29A.84.720	Election Officers – Violation	C	Unranked
29A.84.030	Election or Mail Ballot Violation	C	Unranked
19.300.020	Electronic Communication Devices – Illegal Scanning	C	Unranked
79A.60.090	Eluding a Law Enforcement Vessel	C	Unranked
18.39.350	Embalmers/Funeral Directors Violation	C	Unranked
43.08.140	Embezzlement by State Treasurer	B	Unranked
46.80.020(b)	Engage in Business of Wrecking Vehicles Without a License (Subsequent Offense)	C	Unranked
51.48.103(2)	Engaging in Business After Certificate of Coverage Revocation	C	Unranked
70.345.090	Engaging in Delivery Sales of Vapor Products Without a License, or Without Proper Shipping Documentation	C	Unranked
16.08.100(4)	Entering Dog in a Dog Fight	C	Unranked
9.68.060	Erotic Material (Third or Subsequent Offense)	B	Unranked
9A.76.130(3)(b)	Escape 3 (Third or Subsequent Offense)	C	Unranked
51.48.020(1)	Evading Industrial Insurance Premiums	C	Unranked
82.42.085	Evading the Collection of Aircraft Fuel Tax	C	Unranked

The Caseload Forecast Council is not liable for errors or omissions in the manual, for sentences that may be inappropriately calculated as a result of a practitioner's or court's reliance on the manual, or for any other written or verbal information related to adult or juvenile sentencing. The scoring sheets are intended to provide assistance in most cases but do not cover all permutations of the scoring rules. If you find any errors or omissions, we encourage you to report them to the Caseload Forecast Council.

SECTION 4 - Unranked Offenses

Statute (RCW)	Offense	Class	Seriousness Level
74.09.260	Excessive Charges, Payments	C	Unranked
48.06.190	Exhibiting False Accounts of Insurer	B	Unranked
19.25.040(2)(a)	Failure to Disclose Origin of Certain Recordings (At Least 100 Recordings or Subsequent Conviction)	B	Unranked
19.25.040(2)(b)	Failure to Disclose Origin of Certain Recordings (More than 10 but Less Than 100 Recordings)	C	Unranked
36.18.170	Failure to Pay Over Fees to County Treasurer	C	Unranked
9A.44.132(3)	Failure to Register as a Kidnapping Offender	C	Unranked
9A.44.132(1)(a)	Failure to Register as a Sex Offender (First Violation)	C	Unranked
19.146.050	Failure to Use a Trust Account	C	Unranked
19.142.080	Failure to Use a Trust Account or Furnish Bond for Health Studio	C	Unranked
38.42.050	False Affidavit Under Service Member Civil Relief Act	C	Unranked
74.08.100	False Age and Residency Public Assistance Verification	B	Unranked
42.24.100	False Claim from Municipal Corporation (Charged as Perjury 2)	C	Unranked
42.17A.750	False Documents Registered with Public Disclosure Commission	C	Unranked
48.30.230	False Insurance Claims (Value in Excess of $1,500)	C	Unranked
9.24.050	False Report of Corporation	B	Unranked
74.09.230	False Statement for Medical Assistance	C	Unranked
69.43.080	False Statement in Report of Precursor Drugs	C	Unranked
82.32.290(2)	False Statement to Department of Revenue	C	Unranked
19.230.300	False Statement, Misrepresentation or False Certification of Uniform Money services Record	C	Unranked
41.26.062	False Statements or Records to Defraud Law Enforcement Officers and Firefighters Retirement System	B	Unranked
41.32.055(1)	False Statements or Records to Defraud Teachers Retirement System	B	Unranked
74.09.250	False Statements Regarding Institutions, Facilities	C	Unranked
46.12.750(1)	False Statements, Illegal Transfers, Alterations or Forgeries of Vehicle Title	B	Unranked
26.20.030	Family Abandonment	C	Unranked
76.36.120	Forgery of Forest Product Mark	B	Unranked
65.12.760	Forgery of Registrar's Signature or Seal	B	Unranked
82.24.100	Forgery or Counterfeit Cigarette Tax Stamp	B	Unranked
70.245.200(1)	Forging Request for Medication	A	Unranked
19.100.210	Franchise Investment Protection Violation	B	Unranked
29A.84.711	Fraud in Certification of Nomination or Ballot	C	Unranked
9.45.170	Fraud in Liquor Warehouse Receipts	C	Unranked

The Caseload Forecast Council is not liable for errors or omissions in the manual, for sentences that may be inappropriately calculated as a result of a practitioner's or court's reliance on the manual, or for any other written or verbal information related to adult or juvenile sentencing. The scoring sheets are intended to provide assistance in most cases but do not cover all permutations of the scoring rules. If you find any errors or omissions, we encourage you to report them to the Caseload Forecast Council.

SECTION 4 - Unranked Offenses

Statute (RCW)	Offense	Class	Seriousness Level
9.45.124	Fraud in Measurement of Goods	B	Unranked
9.26A.110(3)	Fraud in Obtaining Telecommunications Services (Value Exceeds $250)	C	Unranked
67.24.010	Fraud in Sporting Contest	B	Unranked
76.48.141(1)(a)	Fraudulent Document as Specialized Forest Products Permit, Sales Invoice, Bill of Lading, etc.	C	Unranked
76.48.141(2)	Fraudulent Document for Specialized Forest Products Buyer	C	Unranked
9.45.270(3)	Fraudulent Filing of Vehicle Report of Sale (Value Exceeds $1,500)	B	Unranked
9.45.270(2)	Fraudulent Filing of Vehicle Report of Sale (Value Exceeds $250)	C	Unranked
9.24.020	Fraudulent Issue of Stock, Scrip, etc.	B	Unranked
48.102.160(3)	Fraudulent Life Insurance Settlement	B	Unranked
65.12.750	Fraudulent Procurement or False Entry on Land Title Registration	C	Unranked
76.48.141(1)(b)	Fraudulent Representation of Authority to Harvest Specialized Forest Products	C	Unranked
82.36.380	Fuel Tax Evasion	C	Unranked
9.46.160	Gambling Without License	B	Unranked
9.46.039	Greyhound Racing	B	Unranked
9A.76.200	Harming a Police Dog/Horse or an Accelerate Detection Dog	C	Unranked
9.94.030	Holding Hostages or Interfering with Officer's Duty	B	Unranked
69.41.040	Illegal Issuance of Legend Drug Prescription	B	Unranked
9.16.020	Imitating Lawful Brands With Intent	C	Unranked
19.146.235(9)	Impairing Mortgage Broker Investigation	B	Unranked
9A.44.100(d-f)	Indecent Liberties - Without Forcible Compulsion	B	Unranked
9.45.126	Inducing Fraud in Measurement of Goods	B	Unranked
40.16.010	Injury to a Public Record	C	Unranked
40.16.020	Injury to and Misappropriation of Public Record by Officer	B	Unranked
88.08.050(1)	Injury to Lighthouses or United States Light	B	Unranked
9.24.030	Insolvent Bank Receiving Deposit	B	Unranked
48.06.030	Insurance Solicitation Permit Violation	B	Unranked
9.91.170(5)	Intentional Infliction, Injury or Death to a Guide Dog or Service Animal	C	Unranked
9.91.175(3)	Intentionally Injures, Disables or Causes Death of an On-Duty Search and Rescue Dog	C	Unranked
9.73.230	Intercepting, Transmitting or Recording Conversations Concerning Controlled Substances	C	Unranked
69.25.155(1)	Interference with Person Performing Official Duties	C	Unranked
69.25.155(2)	Interference with Person Performing Official Duties With a Deadly Weapon	B	Unranked

The Caseload Forecast Council is not liable for errors or omissions in the manual, for sentences that may be inappropriately calculated as a result of a practitioner's or court's reliance on the manual, or for any other written or verbal information related to adult or juvenile sentencing. The scoring sheets are intended to provide assistance in most cases but do not cover all permutations of the scoring rules. If you find any errors or omissions, we encourage you to report them to the Caseload Forecast Council.

SECTION 4 - Unranked Offenses

Statute (RCW)	Offense	Class	Seriousness Level
70.74.275	Intimidation or Harassment With an Explosive	C	Unranked
9A.60.070	Issuing a False Academic Credential	C	Unranked
16.52.320	Kill or Cause Substantial Harm With Malice to Livestock	C	Unranked
46.70.021	Licensing Violation for Car Dealers or Manufacturers (Subsequent Violation)	C	Unranked
30A.12.120	Loan to Officer or Employee from Trust Fund	B	Unranked
67.70.130	Lottery Fraud	B	Unranked
9A.40.090	Luring of a Child or Developmentally Disabled Person	C	Unranked
9A.56.370	Mail Theft	C	Unranked
9.47.090	Maintaining a Bucket Shop	C	Unranked
9.45.220	Making False Sample or Assay of Ore	C	Unranked
9.62.010(1)	Malicious Prosecution	C	Unranked
9.45.260	Malicious Sprinkler Contractor Work	C	Unranked
70.74.022(1)	Manufacture, Purchase, Sell or Store Explosive Device Without License	C	Unranked
46.20.0921(3)(a)	Manufacture, Sell or Deliver Forged Driver's License or Identicard	C	Unranked
82.24.570(2)	Manufacture, Sell or Possess Counterfeit Cigarettes	C	Unranked
82.24.570(3)	Manufacture, Sell or Possess Counterfeit Cigarettes (Subsequent Violation)	B	Unranked
69.51A.060	Medical Marijuana Fraudulent Records (Effective Until 7/1/2016)	C	Unranked
69.51A.240	Medical Marijuana – Unlawful Actions	C	Unranked
9.81.030	Member of Subversive Organization	C	Unranked
42.20.070	Misappropriating and Falsifying Accounts by Public Officer	B	Unranked
42.20.090	Misappropriating and Falsifying Accounts by Treasurer	C	Unranked
9.82.030	Misprision of Treason	C	Unranked
29A.08.740	Misuse of Registered Voter Data	C	Unranked
29A.84.150	Misuse or Alteration of Registration Database	C	Unranked
9.45.070	Mock Auction	C	Unranked
9A.83.020	Money Laundering	B	Unranked
32.04.110	Mutual Savings Bank - Conceal or Destroy Evidence	B	Unranked
32.04.100	Mutual Savings Bank - Falsify Savings Book, Document or Statement	B	Unranked
32.24.080	Mutual Savings Bank - Transfer Bank Assets After Insolvency	B	Unranked
9A.60.030	Obtaining Signature by Deception or Duress	C	Unranked
46.70.180(5)	Odometer Offense	C	Unranked
40.16.030	Offering False Instrument for Filing or Record	C	Unranked
68.50.140(3)	Opening Graves With Intent to Sell or Remove Personal Effects or Human	C	Unranked

The Caseload Forecast Council is not liable for errors or omissions in the manual, for sentences that may be inappropriately calculated as a result of a practitioner's or court's reliance on the manual, or for any other written or verbal information related to adult or juvenile sentencing. The scoring sheets are intended to provide assistance in most cases but do not cover all permutations of the scoring rules. If you find any errors or omissions, we encourage you to report them to the Caseload Forecast Council.

SECTION 4 - Unranked Offenses

Statute (RCW)	Offense	Class	Seriousness Level
	Remains		
90.56.540	Operation of a Vessel While Under the Influence of Intoxicating Liquor or Drugs	C	Unranked
9.46.215	Ownership or Interest in Gambling Device	C	Unranked
69.30.085	Participation in Shellfish Operation or Activities While License is Denied, Revoked or Suspended	C	Unranked
74.09.240(2)	Paying or Offering Bribes, Kickbacks or Rebates	C	Unranked
82.32.290(4)	Phantomware Violation	C	Unranked
69.40.030	Placing Poison or Other Harmful Object or Substance in Food, Drinks, Medicine or Water	B	Unranked
69.40.020	Poison in Milk or Food Product	C	Unranked
9A.58.020	Possessing or Capturing Personal Identification Document	C	Unranked
9.94.041(2)	Possession of Controlled Substance by Prisoner (County or Local Facility)	C	Unranked
9.94.041(1)	Possession of Controlled Substance by Prisoner (State Facility)	C	Unranked
9.94.045	Possession of Controlled Substance in Prison by Non-prisoner	C	Unranked
69.41.350	Possession of Steroids in Excess of 200 tablets or (8) 2cc Bottles Without a Valid Prescription	C	Unranked
9A.56.380	Possession of Stolen Mail	C	Unranked
9.94.040(2)	Possession of Weapons by Prisoners (County or Local Facility)	C	Unranked
9.94.040(1)	Possession of Weapons by Prisoners (State Facility)	B	Unranked
9.94.043	Possession of Weapons in Prison by Non-prisoner	B	Unranked
9.94.010	Prison Riot	B	Unranked
9.46.220	Professional Gambling 1	B	Unranked
9.46.221	Professional Gambling 2	C	Unranked
9A.36.060	Promoting a Suicide Attempt	C	Unranked
67.08.015	Promoting Illegal Boxing, Martial Arts and Wrestling	C	Unranked
9.68.140	Promoting Pornography	C	Unranked
9.68A.102	Promoting Travel for Commercial Sexual Abuse of a Minor	C	Unranked
9A.88.085	Promoting Travel for Prostitution	C	Unranked
29A.84.311	Provides False Information or Conceals or Destroys Candidacy Declaration or Nominating Petition	C	Unranked
26.04.210	Providing False Statements in Affidavits for Marriage	C	Unranked
68.50.140(2)	Purchasing or Receiving Human Remains	C	Unranked
74.09.240(1)	Receiving or Asking for Bribes, Kickbacks or Rebates	C	Unranked
9A.68.030	Receiving or Granting Unlawful Compensation	C	Unranked

The Caseload Forecast Council is not liable for errors or omissions in the manual, for sentences that may be inappropriately calculated as a result of a practitioner's or court's reliance on the manual, or for any other written or verbal information related to adult or juvenile sentencing. The scoring sheets are intended to provide assistance in most cases but do not cover all permutations of the scoring rules. If you find any errors or omissions, we encourage you to report them to the Caseload Forecast Council.

SECTION 4 - Unranked Offenses

Statute (RCW)	Offense	Class	Seriousness Level
81.60.080(2)	Receiving Stolen Railroad Property	C	Unranked
90.56.530	Reckless Operation of a Tank Vessel	C	Unranked
19.110.075(2)	Registration Knowingly Not Obtained Prior to Sale of Business Opportunity (Violation of RCW 19.110.050)	B	Unranked
70.94.430(3)	Releasing Into Ambient Air Hazardous Air Pollutant	C	Unranked
46.12.560	Removal of Sticker on Vehicle Stating Previously Destroyed or Title 1 Loss	C	Unranked
68.50.140(4)	Removal, Disinterment or Mutilation of Human Remains	C	Unranked
68.60.050	Removes, Defaces or Destroys any Historic Grave	C	Unranked
68.50.140(1)	Removing Human Remains	C	Unranked
9.16.010	Removing Lawful Brands	C	Unranked
19.25.020(2)(a)	Reproduction of Sound Recording Without Consent of Owner - Recording Fixed Before 2/15/1972 (At Least 1,000 Recordings or Subsequent Conviction)	B	Unranked
19.25.020(2)(b)	Reproduction of Sound Recording Without Consent of Owner - Recording Fixed Before 2/15/1972 (More Than 100 but Less Than 1,000 Recordings)	C	Unranked
9A.68.020	Requesting Unlawful Compensation	C	Unranked
70.345.030	Retail Sales, Distribution or Delivery Sales of Vapor Products Without a License	C	Unranked
9A.56.360(4)	Retail Theft with Special Circumstances 3	C	Unranked
81.60.080(1)	Sabotaging Rolling Stock	C	Unranked
69.41.030(2)(a)	Sale, Delivery or Possession With Intent to Sell Legend Drug Without Prescription	B	Unranked
33.36.040	Savings and Loan Association - Making False Statement of Assets or Liabilities	C	Unranked
33.36.030	Savings and Loan Association - Preference in Case of Insolvency	C	Unranked
33.36.060	Savings and Loan Association - Suppressing, Secreting or Destroying Evidence or Records	C	Unranked
19.60.067(2)	Second-hand Precious Metal Dealer Violations (Subsequent Violation)	C	Unranked
46.20.0921(2)	Sell or Deliver a Stolen Driver's License or Identicard	C	Unranked
27.44.040(2)	Selling Artifacts or Human Remains from Indian Graves	C	Unranked
48.160.080	Sells Guaranteed Asset Protection Waivers Without Registration	B	Unranked
70.155.140	Shipping or Transporting Tobacco Products Ordered Through Mail or Internet	C	Unranked
82.38.270	Special Fuel Violations	C	Unranked
67.70.160	State Lottery Violations Except Lottery Fraud and Unlicensed Lottery Activity	C	Unranked
30B.12.050	State Trust Company – False Entry, Conceal or Destroy Records	B	Unranked

The Caseload Forecast Council is not liable for errors or omissions in the manual, for sentences that may be inappropriately calculated as a result of a practitioner's or court's reliance on the manual, or for any other written or verbal information related to adult or juvenile sentencing. The scoring sheets are intended to provide assistance in most cases but do not cover all permutations of the scoring rules. If you find any errors or omissions, we encourage you to report them to the Caseload Forecast Council.

SECTION 4 - Unranked Offenses

Statute (RCW)	Offense	Class	Seriousness Level
9.45.020	Substitution of Child	B	Unranked
9.81.020	Subversive Acts	B	Unranked
29A.84.550	Tampering with Election Materials	C	Unranked
9.40.105	Tampering with Fire Alarm, Emergency Signal, or Fire-fighting Equipment with Intent to Commit Arson	B	Unranked
88.08.020	Tampering with Lights or Signals	B	Unranked
29A.84.560	Tampering with Voting Machine	C	Unranked
9A.56.262	Theft of Telecommunication Service	C	Unranked
9A.36.090	Threats Against Governor or Family	C	Unranked
64.36.210	Timeshare Fraud	C	Unranked
64.36.020(5)(b)	Timeshare Registration Requirement Violation	C	Unranked
9A.68.040	Trading in Public Office	C	Unranked
9A.68.050	Trading in Special Influence	C	Unranked
9.46.240	Transmission or Receiving Gambling Information by Internet	C	Unranked
70.105.085(1)(a)	Transport, Disposal or Export of Hazardous Waste That Places Another Person in Danger of Injury or Death	B	Unranked
70.105.085(1)(b)	Transport, Disposal or Export of Hazardous Waste That Places Another Person's Property in Danger of Harm	C	Unranked
82.24.110(2)	Transportation of More Than 10,000 Cigarettes Without Proper Stamps	C	Unranked
68.60.040(3)	Transports Removed Human Remains, Opens a Grave or Removes Personal Effects from Grave	C	Unranked
9.82.010	Treason	A	Unranked
9.91.150(1)	Tree Spiking	C	Unranked
9.02.120	Unauthorized Abortion	C	Unranked
68.44.060	Unauthorized Loans to Cemetery Authority	C	Unranked
29A.84.545	Unauthorized Removal of Paper Record from Electronic Voting Device	C	Unranked
39.62.040	Unauthorized Use of Public Official Facsimile Signature or Seal	B	Unranked
68.05.330	Unfair Practice of Funeral or Cemetery Board	C	Unranked
19.225.110	Uniform Athlete Agent Act Violation	C	Unranked
69.43.070(1)	Unlawful Delivery of Precursor Drug with Intent to Use	B	Unranked
9A.49.020	Unlawful Discharge of a Laser 1	C	Unranked
74.09.290	Unlawful Disclosure of Patient Records or DSHS Information	C	Unranked
69.53.020	Unlawful Fortification of Building for Drug Purposes	C	Unranked
9A.56.264	Unlawful Manufacture of a Telecommunication Device	C	Unranked
88.46.080(2)(b)	Unlawful Operation of a Covered Vessel (Subsequent Violation)	C	Unranked

The Caseload Forecast Council is not liable for errors or omissions in the manual, for sentences that may be inappropriately calculated as a result of a practitioner's or court's reliance on the manual, or for any other written or verbal information related to adult or juvenile sentencing. The scoring sheets are intended to provide assistance in most cases but do not cover all permutations of the scoring rules. If you find any errors or omissions, we encourage you to report them to the Caseload Forecast Council.

SECTION 4 - Unranked Offenses

Statute (RCW)	Offense	Class	Seriousness Level
90.56.300(2)(b)	Unlawful Operation of Onshore or Offshore Facility (Subsequent Conviction)	C	Unranked
9.41.115	Unlawful Private Transfer of a Firearm (Subsequent Offense)	C	Unranked
69.43.070(2)	Unlawful Receipt of Precursor Drug with Intent to Use	B	Unranked
9A.56.266	Unlawful Sale of a Telecommunication Device	C	Unranked
9A.56.230	Unlawful Sale of Subscription Television Services	C	Unranked
46.12.750(3)	Unlawful Sale of Vehicle Certificate of Ownership	C	Unranked
18.64.046(7)	Unlawful Selling of Ephedrine, Pseudoephedrine or Phenylpropanolamine by a Wholesaler	C	Unranked
19.116.080(1)	Unlawful Subleasing of Motor Vehicle	C	Unranked
77.15.770(2)	Unlawful Trade in Shark Fins 1	C	Unranked
77.15.135(4)(d)	Unlawful Trafficking in Species With Extinction 1	C	Unranked
19.116.080(2)	Unlawful Transfer of Ownership of Motor Vehicle	C	Unranked
18.04.370(1)(b)	Unlawful Use of a Professional Title	C	Unranked
18.04.370(1)(c)	Unlawful Use of CPA Title After Suspension	C	Unranked
69.53.030	Unlawful Use of Fortified Building	C	Unranked
77.15.811	Unlawful Use of Invasive Species 1	C	Unranked
66.44.120(2)(b)	Unlawful Use of Liquor Board Seal (Third or Subsequent Offense)	C	Unranked
19.310.120	Unlawfully Engaging in Business as an Exchange Facilitator (RCW 19.310.100(1)-(9))	B	Unranked
82.24.500	Unlawfully Purchase, Sell, Consign or Distribute Cigarettes	C	Unranked
48.102.160(4)	Unlicensed Life Insurance Provider	B	Unranked
67.70.140	Unlicensed Lottery Activity	B	Unranked
48.102.160(5)	Unlicensed Settlement Broker	B	Unranked
29A.84.660	Unqualified Person Voting	C	Unranked
29A.84.140	Unqualified Voting Registration	C	Unranked
19.210.040	Unused Property, Merchants –Prohibited Sales (Third or Subsequent Offense Within 5 Years)	C	Unranked
46.37.673	Use of a Signal Preemption Device Resulting in Property Damage or Less Substantial Bodily Harm	C	Unranked
19.25.030(2)(a)	Use of Recording of Live Performance Without Consent of Owner (At Least 1,000 Recordings or at Least 100 Unauthorized Audiovisual Recordings or Subsequent Offense)	B	Unranked
19.25.030(2)(b)	Use of Recording of Live Performance Without Consent of Owner (At Least 100 but Less Than 1,000 Recordings or More than 10 but Less Than 100 Unauthorized Audiovisual Recording or Subsequent Offense)	C	Unranked
19.144.100(1)	Use or Investment of Proceeds from Mortgage Fraud Activities	B	Unranked

The Caseload Forecast Council is not liable for errors or omissions in the manual, for sentences that may be inappropriately calculated as a result of a practitioner's or court's reliance on the manual, or for any other written or verbal information related to adult or juvenile sentencing. The scoring sheets are intended to provide assistance in most cases but do not cover all permutations of the scoring rules. If you find any errors or omissions, we encourage you to report them to the Caseload Forecast Council.

SECTION 4 - Unranked Offenses

Statute (RCW)	Offense	Class	Seriousness Level
9.68A.075(2)	Viewing Depictions of Minor Engaged in Sexually Explicit Conduct 2	C	Unranked
29A.84.230(1)	Violation by Signer – Initiative or Referendum with False Name	C	Unranked
26.50.110(5)	Violation of a Foreign Protection Order (Third or Subsequent Violation)	C	Unranked
29A.84.240(1)	Violations By Signers – Recall Petition With False Name	B	Unranked
29A.84.130	Voter Violation of Registration Law	C	Unranked
29A.84.650(1)	Voting Repeater – More Than One Vote at Any Election	C	Unranked
48.30.220	Willful Destruction, Injury, Secretion of Insured Property	C	Unranked
10.66.090	Willfully Disobeys an Off-limits Order (Subsequent Violation or Enters Protected Against Drug Trafficking Area)	C	Unranked

The Caseload Forecast Council is not liable for errors or omissions in the manual, for sentences that may be inappropriately calculated as a result of a practitioner's or court's reliance on the manual, or for any other written or verbal information related to adult or juvenile sentencing. The scoring sheets are intended to provide assistance in most cases but do not cover all permutations of the scoring rules. If you find any errors or omissions, we encourage you to report them to the Caseload Forecast Council.

SECTION 4 – MANDATORY REMAND OFFENSES

MANDATORY REMAND OFFENSES

RCW 10.64.025(2)

Statute (RCW)	Offense	Class	Seriousness Level
9A.36.021(2)(b)	Assault 2 With a Finding of Sexual Motivation	A	IV
9A.44.083	Child Molestation 1	A	X
9A.28.020(3)(a)	Child Molestation 1 – Criminal Attempt	A	X
9A.28.030(2)	Child Molestation 1 – Criminal Solicitation	A	X
9A.44.086	Child Molestation 2	B	VII
9A.44.089	Child Molestation 3	C	V
9.68A.090(2)	Communication with Minor for Immoral Purposes (Subsequent Violation or Prior Sex Offense Conviction)	C	III
9A.64.020(1)	Incest 1	B	VI
9A.64.020(2)	Incest 2	C	V
9A.44.100(1)(a)	Indecent Liberties - With Forcible Compulsion	A	X
9A.28.020(3)(a)	Indecent Liberties - With Forcible Compulsion – Criminal Attempt	A	X
9A.28.030(2)	Indecent Liberties - With Forcible Compulsion – Criminal Solicitation	A	X
9A.44.100(1)(b-c)	Indecent Liberties - Without Forcible Compulsion	B	VII
9A.44.100(1)(d-f)	Indecent Liberties - Without Forcible Compulsion	B	Unranked
9A.40.030(3)(b)	Kidnapping 2 With a Finding of Sexual Motivation	A	V
9A.40.090	Luring of a Child or Developmentally Disabled Person	C	Unranked
9.68A.101	Promoting Commercial Sexual Abuse of a Minor	A	XII
9A.44.040	Rape 1	A	XII
9A.28.020(3)(a)	Rape 1 – Criminal Attempt	A	XII
9A.28.030(2)	Rape 1 – Criminal Solicitation	A	XII
9A.44.050	Rape 2	A	XI
9A.28.020(3)(a)	Rape 2 – Criminal Attempt	A	XI
9A.28.030(2)	Rape 2 – Criminal Solicitation	A	XI
9A.44.073	Rape of a Child 1	A	XII
9A.28.020(3)(a)	Rape of a Child 1 – Criminal Attempt	A	XII
9A.28.030(2)	Rape of a Child 1 – Criminal Solicitation	A	XII
9A.44.076	Rape of a Child 2	A	XI
9A.28.020(3)(a)	Rape of a Child 2 – Criminal Attempt	A	XI

The Caseload Forecast Council is not liable for errors or omissions in the manual, for sentences that may be inappropriately calculated as a result of a practitioner's or court's reliance on the manual, or for any other written or verbal information related to adult or juvenile sentencing. The scoring sheets are intended to provide assistance in most cases but do not cover all permutations of the scoring rules. If you find any errors or omissions, we encourage you to report them to the Caseload Forecast Council.

SECTION 4 – MANDATORY REMAND OFFENSES

9A.28.030(2)	Rape of a Child 2 – Criminal Solicitation	A	XI
9A.44.079	Rape of a Child 3	C	VI
9A.44.093	Sexual Misconduct with a Minor 1	C	V
9A.40.100(1)	Trafficking 1	A	XIV
9A.40.100(3)	Trafficking 2	A	XII

Any class A or B felony with a finding of sexual motivation as defined in RCW 9.94A.030(48)

A felony violation of RCW 9.68A.090

Attempt, Solicitation or Conspiracy to commit one of these felonies

---

The Caseload Forecast Council is not liable for errors or omissions in the manual, for sentences that may be inappropriately calculated as a result of a practitioner's or court's reliance on the manual, or for any other written or verbal information related to adult or juvenile sentencing. The scoring sheets are intended to provide assistance in most cases but do not cover all permutations of the scoring rules. If you find any errors or omissions, we encourage you to report them to the Caseload Forecast Council.

SECTION 4 – FELONY INDEX BY OFFENSE

FELONY INDEX BY OFFENSE

Statute (RCW)	Offense	Class	Seriousness Level
9A.42.060	Abandonment of Dependent Persons 1	B	IX
9A.42.070	Abandonment of Dependent Persons 2	C	V
29A.84.680(1)	Absentee Voting Violation	C	Unranked
46.52.130(5)(b)	Abstracts of Driving Records – Intentional Misuse	C	Unranked
20.01.460(2)	Acting as Commission Merchant, Dealer, Cash Buyer Without License	C	Unranked
9A.82.030	Advancing Money or Property for Extortionate Extension of Credit	B	V
69.52.030(3)	Advertising Imitation Controlled Substances	C	Unranked
10.95.020	Aggravated Murder 1	A	XVI
46.37.660(2)(c)	Air Bag Diagnostic Systems	C	V
46.37.660(2)(b)	Air Bag Diagnostic Systems (Causing Bodily Injury or Death)	C	VII
46.37.660(1)(c)	Air Bag Replacement Requirements	C	V
46.37.660(1)(b)	Air Bag Replacement Requirements (Causing Bodily Injury or Death)	C	VII
30A.42.290(3)	Alien Bank or Bureau – Destroy or Secrete Records	B	Unranked
30A.42.290(2)	Alien Bank or Bureau – False Entry, Statements, etc.	B	Unranked
9.41.171	Alien Possession of a Firearm	C	Unranked
9.45.210	Altering Sample or Certificate of Assay	C	Unranked
9A.76.177	Amber Alert – Making False Statements to a Public Servant	C	Unranked
68.64.160	Anatomical Gift - Illegal Financial Gain	C	Unranked
68.64.150	Anatomical Gifts - Illegal Purchase or Sale	C	Unranked
16.52.205(2)	Animal Cruelty 1	C	Unranked
16.52.205(3)	Animal Cruelty 1 - Sexual Contact or Conduct	C	III
16.52.117	Animal Fighting	C	Unranked
9A.48.020	Arson 1	A	VIII
9A.28.020(3)(a)	Arson 1 – Criminal Attempt	A	VIII
9A.28.030(2)	Arson 1 – Criminal Solicitation	A	VIII
9A.48.030	Arson 2	B	IV
9A.36.011	Assault 1	A	XII

The Caseload Forecast Council is not liable for errors or omissions in the manual, for sentences that may be inappropriately calculated as a result of a practitioner's or court's reliance on the manual, or for any other written or verbal information related to adult or juvenile sentencing. The scoring sheets are intended to provide assistance in most cases but do not cover all permutations of the scoring rules. If you find any errors or omissions, we encourage you to report them to the Caseload Forecast Council.

SECTION 4 – FELONY INDEX BY OFFENSE

Statute (RCW)	Offense	Class	Seriousness Level
9A.36.021(2)(a)	Assault 2	B	IV
9A.36.021(2)(b)	Assault 2 With a Finding of Sexual Motivation	A	IV
9A.36.031(1)(a-g) & (i-j)	Assault 3 – Excluding Assault 3 of a Peace Officer with a Projectile Stun Gun	C	III
9A.36.031(1)(h)	Assault 3 - Of a Peace Officer with a Projectile Stun Gun	C	IV
79A.60.060	Assault by Watercraft	B	IV
9A.36.120	Assault of a Child 1	A	XII
9A.36.130	Assault of a Child 2	B	IX
9A.36.140	Assault of a Child 3	C	III
9.05.030	Assembly of Saboteurs	B	Unranked
72.23.170	Assist Escape of Mental Patient	C	Unranked
9A.82.080(3)	Attempt or Conspiracy to Violate RCW 9A.82.080(1) or (2)	C	Unranked
46.61.024	Attempting to Elude Pursuing Police Vehicle	C	I
9A.76.170(3)(b)	Bail Jumping with Class A Felony	B	V
9A.76.170(3)(c)	Bail Jumping with Class B or C Felony	C	III
9A.76.170(3)(a)	Bail Jumping with Murder 1	A	VI
30A.12.100	Bank or Trust Company - Destroy or Secrete Records	B	Unranked
30A.12.090	Bank or Trust Company - False Entry, Statements, etc.	B	Unranked
30A.44.120	Bank or Trust Company - Receiving Deposits When Insolvent	B	Unranked
30A.44.110	Bank or Trust Company - Transfer of Assets Prior to Insolvency	B	Unranked
9A.64.010	Bigamy	C	Unranked
9A.72.100	Bribe Received by Witness	B	IV
9A.68.010	Bribery	B	VI
9A.72.090	Bribing a Witness	B	IV
9.46.155	Bribing to Obtain a License From Public Officials, Employees, Agents	C	Unranked
72.23.300	Bringing Narcotics, Liquor, or Weapons into State Institution or Grounds	B	Unranked
9.47.120	Bunco Steering	B	Unranked
9A.52.020	Burglary 1	A	VII
9A.52.030	Burglary 2	B	III
46.87.260	Cab Card Forgery (Effective Until 7/1/2016)	B	Unranked
9.46.180	Causing Person to Violate Gambling Laws	B	Unranked
9.46.1961	Cheating 1	C	IV
9A.64.030(3)(b)	Child Buying	C	Unranked
49.12.410(2)	Child Labor Law Violation – Death/Disability	C	Unranked

The Caseload Forecast Council is not liable for errors or omissions in the manual, for sentences that may be inappropriately calculated as a result of a practitioner's or court's reliance on the manual, or for any other written or verbal information related to adult or juvenile sentencing. The scoring sheets are intended to provide assistance in most cases but do not cover all permutations of the scoring rules. If you find any errors or omissions, we encourage you to report them to the Caseload Forecast Council.

SECTION 4 – FELONY INDEX BY OFFENSE

Statute (RCW)	Offense	Class	Seriousness Level
9A.44.083	Child Molestation 1	A	X
9A.28.020(3)(a)	Child Molestation 1 – Criminal Attempt	A	X
9A.28.030(2)	Child Molestation 1 – Criminal Solicitation	A	X
9A.44.086	Child Molestation 2	B	VII
9A.44.089	Child Molestation 3	C	V
9A.64.030(3)(a)	Child Selling	C	Unranked
9A.48.120	Civil Disorder Training	B	VII
70.245.200(2)	Coerce Patient to Request Life-ending Medication	A	Unranked
9A.40.110	Coercion of Involuntary Servitude	C	Unranked
9A.82.045	Collection of Unlawful Debt	C	Unranked
9A.68.060	Commercial Bribery	B	IV
77.15.500(3)(b)	Commercial Fishing Without a License 1	C	II
9.68A.100	Commercial Sexual Abuse of a Minor	B	VIII
19.158.160	Commercial Telephone Solicitor Deception (Value of $250 or More)	C	Unranked
30A.04.240	Commingling of Funds or Securities	B	Unranked
21.30.140	Commodity Transaction Violation	B	Unranked
9.68A.090(2)	Communication with Minor for Immoral Purposes (Subsequent Violation or Prior Sex Offense Conviction)	C	III
9A.90.040	Computer Trespass 1	C	II
69.50.465	Conducting or Maintaining a Marijuana Club	C	Unranked
19.144.100(2)	Control of Real Property Resulting from Mortgage Fraud Activities	B	Unranked
69.50.415	Controlled Substance Homicide	B	DG-III
69.50.416	Controlled Substance Label Violation	C	Unranked
9.16.035(4)	Counterfeiting - Endanger Public Health or Safety	C	IV
9.16.035(3)	Counterfeiting – Third Conviction and Value $10,000 or More	C	II
69.50.4011(2)(a-b)	Create, Deliver or Possess a Counterfeit Controlled Substance – Schedule I or II Narcotic or Flunitrazepam or Methamphetamine	B	DG-II
69.50.4011(2)(c-e)	Create, Deliver or Possess a Counterfeit Controlled Substance – Schedule I-II Nonnarcotic, Schedule III-V Except Flunitrazepam or Methamphetamine	C	DG-II
46.87.260	Credential Forgery (Effective 7/1/2016)	B	Unranked
31.12.724(3)	Credit Union - Fraudulent Receipt of Credit Union Deposit	B	Unranked
31.12.724(2)	Credit Union - Transfer of Credit Union Assets Prior to Insolvency	B	Unranked
9.08.090	Crimes Against Animal Facilities	C	Unranked
9A.46.120	Criminal Gang Intimidation	C	III
9A.60.040	Criminal Impersonation 1	C	Unranked

The Caseload Forecast Council is not liable for errors or omissions in the manual, for sentences that may be inappropriately calculated as a result of a practitioner's or court's reliance on the manual, or for any other written or verbal information related to adult or juvenile sentencing. The scoring sheets are intended to provide assistance in most cases but do not cover all permutations of the scoring rules. If you find any errors or omissions, we encourage you to report them to the Caseload Forecast Council.

SECTION 4 – FELONY INDEX BY OFFENSE

Statute (RCW)	Offense	Class	Seriousness Level
9A.84.010(2)(b)	Criminal Mischief	C	Unranked
9A.42.020	Criminal Mistreatment 1	B	X
9A.42.030	Criminal Mistreatment 2	C	V
9A.82.160	Criminal Profiteering Lien After Service of Notice	C	Unranked
9.05.060(2)	Criminal Sabotage	B	Unranked
9A.44.196	Criminal Trespass Against Children	C	Unranked
9A.36.100	Custodial Assault	C	III
9A.40.060	Custodial Interference 1	C	Unranked
9A.40.070	Custodial Interference 2 (Subsequent Offense)	C	Unranked
9A.44.160	Custodial Sexual Misconduct 1	C	V
9.61.260(3)	Cyberstalking (With Prior Harassment Conviction or Threat of Death)	C	III
43.06.230	Damage Property or Cause Personal Injury after State of Emergency Proclaimed	B	Unranked
16.08.100(2)	Dangerous Dog Attack (Subsequent Offense)	C	Unranked
16.08.100(3)	Dangerous Dog Attack Resulting in Severe Injury or Death	C	Unranked
9.68A.050(1)	Dealing in Depictions of Minor Engaged in Sexually Explicit Conduct 1	B	VII
9.68A.050(2)	Dealing in Depictions of Minor Engaged in Sexually Explicit Conduct 2	C	V
22.09.310	Dealing in Unauthorized Warehouse Receipts for Agricultural Commodities	C	Unranked
39.44.101	Defraud a Facsimile Signature on Bonds and Coupons	B	Unranked
87.03.200	Defraud Facsimile Signatures on Bonds and Coupons – Irrigation Districts	B	Unranked
19.110.120	Defraud or Provide Misleading or Untrue Documents Related to a Business Opportunity Sale	B	Unranked
9A.61.030	Defrauding a Public Utility 1	B	Unranked
9A.61.040	Defrauding a Public Utility 2	C	Unranked
19.48.110(1)(b)	Defrauding an Innkeeper (Value of $75.00 or More)	B	Unranked
69.50.401(2)(b)	Deliver or Possess with Intent to Deliver - Methamphetamine	B	DG-II
69.50.4012	Delivery of a Material in Lieu of a Controlled Substance	C	DG-II
9.41.110(8)	Delivery of Firearm by Dealer to Ineligible Person	C	Unranked
9.41.080	Delivery of Firearms to Ineligible Person	C	Unranked
69.52.030(2)	Delivery of Imitation Controlled Substance by Person 18 or Over to Person Under 18	B	DG-III
35A.36.040	Designation of Bonds – Violation (Code Cities)	B	Unranked
35.36.040	Designation of Bonds – Violation (First Class Cities)	B	Unranked
27.44.040(1)	Destroying, Removing or Defacing Indian Graves	C	Unranked
68.60.040(1)	Destruction of Tomb, Plot, Marker, or Cemetery Property	C	Unranked

The Caseload Forecast Council is not liable for errors or omissions in the manual, for sentences that may be inappropriately calculated as a result of a practitioner's or court's reliance on the manual, or for any other written or verbal information related to adult or juvenile sentencing. The scoring sheets are intended to provide assistance in most cases but do not cover all permutations of the scoring rules. If you find any errors or omissions, we encourage you to report them to the Caseload Forecast Council.

SECTION 4 – FELONY INDEX BY OFFENSE

Statute (RCW)	Offense	Class	Seriousness Level
9.38.060	Digital Signatures Fraud	C	Unranked
9A.76.023(2)(a)	Disarming a Law Enforcement or Corrections Officer	C	Unranked
9A.76.023(2)(b)	Disarming a Law Enforcement or Corrections Officer and Firearm is Discharged	B	Unranked
9A.86.010	Disclosing Intimate Images	C	Unranked
19.110.075(2)	Disclosures Knowingly Not Provided at Sale of Business Opportunity (Violation of RCW 19.110.070)	B	Unranked
69.50.402	Dispensing Violation (VUCSA)	C	Unranked
82.26.190	Distributors and Retailer of Tobacco Products License Violation	C	Unranked
27.53.060	Disturbing Archaeological Resources or Site	C	Unranked
43.43.856	Divulging Confidential Investigative Information Pertaining to Organized Crime	B	Unranked
26.50.110	Domestic Violence Court Order Violation	C	V
9A.36.045	Drive-by Shooting	B	VII
46.61.502(6)	Driving While Under the Influence of Intoxicating Liquor or any Drug	B	V
29A.84.270	Duplication of Name – Conspiracy to Mislead	B	Unranked
29A.84.320	Duplication of Names on Declaration of Candidacy	B	Unranked
29A.84.655	Election Officer Permits Repeat Vote	C	Unranked
29A.84.720	Election Officers – Violation	C	Unranked
29A.84.030	Election or Mail Ballot Violation	C	Unranked
19.300.020	Electronic Communication Devices – Illegal Scanning	C	Unranked
9A.90.060	Electronic Data Service Interference	C	II
9A.90.080	Electronic Data Tampering 1	C	II
9A.90.100	Electronic Data Theft	C	II
79A.60.090	Eluding a Law Enforcement Vessel	C	Unranked
18.39.350	Embalmers/Funeral Directors Violation	C	Unranked
43.08.140	Embezzlement by State Treasurer	B	Unranked
9A.42.100	Endangerment With a Controlled Substance	B	IV
46.80.020(b)	Engage in Business of Wrecking Vehicles Without a License (Subsequent Offense)	C	Unranked
51.48.103(2)	Engaging in Business After Certificate of Coverage Revocation	C	Unranked
70.345.090	Engaging in Delivery Sales of Vapor Products Without a License or Proper Shipping Documentation	C	Unranked
77.15.620(3)(b)	Engaging in Fish Dealing Activity Unlicensed 1	C	II
16.08.100(4)	Entering Dog in a Dog Fight	C	Unranked
61.34.030	Equity Skimming	B	II

The Caseload Forecast Council is not liable for errors or omissions in the manual, for sentences that may be inappropriately calculated as a result of a practitioner's or court's reliance on the manual, or for any other written or verbal information related to adult or juvenile sentencing. The scoring sheets are intended to provide assistance in most cases but do not cover all permutations of the scoring rules. If you find any errors or omissions, we encourage you to report them to the Caseload Forecast Council.

SECTION 4 – FELONY INDEX BY OFFENSE

Statute (RCW)	Offense	Class	Seriousness Level
9.68.060	Erotic Material (Third or Subsequent Offense)	B	Unranked
9A.76.110	Escape 1	B	IV
9A.76.120	Escape 2	C	III
9A.76.130(3)(b)	Escape 3 (Third or Subsequent Offense)	C	Unranked
72.09.310	Escape from Community Custody	C	II
51.48.020(1)	Evading Industrial Insurance Premiums	C	Unranked
82.42.085	Evading the Collection of Aircraft Fuel Tax	C	Unranked
74.09.260	Excessive Charges, Payments	C	Unranked
48.06.190	Exhibiting False Accounts of Insurer	B	Unranked
70.74.180	Explosive Devices Prohibited	A	IX
9A.56.120	Extortion 1	B	V
9A.56.130	Extortion 2	C	III
9A.82.020	Extortionate Extension of Credit	B	V
9A.82.040	Extortionate Means to Collect Extensions of Credit	B	V
19.25.040(2)(a)	Failure to Disclose Origin of Certain Recordings (At Least 100 Recordings or Subsequent Conviction)	B	Unranked
19.25.040(2)(b)	Failure to Disclose Origin of Certain Recordings (More than 10 but Less Than 100 Recordings)	C	Unranked
36.18.170	Failure to Pay Over Fees to County Treasurer	C	Unranked
9A.44.132(3)	Failure to Register as a Kidnapping Offender	C	Unranked
9A.44.132(1)(a)	Failure to Register as a Sex Offender (First Violation)	C	Unranked
9A.44.132(1)(a)	Failure to Register as a Sex Offender (Second Violation Committed on or After 6/10/2010)	C	II
9A.44.132(1)(a)	Failure to Register as a Sex Offender (Subsequent Violation Committed on or After 6/7/2006 but Before 6/10/2010)	C	II
9A.44.132(1)(b)	Failure to Register as a Sex Offender (Third or Subsequent Violation Committed on or After 6/10/2010)	B	II
19.146.050	Failure to Use a Trust Account	C	Unranked
19.142.080	Failure to Use a Trust Account or Furnish Bond for Health Studio	C	Unranked
38.42.050	False Affidavit Under Service Member Civil Relief Act	C	Unranked
74.08.100	False Age and Residency Public Assistance Verification	B	Unranked
42.24.100	False Claim from Municipal Corporation (Charged as Perjury 2)	C	Unranked
42.17A.750	False Documents Registered with Public Disclosure Commission	C	Unranked
51.48.020(2)	False Information in Industrial Insurance Claim (Charged as Theft)	*	*
48.30.230	False Insurance Claims (Value in Excess of $1,500)	C	Unranked

The Caseload Forecast Council is not liable for errors or omissions in the manual, for sentences that may be inappropriately calculated as a result of a practitioner's or court's reliance on the manual, or for any other written or verbal information related to adult or juvenile sentencing. The scoring sheets are intended to provide assistance in most cases but do not cover all permutations of the scoring rules. If you find any errors or omissions, we encourage you to report them to the Caseload Forecast Council.

SECTION 4 – FELONY INDEX BY OFFENSE

Statute (RCW)	Offense	Class	Seriousness Level
9.24.050	False Report of Corporation	B	Unranked
74.09.230	False Statement for Medical Assistance	C	Unranked
69.43.080	False Statement in Report of Precursor Drugs	C	Unranked
82.32.290(2)	False Statement to Department of Revenue	C	Unranked
19.230.300	False Statement, Misrepresentation or False Certification of Uniform Money services Record	C	Unranked
41.26.062	False Statements or Records to Defraud Law Enforcement Officers and Firefighters Retirement System	B	Unranked
41.32.055(1)	False Statements or Records to Defraud Teachers Retirement System	B	Unranked
74.09.250	False Statements Regarding Institutions, Facilities	C	Unranked
46.12.750(1)	False Statements, Illegal Transfers, Alterations or Forgeries of Vehicle Title	B	Unranked
65.12.740	False Swearing - Registration of Land Title (Charged as Perjury)	*	*
74.08.055(2)	False Verification for Welfare	B	I
26.20.030	Family Abandonment	C	Unranked
69.41.020	Forged Prescription - Legend Drug	B	DG-I
69.50.403	Forged Prescription for a Controlled Substance	C	DG-I
9A.60.020	Forgery	C	I
76.36.120	Forgery of Forest Product Mark	B	Unranked
65.12.760	Forgery of Registrar's Signature or Seal	B	Unranked
82.24.100	Forgery or Counterfeit Cigarette Tax Stamp	B	Unranked
70.245.200(1)	Forging Request for Medication	A	Unranked
19.100.210	Franchise Investment Protection Violation	B	Unranked
29A.84.711	Fraud in Certification of Nomination or Ballot	C	Unranked
9.45.170	Fraud in Liquor Warehouse Receipts	C	Unranked
9.45.124	Fraud in Measurement of Goods	B	Unranked
9.26A.110(3)	Fraud in Obtaining Telecommunications Services (Value Exceeds $250)	C	Unranked
67.24.010	Fraud in Sporting Contest	B	Unranked
9A.60.060	Fraudulent Creation or Revocation of Mental Health Advance Directive	C	I
76.48.141(1)(a)	Fraudulent Document as Specialized Forest Products Permit, Sales Invoice, Bill of Lading, etc.	C	Unranked
76.48.141(2)	Fraudulent Document for Specialized Forest Products Buyer	C	Unranked
9.45.270(3)	Fraudulent Filing of Vehicle Report of Sale (Value Exceeds $1,500)	B	Unranked
9.45.270(2)	Fraudulent Filing of Vehicle Report of Sale (Value Exceeds $250)	C	Unranked
9.24.020	Fraudulent Issue of Stock, Scrip, etc.	B	Unranked
48.102.160(3)	Fraudulent Life Insurance Settlement	B	Unranked

The Caseload Forecast Council is not liable for errors or omissions in the manual, for sentences that may be inappropriately calculated as a result of a practitioner's or court's reliance on the manual, or for any other written or verbal information related to adult or juvenile sentencing. The scoring sheets are intended to provide assistance in most cases but do not cover all permutations of the scoring rules. If you find any errors or omissions, we encourage you to report them to the Caseload Forecast Council.

SECTION 4 – FELONY INDEX BY OFFENSE

Statute (RCW)	Offense	Class	Seriousness Level
65.12.750	Fraudulent Procurement or False Entry on Land Title Registration	C	Unranked
76.48.141(1)(b)	Fraudulent Representation of Authority to Harvest Specialized Forest Products	C	Unranked
82.36.380	Fuel Tax Evasion	C	Unranked
9.46.160	Gambling Without License	B	Unranked
9.46.039	Greyhound Racing	B	Unranked
9A.46.020(2)(b)	Harassment (Subsequent Conviction or Threat of Death)	C	III
9A.76.200	Harming a Police Dog/Horse or an Accelerate Detection Dog	C	Unranked
48.80.030	Health Care False Claims	C	II
46.52.020(4)(a)	Hit and Run - Death	B	IX
46.52.020(4)(b)	Hit and Run - Injury	C	IV
79A.60.200(3)	Hit and Run with Vessel - Injury Accident	C	IV
9.94.030	Holding Hostages or Interfering with Officer's Duty	B	Unranked
9A.32.055	Homicide by Abuse	A	XV
79A.60.050(1)(c)	Homicide by Watercraft - Disregard for the Safety of Others	A	VII
79A.60.050(1)(b)	Homicide by Watercraft – In a Reckless Manner	A	VIII
79A.60.050(1)(a)	Homicide by Watercraft – While Under the Influence of Intoxicating Liquor or any Drug	A	IX
9.35.020(2)	Identity Theft 1	B	IV
9.35.020(3)	Identity Theft 2	C	II
69.41.040	Illegal Issuance of Legend Drug Prescription	B	Unranked
9.16.020	Imitating Lawful Brands With Intent	C	Unranked
19.146.235(9)	Impairing Mortgage Broker Investigation	B	Unranked
9.35.010	Improperly Obtaining Financial Information	C	II
9A.64.020(1)	Incest 1	B	VI
9A.64.020(2)	Incest 2	C	V
9A.88.010(2)(c)	Indecent Exposure to a Person Under Age 14 (Subsequent Conviction or Has Prior Sex Offense Conviction)	C	IV
9A.44.100(1)(a)	Indecent Liberties - With Forcible Compulsion	A	X
9A.28.020(3)(a)	Indecent Liberties - With Forcible Compulsion – Criminal Attempt	A	X
9A.28.030(2)	Indecent Liberties - With Forcible Compulsion – Criminal Solicitation	A	X
9A.44.100(1)(b-c)	Indecent Liberties - Without Forcible Compulsion	B	VII
9A.44.100(1)(d-f)	Indecent Liberties - Without Forcible Compulsion	B	Unranked
9.45.126	Inducing Fraud in Measurement of Goods	B	Unranked
9A.82.070	Influencing Outcome of Sporting Event	C	IV

The Caseload Forecast Council is not liable for errors or omissions in the manual, for sentences that may be inappropriately calculated as a result of a practitioner's or court's reliance on the manual, or for any other written or verbal information related to adult or juvenile sentencing. The scoring sheets are intended to provide assistance in most cases but do not cover all permutations of the scoring rules. If you find any errors or omissions, we encourage you to report them to the Caseload Forecast Council.

SECTION 4 – FELONY INDEX BY OFFENSE

Statute (RCW)	Offense	Class	Seriousness Level
40.16.010	Injury to a Public Record	C	Unranked
40.16.020	Injury to and Misappropriation of Public Record by Officer	B	Unranked
88.08.050(1)	Injury to Lighthouses or United States Light	B	Unranked
9.24.030	Insolvent Bank Receiving Deposit	B	Unranked
48.06.030	Insurance Solicitation Permit Violation	B	Unranked
9.91.170(5)	Intentional Infliction, Injury or Death to a Guide Dog or Service Animal	C	Unranked
9.91.175(3)	Intentionally Injures, Disables or Causes Death of an On-Duty Search and Rescue Dog	C	Unranked
9.73.230	Intercepting, Transmitting or Recording Conversations Concerning Controlled Substances	C	Unranked
69.25.155(1)	Interference with Person Performing Official Duties	C	Unranked
69.25.155(2)	Interference with Person Performing Official Duties With a Deadly Weapon	B	Unranked
9A.72.160	Intimidating a Judge	B	VI
9A.72.130	Intimidating a Juror	B	VI
9A.76.180	Intimidating a Public Servant	B	III
9A.72.110	Intimidating a Witness	B	VI
70.74.275	Intimidation or Harassment With an Explosive	C	Unranked
9A.76.140	Introducing Contraband 1	B	VII
9A.76.150	Introducing Contraband 2	C	III
69.50.4015	Involving a Minor in Drug Dealing	C	DG-III
9A.60.070	Issuing a False Academic Credential	C	Unranked
9A.40.020	Kidnapping 1	A	X
9A.40.030(3)(a)	Kidnapping 2	B	V
9A.40.030(3)(b)	Kidnapping 2 With a Finding of Sexual Motivation	A	V
16.52.320	Kill or Cause Substantial Harm With Malice to Livestock	C	Unranked
9A.82.060(1)(b)	Leading Organized Crime - Inciting Criminal Profiteering	B	IX
9A.82.060(1)(a)	Leading Organized Crime – Organizing Criminal Profiteering	A	X
46.70.021	Licensing Violation for Car Dealers or Manufacturers (Subsequent Violation)	C	Unranked
30A.12.120	Loan to Officer or Employee from Trust Fund	B	Unranked
67.70.130	Lottery Fraud	B	Unranked
9A.40.090	Luring of a Child or Developmentally Disabled Person	C	Unranked
9A.56.370	Mail Theft	C	Unranked
9.47.090	Maintaining a Bucket Shop	C	Unranked
69.50.402	Maintaining a Dwelling or Place for Controlled Substances	C	DG-II

The Caseload Forecast Council is not liable for errors or omissions in the manual, for sentences that may be inappropriately calculated as a result of a practitioner's or court's reliance on the manual, or for any other written or verbal information related to adult or juvenile sentencing. The scoring sheets are intended to provide assistance in most cases but do not cover all permutations of the scoring rules. If you find any errors or omissions, we encourage you to report them to the Caseload Forecast Council.

SECTION 4 – FELONY INDEX BY OFFENSE

Statute (RCW)	Offense	Class	Seriousness Level
9.45.220	Making False Sample or Assay of Ore	C	Unranked
70.74.280(1)	Malicious Explosion of a Substance 1	A	XV
70.74.280(2)	Malicious Explosion of a Substance 2	A	XIII
70.74.280(3)	Malicious Explosion of a Substance 3	B	X
9A.36.080	Malicious Harassment	C	IV
81.60.070	Malicious Injury to Railroad Property	B	III
9A.48.070	Malicious Mischief 1	B	II
9A.48.080	Malicious Mischief 2	C	I
70.74.270(1)	Malicious Placement of an Explosive 1	A	XIII
70.74.270(2)	Malicious Placement of an Explosive 2	B	IX
70.74.270(3)	Malicious Placement of an Explosive 3	B	VII
70.74.272(1)(a)	Malicious Placement of an Imitation Device 1	B	XII
70.74.272(1)(b)	Malicious Placement of an Imitation Device 2	C	VI
9.62.010(1)	Malicious Prosecution	C	Unranked
9.45.260	Malicious Sprinkler Contractor Work	C	Unranked
9A.32.060	Manslaughter 1	A	XI
9A.32.070	Manslaughter 2	B	VIII
69.50.401(2)(b)	Manufacture Methamphetamine	B	DG-III
46.37.650(1)(c)	Manufacture or Import Counterfeit, Nonfunctional, Damaged, or Previously Deployed Air Bag	C	V
46.37.650(1)(b)	Manufacture or Import Counterfeit, Nonfunctional, Damaged, or Previously Deployed Air Bag (Causing Bodily Injury or Death)	C	VII
69.50.401(2)(b)	Manufacture, Deliver or Possess with Intent to Deliver - Amphetamine	B	DG-II
69.50.401(2)(c)	Manufacture, Deliver or Possess with Intent to Deliver - Marijuana	C	DG-I
69.50.401(2)(a)	Manufacture, Deliver or Possess with Intent to Deliver - Narcotics from Schedule I or II or Flunitrazepam from Schedule IV	B	DG-II
69.50.401(2)(c-e)	Manufacture, Deliver or Possess with Intent to Deliver - Narcotics from Schedule III, IV, or V or Nonnarcotics from Schedule I-V (except Marijuana, Amphetamine, Methamphetamine, or Flunitrazepam)	C	DG-II
69.52.030(1)	Manufacture, Distribute or Possess with Intent to Distribute an Imitation Controlled Substance	C	DG-II
70.74.022(1)	Manufacture, Purchase, Sell or Store Explosive Device Without License	C	Unranked
46.20.0921(3)(a)	Manufacture, Sell or Deliver Forged Driver's License or Identicard	C	Unranked
82.24.570(2)	Manufacture, Sell or Possess Counterfeit Cigarettes	C	Unranked
82.24.570(3)	Manufacture, Sell or Possess Counterfeit Cigarettes (Subsequent Violation)	B	Unranked
69.51A.060	Medical Marijuana Fraudulent Records (Effective Until 7/1/2016)	C	Unranked

The Caseload Forecast Council is not liable for errors or omissions in the manual, for sentences that may be inappropriately calculated as a result of a practitioner's or court's reliance on the manual, or for any other written or verbal information related to adult or juvenile sentencing. The scoring sheets are intended to provide assistance in most cases but do not cover all permutations of the scoring rules. If you find any errors or omissions, we encourage you to report them to the Caseload Forecast Council.

SECTION 4 – FELONY INDEX BY OFFENSE

Statute (RCW)	Offense	Class	Seriousness Level
69.51A.240	Medical Marijuana – Unlawful Actions	C	Unranked
9.81.030	Member of Subversive Organization	C	Unranked
78.44.330	Mineral Trespass	C	I
42.20.070	Misappropriating and Falsifying Accounts by Public Officer	B	Unranked
42.20.090	Misappropriating and Falsifying Accounts by Treasurer	C	Unranked
9.82.030	Misprision of Treason	C	Unranked
29A.08.740	Misuse of Registered Voter Data	C	Unranked
29A.84.150	Misuse or Alteration of Registration Database	C	Unranked
9.45.070	Mock Auction	C	Unranked
9A.83.020	Money Laundering	B	Unranked
19.144.080	Mortgage Fraud	B	III
9A.32.030	Murder 1	A	XV
9A.28.020(3)(a)	Murder 1 – Criminal Attempt	A	XV
9A.28.040(3)(a)	Murder 1 - Criminal Conspiracy	A	XV
9A.28.030(2)	Murder 1 – Criminal Solicitation	A	XV
9A.32.050	Murder 2	A	XIV
9A.28.020(3)(a)	Murder 2 – Criminal Attempt	A	XIV
9A.28.030(2)	Murder 2 – Criminal Solicitation	A	XIV
32.04.110	Mutual Savings Bank - Conceal or Destroy Evidence	B	Unranked
32.04.100	Mutual Savings Bank - Falsify Savings Book, Document or Statement	B	Unranked
32.24.080	Mutual Savings Bank - Transfer Bank Assets After Insolvency	B	Unranked
46.37.675	Negligently Causing Death By Use of a Signal Preemption Device	B	VII
46.37.674	Negligently Causing Substantial Bodily Harm By Use of a Signal Preemption Device	B	III
9A.60.030	Obtaining Signature by Deception or Duress	C	Unranked
46.70.180(5)	Odometer Offense	C	Unranked
40.16.030	Offering False Instrument for Filing or Record	C	Unranked
68.50.140(3)	Opening Graves With Intent to Sell or Remove Personal Effects or Human Remains	C	Unranked
90.56.540	Operation of a Vessel While Under the Influence of Intoxicating Liquor or Drugs	C	Unranked
9A.56.350(2)	Organized Retail Theft 1	B	III
9A.56.350(3)	Organized Retail Theft 2	C	II
69.50.406(1)	Over 18 and Deliver Heroin, Methamphetamine, a Narcotic from Schedule I or II, or Flunitrazepam from Schedule IV to Someone Under 18	A	DG-III

The Caseload Forecast Council is not liable for errors or omissions in the manual, for sentences that may be inappropriately calculated as a result of a practitioner's or court's reliance on the manual, or for any other written or verbal information related to adult or juvenile sentencing. The scoring sheets are intended to provide assistance in most cases but do not cover all permutations of the scoring rules. If you find any errors or omissions, we encourage you to report them to the Caseload Forecast Council.

SECTION 4 – FELONY INDEX BY OFFENSE

Statute (RCW)	Offense	Class	Seriousness Level
69.50.406(2)	Over 18 and Deliver Narcotic from Schedule III, IV or V, or a Nonnarcotic, Except Flunitrazepam or Methamphetamine, from Schedule I-V to Someone Under 18 and 3 Years Junior	B	DG-III
9.46.215	Ownership or Interest in Gambling Device	C	Unranked
69.30.085	Participation in Shellfish Operation or Activities While License is Denied, Revoked or Suspended	C	Unranked
74.09.240(2)	Paying or Offering Bribes, Kickbacks or Rebates	C	Unranked
9A.72.020	Perjury 1	B	V
9A.72.030	Perjury 2	C	III
9.94.070	Persistent Prison Misbehavior	C	V
82.32.290(4)	Phantomware Violation	C	Unranked
46.61.504(6)	Physical Control of a Vehicle While Under the Influence of Intoxicating Liquor or any Drug	C	V
69.40.030	Placing Poison or Other Harmful Object or Substance in Food, Drinks, Medicine or Water	B	Unranked
69.40.020	Poison in Milk or Food Product	C	Unranked
9A.58.020	Possessing or Capturing Personal Identification Document	C	Unranked
9A.56.310	Possession of a Stolen Firearm	B	V
9A.56.068	Possession of a Stolen Vehicle	B	II
9.94.041(2)	Possession of Controlled Substance by Prisoner (County or Local Facility)	C	Unranked
9.94.041(1)	Possession of Controlled Substance by Prisoner (State Facility)	C	Unranked
9.94.045	Possession of Controlled Substance in Prison by Non-prisoner	C	Unranked
69.50.4013	Possession of Controlled Substance That is a Narcotic from Schedule III, IV or V or Nonnarcotic from Schedule I-V	C	DG-I
69.50.4013	Possession of Controlled Substance That is Either Heroin or Narcotics from Schedule I or II	C	DG-I
9.68A.070(1)	Possession of Depictions of Minor Engaged in Sexually Explicit Conduct 1	B	VI
9.68A.070(2)	Possession of Depictions of Minor Engaged in Sexually Explicit Conduct 2	C	IV
69.50.440	Possession of Ephedrine, Pseudoephedrine or Anhydrous Ammonia with Intent to Manufacture Methamphetamine	B	DG-III
9.40.120	Possession of Incendiary Device	B	III
9.41.190	Possession of Machine Gun, Short-barreled Shotgun or Short-barreled Rifle	C	III
69.41.350	Possession of Steroids in Excess of 200 tablets or (8) 2cc Bottles Without a Valid Prescription	C	Unranked
9A.56.380	Possession of Stolen Mail	C	Unranked
9A.56.150	Possession of Stolen Property 1 (Other Than Firearm or Motor Vehicle)	B	II
9A.56.160	Possession of Stolen Property 2 (Other Than Firearm or Motor Vehicle)	C	I

The Caseload Forecast Council is not liable for errors or omissions in the manual, for sentences that may be inappropriately calculated as a result of a practitioner's or court's reliance on the manual, or for any other written or verbal information related to adult or juvenile sentencing. The scoring sheets are intended to provide assistance in most cases but do not cover all permutations of the scoring rules. If you find any errors or omissions, we encourage you to report them to the Caseload Forecast Council.

SECTION 4 – FELONY INDEX BY OFFENSE

Statute (RCW)	Offense	Class	Seriousness Level
9.94.040(2)	Possession of Weapons by Prisoners (County or Local Facility)	C	Unranked
9.94.040(1)	Possession of Weapons by Prisoners (State Facility)	B	Unranked
9.94.043	Possession of Weapons in Prison by Non-prisoner	B	Unranked
9.94.010	Prison Riot	B	Unranked
9.46.220	Professional Gambling 1	B	Unranked
9.46.221	Professional Gambling 2	C	Unranked
9A.36.060	Promoting a Suicide Attempt	C	Unranked
9.68A.101	Promoting Commercial Sexual Abuse of a Minor	A	XII
67.08.015	Promoting Illegal Boxing, Martial Arts and Wrestling	C	Unranked
9.68.140	Promoting Pornography	C	Unranked
9A.88.070	Promoting Prostitution 1	B	VIII
9A.88.080	Promoting Prostitution 2	C	III
9.68A.102	Promoting Travel for Commercial Sexual Abuse of a Minor	C	Unranked
9A.88.085	Promoting Travel for Prostitution	C	Unranked
29A.84.311	Provides False Information or Conceals or Destroys Candidacy Declaration or Nominating Petition	C	Unranked
26.04.210	Providing False Statements in Affidavits for Marriage	C	Unranked
68.50.140(2)	Purchasing or Receiving Human Remains	C	Unranked
9A.44.040	Rape 1	A	XII
9A.28.020(3)(a)	Rape 1 – Criminal Attempt	A	XII
9A.28.030(2)	Rape 1 – Criminal Solicitation	A	XII
9A.44.050	Rape 2	A	XI
9A.28.020(3)(a)	Rape 2 – Criminal Attempt	A	XI
9A.28.030(2)	Rape 2 – Criminal Solicitation	A	XI
9A.44.060	Rape 3	C	V
9A.44.073	Rape of a Child 1	A	XII
9A.28.020(3)(a)	Rape of a Child 1 – Criminal Attempt	A	XII
9A.28.030(2)	Rape of a Child 1 – Criminal Solicitation	A	XII
9A.44.076	Rape of a Child 2	A	XI
9A.28.020(3)(a)	Rape of a Child 2 – Criminal Attempt	A	XI
9A.28.030(2)	Rape of a Child 2 – Criminal Solicitation	A	XI
9A.44.079	Rape of a Child 3	C	VI
74.09.240(1)	Receiving or Asking for Bribes, Kickbacks or Rebates	C	Unranked
9A.68.030	Receiving or Granting Unlawful Compensation	C	Unranked
81.60.080(2)	Receiving Stolen Railroad Property	C	Unranked

The Caseload Forecast Council is not liable for errors or omissions in the manual, for sentences that may be inappropriately calculated as a result of a practitioner's or court's reliance on the manual, or for any other written or verbal information related to adult or juvenile sentencing. The scoring sheets are intended to provide assistance in most cases but do not cover all permutations of the scoring rules. If you find any errors or omissions, we encourage you to report them to the Caseload Forecast Council.

SECTION 4 – FELONY INDEX BY OFFENSE

Statute (RCW)	Offense	Class	Seriousness Level
9A.48.040	Reckless Burning 1	C	I
90.56.530	Reckless Operation of a Tank Vessel	C	Unranked
19.110.075(2)	Registration Knowingly Not Obtained Prior to Sale of Business Opportunity (Violation of RCW 19.110.050)	B	Unranked
70.94.430(3)	Releasing Into Ambient Air Hazardous Air Pollutant	C	Unranked
46.12.560	Removal of Sticker on Vehicle Stating Previously Destroyed or Title 1 Loss	C	Unranked
68.50.140(4)	Removal, Disinterment or Mutilation of Human Remains	C	Unranked
68.60.050	Removes, Defaces or Destroys any Historic Grave	C	Unranked
68.50.140(1)	Removing Human Remains	C	Unranked
9.16.010	Removing Lawful Brands	C	Unranked
9A.76.070(2)(a)	Rendering Criminal Assistance 1	B	V
19.25.020(2)(a)	Reproduction of Sound Recording Without Consent of Owner - Recording Fixed Before 2/15/1972 (At Least 1,000 Recordings or Subsequent Conviction)	B	Unranked
19.25.020(2)(b)	Reproduction of Sound Recording Without Consent of Owner - Recording Fixed Before 2/15/1972 (More Than 100 but Less Than 1,000 Recordings)	C	Unranked
9A.68.020	Requesting Unlawful Compensation	C	Unranked
9A.52.025	Residential Burglary	B	IV
70.345.030	Retail Sales, Distribution or Delivery Sales of Vapor Products Without a License	C	Unranked
9A.56.360(2)	Retail Theft with Special Circumstances 1	B	III
9A.56.360(3)	Retail Theft with Special Circumstances 2	C	II
9A.56.360(4)	Retail Theft with Special Circumstances 3	C	Unranked
9A.56.200	Robbery 1	A	IX
9A.56.210	Robbery 2	B	IV
81.60.080(1)	Sabotaging Rolling Stock	C	Unranked
69.41.030(2)(a)	Sale, Delivery or Possession With Intent to Sell Legend Drug Without Prescription	B	Unranked
46.37.650(2)(b)	Sale, Install, [or] Reinstall Counterfeit, Nonfunctional, Damaged, or Previously Deployed Airbag	C	VII
46.37.650(2)(c)	Sale, Install, [or] Reinstall Counterfeit, Nonfunctional, Damaged, or Previously Deployed Airbag	C	V
33.36.040	Savings and Loan Association - Making False Statement of Assets or Liabilities	C	Unranked
33.36.030	Savings and Loan Association - Preference in Case of Insolvency	C	Unranked
33.36.060	Savings and Loan Association - Suppressing, Secreting or Destroying Evidence or Records	C	Unranked

The Caseload Forecast Council is not liable for errors or omissions in the manual, for sentences that may be inappropriately calculated as a result of a practitioner's or court's reliance on the manual, or for any other written or verbal information related to adult or juvenile sentencing. The scoring sheets are intended to provide assistance in most cases but do not cover all permutations of the scoring rules. If you find any errors or omissions, we encourage you to report them to the Caseload Forecast Council.

SECTION 4 – FELONY INDEX BY OFFENSE

Statute (RCW)	Offense	Class	Seriousness Level
19.290.100	Scrap Processing, Recycling, or Supplying Without a License (Second or Subsequent Offense)	C	II
19.60.067(2)	Second-hand Precious Metal Dealer Violations (Subsequent Violation)	C	Unranked
21.20.400	Securities Act Violation	B	III
46.20.0921(2)	Sell or Deliver a Stolen Driver's License or Identicard	C	Unranked
27.44.040(2)	Selling Artifacts or Human Remains from Indian Graves	C	Unranked
69.50.410	Selling for Profit (Controlled or Counterfeit) any Controlled Substance in Schedule I	C	DG-III
48.160.080	Sells Guaranteed Asset Protection Waivers Without Registration	B	Unranked
9.68A.060(2)	Sending, Bringing into the State Depictions of Minor Engaged in Sexually Explicit Conduct 2	C	V
9.68A.060(1)	Sending, Bringing into the State Depictions of Minor Engaged in Sexually Explicit Conduct 1	B	VII
9.68A.040	Sexual Exploitation of a Minor	B	IX
9A.44.093	Sexual Misconduct with a Minor 1	C	V
9A.44.105	Sexually Violating Human Remains	C	V
9A.76.115	Sexually Violent Predator Escape	A	X
70.155.140	Shipping or Transporting Tobacco Products Ordered Through Mail or Internet	C	Unranked
82.38.270	Special Fuel Violations	C	Unranked
77.15.450(3)(b)	Spotlighting Big Game 1	C	I
9A.46.110	Stalking	B	V
67.70.160	State Lottery Violations Except Lottery Fraud and Unlicensed Lottery Activity	C	Unranked
30B.12.050	State Trust Company – False Entry, Conceal or Destroy Records	B	Unranked
9.45.020	Substitution of Child	B	Unranked
9.81.020	Subversive Acts	B	Unranked
77.15.670(3)(b)	Suspension of Department Privileges 1	C	I
9A.56.070	Taking Motor Vehicle Without Permission 1	B	V
9A.56.075	Taking Motor Vehicle Without Permission 2	C	I
9A.72.120	Tampering with a Witness	C	III
29A.84.550	Tampering with Election Materials	C	Unranked
9.40.105	Tampering with Fire Alarm, Emergency Signal, or Fire-fighting Equipment with Intent to Commit Arson	B	Unranked
88.08.020	Tampering with Lights or Signals	B	Unranked
29A.84.560	Tampering with Voting Machine	C	Unranked

The Caseload Forecast Council is not liable for errors or omissions in the manual, for sentences that may be inappropriately calculated as a result of a practitioner's or court's reliance on the manual, or for any other written or verbal information related to adult or juvenile sentencing. The scoring sheets are intended to provide assistance in most cases but do not cover all permutations of the scoring rules. If you find any errors or omissions, we encourage you to report them to the Caseload Forecast Council.

SECTION 4 – FELONY INDEX BY OFFENSE

Statute (RCW)	Offense	Class	Seriousness Level
9.61.230(2)	Telephone Harassment (With Prior Harassment Conviction or Threat of Death)	C	III
9A.56.030	Theft 1 (Excluding Firearm and Motor Vehicle)	B	II
9A.56.040	Theft 2 (Excluding Firearm and Motor Vehicle)	C	I
9A.56.300	Theft of a Firearm	B	VI
9A.56.065	Theft of a Motor Vehicle	B	II
69.55.010	Theft of Ammonia	C	VIII
9A.56.080	Theft of Livestock 1	B	IV
9A.56.083	Theft of Livestock 2	C	III
9A.56.096(5)(b)	Theft of Rental, Leased, Lease-purchased or Loaned Property (Valued at $750 or More but Less Than $5,000)	C	I
9A.56.096(5)(a)	Theft of Rental, Leased, Lease-purchased or Loaned Property (Valued at $5,000 or More)	B	II
9A.56.262	Theft of Telecommunication Service	C	Unranked
9A.56.340(2)	Theft with Intent to Resell 1	B	III
9A.56.340(3)	Theft with Intent to Resell 2	C	II
9A.36.090	Threats Against Governor or Family	C	Unranked
9.61.160	Threats to Bomb	B	IV
64.36.210	Timeshare Fraud	C	Unranked
64.36.020(5)(b)	Timeshare Registration Requirement Violation	C	Unranked
9A.68.040	Trading in Public Office	C	Unranked
9A.68.050	Trading in Special Influence	C	Unranked
9A.40.100(1)	Trafficking 1	A	XIV
9A.40.100(3)	Trafficking 2	A	XII
48.30A.015	Trafficking in Insurance Claims (Subsequent Violation)	C	II
9A.82.050	Trafficking in Stolen Property 1	B	IV
9A.82.055	Trafficking in Stolen Property 2	C	III
48.17.063(4)	Transaction of Insurance Business Beyond the Scope of Licensure (Violation of RCW 48.17.060)	B	I
9.46.240	Transmission or Receiving Gambling Information by Internet	C	Unranked
70.105.085(1)(a)	Transport, Disposal or Export of Hazardous Waste That Places Another Person in Danger of Injury or Death	B	Unranked
70.105.085(1)(b)	Transport, Disposal or Export of Hazardous Waste That Places Another Person's Property in Danger of Harm	C	Unranked
82.24.110(2)	Transportation of More Than 10,000 Cigarettes Without Proper Stamps	C	Unranked
68.60.040(3)	Transports Removed Human Remains, Opens a Grave or Removes Personal	C	Unranked

The Caseload Forecast Council is not liable for errors or omissions in the manual, for sentences that may be inappropriately calculated as a result of a practitioner's or court's reliance on the manual, or for any other written or verbal information related to adult or juvenile sentencing. The scoring sheets are intended to provide assistance in most cases but do not cover all permutations of the scoring rules. If you find any errors or omissions, we encourage you to report them to the Caseload Forecast Council.

SECTION 4 – FELONY INDEX BY OFFENSE

Statute (RCW)	Offense	Class	Seriousness Level
	Effects from Grave		
9.82.010	Treason	A	Unranked
9.91.150(1)	Tree Spiking	C	Unranked
9.02.120	Unauthorized Abortion	C	Unranked
68.44.060	Unauthorized Loans to Cemetery Authority	C	Unranked
29A.84.545	Unauthorized Removal of Paper Record from Electronic Voting Device	C	Unranked
39.62.040	Unauthorized Use of Public Official Facsimile Signature or Seal	B	Unranked
68.05.330	Unfair Practice of Funeral or Cemetery Board	C	Unranked
19.225.110	Uniform Athlete Agent Act Violation	C	Unranked
69.43.070(1)	Unlawful Delivery of Precursor Drug with Intent to Use	B	Unranked
9A.49.020	Unlawful Discharge of a Laser 1	C	Unranked
74.09.290	Unlawful Disclosure of Patient Records or DSHS Information	C	Unranked
9A.56.290(4)(a)	Unlawful Factoring of a Credit or Payment Card Transaction	C	II
9A.56.290(4)(b)	Unlawful Factoring of a Credit or Payment Card Transaction (Subsequent Violation)	B	IV
69.53.020	Unlawful Fortification of Building for Drug Purposes	C	Unranked
77.15.410(3)(b)	Unlawful Hunting of Big Game 1	C	III
9A.40.040	Unlawful Imprisonment	C	III
9A.56.060(4)	Unlawful Issuance of Checks or Drafts (Value Greater Than $750)	C	I
9A.56.264	Unlawful Manufacture of a Telecommunication Device	C	Unranked
69.04.938(3)	Unlawful Misbranding of Food Fish or Shellfish 1	C	III
88.46.080(2)(b)	Unlawful Operation of a Covered Vessel (Subsequent Violation)	C	Unranked
90.56.300(2)(b)	Unlawful Operation of Onshore or Offshore Facility (Subsequent Conviction)	C	Unranked
77.15.570(2)	Unlawful Participation on Non-Indians in Indian Fishery	C	II
9.41.040(1)	Unlawful Possession of a Firearm 1	B	VII
9.41.040(2)	Unlawful Possession of a Firearm 2	C	III
9A.56.320(3)	Unlawful Possession of a Personal Identification Device	C	I
9A.56.320(4)	Unlawful Possession of Fictitious Identification	C	I
9A.56.320(5)	Unlawful Possession of Instruments of Financial Fraud	C	I
9A.56.320(2)	Unlawful Possession of Payment Instruments	C	I
2.48.180	Unlawful Practice of Law (Subsequent Violation)	C	II
9.41.115	Unlawful Private Transfer of a Firearm (Subsequent Offense)	C	Unranked
9A.56.320(1)	Unlawful Production of Payment Instruments	C	I
77.15.650(3)(b)	Unlawful Purchase or Use of a License 1	C	II

The Caseload Forecast Council is not liable for errors or omissions in the manual, for sentences that may be inappropriately calculated as a result of a practitioner's or court's reliance on the manual, or for any other written or verbal information related to adult or juvenile sentencing. The scoring sheets are intended to provide assistance in most cases but do not cover all permutations of the scoring rules. If you find any errors or omissions, we encourage you to report them to the Caseload Forecast Council.

SECTION 4 – FELONY INDEX BY OFFENSE

Statute (RCW)	Offense	Class	Seriousness Level
69.43.070(2)	Unlawful Receipt of Precursor Drug with Intent to Use	B	Unranked
9.91.144	Unlawful Redemption of Food Stamps	C	I
77.15.250(2)(b)	Unlawful Releasing, Planting, Possessing or Placing Deleterious Exotic Wildlife	C	I
9A.56.266	Unlawful Sale of a Telecommunication Device	C	Unranked
9A.56.230	Unlawful Sale of Subscription Television Services	C	Unranked
46.12.750(3)	Unlawful Sale of Vehicle Certificate of Ownership	C	Unranked
18.64.046(7)	Unlawful Selling of Ephedrine, Pseudoephedrine or Phenylpropanolamine by a Wholesaler	C	Unranked
65.12.730	Unlawful Stealing or Carrying Away Certification of Land Registration (Charged as Theft)	*	*
69.55.020	Unlawful Storage of Ammonia	C	VI
19.116.080(1)	Unlawful Subleasing of Motor Vehicle	C	Unranked
77.15.120(3)(b)	Unlawful Taking of Endangered Fish or Wildlife 1	C	III
77.15.770(2)	Unlawful Trade in Shark Fins 1	C	Unranked
77.15.260(3)(b)	Unlawful Trafficking in Fish, Shellfish or Wildlife 1	B	III
77.15.260(3)(a)	Unlawful Trafficking in Fish, Shellfish or Wildlife 2	C	II
9.91.142(1)	Unlawful Trafficking in Food Stamps	C	I
77.15.135(4)(d)	Unlawful Trafficking in Species With Extinction 1	C	Unranked
48.44.016(3)	Unlawful Transaction of Health Coverage as Health Care Service Contractor	B	IV
48.46.033(3)	Unlawful Transaction of Health Coverage as Health Maintenance Organization	B	IV
48.15.023(3)	Unlawful Transaction of Insurance Business	B	IV
19.116.080(2)	Unlawful Transfer of Ownership of Motor Vehicle	C	Unranked
77.15.530(4)	Unlawful Use of a Nondesignated Vessel	C	III
18.04.370(1)(b)	Unlawful Use of a Professional Title	C	Unranked
69.53.010	Unlawful Use of Building for Drug Purposes	C	DG-I
18.04.370(1)(c)	Unlawful Use of CPA Title After Suspension	C	Unranked
77.15.630(3)(b)	Unlawful Fish and Shellfish Catch Accounting 1	C	I
69.53.030	Unlawful Use of Fortified Building	C	Unranked
77.15.811	Unlawful Use of Invasive Species 1	C	Unranked
66.44.120(2)(b)	Unlawful Use of Liquor Board Seal (Third or Subsequent Offense)	C	Unranked
77.15.580(3)(b)	Unlawful Use of Net to Take Fish	C	I
19.310.120	Unlawfully Engaging in Business as an Exchange Facilitator (RCW 19.310.100(1)-(9))	B	Unranked

The Caseload Forecast Council is not liable for errors or omissions in the manual, for sentences that may be inappropriately calculated as a result of a practitioner's or court's reliance on the manual, or for any other written or verbal information related to adult or juvenile sentencing. The scoring sheets are intended to provide assistance in most cases but do not cover all permutations of the scoring rules. If you find any errors or omissions, we encourage you to report them to the Caseload Forecast Council.

SECTION 4 – FELONY INDEX BY OFFENSE

Statute (RCW)	Offense	Class	Seriousness Level
82.24.500	Unlawfully Purchase, Sell, Consign or Distribute Cigarettes	C	Unranked
48.102.160(4)	Unlicensed Life Insurance Provider	B	Unranked
67.70.140	Unlicensed Lottery Activity	B	Unranked
48.17.063(2)	Unlicensed Practice as an Insurance Professional	B	IV
18.130.190(7)(b)	Unlicensed Practice of a Profession or Business (Subsequent Violation)	C	II
48.102.160(5)	Unlicensed Settlement Broker	B	Unranked
29A.84.660	Unqualified Person Voting	C	Unranked
29A.84.140	Unqualified Voting Registration	C	Unranked
19.210.040	Unused Property, Merchants –Prohibited Sales (Third or Subsequent Offense Within 5 Years)	C	Unranked
46.37.673	Use of a Signal Preemption Device Resulting in Property Damage or Less Substantial Bodily Harm	C	Unranked
9.41.225	Use of Machine Gun in Commission of a Felony	A	VII
9A.82.080(1-2)	Use of Proceeds of Criminal Profiteering	B	IV
19.25.030(2)(a)	Use of Recording of Live Performance Without Consent of Owner (At Least 1,000 Recordings or at Least 100 Unauthorized Audiovisual Recordings or Subsequent Offense)	B	Unranked
19.25.030(2)(b)	Use of Recording of Live Performance Without Consent of Owner (At Least 100 but Less Than 1,000 Recordings or More than 10 but Less Than 100 Unauthorized Audiovisual Recording or Subsequent Offense)	C	Unranked
19.144.100(1)	Use or Investment of Proceeds from Mortgage Fraud Activities	B	Unranked
9A.52.095	Vehicle Prowl 1	C	I
9A.52.100(3)	Vehicle Prowling 2 (Third or Subsequent Offense)	C	IV
46.61.522(1)(c)	Vehicular Assault - Disregard for the Safety of Others	B	III
46.61.522(1)(a-b)	Vehicular Assault – In a Reckless Manner or While Under the Influence of Intoxicating Liquor or any Drug	B	IV
46.61.520(1)(c)	Vehicular Homicide - Disregard for the Safety of Others	A	VII
46.61.520(1)(b)	Vehicular Homicide – In a Reckless Manner	A	XI
46.61.520(1)(a)	Vehicular Homicide – While Under the Influence of Intoxicating Liquor or any Drug	A	XI
9.68A.075(1)	Viewing Depictions of Minor Engaged in Sexually Explicit Conduct 1 (Effective 6/10/2010)	B	IV
9.68A.075(2)	Viewing Depictions of Minor Engaged in Sexually Explicit Conduct 2 (Effective 6/10/2010)	C	Unranked
77.15.550(3)(b)	Violating Commercial Fishing Area or Time 1	C	I
29A.84.230(1)	Violation by Signer – Initiative or Referendum with False Name	C	Unranked

The Caseload Forecast Council is not liable for errors or omissions in the manual, for sentences that may be inappropriately calculated as a result of a practitioner's or court's reliance on the manual, or for any other written or verbal information related to adult or juvenile sentencing. The scoring sheets are intended to provide assistance in most cases but do not cover all permutations of the scoring rules. If you find any errors or omissions, we encourage you to report them to the Caseload Forecast Council.

SECTION 4 – FELONY INDEX BY OFFENSE

Statute (RCW)	Offense	Class	Seriousness Level
26.50.110(5)	Violation of a Foreign Protection Order (Third or Subsequent Violation)	C	Unranked
29A.84.240(1)	Violations By Signers – Recall Petition With False Name	B	Unranked
29A.84.130	Voter Violation of Registration Law	C	Unranked
29A.84.650(1)	Voting Repeater – More Than One Vote at Any Election	C	Unranked
9A.44.115	Voyeurism	C	II
48.30.220	Willful Destruction, Injury, Secretion of Insured Property	C	Unranked
10.66.090	Willfully Disobeys an Off-limits Order (Subsequent Violation or Enters Protected Against Drug Trafficking Area)	C	Unranked

The Caseload Forecast Council is not liable for errors or omissions in the manual, for sentences that may be inappropriately calculated as a result of a practitioner's or court's reliance on the manual, or for any other written or verbal information related to adult or juvenile sentencing. The scoring sheets are intended to provide assistance in most cases but do not cover all permutations of the scoring rules. If you find any errors or omissions, we encourage you to report them to the Caseload Forecast Council.

SECTION 4 – FELONY INDEX BY CLASSIFICATION

FELONY INDEX BY CLASSIFICATION

Statute (RCW)	Offense	Class	Seriousness Level
51.48.020(2)	False Information in Industrial Insurance Claim (Charged as Theft)	*	*
65.12.740	False Swearing - Registration of Land Title (Charged as Perjury)	*	*
65.12.730	Unlawful Stealing or Carrying Away Certification of Land Registration (Charged as Theft)	*	*
10.95.020	Aggravated Murder 1	A	XVI
9A.48.020	Arson 1	A	VIII
9A.28.020(3)(a)	Arson 1 – Criminal Attempt	A	VIII
9A.28.030(2)	Arson 1 – Criminal Solicitation	A	VIII
9A.36.011	Assault 1	A	XII
9A.36.021(2)(b)	Assault 2 With a Finding of Sexual Motivation	A	IV
9A.36.120	Assault of a Child 1	A	XII
9A.76.170(3)(a)	Bail Jumping with Murder 1	A	VI
9A.52.020	Burglary 1	A	VII
9A.44.083	Child Molestation 1	A	X
9A.28.020(3)(a)	Child Molestation 1 – Criminal Attempt	A	X
9A.28.030(2)	Child Molestation 1 – Criminal Solicitation	A	X
70.245.200(2)	Coerce Patient to Request Life-ending Medication	A	Unranked
70.74.180	Explosive Devices Prohibited	A	IX
70.245.200(1)	Forging Request for Medication	A	Unranked
9A.32.055	Homicide by Abuse	A	XV
79A.60.050(1)(c)	Homicide by Watercraft - Disregard for the Safety of Others	A	VII
79A.60.050(1)(b)	Homicide by Watercraft – In a Reckless Manner	A	VIII
79A.60.050(1)(a)	Homicide by Watercraft – While Under the Influence of Intoxicating Liquor or any Drug	A	IX
9A.44.100(1)(a)	Indecent Liberties - With Forcible Compulsion	A	X
9A.28.020(3)(a)	Indecent Liberties - With Forcible Compulsion – Criminal Attempt	A	X
9A.28.030(2)	Indecent Liberties - With Forcible Compulsion – Criminal Solicitation	A	X
9A.40.020	Kidnapping 1	A	X
9A.40.030(3)(b)	Kidnapping 2 With a Finding of Sexual Motivation	A	V

The Caseload Forecast Council is not liable for errors or omissions in the manual, for sentences that may be inappropriately calculated as a result of a practitioner's or court's reliance on the manual, or for any other written or verbal information related to adult or juvenile sentencing. The scoring sheets are intended to provide assistance in most cases but do not cover all permutations of the scoring rules. If you find any errors or omissions, we encourage you to report them to the Caseload Forecast Council.

SECTION 4 – FELONY INDEX BY CLASSIFICATION

Statute (RCW)	Offense	Class	Seriousness Level
9A.82.060(1)(a)	Leading Organized Crime – Organizing Criminal Profiteering	A	X
70.74.280(1)	Malicious Explosion of a Substance 1	A	XV
70.74.280(2)	Malicious Explosion of a Substance 2	A	XIII
70.74.270(1)	Malicious Placement of an Explosive 1	A	XIII
9A.32.060	Manslaughter 1	A	XI
9A.32.030	Murder 1	A	XV
9A.28.020(3)(a)	Murder 1 – Criminal Attempt	A	XV
9A.28.040(3)(a)	Murder 1 - Criminal Conspiracy	A	XV
9A.28.030(2)	Murder 1 – Criminal Solicitation	A	XV
9A.32.050	Murder 2	A	XIV
9A.28.020(3)(a)	Murder 2 – Criminal Attempt	A	XIV
9A.28.030(2)	Murder 2 – Criminal Solicitation	A	XIV
69.50.406(1)	Over 18 and Deliver Heroin, Methamphetamine, a Narcotic from Schedule I or II, or Flunitrazepam from Schedule IV to Someone Under 18	A	DG-III
9.68A.101	Promoting Commercial Sexual Abuse of a Minor	A	XII
9A.44.040	Rape 1	A	XII
9A.28.020(3)(a)	Rape 1 – Criminal Attempt	A	XII
9A.28.030(2)	Rape 1 – Criminal Solicitation	A	XII
9A.44.050	Rape 2	A	XI
9A.28.020(3)(a)	Rape 2 – Criminal Attempt	A	XI
9A.28.030(2)	Rape 2 – Criminal Solicitation	A	XI
9A.44.073	Rape of a Child 1	A	XII
9A.28.020(3)(a)	Rape of a Child 1 – Criminal Attempt	A	XII
9A.28.030(2)	Rape of a Child 1 – Criminal Solicitation	A	XII
9A.44.076	Rape of a Child 2	A	XI
9A.28.020(3)(a)	Rape of a Child 2 – Criminal Attempt	A	XI
9A.28.030(2)	Rape of a Child 2 – Criminal Solicitation	A	XI
9A.56.200	Robbery 1	A	IX
9A.76.115	Sexually Violent Predator Escape	A	X
9A.40.100(1)	Trafficking 1	A	XIV
9A.40.100(3)	Trafficking 2	A	XII
9.82.010	Treason	A	Unranked
9.41.225	Use of Machine Gun in Commission of a Felony	A	VII
46.61.520(1)(c)	Vehicular Homicide - Disregard for the Safety of Others	A	VII
46.61.520(1)(b)	Vehicular Homicide – In a Reckless Manner	A	XI

The Caseload Forecast Council is not liable for errors or omissions in the manual, for sentences that may be inappropriately calculated as a result of a practitioner's or court's reliance on the manual, or for any other written or verbal information related to adult or juvenile sentencing. The scoring sheets are intended to provide assistance in most cases but do not cover all permutations of the scoring rules. If you find any errors or omissions, we encourage you to report them to the Caseload Forecast Council.

SECTION 4 – FELONY INDEX BY CLASSIFICATION

Statute (RCW)	Offense	Class	Seriousness Level
46.61.520(1)(a)	Vehicular Homicide – While Under the Influence of Intoxicating Liquor or any Drug	A	XI
9A.42.060	Abandonment of Dependent Persons 1	B	IX
9A.82.030	Advancing Money or Property for Extortionate Extension of Credit	B	V
30A.42.290(3)	Alien Bank or Bureau – Destroy or Secrete Records	B	Unranked
30A.42.290(2)	Alien Bank or Bureau – False Entry, Statements, etc.	B	Unranked
9A.48.030	Arson 2	B	IV
9A.36.021(2)(a)	Assault 2	B	IV
79A.60.060	Assault by Watercraft	B	IV
9A.36.130	Assault of a Child 2	B	IX
9.05.030	Assembly of Saboteurs	B	Unranked
9A.76.170(3)(b)	Bail Jumping with Class A Felony	B	V
30A.12.100	Bank or Trust Company - Destroy or Secrete Records	B	Unranked
30A.12.090	Bank or Trust Company - False Entry, Statements, etc.	B	Unranked
30A.44.120	Bank or Trust Company - Receiving Deposits When Insolvent	B	Unranked
30A.44.110	Bank or Trust Company - Transfer of Assets Prior to Insolvency	B	Unranked
9A.72.100	Bribe Received by Witness	B	IV
9A.68.010	Bribery	B	VI
9A.72.090	Bribing a Witness	B	IV
72.23.300	Bringing Narcotics, Liquor, or Weapons into State Institution or Grounds	B	Unranked
9.47.120	Bunco Steering	B	Unranked
9A.52.030	Burglary 2	B	III
46.87.260	Cab Card Forgery (Effective Until 7/1/2016)	B	Unranked
9.46.180	Causing Person to Violate Gambling Laws	B	Unranked
9A.44.086	Child Molestation 2	B	VII
9A.48.120	Civil Disorder Training	B	VII
9A.68.060	Commercial Bribery	B	IV
9.68A.100	Commercial Sexual Abuse of a Minor	B	VIII
30A.04.240	Commingling of Funds or Securities	B	Unranked
21.30.140	Commodity Transaction Violation	B	Unranked
19.144.100(2)	Control of Real Property Resulting from Mortgage Fraud Activities	B	Unranked
69.50.415	Controlled Substance Homicide	B	DG-III
69.50.4011(2)(a-b)	Create, Deliver or Possess a Counterfeit Controlled Substance – Schedule I or II Narcotic or Flunitrazepam or Methamphetamine	B	DG-II

The Caseload Forecast Council is not liable for errors or omissions in the manual, for sentences that may be inappropriately calculated as a result of a practitioner's or court's reliance on the manual, or for any other written or verbal information related to adult or juvenile sentencing. The scoring sheets are intended to provide assistance in most cases but do not cover all permutations of the scoring rules. If you find any errors or omissions, we encourage you to report them to the Caseload Forecast Council.

SECTION 4 – FELONY INDEX BY CLASSIFICATION

Statute (RCW)	Offense	Class	Seriousness Level
46.87.260	Credential Forgery (Effective 7/1/2016)	B	Unranked
31.12.724(3)	Credit Union - Fraudulent Receipt of Credit Union Deposit	B	Unranked
31.12.724(2)	Credit Union - Transfer of Credit Union Assets Prior to Insolvency	B	Unranked
9A.42.020	Criminal Mistreatment 1	B	X
9.05.060(2)	Criminal Sabotage	B	Unranked
43.06.230	Damage Property or Cause Personal Injury after State of Emergency Proclaimed	B	Unranked
9.68A.050(1)	Dealing in Depictions of Minor Engaged in Sexually Explicit Conduct 1 (Effective 6/10/2010)	B	VII
39.44.101	Defraud a Facsimile Signature on Bonds and Coupons	B	Unranked
87.03.200	Defraud Facsimile Signatures on Bonds and Coupons – Irrigation Districts	B	Unranked
19.110.120	Defraud or Provide Misleading or Untrue Documents Related to a Business Opportunity Sale	B	Unranked
9A.61.030	Defrauding a Public Utility 1	B	Unranked
19.48.110(1)(b)	Defrauding an Innkeeper (Value of $75.00 or More)	B	Unranked
69.50.401(2)(b)	Deliver or Possess with Intent to Deliver - Methamphetamine	B	DG-II
69.52.030(2)	Delivery of Imitation Controlled Substance by Person 18 or Over to Person Under 18	B	DG-III
35A.36.040	Designation of Bonds – Violation (Code Cities)	B	Unranked
35.36.040	Designation of Bonds – Violation (First Class Cities)	B	Unranked
9A.76.023(2)(b)	Disarming a Law Enforcement or Corrections Officer and Firearm is Discharged	B	Unranked
19.110.075(2)	Disclosures Knowingly Not Provided at Sale of Business Opportunity (Violation of RCW 19.110.070)	B	Unranked
43.43.856	Divulging Confidential Investigative Information Pertaining to Organized Crime	B	Unranked
9A.36.045	Drive-by Shooting	B	VII
46.61.502(6)	Driving While Under the Influence of Intoxicating Liquor or any Drug	B	V
29A.84.270	Duplication of Name – Conspiracy to Mislead	B	Unranked
29A.84.320	Duplication of Names on Declaration of Candidacy	B	Unranked
43.08.140	Embezzlement by State Treasurer	B	Unranked
9A.42.100	Endangerment With a Controlled Substance	B	IV
61.34.030	Equity Skimming	B	II
9.68.060	Erotic Material (Third or Subsequent Offense)	B	Unranked
9A.76.110	Escape 1	B	IV
48.06.190	Exhibiting False Accounts of Insurer	B	Unranked

The Caseload Forecast Council is not liable for errors or omissions in the manual, for sentences that may be inappropriately calculated as a result of a practitioner's or court's reliance on the manual, or for any other written or verbal information related to adult or juvenile sentencing. The scoring sheets are intended to provide assistance in most cases but do not cover all permutations of the scoring rules. If you find any errors or omissions, we encourage you to report them to the Caseload Forecast Council.

SECTION 4 – FELONY INDEX BY CLASSIFICATION

Statute (RCW)	Offense	Class	Seriousness Level
9A.56.120	Extortion 1	B	V
9A.82.020	Extortionate Extension of Credit	B	V
9A.82.040	Extortionate Means to Collect Extensions of Credit	B	V
19.25.040(2)(a)	Failure to Disclose Origin of Certain Recordings (At Least 100 Recordings or Subsequent Conviction)	B	Unranked
9A.44.132(1)(b)	Failure to Register as a Sex Offender (Third or Subsequent Violation Committed on or After 6/10/2010)	B	II
74.08.100	False Age and Residency Public Assistance Verification	B	Unranked
9.24.050	False Report of Corporation	B	Unranked
41.26.062	False Statements or Records to Defraud Law Enforcement Officers and Firefighters Retirement System	B	Unranked
41.32.055(1)	False Statements or Records to Defraud Teachers Retirement System	B	Unranked
46.12.750(1)	False Statements, Illegal Transfers, Alterations or Forgeries of Vehicle Title	B	Unranked
74.08.055(2)	False Verification for Welfare	B	I
69.41.020	Forged Prescription - Legend Drug	B	DG-I
76.36.120	Forgery of Forest Product Mark	B	Unranked
65.12.760	Forgery of Registrar's Signature or Seal	B	Unranked
82.24.100	Forgery or Counterfeit Cigarette Tax Stamp	B	Unranked
19.100.210	Franchise Investment Protection Violation	B	Unranked
9.45.124	Fraud in Measurement of Goods	B	Unranked
67.24.010	Fraud in Sporting Contest	B	Unranked
9.45.270(3)	Fraudulent Filing of Vehicle Report of Sale (Value Exceeds $1,500)	B	Unranked
9.24.020	Fraudulent Issue of Stock, Scrip, etc.	B	Unranked
48.102.160(3)	Fraudulent Life Insurance Settlement	B	Unranked
9.46.160	Gambling Without License	B	Unranked
9.46.039	Greyhound Racing	B	Unranked
46.52.020(4)(a)	Hit and Run - Death	B	IX
9.94.030	Holding Hostages or Interfering with Officer's Duty	B	Unranked
9.35.020(2)	Identity Theft 1	B	IV
69.41.040	Illegal Issuance of Legend Drug Prescription	B	Unranked
19.146.235(9)	Impairing Mortgage Broker Investigation	B	Unranked
9A.64.020(1)	Incest 1	B	VI
9A.44.100(1)(b-c)	Indecent Liberties - Without Forcible Compulsion	B	VII
9A.44.100(1)(d-f)	Indecent Liberties - Without Forcible Compulsion	B	Unranked
9.45.126	Inducing Fraud in Measurement of Goods	B	Unranked

The Caseload Forecast Council is not liable for errors or omissions in the manual, for sentences that may be inappropriately calculated as a result of a practitioner's or court's reliance on the manual, or for any other written or verbal information related to adult or juvenile sentencing. The scoring sheets are intended to provide assistance in most cases but do not cover all permutations of the scoring rules. If you find any errors or omissions, we encourage you to report them to the Caseload Forecast Council.

SECTION 4 – FELONY INDEX BY CLASSIFICATION

Statute (RCW)	Offense	Class	Seriousness Level
40.16.020	Injury to and Misappropriation of Public Record by Officer	B	Unranked
88.08.050(1)	Injury to Lighthouses or United States Light	B	Unranked
9.24.030	Insolvent Bank Receiving Deposit	B	Unranked
48.06.030	Insurance Solicitation Permit Violation	B	Unranked
69.25.155(2)	Interference with Person Performing Official Duties With a Deadly Weapon	B	Unranked
9A.72.160	Intimidating a Judge	B	VI
9A.72.130	Intimidating a Juror	B	VI
9A.76.180	Intimidating a Public Servant	B	III
9A.72.110	Intimidating a Witness	B	VI
9A.76.140	Introducing Contraband 1	B	VII
9A.40.030(3)(a)	Kidnapping 2	B	V
9A.82.060(1)(b)	Leading Organized Crime - Inciting Criminal Profiteering	B	IX
30A.12.120	Loan to Officer or Employee from Trust Fund	B	Unranked
67.70.130	Lottery Fraud	B	Unranked
70.74.280(3)	Malicious Explosion of a Substance 3	B	X
81.60.070	Malicious Injury to Railroad Property	B	III
9A.48.070	Malicious Mischief 1	B	II
70.74.270(2)	Malicious Placement of an Explosive 2	B	IX
70.74.270(3)	Malicious Placement of an Explosive 3	B	VII
70.74.272(1)(a)	Malicious Placement of an Imitation Device 1	B	XII
9A.32.070	Manslaughter 2	B	VIII
69.50.401(2)(b)	Manufacture Methamphetamine	B	DG-III
69.50.401(2)(b)	Manufacture, Deliver or Possess with Intent to Deliver - Amphetamine	B	DG-II
69.50.401(2)(a)	Manufacture, Deliver or Possess with Intent to Deliver - Narcotics from Schedule I or II or Flunitrazepam from Schedule IV	B	DG-II
82.24.570(3)	Manufacture, Sell or Possess Counterfeit Cigarettes (Subsequent Violation)	B	Unranked
42.20.070	Misappropriating and Falsifying Accounts by Public Officer	B	Unranked
9A.83.020	Money Laundering	B	Unranked
19.144.080	Mortgage Fraud	B	III
32.04.110	Mutual Savings Bank - Conceal or Destroy Evidence	B	Unranked
32.04.100	Mutual Savings Bank - Falsify Savings Book, Document or Statement	B	Unranked
32.24.080	Mutual Savings Bank - Transfer Bank Assets After Insolvency	B	Unranked
46.37.675	Negligently Causing Death By Use of a Signal Preemption Device	B	VII
46.37.674	Negligently Causing Substantial Bodily Harm By Use of a Signal Preemption Device	B	III

The Caseload Forecast Council is not liable for errors or omissions in the manual, for sentences that may be inappropriately calculated as a result of a practitioner's or court's reliance on the manual, or for any other written or verbal information related to adult or juvenile sentencing. The scoring sheets are intended to provide assistance in most cases but do not cover all permutations of the scoring rules. If you find any errors or omissions, we encourage you to report them to the Caseload Forecast Council.

SECTION 4 – FELONY INDEX BY CLASSIFICATION

Statute (RCW)	Offense	Class	Seriousness Level
9A.56.350(2)	Organized Retail Theft 1	B	III
69.50.406(2)	Over 18 and Deliver Narcotic from Schedule III, IV or V, or a Nonnarcotic, Except Flunitrazepam or Methamphetamine, from Schedule I-V to Someone Under 18 and 3 Years Junior	B	DG-III
9A.72.020	Perjury 1	B	V
69.40.030	Placing Poison or Other Harmful Object or Substance in Food, Drinks, Medicine or Water	B	Unranked
9A.56.310	Possession of a Stolen Firearm	B	V
9A.56.068	Possession of a Stolen Vehicle	B	II
9.68A.070(1)	Possession of Depictions of Minor Engaged in Sexually Explicit Conduct 1	B	VI
69.50.440	Possession of Ephedrine, Pseudoephedrine or Anhydrous Ammonia with Intent to Manufacture Methamphetamine	B	DG-III
9.40.120	Possession of Incendiary Device	B	III
9A.56.150	Possession of Stolen Property 1 (Other Than Firearm or Motor Vehicle)	B	II
9.94.040(1)	Possession of Weapons by Prisoners (State Facility)	B	Unranked
9.94.043	Possession of Weapons in Prison by Non-prisoner	B	Unranked
9.94.010	Prison Riot	B	Unranked
9.46.220	Professional Gambling 1	B	Unranked
9A.88.070	Promoting Prostitution 1	B	VIII
19.110.075(2)	Registration Knowingly Not Obtained Prior to Sale of Business Opportunity (Violation of RCW 19.110.050)	B	Unranked
9A.76.070(2)(a)	Rendering Criminal Assistance 1	B	V
19.25.020(2)(a)	Reproduction of Sound Recording Without Consent of Owner - Recording Fixed Before 2/15/1972 (At Least 1,000 Recordings or Subsequent Conviction)	B	Unranked
9A.52.025	Residential Burglary	B	IV
9A.56.360(2)	Retail Theft with Special Circumstances 1	B	III
9A.56.210	Robbery 2	B	IV
69.41.030(2)(a)	Sale, Delivery or Possession With Intent to Sell Legend Drug Without Prescription	B	Unranked
21.20.400	Securities Act Violation	B	III
48.160.080	Sells Guaranteed Asset Protection Waivers Without Registration	B	Unranked
9.68A.060(1)	Sending, Bringing into the State Depictions of Minor Engaged in Sexually Explicit Conduct 1	B	VII
9.68A.040	Sexual Exploitation of a Minor	B	IX
9A.46.110	Stalking	B	V
30B.12.050	State Trust Company – False Entry, Conceal or Destroy Records	B	Unranked

The Caseload Forecast Council is not liable for errors or omissions in the manual, for sentences that may be inappropriately calculated as a result of a practitioner's or court's reliance on the manual, or for any other written or verbal information related to adult or juvenile sentencing. The scoring sheets are intended to provide assistance in most cases but do not cover all permutations of the scoring rules. If you find any errors or omissions, we encourage you to report them to the Caseload Forecast Council.

SECTION 4 – FELONY INDEX BY CLASSIFICATION

Statute (RCW)	Offense	Class	Seriousness Level
29.45.020	Substitution of Child	B	Unranked
9.81.020	Subversive Acts	B	Unranked
9A.56.070	Taking Motor Vehicle Without Permission 1	B	V
9.40.105	Tampering with Fire Alarm, Emergency Signal, or Fire-fighting Equipment with Intent to Commit Arson	B	Unranked
88.08.020	Tampering with Lights or Signals	B	Unranked
9A.56.030	Theft 1 (Excluding Firearm and Motor Vehicle)	B	II
9A.56.300	Theft of a Firearm	B	VI
9A.56.065	Theft of a Motor Vehicle	B	II
9A.56.080	Theft of Livestock 1	B	IV
9A.56.096(5)(a)	Theft of Rental, Leased, Lease-purchased or Loaned Property (Valued at $5,000 or More)	B	II
9A.56.340(2)	Theft with Intent to Resell 1	B	III
9.61.160	Threats to Bomb	B	IV
9A.82.050	Trafficking in Stolen Property 1	B	IV
48.17.063(4)	Transaction of Insurance Business Beyond the Scope of Licensure (Violation of RCW 48.17.060)	B	I
70.105.085(1)(a)	Transport, Disposal or Export of Hazardous Waste That Places Another Person in Danger of Injury or Death	B	Unranked
39.62.040	Unauthorized Use of Public Official Facsimile Signature or Seal	B	Unranked
69.43.070(1)	Unlawful Delivery of Precursor Drug with Intent to Use	B	Unranked
9A.56.290(4)(b)	Unlawful Factoring of a Credit or Payment Card Transaction (Subsequent Violation)	B	IV
9.41.040(1)	Unlawful Possession of a Firearm 1	B	VII
69.43.070(2)	Unlawful Receipt of Precursor Drug with Intent to Use	B	Unranked
77.15.260(3)(b)	Unlawful Trafficking in Fish, Shellfish or Wildlife 1	B	III
48.44.016(3)	Unlawful Transaction of Health Coverage as Health Care Service Contractor	B	IV
48.46.033(3)	Unlawful Transaction of Health Coverage as Health Maintenance Organization	B	IV
48.15.023(3)	Unlawful Transaction of Insurance Business	B	IV
19.310.120	Unlawfully Engaging in Business as an Exchange Facilitator (RCW 19.310.100(1)-(9))	B	Unranked
48.102.160(4)	Unlicensed Life Insurance Provider	B	Unranked
67.70.140	Unlicensed Lottery Activity	B	Unranked
48.17.063(2)	Unlicensed Practice as an Insurance Professional	B	IV
48.102.160(5)	Unlicensed Settlement Broker	B	Unranked

The Caseload Forecast Council is not liable for errors or omissions in the manual, for sentences that may be inappropriately calculated as a result of a practitioner's or court's reliance on the manual, or for any other written or verbal information related to adult or juvenile sentencing. The scoring sheets are intended to provide assistance in most cases but do not cover all permutations of the scoring rules. If you find any errors or omissions, we encourage you to report them to the Caseload Forecast Council.

SECTION 4 – FELONY INDEX BY CLASSIFICATION

Statute (RCW)	Offense	Class	Seriousness Level
9A.82.080(1-2)	Use of Proceeds of Criminal Profiteering	B	IV
19.25.030(2)(a)	Use of Recording of Live Performance Without Consent of Owner (At Least 1,000 Recordings or at Least 100 Unauthorized Audiovisual Recordings or Subsequent Offense)	B	Unranked
19.144.100(1)	Use or Investment of Proceeds from Mortgage Fraud Activities	B	Unranked
46.61.522(1)(c)	Vehicular Assault - Disregard for the Safety of Others	B	III
46.61.522(1)(a-b)	Vehicular Assault – In a Reckless Manner or While Under the Influence of Intoxicating Liquor or any Drug	B	IV
9.68A.075(1)	Viewing Depictions of Minor Engaged in Sexually Explicit Conduct 1	B	IV
29A.84.240(1)	Violations By Signers – Recall Petition With False Name	B	Unranked
9A.42.070	Abandonment of Dependent Persons 2	C	V
29A.84.680(1)	Absentee Voting Violation	C	Unranked
46.52.130(5)(b)	Abstracts of Driving Records – Intentional Misuse	C	Unranked
20.01.460(2)	Acting as Commission Merchant, Dealer, Cash Buyer Without License	C	Unranked
69.52.030(3)	Advertising Imitation Controlled Substances	C	Unranked
46.37.660(2)(c)	Air Bag Diagnostic Systems	C	V
46.37.660(2)(b)	Air Bag Diagnostic Systems (Causing Bodily Injury or Death)	C	VII
46.37.660(1)(c)	Air Bag Replacement Requirements	C	V
46.37.660(1)(b)	Air Bag Replacement Requirements (Causing Bodily Injury or Death)	C	VII
9.41.171	Alien Possession of a Firearm	C	Unranked
9.45.210	Altering Sample or Certificate of Assay	C	Unranked
9A.76.177	Amber Alert – Making False Statements to a Public Servant	C	Unranked
68.64.160	Anatomical Gift - Illegal Financial Gain	C	Unranked
68.64.150	Anatomical Gifts - Illegal Purchase or Sale	C	Unranked
16.52.205(2)	Animal Cruelty 1	C	Unranked
16.52.205(3)	Animal Cruelty 1 - Sexual Contact or Conduct	C	III
16.52.117	Animal Fighting	C	Unranked
9A.36.031(1)(a-g) & (i-j)	Assault 3 – Excluding Assault 3 of a Peace Officer with a Projectile Stun Gun	C	III
9A.36.031(1)(h)	Assault 3 - Of a Peace Officer with a Projectile Stun Gun	C	IV
9A.36.140	Assault of a Child 3	C	III
72.23.170	Assist Escape of Mental Patient	C	Unranked
9A.82.080(3)	Attempt or Conspiracy to Violate RCW 9A.82.080(1) or (2)	C	Unranked
46.61.024	Attempting to Elude Pursuing Police Vehicle	C	I
9A.76.170(3)(c)	Bail Jumping with Class B or C Felony	C	III

The Caseload Forecast Council is not liable for errors or omissions in the manual, for sentences that may be inappropriately calculated as a result of a practitioner's or court's reliance on the manual, or for any other written or verbal information related to adult or juvenile sentencing. The scoring sheets are intended to provide assistance in most cases but do not cover all permutations of the scoring rules. If you find any errors or omissions, we encourage you to report them to the Caseload Forecast Council.

SECTION 4 – FELONY INDEX BY CLASSIFICATION

Statute (RCW)	Offense	Class	Seriousness Level
9A.64.010	Bigamy	C	Unranked
9.46.155	Bribing to Obtain a License From Public Officials, Employees, Agents	C	Unranked
9.46.1961	Cheating 1	C	IV
9A.64.030(3)(b)	Child Buying	C	Unranked
49.12.410(2)	Child Labor Law Violation – Death/Disability	C	Unranked
9A.44.089	Child Molestation 3	C	V
9A.64.030(3)(a)	Child Selling	C	Unranked
9A.40.110	Coercion of Involuntary Servitude	C	Unranked
9A.82.045	Collection of Unlawful Debt	C	Unranked
77.15.500(3)(b)	Commercial Fishing Without a License 1	C	II
19.158.160	Commercial Telephone Solicitor Deception (Value of $250 or More)	C	Unranked
9.68A.090(2)	Communication with Minor for Immoral Purposes (Subsequent Violation or Prior Sex Offense Conviction)	C	III
9A.90.040	Computer Trespass 1	C	II
69.50.465	Conducting or Maintaining a Marijuana Club	C	Unranked
69.50.416	Controlled Substance Label Violation	C	Unranked
9.16.035(4)	Counterfeiting – Endanger Public Health or Safety	C	IV
9.16.035(3)	Counterfeiting – Third Conviction and Value $10,000 or More	C	II
69.50.4011(2)(c-e)	Create, Deliver or Possess a Counterfeit Controlled Substance – Schedule I-II Nonnarcotic, Schedule III-V Except Flunitrazepam or Methamphetamine	C	DG-II
9.08.090	Crimes Against Animal Facilities	C	Unranked
9A.46.120	Criminal Gang Intimidation	C	III
9A.60.040	Criminal Impersonation 1	C	Unranked
9A.84.010(2)(b)	Criminal Mischief	C	Unranked
9A.42.030	Criminal Mistreatment 2	C	V
9A.82.160	Criminal Profiteering Lien After Service of Notice	C	Unranked
9A.44.196	Criminal Trespass Against Children	C	Unranked
9A.36.100	Custodial Assault	C	III
9A.40.060	Custodial Interference 1	C	Unranked
9A.40.070	Custodial Interference 2 (Subsequent Offense)	C	Unranked
9A.44.160	Custodial Sexual Misconduct 1	C	V
9.61.260(3)	Cyberstalking (With Prior Harassment Conviction or Threat of Death)	C	III
16.08.100(2)	Dangerous Dog Attack (Subsequent Offense)	C	Unranked
16.08.100(3)	Dangerous Dog Attack Resulting in Severe Injury or Death	C	Unranked

The Caseload Forecast Council is not liable for errors or omissions in the manual, for sentences that may be inappropriately calculated as a result of a practitioner's or court's reliance on the manual, or for any other written or verbal information related to adult or juvenile sentencing. The scoring sheets are intended to provide assistance in most cases but do not cover all permutations of the scoring rules. If you find any errors or omissions, we encourage you to report them to the Caseload Forecast Council.

SECTION 4 – FELONY INDEX BY CLASSIFICATION

Statute (RCW)	Offense	Class	Seriousness Level
9.68A.050(2)	Dealing in Depictions of Minor Engaged in Sexually Explicit Conduct 2	C	V
22.09.310	Dealing in Unauthorized Warehouse Receipts for Agricultural Commodities	C	Unranked
9A.61.040	Defrauding a Public Utility 2	C	Unranked
69.50.4012	Delivery of a Material in Lieu of a Controlled Substance	C	DG-II
9.41.110(8)	Delivery of Firearm by Dealer to Ineligible Person	C	Unranked
9.41.080	Delivery of Firearms to Ineligible Person	C	Unranked
27.44.040(1)	Destroying, Removing or Defacing Indian Graves	C	Unranked
68.60.040(1)	Destruction of Tomb, Plot, Marker, or Cemetery Property	C	Unranked
9.38.060	Digital Signatures Fraud	C	Unranked
9A.76.023(2)(a)	Disarming a Law Enforcement or Corrections Officer	C	Unranked
9A.86.010	Disclosing Intimate Images	C	Unranked
69.50.402	Dispensing Violation (VUCSA)	C	Unranked
82.26.190	Distributors and Retailer of Tobacco Products License Violation	C	Unranked
27.53.060	Disturbing Archaeological Resources or Site	C	Unranked
26.50.110	Domestic Violence Court Order Violation	C	V
29A.84.655	Election Officer Permits Repeat Vote	C	Unranked
29A.84.720	Election Officers – Violation	C	Unranked
29A.84.030	Election or Mail Ballot Violation	C	Unranked
19.300.020	Electronic Communication Devices – Illegal Scanning	C	Unranked
9A.90.060	Electronic Data Service Interference	C	II
9A.90.080	Electronic Data Tampering 1	C	II
9A.90.100	Electronic Data Theft	C	II
79A.60.090	Eluding a Law Enforcement Vessel	C	Unranked
18.39.350	Embalmers/Funeral Directors Violation	C	Unranked
46.80.020(b)	Engage in Business of Wrecking Vehicles Without a License (Subsequent Offense)	C	Unranked
51.48.103(2)	Engaging in Business After Certificate of Coverage Revocation	C	Unranked
70.345.090	Engaging in Delivery Sales of Vapor Products Without a License or Without Proper Shipping Documentation	C	Unranked
77.15.620(3)(b)	Engaging in Fish Dealing Activity Unlicensed 1	C	II
16.08.100(4)	Entering Dog in a Dog Fight	C	Unranked
9A.76.120	Escape 2	C	III
9A.76.130(3)(b)	Escape 3 (Third or Subsequent Offense)	C	Unranked
72.09.310	Escape from Community Custody	C	II

The Caseload Forecast Council is not liable for errors or omissions in the manual, for sentences that may be inappropriately calculated as a result of a practitioner's or court's reliance on the manual, or for any other written or verbal information related to adult or juvenile sentencing. The scoring sheets are intended to provide assistance in most cases but do not cover all permutations of the scoring rules. If you find any errors or omissions, we encourage you to report them to the Caseload Forecast Council.

SECTION 4 – FELONY INDEX BY CLASSIFICATION

Statute (RCW)	Offense	Class	Seriousness Level
51.48.020(1)	Evading Industrial Insurance Premiums	C	Unranked
82.42.085	Evading the Collection of Aircraft Fuel Tax	C	Unranked
74.09.260	Excessive Charges, Payments	C	Unranked
9A.56.130	Extortion 2	C	III
19.25.040(2)(b)	Failure to Disclose Origin of Certain Recordings (More than 10 but Less Than 100 Recordings)	C	Unranked
36.18.170	Failure to Pay Over Fees to County Treasurer	C	Unranked
9A.44.132(3)	Failure to Register as a Kidnapping Offender	C	Unranked
9A.44.132(1)(a)	Failure to Register as a Sex Offender (First Violation)	C	Unranked
9A.44.132(1)(a)	Failure to Register as a Sex Offender (Second Violation Committed on or After 6/10/2010)	C	II
9A.44.132(1)(a)	Failure to Register as a Sex Offender (Subsequent Violation Committed on or After 6/7/2006 but Before 6/10/2010)	C	II
19.146.050	Failure to Use a Trust Account	C	Unranked
19.142.080	Failure to Use a Trust Account or Furnish Bond for Health Studio	C	Unranked
38.42.050	False Affidavit Under Service Member Civil Relief Act	C	Unranked
42.24.100	False Claim from Municipal Corporation (Charged as Perjury 2)	C	Unranked
42.17A.750	False Documents Registered with Public Disclosure Commission	C	Unranked
48.30.230	False Insurance Claims (Value in Excess of $1,500)	C	Unranked
74.09.230	False Statement for Medical Assistance	C	Unranked
69.43.080	False Statement in Report of Precursor Drugs	C	Unranked
82.32.290(2)	False Statement to Department of Revenue	C	Unranked
19.230.300	False Statement, Misrepresentation or False Certification of Uniform Money services Record	C	Unranked
74.09.250	False Statements Regarding Institutions, Facilities	C	Unranked
26.20.030	Family Abandonment	C	Unranked
69.50.403	Forged Prescription for a Controlled Substance	C	DG-I
9A.60.020	Forgery	C	I
29A.84.711	Fraud in Certification of Nomination or Ballot	C	Unranked
9.45.170	Fraud in Liquor Warehouse Receipts	C	Unranked
9.26A.110(3)	Fraud in Obtaining Telecommunications Services (Value Exceeds $250)	C	Unranked
9A.60.060	Fraudulent Creation or Revocation of Mental Health Advance Directive	C	I
76.48.141(1)(a)	Fraudulent Document as Specialized Forest Products Permit, Sales Invoice, Bill of Lading, etc.	C	Unranked
76.48.141(2)	Fraudulent Document for Specialized Forest Products Buyer	C	Unranked

The Caseload Forecast Council is not liable for errors or omissions in the manual, for sentences that may be inappropriately calculated as a result of a practitioner's or court's reliance on the manual, or for any other written or verbal information related to adult or juvenile sentencing. The scoring sheets are intended to provide assistance in most cases but do not cover all permutations of the scoring rules. If you find any errors or omissions, we encourage you to report them to the Caseload Forecast Council.

SECTION 4 – FELONY INDEX BY CLASSIFICATION

Statute (RCW)	Offense	Class	Seriousness Level
9.45.270(2)	Fraudulent Filing of Vehicle Report of Sale (Value Exceeds $250)	C	Unranked
65.12.750	Fraudulent Procurement or False Entry on Land Title Registration	C	Unranked
76.48.141(1)(b)	Fraudulent Representation of Authority to Harvest Specialized Forest Products	C	Unranked
82.36.380	Fuel Tax Evasion	C	Unranked
9A.46.020(2)(b)	Harassment (Subsequent Conviction or Threat of Death)	C	III
9A.76.200	Harming a Police Dog/Horse or an Accelerate Detection Dog	C	Unranked
48.80.030	Health Care False Claims	C	II
46.52.020(4)(b)	Hit and Run - Injury	C	IV
79A.60.200(3)	Hit and Run with Vessel - Injury Accident	C	IV
9.35.020(3)	Identity Theft 2	C	II
9.16.020	Imitating Lawful Brands With Intent	C	Unranked
9.35.010	Improperly Obtaining Financial Information	C	II
9A.64.020(2)	Incest 2	C	V
9A.88.010(2)(c)	Indecent Exposure to a Person Under Age 14 (Subsequent Conviction or Has Prior Sex Offense Conviction)	C	IV
9A.82.070	Influencing Outcome of Sporting Event	C	IV
40.16.010	Injury to a Public Record	C	Unranked
9.91.170(5)	Intentional Infliction, Injury or Death to a Guide Dog or Service Animal	C	Unranked
9.91.175(3)	Intentionally Injures, Disables or Causes Death of an On-Duty Search and Rescue Dog	C	Unranked
9.73.230	Intercepting, Transmitting or Recording Conversations Concerning Controlled Substances	C	Unranked
69.25.155(1)	Interference with Person Performing Official Duties	C	Unranked
70.74.275	Intimidation or Harassment With an Explosive	C	Unranked
9A.76.150	Introducing Contraband 2	C	III
69.50.4015	Involving a Minor in Drug Dealing	C	DG-III
9A.60.070	Issuing a False Academic Credential	C	Unranked
16.52.320	Kill or Cause Substantial Harm With Malice to Livestock	C	Unranked
46.70.021	Licensing Violation for Car Dealers or Manufacturers (Subsequent Violation)	C	Unranked
9A.40.090	Luring of a Child or Developmentally Disabled Person	C	Unranked
9A.56.370	Mail Theft	C	Unranked
9.47.090	Maintaining a Bucket Shop	C	Unranked
69.50.402	Maintaining a Dwelling or Place for Controlled Substances	C	DG-II
9.45.220	Making False Sample or Assay of Ore	C	Unranked

The Caseload Forecast Council is not liable for errors or omissions in the manual, for sentences that may be inappropriately calculated as a result of a practitioner's or court's reliance on the manual, or for any other written or verbal information related to adult or juvenile sentencing. The scoring sheets are intended to provide assistance in most cases but do not cover all permutations of the scoring rules. If you find any errors or omissions, we encourage you to report them to the Caseload Forecast Council.

SECTION 4 – FELONY INDEX BY CLASSIFICATION

Statute (RCW)	Offense	Class	Seriousness Level
9A.36.080	Malicious Harassment	C	IV
9A.48.080	Malicious Mischief 2	C	I
70.74.272(1)(b)	Malicious Placement of an Imitation Device 2	C	VI
9.62.010(1)	Malicious Prosecution	C	Unranked
9.45.260	Malicious Sprinkler Contractor Work	C	Unranked
69.50.401(2)(c)	Manufacture, Deliver or Possess with Intent to Deliver - Marijuana	C	DG-I
46.37.650(1)(c)	Manufacture or Import Counterfeit, Nonfunctional, Damaged, or Previously Deployed Air Bag	C	V
46.37.650(1)(b)	Manufacture or Import Counterfeit, Nonfunctional, Damaged, or Previously Deployed Air Bag (Causing Bodily Injury or Death)	C	VII
69.50.401(2)(c-e)	Manufacture, Deliver or Possess with Intent to Deliver - Narcotics from Schedule III, IV, or V or Nonnarcotics from Schedule I-V (except Marijuana, Amphetamine, Methamphetamine, or Flunitrazepam)	C	DG-II
69.52.030(1)	Manufacture, Distribute or Possess with Intent to Distribute an Imitation Controlled Substance	C	DG-II
70.74.022(1)	Manufacture, Purchase, Sell or Store Explosive Device Without License	C	Unranked
46.20.0921(3)(a)	Manufacture, Sell or Deliver Forged Driver's License or Identicard	C	Unranked
82.24.570(2)	Manufacture, Sell or Possess Counterfeit Cigarettes	C	Unranked
69.51A.060	Medical Marijuana Fraudulent Records (Effective Until 7/1/2016)	C	Unranked
69.51A.240	Medical Marijuana – Unlawful Actions	C	Unranked
9.81.030	Member of Subversive Organization	C	Unranked
78.44.330	Mineral Trespass	C	I
42.20.090	Misappropriating and Falsifying Accounts by Treasurer	C	Unranked
9.82.030	Misprision of Treason	C	Unranked
29A.08.740	Misuse of Registered Voter Data	C	Unranked
29A.84.150	Misuse or Alteration of Registration Database	C	Unranked
9.45.070	Mock Auction	C	Unranked
9A.60.030	Obtaining Signature by Deception or Duress	C	Unranked
46.70.180(5)	Odometer Offense	C	Unranked
40.16.030	Offering False Instrument for Filing or Record	C	Unranked
68.50.140(3)	Opening Graves With Intent to Sell or Remove Personal Effects or Human Remains	C	Unranked
90.56.540	Operation of a Vessel While Under the Influence of Intoxicating Liquor or Drugs	C	Unranked
9A.56.350(3)	Organized Retail Theft 2	C	II
9.46.215	Ownership or Interest in Gambling Device	C	Unranked

The Caseload Forecast Council is not liable for errors or omissions in the manual, for sentences that may be inappropriately calculated as a result of a practitioner's or court's reliance on the manual, or for any other written or verbal information related to adult or juvenile sentencing. The scoring sheets are intended to provide assistance in most cases but do not cover all permutations of the scoring rules. If you find any errors or omissions, we encourage you to report them to the Caseload Forecast Council.

SECTION 4 – FELONY INDEX BY CLASSIFICATION

Statute (RCW)	Offense	Class	Seriousness Level
69.30.085	Participation in Shellfish Operation or Activities While License is Denied, Revoked or Suspended	C	Unranked
74.09.240(2)	Paying or Offering Bribes, Kickbacks or Rebates	C	Unranked
9A.72.030	Perjury 2	C	III
9.94.070	Persistent Prison Misbehavior	C	V
82.32.290(4)	Phantomware Violation	C	Unranked
46.61.504(6)	Physical Control of a Vehicle While Under the Influence of Intoxicating Liquor or any Drug	C	V
69.40.020	Poison in Milk or Food Product	C	Unranked
9A.58.020	Possessing or Capturing Personal Identification Document	C	Unranked
9.94.041(2)	Possession of Controlled Substance by Prisoner (County or Local Facility)	C	Unranked
9.94.041(1)	Possession of Controlled Substance by Prisoner (State Facility)	C	Unranked
9.94.045	Possession of Controlled Substance in Prison by Non-prisoner	C	Unranked
69.50.4013	Possession of Controlled Substance That is a Narcotic from Schedule III, IV or V or Nonnarcotic from Schedule I-V	C	DG-I
69.50.4013	Possession of Controlled Substance That is Either Heroin or Narcotics from Schedule I or II	C	DG-I
9.68A.070(2)	Possession of Depictions of Minor Engaged in Sexually Explicit Conduct 2	C	IV
9.41.190	Possession of Machine Gun, Short-barreled Shotgun or Short-barreled Rifle	C	III
69.41.350	Possession of Steroids in Excess of 200 tablets or (8) 2cc Bottles Without a Valid Prescription	C	Unranked
9A.56.380	Possession of Stolen Mail	C	Unranked
9A.56.160	Possession of Stolen Property 2 (Other Than Firearm or Motor Vehicle)	C	I
9.94.040(2)	Possession of Weapons by Prisoners (County or Local Facility)	C	Unranked
9.46.221	Professional Gambling 2	C	Unranked
9A.36.060	Promoting a Suicide Attempt	C	Unranked
67.08.015	Promoting Illegal Boxing, Martial Arts and Wrestling	C	Unranked
9.68.140	Promoting Pornography	C	Unranked
9A.88.080	Promoting Prostitution 2	C	III
9.68A.102	Promoting Travel for Commercial Sexual Abuse of a Minor	C	Unranked
9A.88.085	Promoting Travel for Prostitution	C	Unranked
29A.84.311	Provides False Information or Conceals or Destroys Candidacy Declaration or Nominating Petition	C	Unranked
26.04.210	Providing False Statements in Affidavits for Marriage	C	Unranked
68.50.140(2)	Purchasing or Receiving Human Remains	C	Unranked
9A.44.060	Rape 3	C	V

The Caseload Forecast Council is not liable for errors or omissions in the manual, for sentences that may be inappropriately calculated as a result of a practitioner's or court's reliance on the manual, or for any other written or verbal information related to adult or juvenile sentencing. The scoring sheets are intended to provide assistance in most cases but do not cover all permutations of the scoring rules. If you find any errors or omissions, we encourage you to report them to the Caseload Forecast Council.

SECTION 4 – FELONY INDEX BY CLASSIFICATION

Statute (RCW)	Offense	Class	Seriousness Level
9A.44.079	Rape of a Child 3	C	VI
74.09.240(1)	Receiving or Asking for Bribes, Kickbacks or Rebates	C	Unranked
9A.68.030	Receiving or Granting Unlawful Compensation	C	Unranked
81.60.080(2)	Receiving Stolen Railroad Property	C	Unranked
9A.48.040	Reckless Burning 1	C	I
90.56.530	Reckless Operation of a Tank Vessel	C	Unranked
70.94.430(3)	Releasing Into Ambient Air Hazardous Air Pollutant	C	Unranked
46.12.560	Removal of Sticker on Vehicle Stating Previously Destroyed or Title 1 Loss	C	Unranked
68.50.140(4)	Removal, Disinterment or Mutilation of Human Remains	C	Unranked
68.60.050	Removes, Defaces or Destroys any Historic Grave	C	Unranked
68.50.140(1)	Removing Human Remains	C	Unranked
9.16.010	Removing Lawful Brands	C	Unranked
19.25.020(2)(b)	Reproduction of Sound Recording Without Consent of Owner - Recording Fixed Before 2/15/1972 (More Than 100 but Less Than 1,000 Recordings)	C	Unranked
9A.68.020	Requesting Unlawful Compensation	C	Unranked
70.345.030	Retail Sales, Distribution or Delivery Sales of Vapor Products Without a License	C	Unranked
9A.56.360(3)	Retail Theft with Special Circumstances 2	C	II
9A.56.360(4)	Retail Theft with Special Circumstances 3	C	Unranked
81.60.080(1)	Sabotaging Rolling Stock	C	Unranked
46.37.650(2)(b)	Sale, Install, [or] Reinstall Counterfeit, Nonfunctional, Damaged, or Previously Deployed Airbag	C	VII
46.37.650(2)(c)	Sale, Install, [or] Reinstall Counterfeit, Nonfunctional, Damaged, or Previously Deployed Airbag	C	V
33.36.040	Savings and Loan Association - Making False Statement of Assets or Liabilities	C	Unranked
33.36.030	Savings and Loan Association - Preference in Case of Insolvency	C	Unranked
33.36.060	Savings and Loan Association - Suppressing, Secreting or Destroying Evidence or Records	C	Unranked
19.290.100	Scrap Processing, Recycling, or Supplying Without a License (Second or Subsequent Offense)	C	II
19.60.067(2)	Second-hand Precious Metal Dealer Violations (Subsequent Violation)	C	Unranked
46.20.0921(2)	Sell or Deliver a Stolen Driver's License or Identicard	C	Unranked
27.44.040(2)	Selling Artifacts or Human Remains from Indian Graves	C	Unranked
69.50.410	Selling for Profit (Controlled or Counterfeit) any Controlled Substance in Schedule I	C	DG-III
9.68A.060(2)	Sending, Bringing into the State Depictions of Minor Engaged in Sexually	C	V

The Caseload Forecast Council is not liable for errors or omissions in the manual, for sentences that may be inappropriately calculated as a result of a practitioner's or court's reliance on the manual, or for any other written or verbal information related to adult or juvenile sentencing. The scoring sheets are intended to provide assistance in most cases but do not cover all permutations of the scoring rules. If you find any errors or omissions, we encourage you to report them to the Caseload Forecast Council.

SECTION 4 – FELONY INDEX BY CLASSIFICATION

Statute (RCW)	Offense	Class	Seriousness Level
	Explicit Conduct 2		
9A.44.093	Sexual Misconduct with a Minor 1	C	V
9A.44.105	Sexually Violating Human Remains	C	V
70.155.140	Shipping or Transporting Tobacco Products Ordered Through Mail or Internet	C	Unranked
82.38.270	Special Fuel Violations	C	Unranked
77.15.450(3)(b)	Spotlighting Big Game 1	C	I
67.70.160	State Lottery Violations Except Lottery Fraud and Unlicensed Lottery Activity	C	Unranked
77.15.670(3)(b)	Suspension of Department Privileges 1	C	I
9A.56.075	Taking Motor Vehicle Without Permission 2	C	I
9A.72.120	Tampering with a Witness	C	III
29A.84.550	Tampering with Election Materials	C	Unranked
29A.84.560	Tampering with Voting Machine	C	Unranked
9.61.230(2)	Telephone Harassment (With Prior Harassment Conviction or Threat of Death)	C	III
9A.56.040	Theft 2 (Excluding Firearm and Motor Vehicle)	C	I
69.55.010	Theft of Ammonia	C	VIII
9A.56.083	Theft of Livestock 2	C	III
9A.56.096(5)(b)	Theft of Rental, Leased, Lease-purchased or Loaned Property (Valued at $750 or More but Less Than $5,000)	C	I
9A.56.262	Theft of Telecommunication Service	C	Unranked
9A.56.340(3)	Theft with Intent to Resell 2	C	II
9A.36.090	Threats Against Governor or Family	C	Unranked
64.36.210	Timeshare Fraud	C	Unranked
64.36.020(5)(b)	Timeshare Registration Requirement Violation	C	Unranked
9A.68.040	Trading in Public Office	C	Unranked
9A.68.050	Trading in Special Influence	C	Unranked
48.30A.015	Trafficking in Insurance Claims (Subsequent Violation)	C	II
9A.82.055	Trafficking in Stolen Property 2	C	III
9.46.240	Transmission or Receiving Gambling Information by Internet	C	Unranked
70.105.085(1)(b)	Transport, Disposal or Export of Hazardous Waste That Places Another Person's Property in Danger of Harm	C	Unranked
82.24.110(2)	Transportation of More Than 10,000 Cigarettes Without Proper Stamps	C	Unranked
68.60.040(3)	Transports Removed Human Remains, Opens a Grave or Removes Personal Effects from Grave	C	Unranked

The Caseload Forecast Council is not liable for errors or omissions in the manual, for sentences that may be inappropriately calculated as a result of a practitioner's or court's reliance on the manual, or for any other written or verbal information related to adult or juvenile sentencing. The scoring sheets are intended to provide assistance in most cases but do not cover all permutations of the scoring rules. If you find any errors or omissions, we encourage you to report them to the Caseload Forecast Council.

SECTION 4 – FELONY INDEX BY CLASSIFICATION

Statute (RCW)	Offense	Class	Seriousness Level
9.91.150(1)	Tree Spiking	C	Unranked
9.02.120	Unauthorized Abortion	C	Unranked
68.44.060	Unauthorized Loans to Cemetery Authority	C	Unranked
29A.84.545	Unauthorized Removal of Paper Record from Electronic Voting Device	C	Unranked
68.05.330	Unfair Practice of Funeral or Cemetery Board	C	Unranked
19.225.110	Uniform Athlete Agent Act Violation	C	Unranked
9A.49.020	Unlawful Discharge of a Laser 1	C	Unranked
74.09.290	Unlawful Disclosure of Patient Records or DSHS Information	C	Unranked
9A.56.290(4)(a)	Unlawful Factoring of a Credit or Payment Card Transaction	C	II
69.53.020	Unlawful Fortification of Building for Drug Purposes	C	Unranked
77.15.410(3)(b)	Unlawful Hunting of Big Game 1	C	III
9A.40.040	Unlawful Imprisonment	C	III
9A.56.060(4)	Unlawful Issuance of Checks or Drafts (Value Greater Than $750)	C	I
9A.56.264	Unlawful Manufacture of a Telecommunication Device	C	Unranked
69.04.938(3)	Unlawful Misbranding of Food Fish or Shellfish 1	C	III
88.46.080(2)(b)	Unlawful Operation of a Covered Vessel (Subsequent Violation)	C	Unranked
90.56.300(2)(b)	Unlawful Operation of Onshore or Offshore Facility (Subsequent Conviction)	C	Unranked
77.15.570(2)	Unlawful Participation on Non-Indians in Indian Fishery	C	II
9.41.040(2)	Unlawful Possession of a Firearm 2	C	III
9A.56.320(3)	Unlawful Possession of a Personal Identification Device	C	I
9A.56.320(4)	Unlawful Possession of Fictitious Identification	C	I
9A.56.320(5)	Unlawful Possession of Instruments of Financial Fraud	C	I
9A.56.320(2)	Unlawful Possession of Payment Instruments	C	I
2.48.180	Unlawful Practice of Law (Subsequent Violation)	C	II
9.41.115	Unlawful Private Transfer of a Firearm (Subsequent Offense)	C	Unranked
9A.56.320(1)	Unlawful Production of Payment Instruments	C	I
77.15.650(3)(b)	Unlawful Purchase or Use of a License 1	C	II
9.91.144	Unlawful Redemption of Food Stamps	C	I
77.15.250(2)(b)	Unlawful Releasing, Planting, Possessing or Placing Deleterious Exotic Wildlife	C	I
9A.56.266	Unlawful Sale of a Telecommunication Device	C	Unranked
9A.56.230	Unlawful Sale of Subscription Television Services	C	Unranked
46.12.750(3)	Unlawful Sale of Vehicle Certificate of Ownership	C	Unranked

The Caseload Forecast Council is not liable for errors or omissions in the manual, for sentences that may be inappropriately calculated as a result of a practitioner's or court's reliance on the manual, or for any other written or verbal information related to adult or juvenile sentencing. The scoring sheets are intended to provide assistance in most cases but do not cover all permutations of the scoring rules. If you find any errors or omissions, we encourage you to report them to the Caseload Forecast Council.

SECTION 4 – FELONY INDEX BY CLASSIFICATION

Statute (RCW)	Offense	Class	Seriousness Level
18.64.046(7)	Unlawful Selling of Ephedrine, Pseudoephedrine or Phenylpropanolamine by a Wholesaler	C	Unranked
69.55.020	Unlawful Storage of Ammonia	C	VI
19.116.080(1)	Unlawful Subleasing of Motor Vehicle	C	Unranked
77.15.120(3)(b)	Unlawful Taking of Endangered Fish or Wildlife 1	C	III
77.15.770(2)	Unlawful Trade in Shark Fins 1	C	Unranked
77.15.260(3)(a)	Unlawful Trafficking in Fish, Shellfish or Wildlife 2	C	II
9.91.142(1)	Unlawful Trafficking in Food Stamps	C	I
77.15.135(4)(d)	Unlawful Trafficking in Species With Extinction 1	C	Unranked
19.116.080(2)	Unlawful Transfer of Ownership of Motor Vehicle	C	Unranked
77.15.530(4)	Unlawful Use of a Nondesignated Vessel	C	III
18.04.370(1)(b)	Unlawful Use of a Professional Title	C	Unranked
69.53.010	Unlawful Use of Building for Drug Purposes	C	DG-I
18.04.370(1)(c)	Unlawful Use of CPA Title After Suspension	C	Unranked
77.15.630(3)(b)	Unlawful Fish and Shellfish Catch Accounting 1	C	I
69.53.030	Unlawful Use of Fortified Building	C	Unranked
77.15.811	Unlawful Use of Invasive Species 1	C	Unranked
66.44.120(2)(b)	Unlawful Use of Liquor Board Seal (Third or Subsequent Offense)	C	Unranked
77.15.580(3)(b)	Unlawful Use of Net to Take Fish	C	I
82.24.500	Unlawfully Purchase, Sell, Consign or Distribute Cigarettes	C	Unranked
18.130.190(7)(b)	Unlicensed Practice of a Profession or Business (Subsequent Violation)	C	II
29A.84.660	Unqualified Person Voting	C	Unranked
29A.84.140	Unqualified Voting Registration	C	Unranked
19.210.040	Unused Property, Merchants –Prohibited Sales (Third or Subsequent Offense Within 5 Years)	C	Unranked
46.37.673	Use of a Signal Preemption Device Resulting in Property Damage or Less Substantial Bodily Harm	C	Unranked
19.25.030(2)(b)	Use of Recording of Live Performance Without Consent of Owner (At Least 100 but Less Than 1,000 Recordings or More than 10 but Less Than 100 Unauthorized Audiovisual Recording or Subsequent Offense)	C	Unranked
9A.52.095	Vehicle Prowl 1	C	I
9A.52.100(3)	Vehicle Prowling 2 (Third or Subsequent Offense)	C	IV
9.68A.075(2)	Viewing Depictions of Minor Engaged in Sexually Explicit Conduct 2	C	Unranked
77.15.550(3)(b)	Violating Commercial Fishing Area or Time 1	C	I
29A.84.230(1)	Violation by Signer – Initiative or Referendum with False Name	C	Unranked
26.50.110(5)	Violation of a Foreign Protection Order (Third or Subsequent Violation)	C	Unranked

The Caseload Forecast Council is not liable for errors or omissions in the manual, for sentences that may be inappropriately calculated as a result of a practitioner's or court's reliance on the manual, or for any other written or verbal information related to adult or juvenile sentencing. The scoring sheets are intended to provide assistance in most cases but do not cover all permutations of the scoring rules. If you find any errors or omissions, we encourage you to report them to the Caseload Forecast Council.

SECTION 4 – FELONY INDEX BY CLASSIFICATION

Statute (RCW)	Offense	Class	Seriousness Level
29A.84.130	Voter Violation of Registration Law	C	Unranked
29A.84.650(1)	Voting Repeater – More Than One Vote at Any Election	C	Unranked
9A.44.115	Voyeurism	C	II
48.30.220	Willful Destruction, Injury, Secretion of Insured Property	C	Unranked
10.66.090	Willfully Disobeys an Off-limits Order (Subsequent Violation or Enters Protected Against Drug Trafficking Area)	C	Unranked

The Caseload Forecast Council is not liable for errors or omissions in the manual, for sentences that may be inappropriately calculated as a result of a practitioner's or court's reliance on the manual, or for any other written or verbal information related to adult or juvenile sentencing. The scoring sheets are intended to provide assistance in most cases but do not cover all permutations of the scoring rules. If you find any errors or omissions, we encourage you to report them to the Caseload Forecast Council.

SECTION 4 - FELONY INDEX BY RCW

FELONY INDEX BY RCW

Statute (RCW)	Offense	Class	Seriousness Level
2.48.180	Unlawful Practice of Law (Subsequent Violation)	C	II
9.02.120	Unauthorized Abortion	C	Unranked
9.05.030	Assembly of Saboteurs	B	Unranked
9.05.060(2)	Criminal Sabotage	B	Unranked
9.08.090	Crimes Against Animal Facilities	C	Unranked
9.16.010	Removing Lawful Brands	C	Unranked
9.16.020	Imitating Lawful Brands With Intent	C	Unranked
9.16.035(3)	Counterfeiting – Third Conviction and Value $10,000 or More	C	II
9.16.035(4)	Counterfeiting – Endanger Public Health or Safety	C	IV
9.24.020	Fraudulent Issue of Stock, Scrip, etc.	B	Unranked
9.24.030	Insolvent Bank Receiving Deposit	B	Unranked
9.24.050	False Report of Corporation	B	Unranked
9.26A.110(3)	Fraud in Obtaining Telecommunications Services (Value Exceeds $250)	C	Unranked
9.35.010	Improperly Obtaining Financial Information	C	II
9.35.020(2)	Identity Theft 1	B	IV
9.35.020(3)	Identity Theft 2	C	II
9.38.060	Digital Signatures Fraud	C	Unranked
9.40.105	Tampering with Fire Alarm, Emergency Signal, or Fire-fighting Equipment with Intent to Commit Arson	B	Unranked
9.40.120	Possession of Incendiary Device	B	III
9.41.040(1)	Unlawful Possession of a Firearm 1	B	VII
9.41.040(2)	Unlawful Possession of a Firearm 2	C	III
9.41.080	Delivery of Firearms to Ineligible Person	C	Unranked
9.41.110(8)	Delivery of Firearm by Dealer to Ineligible Person	C	Unranked
9.41.115	Unlawful Private Transfer of a Firearm (Subsequent Offense)	C	Unranked
9.41.171	Alien Possession of a Firearm	C	Unranked
9.41.190	Possession of Machine Gun, Short-barreled Shotgun or Short-barreled Rifle	C	III
9.41.225	Use of Machine Gun in Commission of a Felony	A	VII
9.45.020	Substitution of Child	B	Unranked
9.45.070	Mock Auction	C	Unranked

The Caseload Forecast Council is not liable for errors or omissions in the manual, for sentences that may be inappropriately calculated as a result of a practitioner's or court's reliance on the manual, or for any other written or verbal information related to adult or juvenile sentencing. The scoring sheets are intended to provide assistance in most cases but do not cover all permutations of the scoring rules. If you find any errors or omissions, we encourage you to report them to the Caseload Forecast Council.

SECTION 4 - Felony Index By RCW

Statute (RCW)	Offense	Class	Seriousness Level
9.45.124	Fraud in Measurement of Goods	B	Unranked
9.45.126	Inducing Fraud in Measurement of Goods	B	Unranked
9.45.170	Fraud in Liquor Warehouse Receipts	C	Unranked
9.45.210	Altering Sample or Certificate of Assay	C	Unranked
9.45.220	Making False Sample or Assay of Ore	C	Unranked
9.45.260	Malicious Sprinkler Contractor Work	C	Unranked
9.45.270(2)	Fraudulent Filing of Vehicle Report of Sale (Value Exceeds $250)	C	Unranked
9.45.270(3)	Fraudulent Filing of Vehicle Report of Sale (Value Exceeds $1,500)	B	Unranked
9.46.039	Greyhound Racing	B	Unranked
9.46.155	Bribing to Obtain a License From Public Officials, Employees, Agents	C	Unranked
9.46.160	Gambling Without License	B	Unranked
9.46.180	Causing Person to Violate Gambling Laws	B	Unranked
9.46.1961	Cheating 1	C	IV
9.46.215	Ownership or Interest in Gambling Device	C	Unranked
9.46.220	Professional Gambling 1	B	Unranked
9.46.221	Professional Gambling 2	C	Unranked
9.46.240	Transmission or Receiving Gambling Information by Internet	C	Unranked
9.47.090	Maintaining a Bucket Shop	C	Unranked
9.47.120	Bunco Steering	B	Unranked
9.61.160	Threats to Bomb	B	IV
9.61.230(2)	Telephone Harassment (With Prior Harassment Conviction or Threat of Death)	C	III
9.61.260(3)	Cyberstalking (With Prior Harassment Conviction or Threat of Death)	C	III
9.62.010(1)	Malicious Prosecution	C	Unranked
9.68.060	Erotic Material (Third or Subsequent Offense)	B	Unranked
9.68.140	Promoting Pornography	C	Unranked
9.68A.040	Sexual Exploitation of a Minor	B	IX
9.68A.050(1)	Dealing in Depictions of Minor Engaged in Sexually Explicit Conduct 1	B	VII
9.68A.050(2)	Dealing in Depictions of Minor Engaged in Sexually Explicit Conduct 2	C	V
9.68A.060(1)	Sending, Bringing into the State Depictions of Minor Engaged in Sexually Explicit Conduct 1	B	VII
9.68A.060(2)	Sending, Bringing into the State Depictions of Minor Engaged in Sexually Explicit Conduct 2	C	V
9.68A.070(1)	Possession of Depictions of Minor Engaged in Sexually Explicit Conduct 1	B	VI
9.68A.070(2)	Possession of Depictions of Minor Engaged in Sexually Explicit Conduct 2	C	IV

The Caseload Forecast Council is not liable for errors or omissions in the manual, for sentences that may be inappropriately calculated as a result of a practitioner's or court's reliance on the manual, or for any other written or verbal information related to adult or juvenile sentencing. The scoring sheets are intended to provide assistance in most cases but do not cover all permutations of the scoring rules. If you find any errors or omissions, we encourage you to report them to the Caseload Forecast Council.

SECTION 4 - Felony Index By RCW

Statute (RCW)	Offense	Class	Seriousness Level
9.68A.075(1)	Viewing Depictions of Minor Engaged in Sexually Explicit Conduct 1	B	IV
9.68A.075(2)	Viewing Depictions of Minor Engaged in Sexually Explicit Conduct 2	C	Unranked
9.68A.090(2)	Communication with Minor for Immoral Purposes (Subsequent Violation or Prior Sex Offense Conviction)	C	III
9.68A.100	Commercial Sexual Abuse of a Minor	B	VIII
9.68A.101	Promoting Commercial Sexual Abuse of a Minor	A	XII
9.68A.102	Promoting Travel for Commercial Sexual Abuse of a Minor	C	Unranked
9.73.230	Intercepting, Transmitting or Recording Conversations Concerning Controlled Substances	C	Unranked
9.81.020	Subversive Acts	B	Unranked
9.81.030	Member of Subversive Organization	C	Unranked
9.82.010	Treason	A	Unranked
9.82.030	Misprision of Treason	C	Unranked
9.91.142(1)	Unlawful Trafficking in Food Stamps	C	I
9.91.144	Unlawful Redemption of Food Stamps	C	I
9.91.150(1)	Tree Spiking	C	Unranked
9.91.170(5)	Intentional Infliction, Injury or Death to a Guide Dog or Service Animal	C	Unranked
9.91.175(3)	Intentionally Injures, Disables or Causes Death of an On-Duty Search and Rescue Dog	C	Unranked
9.94.010	Prison Riot	B	Unranked
9.94.030	Holding Hostages or Interfering with Officer's Duty	B	Unranked
9.94.040(1)	Possession of Weapons by Prisoners (State Facility)	B	Unranked
9.94.040(2)	Possession of Weapons by Prisoners (County or Local Facility)	C	Unranked
9.94.041(1)	Possession of Controlled Substance by Prisoner (State Facility)	C	Unranked
9.94.041(2)	Possession of Controlled Substance by Prisoner (County or Local Facility)	C	Unranked
9.94.043	Possession of Weapons in Prison by Non-prisoner	B	Unranked
9.94.045	Possession of Controlled Substance in Prison by Non-prisoner	C	Unranked
9.94.070	Persistent Prison Misbehavior	C	V
9A.28.020(3)(a)	Arson 1 – Criminal Attempt	A	VIII
9A.28.020(3)(a)	Child Molestation 1 – Criminal Attempt	A	X
9A.28.020(3)(a)	Indecent Liberties - With Forcible Compulsion – Criminal Attempt	A	X
9A.28.020(3)(a)	Murder 1 – Criminal Attempt	A	XV
9A.28.020(3)(a)	Murder 2 – Criminal Attempt	A	XIV
9A.28.020(3)(a)	Rape 1 – Criminal Attempt	A	XII
9A.28.020(3)(a)	Rape 2 – Criminal Attempt	A	XI
9A.28.020(3)(a)	Rape of a Child 1 – Criminal Attempt	A	XII

The Caseload Forecast Council is not liable for errors or omissions in the manual, for sentences that may be inappropriately calculated as a result of a practitioner's or court's reliance on the manual, or for any other written or verbal information related to adult or juvenile sentencing. The scoring sheets are intended to provide assistance in most cases but do not cover all permutations of the scoring rules. If you find any errors or omissions, we encourage you to report them to the Caseload Forecast Council.

SECTION 4 - Felony Index By RCW

Statute (RCW)	Offense	Class	Seriousness Level
9A.28.020(3)(a)	Rape of a Child 2 – Criminal Attempt	A	XI
9A.28.030(2)	Arson 1 – Criminal Solicitation	A	VIII
9A.28.030(2)	Child Molestation 1 – Criminal Solicitation	A	X
9A.28.030(2)	Indecent Liberties - With Forcible Compulsion – Criminal Solicitation	A	X
9A.28.030(2)	Murder 1 – Criminal Solicitation	A	XV
9A.28.030(2)	Murder 2 – Criminal Solicitation	A	XIV
9A.28.030(2)	Rape 1 – Criminal Solicitation	A	XII
9A.28.030(2)	Rape 2 – Criminal Solicitation	A	XI
9A.28.030(2)	Rape of a Child 1 – Criminal Solicitation	A	XII
9A.28.030(2)	Rape of a Child 2 – Criminal Solicitation	A	XI
9A.28.040(3)(a)	Murder 1 - Criminal Conspiracy	A	XV
9A.32.030	Murder 1	A	XV
9A.32.050	Murder 2	A	XIV
9A.32.055	Homicide by Abuse	A	XV
9A.32.060	Manslaughter 1	A	XI
9A.32.070	Manslaughter 2	B	VIII
9A.36.011	Assault 1	A	XII
9A.36.021(2)(a)	Assault 2	B	IV
9A.36.021(2)(b)	Assault 2 With a Finding of Sexual Motivation	A	IV
9A.36.031(1)(a-g) & (i-j)	Assault 3 – Excluding Assault 3 of a Peace Officer with a Projectile Stun Gun	C	III
9A.36.031(1)(h)	Assault 3 - Of a Peace Officer with a Projectile Stun Gun	C	IV
9A.36.045	Drive-by Shooting	B	VII
9A.36.060	Promoting a Suicide Attempt	C	Unranked
9A.36.080	Malicious Harassment	C	IV
9A.36.090	Threats Against Governor or Family	C	Unranked
9A.36.100	Custodial Assault	C	III
9A.36.120	Assault of a Child 1	A	XII
9A.36.130	Assault of a Child 2	B	IX
9A.36.140	Assault of a Child 3	C	III
9A.40.020	Kidnapping 1	A	X
9A.40.030(3)(a)	Kidnapping 2	B	V
9A.40.030(3)(b)	Kidnapping 2 With a Finding of Sexual Motivation	A	V
9A.40.040	Unlawful Imprisonment	C	III
9A.40.060	Custodial Interference 1	C	Unranked

The Caseload Forecast Council is not liable for errors or omissions in the manual, for sentences that may be inappropriately calculated as a result of a practitioner's or court's reliance on the manual, or for any other written or verbal information related to adult or juvenile sentencing. The scoring sheets are intended to provide assistance in most cases but do not cover all permutations of the scoring rules. If you find any errors or omissions, we encourage you to report them to the Caseload Forecast Council.

SECTION 4 - Felony Index By RCW

Statute (RCW)	Offense	Class	Seriousness Level
9A.40.070	Custodial Interference 2 (Subsequent Offense)	C	Unranked
9A.40.090	Luring of a Child or Developmentally Disabled Person	C	Unranked
9A.40.100(1)	Trafficking 1	A	XIV
9A.40.100(3)	Trafficking 2	A	XII
9A.40.110	Coercion of Involuntary Servitude	C	Unranked
9A.42.020	Criminal Mistreatment 1	B	X
9A.42.030	Criminal Mistreatment 2	C	V
9A.42.060	Abandonment of Dependent Persons 1	B	IX
9A.42.070	Abandonment of Dependent Persons 2	C	V
9A.42.100	Endangerment With a Controlled Substance	B	IV
9A.44.040	Rape 1	A	XII
9A.44.050	Rape 2	A	XI
9A.44.060	Rape 3	C	V
9A.44.073	Rape of a Child 1	A	XII
9A.44.076	Rape of a Child 2	A	XI
9A.44.079	Rape of a Child 3	C	VI
9A.44.083	Child Molestation 1	A	X
9A.44.086	Child Molestation 2	B	VII
9A.44.089	Child Molestation 3	C	V
9A.44.093	Sexual Misconduct with a Minor 1	C	V
9A.44.100(1)(a)	Indecent Liberties - With Forcible Compulsion	A	X
9A.44.100(1)(b-c)	Indecent Liberties - Without Forcible Compulsion	B	VII
9A.44.100(1)(d-f)	Indecent Liberties - Without Forcible Compulsion	B	Unranked
9A.44.105	Sexually Violating Human Remains	C	V
9A.44.115	Voyeurism	C	II
9A.44.132(1)(a)	Failure to Register as a Sex Offender (First Violation)	C	Unranked
9A.44.132(1)(a)	Failure to Register as a Sex Offender (Second Violation Committed on or After 6/10/2010)	C	II
9A.44.132(1)(a)	Failure to Register as a Sex Offender (Subsequent Violation Committed on or After 6/7/2006 but Before 6/10/2010)	C	II
9A.44.132(1)(b)	Failure to Register as a Sex Offender (Third or Subsequent Violation Committed on or After 6/10/2010)	B	II
9A.44.132(3)	Failure to Register as a Kidnapping Offender	C	Unranked
9A.44.160	Custodial Sexual Misconduct 1	C	V
9A.44.196	Criminal Trespass Against Children	C	Unranked

The Caseload Forecast Council is not liable for errors or omissions in the manual, for sentences that may be inappropriately calculated as a result of a practitioner's or court's reliance on the manual, or for any other written or verbal information related to adult or juvenile sentencing. The scoring sheets are intended to provide assistance in most cases but do not cover all permutations of the scoring rules. If you find any errors or omissions, we encourage you to report them to the Caseload Forecast Council.

SECTION 4 - Felony Index By RCW

Statute (RCW)	Offense	Class	Seriousness Level
9A.46.020(2)(b)	Harassment (Subsequent Conviction or Threat of Death)	C	III
9A.46.110	Stalking	B	V
9A.46.120	Criminal Gang Intimidation	C	III
9A.48.020	Arson 1	A	VIII
9A.48.030	Arson 2	B	IV
9A.48.040	Reckless Burning 1	C	I
9A.48.070	Malicious Mischief 1	B	II
9A.48.080	Malicious Mischief 2	C	I
9A.48.120	Civil Disorder Training	B	VII
9A.49.020	Unlawful Discharge of a Laser 1	C	Unranked
9A.52.020	Burglary 1	A	VII
9A.52.025	Residential Burglary	B	IV
9A.52.030	Burglary 2	B	III
9A.52.095	Vehicle Prowl 1	C	I
9A.52.100(3)	Vehicle Prowling 2 (Third or Subsequent Offense)	C	IV
9A.56.030	Theft 1 (Excluding Firearm and Motor Vehicle)	B	II
9A.56.040	Theft 2 (Excluding Firearm and Motor Vehicle)	C	I
9A.56.060(4)	Unlawful Issuance of Checks or Drafts (Value Greater Than $750)	C	I
9A.56.065	Theft of a Motor Vehicle	B	II
9A.56.068	Possession of a Stolen Vehicle	B	II
9A.56.070	Taking Motor Vehicle Without Permission 1	B	V
9A.56.075	Taking Motor Vehicle Without Permission 2	C	I
9A.56.080	Theft of Livestock 1	B	IV
9A.56.083	Theft of Livestock 2	C	III
9A.56.096(5)(a)	Theft of Rental, Leased, Lease-purchased or Loaned Property (Valued at $5,000 or More)	B	II
9A.56.096(5)(b)	Theft of Rental, Leased, Lease-purchased or Loaned Property (Valued at $750 or More but Less Than $5,000)	C	I
9A.56.120	Extortion 1	B	V
9A.56.130	Extortion 2	C	III
9A.56.150	Possession of Stolen Property 1 (Other Than Firearm or Motor Vehicle)	B	II
9A.56.160	Possession of Stolen Property 2 (Other Than Firearm or Motor Vehicle)	C	I
9A.56.200	Robbery 1	A	IX
9A.56.210	Robbery 2	B	IV
9A.56.230	Unlawful Sale of Subscription Television Services	C	Unranked

The Caseload Forecast Council is not liable for errors or omissions in the manual, for sentences that may be inappropriately calculated as a result of a practitioner's or court's reliance on the manual, or for any other written or verbal information related to adult or juvenile sentencing. The scoring sheets are intended to provide assistance in most cases but do not cover all permutations of the scoring rules. If you find any errors or omissions, we encourage you to report them to the Caseload Forecast Council.

SECTION 4 - Felony Index By RCW

Statute (RCW)	Offense	Class	Seriousness Level
9A.56.262	Theft of Telecommunication Service	C	Unranked
9A.56.264	Unlawful Manufacture of a Telecommunication Device	C	Unranked
9A.56.266	Unlawful Sale of a Telecommunication Device	C	Unranked
9A.56.290(4)(a)	Unlawful Factoring of a Credit or Payment Card Transaction	C	II
9A.56.290(4)(b)	Unlawful Factoring of a Credit or Payment Card Transaction (Subsequent Violation)	B	IV
9A.56.300	Theft of a Firearm	B	VI
9A.56.310	Possession of a Stolen Firearm	B	V
9A.56.320(1)	Unlawful Production of Payment Instruments	C	I
9A.56.320(2)	Unlawful Possession of Payment Instruments	C	I
9A.56.320(3)	Unlawful Possession of a Personal Identification Device	C	I
9A.56.320(4)	Unlawful Possession of Fictitious Identification	C	I
9A.56.320(5)	Unlawful Possession of Instruments of Financial Fraud	C	I
9A.56.340(2)	Theft with Intent to Resell 1	B	III
9A.56.340(3)	Theft with Intent to Resell 2	C	II
9A.56.350(2)	Organized Retail Theft 1	B	III
9A.56.350(3)	Organized Retail Theft 2	C	II
9A.56.360(2)	Retail Theft with Special Circumstances 1	B	III
9A.56.360(3)	Retail Theft with Special Circumstances 2	C	II
9A.56.360(4)	Retail Theft with Special Circumstances 3	C	Unranked
9A.56.370	Mail Theft	C	Unranked
9A.56.380	Possession of Stolen Mail	C	Unranked
9A.58.020	Possessing or Capturing Personal Identification Document	C	Unranked
9A.60.020	Forgery	C	I
9A.60.030	Obtaining Signature by Deception or Duress	C	Unranked
9A.60.040	Criminal Impersonation 1	C	Unranked
9A.60.060	Fraudulent Creation or Revocation of Mental Health Advance Directive	C	I
9A.60.070	Issuing a False Academic Credential	C	Unranked
9A.61.030	Defrauding a Public Utility 1	B	Unranked
9A.61.040	Defrauding a Public Utility 2	C	Unranked
9A.64.010	Bigamy	C	Unranked
9A.64.020(1)	Incest 1	B	VI
9A.64.020(2)	Incest 2	C	V
9A.64.030(3)(a)	Child Selling	C	Unranked
9A.64.030(3)(b)	Child Buying	C	Unranked

The Caseload Forecast Council is not liable for errors or omissions in the manual, for sentences that may be inappropriately calculated as a result of a practitioner's or court's reliance on the manual, or for any other written or verbal information related to adult or juvenile sentencing. The scoring sheets are intended to provide assistance in most cases but do not cover all permutations of the scoring rules. If you find any errors or omissions, we encourage you to report them to the Caseload Forecast Council.

SECTION 4 - Felony Index By RCW

Statute (RCW)	Offense	Class	Seriousness Level
9A.68.010	Bribery	B	VI
9A.68.020	Requesting Unlawful Compensation	C	Unranked
9A.68.030	Receiving or Granting Unlawful Compensation	C	Unranked
9A.68.040	Trading in Public Office	C	Unranked
9A.68.050	Trading in Special Influence	C	Unranked
9A.68.060	Commercial Bribery	B	IV
9A.72.020	Perjury 1	B	V
9A.72.030	Perjury 2	C	III
9A.72.090	Bribing a Witness	B	IV
9A.72.100	Bribe Received by Witness	B	IV
9A.72.110	Intimidating a Witness	B	VI
9A.72.120	Tampering with a Witness	C	III
9A.72.130	Intimidating a Juror	B	VI
9A.72.160	Intimidating a Judge	B	VI
9A.76.023(2)(a)	Disarming a Law Enforcement or Corrections Officer	C	Unranked
9A.76.023(2)(b)	Disarming a Law Enforcement or Corrections Officer and Firearm is Discharged	B	Unranked
9A.76.070(2)(a)	Rendering Criminal Assistance 1	B	V
9A.76.110	Escape 1	B	IV
9A.76.115	Sexually Violent Predator Escape	A	X
9A.76.120	Escape 2	C	III
9A.76.130(3)(b)	Escape 3 (Third or Subsequent Offense)	C	Unranked
9A.76.140	Introducing Contraband 1	B	VII
9A.76.150	Introducing Contraband 2	C	III
9A.76.170(3)(a)	Bail Jumping with Murder 1	A	VI
9A.76.170(3)(b)	Bail Jumping with Class A Felony	B	V
9A.76.170(3)(c)	Bail Jumping with Class B or C Felony	C	III
9A.76.177	Amber Alert – Making False Statements to a Public Servant	C	Unranked
9A.76.180	Intimidating a Public Servant	B	III
9A.76.200	Harming a Police Dog/Horse or an Accelerate Detection Dog	C	Unranked
9A.82.020	Extortionate Extension of Credit	B	V
9A.82.030	Advancing Money or Property for Extortionate Extension of Credit	B	V
9A.82.040	Extortionate Means to Collect Extensions of Credit	B	V
9A.82.045	Collection of Unlawful Debt	C	Unranked
9A.82.050	Trafficking in Stolen Property 1	B	IV

The Caseload Forecast Council is not liable for errors or omissions in the manual, for sentences that may be inappropriately calculated as a result of a practitioner's or court's reliance on the manual, or for any other written or verbal information related to adult or juvenile sentencing. The scoring sheets are intended to provide assistance in most cases but do not cover all permutations of the scoring rules. If you find any errors or omissions, we encourage you to report them to the Caseload Forecast Council.

SECTION 4 - Felony Index By RCW

Statute (RCW)	Offense	Class	Seriousness Level
9A.82.055	Trafficking in Stolen Property 2	C	III
9A.82.060(1)(a)	Leading Organized Crime – Organizing Criminal Profiteering	A	X
9A.82.060(1)(b)	Leading Organized Crime - Inciting Criminal Profiteering	B	IX
9A.82.070	Influencing Outcome of Sporting Event	C	IV
9A.82.080(1-2)	Use of Proceeds of Criminal Profiteering	B	IV
9A.82.080(3)	Attempt or Conspiracy to Violate RCW 9A.82.080(1) or (2)	C	Unranked
9A.82.160	Criminal Profiteering Lien After Service of Notice	C	Unranked
9A.83.020	Money Laundering	B	Unranked
9A.84.010(2)(b)	Criminal Mischief	C	Unranked
9A.86.010	Disclosing Intimate Images	C	Unranked
9A.88.010(2)(c)	Indecent Exposure to a Person Under Age 14 (Subsequent Conviction or Has Prior Sex Offense Conviction)	C	IV
9A.88.070	Promoting Prostitution 1	B	VIII
9A.88.080	Promoting Prostitution 2	C	III
9A.88.085	Promoting Travel for Prostitution	C	Unranked
9A.90.040	Computer Trespass 1	C	II
9A.90.060	Electronic Data Service Interference	C	II
9A.90.080	Electronic Data Tampering 1	C	II
9A.90.100	Electronic Data Theft	C	II
10.66.090	Willfully Disobeys an Off-limits Order (Subsequent Violation or Enters Protected Against Drug Trafficking Area)	C	Unranked
10.95.020	Aggravated Murder 1	A	XVI
16.08.100(2)	Dangerous Dog Attack (Subsequent Offense)	C	Unranked
16.08.100(3)	Dangerous Dog Attack Resulting in Severe Injury or Death	C	Unranked
16.08.100(4)	Entering Dog in a Dog Fight	C	Unranked
16.52.117	Animal Fighting	C	Unranked
16.52.205(2)	Animal Cruelty 1	C	Unranked
16.52.205(3)	Animal Cruelty 1 - Sexual Contact or Conduct	C	III
16.52.320	Kill or Cause Substantial Harm With Malice to Livestock	C	Unranked
18.04.370(1)(b)	Unlawful Use of a Professional Title	C	Unranked
18.04.370(1)(c)	Unlawful Use of CPA Title After Suspension	C	Unranked
18.39.350	Embalmers/Funeral Directors Violation	C	Unranked
18.64.046(7)	Unlawful Selling of Ephedrine, Pseudoephedrine or Phenylpropanolamine by a Wholesaler	C	Unranked
18.130.190(7)(b)	Unlicensed Practice of a Profession or Business (Subsequent Violation)	C	II
19.25.020(2)(a)	Reproduction of Sound Recording Without Consent of Owner - Recording	B	Unranked

The Caseload Forecast Council is not liable for errors or omissions in the manual, for sentences that may be inappropriately calculated as a result of a practitioner's or court's reliance on the manual, or for any other written or verbal information related to adult or juvenile sentencing. The scoring sheets are intended to provide assistance in most cases but do not cover all permutations of the scoring rules. If you find any errors or omissions, we encourage you to report them to the Caseload Forecast Council.

SECTION 4 - Felony Index By RCW

Statute (RCW)	Offense	Class	Seriousness Level
	Fixed Before 2/15/1972 (At Least 1,000 Recordings or Subsequent Conviction)		
19.25.020(2)(b)	Reproduction of Sound Recording Without Consent of Owner - Recording Fixed Before 2/15/1972 (More Than 100 but Less Than 1,000 Recordings)	C	Unranked
19.25.030(2)(a)	Use of Recording of Live Performance Without Consent of Owner (At Least 1,000 Recordings or at Least 100 Unauthorized Audiovisual Recordings or Subsequent Offense)	B	Unranked
19.25.030(2)(b)	Use of Recording of Live Performance Without Consent of Owner (At Least 100 but Less Than 1,000 Recordings or More than 10 but Less Than 100 Unauthorized Audiovisual Recording or Subsequent Offense)	C	Unranked
19.25.040(2)(a)	Failure to Disclose Origin of Certain Recordings (At Least 100 Recordings or Subsequent Conviction)	B	Unranked
19.25.040(2)(b)	Failure to Disclose Origin of Certain Recordings (More than 10 but Less Than 100 Recordings)	C	Unranked
19.48.110(1)(b)	Defrauding an Innkeeper (Value of $75.00 or More)	B	Unranked
19.60.067(2)	Second-hand Precious Metal Dealer Violations (Subsequent Violation)	C	Unranked
19.100.210	Franchise Investment Protection Violation	B	Unranked
19.110.075(2)	Disclosures Knowingly Not Provided at Sale of Business Opportunity (Violation of RCW 19.110.070)	B	Unranked
19.110.075(2)	Registration Knowingly Not Obtained Prior to Sale of Business Opportunity (Violation of RCW 19.110.050)	B	Unranked
19.110.120	Defraud or Provide Misleading or Untrue Documents Related to a Business Opportunity Sale	B	Unranked
19.116.080(1)	Unlawful Subleasing of Motor Vehicle	C	Unranked
19.116.080(2)	Unlawful Transfer of Ownership of Motor Vehicle	C	Unranked
19.142.080	Failure to Use a Trust Account or Furnish Bond for Health Studio	C	Unranked
19.144.080	Mortgage Fraud	B	III
19.144.100(1)	Use or Investment of Proceeds from Mortgage Fraud Activities	B	Unranked
19.144.100(2)	Control of Real Property Resulting from Mortgage Fraud Activities	B	Unranked
19.146.050	Failure to Use a Trust Account	C	Unranked
19.158.160	Commercial Telephone Solicitor Deception (Value of $250 or More)	C	Unranked
19.210.040	Unused Property, Merchants –Prohibited Sales (Third or Subsequent Offense Within 5 Years)	C	Unranked
19.225.110	Uniform Athlete Agent Act Violation	C	Unranked
19.230.300	False Statement, Misrepresentation or False Certification of Uniform Money services Record	C	Unranked
19.290.100	Scrap Processing, Recycling, or Supplying Without a License (Second or Subsequent Offense)	C	II
19.300.020	Electronic Communication Devices – Illegal Scanning	C	Unranked
19.310.120	Unlawfully Engaging in Business as an Exchange Facilitator (RCW	B	Unranked

The Caseload Forecast Council is not liable for errors or omissions in the manual, for sentences that may be inappropriately calculated as a result of a practitioner's or court's reliance on the manual, or for any other written or verbal information related to adult or juvenile sentencing. The scoring sheets are intended to provide assistance in most cases but do not cover all permutations of the scoring rules. If you find any errors or omissions, we encourage you to report them to the Caseload Forecast Council.

SECTION 4 - Felony Index By RCW

Statute (RCW)	Offense	Class	Seriousness Level
	19.310.100(1)-(9))		
20.01.460(2)	Acting as Commission Merchant, Dealer, Cash Buyer Without License	C	Unranked
21.20.400	Securities Act Violation	B	III
21.30.140	Commodity Transaction Violation	B	Unranked
22.09.310	Dealing in Unauthorized Warehouse Receipts for Agricultural Commodities	C	Unranked
26.04.210	Providing False Statements in Affidavits for Marriage	C	Unranked
26.20.030	Family Abandonment	C	Unranked
26.50.110	Domestic Violence Court Order Violation	C	V
26.50.110(5)	Violation of a Foreign Protection Order (Third or Subsequent Violation)	C	Unranked
27.44.040(1)	Destroying, Removing or Defacing Indian Graves	C	Unranked
27.44.040(2)	Selling Artifacts or Human Remains from Indian Graves	C	Unranked
27.53.060	Disturbing Archaeological Resources or Site	C	Unranked
29A.08.740	Misuse of Registered Voter Data	C	Unranked
29A.84.030	Election or Mail Ballot Violation	C	Unranked
29A.84.130	Voter Violation of Registration Law	C	Unranked
29A.84.140	Unqualified Voting Registration	C	Unranked
29A.84.150	Misuse or Alteration of Registration Database	C	Unranked
29A.84.230(1)	Violation by Signer – Initiative or Referendum with False Name	C	Unranked
29A.84.240(1)	Violations By Signers – Recall Petition With False Name	B	Unranked
29A.84.270	Duplication of Name – Conspiracy to Mislead	B	Unranked
29A.84.311	Provides False Information or Conceals or Destroys Candidacy Declaration or Nominating Petition	C	Unranked
29A.84.320	Duplication of Names on Declaration of Candidacy	B	Unranked
29A.84.545	Unauthorized Removal of Paper Record from Electronic Voting Device	C	Unranked
29A.84.550	Tampering with Election Materials	C	Unranked
29A.84.560	Tampering with Voting Machine	C	Unranked
29A.84.650(1)	Voting Repeater – More Than One Vote at Any Election	C	Unranked
29A.84.655	Election Officer Permits Repeat Vote	C	Unranked
29A.84.660	Unqualified Person Voting	C	Unranked
29A.84.680(1)	Absentee Voting Violation	C	Unranked
29A.84.711	Fraud in Certification of Nomination or Ballot	C	Unranked
29A.84.720	Election Officers – Violation	C	Unranked
30A.04.240	Commingling of Funds or Securities	B	Unranked
30A.12.090	Bank or Trust Company - False Entry, Statements, etc.	B	Unranked
30A.12.100	Bank or Trust Company - Destroy or Secrete Records	B	Unranked

The Caseload Forecast Council is not liable for errors or omissions in the manual, for sentences that may be inappropriately calculated as a result of a practitioner's or court's reliance on the manual, or for any other written or verbal information related to adult or juvenile sentencing. The scoring sheets are intended to provide assistance in most cases but do not cover all permutations of the scoring rules. If you find any errors or omissions, we encourage you to report them to the Caseload Forecast Council.

SECTION 4 - Felony Index By RCW

Statute (RCW)	Offense	Class	Seriousness Level
30A.12.120	Loan to Officer or Employee from Trust Fund	B	Unranked
30A.42.290(2)	Alien Bank or Bureau – False Entry, Statements, etc.	B	Unranked
30A.42.290(3)	Alien Bank or Bureau – Destroy or Secrete Records	B	Unranked
30A.44.110	Bank or Trust Company - Transfer of Assets Prior to Insolvency	B	Unranked
30A.44.120	Bank or Trust Company - Receiving Deposits When Insolvent	B	Unranked
30B.12.050	State Trust Company – False Entry, Conceal or Destroy Records	B	Unranked
31.12.724(2)	Credit Union - Transfer of Credit Union Assets Prior to Insolvency	B	Unranked
31.12.724(3)	Credit Union - Fraudulent Receipt of Credit Union Deposit	B	Unranked
32.04.100	Mutual Savings Bank - Falsify Savings Book, Document or Statement	B	Unranked
32.04.110	Mutual Savings Bank - Conceal or Destroy Evidence	B	Unranked
32.24.080	Mutual Savings Bank - Transfer Bank Assets After Insolvency	B	Unranked
33.36.030	Savings and Loan Association - Preference in Case of Insolvency	C	Unranked
33.36.040	Savings and Loan Association - Making False Statement of Assets or Liabilities	C	Unranked
33.36.060	Savings and Loan Association - Suppressing, Secreting or Destroying Evidence or Records	C	Unranked
35.36.040	Designation of Bonds – Violation (First Class Cities)	B	Unranked
35A.36.040	Designation of Bonds – Violation (Code Cities)	B	Unranked
36.18.170	Failure to Pay Over Fees to County Treasurer	C	Unranked
38.42.050	False Affidavit Under Service Member Civil Relief Act	C	Unranked
39.44.101	Defraud a Facsimile Signature on Bonds and Coupons	B	Unranked
39.62.040	Unauthorized Use of Public Official Facsimile Signature or Seal	B	Unranked
40.16.010	Injury to a Public Record	C	Unranked
40.16.020	Injury to and Misappropriation of Public Record by Officer	B	Unranked
40.16.030	Offering False Instrument for Filing or Record	C	Unranked
41.26.062	False Statements or Records to Defraud Law Enforcement Officers and Firefighters Retirement System	B	Unranked
41.32.055(1)	False Statements or Records to Defraud Teachers Retirement System	B	Unranked
42.17A.750	False Documents Registered with Public Disclosure Commission	C	Unranked
42.20.070	Misappropriating and Falsifying Accounts by Public Officer	B	Unranked
42.20.090	Misappropriating and Falsifying Accounts by Treasurer	C	Unranked
42.24.100	False Claim from Municipal Corporation (Charged as Perjury 2)	C	Unranked
43.06.230	Damage Property or Cause Personal Injury after State of Emergency Proclaimed	B	Unranked
43.08.140	Embezzlement by State Treasurer	B	Unranked
43.43.856	Divulging Confidential Investigative Information Pertaining to Organized	B	Unranked

The Caseload Forecast Council is not liable for errors or omissions in the manual, for sentences that may be inappropriately calculated as a result of a practitioner's or court's reliance on the manual, or for any other written or verbal information related to adult or juvenile sentencing. The scoring sheets are intended to provide assistance in most cases but do not cover all permutations of the scoring rules. If you find any errors or omissions, we encourage you to report them to the Caseload Forecast Council.

SECTION 4 - Felony Index By RCW

Statute (RCW)	Offense Crime	Class	Seriousness Level
46.12.560	Removal of Sticker on Vehicle Stating Previously Destroyed or Title 1 Loss	C	Unranked
46.12.750(1)	False Statements, Illegal Transfers, Alterations or Forgeries of Vehicle Title	B	Unranked
46.12.750(3)	Unlawful Sale of Vehicle Certificate of Ownership	C	Unranked
46.20.0921(2)	Sell or Deliver a Stolen Driver's License or Identicard	C	Unranked
46.20.0921(3)(a)	Manufacture, Sell or Deliver Forged Driver's License or Identicard	C	Unranked
46.37.650(1)(b)	Manufacture or Import Counterfeit, Nonfunctional, Damaged, or Previously Deployed Air Bag (Causing Bodily Injury or Death)	C	VII
46.37.650(1)(c)	Manufacture or Import Counterfeit, Nonfunctional, Damaged, or Previously Deployed Air Bag	C	V
46.37.650(2)(b)	Sale, Install, [or] Reinstall Counterfeit, Nonfunctional, Damaged, or Previously Deployed Airbag	C	VII
46.37.650(2)(c)	Sale, Install, [or] Reinstall Counterfeit, Nonfunctional, Damaged, or Previously Deployed Airbag	C	V
46.37.660(1)(b)	Air Bag Replacement Requirements (Causing Bodily Injury or Death)	C	VII
46.37.660(1)(c)	Air Bag Replacement Requirements	C	V
46.37.660(2)(b)	Air Bag Diagnostic Systems (Causing Bodily Injury or Death)	C	VII
46.37.660(2)(c)	Air Bag Diagnostic Systems	C	V
46.37.673	Use of a Signal Preemption Device Resulting in Property Damage or Less Substantial Bodily Harm	C	Unranked
46.37.674	Negligently Causing Substantial Bodily Harm By Use of a Signal Preemption Device	B	III
46.37.675	Negligently Causing Death By Use of a Signal Preemption Device	B	VII
46.52.020(4)(a)	Hit and Run - Death	B	IX
46.52.020(4)(b)	Hit and Run - Injury	C	IV
46.52.130(5)(b)	Abstracts of Driving Records – Intentional Misuse	C	Unranked
46.61.024	Attempting to Elude Pursuing Police Vehicle	C	I
46.61.502(6)	Driving While Under the Influence of Intoxicating Liquor or any Drug	B	V
46.61.504(6)	Physical Control of a Vehicle While Under the Influence of Intoxicating Liquor or any Drug	C	V
46.61.520(1)(a)	Vehicular Homicide – While Under the Influence of Intoxicating Liquor or any Drug	A	XI
46.61.520(1)(b)	Vehicular Homicide – In a Reckless Manner	A	XI
46.61.520(1)(c)	Vehicular Homicide - Disregard for the Safety of Others	A	VII
46.61.522(1)(a-b)	Vehicular Assault – In a Reckless Manner or While Under the Influence of Intoxicating Liquor or any Drug	B	IV
46.61.522(1)(c)	Vehicular Assault - Disregard for the Safety of Others	B	III
46.70.021	Licensing Violation for Car Dealers or Manufacturers (Subsequent	C	Unranked

The Caseload Forecast Council is not liable for errors or omissions in the manual, for sentences that may be inappropriately calculated as a result of a practitioner's or court's reliance on the manual, or for any other written or verbal information related to adult or juvenile sentencing. The scoring sheets are intended to provide assistance in most cases but do not cover all permutations of the scoring rules. If you find any errors or omissions, we encourage you to report them to the Caseload Forecast Council.

SECTION 4 - Felony Index By RCW

Statute (RCW)	Offense	Class	Seriousness Level
	Violation)		
46.70.180(5)	Odometer Offense	C	Unranked
46.80.020(b)	Engage in Business of Wrecking Vehicles Without a License (Subsequent Offense)	C	Unranked
46.87.260	Cab Card Forgery (Effective Until 7/1/2016)	B	Unranked
46.87.260	Credential Forgery (Effective 7/1/2016)	B	Unranked
48.06.030	Insurance Solicitation Permit Violation	B	Unranked
48.06.190	Exhibiting False Accounts of Insurer	B	Unranked
48.15.023(3)	Unlawful Transaction of Insurance Business	B	IV
48.17.063(2)	Unlicensed Practice as an Insurance Professional	B	IV
48.17.063(4)	Transaction of Insurance Business Beyond the Scope of Licensure (Violation of RCW 48.17.060)	B	I
48.30.220	Willful Destruction, Injury, Secretion of Insured Property	C	Unranked
48.30.230	False Insurance Claims (Value in Excess of $1,500)	C	Unranked
48.30A.015	Trafficking in Insurance Claims (Subsequent Violation)	C	II
48.44.016(3)	Unlawful Transaction of Health Coverage as Health Care Service Contractor	B	IV
48.46.033(3)	Unlawful Transaction of Health Coverage as Health Maintenance Organization	B	IV
48.80.030	Health Care False Claims	C	II
48.102.160(3)	Fraudulent Life Insurance Settlement	B	Unranked
48.102.160(4)	Unlicensed Life Insurance Provider	B	Unranked
48.102.160(5)	Unlicensed Settlement Broker	B	Unranked
48.160.080	Sells Guaranteed Asset Protection Waivers Without Registration	B	Unranked
49.12.410(2)	Child Labor Law Violation – Death/Disability	C	Unranked
51.48.020(1)	Evading Industrial Insurance Premiums	C	Unranked
51.48.020(2)	False Information in Industrial Insurance Claim (Charged as Theft)	*	*
51.48.103(2)	Engaging in Business After Certificate of Coverage Revocation	C	Unranked
61.34.030	Equity Skimming	B	II
64.36.020(5)(b)	Timeshare Registration Requirement Violation	C	Unranked
64.36.210	Timeshare Fraud	C	Unranked
65.12.730	Unlawful Stealing or Carrying Away Certification of Land Registration (Charged as Theft)	*	*
65.12.740	False Swearing - Registration of Land Title (Charged as Perjury)	*	*
65.12.750	Fraudulent Procurement or False Entry on Land Title Registration	C	Unranked
65.12.760	Forgery of Registrar's Signature or Seal	B	Unranked
66.44.120(2)(b)	Unlawful Use of Liquor Board Seal (Third or Subsequent Offense)	C	Unranked

The Caseload Forecast Council is not liable for errors or omissions in the manual, for sentences that may be inappropriately calculated as a result of a practitioner's or court's reliance on the manual, or for any other written or verbal information related to adult or juvenile sentencing. The scoring sheets are intended to provide assistance in most cases but do not cover all permutations of the scoring rules. If you find any errors or omissions, we encourage you to report them to the Caseload Forecast Council.

SECTION 4 - Felony Index By RCW

Statute (RCW)	Offense	Class	Seriousness Level
67.08.015	Promoting Illegal Boxing, Martial Arts and Wrestling	C	Unranked
67.24.010	Fraud in Sporting Contest	B	Unranked
67.70.130	Lottery Fraud	B	Unranked
67.70.140	Unlicensed Lottery Activity	B	Unranked
67.70.160	State Lottery Violations Except Lottery Fraud and Unlicensed Lottery Activity	C	Unranked
68.05.330	Unfair Practice of Funeral or Cemetery Board	C	Unranked
68.44.060	Unauthorized Loans to Cemetery Authority	C	Unranked
68.50.140(1)	Removing Human Remains	C	Unranked
68.50.140(2)	Purchasing or Receiving Human Remains	C	Unranked
68.50.140(3)	Opening Graves With Intent to Sell or Remove Personal Effects or Human Remains	C	Unranked
68.50.140(4)	Removal, Disinterment or Mutilation of Human Remains	C	Unranked
68.60.040(1)	Destruction of Tomb, Plot, Marker, or Cemetery Property	C	Unranked
68.60.040(3)	Transports Removed Human Remains, Opens a Grave or Removes Personal Effects from Grave	C	Unranked
68.60.050	Removes, Defaces or Destroys any Historic Grave	C	Unranked
68.64.150	Anatomical Gifts - Illegal Purchase or Sale	C	Unranked
68.64.160	Anatomical Gift - Illegal Financial Gain	C	Unranked
69.04.938(3)	Unlawful Misbranding of Food Fish or Shellfish 1	C	III
69.25.155(1)	Interference with Person Performing Official Duties	C	Unranked
69.25.155(2)	Interference with Person Performing Official Duties With a Deadly Weapon	B	Unranked
69.30.085	Participation in Shellfish Operation or Activities While License is Denied, Revoked or Suspended	C	Unranked
69.40.020	Poison in Milk or Food Product	C	Unranked
69.40.030	Placing Poison or Other Harmful Object or Substance in Food, Drinks, Medicine or Water	B	Unranked
69.41.020	Forged Prescription - Legend Drug	B	DG-I
69.41.030(2)(a)	Sale, Delivery or Possession With Intent to Sell Legend Drug Without Prescription	B	Unranked
69.41.040	Illegal Issuance of Legend Drug Prescription	B	Unranked
69.41.350	Possession of Steroids in Excess of 200 tablets or (8) 2cc Bottles Without a Valid Prescription	C	Unranked
69.43.070(1)	Unlawful Delivery of Precursor Drug with Intent to Use	B	Unranked
69.43.070(2)	Unlawful Receipt of Precursor Drug with Intent to Use	B	Unranked
69.43.080	False Statement in Report of Precursor Drugs	C	Unranked
69.50.401(2)(c-e)	Manufacture, Deliver or Possess with Intent to Deliver - Narcotics from	C	DG-II

The Caseload Forecast Council is not liable for errors or omissions in the manual, for sentences that may be inappropriately calculated as a result of a practitioner's or court's reliance on the manual, or for any other written or verbal information related to adult or juvenile sentencing. The scoring sheets are intended to provide assistance in most cases but do not cover all permutations of the scoring rules. If you find any errors or omissions, we encourage you to report them to the Caseload Forecast Council.

SECTION 4 - Felony Index By RCW

Statute (RCW)	Offense	Class	Seriousness Level
	Schedule III, IV, or V or Nonnarcotics from Schedule I-V (except Marijuana, Amphetamine, Methamphetamine, or Flunitrazepam)		
69.50.401(2)(a)	Manufacture, Deliver or Possess with Intent to Deliver - Narcotics from Schedule I or II or Flunitrazepam from Schedule IV	B	DG-II
69.50.401(2)(b)	Deliver or Possess with Intent to Deliver - Methamphetamine	B	DG-II
69.50.401(2)(b)	Manufacture Methamphetamine	B	DG-III
69.50.401(2)(b)	Manufacture, Deliver or Possess with Intent to Deliver - Amphetamine	B	DG-II
69.50.401(2)(c)	Manufacture, Deliver or Possess with Intent to Deliver - Marijuana	C	DG-I
69.50.4011(2)(a-b)	Create, Deliver or Possess a Counterfeit Controlled Substance – Schedule I or II Narcotic or Flunitrazepam or Methamphetamine	B	DG-II
69.50.4011(2)(c-e)	Create, Deliver or Possess a Counterfeit Controlled Substance – Schedule I-II Nonnarcotic, Schedule III-V Except Flunitrazepam or Methamphetamine	C	DG-II
69.50.4012	Delivery of a Material in Lieu of a Controlled Substance	C	DG-II
69.50.4013	Possession of Controlled Substance That is a Narcotic from Schedule III, IV or V or Nonnarcotic from Schedule I-V	C	DG-I
69.50.4013	Possession of Controlled Substance That is Either Heroin or Narcotics from Schedule I or II	C	DG-I
69.50.4015	Involving a Minor in Drug Dealing	C	DG-III
69.50.402	Dispensing Violation (VUCSA)	C	Unranked
69.50.402	Maintaining a Dwelling or Place for Controlled Substances	C	DG-II
69.50.403	Forged Prescription for a Controlled Substance	C	DG-I
69.50.406(1)	Over 18 and Deliver Heroin, Methamphetamine, a Narcotic from Schedule I or II, or Flunitrazepam from Schedule IV to Someone Under 18	A	DG-III
69.50.406(2)	Over 18 and Deliver Narcotic from Schedule III, IV or V, or a Nonnarcotic, Except Flunitrazepam or Methamphetamine, from Schedule I-V to Someone Under 18 and 3 Years Junior	B	DG-III
69.50.410	Selling for Profit (Controlled or Counterfeit) any Controlled Substance in Schedule I	C	DG-III
69.50.415	Controlled Substance Homicide	B	DG-III
69.50.416	Controlled Substance Label Violation	C	Unranked
69.50.440	Possession of Ephedrine, Pseudoephedrine or Anhydrous Ammonia with Intent to Manufacture Methamphetamine	B	DG-III
69.50.465	Conducting or Maintaining a Marijuana Club	C	Unranked
69.51A.060	Medical Marijuana Fraudulent Records (Effective Until 7/1/2016)	C	Unranked
69.51A.240	Medical Marijuana – Unlawful Actions	C	Unranked
69.52.030(1)	Manufacture, Distribute or Possess with Intent to Distribute an Imitation Controlled Substance	C	DG-II
69.52.030(2)	Delivery of Imitation Controlled Substance by Person 18 or Over to Person	B	DG-III

The Caseload Forecast Council is not liable for errors or omissions in the manual, for sentences that may be inappropriately calculated as a result of a practitioner's or court's reliance on the manual, or for any other written or verbal information related to adult or juvenile sentencing. The scoring sheets are intended to provide assistance in most cases but do not cover all permutations of the scoring rules. If you find any errors or omissions, we encourage you to report them to the Caseload Forecast Council.

SECTION 4 - Felony Index By RCW

Statute (RCW)	Offense	Class	Seriousness Level
	Under 18		
69.52.030(3)	Advertising Imitation Controlled Substances	C	Unranked
69.53.010	Unlawful Use of Building for Drug Purposes	C	DG-I
69.53.020	Unlawful Fortification of Building for Drug Purposes	C	Unranked
69.53.030	Unlawful Use of Fortified Building	C	Unranked
69.55.010	Theft of Ammonia	C	VIII
69.55.020	Unlawful Storage of Ammonia	C	VI
70.74.022(1)	Manufacture, Purchase, Sell or Store Explosive Device Without License	C	Unranked
70.74.180	Explosive Devices Prohibited	A	IX
70.74.270(1)	Malicious Placement of an Explosive 1	A	XIII
70.74.270(2)	Malicious Placement of an Explosive 2	B	IX
70.74.270(3)	Malicious Placement of an Explosive 3	B	VII
70.74.272(1)(a)	Malicious Placement of an Imitation Device 1	B	XII
70.74.272(1)(b)	Malicious Placement of an Imitation Device 2	C	VI
70.74.275	Intimidation or Harassment With an Explosive	C	Unranked
70.74.280(1)	Malicious Explosion of a Substance 1	A	XV
70.74.280(2)	Malicious Explosion of a Substance 2	A	XIII
70.74.280(3)	Malicious Explosion of a Substance 3	B	X
70.94.430(3)	Releasing Into Ambient Air Hazardous Air Pollutant	C	Unranked
70.105.085(1)(a)	Transport, Disposal or Export of Hazardous Waste That Places Another Person in Danger of Injury or Death	B	Unranked
70.105.085(1)(b)	Transport, Disposal or Export of Hazardous Waste That Places Another Person's Property in Danger of Harm	C	Unranked
70.155.140	Shipping or Transporting Tobacco Products Ordered Through Mail or Internet	C	Unranked
70.245.200(1)	Forging Request for Medication	A	Unranked
70.245.200(2)	Coerce Patient to Request Life-ending Medication	A	Unranked
70.345.030	Retail Sales, Distribution or Delivery Sales of Vapor Products Without a License	C	Unranked
70.345.090	Engaging in Delivery Sales of Vapor Products Without a License, or Without Proper Documentation	C	Unranked
72.09.310	Escape from Community Custody	C	II
72.23.170	Assist Escape of Mental Patient	C	Unranked
72.23.300	Bringing Narcotics, Liquor, or Weapons into State Institution or Grounds	B	Unranked
74.08.055(2)	False Verification for Welfare	B	I
74.08.100	False Age and Residency Public Assistance Verification	B	Unranked
74.09.230	False Statement for Medical Assistance	C	Unranked

The Caseload Forecast Council is not liable for errors or omissions in the manual, for sentences that may be inappropriately calculated as a result of a practitioner's or court's reliance on the manual, or for any other written or verbal information related to adult or juvenile sentencing. The scoring sheets are intended to provide assistance in most cases but do not cover all permutations of the scoring rules. If you find any errors or omissions, we encourage you to report them to the Caseload Forecast Council.

SECTION 4 - Felony Index By RCW

Statute (RCW)	Offense	Class	Seriousness Level
74.09.240(1)	Receiving or Asking for Bribes, Kickbacks or Rebates	C	Unranked
74.09.240(2)	Paying or Offering Bribes, Kickbacks or Rebates	C	Unranked
74.09.250	False Statements Regarding Institutions, Facilities	C	Unranked
74.09.260	Excessive Charges, Payments	C	Unranked
74.09.290	Unlawful Disclosure of Patient Records or DSHS Information	C	Unranked
76.36.120	Forgery of Forest Product Mark	B	Unranked
76.48.141(1)(a)	Fraudulent Document as Specialized Forest Products Permit, Sales Invoice, Bill of Lading, etc.	C	Unranked
76.48.141(1)(b)	Fraudulent Representation of Authority to Harvest Specialized Forest Products	C	Unranked
76.48.141(2)	Fraudulent Document for Specialized Forest Products Buyer	C	Unranked
77.15.120(3)(b)	Unlawful Taking of Endangered Fish or Wildlife 1	C	III
77.15.135(4)(d)	Unlawful Trafficking in Species With Extinction 1	C	Unranked
77.15.250(2)(b)	Unlawful Releasing, Planting, Possessing or Placing Deleterious Exotic Wildlife	C	I
77.15.260(3)(a)	Unlawful Trafficking in Fish, Shellfish or Wildlife 2	C	II
77.15.260(3)(b)	Unlawful Trafficking in Fish, Shellfish or Wildlife 1	B	III
77.15.410(3)(b)	Unlawful Hunting of Big Game 1	C	III
77.15.450(3)(b)	Spotlighting Big Game 1	C	I
77.15.500(3)(b)	Commercial Fishing Without a License 1	C	II
77.15.530(4)	Unlawful Use of a Nondesignated Vessel	C	III
77.15.550(3)(b)	Violating Commercial Fishing Area or Time 1	C	I
77.15.570(2)	Unlawful Participation on Non-Indians in Indian Fishery	C	II
77.15.580(3)(b)	Unlawful Use of Net to Take Fish	C	I
77.15.620(3)(b)	Engaging in Fish Dealing Activity Unlicensed 1	C	II
77.15.630(3)(b)	Unlawful Fish and Shellfish Catch Accounting 1	C	I
77.15.650(3)(b)	Unlawful Purchase or Use of a License 1	C	II
77.15.670(3)(b)	Suspension of Department Privileges 1	C	I
77.15.770(2)	Unlawful Trade in Shark Fins 1	C	Unranked
77.15.811	Unlawful Use of Invasive Species 1	C	Unranked
78.44.330	Mineral Trespass	C	I
79A.60.050(1)(a)	Homicide by Watercraft – While Under the Influence of Intoxicating Liquor or any Drug	A	IX
79A.60.050(1)(b)	Homicide by Watercraft – In a Reckless Manner	A	VIII
79A.60.050(1)(c)	Homicide by Watercraft - Disregard for the Safety of Others	A	VII

The Caseload Forecast Council is not liable for errors or omissions in the manual, for sentences that may be inappropriately calculated as a result of a practitioner's or court's reliance on the manual, or for any other written or verbal information related to adult or juvenile sentencing. The scoring sheets are intended to provide assistance in most cases but do not cover all permutations of the scoring rules. If you find any errors or omissions, we encourage you to report them to the Caseload Forecast Council.

SECTION 4 - Felony Index By RCW

Statute (RCW)	Offense	Class	Seriousness Level
79A.60.060	Assault by Watercraft	B	IV
79A.60.090	Eluding a Law Enforcement Vessel	C	Unranked
79A.60.200(3)	Hit and Run with Vessel - Injury Accident	C	IV
81.60.070	Malicious Injury to Railroad Property	B	III
81.60.080(1)	Sabotaging Rolling Stock	C	Unranked
81.60.080(2)	Receiving Stolen Railroad Property	C	Unranked
82.24.100	Forgery or Counterfeit Cigarette Tax Stamp	B	Unranked
82.24.110(2)	Transportation of More Than 10,000 Cigarettes Without Proper Stamps	C	Unranked
82.24.500	Unlawfully Purchase, Sell, Consign or Distribute Cigarettes	C	Unranked
82.24.570(2)	Manufacture, Sell or Possess Counterfeit Cigarettes	C	Unranked
82.24.570(3)	Manufacture, Sell or Possess Counterfeit Cigarettes (Subsequent Violation)	B	Unranked
82.26.190	Distributors and Retailer of Tobacco Products License Violation	C	Unranked
82.32.290(2)	False Statement to Department of Revenue	C	Unranked
82.32.290(4)	Phantomware Violation	C	Unranked
82.42.085	Evading the Collection of Aircraft Fuel Tax	C	Unranked
82.36.380	Fuel Tax Evasion	C	Unranked
82.38.270	Special Fuel Violations	C	Unranked
87.03.200	Defraud Facsimile Signatures on Bonds and Coupons – Irrigation Districts	B	Unranked
88.08.020	Tampering with Lights or Signals	B	Unranked
88.08.050(1)	Injury to Lighthouses or United States Light	B	Unranked
88.46.080(2)(b)	Unlawful Operation of a Covered Vessel (Subsequent Violation)	C	Unranked
90.56.300(2)(b)	Unlawful Operation of Onshore or Offshore Facility (Subsequent Conviction)	C	Unranked
90.56.530	Reckless Operation of a Tank Vessel	C	Unranked
90.56.540	Operation of a Vessel While Under the Influence of Intoxicating Liquor or Drugs	C	Unranked

The Caseload Forecast Council is not liable for errors or omissions in the manual, for sentences that may be inappropriately calculated as a result of a practitioner's or court's reliance on the manual, or for any other written or verbal information related to adult or juvenile sentencing. The scoring sheets are intended to provide assistance in most cases but do not cover all permutations of the scoring rules. If you find any errors or omissions, we encourage you to report them to the Caseload Forecast Council.

The Caseload Forecast Council is not liable for errors or omissions in the manual, for sentences that may be inappropriately calculated as a result of a practitioner's or court's reliance on the manual, or for any other written or verbal information related to adult or juvenile sentencing. The scoring sheets are intended to provide assistance in most cases but do not cover all permutations of the scoring rules. If you find any errors or omissions, we encourage you to report them to the Caseload Forecast Council.

SECTION 5 - QUICK REFERENCE SHEETS

SENTENCING ALTERNATIVES

FIRST-TIME OFFENDER WAIVER (FTOW) (RCW 9.94A.650)

Offender Eligibility
- No prior conviction of a felony in this state, federal court, or another state; and
- Never participated in a program of deferred prosecution for a felony.

Certain felony offenses are *not* eligible for a FTOW sentence.
- Any offense classified as violent or sex under this chapter;
- Manufacture, delivery, or possession with intent to manufacture or deliver a controlled substance classified in Schedule I or II that is a narcotic drug or flunitrazepam classified in Schedule IV;
- Manufacture, delivery, or possession with intent to deliver a methamphetamine, its salts, isomers, and salts of its isomers as defined in RCW 69.50.206(d)(2);
- Selling for profit of any controlled substance or counterfeit substance classified in Schedule I, RCW 69.50.204, except leaves and flowering tops of marihuana;
- Felony driving while under the influence of intoxicating liquor or any drug; or
- Felony physical control of a vehicle while under the influence of intoxicating liquor or any drug.

Sentencing
- The court may waive the imposition of a sentence within the standard sentence range and impose a sentence which may include up to ninety days of confinement in a facility operated or utilized under contract by the county and a requirement that the offender refrain from committing new offenses.

Community Custody
In 2011, the legislature reduced the duration of community custody for FTOW sentences.
- Up to 6 months of community custody;
- Up to 12 months of community custody if treatment is ordered.

For further information on community custody conditions of an FTOW, see RCW 9.94A.703.

PARENTING SENTENCING ALTERNATIVE (RCW 9.94A.655)

Offender Eligibility
- The high end of the standard sentence range for the current offense is greater than one year;
- No prior or current conviction for a felony that is a sex offense or a violent offense;
- Not subject to a deportation detainer order and does not become subject to a deportation order during the period of the sentence;
- The offender signs any release of information waivers required to allow information regarding current or prior child welfare cases to be shared with the department and the court; and

---

The Caseload Forecast Council is not liable for errors or omissions in the manual, for sentences that may be inappropriately calculated as a result of a practitioner's or court's reliance on the manual, or for any other written or verbal information related to adult or juvenile sentencing. The scoring sheets are intended to provide assistance in most cases but do not cover all permutations of the scoring rules. If you find any errors or omissions, we encourage you to report them to the Caseload Forecast Council.

SECTION 5: Quick Reference Sheets

- The offender has physical custody of his or her minor child or is a legal guardian or custodian with physical custody of a child under the age of eighteen at the time of the current offense.

In making its determination, the court may order the department to complete either a risk assessment report or a chemical dependency screening report as provided in RCW 9.94A.500, or both reports prior to sentencing.

Open or prior child welfare cases:
- If the offender has an open child welfare case, the children's administration or the tribal child welfare agency shall provide a report within seven business days. See RCW 9.94A.655(3)(a) for minimum requirements of the report.
- Prior child welfare case: If the offender has a prior child welfare case with the children's administration or with a tribal child welfare agency, the department will obtain information from the children's administration on the number and type of past substantiated referrals of abuse or neglect and report that information to the court.

Sentencing
- <u>Imposing The Parenting Sentencing Alternative:</u>
    - The court shall waive imposition of a sentence within the standard sentence range and impose a sentence consisting of twelve months of community custody.
    - The court shall consider the offender's criminal history when determining if the alternative is appropriate.
- When a Court Imposes a Sentence Of Community Custody Under This Section:
    - The court may impose conditions as provided in RCW 9.94A.703 and may impose other affirmative conditions as the court considers appropriate.
    - The department may impose conditions as authorized in RCW 9.94A.704 that may include, but are not limited to:
        - Parenting classes;
        - Chemical dependency treatment;
        - Mental health treatment;
        - Vocational training;
        - Offender change programs;
        - Life skills classes.
    - The department shall report to the court if the offender commits any violations of his or her sentence conditions.

Community Custody
- <u>The department shall provide the court with quarterly progress reports</u> regarding the offender's progress in required programming, treatment, and other supervision conditions. When an offender has an open child welfare case, the department will seek to coordinate services with the children's administration.
- <u>Violations and Sanctions</u>

The Caseload Forecast Council is not liable for errors or omissions in the manual, for sentences that may be inappropriately calculated as a result of a practitioner's or court's reliance on the manual, or for any other written or verbal information related to adult or juvenile sentencing. The scoring sheets are intended to provide assistance in most cases but do not cover all permutations of the scoring rules. If you find any errors or omissions, we encourage you to report them to the Caseload Forecast Council.

SECTION 5: Quick Reference Sheets

- o If the offender is brought back to court, the court may modify the conditions of community custody or impose sanctions under RCW 9.94A.655(7)(c).
- o The court may order the offender to serve a term of total confinement within the standard range of the offender's current offense at any time during the period of community custody. RCW 9.94A.655(7)(c).

Alternative to Sentencing Under RCW 9.94A.6551: Partial Confinement As Part Of A Parenting Program
For offenders not sentenced under RCW 9.94A.655, but otherwise eligible under this section, no more than the final twelve months of the offender's term of confinement may be served in partial confinement as home detention as part of the parenting program developed by the department.

- Eligibility requirements - The secretary may transfer an offender from a correctional facility to home detention in the community if it is determined that the parenting program is an appropriate placement and when all of the following conditions exist:
    - o The offender is serving a sentence in which the high end of the range is greater than one year;
    - o The offender has no current conviction for a felony that is a sex offense or a violent offense;
    - o The offender has not been found by the United States attorney general to be subject to a deportation detainer or order and does not become subject to a deportation order during the period of the sentence;
    - o The offender signs any release of information waivers required to allow information regarding current or prior child welfare cases to be shared with the department and the court;
    - o The offender:
        - Has physical or legal custody of a minor child;
        - Has a proven, established, ongoing, and substantial relationship with his or her minor child that existed prior to the commission of the current offense; or
        - Is a legal guardian of a child that was under the age of eighteen at the time of the current offense; and
        - The department determines that such a placement is in the best interests of the child.

When the department is considering partial confinement as part of the parenting program for an offender, the department shall inquire of the individual and the children's administration with the Washington state department of social and health services whether the agency has an open child welfare case or prior substantiated referral for abuse or neglect involving the offender. If the children's administration or a tribal jurisdiction has an open child welfare case, the department will seek input from the children's administration or the involved tribal jurisdiction as to: (a) The status of the child welfare case; and (b) recommendations regarding placement of the offender and services required of the department and the court governing the individual's child welfare case. The department and its officers, agents, and employees are not liable for the acts of offenders participating in the parenting program unless the department or its officers, agents, and employees acted with willful and wanton disregard.

- Conditions for partial confinement
    - o All offenders placed on home detention as part of the parenting program shall provide an approved residence and living arrangement prior to transfer to home detention.

The Caseload Forecast Council is not liable for errors or omissions in the manual, for sentences that may be inappropriately calculated as a result of a practitioner's or court's reliance on the manual, or for any other written or verbal information related to adult or juvenile sentencing. The scoring sheets are intended to provide assistance in most cases but do not cover all permutations of the scoring rules. If you find any errors or omissions, we encourage you to report them to the Caseload Forecast Council.

SECTION 5: Quick Reference Sheets

- o While in the community on home detention as part of the parenting program, the department shall:
  - Require the offender to be placed on electronic home monitoring;
  - Require the offender to participate in programming and treatment that the department determines is needed;
  - Assign a community corrections officer who will monitor the offender's compliance with conditions of partial confinement and programming requirements; and
  - If the offender has an open child welfare case with the children's administration, collaborate and communicate with the identified social worker in the provision of services.
- o The department has the authority to return any offender serving partial confinement in the parenting program to total confinement if the offender is not complying with sentence requirements.

DRUG OFFENDER SENTENCING ALTERNATIVE (DOSA) (RCW 9.94A.660)

Prison – Based Option (RCW 9.94A.662) or Residential-Based Treatment Option (RCW 9.94A.664)

Offender Eligibility
An offender is eligible for the special drug offender sentencing alternative if:
- The offender is convicted of a felony that is not a violent offense or sex offense and the violation does not involve a sentence enhancement under RCW 9.94A.533(3) or (4);
- The offender is convicted of a felony that is not a felony Driving While Under the Influence of Intoxicating Liquor or Any Drug (RCW 46.61.502(6)) or felony Physical Control of a Vehicle While Under The Influence of Intoxicating Liquor or Any Drug (RCW 46.61.504(6));
- The offender has no current or prior convictions for a sex offense at any time or violent offense within ten years before conviction of the current offense, in this state, another state, or the United States;
- For a violation of the Uniform Controlled Substances Act under Chapter 69.50 RCW or a criminal solicitation to commit such a violation under Chapter 9A.28 RCW, the offense involved only a small quantity of the particular controlled substance as determined by the judge upon consideration of such factors as the weight, purity, packaging, sale price, and street value of the controlled substance;
- The offender has not been found by the United States attorney general to be subject to a deportation detainer or order and does not become subject to a deportation order during the period of the sentence;
- The standard range meets certain qualifications:
  - o Prison-based option - the end of the standard sentence range for the current offense is greater than one year;
  - o Residential-based option – the end of the standard sentence range for the current offense is greater than one year and the midpoint of the standard range is 24 months or less; and
- The offender has not received a drug offender sentencing alternative more than once in the prior ten years before the current offense.

Sentencing
- If the sentencing court determines that the offender is eligible for an alternative sentence under this section and that the alternative sentence is appropriate, the court shall:

SECTION 5: Quick Reference Sheets

- o Waive imposition of a sentence within the standard sentence range; and
- o Impose a sentence consisting of either a prison-based alternative or a residential chemical dependency treatment-based alternative.
- To assist the court in making its determination, the court may order the department to complete a risk assessment report, a chemical dependency screening report or both. Refer to RCW 9.94A.500 for minimum requirements of both prison-based and residential treatment examinations.
- Prison-based option will include a period of total confinement in a state facility for one-half the midpoint of the standard sentence range or 12 months, whichever is greater.

Community Custody
- The court may bring any offender sentenced under this section back into court at any time on its own initiative to evaluate the offender's progress in treatment or to determine if any violations of the conditions of the sentence have occurred.
- If the offender is brought back to court, the court may modify the conditions of the community custody or impose sanctions under RCW 9.94A.660(7)(c).
- The court may order the offender to serve a term of total confinement within the standard range of the offender's current offense at any time during the period of community custody if the offender violates the conditions or requirements of the sentence or if the offender is failing to make satisfactory progress in treatment. RCW 9.94A.660(7)(c).
- Prison-based option includes:
  o A term of community custody equal to one-half of the midpoint of the standard sentence range;
  o Appropriate substance abuse treatment in a program approved by DSHS-DASA;
  o Crime-related prohibitions, including a condition not to use illegal controlled substances;
  o A requirement to submit to urinalysis or other testing;
  o Upon failure to complete or administrative termination from the program, a term of community custody pursuant to RCW 9.94A.701 is to be imposed.
- Residential-based option includes:
  o A term of community custody equal to one-half of the midpoint of the standard range or two years, whichever is greater;
  o Entrance and remaining in residential chemical dependency treatment certified under Chapter 70.96A RCW for a period between three and six months as set by the court.

SPECIAL SEX OFFENDER SENTENCING ALTERNATIVE (SSOSA) (RCW 9.94A.670)

Offender Eligibility
An offender is eligible for the special sex offender sentencing alternative if:
- The offender is convicted of a sex offense that is not:
  o Serious violent offense
  o Rape 2nd degree; and
- The offender has no prior:
  o Convictions for a felony sex offense in this or any other state; and
  o Adult conviction for a violent offense in the five years prior to the date the current offense was committed; and
- The offense did not result in substantial bodily harm to the victim; and

SECTION 5: Quick Reference Sheets

- There was an established relationship/connection to the victim other than that resulting from the crime; and
- If the conviction results from a guilty plea, the offender must voluntarily and affirmatively admit to committing all of the elements of the crime (Alford and Newton pleas are not eligible); and
- The standard sentence range for the offense includes the possibility of confinement of less than 11 years.

If the court finds the offender is eligible for this alternative, it may order an examination to determine whether the offender is amenable to treatment. After receipt of the reports, the court shall determine whether this alternative is appropriate. If the sentencing court determines that the offender is eligible for an alternative sentence under this section and that the alternative sentence is appropriate, the court shall impose a sentence or minimum term (RCW 9.94A.507) within the standard range. If the sentencing imposed is less than 11 years, the court may suspend the execution of the sentence.

Suspended Sentence Sentencing
- The court must impose:
    - A term of confinement up to 12 months or the maximum term within the standard range, whichever is less.
    - A term of confinement greater than 12 months or the maximum term within the standard range if an aggravating circumstance is present.
- The court may order the offender to serve all or part of the sentence in partial confinement.
- SSOSA sentences are not eligible for earned release.
- The court may revoke the suspended sentence at any time during the period of community custody and order execution of the sentence if:
    - The offender violate conditions of suspended sentence; or
    - The court finds the offender is failing to make satisfactory progress in treatment.

Suspended Sentencing Treatment
The court must impose outpatient or inpatient sex offender treatment for any period up to five years.

Suspended Sentence Community Custody
- The court must impose:
    - A term of community custody equal to the length of the suspended sentence, the length of the maximum term imposed per RCW 9.94A.507, or three years, whichever is greater; and
    - Specific prohibitions and affirmative conditions related to precursor behaviors or activities.
- Conditions of the suspended sentence may include one or more of the following:
    - Crime-related prohibitions;
    - Require the offender to devote time to a specific employment or occupation;
    - Remain within prescribed geographical boundaries and
    - Notify the court or community corrections officer prior to any address or employment change;
    - Report as directed to the court and a community corrections officer;
    - Pay all court-ordered legal financial obligations;
    - Perform community restitution work; or
    - Reimburse victim for any counseling costs as a result of the crime.

The Caseload Forecast Council is not liable for errors or omissions in the manual, for sentences that may be inappropriately calculated as a result of a practitioner's or court's reliance on the manual, or for any other written or verbal information related to adult or juvenile sentencing. The scoring sheets are intended to provide assistance in most cases but do not cover all permutations of the scoring rules. If you find any errors or omissions, we encourage you to report them to the Caseload Forecast Council.

SECTION 5: Quick Reference Sheets

- The Department of Corrections may impose sanctions for a violation of a requirement that is not a condition of the suspended sentence.
- For violations of the prohibited or affirmative conditions relating to precursor behaviors or activities, the Department of Corrections shall:
    - First violation
        - Impose sanctions per RCW 9.94A.633(1) or
        - Refer violation to the court and recommend revocation of suspended sentence
    - Second violation – refer the violation to the court and recommend revocation of suspended sentence.
- If the suspended sentence is revoked, all confinement time served during community custody shall be credited to the offender.

SENTENCING ENHANCEMENTS

Felony Traffic Enhancements

- Vehicular Homicide While Under the Influence of Intoxicating Liquor or Any Drug (RCW 9.94A.533(7))
    - Enhancement duration of 24 months for each prior offense under RCW 46.61.5055 in a person's criminal history.
    - These prior offenses used to enhance a sentence do not count towards the offender's score.
    - The enhancement portion is subject to earned release time.
    - Shall be served in total confinement and shall run consecutive to all other sentencing provisions, including other impaired driving enhancements, for all offenses sentenced under this chapter.
- Attempting to Elude a Police Vehicle (RCW 9.94A.533(11))
    - Resulting in the threat of physical injury or harm to one or more persons other than the defendant or the pursuing law enforcement officer.
    - Enhancement duration is a *12 months and 1 day enhancement* to the presumptive sentence.
    - In order to obtain the enhancement, the State must file a special allegation and a judge or jury must find that it occurred beyond a reasonable doubt.
- Minor Child (RCW 9.94A.533(13))
    - Applies to the following traffic offenses:
        - Vehicular Homicide While Under the Influence of Intoxicating Liquor or Any Drug;
        - Vehicular Assault While Under the Influence of Intoxicating Liquor or Any Drug;
        - Any Felony Driving Under the Influence; or
        - Felony Physical Control Under the Influence.
    - 12 month enhancement for each child passenger under 16 in the defendant's vehicle.
    - Shall be served in total confinement and shall run consecutively to all other sentencing provisions.
    - If the minor child enhancement increases the sentence so that it would exceed the statutory maximum for the offense, the portion representing the enhancement may not be reduced.

The Caseload Forecast Council is not liable for errors or omissions in the manual, for sentences that may be inappropriately calculated as a result of a practitioner's or court's reliance on the manual, or for any other written or verbal information related to adult or juvenile sentencing. The scoring sheets are intended to provide assistance in most cases but do not cover all permutations of the scoring rules. If you find any errors or omissions, we encourage you to report them to the Caseload Forecast Council.

SECTION 5: Quick Reference Sheets

Firearm and Deadly Weapon Enhancements

All felony offenses, except where the use of a firearm is an element of the offense, are eligible for firearm (RCW 9.94A.533(3)) and deadly weapon (RCW 9.94A.533(4)) enhancements.
- Anytime a court makes a finding of fact or a jury returns a special verdict that the accused or accomplice was armed with a deadly weapon at the time of the commission of the crime, the court must apply the enhancement to the sentence.
- Enhancements apply to both the accused and any accomplice(s).
- All firearm and deadly weapon enhancements shall be served in total confinement, and shall run consecutively to all other offenses included in the sentence.
- This applies to anticipatory offenses, including attempts, conspiracies and solicitations to commit a crime.
- If the addition of a firearm enhancement increases the sentence so that it would exceed the statutory maximum for the offense, the portion of the sentence representing the enhancement may not be reduced. RCW 9.94A.599.

For the amounts of each enhancement and the applicable offenses by effective date, please go to the Deadly Weapon Enhancement scoring form under General Scoring Forms in Section 7.

Drug-Related Enhancements

Certain drug offenses are subject to enhancements when the offense takes place in a protected zone, in the presence of a child, or in a correctional facility.
- Protected Zone (RCW 9.94A.533(6))
  - If an offender is sentenced for committing certain drug offenses committed in a protected zone; and
  - Committed in a protected zones:
    - Schools or school buses;
    - 1,000 feet of a school bus route or a school ground perimeter;
    - Public parks;
    - Public transit vehicles or public transit stops;
    - Civic centers designated as a drug-free zone by the governing authority or 1,000 feet of the perimeter of the facility, if the local governing authority specifically designates the 1,000 foot perimeter;
    - In a public housing project designated by a local governing authority as a drug-free zone.
  - Enhancement duration of 24 months is added to the presumptive sentence and the maximum imprisonment and fine are doubled (RCW 69.50.406 offenses are excluded).
- Presence of a Child (RCW 9.94A.533(6))
  - Convicted of manufacture of methamphetamine or of the possession of ephedrine or pseudo-ephedrine with intent to manufacture; and

SECTION 5: Quick Reference Sheets

- o There was a special allegation proven that a person under the age of 18 years old was present in or upon the premises.
- o Enhancement duration is 24 months to the presumptive sentence.
- Correctional Facility (RCW 9.94A.533(5))
    - o If an offender or accomplice committed certain violations of the VUCSA statute while in county or state correctional facility, an enhancement must be added to the presumptive range.
    - o **18 month enhancement for offenses under RCW 69.50.401(2)(a) or (b), 69.50.410**:
        - Manufacture, Possess w/Intent to Deliver Heroin or Cocaine;
        - Manufacture, Deliver, Possess with Intent to Deliver Schedule I or II Narcotics (Except Heroin or Cocaine) or Flunitrazepam from Schedule IV;
        - Selling for Profit (Controlled or Counterfeit) Any Controlled Substance; Deliver or Possess with Intent to Deliver Methamphetamine;
        - Manufacture of Methamphetamine; Manufacture, Deliver, Possess with Intent to Deliver Amphetamine.
    - o **15 month enhancement for offenses under RCW 69.50.401(c), (d) or (e)**:
        - Manufacture, Deliver, Possess with Intent to Deliver Schedule III-V Narcotics or Schedule I-V Nonnarcotic (Except Marijuana, Amphetamine, Methamphetamine or Flunitrazepam);
        - Manufacture, Deliver, Possess with Intent to Deliver Marijuana;
    - o **12 month enhancement for offenses under RCW 69.50.4013**:
        - Possession of Controlled Substance that is either Heroin or Narcotics from Schedule I or II or Flunitrazepam from Schedule IV;
        - Possession of Phencyclidine (PCP);
        - Possession of a Controlled Substance that is a Narcotic from Schedule III-V or Nonnarcotic from Schedule I-V (Except Phencyclidine).

Sex Offense Enhancements

- Sexual Conduct in Return for a Fee (RCW 9.94A.533(9))
    - o Anticipatory offenses receive the same enhancement as if completed.
    - o Rape of a Child or Child Molestation in exchange for a fee with the victim if committed after July 22, 2007.
    - o Duration of enhancement is 12 months.
- Sexual Motivation (RCW 9.94A.533(8))
    - o This enhancement is applicable to any felony offense committed after July 1, 2006.
    - o Anticipatory offenses receive same enhancement as if completed.
    - o Enhancement duration:
        - Class A = 24 mos.;
        - Class B = 18 mos.;
        - Class C = 12 mos.
    - o Prior sexual motivation enhancements: if the offender has any prior SM enhancements after July 1, 2006, the subsequent sexual motivation enhancement duration is doubled.
    - o Enhancement served in total confinement.

The Caseload Forecast Council is not liable for errors or omissions in the manual, for sentences that may be inappropriately calculated as a result of a practitioner's or court's reliance on the manual, or for any other written or verbal information related to adult or juvenile sentencing. The scoring sheets are intended to provide assistance in most cases but do not cover all permutations of the scoring rules. If you find any errors or omissions, we encourage you to report them to the Caseload Forecast Council.

SECTION 5: Quick Reference Sheets

- If the addition of a sexual motivation enhancement increases the sentence so that it would exceed the statutory maximum for the offense, the portion of the sentence representing the enhancement may not be reduced.
- Sex offense enhancements shall run consecutively to all other sentencing provisions.

Law Enforcement Enhancement

Assault of law enforcement officer or other employee of a law enforcement agency (RCW 9.94A.533(12)).
- Any person found guilty of assaulting a law enforcement officer, or other employee of a law enforcement agency who was performing his or her duties at the time of the assault
- Duration of enhancement is 12 months.
- In order to obtain the enhancement, the State must file a special allegation and a judge or jury must find that it occurred beyond a reasonable doubt.

Criminal Street Gang-Related Enhancement

Felony offense involving the compensation, threatening, or solicitation of a minor in order to involve that minor in the commission of a felony offense (RCW 9.94A.533(10)).
- This enhancement increases the standard range sentence for the underlying crime.
- When the State files a special allegation and proves that a felony offense involved the compensation, threatening, or solicitation of a minor in order to involve that minor in the commission of the felony offense, the standard range for that felony is determined by multiplying the grid range by 125%. RCW 9.94A.533(10)(a).
- The enhancement does not apply to any criminal street gang-related felony for which involving a minor in the commission of the felony is already an element of the offense. RCW 9.94A.533(10)(b).
- This enhancement is unavailable in the event that the prosecution gives notice that it will seek an exceptional sentence based on an aggravating factor under RCW 9.94A.535.

Robbery of a Pharmacy Enhancement

The robbery of a pharmacy special enhancement applies to convictions for first or second degree robbery where a special allegation is pleaded and proven beyond a reasonable doubt that the defendant committed a robbery of a pharmacy. This enhancement adds an additional 12 months to the standard range (RCW 9.94A.533(14)).

SECTION 5: Quick Reference Sheets

COMMUNITY CUSTODY

Offense	Sentenced to a term of confinement for one year or less. *See RCW 9.94A.702*	Sentenced to the Department of Corrections. *See 9.94A.701*
Sex offenses (see page 70)	Up to 12 months	36 months (if not sentenced under RCW 9.94A.507)
Violent offenses (see page 68)	Up to 12 months	18 months
A crime against a person under RCW 9.94A.411(2) (see page 77)	Up to 12 months	12 months
A felony offense under Chapter 69.50 or 69.52 RCW	Up to 12 months (includes solicitation)	12 months (excludes solicitation)
A felony violation of RCW9.A.44.132(1)(Failure to Register)	Up to 12 months	12 months
A serious violent offense (see page 67)		36 months
Offense involving the Unlawful Possession of a Firearm (RCW 9.41.040) where the offender is a criminal street gang member/associate		12 months

The Caseload Forecast Council is not liable for errors or omissions in the manual, for sentences that may be inappropriately calculated as a result of a practitioner's or court's reliance on the manual, or for any other written or verbal information related to adult or juvenile sentencing. The scoring sheets are intended to provide assistance in most cases but do not cover all permutations of the scoring rules. If you find any errors or omissions, we encourage you to report them to the Caseload Forecast Council.

SECTION 6 – GENERAL FELONY SCORING FORMS

General scoring forms are provided at the beginning of this section and are followed by the individual offense scoring forms. The General scoring forms include scoring sheets intended to assist in the calculation of offender scores and sentence ranges for offenses imposed with a deadly weapon enhancement, a sexual motivation finding or a domestic violence finding.

Individual offense scoring forms are arranged alphabetically in Section 8 and include forms for controlled substances, imitation controlled substances and legend drug crimes. Please note that the scoring forms do not present sentencing options eligibility (*e.g.,* work release, work ethic camp). Please refer to Sentencing Alternatives in Section 6 of this manual for clarification of eligibility rules or conditions for each sentencing option.

In past manuals, if a sentence range extended past the statutory maximum of the offense, the sentence range was truncated and displayed an asterisk that referenced what the statutory maximum was. In this manual, the sentence range will still be truncated where available and display an asterisk. The corresponding asterisk will be next to the classification at the top of the page, *i.e.,* Class C*.

The Caseload Forecast Council is not liable for errors or omissions in the manual, for sentences that may be inappropriately calculated as a result of a practitioner's or court's reliance on the manual, or for any other written or verbal information related to adult or juvenile sentencing. The scoring sheets are intended to provide assistance in most cases but do not cover all permutations of the scoring rules. If you find any errors or omissions, we encourage you to report them to the Caseload Forecast Council.

Deadly Weapon Enhancement

If offense was committed <u>after July 23, 1995</u> with a firearm or other deadly weapon finding

CLASS A FELONY
First Deadly Weapon/Firearm Offense
    Firearm   5 years
    Other Deadly Weapon   2 years

Subsequent Deadly Weapon/Firearm Offense
    Firearm   10 years
    Other Deadly Weapon   4 years

CLASS B FELONY
First Deadly Weapon/Firearm Offense
    Firearm   3 years
    Other Deadly Weapon   1 years

Subsequent Deadly Weapon/Firearm Offense
    Firearm   6 years
    Other Deadly Weapon   2 years

CLASS C FELONY
First Deadly Weapon/Firearm Offense
    Firearm   18 months
    Other Deadly Weapon   6 months

Subsequent Deadly Weapon/Firearm Offense
    Firearm   3 years
    Other Deadly Weapon   1 year

Excluded offenses: Possession of a Machine gun, Possessing a Stolen Firearm, Drive-by Shooting, Theft of a Firearm, Unlawful Possession of a Firearm 1 and 2, Use of a Machine Gun in a felony.

To be sentenced to a subsequent deadly weapon finding, the offense in history with a deadly weapon finding must also have been committed after July 23, 1995.

If offense was committed <u>after June 12, 1994 and before July 24, 1995</u> with a deadly weapon finding

OFFENSES ELIGIBLE FOR A SPECIFIC DEADLY WEAPON ENHANCEMENT:

Kidnapping 1   24 months
Rape 1
Robbery 1

Burglary 1   18 months

Assault 2   12 months
Assault of a Child 2
Escape 1
Kidnapping 2
Burglary 2
Drug offense
Theft of Livestock 1
Theft of Livestock 2
Any Serious Violent or Violent Offense Not Listed Above.

The standard range may in no case exceed the statutory maximum.

STANDARD RANGE CALCULATION

OFFENDER SCORE .... ☐

SERIOUSNESS LEVEL .... ☐

STANDARD SENTENCE RANGE .... [Low] to [High]

DEADLY WEAPON ENHANCEMENT .... ☐

STANDARD SENTENCE RANGE PLUS ENHANCEMENT .... [Low] to [High]

✓ ....For anticipatory offenses, add the enhancement after reducing the standard sentence range

---

The Caseload Forecast Council is not liable for errors or omissions in the manual, for sentences that may be inappropriately calculated as a result of a practitioner's or court's reliance on the manual, or for any other written or verbal information related to adult or juvenile sentencing. The scoring sheets are intended to provide assistance in most cases but do not cover all permutations of the scoring rules. If you find any errors or omissions, we encourage you to report them to the Caseload Forecast Council.

General Nonviolent Offense Where Domestic Violence Has Been Plead And Proven

NONVIOLENT

OFFENDER SCORING RCW 9.94A.525(21)

CURRENT OFFENSE BEING SCORED:
_____

ADULT HISTORY:
Enter number of domestic violence felony convictions as listed below* .... _____ x 2 = _____

Enter number of repetitive domestic violence offense convictions (RCW 9.94A.030(42)) plead and proven after 8/1/11 .... _____ x 1 = _____

Enter number of felony convictions .... _____ x 1 = _____

JUVENILE HISTORY:
Enter number of subsequent domestic violence felony dispositions as listed below* .... _____ x 1 = _____

Enter number of serious violent and violent felony dispositions .... _____ x 1 = _____

Enter number of nonviolent felony dispositions .... _____ x ½ = _____

OTHER CURRENT OFFENSES:
(Other current offenses that do not encompass the same conduct count in offender score)
Enter number of other domestic violence felony convictions as listed below* .... _____ x 2 = _____

Enter number of other repetitive domestic violence offense convictions plead and proven after 8/1/11 .... _____ x 1 = _____

Enter number of other felony convictions .... _____ x 1 = _____

STATUS:
Was the offender on community custody on the date the current offense was committed? (if yes) ...... + 1 = _____

*If domestic violence was pleaded and proven after 8/1/2011 for the following felony offenses:
Violation of a No-Contact Order, Violation of a Protection Order, Domestic Violence Harassment, Domestic Violence Stalking, Domestic Violence Burglary 1, Domestic Violence Kidnapping 1, Domestic Violence Kidnapping 2, Domestic Violence Unlawful Imprisonment, Domestic Violence Robbery 1, Domestic Violence Robbery 2, Domestic Violence Assault 1, Domestic Violence Assault 2, Domestic Violence Assault 3, Domestic Violence Arson 1, Domestic Violence Arson 2.

STANDARD RANGE CALCULATION

Total the last column to get the **Offender Score** (Round down to the nearest whole number)

SERIOUSNESS LEVEL ....

STANDARD SENTENCE RANGE .... [Low] to [High]

- ✓ For attempt, solicitation, conspiracy (RCW 9.94A.595) see page 23 or for gang-related felonies where the court found the offender involved a minor (RCW 9.94A.833) see page 186 for standard range adjustments.
- ✓ For deadly weapon enhancement, see page 190.
- ✓ For sentencing alternatives, see page 177.
- ✓ For community custody eligibility, see page 187.
- ✓ For any applicable enhancements other than deadly weapon enhancement, see page 183.

The Caseload Forecast Council is not liable for errors or omissions in the manual, for sentences that may be inappropriately calculated as a result of a practitioner's or court's reliance on the manual, or for any other written or verbal information related to adult or juvenile sentencing. The scoring sheets are intended to provide assistance in most cases but do not cover all permutations of the scoring rules. If you find any errors or omissions, we encourage you to report them to the Caseload Forecast Council.

General Nonviolent/Sex Offense Where Domestic Violence Has Been Plead And Proven

NONVIOLENT/SEX

OFFENDER SCORING RCW 9.94A.525(17)

CURRENT OFFENSE BEING SCORED: _____

ADULT HISTORY:
    Enter number of sex offense felony convictions .... _____ x 3 = _____
    Enter number of domestic violence felony convictions as listed below* .... _____ x 2 = _____
    Enter number of repetitive domestic violence offense convictions (RCW 9.94A.030(42)) plead and proven after 8/1/11 .... _____ x 1 = _____
    Enter number of felony convictions .... _____ x 1 = _____

JUVENILE HISTORY:
    Enter number of sex offense felony dispositions .... _____ x 3 = _____
    Enter number of subsequent domestic violence felony dispositions as listed below* .... _____ x 1 = _____
    Enter number of serious violent and violent felony dispositions .... _____ x 1 = _____
    Enter number of nonviolent felony dispositions .... _____ x ½ = _____

OTHER CURRENT OFFENSES:
(Other current offenses that do not encompass the same conduct count in offender score)
    Enter number of other sex offense felony convictions .... _____ x 3 = _____
    Enter number of other domestic violence felony convictions as listed below* ... _____ x 2 = _____
    Enter number of other repetitive domestic violence offense convictions plead and proven after 8/1/11 .... _____ x 1 = _____
    Enter number of other felony convictions .... _____ x 1 = _____

STATUS:
    Was the offender on community custody on the date the current offense was committed? (if yes) .... + 1 = _____

*If domestic violence was plead and proven after 8/1/2011 for the following felony offenses:
    Violation of a No-Contact Order, Violation of a Protection Order, Domestic Violence Harassment, Domestic Violence Stalking, Domestic Violence Burglary 1, Domestic Violence Kidnapping 1, Domestic Violence Kidnapping 2, Domestic Violence Unlawful Imprisonment, Domestic Violence Robbery 1, Domestic Violence Robbery 2, Domestic Violence Assault 1, Domestic Violence Assault 2, Domestic Violence Assault 3, Domestic Violence Arson 1, Domestic Violence Arson 2.

STANDARD RANGE CALCULATION

Total the last column to get the **Offender Score** (Round down to the nearest whole number)

SERIOUSNESS LEVEL ....

STANDARD SENTENCE RANGE .... Low _____ to High _____

- ✓ For attempt, solicitation, conspiracy (RCW 9.94A.595) see page 23 or for gang-related felonies where the court found the offender involved a minor (RCW 9.94A.833) see page 186 for standard range adjustments.
- ✓ For deadly weapon enhancement, see page 190.
- ✓ For sentencing alternatives, see page 177.
- ✓ For community custody eligibility, see page 187.
- ✓ For any applicable enhancements other than deadly weapon enhancement, see page 183.
- ✓ If the offender is not a persistent offender and has a prior conviction for an offense listed in RCW 9.94A.030(38)(b), then the sentence is subject to the requirements of RCW 9.94A.507.

The Caseload Forecast Council is not liable for errors or omissions in the manual, for sentences that may be inappropriately calculated as a result of a practitioner's or court's reliance on the manual, or for any other written or verbal information related to adult or juvenile sentencing. The scoring sheets are intended to provide assistance in most cases but do not cover all permutations of the scoring rules. If you find any errors or omissions, we encourage you to report them to the Caseload Forecast Council.

General Nonviolent Offense With A Sexual Motivation Finding

NONVIOLENT/SEX

OFFENDER SCORING RCW 9.94A.525(17)

CURRENT OFFENSE BEING SCORED:
_____

ADULT HISTORY:
    Enter number of sex offense felony convictions .... _____   x 3 = _____

    Enter number of felony convictions .... _____   x 1 = _____

JUVENILE HISTORY:
    Enter number of sex offense felony dispositions .... _____   x 3 = _____

    Enter number of serious violent and violent felony dispositions .... _____   x 1 = _____

    Enter number of nonviolent felony dispositions .... _____   x ½ = _____

OTHER CURRENT OFFENSES:
(Other current offenses that do not encompass the same conduct count in offender score)
    Enter number of other sex offense felony convictions .... _____   x 3 = _____

    Enter number of other felony convictions .... _____   x 1 = _____

STATUS:
    Was the offender on community custody on the date the current offense was committed? (if yes) ......   + 1 = _____

STANDARD RANGE CALCULATION

Total the last column to get the **Offender Score** (Round down to the nearest whole number)   [ ]

SERIOUSNESS LEVEL ....   [ ]

STANDARD SENTENCE RANGE .... [Low] to [High]

SEXUAL MOTIVATION ENHANCEMENT (Per Sexual Motivation Enhancement, page 185)   [ ]

STANDARD SENTENCE RANGE PLUS ENHANCEMENT .... [Low] to [High]

- ✓ For attempt, solicitation, conspiracy (RCW 9.94A.595) see page 23 or for gang-related felonies where the court found the offender involved a minor (RCW 9.94A.833) see page 186 for standard range adjustments.
- ✓ For deadly weapon enhancement, see page 190.
- ✓ For sentencing alternatives, see page 177.
- ✓ For community custody eligibility, see page 187.
- ✓ For any applicable enhancements other than deadly weapon enhancement, see page 183.
- ✓ If the offender is not a persistent offender and has a prior conviction for an offense listed in RCW 9.94A.030(38)(b), then the sentence is subject to the requirements of RCW 9.94A.507.

The Caseload Forecast Council is not liable for errors or omissions in the manual, for sentences that may be inappropriately calculated as a result of a practitioner's or court's reliance on the manual, or for any other written or verbal information related to adult or juvenile sentencing. The scoring sheets are intended to provide assistance in most cases but do not cover all permutations of the scoring rules. If you find any errors or omissions, we encourage you to report them to the Caseload Forecast Council.

General Drug Offense Where Domestic Violence Has Been Plead And Proven

NONVIOLENT/DRUG

OFFENDER SCORING RCW 9.94A.525(21)

CURRENT OFFENSE BEING SCORED:
_____

ADULT HISTORY:
- Enter number of domestic violence felony convictions as listed below* .... _____ x 2 = _____
- Enter number of repetitive domestic violence offense convictions (RCW 9.94A.030(42)) plead and proven after 8/1/11 .... _____ x 1 = _____
- Does the offender have a prior sex or serious violent offense in history?
  - **YES** Enter number of felony drug convictions .... _____ x 3 = _____
  - **NO** Enter number of felony drug convictions .... _____ x 1 = _____
- Enter number of felony convictions .... _____ x 1 = _____

JUVENILE HISTORY:
- Enter number of subsequent domestic violence felony dispositions as listed below* .... _____ x 1 = _____
- Does the offender have a prior sex or serious violent offense in history?
  - **YES** Enter number of felony drug dispositions .... _____ x 2 = _____
  - **NO** Enter number of felony drug dispositions .... _____ x ½ = _____
- Enter number of serious violent and violent felony dispositions .... _____ x 1 = _____
- Enter number of nonviolent felony dispositions .... _____ x ½ = _____

OTHER CURRENT OFFENSES:
(Other current offenses that do not encompass the same conduct count in offender score)
- Enter number of other domestic violence felony convictions as listed below* .... _____ x 2 = _____
- Enter number of other repetitive domestic violence offense convictions plead and proven after 8/1/11 .... _____ x 1 = _____
- Does the offender have other prior sex or serious violent offense in history?
  - **YES** Enter number of other felony drug convictions .... _____ x 3 = _____
  - **NO** Enter number of other felony drug convictions .... _____ x 1 = _____
- Enter number of other felony convictions .... _____ x 1 = _____

STATUS:
- Was the offender on community custody on the date the current offense was committed? (if yes) .... + 1 = _____

*If domestic violence was plead and proven after 8/1/2011 for the following felony offenses: Violation of a No-Contact Order, Violation of a Protection Order, Domestic Violence Harassment, Domestic Violence Stalking, Domestic Violence Burglary 1, Domestic Violence Kidnapping 1, Domestic Violence Kidnapping 2, Domestic Violence Unlawful Imprisonment, Domestic Violence Robbery 1, Domestic Violence Robbery 2, Domestic Violence Assault 1, Domestic Violence Assault 2, Domestic Violence Assault 3, Domestic Violence Arson 1, Domestic Violence Arson 2.

STANDARD RANGE CALCULATION

Total the last column to get the **Offender Score** (Round down to the nearest whole number) .... [ ]

SERIOUSNESS LEVEL .... [ ]

STANDARD SENTENCE RANGE .... [Low] to [High]

- ✓ For attempt, solicitation, conspiracy (RCW 9.94A.595) see page 23 or for gang-related felonies where the court found the offender involved a minor (RCW 9.94A.833) see page 186 for standard range adjustments.
- ✓ For deadly weapon enhancement, see page 190.
- ✓ For sentencing alternatives, see page 177.
- ✓ For community custody eligibility, see page 187.
- ✓ For any applicable enhancements other than deadly weapon enhancement, see page 183.

The Caseload Forecast Council is not liable for errors or omissions in the manual, for sentences that may be inappropriately calculated as a result of a practitioner's or court's reliance on the manual, or for any other written or verbal information related to adult or juvenile sentencing. The scoring sheets are intended to provide assistance in most cases but do not cover all permutations of the scoring rules. If you find any errors or omissions, we encourage you to report them to the Caseload Forecast Council.

General Drug Offense With A Sexual Motivation Finding

NONVIOLENT/DRUG/SEX

OFFENDER SCORING RCW 9.94A.525(17)

CURRENT OFFENSE BEING SCORED:
_____

ADULT HISTORY:
Enter number of sex offense felony convictions .... _____ x 3 = _____

Does the offender have a prior sex or serious violent offense in history?
    YES Enter number of felony drug convictions .... _____ x 3 = _____
    NO Enter number of felony drug convictions .... _____ x 1 = _____

Enter number of felony convictions .... _____ x 1 = _____

JUVENILE HISTORY:
Enter number of sex offense felony dispositions .... _____ x 3 = _____

Does the offender have a prior sex or serious violent offense in history?
    YES Enter number of felony drug dispositions .... _____ x 2 = _____
    NO Enter number of felony drug dispositions .... _____ x ½ = _____

Enter number of serious violent and violent felony dispositions .... _____ x 1 = _____

Enter number of nonviolent felony dispositions .... _____ x ½ = _____

OTHER CURRENT OFFENSES:
(Other current offenses that do not encompass the same conduct count in offender score)
Enter number of other sex offense felony convictions .... _____ x 3 = _____

Does the offender have other prior sex or serious violent offense in history?
    YES Enter number of other felony drug convictions .... _____ x 3 = _____
    NO Enter number of other felony drug convictions .... _____ x 1 = _____

Enter number of other felony convictions .... _____ x 1 = _____

STATUS:
Was the offender on community custody on the date the current offense was committed? (if yes) .... + 1 = _____

STANDARD RANGE CALCULATION

Total the last column to get the **Offender Score** (Round down to the nearest whole number) .... [ ]

SERIOUSNESS LEVEL .... [ ]

STANDARD SENTENCE RANGE .... [Low] to [High]

SEXUAL MOTIVATION ENHANCEMENT (Per Sexual Motivation Enhancement, page 185) .... [ ]

STANDARD SENTENCE RANGE PLUS ENHANCEMENT .... [Low] to [High]

- ✓ For attempt, solicitation, conspiracy (RCW 9.94A.595) see page 23 or for gang-related felonies where the court found the offender involved a minor (RCW 9.94A.833) see page 186 for standard range adjustments.
- ✓ For deadly weapon enhancement, see page 190.
- ✓ For sentencing alternatives, see page 177.
- ✓ For community custody eligibility, see page 187.
- ✓ For any applicable enhancements other than deadly weapon enhancement, see page 183.
- ✓ If the offender is not a persistent offender and has a prior conviction for an offense listed in RCW 9.94A.030(38)(b), then the sentence is subject to the requirements of RCW 9.94A.507.

The Caseload Forecast Council is not liable for errors or omissions in the manual, for sentences that may be inappropriately calculated as a result of a practitioner's or court's reliance on the manual, or for any other written or verbal information related to adult or juvenile sentencing. The scoring sheets are intended to provide assistance in most cases but do not cover all permutations of the scoring rules. If you find any errors or omissions, we encourage you to report them to the Caseload Forecast Council.

General Serious Violent Offense Where Domestic Violence Has Been Plead And Proven

SERIOUS VIOLENT
OFFENDER SCORING RCW 9.94A.525(21)

CURRENT OFFENSE BEING SCORED: _____

ADULT HISTORY:
- Enter number of domestic violence felony convictions as listed below* .... _____ x 2 = _____
- Enter number of repetitive domestic violence offense convictions (RCW 9.94A.030(42)) plead and proven after 8/1/11 .... _____ x 1 = _____
- Enter number of serious violent felony convictions .... _____ x 3 = _____
- Enter number of violent felony convictions .... _____ x 2 = _____
- Enter number of nonviolent felony convictions .... _____ x 1 = _____

JUVENILE HISTORY:
- Enter number of subsequent domestic violence felony dispositions as listed below* .... _____ x 1 = _____
- Enter number of serious violent felony dispositions .... _____ x 3 = _____
- Enter number of violent felony dispositions .... _____ x 2 = _____
- Enter number of nonviolent felony dispositions .... _____ x ½ = _____

OTHER CURRENT OFFENSES:
(Other current offenses that do not encompass the same conduct count in offender score)
- Enter number of other domestic violence felony convictions as listed below* .... _____ x 2 = _____
- Enter number of other repetitive domestic violence offense convictions plead and proven after 8/1/11 .... _____ x 1 = _____
- Enter number of other violent felony convictions .... _____ x 2 = _____
- Enter number of other nonviolent felony convictions .... _____ x 1 = _____

STATUS:
- Was the offender on community custody on the date the current offense was committed? .... + 1 = _____

*If domestic violence was plead and proven after 8/1/2011 for the following felony offenses: Violation of a No-Contact Order, Violation of a Protection Order, Domestic Violence Harassment, Domestic Violence Stalking, Domestic Violence Burglary 1, Domestic Violence Kidnapping 1, Domestic Violence Kidnapping 2, Domestic Violence Unlawful Imprisonment, Domestic Violence Robbery 1, Domestic Violence Robbery 2, Domestic Violence Assault 1, Domestic Violence Assault 2, Domestic Violence Assault 3, Domestic Violence Arson 1, Domestic Violence Arson 2.

STANDARD RANGE CALCULATION

Total the last column to get the **Offender Score** (Round down to the nearest whole number)

SERIOUSNESS LEVEL ....

STANDARD SENTENCE RANGE .... [Low] to [High]

- ✓ For attempt, solicitation, conspiracy (RCW 9.94A.595) see page 23 or for gang-related felonies where the court found the offender involved a minor (RCW 9.94A.833) see page 186 for standard range adjustments.
- ✓ For deadly weapon enhancement, see page 190.
- ✓ For sentencing alternatives, see page 177.
- ✓ For community custody eligibility, see page 187.
- ✓ For any applicable enhancements other than deadly weapon enhancement, see page 183.

The Caseload Forecast Council is not liable for errors or omissions in the manual, for sentences that may be inappropriately calculated as a result of a practitioner's or court's reliance on the manual, or for any other written or verbal information related to adult or juvenile sentencing. The scoring sheets are intended to provide assistance in most cases but do not cover all permutations of the scoring rules. If you find any errors or omissions, we encourage you to report them to the Caseload Forecast Council.

General Serious Violent/Sex Offense Where Domestic Violence Has Been Plead And Proven

SERIOUS VIOLENT/SEX

OFFENDER SCORING RCW 9.94A.525(17)

CURRENT OFFENSE BEING SCORED: _____

ADULT HISTORY:
    Enter number of sex offense convictions .... _____ x 3 = _____
    Enter number of domestic violence felony convictions as listed below* .... _____ x 2 = _____
    Enter number of <u>repetitive domestic violence offense</u> convictions (RCW 9.94A.030(42)) plead and proven after 8/1/11 .... _____ x 1 = _____
    Enter number of serious violent felony convictions .... _____ x 3 = _____
    Enter number of violent felony convictions .... _____ x 2 = _____
    Enter number of nonviolent felony convictions .... _____ x 1 = _____

JUVENILE HISTORY:
    Enter number of sex offense dispositions .... _____ x 3 = _____
    Enter number of <u>subsequent</u> domestic violence felony dispositions as listed below* .... _____ x 1 = _____
    Enter number of serious violent felony dispositions .... _____ x 3 = _____
    Enter number of violent felony dispositions .... _____ x 2 = _____
    Enter number of nonviolent felony dispositions .... _____ x ½ = _____

OTHER CURRENT OFFENSES:
(Other current offenses that do not encompass the same conduct count in offender score)
    Enter number of other sex offense convictions .... _____ x 3 = _____
    Enter number of other domestic violence felony convictions as listed below* .... _____ x 2 = _____
    Enter number of other <u>repetitive domestic violence offense</u> convictions plead and proven after 8/1/11 .... _____ x 1 = _____
    Enter number of other violent felony convictions .... _____ x 2 = _____
    Enter number of other nonviolent felony convictions .... _____ x 1 = _____

STATUS:
    Was the offender on community custody on the date the current offense was committed? .... + 1 = _____

*If domestic violence was plead and proven after 8/1/2011 for the following felony offenses:
Violation of a No-Contact Order, Violation of a Protection Order, Domestic Violence Harassment, Domestic Violence Stalking, Domestic Violence Burglary 1, Domestic Violence Kidnapping 1, Domestic Violence Kidnapping 2, Domestic Violence Unlawful Imprisonment, Domestic Violence Robbery 1, Domestic Violence Robbery 2, Domestic Violence Assault 1, Domestic Violence Assault 2, Domestic Violence Assault 3, Domestic Violence Arson 1, Domestic Violence Arson 2.

STANDARD RANGE CALCULATION

Total the last column to get the **Offender Score** (Round down to the nearest whole number) .... [ ]

SERIOUSNESS LEVEL .... [ ]

STANDARD SENTENCE RANGE .... [Low] to [High]

- ✓ For attempt, solicitation, conspiracy (RCW 9.94A.595) see page 23 or for gang-related felonies where the court found the offender involved a minor (RCW 9.94A.833) see page 186 for standard range adjustments.
- ✓ For deadly weapon enhancement, see page 190.
- ✓ For sentencing alternatives, see page 177.
- ✓ For community custody eligibility, see page 187.
- ✓ For any applicable enhancements other than deadly weapon enhancement, see page 183.
- ✓ If the offender is not a persistent offender and has a prior conviction for an offense listed in RCW 9.94A.030(38)(b), then the sentence is subject to the requirements of RCW 9.94A.507.

The Caseload Forecast Council is not liable for errors or omissions in the manual, for sentences that may be inappropriately calculated as a result of a practitioner's or court's reliance on the manual, or for any other written or verbal information related to adult or juvenile sentencing. The scoring sheets are intended to provide assistance in most cases but do not cover all permutations of the scoring rules. If you find any errors or omissions, we encourage you to report them to the Caseload Forecast Council.

General Serious Violent Offense With A Sexual Motivation Finding

SERIOUS VIOLENT/SEX

OFFENDER SCORING RCW 9.94A.525(17)

CURRENT OFFENSE BEING SCORED:
_____

ADULT HISTORY:
Enter number of sex offense convictions .... _____ x 3 = _____
Enter number of serious violent felony convictions .... _____ x 3 = _____
Enter number of violent felony convictions .... _____ x 2 = _____
Enter number of nonviolent felony convictions .... _____ x 1 = _____

JUVENILE HISTORY:
Enter number of sex offense dispositions .... _____ x 3 = _____
Enter number of serious violent felony dispositions .... _____ x 3 = _____
Enter number of violent felony dispositions .... _____ x 2 = _____
Enter number of nonviolent felony dispositions .... _____ x ½ = _____

OTHER CURRENT OFFENSES:
(Other current offenses that do not encompass the same conduct count in offender score)
Enter number of other sex offense convictions .... _____ x 3 = _____
Enter number of other violent felony convictions .... _____ x 2 = _____
Enter number of other nonviolent felony convictions .... _____ x 1 = _____

STATUS:
Was the offender on community custody on the date the current offense was committed? .... + 1 = _____

STANDARD RANGE CALCULATION

Total the last column to get the **Offender Score** (Round down to the nearest whole number) [ ]

SERIOUSNESS LEVEL .... [ ]

STANDARD SENTENCE RANGE .... [Low] to [High]

SEXUAL MOTIVATION ENHANCEMENT (Per Sexual Motivation Enhancement, page 185) [ ]

STANDARD SENTENCE RANGE PLUS ENHANCEMENT .... [Low] to [High]

- ✓ For attempt, solicitation, conspiracy (RCW 9.94A.595) see page 23 or for gang-related felonies where the court found the offender involved a minor (RCW 9.94A.833) see page 186 for standard range adjustments.
- ✓ For deadly weapon enhancement, see page 190.
- ✓ For sentencing alternatives, see page 177.
- ✓ For community custody eligibility, see page 187.
- ✓ For any applicable enhancements other than deadly weapon enhancement, see page 183.
- ✓ If the offender is not a persistent offender and has a prior conviction for an offense listed in RCW 9.94A.030(38)(b), then the sentence is subject to the requirements of RCW 9.94A.507.

The Caseload Forecast Council is not liable for errors or omissions in the manual, for sentences that may be inappropriately calculated as a result of a practitioner's or court's reliance on the manual, or for any other written or verbal information related to adult or juvenile sentencing. The scoring sheets are intended to provide assistance in most cases but do not cover all permutations of the scoring rules. If you find any errors or omissions, we encourage you to report them to the Caseload Forecast Council.

General Violent Offense Where Domestic Violence Has Been Plead And Proven

VIOLENT
OFFENDER SCORING RCW 9.94A.525(21)

CURRENT OFFENSE BEING SCORED:
_____

ADULT HISTORY:

Enter number of domestic violence felony convictions as listed below* .... _____ x 2 = _____

Enter number of <u>repetitive domestic violence offense</u> convictions (RCW 9.94A.030(42)) plead and proven after 8/1/11 .... _____ x 1 = _____

Enter number of serious violent and violent felony convictions .... _____ x 2 = _____

Enter number of nonviolent felony convictions .... _____ x 1 = _____

JUVENILE HISTORY:

Enter number of <u>subsequent</u> domestic violence felony dispositions as listed below* .... _____ x 1 = _____

Enter number of serious violent and violent felony dispositions .... _____ x 2 = _____

Enter number of nonviolent felony dispositions .... _____ x ½ = _____

OTHER CURRENT OFFENSES:
(Other current offenses that do not encompass the same conduct count in offender score)

Enter number of other domestic violence felony convictions as listed below* .... _____ x 2 = _____

Enter number of <u>repetitive domestic violence offense</u> convictions plead and proven after 8/1/11 .... _____ x 1 = _____

Enter number of other serious violent and violent felony convictions .... _____ x 2 = _____

Enter number of other nonviolent felony convictions .... _____ x 1 = _____

STATUS:

Was the offender on community custody on the date the current offense was committed? ... + 1 = _____

*If domestic violence was plead and proven after 8/1/2011 for the following felony offenses:
Violation of a No-Contact Order, Violation of a Protection Order, Domestic Violence Harassment, Domestic Violence Stalking, Domestic Violence Burglary 1, Domestic Violence Kidnapping 1, Domestic Violence Kidnapping 2, Domestic Violence Unlawful Imprisonment, Domestic Violence Robbery 1, Domestic Violence Robbery 2, Domestic Violence Assault 1, Domestic Violence Assault 2, Domestic Violence Assault 3, Domestic Violence Arson 1, Domestic Violence Arson 2.

STANDARD RANGE CALCULATION

Total the last column to get the **Offender Score** (Round down to the nearest whole number)

SERIOUSNESS LEVEL ....

STANDARD SENTENCE RANGE .... [Low] to [High]

- ✓ For attempt, solicitation, conspiracy (RCW 9.94A.595) see page 23 or for gang-related felonies where the court found the offender involved a minor (RCW 9.94A.833) see page 186 for standard range adjustments.
- ✓ For deadly weapon enhancement, see page 190.
- ✓ For sentencing alternatives, see page 177.
- ✓ For community custody eligibility, see page 187.
- ✓ For any applicable enhancements other than deadly weapon enhancement, see page 183.

The Caseload Forecast Council is not liable for errors or omissions in the manual, for sentences that may be inappropriately calculated as a result of a practitioner's or court's reliance on the manual, or for any other written or verbal information related to adult or juvenile sentencing. The scoring sheets are intended to provide assistance in most cases but do not cover all permutations of the scoring rules. If you find any errors or omissions, we encourage you to report them to the Caseload Forecast Council.

General Violent/Sex Offense Where Domestic Violence Has Been Plead And Proven

VIOLENT/SEX

OFFENDER SCORING RCW 9.94A.525(17)

CURRENT OFFENSE BEING SCORED: _____

ADULT HISTORY:
Enter number of sex offense convictions .... _____ x 3 = _____
Enter number of domestic violence felony convictions as listed below* .... _____ x 2 = _____
Enter number of repetitive domestic violence offense convictions (RCW 9.94A.030(42)) plead and proven after 8/1/11 .... _____ x 1 = _____
Enter number of serious violent and violent felony convictions .... _____ x 2 = _____
Enter number of nonviolent felony convictions .... _____ x 1 = _____

JUVENILE HISTORY:
Enter number of sex offense dispositions .... _____ x 3 = _____
Enter number of subsequent domestic violence felony dispositions as listed below* .... _____ x 1 = _____
Enter number of serious violent and violent felony dispositions .... _____ x 2 = _____
Enter number of nonviolent felony dispositions .... _____ x ½ = _____

OTHER CURRENT OFFENSES:
(Other current offenses that do not encompass the same conduct count in offender score)
Enter number of other sex offense convictions .... _____ x 3 = _____
Enter number of other domestic violence felony convictions as listed below* .... _____ x 2 = _____
Enter number of repetitive domestic violence offense convictions plead and proven after 8/1/11 .... _____ x 1 = _____
Enter number of other serious violent and violent felony convictions .... _____ x 2 = _____
Enter number of other nonviolent felony convictions .... _____ x 1 = _____

STATUS:
Was the offender on community custody on the date the current offense was committed? .... + 1 = _____

*If domestic violence was plead and proven after 8/1/2011 for the following felony offenses: Violation of a No-Contact Order, Violation of a Protection Order, Domestic Violence Harassment, Domestic Violence Stalking, Domestic Violence Burglary 1, Domestic Violence Kidnapping 1, Domestic Violence Kidnapping 2, Domestic Violence Unlawful Imprisonment, Domestic Violence Robbery 1, Domestic Violence Robbery 2, Domestic Violence Assault 1, Domestic Violence Assault 2, Domestic Violence Assault 3, Domestic Violence Arson 1, Domestic Violence Arson 2.

STANDARD RANGE CALCULATION

Total the last column to get the **Offender Score** (Round down to the nearest whole number) ....

SERIOUSNESS LEVEL ....

STANDARD SENTENCE RANGE .... [Low] to [High]

- ✓ For attempt, solicitation, conspiracy (RCW 9.94A.595) see page 23 or for gang-related felonies where the court found the offender involved a minor (RCW 9.94A.833) see page 186 for standard range adjustments.
- ✓ For deadly weapon enhancement, see page 190.
- ✓ For sentencing alternatives, see page 177.
- ✓ For community custody eligibility, see page 187.
- ✓ For any applicable enhancements other than deadly weapon enhancement, see page 183.
- ✓ If the offender is not a persistent offender and has a prior conviction for an offense listed in RCW 9.94A.030(38)(b), then the sentence is subject to the requirements of RCW 9.94A.507.

The Caseload Forecast Council is not liable for errors or omissions in the manual, for sentences that may be inappropriately calculated as a result of a practitioner's or court's reliance on the manual, or for any other written or verbal information related to adult or juvenile sentencing. The scoring sheets are intended to provide assistance in most cases but do not cover all permutations of the scoring rules. If you find any errors or omissions, we encourage you to report them to the Caseload Forecast Council.

General Violent Offense With A Sexual Motivation Finding

VIOLENT/SEX

OFFENDER SCORING RCW 9.94A.525(17)

CURRENT OFFENSE BEING SCORED:
_____

ADULT HISTORY:
Enter number of sex offense convictions .... _____ x 3 = _____
Enter number of serious violent and violent felony convictions .... _____ x 2 = _____
Enter number of nonviolent felony convictions .... _____ x 1 = _____

JUVENILE HISTORY:
Enter number of sex offense dispositions .... _____ x 3 = _____
Enter number of serious violent and violent felony dispositions .... _____ x 2 = _____
Enter number of nonviolent felony dispositions .... _____ x ½ = _____

OTHER CURRENT OFFENSES:
(Other current offenses that do not encompass the same conduct count in offender score)
Enter number of other sex offense convictions .... _____ x 3 = _____
Enter number of other serious violent and violent felony convictions .... _____ x 2 = _____
Enter number of other nonviolent felony convictions .... _____ x 1 = _____

STATUS:
Was the offender on community custody on the date the current offense was committed?.................. + 1 = _____

STANDARD RANGE CALCULATION

Total the last column to get the **Offender Score** (Round down to the nearest whole number) [____]

SERIOUSNESS LEVEL .... [____]

STANDARD SENTENCE RANGE .... [Low] to [High]

SEXUAL MOTIVATION ENHANCEMENT (Per Sexual Motivation Enhancement, page 185) [____]

STANDARD SENTENCE RANGE PLUS ENHANCEMENT .... [Low] to [High]

- ✓ For attempt, solicitation, conspiracy (RCW 9.94A.595) see page 23 or for gang-related felonies where the court found the offender involved a minor (RCW 9.94A.833) see page 186 for standard range adjustments.
- ✓ For deadly weapon enhancement, see page 190.
- ✓ For sentencing alternatives, see page 177.
- ✓ For community custody eligibility, see page 187.
- ✓ For any applicable enhancements other than deadly weapon enhancement, see page 183.
- ✓ If the offender is not a persistent offender and has a prior conviction for an offense listed in RCW 9.94A.030(38)(b), then the sentence is subject to the requirements of RCW 9.94A.507.

The Caseload Forecast Council is not liable for errors or omissions in the manual, for sentences that may be inappropriately calculated as a result of a practitioner's or court's reliance on the manual, or for any other written or verbal information related to adult or juvenile sentencing. The scoring sheets are intended to provide assistance in most cases but do not cover all permutations of the scoring rules. If you find any errors or omissions, we encourage you to report them to the Caseload Forecast Council.

General Burglary First Degree Offense Where Domestic Violence Has Been Plead And Proven

VIOLENT

OFFENDER SCORING RCW 9.94A.525(21)

CURRENT OFFENSE BEING SCORED:
_____

ADULT HISTORY:
Enter number of domestic violence felony convictions as listed below* .... _____ x 2 = _____
Enter number of <u>repetitive domestic violence offense</u> convictions (RCW 9.94A.030(42)) plead and proven after 8/1/11 .... _____ x 1 = _____
Enter number of Burglary 2 and Residential Burglary felony convictions .... _____ x 2 = _____
Enter number of serious violent and violent felony convictions .... _____ x 2 = _____
Enter number of nonviolent felony convictions .... _____ x 1 = _____

JUVENILE HISTORY:
Enter number of <u>subsequent</u> domestic violence felony dispositions as listed below* .... _____ x 1 = _____
Enter number of Burglary 2 and Residential Burglary felony dispositions .... _____ x 1 = _____
Enter number of serious violent and violent felony dispositions .... _____ x 2 = _____
Enter number of nonviolent felony dispositions .... _____ x ½ = _____

OTHER CURRENT OFFENSES:
(Other current offenses that do not encompass the same conduct count in offender score)
Enter number of other domestic violence felony convictions as listed below* .... _____ x 2 = _____
Enter number of <u>repetitive domestic violence offense</u> convictions plead and proven after 8/1/11 .... _____ x 1 = _____
Enter number of Burglary 2 and Residential Burglary felony convictions .... _____ x 2 = _____
Enter number of other serious violent and violent felony convictions .... _____ x 2 = _____
Enter number of other nonviolent felony convictions .... _____ x 1 = _____

STATUS:
Was the offender on community custody on the date the current offense was committed? .... + 1 = _____

*If domestic violence was plead and proven after 8/1/2011 for the following felony offenses:
Violation of a No-Contact Order, Violation of a Protection Order, Domestic Violence Harassment, Domestic Violence Stalking, Domestic Violence Burglary 1, Domestic Violence Kidnapping 1, Domestic Violence Kidnapping 2, Domestic Violence Unlawful Imprisonment, Domestic Violence Robbery 1, Domestic Violence Robbery 2, Domestic Violence Assault 1, Domestic Violence Assault 2, Domestic Violence Assault 3, Domestic Violence Arson 1, Domestic Violence Arson 2.

STANDARD RANGE CALCULATION

Total the last column to get the **Offender Score** (Round down to the nearest whole number)

SERIOUSNESS LEVEL ....

STANDARD SENTENCE RANGE .... [Low] to [High]

- ✓ For attempt, solicitation, conspiracy (RCW 9.94A.595) see page 23 or for gang-related felonies where the court found the offender involved a minor (RCW 9.94A.833) see page 186 for standard range adjustments.
- ✓ For deadly weapon enhancement, see page 190.
- ✓ For sentencing alternatives, see page 177.
- ✓ For community custody eligibility, see page 187.
- ✓ For any applicable enhancements other than deadly weapon enhancement, see page 183.

The Caseload Forecast Council is not liable for errors or omissions in the manual, for sentences that may be inappropriately calculated as a result of a practitioner's or court's reliance on the manual, or for any other written or verbal information related to adult or juvenile sentencing. The scoring sheets are intended to provide assistance in most cases but do not cover all permutations of the scoring rules. If you find any errors or omissions, we encourage you to report them to the Caseload Forecast Council.

General Burglary Second Degree Or Residential Burglary Offense Where Domestic Violence Has Been Plead and Proven

NONVIOLENT

OFFENDER SCORING RCW 9.94A.525(21)

CURRENT OFFENSE BEING SCORED:
_____

ADULT HISTORY:
- Enter number of domestic violence felony convictions as listed below* .... _____ x 2 = _____
- Enter number of <u>repetitive domestic violence offense</u> convictions (RCW 9.94A.030(42)) plead and proven after 8/1/11 .... _____ x 1 = _____
- Enter number of Burglary 1 felony convictions .... _____ x 2 = _____
- Enter number of Burglary 2 and Residential Burglary felony convictions .... _____ x 2 = _____
- Enter number of felony convictions .... _____ x 1 = _____

JUVENILE HISTORY:
- Enter number of <u>subsequent</u> domestic violence felony dispositions as listed below* .... _____ x 1 = _____
- Enter number of Burglary 1 felony dispositions .... _____ x 2 = _____
- Enter number of Burglary 2 and Residential Burglary felony dispositions .... _____ x 1 = _____
- Enter number of serious violent and violent felony dispositions .... _____ x 1 = _____
- Enter number of nonviolent felony dispositions .... _____ x ½ = _____

OTHER CURRENT OFFENSES:
(Other current offenses that do not encompass the same conduct count in offender score)
- Enter number of other domestic violence felony convictions as listed below* .... _____ x 2 = _____
- Enter number of other <u>repetitive domestic violence offense</u> convictions plead and proven after 8/1/11 .... _____ x 1 = _____
- Enter number of Burglary 1 felony convictions .... _____ x 2 = _____
- Enter number of Burglary 2 and Residential Burglary felony convictions .... _____ x 2 = _____
- Enter number of other felony convictions .... _____ x 1 = _____

STATUS:
- Was the offender on community custody on the date the current offense was committed? (if yes) .... + 1 = _____

*If domestic violence was plead and proven after 8/1/2011 for the following felony offenses:
Violation of a No-Contact Order, Violation of a Protection Order, Domestic Violence Harassment, Domestic Violence Stalking, Domestic Violence Burglary 1, Domestic Violence Kidnapping 1, Domestic Violence Kidnapping 2, Domestic Violence Unlawful Imprisonment, Domestic Violence Robbery 1, Domestic Violence Robbery 2, Domestic Violence Assault 1, Domestic Violence Assault 2, Domestic Violence Assault 3, Domestic Violence Arson 1, Domestic Violence Arson 2.

STANDARD RANGE CALCULATION

Total the last column to get the **Offender Score** (Round down to the nearest whole number)   [ ]

SERIOUSNESS LEVEL ....   [ ]

STANDARD SENTENCE RANGE .... [Low] to [High]

- ✓ For attempt, solicitation, conspiracy (RCW 9.94A.595) see page 23 or for gang-related felonies where the court found the offender involved a minor (RCW 9.94A.833) see page 186 for standard range adjustments.
- ✓ For deadly weapon enhancement, see page 190.
- ✓ For sentencing alternatives, see page 177.
- ✓ For community custody eligibility, see page 187.
- ✓ For any applicable enhancements other than deadly weapon enhancement, see page 183.

General Unranked Offense With A Sexual Motivation Finding

NONVIOLENT/SEX

OFFENDER SCORING RCW 9.94A.525(17)

CURRENT OFFENSE BEING SCORED: _____

ADULT HISTORY:
Not scored

JUVENILE HISTORY:
Not scored

OTHER CURRENT OFFENSES:
Not scored

STATUS:
Not scored

STANDARD RANGE CALCULATION

STANDARD SENTENCE RANGE .... [Low] to [High]

SEXUAL MOTIVATION ENHANCEMENT (Per Sexual Motivation Enhancement, page 185) [ ]

STANDARD SENTENCE RANGE PLUS ENHANCEMENT .... [Low] to [High]

- ✓ For gang-related felonies where the court found the offender involved a minor (RCW 9.94A.833) see page 186 for standard range adjustment.
- ✓ For deadly weapon enhancement, see page 190.
- ✓ For sentencing alternatives, see page 177.
- ✓ For community custody eligibility, see page 187.
- ✓ For any applicable enhancements other than deadly weapon enhancement, see page 183.
- ✓ If the offender is not a persistent offender and has a prior conviction for an offense listed in RCW 9.94A.030(38)(b), then the sentence is subject to the requirements of RCW 9.94A.507.

The Caseload Forecast Council is not liable for errors or omissions in the manual, for sentences that may be inappropriately calculated as a result of a practitioner's or court's reliance on the manual, or for any other written or verbal information related to adult or juvenile sentencing. The scoring sheets are intended to provide assistance in most cases but do not cover all permutations of the scoring rules. If you find any errors or omissions, we encourage you to report them to the Caseload Forecast Council.

SECTION 7 – ALPHABETIZED FELONY SCORING FORMS

General scoring forms are provided at the beginning of this section and are followed by the individual offense scoring. The individual offense scoring forms are arranged alphabetically and include forms for controlled substances, imitation controlled substances and legend drug crimes. Please note that the scoring forms do not present sentencing options eligibility (*e.g.*, work release, work ethic camp). Please refer to Sentencing Alternatives in Section 6 of this manual for clarification of eligibility rules or conditions for each sentencing option.

In past manuals, if a sentence range extended past the statutory maximum of the offense, the sentence range was truncated and displayed an asterisk that referenced what the statutory maximum was. In this manual, the sentence range will still be truncated where available and display an asterisk. The corresponding asterisk will be next to the classification at the top of the page, *i.e.*, Class C*.

Abandonment Of Dependent Persons First Degree

RCW 9A.42.060
CLASS B* – NONVIOLENT

OFFENDER SCORING RCW 9.94A.525(7)

If it was found that this offense was committed with sexual motivation (RCW 9.94A.533(8)) on or after 7/01/2006, use the General Nonviolent Offense with a Sexual Motivation Finding scoring form on page 193.

If the present conviction is for a felony domestic violence offense where domestic violence was plead and proven, use the General Nonviolent Offense Where Domestic Violence Has Been Plead and Proven scoring form on page 191.

ADULT HISTORY:
  Enter number of felony convictions .... _____ x 1 = _____

JUVENILE HISTORY:
  Enter number of serious violent and violent felony dispositions .... _____ x 1 = _____
  Enter number of nonviolent felony dispositions .... _____ x ½ = _____

OTHER CURRENT OFFENSES:
(Other current offenses that do not encompass the same conduct count in offender score)
  Enter number of other felony convictions .... _____ x 1 = _____

STATUS:
  Was the offender on community custody on the date the current offense was committed? (if yes) ...... + 1 = _____

Total the last column to get the **Offender Score** (Round down to the nearest whole number)

SENTENCE RANGE

	Offender Score									
	0	1	2	3	4	5	6	7	8	9+
LEVEL IX	36m	42m	47.5m	53.5m	59.5m	66m	89.5m	101.5m	114m	
	31 - 41	36 - 48	41 - 54	46 - 61	51 - 68	57 - 75	77 - 102	87 - 116	108 - 120*	120 - 120*

- ✓ For attempt, solicitation, conspiracy (RCW 9.94A.595) see page 23 or for gang-related felonies where the court found the offender involved a minor (RCW 9.94A.833) see page 186 for standard range adjustments.
- ✓ For deadly weapon enhancement, see page 190.
- ✓ For sentencing alternatives, see page 177.
- ✓ For community custody eligibility, see page 187.
- ✓ For any applicable enhancements other than deadly weapon enhancement, see page 183.

Abandonment Of Dependent Persons Second Degree

RCW 9A.42.070
CLASS C* – NONVIOLENT
OFFENDER SCORING RCW 9.94A.525(7)

If it was found that this offense was committed with sexual motivation (RCW 9.94A.533(8)) on or after 7/01/2006, use the General Nonviolent Offense with a Sexual Motivation Finding scoring form on page 193.

If the present conviction is for a felony domestic violence offense where domestic violence was plead and proven, use the General Nonviolent Offense Where Domestic Violence Has Been Plead and Proven scoring form on page 191.

ADULT HISTORY:
Enter number of felony convictions .... _____ x 1 = _____

JUVENILE HISTORY:
Enter number of serious violent and violent felony dispositions .... _____ x 1 = _____

Enter number of nonviolent felony dispositions .... _____ x ½ = _____

OTHER CURRENT OFFENSES:
(Other current offenses that do not encompass the same conduct count in offender score)
Enter number of other felony convictions .... _____ x 1 = _____

STATUS:
Was the offender on community custody on the date the current offense was committed? (if yes) .... + 1 = _____

Total the last column to get the **Offender Score** (Round down to the nearest whole number)

SENTENCE RANGE

	Offender Score									
	0	1	2	3	4	5	6	7	8	9+
LEVEL V	9m	13m	15m	17.5m	25.5m	38m	47.5m	55.5m		
	6 - 12	12+ - 14	13 - 17	15 - 20	22 - 29	33 - 43	41 - 54	51 - 60*	60 - 60*	60 - 60*

✓ For gang-related felonies where the court found the offender involved a minor (RCW 9.94A.833) see page 186 for standard range adjustment.

✓ For deadly weapon enhancement, see page 190.

✓ For sentencing alternatives, see page 177.

✓ For community custody eligibility, see page 187.

✓ For any applicable enhancements other than deadly weapon enhancement, see page 183.

Advancing Money Or Property For Extortionate Extension Of Credit

RCW 9A.82.030

CLASS B – NONVIOLENT

OFFENDER SCORING RCW 9.94A.525(7)

If it was found that this offense was committed with sexual motivation (RCW 9.94A.533(8)) on or after 7/01/2006, use the General Nonviolent Offense with a Sexual Motivation Finding scoring form on page 193.

If the present conviction is for a felony domestic violence offense where domestic violence was plead and proven, use the General Nonviolent Offense Where Domestic Violence Has Been Plead and Proven scoring form on page 191.

ADULT HISTORY:
  Enter number of felony convictions .... _____   x 1 = _____

JUVENILE HISTORY:
  Enter number of serious violent and violent felony dispositions .... _____   x 1 = _____

  Enter number of nonviolent felony dispositions .... _____   x ½ = _____

OTHER CURRENT OFFENSES:
(Other current offenses that do not encompass the same conduct count in offender score)
  Enter number of other felony convictions .... _____   x 1 = _____

STATUS:
  Was the offender on community custody on the date the current offense was committed? (if yes) ......   + 1 = _____

Total the last column to get the **Offender Score** (Round down to the nearest whole number)

SENTENCE RANGE

	\multicolumn{10}{c}{Offender Score}
	0	1	2	3	4	5	6	7	8	9+
LEVEL V	9m 6 - 12	13m 12+ - 14	15m 13 - 17	17.5m 15 - 20	25.5m 22 - 29	38m 33 - 43	47.5m 41 - 54	59.5m 51 - 68	72m 62 - 82	84m 72 - 96

✓ For attempt, solicitation, conspiracy (RCW 9.94A.595) see page 23 or for gang-related felonies where the court found the offender involved a minor (RCW 9.94A.833) see page 186 for standard range adjustments.

✓ For deadly weapon enhancement, see page 190.

✓ For sentencing alternatives, see page 177.

✓ For community custody eligibility, see page 187.

✓ For any applicable enhancements other than deadly weapon enhancement, see page 183.

The Caseload Forecast Council is not liable for errors or omissions in the manual, for sentences that may be inappropriately calculated as a result of a practitioner's or court's reliance on the manual, or for any other written or verbal information related to adult or juvenile sentencing. The scoring sheets are intended to provide assistance in most cases but do not cover all permutations of the scoring rules. If you find any errors or omissions, we encourage you to report them to the Caseload Forecast Council.

Aggravated Murder First Degree

RCW 10.95.020 & RCW 10.95.030(1)
CLASS A – SERIOUS VIOLENT

OFFENDER SCORING

ADULT HISTORY: Not scored

JUVENILE HISTORY: Not scored

OTHER CURRENT OFFENSES: Not scored

STATUS: Not scored

SENTENCE RANGE

	Offender Score									
	0	1	2	3	4	5	6	7	8	9+
LEVEL XVI	Life sentence without parole/death penalty for offenders at or over the age of eighteen. For offenders under the age of eighteen, a term of twenty-five years to life.									

- ✓ A person found to be intellectually disabled under RCW 10.95.030 may in no case be sentenced to death (RCW 10.95.070).

- ✓ A person who was at least 16 years old but less than 18 years old shall be sentenced to a maximum term of life imprisonment and a minimum term of total confinement of no less than 25 years. A minimum term of life may be imposed, in which case the person will be ineligible for parole or early release. (In setting the minimum term, the court must take into account mitigating factors that account for the diminished culpability of youth as provided in *Miller v. Alabama*, 132 S. Ct. 2455 (2012)).

- ✓ A person who was younger than 16 years old shall be sentenced to a maximum term of life imprisonment and a minimum term of total confinement of 25 years.

The Caseload Forecast Council is not liable for errors or omissions in the manual, for sentences that may be inappropriately calculated as a result of a practitioner's or court's reliance on the manual, or for any other written or verbal information related to adult or juvenile sentencing. The scoring sheets are intended to provide assistance in most cases but do not cover all permutations of the scoring rules. If you find any errors or omissions, we encourage you to report them to the Caseload Forecast Council.

Animal Cruelty First Degree Sexual Contact Or Conduct

RCW 16.52.205(3)
CLASS C* – NONVIOLENT

OFFENDER SCORING RCW 9.94A.525(7)

If it was found that this offense was committed with sexual motivation (RCW 9.94A.533(8)) on or after 7/01/2006, use the General Nonviolent Offense with a Sexual Motivation Finding scoring form on page 193.

If the present conviction is for a felony domestic violence offense where domestic violence was plead and proven, use the General Nonviolent Offense Where Domestic Violence Has Been Plead and Proven scoring form on page 191.

ADULT HISTORY:
    Enter number of felony convictions .... _____ x 1 = _____

JUVENILE HISTORY:
    Enter number of serious violent and violent felony dispositions .... _____ x 1 = _____
    Enter number of nonviolent felony dispositions .... _____ x ½ = _____

OTHER CURRENT OFFENSES:
(Other current offenses that do not encompass the same conduct count in offender score)
    Enter number of other felony convictions .... _____ x 1 = _____

STATUS:
    Was the offender on community custody on the date the current offense was committed? (if yes) ...... + 1 = _____

Total the last column to get the **Offender Score** (Round down to the nearest whole number)

SENTENCE RANGE

	Offender Score									
	0	1	2	3	4	5	6	7	8	9+
LEVEL III	2m	5m	8m	11m	14m	19.5m	25.5m	38m	50m	55.5m
	1 - 3	3 - 8	4 - 12	9 - 12	12+ - 16	17 - 22	22 - 29	33 - 43	43 - 57	51 - 60*

- ✓ For gang-related felonies where the court found the offender involved a minor (RCW 9.94A.833) see page 186 for standard range adjustment.
- ✓ For deadly weapon enhancement, see page 190.
- ✓ For sentencing alternatives, see page 177.
- ✓ For community custody eligibility, see page 187.
- ✓ For any applicable enhancements other than deadly weapon enhancement, see page 183.

The Caseload Forecast Council is not liable for errors or omissions in the manual, for sentences that may be inappropriately calculated as a result of a practitioner's or court's reliance on the manual, or for any other written or verbal information related to adult or juvenile sentencing. The scoring sheets are intended to provide assistance in most cases but do not cover all permutations of the scoring rules. If you find any errors or omissions, we encourage you to report them to the Caseload Forecast Council.

Arson First Degree

RCW 9A.48.020
CLASS A – VIOLENT
ATTEMPT/SOLICITATION = CLASS A
CONSPIRACY = CLASS B

OFFENDER SCORING RCW 9.94A.525(8)

If it was found that this offense was committed with sexual motivation (RCW 9.94A.533(8)) on or after 7/01/2006, use the General Violent Offense with a Sexual Motivation Finding scoring form on page 201.

If the present conviction is for a felony domestic violence offense where domestic violence was plead and proven, use the General Violent Offense Where Domestic Violence Has Been Plead and Proven scoring form on page 199.

ADULT HISTORY:
   Enter number of serious violent and violent felony convictions .... _____ x 2 = _____
   Enter number of nonviolent felony convictions .... _____ x 1 = _____

JUVENILE HISTORY:
   Enter number of serious violent and violent felony dispositions .... _____ x 2 = _____
   Enter number of nonviolent felony dispositions .... _____ x ½ = _____

OTHER CURRENT OFFENSES:
(Other current offenses that do not encompass the same conduct count in offender score)
   Enter number of other serious violent and violent felony convictions .... _____ x 2 = _____
   Enter number of other nonviolent felony convictions .... _____ x 1 = _____

STATUS:
   Was the offender on community custody on the date the current offense was committed? (if yes) .... + 1 = _____

Total the last column to get the **Offender Score** (Round down to the nearest whole number)

SENTENCE RANGE

	_	Offender Score								
	0	**1**	**2**	**3**	**4**	**5**	**6**	**7**	**8**	**9+**
LEVEL VIII	24m 21 - 27	30m 26 - 34	36m 31 - 41	42m 36 - 48	47.5m 41 - 54	53.5m 46 - 61	78m 67 - 89	89.5m 77 - 102	101.5m 87 - 116	126m 108 - 144

- ✓ For attempt, solicitation, conspiracy (RCW 9.94A.595) see page 23 or for gang-related felonies where the court found the offender involved a minor (RCW 9.94A.833) see page 186 for standard range adjustments.
- ✓ For deadly weapon enhancement, see page 190.
- ✓ For sentencing alternatives, see page 177.
- ✓ For community custody eligibility, see page 187.
- ✓ For any applicable enhancements other than deadly weapon enhancement, see page 183.

The Caseload Forecast Council is not liable for errors or omissions in the manual, for sentences that may be inappropriately calculated as a result of a practitioner's or court's reliance on the manual, or for any other written or verbal information related to adult or juvenile sentencing. The scoring sheets are intended to provide assistance in most cases but do not cover all permutations of the scoring rules. If you find any errors or omissions, we encourage you to report them to the Caseload Forecast Council.

Arson Second Degree

RCW 9A.48.030
CLASS B – VIOLENT

OFFENDER SCORING RCW 9.94A.525(8)

If it was found that this offense was committed with sexual motivation (RCW 9.94A.533(8)) on or after 7/01/2006, use the General Violent Offense with a Sexual Motivation Finding scoring form on page 201.

If the present conviction is for a felony domestic violence offense where domestic violence was plead and proven, use the General Violent Offense Where Domestic Violence Has Been Plead and Proven scoring form on page 199.

ADULT HISTORY:
    Enter number of serious violent and violent felony convictions .... _____ x 2 = _____
    Enter number of nonviolent felony convictions .... _____ x 1 = _____

JUVENILE HISTORY:
    Enter number of serious violent and violent felony dispositions .... _____ x 2 = _____
    Enter number of nonviolent felony dispositions .... _____ x ½ = _____

OTHER CURRENT OFFENSES:
(Other current offenses that do not encompass the same conduct count in offender score)
    Enter number of other serious violent and violent felony convictions .... _____ x 2 = _____
    Enter number of other nonviolent felony convictions .... _____ x 1 = _____

STATUS:
    Was the offender on community custody on the date the current offense was committed? (if yes) ...... + 1 = _____

Total the last column to get the **Offender Score** (Round down to the nearest whole number)

SENTENCE RANGE

	Offender Score									
	0	1	2	3	4	5	6	7	8	9+
LEVEL IV	6m	9m	13m	15m	17.5m	25.5m	38m	50m	61.5m	73.5m
	3 - 9	6 - 12	12+ - 14	13 - 17	15 - 20	22 - 29	33 - 43	43 - 57	53 - 70	63 - 84

- ✓ For attempt, solicitation, conspiracy (RCW 9.94A.595) see page 23 or for gang-related felonies where the court found the offender involved a minor (RCW 9.94A.833) see page 186 for standard range adjustments.
- ✓ For deadly weapon enhancement, see page 190.
- ✓ For sentencing alternatives, see page 177.
- ✓ For community custody eligibility, see page 187.
- ✓ For any applicable enhancements other than deadly weapon enhancement, see page 183.

The Caseload Forecast Council is not liable for errors or omissions in the manual, for sentences that may be inappropriately calculated as a result of a practitioner's or court's reliance on the manual, or for any other written or verbal information related to adult or juvenile sentencing. The scoring sheets are intended to provide assistance in most cases but do not cover all permutations of the scoring rules. If you find any errors or omissions, we encourage you to report them to the Caseload Forecast Council.

Assault First Degree

RCW 9A.36.011
CLASS A – SERIOUS VIOLENT

OFFENDER SCORING RCW 9.94A.525(9)

If the present conviction is for a felony domestic violence offense where domestic violence was plead and proven, use the General Serious Violent Offense Where Domestic Violence Has Been Plead and Proven scoring form on page 196.

ADULT HISTORY:
    Enter number of serious violent felony convictions .... _____ x 3 = _____
    Enter number of violent felony convictions .... _____ x 2 = _____
    Enter number of nonviolent felony convictions .... _____ x 1 = _____

JUVENILE HISTORY:
    Enter number of serious violent felony dispositions .... _____ x 3 = _____
    Enter number of violent felony dispositions .... _____ x 2 = _____
    Enter number of nonviolent felony dispositions .... _____ x ½ = _____

OTHER CURRENT OFFENSES:
(Other current offenses that do not encompass the same conduct count in offender score)
    Enter number of other violent felony convictions .... _____ x 2 = _____
    Enter number of other nonviolent felony convictions .... _____ x 1 = _____

STATUS:
    Was the offender on community custody on the date the current offense was committed? .... + 1 = _____

Total the last column to get the **Offender Score** (Round down to the nearest whole number)

SENTENCE RANGE

	Offender Score									
	0	1	2	3	4	5	6	7	8	9+
LEVEL XII	108m 93 - 123	119m 102 - 136	129m 111 - 147	140m 120 - 160	150m 129 - 171	161m 138 - 184	189m 162 - 216	207m 178 - 236	243m 209 - 277	279m 240 - 318

- ✓ For attempt, solicitation, conspiracy (RCW 9.94A.595) see page 23 or for gang-related felonies where the court found the offender involved a minor (RCW 9.94A.833) see page 186 for standard range adjustments.
- ✓ For deadly weapon enhancement, see page 190.
- ✓ For sentencing alternatives, see page 177.
- ✓ For community custody eligibility, see page 187.
- ✓ For any applicable enhancements other than deadly weapon enhancement, see page 183.
- ✓ Multiple current serious violent offenses shall have consecutive sentences imposed per the rules of RCW 9.94A.589(1)(b).
- ✓ Statutory <u>minimum</u> sentence is 60 months (RCW 9.94A.540) if the offender used force or means likely to result in death or intended to kill the victim. The statutory minimum sentence shall not be varied or modified under RCW 9.94A.535.

The Caseload Forecast Council is not liable for errors or omissions in the manual, for sentences that may be inappropriately calculated as a result of a practitioner's or court's reliance on the manual, or for any other written or verbal information related to adult or juvenile sentencing. The scoring sheets are intended to provide assistance in most cases but do not cover all permutations of the scoring rules. If you find any errors or omissions, we encourage you to report them to the Caseload Forecast Council.

Assault First Degree With A Finding Of Sexual Motivation

RCW 9A.36.011
CLASS A – SERIOUS VIOLENT/SEX

OFFENDER SCORING RCW 9.94A.525(17)

ADULT HISTORY:
    Enter number of sex offense convictions .... _____ x 3 = _____
    Enter number of serious violent felony convictions .... _____ x 3 = _____
    Enter number of violent felony convictions .... _____ x 2 = _____
    Enter number of nonviolent felony convictions .... _____ x 1 = _____

JUVENILE HISTORY:
    Enter number of sex offense dispositions .... _____ x 3 = _____
    Enter number of serious violent felony dispositions .... _____ x 3 = _____
    Enter number of violent felony dispositions .... _____ x 2 = _____
    Enter number of nonviolent felony dispositions .... _____ x ½ = _____

OTHER CURRENT OFFENSES:
(Other current offenses that do not encompass the same conduct count in offender score)
    Enter number of other sex offense convictions .... _____ x 3 = _____
    Enter number of other violent felony convictions .... _____ x 2 = _____
    Enter number of other nonviolent felony convictions .... _____ x 1 = _____

STATUS:
    Was the offender on community custody on the date the current offense was committed?................. + 1 = _____

Total the last column to get the **Offender Score** (Round down to the nearest whole number)

SENTENCE RANGE

	Offender Score									
	0	1	2	3	4	5	6	7	8	9+
LEVEL XII	108m	119m	129m	140m	150m	161m	189m	207m	243m	279m
	93 - 123	102 - 136	111 - 147	120 - 160	129 - 171	138 - 184	162 - 216	178 - 236	209 - 277	240 - 318

Add Sexual Motivation Enhancement (see page 185) \[____\] Standard Range = \[Low \] to \[High \]

- ✓ For attempt, solicitation, conspiracy (RCW 9.94A.595) see page 23 or for gang-related felonies where the court found the offender involved a minor (RCW 9.94A.833) see page 186 for standard range adjustments.
- ✓ For deadly weapon enhancement, see page 190.
- ✓ For sentencing alternatives, see page 177.
- ✓ For community custody eligibility, see page 187.
- ✓ For any applicable enhancements other than deadly weapon enhancement, see page 183.
- ✓ If the offender is not a persistent offender and the current offense was committed on or after 9/1/2001, then the offender is subject to the requirements under RCW 9.94A.507.
- ✓ Multiple current serious violent offenses shall have consecutive sentences imposed per the rules of RCW 9.94A.589(1)(b).
- ✓ Statutory minimum sentence is 60 months per RCW 9.94A.540 if the offender used force or means likely to result in death or intended to kill the victim. The statutory minimum sentence shall not be varied or modified under RCW 9.94A.535.

The Caseload Forecast Council is not liable for errors or omissions in the manual, for sentences that may be inappropriately calculated as a result of a practitioner's or court's reliance on the manual, or for any other written or verbal information related to adult or juvenile sentencing. The scoring sheets are intended to provide assistance in most cases but do not cover all permutations of the scoring rules. If you find any errors or omissions, we encourage you to report them to the Caseload Forecast Council.

Assault Second Degree

RCW 9A.36.021(2)(a)
CLASS B – VIOLENT
OFFENDER SCORING RCW 9.94A.525(8)

If the present conviction is for a felony domestic violence offense where domestic violence was plead and proven, use the General Violent Offense Where Domestic Violence Has Been Plead and Proven scoring form on page 199.

ADULT HISTORY:
    Enter number of serious violent and violent felony convictions .... _____ x 2 = _____

    Enter number of nonviolent felony convictions .... _____ x 1 = _____

JUVENILE HISTORY:
    Enter number of serious violent and violent felony dispositions .... _____ x 2 = _____

    Enter number of nonviolent felony dispositions .... _____ x ½ = _____

OTHER CURRENT OFFENSES:
(Other current offenses that do not encompass the same conduct count in offender score)
    Enter number of other serious violent and violent felony convictions .... _____ x 2 = _____

    Enter number of other nonviolent felony convictions .... _____ x 1 = _____

STATUS:
    Was the offender on community custody on the date the current offense was committed? .... + 1 = _____

Total the last column to get the **Offender Score** (Round down to the nearest whole number)

SENTENCE RANGE

	\multicolumn{10}{c}{Offender Score}									
	0	1	2	3	4	5	6	7	8	9+
LEVEL IV	6m 3 - 9	9m 6 - 12	13m 12+ - 14	15m 13 - 17	17.5m 15 - 20	25.5m 22 - 29	38m 33 - 43	50m 43 - 57	61.5m 53 - 70	73.5m 63 - 84

- ✓ For attempt, solicitation, conspiracy (RCW 9.94A.595) see page 23 or for gang-related felonies where the court found the offender involved a minor (RCW 9.94A.833) see page 186 for standard range adjustments.
- ✓ For deadly weapon enhancement, see page 190.
- ✓ For sentencing alternatives, see page 177.
- ✓ For community custody eligibility, see page 187.
- ✓ For any applicable enhancements other than deadly weapon enhancement, see page 183.

The Caseload Forecast Council is not liable for errors or omissions in the manual, for sentences that may be inappropriately calculated as a result of a practitioner's or court's reliance on the manual, or for any other written or verbal information related to adult or juvenile sentencing. The scoring sheets are intended to provide assistance in most cases but do not cover all permutations of the scoring rules. If you find any errors or omissions, we encourage you to report them to the Caseload Forecast Council.

Assault Second Degree With A Finding Of Sexual Motivation

RCW 9A.36.021(2)(b)
CLASS A – VIOLENT/SEX

OFFENDER SCORING RCW 9.94A.525(17)

ADULT HISTORY:
    Enter number of sex offense convictions .... _____ x 3 = _____

    Enter number of serious violent and violent felony convictions .... _____ x 2 = _____

    Enter number of nonviolent felony convictions .... _____ x 1 = _____

JUVENILE HISTORY:
    Enter number of sex offense dispositions .... _____ x 3 = _____

    Enter number of serious violent and violent felony dispositions .... _____ x 2 = _____

    Enter number of nonviolent felony dispositions .... _____ x ½ = _____

OTHER CURRENT OFFENSES:
(Other current offenses that do not encompass the same conduct count in offender score)
    Enter number of other sex offense convictions .... _____ x 3 = _____

    Enter number of other serious violent and violent felony convictions .... _____ x 2 = _____

    Enter number of other nonviolent felony convictions .... _____ x 1 = _____

STATUS:
    Was the offender on community custody on the date the current offense was committed?.................. + 1 = _____

Total the last column to get the **Offender Score** (Round down to the nearest whole number)

SENTENCE RANGE

	Offender Score									
	0	1	2	3	4	5	6	7	8	9+
LEVEL IV	6m	9m	13m	15m	17.5m	25.5m	38m	50m	61.5m	73.5m
	3 - 9	6 - 12	12+ - 14	13 - 17	15 - 20	22 - 29	33 - 43	43 - 57	53 - 70	63 - 84

Add Sexual Motivation Enhancement (see page 185) [____] o Standard Range = [Low] to [High]

- ✓ For attempt, solicitation, conspiracy (RCW 9.94A.595) see page 23 or for gang-related felonies where the court found the offender involved a minor (RCW 9.94A.833) see page 186 for standard range adjustments.
- ✓ For deadly weapon enhancement, see page 190.
- ✓ For sentencing alternatives, see page 177.
- ✓ For community custody eligibility, see page 187.
- ✓ For any applicable enhancements other than deadly weapon enhancement, see page 183.
- ✓ If the offender is not a persistent offender and the current offense was committed on or after 9/1/2001, then the offender is subject to the requirements under RCW 9.94A.507.

The Caseload Forecast Council is not liable for errors or omissions in the manual, for sentences that may be inappropriately calculated as a result of a practitioner's or court's reliance on the manual, or for any other written or verbal information related to adult or juvenile sentencing. The scoring sheets are intended to provide assistance in most cases but do not cover all permutations of the scoring rules. If you find any errors or omissions, we encourage you to report them to the Caseload Forecast Council.

Assault Third Degree Excluding Assault 3 Of A Peace Officer With A Projectile Stun Gun

RCW 9A.36.031(1)(a)-(g) & (i)-(j)
CLASS C* – NONVIOLENT

OFFENDER SCORING RCW 9.94A.525(7)

If it was found that this offense was committed with sexual motivation (RCW 9.94A.533(8)) on or after 7/01/2006, use the General Nonviolent Offense with a Sexual Motivation Finding scoring form on page 193.

If the present conviction is for a felony domestic violence offense where domestic violence was plead and proven, use the General Nonviolent Offense Where Domestic Violence Has Been Plead and Proven scoring form on page 191.

ADULT HISTORY:
  Enter number of felony convictions .... _____ x 1 = _____

JUVENILE HISTORY:
  Enter number of serious violent and violent felony dispositions .... _____ x 1 = _____
  Enter number of nonviolent felony dispositions .... _____ x ½ = _____

OTHER CURRENT OFFENSES:
(Other current offenses that do not encompass the same conduct count in offender score)
  Enter number of other felony convictions .... _____ x 1 = _____

STATUS:
  Was the offender on community custody on the date the current offense was committed? .... + 1 = _____

Total the last column to get the **Offender Score** (Round down to the nearest whole number)

SENTENCE RANGE

	Offender Score									
	0	1	2	3	4	5	6	7	8	9+
LEVEL III	2m	5m	8m	11m	14m	19.5m	25.5m	38m	50m	55.5m
	1 - 3	3 - 8	4 - 12	9 - 12	12+ - 16	17 - 22	22 - 29	33 - 43	43 - 57	51 - 60*

- ✓ For gang-related felonies where the court found the offender involved a minor (RCW 9.94A.833) see page 186 for standard range adjustment.
- ✓ For deadly weapon enhancement, see page 190.
- ✓ For sentencing alternatives, see page 177.
- ✓ For community custody eligibility, see page 187.
- ✓ For any applicable enhancements other than deadly weapon enhancement, see page 183.

The Caseload Forecast Council is not liable for errors or omissions in the manual, for sentences that may be inappropriately calculated as a result of a practitioner's or court's reliance on the manual, or for any other written or verbal information related to adult or juvenile sentencing. The scoring sheets are intended to provide assistance in most cases but do not cover all permutations of the scoring rules. If you find any errors or omissions, we encourage you to report them to the Caseload Forecast Council.

Assault Third Degree Of A Peace Officer With A Projectile Stun Gun

RCW 9A.36.031(1)(h)
CLASS C* – NONVIOLENT

OFFENDER SCORING RCW 9.94A.525(7)

If it was found that this offense was committed with sexual motivation (RCW 9.94A.533(8)) on or after 7/01/2006, use the General Nonviolent Offense with a Sexual Motivation Finding scoring form on page 193.

If the present conviction is for a felony domestic violence offense where domestic violence was plead and proven, use the General Nonviolent Offense Where Domestic Violence Has Been Plead and Proven scoring form on page 191.

ADULT HISTORY:
    Enter number of felony convictions .... _____ x 1 = _____

JUVENILE HISTORY:
    Enter number of serious violent and violent felony dispositions .... _____ x 1 = _____
    Enter number of nonviolent felony dispositions .... _____ x ½ = _____

OTHER CURRENT OFFENSES:
(Other current offenses that do not encompass the same conduct count in offender score)
    Enter number of other felony convictions .... _____ x 1 = _____

STATUS:
    Was the offender on community custody on the date the current offense was committed?.............. + 1 = _____

Total the last column to get the **Offender Score** (Round down to the nearest whole number)

SENTENCE RANGE

	Offender Score									
	0	1	2	3	4	5	6	7	8	9+
LEVEL IV	6m	9m	13m	15m	17.5m	25.5m	38m	50m	56.5m	
	3 - 9	6 - 12	12+ - 14	13 - 17	15 - 20	22 - 29	33 - 43	43 - 57	53 - 60*	60 - 60*

- ✓ For gang-related felonies where the court found the offender involved a minor (RCW 9.94A.833) see page 186 for standard range adjustment.
- ✓ For deadly weapon enhancement, see page 190.
- ✓ For sentencing alternatives, see page 177.
- ✓ For community custody eligibility, see page 187.
- ✓ For any applicable enhancements other than deadly weapon enhancement, see page 183.

The Caseload Forecast Council is not liable for errors or omissions in the manual, for sentences that may be inappropriately calculated as a result of a practitioner's or court's reliance on the manual, or for any other written or verbal information related to adult or juvenile sentencing. The scoring sheets are intended to provide assistance in most cases but do not cover all permutations of the scoring rules. If you find any errors or omissions, we encourage you to report them to the Caseload Forecast Council.

Assault By Watercraft

RCW 79A.60.060
CLASS B – NONVIOLENT
OFFENDER SCORING RCW 9.94A.525(12)

If it was found that this offense was committed with sexual motivation (RCW 9.94A.533(8)) on or after 7/01/2006, use the General Nonviolent Offense with a Sexual Motivation Finding scoring form on page 193.

If the present conviction is for a felony domestic violence offense where domestic violence was plead and proven, use the General Nonviolent Offense Where Domestic Violence Has Been Plead and Proven scoring form on page 191.

ADULT HISTORY:
Enter number of Homicide by Watercraft and Assault by Watercraft convictions .... _____ x 2 = _____

Enter number of Driving Under the Influence of Intoxicating Liquor or Any Drug and Actual Physical Control of a Motor Vehicle While Under the Influence of Intoxicating Liquor or Any Drug and Operation of a Vessel While Under the Influence of Intoxicating Liquor or Any Drug convictions ..... _____ x 1 = _____

Enter number of felony convictions .... _____ x 1 = _____

JUVENILE HISTORY:
Enter number of Homicide by Watercraft and Assault by Watercraft convictions .... _____ x 2 = _____

Enter number of Driving Under the Influence of Intoxicating Liquor or Any Drug and Actual Physical Control of a Motor Vehicle While Under the Influence of Intoxicating Liquor or Any Drug and Operation of a Vessel While Under the Influence of Intoxicating Liquor or Any Drug convictions ..... _____ x ½ = _____

Enter number of felony dispositions .... _____ x ½ = _____

OTHER CURRENT OFFENSES:
(Other current offenses that do not encompass the same conduct count in offender score)
Enter number of other Homicide by Watercraft and Assault by Watercraft convictions ..... _____ x 2 = _____

Enter number of Driving Under the Influence of Intoxicating Liquor or Any Drug and Actual Physical Control of a Motor Vehicle While Under the Influence of Intoxicating Liquor or Any Drug and Operation of a Vessel While Under the Influence of Intoxicating Liquor or Any Drug convictions ..... _____ x 1 = _____

Enter number of other felony convictions .... _____ x 1 = _____

STATUS:
Was the offender on community custody on the date the current offense was committed? .... + 1 = _____

Total the last column to get the **Offender Score** (Round down to the nearest whole number)

SENTENCE RANGE

	\multicolumn{10}{c	}{Offender Score}
	0	1	2	3	4	5	6	7	8	9+
LEVEL IV	6m 3 - 9	9m 6 - 12	13m 12+ - 14	15m 13 - 17	17.5m 15 - 20	25.5m 22 - 29	38m 33 - 43	50m 43 - 57	61.5m 53 - 70	73.5m 63 - 84

- ✓ For attempt, solicitation, conspiracy (RCW 9.94A.595) see page 23 or for gang-related felonies where the court found the offender involved a minor (RCW 9.94A.833) see page 186 for standard range adjustments.
- ✓ For deadly weapon enhancement, see page 190.
- ✓ For sentencing alternatives, see page 177.
- ✓ For community custody eligibility, see page 187.
- ✓ For any applicable enhancements other than deadly weapon enhancement, see page 183.

The Caseload Forecast Council is not liable for errors or omissions in the manual, for sentences that may be inappropriately calculated as a result of a practitioner's or court's reliance on the manual, or for any other written or verbal information related to adult or juvenile sentencing. The scoring sheets are intended to provide assistance in most cases but do not cover all permutations of the scoring rules. If you find any errors or omissions, we encourage you to report them to the Caseload Forecast Council.

Assault Of A Child First Degree

RCW 9A.36.120
CLASS A – SERIOUS VIOLENT
OFFENDER SCORING RCW 9.94A.525(9)

If the present conviction is for a felony domestic violence offense where domestic violence was plead and proven, use the General Serious Violent Offense Where Domestic Violence Has Been Plead and Proven scoring form on page 196.

ADULT HISTORY:
    Enter number of serious violent felony convictions .... _____ x 3 = _____
    Enter number of violent felony convictions .... _____ x 2 = _____
    Enter number of nonviolent felony convictions .... _____ x 1 = _____

JUVENILE HISTORY:
    Enter number of serious violent felony dispositions .... _____ x 3 = _____
    Enter number of violent felony dispositions .... _____ x 2 = _____
    Enter number of nonviolent felony dispositions .... _____ x ½ = _____

OTHER CURRENT OFFENSES:
(Other current offenses that do not encompass the same conduct count in offender score)
    Enter number of other violent felony convictions .... _____ x 2 = _____
    Enter number of other nonviolent felony convictions .... _____ x 1 = _____

STATUS:
    Was the offender on community custody on the date the current offense was committed? .... + 1 = _____

Total the last column to get the **Offender Score** (Round down to the nearest whole number)

SENTENCE RANGE

	\multicolumn{10}{c}{Offender Score}
	0	1	2	3	4	5	6	7	8	9+
LEVEL XII	108m 93 - 123	119m 102 - 136	129m 111 - 147	140m 120 - 160	150m 129 - 171	161m 138 - 184	189m 162 - 216	207m 178 - 236	243m 209 - 277	279m 240 - 318

- ✓ For attempt, solicitation, conspiracy (RCW 9.94A.595) see page 23 or for gang-related felonies where the court found the offender involved a minor (RCW 9.94A.833) see page 186 for standard range adjustments.
- ✓ For deadly weapon enhancement, see page 190.
- ✓ For sentencing alternatives, see page 177.
- ✓ For community custody eligibility, see page 187.
- ✓ For any applicable enhancements other than deadly weapon enhancement, see page 183.
- ✓ Multiple current serious violent offenses shall have consecutive sentences imposed per the rules of RCW 9.94A.589(1)(b).
- ✓ Statutory <u>minimum</u> sentence is 60 months (RCW 9.94A.540) if the offender used force or means likely to result in death or intended to kill the victim. The statutory minimum sentence shall not be varied or modified under RCW 9.94A.535.

The Caseload Forecast Council is not liable for errors or omissions in the manual, for sentences that may be inappropriately calculated as a result of a practitioner's or court's reliance on the manual, or for any other written or verbal information related to adult or juvenile sentencing. The scoring sheets are intended to provide assistance in most cases but do not cover all permutations of the scoring rules. If you find any errors or omissions, we encourage you to report them to the Caseload Forecast Council.

Assault Of A Child First Degree With A Finding Of Sexual Motivation

RCW 9A.36.120
CLASS A – SERIOUS VIOLENT/SEX

OFFENDER SCORING RCW 9.94A.525(17)

ADULT HISTORY:
- Enter number of sex offense convictions .... _____ x 3 = _____
- Enter number of serious violent felony convictions .... _____ x 3 = _____
- Enter number of violent felony convictions .... _____ x 2 = _____
- Enter number of nonviolent felony convictions .... _____ x 1 = _____

JUVENILE HISTORY:
- Enter number of sex offense dispositions .... _____ x 3 = _____
- Enter number of serious violent felony dispositions .... _____ x 3 = _____
- Enter number of violent felony dispositions .... _____ x 2 = _____
- Enter number of nonviolent felony dispositions .... _____ x ½ = _____

OTHER CURRENT OFFENSES:
(Other current offenses that do not encompass the same conduct count in offender score)
- Enter number of other sex offense convictions .... _____ x 3 = _____
- Enter number of other violent felony convictions .... _____ x 2 = _____
- Enter number of other nonviolent felony convictions .... _____ x 1 = _____

STATUS:
- Was the offender on community custody on the date the current offense was committed? .... + 1 = _____

Total the last column to get the **Offender Score** (Round down to the nearest whole number) [____]

SENTENCE RANGE

	\multicolumn{10}{c}{Offender Score}
	0	1	2	3	4	5	6	7	8	9+
LEVEL XII	108m	119m	129m	140m	150m	161m	189m	207m	243m	279m
	93 - 123	102 - 136	111 - 147	120 - 160	129 - 171	138 - 184	162 - 216	178 - 236	209 - 277	240 - 318

Add Sexual Motivation Enhancement (see page 185) [____] to Standard Range = [Low] to [High]

- ✓ For attempt, solicitation, conspiracy (RCW 9.94A.595) see page 23 or for gang-related felonies where the court found the offender involved a minor (RCW 9.94A.833) see page 186 for standard range adjustments.
- ✓ For deadly weapon enhancement, see page 190.
- ✓ For sentencing alternatives, see page 177.
- ✓ For community custody eligibility, see page 187.
- ✓ For any applicable enhancements other than deadly weapon enhancement, see page 183.
- ✓ If the offender is not a persistent offender and the current offense was committed on or after 9/1/2001, then the offender is subject to the requirements under RCW 9.94A.507.
- ✓ Multiple current serious violent offenses shall have consecutive sentences imposed per the rules of RCW 9.94A.589(1)(b).
- ✓ Statutory minimum sentence is 60 months per RCW 9.94A.540 if the offender used force or means likely to result in death or intended to kill the victim. The statutory minimum sentence shall not be varied or modified under RCW 9.94A.535.

The Caseload Forecast Council is not liable for errors or omissions in the manual, for sentences that may be inappropriately calculated as a result of a practitioner's or court's reliance on the manual, or for any other written or verbal information related to adult or juvenile sentencing. The scoring sheets are intended to provide assistance in most cases but do not cover all permutations of the scoring rules. If you find any errors or omissions, we encourage you to report them to the Caseload Forecast Council.

Assault Of A Child Second Degree

RCW 9A.36.130
CLASS B* – VIOLENT

OFFENDER SCORING RCW 9.94A.525(8)

If the present conviction is for a felony domestic violence offense where domestic violence was plead and proven, use the General Violent Offense Where Domestic Violence Has Been Plead and Proven scoring form on page 199.

ADULT HISTORY:
    Enter number of serious violent and violent felony convictions .... _____ x 2 = _____

    Enter number of nonviolent felony convictions .... _____ x 1 = _____

JUVENILE HISTORY:
    Enter number of serious violent and violent felony dispositions .... _____ x 2 = _____

    Enter number of nonviolent felony dispositions .... _____ x ½ = _____

OTHER CURRENT OFFENSES:
(Other current offenses that do not encompass the same conduct count in offender score)
    Enter number of other serious violent and violent felony convictions .... _____ x 2 = _____

    Enter number of other nonviolent felony convictions .... _____ x 1 = _____

STATUS:
    Was the offender on community custody on the date the current offense was committed? .... + 1 = _____

Total the last column to get the **Offender Score** (Round down to the nearest whole number)

SENTENCE RANGE

	Offender Score									
	0	1	2	3	4	5	6	7	8	9+
LEVEL IX	36m	42m	47.5m	53.5m	59.5m	66m	89.5m	101.5m	114m	
	31 - 41	36 - 48	41 - 54	46 - 61	51 - 68	57 - 75	77 - 102	87 - 116	108 - 120*	120 - 120*

✓ For attempt, solicitation, conspiracy (RCW 9.94A.595) see page 23 or for gang-related felonies where the court found the offender involved a minor (RCW 9.94A.833) see page 186 for standard range adjustments.

✓ For deadly weapon enhancement, see page 190.

✓ For sentencing alternatives, see page 177.

✓ For community custody eligibility, see page 187.

✓ For any applicable enhancements other than deadly weapon enhancement, see page 183.

Assault Of A Child Second Degree With A Finding Of Sexual Motivation

RCW 9A.36.130
CLASS B* – VIOLENT/SEX

OFFENDER SCORING RCW 9.94A.525(17)

ADULT HISTORY:
Enter number of sex offense convictions .... _____ x 3 = _____
Enter number of serious violent felony convictions .... _____ x 3 = _____
Enter number of violent felony convictions .... _____ x 2 = _____
Enter number of nonviolent felony convictions .... _____ x 1 = _____

JUVENILE HISTORY:
Enter number of sex offense dispositions .... _____ x 3 = _____
Enter number of serious violent felony dispositions .... _____ x 3 = _____
Enter number of violent felony dispositions .... _____ x 2 = _____
Enter number of nonviolent felony dispositions .... _____ x ½ = _____

OTHER CURRENT OFFENSES:
(Other current offenses that do not encompass the same conduct count in offender score)
Enter number of other sex offense convictions .... _____ x 3 = _____
Enter number of other violent felony convictions .... _____ x 2 = _____
Enter number of other nonviolent felony convictions .... _____ x 1 = _____

STATUS:
Was the offender on community custody on the date the current offense was committed? .... + 1 = _____

Total the last column to get the **Offender Score** (Round down to the nearest whole number)

SENTENCE RANGE

	Offender Score									
	0	**1**	**2**	**3**	**4**	**5**	**6**	**7**	**8**	**9+**
LEVEL IX	36m	42m	47.5m	53.5m	59.5m	66m	89.5m	101.5m	114m	
	31 - 41	36 - 48	41 - 54	46 - 61	51 - 68	57 - 75	77 - 102	87 - 116	108 - 120*	120 - 120*

Add Sexual Motivation Enhancement (see page 185) [____] to Standard Range = [Low] to [High]

- ✓ For attempt, solicitation, conspiracy (RCW 9.94A.595) see page 23 or for gang-related felonies where the court found the offender involved a minor (RCW 9.94A.833) see page 186 for standard range adjustments.
- ✓ For deadly weapon enhancement, see page 190.
- ✓ For sentencing alternatives, see page 177.
- ✓ For community custody eligibility, see page 187.
- ✓ For any applicable enhancements other than deadly weapon enhancement, see page 183.
- ✓ If the offender is not a persistent offender and the current offense was committed on or after 9/1/2001, then the offender is subject to the requirements under RCW 9.94A.507.

The Caseload Forecast Council is not liable for errors or omissions in the manual, for sentences that may be inappropriately calculated as a result of a practitioner's or court's reliance on the manual, or for any other written or verbal information related to adult or juvenile sentencing. The scoring sheets are intended to provide assistance in most cases but do not cover all permutations of the scoring rules. If you find any errors or omissions, we encourage you to report them to the Caseload Forecast Council.

Assault Of A Child Third Degree

RCW 9A.36.140
CLASS C* – NONVIOLENT

OFFENDER SCORING RCW 9.94A.525(7)

If it was found that this offense was committed with sexual motivation (RCW 9.94A.533(8)) on or after 7/01/2006, use the General Nonviolent Offense with a Sexual Motivation Finding scoring form on page 193.

If the present conviction is for a felony domestic violence offense where domestic violence was plead and proven, use the General Nonviolent Offense Where Domestic Violence Has Been Plead and Proven scoring form on page 191.

ADULT HISTORY:
    Enter number of felony convictions .... _____ x 1 = _____

JUVENILE HISTORY:
    Enter number of serious violent and violent felony dispositions .... _____ x 1 = _____
    Enter number of nonviolent felony dispositions .... _____ x ½ = _____

OTHER CURRENT OFFENSES:
(Other current offenses that do not encompass the same conduct count in offender score)
    Enter number of other felony convictions .... _____ x 1 = _____

STATUS:
    Was the offender on community custody on the date the current offense was committed?........... + 1 = _____

Total the last column to get the **Offender Score** (Round down to the nearest whole number)

SENTENCE RANGE

	Offender Score									
	0	1	2	3	4	5	6	7	8	9+
LEVEL III	2m	5m	8m	11m	14m	19.5m	25.5m	38m	50m	55.5m
	1 - 3	3 - 8	4 - 12	9 - 12	12+ - 16	17 - 22	22 - 29	33 - 43	43 - 57	51 - 60*

✓ For gang-related felonies where the court found the offender involved a minor (RCW 9.94A.833) see page 186 for standard range adjustment.

✓ For deadly weapon enhancement, see page 190.

✓ For sentencing alternatives, see page 177.

✓ For community custody eligibility, see page 187.

✓ For any applicable enhancements other than deadly weapon enhancement, see page 183.

Attempting To Elude Pursuing Police Vehicle

RCW 46.61.024

CLASS C – FELONY TRAFFIC OFFENSE

OFFENDER SCORING RCW 9.94A.525(11)

ADULT HISTORY:
    Enter number of Vehicular Homicide and Vehicular Assault convictions .... _____ x 2 = _____

    Enter number of Operation of a Vessel While Under the Influence of Intoxicating Liquor or Any Drug felony convictions .... _____ x 1 = _____

    Enter number of felony convictions .... _____ x 1 = _____

    Enter number of Driving While Under the Influence of Intoxicating Liquor or Any Drug and Actual Physical Control While Under the Influence of Intoxicating Liquor or Any Drug and Reckless Driving and Hit-And-Run Attended Vehicle <u>non-felony</u> convictions .... _____ x 1 = _____

JUVENILE HISTORY:
    Enter number of Vehicular Homicide and Vehicular Assault dispositions .... _____ x 2 = _____

    Enter number of Operation of a Vessel While Under the Influence of Intoxicating Liquor or Any Drug felony dispositions .... _____ x ½ = _____

    Enter number of felony dispositions .... _____ x ½ = _____

    Enter number of Driving While Under the Influence of Intoxicating Liquor or Any Drug and Actual Physical Control While Under the Influence of Intoxicating Liquor or Any Drug and Reckless Driving and Hit-And-Run Attended Vehicle <u>non-felony</u> convictions .... _____ x ½ = _____

OTHER CURRENT OFFENSES:
(Other current offenses that do not encompass the same conduct count in offender score)

    Enter number of Vehicular Homicide and Vehicular Assault convictions .... _____ x 2 = _____

    Enter number of other Operation of a Vessel While Under the Influence of Intoxicating Liquor or Any Drug felony convictions .... _____ x 1 = _____

    Enter number of other felony convictions .... _____ x 1 = _____

    Enter number of Driving While Under the Influence of Intoxicating Liquor or Any Drug and Actual Physical Control While Under the Influence of Intoxicating Liquor or Any Drug and Reckless Driving and Hit-And-Run Attended Vehicle <u>non-felony</u> convictions .... _____ x 1 = _____

STATUS:
    Was the offender on community custody on the date the current offense was committed? .... + 1 = _____

Total the last column to get the **Offender Score** (Round down to the nearest whole number)

SENTENCE RANGE

	Offender Score									
	0	1	2	3	4	5	6	7	8	9+
LEVEL I	0-60 days	0-90 days	3m 2 - 5	4m 2 - 6	5.5m 3 - 8	8m 4 - 12	13m 12+ - 14	16m 14 - 18	19.5m 17 - 22	25.5m 22 - 29

- ✓ For gang-related felonies where the court found the offender involved a minor (RCW 9.94A.833) see page 186 for standard range adjustment.
- ✓ For deadly weapon enhancement, see page 190.
- ✓ For sentencing alternatives, see page 177.
- ✓ For community custody eligibility, see page 187.
- ✓ For any applicable enhancements other than deadly weapon enhancement, see page 183.
- ✓ If the conviction includes a finding by special allegation of 'endangering one or more persons' under RCW 9.94A.834, add 12 months and 1 day to the entire standard sentencing range for the current offense. Effective 06/12/2008.

The Caseload Forecast Council is not liable for errors or omissions in the manual, for sentences that may be inappropriately calculated as a result of a practitioner's or court's reliance on the manual, or for any other written or verbal information related to adult or juvenile sentencing. The scoring sheets are intended to provide assistance in most cases but do not cover all permutations of the scoring rules. If you find any errors or omissions, we encourage you to report them to the Caseload Forecast Council.

Bail Jumping With Class A Felony

RCW 9A.76.170(3)(b)
CLASS B – NONVIOLENT

OFFENDER SCORING RCW 9.94A.525(7)

If it was found that this offense was committed with sexual motivation (RCW 9.94A.533(8)) on or after 7/01/2006, use the General Nonviolent Offense with a Sexual Motivation Finding scoring form on page 193.

If the present conviction is for a felony domestic violence offense where domestic violence was plead and proven, use the General Nonviolent Offense Where Domestic Violence Has Been Plead and Proven scoring form on page 191.

ADULT HISTORY:
   Enter number of felony convictions .... _____ x 1 = _____

JUVENILE HISTORY:
   Enter number of serious violent and violent felony dispositions .... _____ x 1 = _____
   Enter number of nonviolent felony dispositions .... _____ x ½ = _____

OTHER CURRENT OFFENSES:
(Other current offenses that do not encompass the same conduct count in offender score)
   Enter number of other felony convictions .... _____ x 1 = _____

STATUS:
   Was the offender on community custody on the date the current offense was committed?........... + 1 = _____

Total the last column to get the **Offender Score** (Round down to the nearest whole number)

SENTENCE RANGE

Offender Score	0	1	2	3	4	5	6	7	8	9+
LEVEL V	9m 6 - 12	13m 12+ - 14	15m 13 - 17	17.5m 15 - 20	25.5m 22 - 29	38m 33 - 43	47.5m 41 - 54	59.5m 51 - 68	72m 62 - 82	84m 72 - 96

- ✓ For attempt, solicitation, conspiracy (RCW 9.94A.595) see page 23 or for gang-related felonies where the court found the offender involved a minor (RCW 9.94A.833) see page 186 for standard range adjustments.
- ✓ For deadly weapon enhancement, see page 190.
- ✓ For sentencing alternatives, see page 177.
- ✓ For community custody eligibility, see page 187.
- ✓ For any applicable enhancements other than deadly weapon enhancement, see page 183.

The Caseload Forecast Council is not liable for errors or omissions in the manual, for sentences that may be inappropriately calculated as a result of a practitioner's or court's reliance on the manual, or for any other written or verbal information related to adult or juvenile sentencing. The scoring sheets are intended to provide assistance in most cases but do not cover all permutations of the scoring rules. If you find any errors or omissions, we encourage you to report them to the Caseload Forecast Council.

Bail Jumping With Class B Or C Felony

RCW 9A.76.170(3)(c)
CLASS C* – NONVIOLENT

OFFENDER SCORING RCW 9.94A.525(7)

If it was found that this offense was committed with sexual motivation (RCW 9.94A.533(8)) on or after 7/01/2006, use the General Nonviolent Offense with a Sexual Motivation Finding scoring form on page 193.

If the present conviction is for a felony domestic violence offense where domestic violence was plead and proven, use the General Nonviolent Offense Where Domestic Violence Has Been Plead and Proven scoring form on page 191.

ADULT HISTORY:
    Enter number of felony convictions .... _____ x 1 = _____

JUVENILE HISTORY:
    Enter number of serious violent and violent felony dispositions .... _____ x 1 = _____

    Enter number of nonviolent felony dispositions .... _____ x ½ = _____

OTHER CURRENT OFFENSES:
(Other current offenses that do not encompass the same conduct count in offender score)
    Enter number of other felony convictions .... _____ x 1 = _____

STATUS:
    Was the offender on community custody on the date the current offense was committed? .... + 1 = _____

Total the last column to get the **Offender Score** (Round down to the nearest whole number)

SENTENCE RANGE

	__	__	__	__	__	__	__	__	__	__
Offender Score	0	1	2	3	4	5	6	7	8	9+
LEVEL III	2m	5m	8m	11m	14m	19.5m	25.5m	38m	50m	55.5m
	1 - 3	3 - 8	4 - 12	9 - 12	12+ - 16	17 - 22	22 - 29	33 - 43	43 - 57	51 - 60*

- ✓ For gang-related felonies where the court found the offender involved a minor (RCW 9.94A.833) see page 186 for standard range adjustment.
- ✓ For deadly weapon enhancement, see page 190.
- ✓ For sentencing alternatives, see page 177.
- ✓ For community custody eligibility, see page 187.
- ✓ For any applicable enhancements other than deadly weapon enhancement, see page 183.

The Caseload Forecast Council is not liable for errors or omissions in the manual, for sentences that may be inappropriately calculated as a result of a practitioner's or court's reliance on the manual, or for any other written or verbal information related to adult or juvenile sentencing. The scoring sheets are intended to provide assistance in most cases but do not cover all permutations of the scoring rules. If you find any errors or omissions, we encourage you to report them to the Caseload Forecast Council.

Bail Jumping With Murder 1

RCW 9A.76.170(3)(a)
CLASS A – VIOLENT

OFFENDER SCORING RCW 9.94A.525(8)

If it was found that this offense was committed with sexual motivation (RCW 9.94A.533(8)) on or after 7/01/2006, use the General Violent Offense with a Sexual Motivation Finding scoring form on page 201.

If the present conviction is for a felony domestic violence offense where domestic violence was plead and proven, use the General Violent Offense Where Domestic Violence Has Been Plead and Proven scoring form on page 199.

ADULT HISTORY:
    Enter number of serious violent and violent felony convictions .... _____ x 2 = _____

    Enter number of nonviolent felony convictions .... _____ x 1 = _____

JUVENILE HISTORY:
    Enter number of serious violent and violent felony dispositions .... _____ x 2 = _____

    Enter number of nonviolent felony dispositions .... _____ x ½ = _____

OTHER CURRENT OFFENSES:
(Other current offenses that do not encompass the same conduct count in offender score)
    Enter number of other serious violent and violent felony convictions .... _____ x 2 = _____

    Enter number of other nonviolent felony convictions .... _____ x 1 = _____

STATUS:
    Was the offender on community custody on the date the current offense was committed?......... + 1 = _____

Total the last column to get the **Offender Score** (Round down to the nearest whole number)

SENTENCE RANGE

	Offender Score									
	0	1	2	3	4	5	6	7	8	9+
LEVEL VI	13m	17.5m	24m	30m	36m	42m	53.5m	66m	78m	89.5m
	12+ - 14	15 - 20	21 - 27	26 - 34	31 - 41	36 - 48	46 - 61	57 - 75	67 - 89	77 - 102

- ✓ For attempt, solicitation, conspiracy (RCW 9.94A.595) see page 23 or for gang-related felonies where the court found the offender involved a minor (RCW 9.94A.833) see page 186 for standard range adjustments.
- ✓ For deadly weapon enhancement, see page 190.
- ✓ For sentencing alternatives, see page 177.
- ✓ For community custody eligibility, see page 187.
- ✓ For any applicable enhancements other than deadly weapon enhancement, see page 183.

The Caseload Forecast Council is not liable for errors or omissions in the manual, for sentences that may be inappropriately calculated as a result of a practitioner's or court's reliance on the manual, or for any other written or verbal information related to adult or juvenile sentencing. The scoring sheets are intended to provide assistance in most cases but do not cover all permutations of the scoring rules. If you find any errors or omissions, we encourage you to report them to the Caseload Forecast Council.

Bribe Received By Witness Bribing A Witness

RCW 9A.72.100 & 9A.72.090
CLASS B – NONVIOLENT

OFFENDER SCORING RCW 9.94A.525(7)

If it was found that this offense was committed with sexual motivation (RCW 9.94A.533(8)) on or after 7/01/2006, use the General Nonviolent Offense with a Sexual Motivation Finding scoring form on page 193.

If the present conviction is for a felony domestic violence offense where domestic violence was plead and proven, use the General Nonviolent Offense Where Domestic Violence Has Been Plead and Proven scoring form on page 191.

ADULT HISTORY:
    Enter number of felony convictions .... _____ x 1 = _____

JUVENILE HISTORY:
    Enter number of serious violent and violent felony dispositions .... _____ x 1 = _____
    Enter number of nonviolent felony dispositions .... _____ x ½ = _____

OTHER CURRENT OFFENSES:
(Other current offenses that do not encompass the same conduct count in offender score)
    Enter number of other felony convictions .... _____ x 1 = _____

STATUS:
    Was the offender on community custody on the date the current offense was committed? .... + 1 = _____

Total the last column to get the **Offender Score** (Round down to the nearest whole number)

SENTENCE RANGE

	Offender Score									
	0	1	2	3	4	5	6	7	8	9+
LEVEL IV	6m	9m	13m	15m	17.5m	25.5m	38m	50m	61.5m	73.5m
	3 - 9	6 - 12	12+ - 14	13 - 17	15 - 20	22 - 29	33 - 43	43 - 57	53 - 70	63 - 84

- ✓ For attempt, solicitation, conspiracy (RCW 9.94A.595) see page 23 or for gang-related felonies where the court found the offender involved a minor (RCW 9.94A.833) see page 186 for standard range adjustments.
- ✓ For deadly weapon enhancement, see page 190.
- ✓ For sentencing alternatives, see page 177.
- ✓ For community custody eligibility, see page 187.
- ✓ For any applicable enhancements other than deadly weapon enhancement, see page 183.

The Caseload Forecast Council is not liable for errors or omissions in the manual, for sentences that may be inappropriately calculated as a result of a practitioner's or court's reliance on the manual, or for any other written or verbal information related to adult or juvenile sentencing. The scoring sheets are intended to provide assistance in most cases but do not cover all permutations of the scoring rules. If you find any errors or omissions, we encourage you to report them to the Caseload Forecast Council.

Bribery

RCW 9A.68.010
CLASS B – NONVIOLENT

OFFENDER SCORING RCW 9.94A.525(7)

If it was found that this offense was committed with sexual motivation (RCW 9.94A.533(8)) on or after 7/01/2006, use the General Nonviolent Offense with a Sexual Motivation Finding scoring form on page 193.

If the present conviction is for a felony domestic violence offense where domestic violence was plead and proven, use the General Nonviolent Offense Where Domestic Violence Has Been Plead and Proven scoring form on page 191.

ADULT HISTORY:
    Enter number of felony convictions .... _____ x 1 = _____

JUVENILE HISTORY:
    Enter number of serious violent and violent felony dispositions .... _____ x 1 = _____
    Enter number of nonviolent felony dispositions .... _____ x ½ = _____

OTHER CURRENT OFFENSES:
(Other current offenses that do not encompass the same conduct count in offender score)
    Enter number of other felony convictions .... _____ x 1 = _____

STATUS:
    Was the offender on community custody on the date the current offense was committed?.......... + 1 = _____

Total the last column to get the **Offender Score** (Round down to the nearest whole number)

SENTENCE RANGE

	\multicolumn{10}{c}{Offender Score}
	0	1	2	3	4	5	6	7	8	9+
LEVEL VI	13m	17.5m	24m	30m	36m	42m	53.5m	66m	78m	89.5m
	12+ - 14	15 - 20	21 - 27	26 - 34	31 - 41	36 - 48	46 - 61	57 - 75	67 - 89	77 - 102

✓ For attempt, solicitation, conspiracy (RCW 9.94A.595) see page 23 or for gang-related felonies where the court found the offender involved a minor (RCW 9.94A.833) see page 186 for standard range adjustments.

✓ For deadly weapon enhancement, see page 190.

✓ For sentencing alternatives, see page 177.

✓ For community custody eligibility, see page 187.

✓ For any applicable enhancements other than deadly weapon enhancement, see page 183.

Burglary First Degree

RCW 9A.52.020
CLASS A – VIOLENT

OFFENDER SCORING RCW 9.94A.525(10)

If the present conviction is for a felony domestic violence offense where domestic violence was plead and proven, use the General Burglary 1 Offense Where Domestic Violence Has Been Plead and Proven scoring form on page 202.

ADULT HISTORY:
Enter number of serious violent and violent felony convictions .... _____ x 2 = _____
Enter number of Burglary 2 and Residential Burglary felony convictions .... _____ x 2 = _____
Enter number of nonviolent felony convictions .... _____ x 1 = _____

JUVENILE HISTORY:
Enter number of serious violent and violent felony dispositions .... _____ x 2 = _____
Enter number of Burglary 2 and Residential Burglary felony dispositions .... _____ x 1 = _____
Enter number of nonviolent felony dispositions .... _____ x ½ = _____

OTHER CURRENT OFFENSES:
(Other current offenses that do not encompass the same conduct count in offender score)
Enter number of other serious violent and violent felony convictions .... _____ x 2 = _____
Enter number of other Burglary 2 and Residential Burglary felony convictions .... _____ x 2 = _____
Enter number of other nonviolent felony convictions .... _____ x 1 = _____

STATUS:
Was the offender on community custody on the date the current offense was committed? .... + 1 = _____

Total the last column to get the **Offender Score** (Round down to the nearest whole number)

SENTENCE RANGE

	\multicolumn{10}{c	}{Offender Score}

	0	1	2	3	4	5	6	7	8	9+
LEVEL VII	17.5m	24m	30m	36m	42m	47.5m	66m	78m	89.5m	101.5m
	15 - 20	21 - 27	26 - 34	31 - 41	36 - 48	41 - 54	57 - 75	67 - 89	77 - 102	87 - 116

- ✓ For attempt, solicitation, conspiracy (RCW 9.94A.595) see page 23 or for gang-related felonies where the court found the offender involved a minor (RCW 9.94A.833) see page 186 for standard range adjustments.
- ✓ For deadly weapon enhancement, see page 190.
- ✓ For sentencing alternatives, see page 177.
- ✓ For community custody eligibility, see page 187.
- ✓ For any applicable enhancements other than deadly weapon enhancement, see page 183.

The Caseload Forecast Council is not liable for errors or omissions in the manual, for sentences that may be inappropriately calculated as a result of a practitioner's or court's reliance on the manual, or for any other written or verbal information related to adult or juvenile sentencing. The scoring sheets are intended to provide assistance in most cases but do not cover all permutations of the scoring rules. If you find any errors or omissions, we encourage you to report them to the Caseload Forecast Council.

Burglary First Degree With A Finding Of Sexual Motivation

RCW 9A.52.020
CLASS A – VIOLENT/SEX

OFFENDER SCORING RCW 9.94A.525(17)

ADULT HISTORY:
Enter number of sex offense felony convictions .... _____ x 3 = _____

Enter number of serious violent and violent felony convictions .... _____ x 2 = _____

Enter number of Burglary 2 and Residential Burglary felony convictions .... _____ x 2 = _____

Enter number of nonviolent felony convictions .... _____ x 1 = _____

JUVENILE HISTORY:
Enter number of sex offense felony dispositions .... _____ x 3 = _____

Enter number of serious violent and violent felony dispositions .... _____ x 2 = _____

Enter number of Burglary 2 and Residential Burglary felony dispositions .... _____ x 1 = _____

Enter number of nonviolent felony dispositions .... _____ x ½ = _____

OTHER CURRENT OFFENSES:
(Other current offenses that do not encompass the same conduct count in offender score)
Enter number of other sex offense felony convictions .... _____ x 3 = _____

Enter number of other serious violent and violent felony convictions .... _____ x 2 = _____

Enter number of other Burglary 2 and Residential Burglary felony convictions .... _____ x 2 = _____

Enter number of other nonviolent felony convictions .... _____ x 1 = _____

STATUS:
Was the offender on community custody on the date the current offense was committed?................... + 1 = _____

Total the last column to get the **Offender Score** (Round down to the nearest whole number)

SENTENCE RANGE

	Offender Score									
	0	1	2	3	4	5	6	7	8	9+
LEVEL VII	17.5m	24m	30m	36m	42m	47.5m	66m	78m	89.5m	101.5m
	15 - 20	21 - 27	26 - 34	31 - 41	36 - 48	41 - 54	57 - 75	67 - 89	77 - 102	87 - 116

Add Sexual Motivation Enhancement (see page 185) _____ to Standard Range = Low ____ to High ____

- ✓ For attempt, solicitation, conspiracy (RCW 9.94A.595) see page 23 or for gang-related felonies where the court found the offender involved a minor (RCW 9.94A.833) see page 186 for standard range adjustments.
- ✓ For deadly weapon enhancement, see page 190.
- ✓ For sentencing alternatives, see page 177.
- ✓ For community custody eligibility, see page 187.
- ✓ For any applicable enhancements other than deadly weapon enhancement, see page 183.
- ✓ If the offender is not a persistent offender and the <u>current offense</u> was committed on or after 9/1/2001, then the offender is subject to the requirements under RCW 9.94A.507.

The Caseload Forecast Council is not liable for errors or omissions in the manual, for sentences that may be inappropriately calculated as a result of a practitioner's or court's reliance on the manual, or for any other written or verbal information related to adult or juvenile sentencing. The scoring sheets are intended to provide assistance in most cases but do not cover all permutations of the scoring rules. If you find any errors or omissions, we encourage you to report them to the Caseload Forecast Council.

Burglary Second Degree

RCW 9A.52.030
CLASS B – NONVIOLENT

OFFENDER SCORING RCW 9.94A.525(16)

If the present conviction is for a felony domestic violence offense where domestic violence was plead and proven, use the General Burglary Second Degree or Residential Burglary Offense Where Domestic Violence Has Been Plead and Proven scoring form on page 203.

ADULT HISTORY:
    Enter number of Burglary 1 felony convictions .... _____ x 2 = _____
    Enter number of Burglary 2 and Residential Burglary felony convictions .... _____ x 2 = _____
    Enter number of felony convictions .... _____ x 1 = _____

JUVENILE HISTORY:
    Enter number of Burglary 1 felony dispositions .... _____ x 2 = _____
    Enter number of Burglary 2 and Residential Burglary felony dispositions .... _____ x 1 = _____
    Enter number of serious violent and violent felony dispositions .... _____ x 1 = _____
    Enter number of nonviolent felony dispositions .... _____ x ½ = _____

OTHER CURRENT OFFENSES:
(Other current offenses that do not encompass the same conduct count in offender score)
    Enter number of other Burglary 1 felony convictions .... _____ x 2 = _____
    Enter number of other Burglary 2 and Residential Burglary felony convictions .... _____ x 2 = _____
    Enter number of other felony convictions .... _____ x 1 = _____

STATUS:
    Was the offender on community custody on the date the current offense was committed? .... + 1 = _____

Total the last column to get the **Offender Score** (Round down to the nearest whole number)

SENTENCE RANGE

	Offender Score									
	0	1	2	3	4	5	6	7	8	9+
LEVEL III	2m 1 - 3	5m 3 - 8	8m 4 - 12	11m 9 - 12	14m 12+ - 16	19.5m 17 - 22	25.5m 22 - 29	38m 33 - 43	50m 43 - 57	59.5m 51 - 68

- ✓ For attempt, solicitation, conspiracy (RCW 9.94A.595) see page 23 or for gang-related felonies where the court found the offender involved a minor (RCW 9.94A.833) see page 186 for standard range adjustments.
- ✓ For deadly weapon enhancement, see page 190.
- ✓ For sentencing alternatives, see page 177.
- ✓ For community custody eligibility, see page 187.
- ✓ For any applicable enhancements other than deadly weapon enhancement, see page 183.

The Caseload Forecast Council is not liable for errors or omissions in the manual, for sentences that may be inappropriately calculated as a result of a practitioner's or court's reliance on the manual, or for any other written or verbal information related to adult or juvenile sentencing. The scoring sheets are intended to provide assistance in most cases but do not cover all permutations of the scoring rules. If you find any errors or omissions, we encourage you to report them to the Caseload Forecast Council.

Burglary Second Degree With A Finding Of Sexual Motivation

RCW 9A.52.030
CLASS B – NONVIOLENT/SEX
OFFENDER SCORING RCW 9.94A.525(17)

ADULT HISTORY:
Enter number of sex offense felony convictions .... _____ x 3 = _____
Enter number of Burglary 1 felony convictions .... _____ x 2 = _____
Enter number of Burglary 2 and Residential Burglary felony convictions .... _____ x 2 = _____
Enter number of felony convictions .... _____ x 1 = _____

JUVENILE HISTORY:
Enter number of sex offense felony dispositions .... _____ x 3 = _____
Enter number of Burglary 1 felony dispositions .... _____ x 2 = _____
Enter number of Burglary 2 and Residential Burglary felony dispositions .... _____ x 1 = _____
Enter number of serious violent and violent felony dispositions .... _____ x 1 = _____
Enter number of nonviolent felony dispositions .... _____ x ½ = _____

OTHER CURRENT OFFENSES:
(Other current offenses that do not encompass the same conduct count in offender score)
Enter number of other sex offense felony convictions .... _____ x 3 = _____
Enter number of other Burglary 1 felony convictions .... _____ x 2 = _____
Enter number of other Burglary 2 and Residential Burglary felony convictions _____ x 2 = _____
Enter number of other felony convictions .... _____ x 1 = _____

STATUS:
Was the offender on community custody on the date the current offense was committed?.......... + 1 = _____

Total the last column to get the **Offender Score** (Round down to the nearest whole number) [____]

SENTENCE RANGE

Offender Score	0	1	2	3	4	5	6	7	8	9+
LEVEL III	2m 1 - 3	5m 3 - 8	8m 4 - 12	11m 9 - 12	14m 12+ - 16	19.5m 17 - 22	25.5m 22 - 29	38m 33 - 43	50m 43 - 57	59.5m 51 - 68

Add Sexual Motivation Enhancement (see page 185) [____] to Standard Range = [Low] to [High]

- ✓ For attempt, solicitation, conspiracy (RCW 9.94A.595) see page 23 or for gang-related felonies where the court found the offender involved a minor (RCW 9.94A.833) see page 186 for standard range adjustments.
- ✓ For deadly weapon enhancement, see page 190.
- ✓ For sentencing alternatives, see page 177.
- ✓ For community custody eligibility, see page 187.
- ✓ For any applicable enhancements other than deadly weapon enhancement, see page 183.
- ✓ If the offender is not a persistent offender and has a prior conviction for an offense listed in RCW 9.94A.030(38)(b), then the sentence is subject to the requirements of RCW 9.94A.507.

The Caseload Forecast Council is not liable for errors or omissions in the manual, for sentences that may be inappropriately calculated as a result of a practitioner's or court's reliance on the manual, or for any other written or verbal information related to adult or juvenile sentencing. The scoring sheets are intended to provide assistance in most cases but do not cover all permutations of the scoring rules. If you find any errors or omissions, we encourage you to report them to the Caseload Forecast Council.

Cheating First Degree

RCW 9.46.1961
CLASS C* – NONVIOLENT
OFFENDER SCORING RCW 9.94A.525(7)

If it was found that this offense was committed with sexual motivation (RCW 9.94A.533(8)) on or after 7/01/2006, use the General Nonviolent Offense with a Sexual Motivation Finding scoring form on page 193.

If the present conviction is for a felony domestic violence offense where domestic violence was plead and proven, use the General Nonviolent Offense Where Domestic Violence Has Been Plead and Proven scoring form on page 191.

ADULT HISTORY:
Enter number of felony convictions .... _____ x 1 = _____

JUVENILE HISTORY:
Enter number of serious violent and violent felony dispositions .... _____ x 1 = _____

Enter number of nonviolent felony dispositions .... _____ x ½ = _____

OTHER CURRENT OFFENSES:
(Other current offenses that do not encompass the same conduct count in offender score)
Enter number of other felony convictions .... _____ x 1 = _____

STATUS:
Was the offender on community custody on the date the current offense was committed? (if yes)....... + 1 = _____

Total the last column to get the **Offender Score** (Round down to the nearest whole number)

SENTENCE RANGE

	Offender Score									
	0	1	2	3	4	5	6	7	8	9+
LEVEL IV	6m	9m	13m	15m	17.5m	25.5m	38m	50m	56.5m	
	3 - 9	6 - 12	12+ - 14	13 - 17	15 - 20	22 - 29	33 - 43	43 - 57	53 - 60*	60 - 60*

- ✓ For gang-related felonies where the court found the offender involved a minor (RCW 9.94A.833) see page 186 for standard range adjustment.
- ✓ For deadly weapon enhancement, see page 190.
- ✓ For sentencing alternatives, see page 177.
- ✓ For community custody eligibility, see page 187.
- ✓ For any applicable enhancements other than deadly weapon enhancement, see page 183.

The Caseload Forecast Council is not liable for errors or omissions in the manual, for sentences that may be inappropriately calculated as a result of a practitioner's or court's reliance on the manual, or for any other written or verbal information related to adult or juvenile sentencing. The scoring sheets are intended to provide assistance in most cases but do not cover all permutations of the scoring rules. If you find any errors or omissions, we encourage you to report them to the Caseload Forecast Council.

Child Molestation First Degree

RCW 9A.44.083
CLASS A – VIOLENT/SEX
ATTEMPT/SOLICITATION = CLASS A
CONSPIRACY = CLASS B

OFFENDER SCORING RCW 9.94A.525(17)

If the present conviction is for a felony domestic violence offense where domestic violence was plead and proven, use the General Violent/Sex Offense Where Domestic Violence Has Been Plead and Proven scoring form on page 200.

ADULT HISTORY:
- Enter number of sex offense felony convictions .... _____ x 3 = _____
- Enter number of serious violent and violent felony convictions .... _____ x 2 = _____
- Enter number of nonviolent felony convictions .... _____ x 1 = _____

JUVENILE HISTORY:
- Enter number of sex offense felony dispositions .... _____ x 3 = _____
- Enter number of serious violent and violent felony dispositions .... _____ x 2 = _____
- Enter number of nonviolent felony dispositions .... _____ x ½ = _____

OTHER CURRENT OFFENSES:
(Other current offenses that do not encompass the same conduct count in offender score)
- Enter number of other sex offense felony convictions .... _____ x 3 = _____
- Enter number of other serious violent and violent felony convictions .... _____ x 2 = _____
- Enter number of other nonviolent felony convictions .... _____ x 1 = _____

STATUS:
- Was the offender on community custody on the date the current offense was committed?............ + 1 = _____

Total the last column to get the **Offender Score** (Round down to the nearest whole number)

SENTENCE RANGE

Offender Score	0	1	2	3	4	5	6	7	8	9+
LEVEL X	59.5m 51 - 68	66m 57 - 75	72m 62 - 82	78m 67 - 89	84m 72 - 96	89.5m 77 - 102	114m 98 - 130	126m 108 - 144	150m 129 - 171	230.5m 149 - 198

- ✓ For attempt, solicitation, conspiracy (RCW 9.94A.595) see page 23 or for gang-related felonies where the court found the offender involved a minor (RCW 9.94A.833) see page 186 for standard range adjustments.
- ✓ For deadly weapon enhancement, see page 190.
- ✓ For sentencing alternatives, see page 177.
- ✓ For community custody eligibility, see page 187.
- ✓ For any applicable enhancements other than deadly weapon enhancement, see page 183.
- ✓ If the offender is greater than 17 years of age and is not a persistent offender and the <u>current offense</u> was committed on or after 9/1/2001, then the offender is subject to the requirements under RCW 9.94A.507.
- ✓ If the offender engaged the victim in sexual conduct in exchange for a fee, an additional 12 months shall be added to the standard sentence range (RCW 9.94A.533(9)).
- ✓ Per RCW 9.94A.507(3)(c)(ii), <u>excluding attempt, solicitation and conspiracy convictions</u>, the <u>minimum</u> term shall be either the maximum of the standard sentence range for the offense or 25 years, whichever is greater, for a finding that the offense was **predatory**.

The Caseload Forecast Council is not liable for errors or omissions in the manual, for sentences that may be inappropriately calculated as a result of a practitioner's or court's reliance on the manual, or for any other written or verbal information related to adult or juvenile sentencing. The scoring sheets are intended to provide assistance in most cases but do not cover all permutations of the scoring rules. If you find any errors or omissions, we encourage you to report them to the Caseload Forecast Council.

Child Molestation Second Degree

RCW 9A.44.086
CLASS B – NONVIOLENT/SEX

OFFENDER SCORING RCW 9.94A.525(17)

If the present conviction is for a felony domestic violence offense where domestic violence was plead and proven, use the General Nonviolent/Sex Offense Where Domestic Violence Has Been Plead and Proven scoring form on page 192.

ADULT HISTORY:
    Enter number of sex offense felony convictions .... _____ x 3 = _____

    Enter number of felony convictions .... _____ x 1 = _____

JUVENILE HISTORY:
    Enter number of sex offense felony dispositions .... _____ x 3 = _____

    Enter number of serious violent and violent felony dispositions .... _____ x 1 = _____

    Enter number of nonviolent felony dispositions .... _____ x ½ = _____

OTHER CURRENT OFFENSES:
(Other current offenses that do not encompass the same conduct count in offender score)
    Enter number of other sex offense felony convictions .... _____ x 3 = _____

    Enter number of other felony convictions .... _____ x 1 = _____

STATUS:
    Was the offender on community custody on the date the current offense was committed? .... + 1 = _____

Total the last column to get the **Offender Score** (Round down to the nearest whole number)

SENTENCE RANGE

	Offender Score									
	0	1	2	3	4	5	6	7	8	9+
LEVEL VII	17.5m 15 - 20	24m 21 - 27	30m 26 - 34	36m 31 - 41	42m 36 - 48	47.5m 41 - 54	66m 57 - 75	78m 67 - 89	89.5m 77 - 102	101.5m 87 - 116

- ✓ For attempt, solicitation, conspiracy (RCW 9.94A.595) see page 23 or for gang-related felonies where the court found the offender involved a minor (RCW 9.94A.833) see page 186 for standard range adjustments.
- ✓ For deadly weapon enhancement, see page 190.
- ✓ For sentencing alternatives, see page 177.
- ✓ For community custody eligibility, see page 187.
- ✓ For any applicable enhancements other than deadly weapon enhancement, see page 183.
- ✓ If the offender is not a persistent offender and has a prior conviction for an offense listed in RCW 9.94A.030(38)(b), then the sentence is subject to the requirements of RCW 9.94A.507.
- ✓ If the offender engaged the victim in sexual conduct in exchange for a fee, an additional 12 months shall be added to the standard sentence range (RCW 9.94A.533(9)).

The Caseload Forecast Council is not liable for errors or omissions in the manual, for sentences that may be inappropriately calculated as a result of a practitioner's or court's reliance on the manual, or for any other written or verbal information related to adult or juvenile sentencing. The scoring sheets are intended to provide assistance in most cases but do not cover all permutations of the scoring rules. If you find any errors or omissions, we encourage you to report them to the Caseload Forecast Council.

Child Molestation Third Degree

RCW 9A.44.089
CLASS C* – NONVIOLENT/SEX
OFFENDER SCORING RCW 9.94A.525(17)

If the present conviction is for a felony domestic violence offense where domestic violence was plead and proven, use the General Nonviolent/Sex Offense Where Domestic Violence Has Been Plead and Proven scoring form on page 192.

ADULT HISTORY:
    Enter number of sex offense felony convictions .... _____ x 3 = _____
    Enter number of felony convictions .... _____ x 1 = _____

JUVENILE HISTORY:
    Enter number of sex offense felony dispositions .... _____ x 3 = _____
    Enter number of serious violent and violent felony dispositions .... _____ x 1 = _____
    Enter number of nonviolent felony dispositions .... _____ x ½ = _____

OTHER CURRENT OFFENSES:
(Other current offenses that do not encompass the same conduct count in offender score)
    Enter number of other sex offense felony convictions .... _____ x 3 = _____
    Enter number of other felony convictions .... _____ x 1 = _____

STATUS:
    Was the offender on community custody on the date the current offense was committed?.......... + 1 = _____

Total the last column to get the **Offender Score** (Round down to the nearest whole number)

SENTENCE RANGE

	\multicolumn{10}{c}{Offender Score}
	0	1	2	3	4	5	6	7	8	9+
LEVEL V	9m	13m	15m	17.5m	25.5m	38m	47.5m	55.5m		
	6 - 12	12+ - 14	13 - 17	15 - 20	22 - 29	33 - 43	41 - 54	51 - 60*	60 - 60*	60 - 60*

- ✓ For gang-related felonies where the court found the offender involved a minor (RCW 9.94A.833) see page 186 for standard range adjustment.
- ✓ For deadly weapon enhancement, see page 190.
- ✓ For sentencing alternatives, see page 177.
- ✓ For community custody eligibility, see page 187.
- ✓ For any applicable enhancements other than deadly weapon enhancement, see page 183.
- ✓ If the offender is not a persistent offender and has a prior conviction for an offense listed in RCW 9.94A.030(38)(b), then the sentence is subject to the requirements of RCW 9.94A.507.
- ✓ If the offender engaged the victim in sexual conduct in exchange for a fee, an additional 12 months shall be added to the standard sentence range (RCW 9.94A.533(9)).

The Caseload Forecast Council is not liable for errors or omissions in the manual, for sentences that may be inappropriately calculated as a result of a practitioner's or court's reliance on the manual, or for any other written or verbal information related to adult or juvenile sentencing. The scoring sheets are intended to provide assistance in most cases but do not cover all permutations of the scoring rules. If you find any errors or omissions, we encourage you to report them to the Caseload Forecast Council.

Civil Disorder Training

RCW 9A.48.120
CLASS B – NONVIOLENT
OFFENDER SCORING RCW 9.94A.525(7)

If it was found that this offense was committed with sexual motivation (RCW 9.94A.533(8)) on or after 7/01/2006, use the General Nonviolent Offense with a Sexual Motivation Finding scoring form on page 193.

If the present conviction is for a felony domestic violence offense where domestic violence was plead and proven, use the General Nonviolent Offense Where Domestic Violence Has Been Plead and Proven scoring form on page 191.

ADULT HISTORY:
   Enter number of felony convictions .... _____ x 1 = _____

JUVENILE HISTORY:
   Enter number of serious violent and violent felony dispositions .... _____ x 1 = _____

   Enter number of nonviolent felony dispositions .... _____ x ½ = _____

OTHER CURRENT OFFENSES:
(Other current offenses that do not encompass the same conduct count in offender score)
   Enter number of other felony convictions .... _____ x 1 = _____

STATUS:
   Was the offender on community custody on the date the current offense was committed? (if yes) .... + 1 = _____

Total the last column to get the **Offender Score** (Round down to the nearest whole number)

SENTENCE RANGE

	Offender Score									
	0	1	2	3	4	5	6	7	8	9+
LEVEL VII	17.5m	24m	30m	36m	42m	47.5m	66m	78m	89.5m	101.5m
	15 - 20	21 - 27	26 - 34	31 - 41	36 - 48	41 - 54	57 - 75	67 - 89	77 - 102	87 - 116

- ✓ For attempt, solicitation, conspiracy (RCW 9.94A.595) see page 23 or for gang-related felonies where the court found the offender involved a minor (RCW 9.94A.833) see page 186 for standard range adjustments.
- ✓ For deadly weapon enhancement, see page 190.
- ✓ For sentencing alternatives, see page 177.
- ✓ For community custody eligibility, see page 187.
- ✓ For any applicable enhancements other than deadly weapon enhancement, see page 183.

The Caseload Forecast Council is not liable for errors or omissions in the manual, for sentences that may be inappropriately calculated as a result of a practitioner's or court's reliance on the manual, or for any other written or verbal information related to adult or juvenile sentencing. The scoring sheets are intended to provide assistance in most cases but do not cover all permutations of the scoring rules. If you find any errors or omissions, we encourage you to report them to the Caseload Forecast Council.

Commercial Bribery

RCW 9A.68.060
CLASS B – NONVIOLENT
OFFENDER SCORING RCW 9.94A.525(7)

If it was found that this offense was committed with sexual motivation (RCW 9.94A.533(8)) on or after 7/01/2006, use the General Nonviolent Offense with a Sexual Motivation Finding scoring form on page 193.

If the present conviction is for a felony domestic violence offense where domestic violence was plead and proven, use the General Nonviolent Offense Where Domestic Violence Has Been Plead and Proven scoring form on page 191.

ADULT HISTORY:
    Enter number of felony convictions .... _____ x 1 = _____

JUVENILE HISTORY:
    Enter number of serious violent and violent felony dispositions .... _____ x 1 = _____
    Enter number of nonviolent felony dispositions .... _____ x ½ = _____

OTHER CURRENT OFFENSES:
(Other current offenses that do not encompass the same conduct count in offender score)
    Enter number of other felony convictions .... _____ x 1 = _____

STATUS:
    Was the offender on community custody on the date the current offense was committed? (if yes) ...... + 1 = _____

Total the last column to get the **Offender Score** (Round down to the nearest whole number)

SENTENCE RANGE

	\multicolumn{10}{c}{Offender Score}
	0	1	2	3	4	5	6	7	8	9+
LEVEL IV	6m 3 - 9	9m 6 - 12	13m 12+ - 14	15m 13 - 17	17.5m 15 - 20	25.5m 22 - 29	38m 33 - 43	50m 43 - 57	61.5m 53 - 70	73.5m 63 - 84

- ✓ For attempt, solicitation, conspiracy (RCW 9.94A.595) see page 23 or for gang-related felonies where the court found the offender involved a minor (RCW 9.94A.833) see page 186 for standard range adjustments.
- ✓ For deadly weapon enhancement, see page 190.
- ✓ For sentencing alternatives, see page 177.
- ✓ For community custody eligibility, see page 187.
- ✓ For any applicable enhancements other than deadly weapon enhancement, see page 183.

The Caseload Forecast Council is not liable for errors or omissions in the manual, for sentences that may be inappropriately calculated as a result of a practitioner's or court's reliance on the manual, or for any other written or verbal information related to adult or juvenile sentencing. The scoring sheets are intended to provide assistance in most cases but do not cover all permutations of the scoring rules. If you find any errors or omissions, we encourage you to report them to the Caseload Forecast Council.

Commercial Sexual Abuse Of A Minor Known As Patronizing A Juvenile Prostitute Prior To 7/22/2007

RCW 9.68A.100
CLASS B* – NONVIOLENT/SEX

OFFENDER SCORING RCW 9.94A.525(17)

If the present conviction is for a felony domestic violence offense where domestic violence was plead and proven, use the General Nonviolent/Sex Offense Where Domestic Violence Has Been Plead and Proven scoring form on page 192.

ADULT HISTORY:
    Enter number of sex offense felony convictions .... _____ x 3 = _____
    Enter number of felony convictions .... _____ x 1 = _____

JUVENILE HISTORY:
    Enter number of sex offense felony dispositions .... _____ x 3 = _____
    Enter number of serious violent and violent felony dispositions .... _____ x 1 = _____
    Enter number of nonviolent felony dispositions .... _____ x ½ = _____

OTHER CURRENT OFFENSES:
(Other current offenses that do not encompass the same conduct count in offender score)
    Enter number of other sex offense felony convictions .... _____ x 3 = _____
    Enter number of other felony convictions .... _____ x 1 = _____

STATUS:
    Was the offender on community custody on the date the current offense was committed? (if yes) .... + 1 = _____

Total the last column to get the **Offender Score** (Round down to the nearest whole number)

SENTENCE RANGE

	\multicolumn{10}{c}{Offender Score}

	0	1	2	3	4	5	6	7	8	9+
LEVEL VIII	24m 21 - 27	30m 26 - 34	36m 31 - 41	42m 36 - 48	47.5m 41 - 54	53.5m 46 - 61	78m 67 - 89	89.5m 77 - 102	101.5m 87 - 116	114m 108 - 120*

- ✓ For attempt, solicitation, conspiracy (RCW 9.94A.595) see page 23 or for gang-related felonies where the court found the offender involved a minor (RCW 9.94A.833) see page 186 for standard range adjustments.
- ✓ For deadly weapon enhancement, see page 190.
- ✓ For sentencing alternatives, see page 177.
- ✓ For community custody eligibility, see page 187.
- ✓ For any applicable enhancements other than deadly weapon enhancement, see page 183.
- ✓ If the offender is not a persistent offender and has a prior conviction for an offense listed in RCW 9.94A.030(38)(b), then the sentence is subject to the requirements of RCW 9.94A.507.

The Caseload Forecast Council is not liable for errors or omissions in the manual, for sentences that may be inappropriately calculated as a result of a practitioner's or court's reliance on the manual, or for any other written or verbal information related to adult or juvenile sentencing. The scoring sheets are intended to provide assistance in most cases but do not cover all permutations of the scoring rules. If you find any errors or omissions, we encourage you to report them to the Caseload Forecast Council.

Communication With A Minor For Immoral Purposes Subsequent Violation Or Prior Sex Offense Conviction

RCW 9.68A.090(2)
CLASS C – NONVIOLENT/SEX
OFFENDER SCORING RCW 9.94A.525(17)

If the present conviction is for a felony domestic violence offense where domestic violence was plead and proven, use the General Nonviolent/Sex Offense Where Domestic Violence Has Been Plead and Proven scoring form on page 192.

ADULT HISTORY:
    Enter number of sex offense felony convictions .... _____ x 3 = _____
    Enter number of felony convictions .... _____ x 1 = _____

JUVENILE HISTORY:
    Enter number of sex offense felony dispositions .... _____ x 3 = _____
    Enter number of serious violent and violent felony dispositions .... _____ x 1 = _____
    Enter number of nonviolent felony dispositions .... _____ x ½ = _____

OTHER CURRENT OFFENSES:
(Other current offenses that do not encompass the same conduct count in offender score)
    Enter number of other sex offense felony convictions .... _____ x 3 = _____
    Enter number of other felony convictions .... _____ x 1 = _____

STATUS:
    Was the offender on community custody on the date the current offense was committed? (if yes) ...... + 1 = _____

Total the last column to get the **Offender Score** (Round down to the nearest whole number)

SENTENCE RANGE

	\multicolumn{10}{c}{Offender Score}
	0	1	2	3	4	5	6	7	8	9+
LEVEL III	2m 1 - 3	5m 3 - 8	8m 4 - 12	11m 9 - 12	14m 12+ - 16	19.5m 17 - 22	25.5m 22 - 29	38m 33 - 43	50m 43 - 57	55.5m 51 - 60*

- ✓ For gang-related felonies where the court found the offender involved a minor (RCW 9.94A.833) see page 186 for standard range adjustment.
- ✓ For deadly weapon enhancement, see page 190.
- ✓ For sentencing alternatives, see page 177.
- ✓ For community custody eligibility, see page 187.
- ✓ For any applicable enhancements other than deadly weapon enhancement, see page 183.
- ✓ If the offender is not a persistent offender and has a prior conviction for an offense listed in RCW 9.94A.030(38)(b), then the sentence is subject to the requirements of RCW 9.94A.507.

The Caseload Forecast Council is not liable for errors or omissions in the manual, for sentences that may be inappropriately calculated as a result of a practitioner's or court's reliance on the manual, or for any other written or verbal information related to adult or juvenile sentencing. The scoring sheets are intended to provide assistance in most cases but do not cover all permutations of the scoring rules. If you find any errors or omissions, we encourage you to report them to the Caseload Forecast Council.

Computer Trespass First Degree

RCW 9A.90.040
CLASS C – NONVIOLENT
OFFENDER SCORING RCW 9.94A.525(7)

If it was found that this offense was committed with sexual motivation (RCW 9.94A.533(8)) on or after 7/01/2006, use the General Nonviolent Offense with a Sexual Motivation Finding scoring form on page 193.

If the present conviction is for a felony domestic violence offense where domestic violence was plead and proven, use the General Nonviolent Offense Where Domestic Violence Has Been Plead and Proven scoring form on page 191.

ADULT HISTORY:
  Enter number of felony convictions .... _____ x 1 = _____

JUVENILE HISTORY:
  Enter number of serious violent and violent felony dispositions .... _____ x 1 = _____
  Enter number of nonviolent felony dispositions .... _____ x ½ = _____

OTHER CURRENT OFFENSES:
(Other current offenses that do not encompass the same conduct count in offender score)
  Enter number of other felony convictions .... _____ x 1 = _____

STATUS:
  Was the offender on community custody on the date the current offense was committed? (if yes) .... + 1 = _____

Total the last column to get the **Offender Score** (Round down to the nearest whole number)

SENTENCE RANGE

	\multicolumn{11}{c}{Offender Score}
	0	1	2	3	4	5	6	7	8	9+
LEVEL II	0-90 days	4m 2 - 6	6m 3 - 9	8m 4 - 12	13m 12+ - 14	16m 14 - 18	19.5m 17 - 22	25.5m 22 - 29	38m 33 - 43	50m 43 - 57

- ✓ For gang-related felonies where the court found the offender involved a minor (RCW 9.94A.833) see page 186 for standard range adjustment.
- ✓ For deadly weapon enhancement, see page 190.
- ✓ For sentencing alternatives, see page 177.
- ✓ For community custody eligibility, see page 187.
- ✓ For any applicable enhancements other than deadly weapon enhancement, see page 183.

The Caseload Forecast Council is not liable for errors or omissions in the manual, for sentences that may be inappropriately calculated as a result of a practitioner's or court's reliance on the manual, or for any other written or verbal information related to adult or juvenile sentencing. The scoring sheets are intended to provide assistance in most cases but do not cover all permutations of the scoring rules. If you find any errors or omissions, we encourage you to report them to the Caseload Forecast Council.

Controlled Substance Homicide

RCW 69.50.415
CLASS B – NONVIOLENT/DRUG

OFFENDER SCORING RCW 9.94A.525(13)

If it was found that this offense was committed with sexual motivation (RCW 9.94A.533(8)) on or after 7/01/2006, use the General Drug Offense with a Sexual Motivation Finding scoring form on page 195.

If the present conviction is for a felony domestic violence offense where domestic violence was plead and proven, use the General Drug Offense Where Domestic Violence Has Been Plead and Proven scoring form on page 194.

ADULT HISTORY:
    Does the offender have a prior sex or serious violent offense in history?
        YES Enter number of felony drug convictions .... _____   x 3 = _____
        NO Enter number of felony drug convictions .... _____   x 1 = _____
    Enter number of felony convictions .... _____   x 1 = _____

JUVENILE HISTORY:
    Does the offender have a prior sex or serious violent offense in history?
        YES Enter number of felony drug dispositions .... _____   x 2 = _____
        NO Enter number of felony drug dispositions .... _____   x ½ = _____
    Enter number of serious violent and violent felony dispositions .... _____   x 1 = _____
    Enter number of nonviolent felony dispositions .... _____   x ½ = _____

OTHER CURRENT OFFENSES:
(Other current offenses that do not encompass the same conduct count in offender score)
    Does the offender have other prior sex or serious violent offense in history?
        YES Enter number of other felony drug convictions .... _____   x 3 = _____
        NO Enter number of other felony drug convictions .... _____   x 1 = _____
    Enter number of other felony convictions .... _____   x 1 = _____

STATUS:
    Was the offender on community custody on the date the current offense was committed? (if yes) ...... + 1 = _____

Total the last column to get the **Offender Score** (Round down to the nearest whole number)

SENTENCE RANGE – DRUG

	Offender Score		
	0 to 2	**3 to 5**	**6 to 9+**
LEVEL III	59.5m 51 - 68	84m 68+ - 100	110m 100+ - 120

- ✓ For attempt, solicitation or conspiracy drug felonies see page 25 or for gang-related felonies where the court found the offender involved a minor (RCW 9.94A.833) see page 186 for standard range adjustments.
- ✓ Per RCW 9.94A.518, any felony offense under chapter 69.50 RCW with a deadly weapon special verdict under RCW 9.94A.602 becomes a level III offense.
- ✓ For deadly weapon enhancement, see page 190.
- ✓ For sentencing alternatives, see page 177.
- ✓ For community custody eligibility, see page 187.
- ✓ For any applicable enhancements other than deadly weapon enhancement, see page 183.
- ✓ Per RCW 69.50.408, the statutory maximum for a **subsequent conviction** under chapter 69.50 RCW is 240 months.

The Caseload Forecast Council is not liable for errors or omissions in the manual, for sentences that may be inappropriately calculated as a result of a practitioner's or court's reliance on the manual, or for any other written or verbal information related to adult or juvenile sentencing. The scoring sheets are intended to provide assistance in most cases but do not cover all permutations of the scoring rules. If you find any errors or omissions, we encourage you to report them to the Caseload Forecast Council.

Counterfeiting Third Conviction And Value $10,000 Or More

RCW 9.16.035(3)
CLASS C– NONVIOLENT

OFFENDER SCORING RCW 9.94A.525(7)

If it was found that this offense was committed with sexual motivation (RCW 9.94A.533(8)) on or after 7/01/2006, use the General Nonviolent Offense with a Sexual Motivation Finding scoring form on page 193.

If the present conviction is for a felony domestic violence offense where domestic violence was plead and proven, use the General Nonviolent Offense Where Domestic Violence Has Been Plead and Proven scoring form on page 191.

ADULT HISTORY:
    Enter number of felony convictions .... _____ x 1 = _____

JUVENILE HISTORY:
    Enter number of serious violent and violent felony dispositions .... _____ x 1 = _____

    Enter number of nonviolent felony dispositions .... _____ x ½ = _____

OTHER CURRENT OFFENSES:
(Other current offenses that do not encompass the same conduct count in offender score)
    Enter number of other felony convictions .... _____ x 1 = _____

STATUS:
    Was the offender on community custody on the date the current offense was committed? (if yes) .... + 1 = _____

Total the last column to get the **Offender Score** (Round down to the nearest whole number)

SENTENCE RANGE

	\multicolumn{11}{c}{Offender Score}										
	0	1	2	3	4	5	6	7	8	9+
LEVEL II	0-90 days	4m 2 - 6	6m 3 - 9	8m 4 - 12	13m 12+ - 14	16m 14 - 18	19.5m 17 - 22	25.5m 22 - 29	38m 33 - 43	50m 43 - 57

- ✓ For gang-related felonies where the court found the offender involved a minor (RCW 9.94A.833) see page 186 for standard range adjustment.
- ✓ For deadly weapon enhancement, see page 190.
- ✓ For sentencing alternatives, see page 177.
- ✓ For community custody eligibility, see page 187.
- ✓ For any applicable enhancements other than deadly weapon enhancement, see page 183.

Counterfeiting - Endanger Public Health Or Safety

RCW 9.16.035(4)
CLASS C* – NONVIOLENT

OFFENDER SCORING RCW 9.94A.525(7)

If it was found that this offense was committed with sexual motivation (RCW 9.94A.533(8)) on or after 7/01/2006, use the General Nonviolent Offense with a Sexual Motivation Finding scoring form on page 193.

If the present conviction is for a felony domestic violence offense where domestic violence was plead and proven, use the General Nonviolent Offense Where Domestic Violence Has Been Plead and Proven scoring form on page 191.

ADULT HISTORY:
    Enter number of felony convictions .... _____ x 1 = _____

JUVENILE HISTORY:
    Enter number of serious violent and violent felony dispositions .... _____ x 1 = _____
    Enter number of nonviolent felony dispositions .... _____ x ½ = _____

OTHER CURRENT OFFENSES:
(Other current offenses that do not encompass the same conduct count in offender score)
    Enter number of other felony convictions .... _____ x 1 = _____

STATUS:
    Was the offender on community custody on the date the current offense was committed? (if yes) ...... + 1 = _____

Total the last column to get the **Offender Score** (Round down to the nearest whole number)

SENTENCE RANGE

	Offender Score									
	0	1	2	3	4	5	6	7	8	9+
LEVEL IV	6m 3 - 9	9m 6 - 12	13m 12+ - 14	15m 13 - 17	17.5m 15 - 20	25.5m 22 - 29	38m 33 - 43	50m 43 - 57	56.5m 53 - 60*	60 - 60*

- ✓ For gang-related felonies where the court found the offender involved a minor (RCW 9.94A.833) see page 186 for standard range adjustment.
- ✓ For deadly weapon enhancement, see page 190.
- ✓ For sentencing alternatives, see page 177.
- ✓ For community custody eligibility, see page 187.
- ✓ For any applicable enhancements other than deadly weapon enhancement, see page 183.

The Caseload Forecast Council is not liable for errors or omissions in the manual, for sentences that may be inappropriately calculated as a result of a practitioner's or court's reliance on the manual, or for any other written or verbal information related to adult or juvenile sentencing. The scoring sheets are intended to provide assistance in most cases but do not cover all permutations of the scoring rules. If you find any errors or omissions, we encourage you to report them to the Caseload Forecast Council.

Create, Deliver Or Possess A Counterfeit Controlled Substance Schedule I Or II Narcotic Or Flunitrazepam Or Methamphetamine

RCW 69.50.4011(2)(a-b)
CLASS B – NONVIOLENT/DRUG

OFFENDER SCORING RCW 9.94A.525(13)

If it was found that this offense was committed with sexual motivation (RCW 9.94A.533(8)) on or after 7/01/2006, use the General Drug Offense with a Sexual Motivation Finding scoring form on page 195.

If the present conviction is for a felony domestic violence offense where domestic violence was plead and proven, use the General Drug Offense Where Domestic Violence Has Been Plead and Proven scoring form on page 194.

ADULT HISTORY:
Does the offender have a prior sex or serious violent offense in history?
    YES Enter number of felony drug convictions .... _____ x 3 = _____
    NO Enter number of felony drug convictions .... _____ x 1 = _____
Enter number of felony convictions .... _____ x 1 = _____

JUVENILE HISTORY:
Does the offender have a prior sex or serious violent offense in history?
    YES Enter number of felony drug dispositions .... _____ x 2 = _____
    NO Enter number of felony drug dispositions .... _____ x ½ = _____
Enter number of serious violent and violent felony dispositions .... _____ x 1 = _____
Enter number of nonviolent felony dispositions .... _____ x ½ = _____

OTHER CURRENT OFFENSES:
(Other current offenses that do not encompass the same conduct count in offender score)
Does the offender have other prior sex or serious violent offense in history?
    YES Enter number of other felony drug convictions .... _____ x 3 = _____
    NO Enter number of other felony drug convictions .... _____ x 1 = _____
Enter number of other felony convictions .... _____ x 1 = _____

STATUS:
Was the offender on community custody on the date the current offense was committed? (if yes) .... + 1 = _____

Total the last column to get the **Offender Score** (Round down to the nearest whole number)

SENTENCE RANGE – DRUG

	Offender Score		
	0 to 2	3 to 5	6 to 9+
LEVEL II	16m 12+ - 20	40m 20+ - 60	90m 60+ - 120

- ✓ For attempt, solicitation or conspiracy drug felonies see page 25 or for gang-related felonies where the court found the offender involved a minor (RCW 9.94A.833) see page 186 for standard range adjustments.
- ✓ Per RCW 9.94A.518, any felony offense under chapter 69.50 RCW with a deadly weapon special verdict under RCW 9.94A.602 becomes a level III offense.
- ✓ For deadly weapon enhancement, see page 190.
- ✓ For sentencing alternatives, see page 177.
- ✓ For community custody eligibility, see page 187.
- ✓ For any applicable enhancements other than deadly weapon enhancement, see page 183.
- ✓ Per RCW 69.50.408, the statutory maximum for a **subsequent conviction** under chapter 69.50 RCW is 240 months.

The Caseload Forecast Council is not liable for errors or omissions in the manual, for sentences that may be inappropriately calculated as a result of a practitioner's or court's reliance on the manual, or for any other written or verbal information related to adult or juvenile sentencing. The scoring sheets are intended to provide assistance in most cases but do not cover all permutations of the scoring rules. If you find any errors or omissions, we encourage you to report them to the Caseload Forecast Council.

Create, Deliver Or Possess A Counterfeit Controlled Substance Schedule I-II Nonnarcotic, Schedule III-V Except Flunitrazepam Or Methamphetamine

RCW 69.50.4011(2)(c-e)
CLASS C* – NONVIOLENT/DRUG

OFFENDER SCORING RCW 9.94A.525(13)

If it was found that this offense was committed with sexual motivation (RCW 9.94A.533(8)) on or after 7/01/2006, use the General Drug Offense with a Sexual Motivation Finding scoring form on page 195.

If the present conviction is for a felony domestic violence offense where domestic violence was plead and proven, use the General Drug Offense Where Domestic Violence Has Been Plead and Proven scoring form on page 194.

ADULT HISTORY:
Does the offender have a prior sex or serious violent offense in history?
    YES Enter number of felony drug convictions.. _____ x 3 = _____
    NO Enter number of felony drug convictions .... _____ x 1 = _____

Enter number of felony convictions .... _____ x 1 = _____

JUVENILE HISTORY:
Does the offender have a prior sex or serious violent offense in history?
    YES Enter number of felony drug dispositions.. _____ x 2 = _____
    NO Enter number of felony drug dispositions.. _____ x ½ = _____

Enter number of serious violent and violent felony dispositions .... _____ x 1 = _____

Enter number of nonviolent felony dispositions .... _____ x ½ = _____

OTHER CURRENT OFFENSES:
(Other current offenses that do not encompass the same conduct count in offender score)
Does the offender have other prior sex or serious violent offense in history?
    YES Enter number of other felony drug convictions .... _____ x 3 = _____
    NO Enter number of other felony drug convictions .... _____ x 1 = _____

Enter number of other felony convictions .... _____ x 1 = _____

STATUS:
Was the offender on community custody on the date the current offense was committed? (if yes).......... + 1 = _____

Total the last column to get the **Offender Score** (Round down to the nearest whole number)

SENTENCE RANGE – DRUG

	Offender Score		
	0 to 2	3 to 5	6 to 9+
LEVEL II	16m 12+ - 20	40m 20+ - 60	60 - 60*

✓ For attempt, solicitation or conspiracy drug felonies see page 25 or for gang-related felonies where the court found the offender involved a minor (RCW 9.94A.833) see page 186 for standard range adjustments.

✓ Per RCW 9.94A.518, any felony offense under chapter 69.50 RCW with a deadly weapon special verdict under RCW 9.94A.602 becomes a level III offense.

✓ For deadly weapon enhancement, see page 190.

✓ For sentencing alternatives, see page 177.

✓ For community custody eligibility, see page 187.

✓ For any applicable enhancements other than deadly weapon enhancement, see page 183.

✓ Per RCW 69.50.408, the statutory maximum for a **subsequent conviction** under chapter 69.50 RCW is 120 months.

The Caseload Forecast Council is not liable for errors or omissions in the manual, for sentences that may be inappropriately calculated as a result of a practitioner's or court's reliance on the manual, or for any other written or verbal information related to adult or juvenile sentencing. The scoring sheets are intended to provide assistance in most cases but do not cover all permutations of the scoring rules. If you find any errors or omissions, we encourage you to report them to the Caseload Forecast Council.

Criminal Gang Intimidation

RCW 9A.46.120

CLASS C* – NONVIOLENT

OFFENDER SCORING RCW 9.94A.525(7)

If it was found that this offense was committed with sexual motivation (RCW 9.94A.533(8)) on or after 7/01/2006, use the General Nonviolent Offense with a Sexual Motivation Finding scoring form on page 193.

If the present conviction is for a felony domestic violence offense where domestic violence was plead and proven, use the General Nonviolent Offense Where Domestic Violence Has Been Plead and Proven scoring form on page 191.

ADULT HISTORY:
　Enter number of felony convictions .... _____ x 1 = _____

JUVENILE HISTORY:
　Enter number of serious violent and violent felony dispositions .... _____ x 1 = _____
　Enter number of nonviolent felony dispositions .... _____ x ½ = _____

OTHER CURRENT OFFENSES:
(Other current offenses that do not encompass the same conduct count in offender score)
　Enter number of other felony convictions .... _____ x 1 = _____

STATUS:
　Was the offender on community custody on the date the current offense was committed? (if yes)....... + 1 = _____

Total the last column to get the **Offender Score** (Round down to the nearest whole number)

SENTENCE RANGE

	| Offender Score									
	0	**1**	**2**	**3**	**4**	**5**	**6**	**7**	**8**	**9+**
LEVEL III	2m 1 - 3	5m 3 - 8	8m 4 - 12	11m 9 - 12	14m 12+ - 16	19.5m 17 - 22	25.5m 22 - 29	38m 33 - 43	50m 43 - 57	55.5m 51 - 60*

- ✓ For gang-related felonies where the court found the offender involved a minor (RCW 9.94A.833) see page 186 for standard range adjustment.
- ✓ For deadly weapon enhancement, see page 190.
- ✓ For sentencing alternatives, see page 177.
- ✓ For community custody eligibility, see page 187.
- ✓ For any applicable enhancements other than deadly weapon enhancement, see page 183.

Criminal Mistreatment First Degree

RCW 9A.42.020
CLASS B* – NONVIOLENT
OFFENDER SCORING RCW 9.94A.525(7)

If it was found that this offense was committed with sexual motivation (RCW 9.94A.533(8)) on or after 7/01/2006, use the General Nonviolent Offense with a Sexual Motivation Finding scoring form on page 193.

If the present conviction is for a felony domestic violence offense where domestic violence was plead and proven, use the General Nonviolent Offense Where Domestic Violence Has Been Plead and Proven scoring form on page 191.

ADULT HISTORY:
    Enter number of felony convictions .... _____ x 1 = _____

JUVENILE HISTORY:
    Enter number of serious violent and violent felony dispositions .... _____ x 1 = _____
    Enter number of nonviolent felony dispositions .... _____ x ½ = _____

OTHER CURRENT OFFENSES:
(Other current offenses that do not encompass the same conduct count in offender score)
    Enter number of other felony convictions .... _____ x 1 = _____

STATUS:
    Was the offender on community custody on the date the current offense was committed? (if yes) ...... + 1 = _____

Total the last column to get the **Offender Score** (Round down to the nearest whole number)

SENTENCE RANGE

	Offender Score									
	0	**1**	**2**	**3**	**4**	**5**	**6**	**7**	**8**	**9+**
LEVEL X	59.5m 51 - 68	66m 57 - 75	72m 62 - 82	78m 67 - 89	84m 72 - 96	89.5m 77 - 102	109m 98 - 120*	120 - 120*	120 - 120*	120 - 120*

- ✓ For attempt, solicitation, conspiracy (RCW 9.94A.595) see page 23 or for gang-related felonies where the court found the offender involved a minor (RCW 9.94A.833) see page 186 for standard range adjustments.
- ✓ For deadly weapon enhancement, see page 190.
- ✓ For sentencing alternatives, see page 177.
- ✓ For community custody eligibility, see page 187.
- ✓ For any applicable enhancements other than deadly weapon enhancement, see page 183.

Criminal Mistreatment Second Degree

RCW 9A.42.030

CLASS C* – NONVIOLENT

OFFENDER SCORING RCW 9.94A.525(7)

If it was found that this offense was committed with sexual motivation (RCW 9.94A.533(8)) on or after 7/01/2006, use the General Nonviolent Offense with a Sexual Motivation Finding scoring form on page 193.

If the present conviction is for a felony domestic violence offense where domestic violence was plead and proven, use the General Nonviolent Offense Where Domestic Violence Has Been Plead and Proven scoring form on page 191.

ADULT HISTORY:
    Enter number of felony convictions .... _____ x 1 = _____

JUVENILE HISTORY:
    Enter number of serious violent and violent felony dispositions .... _____ x 1 = _____

    Enter number of nonviolent felony dispositions .... _____ x ½ = _____

OTHER CURRENT OFFENSES:
(Other current offenses that do not encompass the same conduct count in offender score)
    Enter number of other felony convictions .... _____ x 1 = _____

STATUS:
    Was the offender on community custody on the date the current offense was committed? (if yes)....... + 1 = _____

Total the last column to get the **Offender Score** (Round down to the nearest whole number)

SENTENCE RANGE

	_	_	_	_	Offender Score	_	_	_	_	_
	0	1	2	3	4	5	6	7	8	9+
LEVEL V	9m	13m	15m	17.5m	25.5m	38m	47.5m	55.5m		
	6 - 12	12+ - 14	13 - 17	15 - 20	22 - 29	33 - 43	41 - 54	51 - 60*	60 - 60*	60 - 60*

- ✓ For gang-related felonies where the court found the offender involved a minor (RCW 9.94A.833) see page 186 for standard range adjustment.
- ✓ For deadly weapon enhancement, see page 190.
- ✓ For sentencing alternatives, see page 177.
- ✓ For community custody eligibility, see page 187.
- ✓ For any applicable enhancements other than deadly weapon enhancement, see page 183.

The Caseload Forecast Council is not liable for errors or omissions in the manual, for sentences that may be inappropriately calculated as a result of a practitioner's or court's reliance on the manual, or for any other written or verbal information related to adult or juvenile sentencing. The scoring sheets are intended to provide assistance in most cases but do not cover all permutations of the scoring rules. If you find any errors or omissions, we encourage you to report them to the Caseload Forecast Council.

Custodial Assault

RCW 9A.36.100

CLASS C* – NONVIOLENT

OFFENDER SCORING RCW 9.94A.525(7)

If it was found that this offense was committed with sexual motivation (RCW 9.94A.533(8)) on or after 7/01/2006, use the General Nonviolent Offense with a Sexual Motivation Finding scoring form on page 193.

If the present conviction is for a felony domestic violence offense where domestic violence was plead and proven, use the General Nonviolent Offense Where Domestic Violence Has Been Plead and Proven scoring form on page 191.

ADULT HISTORY:
    Enter number of felony convictions .... _____   x 1 = _____

JUVENILE HISTORY:
    Enter number of serious violent and violent felony dispositions .... _____   x 1 = _____
    Enter number of nonviolent felony dispositions .... _____   x ½ = _____

OTHER CURRENT OFFENSES:
(Other current offenses that do not encompass the same conduct count in offender score)
    Enter number of other felony convictions .... _____   x 1 = _____

STATUS:
    Was the offender on community custody on the date the current offense was committed? (if yes) ...... + 1 = _____

Total the last column to get the **Offender Score** (Round down to the nearest whole number)

SENTENCE RANGE

	Offender Score									
	0	1	2	3	4	5	6	7	8	9+
LEVEL III	2m	5m	8m	11m	14m	19.5m	25.5m	38m	50m	55.5m
	1 - 3	3 - 8	4 - 12	9 - 12	12+ - 16	17 - 22	22 - 29	33 - 43	43 - 57	51 - 60*

✓ For gang-related felonies where the court found the offender involved a minor (RCW 9.94A.833) see page 186 for standard range adjustment.

✓ For deadly weapon enhancement, see page 190.

✓ For sentencing alternatives, see page 177.

✓ For community custody eligibility, see page 187.

✓ For any applicable enhancements other than deadly weapon enhancement, see page 183.

Custodial Sexual Misconduct First Degree

RCW 9A.44.160
CLASS C* – NONVIOLENT/SEX
OFFENDER SCORING RCW 9.94A.525(17)

If the present conviction is for a felony domestic violence offense where domestic violence was plead and proven, use the General Nonviolent/Sex Offense Where Domestic Violence Has Been Plead and Proven scoring form on page 192.

ADULT HISTORY:
    Enter number of sex offense felony convictions .... _____ x 3 = _____
    Enter number of felony convictions .... _____ x 1 = _____

JUVENILE HISTORY:
    Enter number of sex offense felony dispositions .... _____ x 3 = _____
    Enter number of serious violent and violent felony dispositions .... _____ x 1 = _____
    Enter number of nonviolent felony dispositions .... _____ x ½ = _____

OTHER CURRENT OFFENSES:
(Other current offenses that do not encompass the same conduct count in offender score)
    Enter number of other sex offense felony convictions .... _____ x 3 = _____
    Enter number of other felony convictions .... _____ x 1 = _____

STATUS:
    Was the offender on community custody on the date the current offense was committed? (if yes)....... + 1 = _____

Total the last column to get the **Offender Score** (Round down to the nearest whole number)

SENTENCE RANGE

	Offender Score									
	0	**1**	**2**	**3**	**4**	**5**	**6**	**7**	**8**	**9+**
LEVEL V	9m	13m	15m	17.5m	25.5m	38m	47.5m	55.5m		
	6 - 12	12+ - 14	13 - 17	15 - 20	22 - 29	33 - 43	41 - 54	51 - 60*	60 - 60*	60 - 60*

- ✓ For gang-related felonies where the court found the offender involved a minor (RCW 9.94A.833) see page 186 for standard range adjustment.
- ✓ For deadly weapon enhancement, see page 190.
- ✓ For sentencing alternatives, see page 177.
- ✓ For community custody eligibility, see page 187.
- ✓ For any applicable enhancements other than deadly weapon enhancement, see page 183.
- ✓ If the offender is not a persistent offender and has a prior conviction for an offense listed in RCW 9.94A.030(38)(b), then the sentence is subject to the requirements of RCW 9.94A.507.

The Caseload Forecast Council is not liable for errors or omissions in the manual, for sentences that may be inappropriately calculated as a result of a practitioner's or court's reliance on the manual, or for any other written or verbal information related to adult or juvenile sentencing. The scoring sheets are intended to provide assistance in most cases but do not cover all permutations of the scoring rules. If you find any errors or omissions, we encourage you to report them to the Caseload Forecast Council.

Cyberstalking With Prior Harassment Conviction Or Threat Of Death

RCW 9.61.260(3)
CLASS C* – NONVIOLENT

OFFENDER SCORING RCW 9.94A.525(7)

If it was found that this offense was committed with sexual motivation (RCW 9.94A.533(8)) on or after 7/01/2006, use the General Nonviolent Offense with a Sexual Motivation Finding scoring form on page 193.

If the present conviction is for a felony domestic violence offense where domestic violence was plead and proven, use the General Nonviolent Offense Where Domestic Violence Has Been Plead and Proven scoring form on page 191.

ADULT HISTORY:
  Enter number of felony convictions .... _____ x 1 = _____

JUVENILE HISTORY:
  Enter number of serious violent and violent felony dispositions .... _____ x 1 = _____
  Enter number of nonviolent felony dispositions .... _____ x ½ = _____

OTHER CURRENT OFFENSES:
(Other current offenses that do not encompass the same conduct count in offender score)
  Enter number of other felony convictions .... _____ x 1 = _____

STATUS:
  Was the offender on community custody on the date the current offense was committed? (if yes) ...... + 1 = _____

Total the last column to get the **Offender Score** (Round down to the nearest whole number)

SENTENCE RANGE

	Offender Score									
	0	1	2	3	4	5	6	7	8	9+
LEVEL III	2m	5m	8m	11m	14m	19.5m	25.5m	38m	50m	55.5m
	1 - 3	3 - 8	4 - 12	9 - 12	12+ - 16	17 - 22	22 - 29	33 - 43	43 - 57	51 - 60*

- ✓ For gang-related felonies where the court found the offender involved a minor (RCW 9.94A.833) see page 186 for standard range adjustment.
- ✓ For deadly weapon enhancement, see page 190.
- ✓ For sentencing alternatives, see page 177.
- ✓ For community custody eligibility, see page 187.
- ✓ For any applicable enhancements other than deadly weapon enhancement, see page 183.

Dealing In Depictions Of A Minor Engaged In Sexually Explicit Conduct First Degree

RCW 9.68A.050(1)
CLASS B – NONVIOLENT/SEX
OFFENDER SCORING RCW 9.94A.525(17)

If the present conviction is for a felony domestic violence offense where domestic violence was plead and proven, use the General Nonviolent/Sex Offense Where Domestic Violence Has Been Plead and Proven scoring form on page 192.

ADULT HISTORY:
Enter number of sex offense felony convictions .... _____ x 3 = _____
Enter number of felony convictions .... _____ x 1 = _____

JUVENILE HISTORY:
Enter number of sex offense felony dispositions .... _____ x 3 = _____
Enter number of serious violent and violent felony dispositions .... _____ x 1 = _____
Enter number of nonviolent felony dispositions .... _____ x ½ = _____

OTHER CURRENT OFFENSES:
(Other current offenses that do not encompass the same conduct count in offender score)
Enter number of other sex offense felony convictions .... _____ x 3 = _____
Enter number of other felony convictions .... _____ x 1 = _____

STATUS:
Was the offender on community custody on the date the current offense was committed? (if yes) .... + 1 = _____

Total the last column to get the **Offender Score** (Round down to the nearest whole number)

SENTENCE RANGE

	Offender Score									
	0	1	2	3	4	5	6	7	8	9+
LEVEL VII	17.5m	24m	30m	36m	42m	47.5m	66m	78m	89.5m	101.5m
	15 - 20	21 - 27	26 - 34	31 - 41	36 - 48	41 - 54	57 - 75	67 - 89	77 - 102	87 - 116

- ✓ For attempt, solicitation, conspiracy (RCW 9.94A.595) see page 23 or for gang-related felonies where the court found the offender involved a minor (RCW 9.94A.833) see page 186 for standard range adjustments.
- ✓ For deadly weapon enhancement, see page 190.
- ✓ For sentencing alternatives, see page 177.
- ✓ For community custody eligibility, see page 187.
- ✓ For any applicable enhancements other than deadly weapon enhancement, see page 183.
- ✓ If the offender is not a persistent offender and has a prior conviction for an offense listed in RCW 9.94A.030(38)(b), then the sentence is subject to the requirements of RCW 9.94A.507.

The Caseload Forecast Council is not liable for errors or omissions in the manual, for sentences that may be inappropriately calculated as a result of a practitioner's or court's reliance on the manual, or for any other written or verbal information related to adult or juvenile sentencing. The scoring sheets are intended to provide assistance in most cases but do not cover all permutations of the scoring rules. If you find any errors or omissions, we encourage you to report them to the Caseload Forecast Council.

Dealing In Depictions Of A Minor Engaged In Sexually Explicit Conduct Second Degree

RCW 9.68A.050(2)
CLASS C* – NONVIOLENT/SEX

OFFENDER SCORING RCW 9.94A.525(17)

If the present conviction is for a felony domestic violence offense where domestic violence was plead and proven, use the General Nonviolent/Sex Offense Where Domestic Violence Has Been Plead and Proven scoring form on page 192.

ADULT HISTORY:
    Enter number of sex offense felony convictions .... _____ x 3 = _____
    Enter number of felony convictions .... _____ x 1 = _____

JUVENILE HISTORY:
    Enter number of sex offense felony dispositions .... _____ x 3 = _____
    Enter number of serious violent and violent felony dispositions .... _____ x 1 = _____
    Enter number of nonviolent felony dispositions .... _____ x ½ = _____

OTHER CURRENT OFFENSES:
(Other current offenses that do not encompass the same conduct count in offender score)
    Enter number of other sex offense felony convictions .... _____ x 3 = _____
    Enter number of other felony convictions .... _____ x 1 = _____

STATUS:
    Was the offender on community custody on the date the current offense was committed? (if yes) ...... + 1 = _____

Total the last column to get the **Offender Score** (Round down to the nearest whole number)

SENTENCE RANGE

	\multicolumn{10}{c}{Offender Score}
	0	1	2	3	4	5	6	7	8	9+
LEVEL V	9m 6 - 12	13m 12+ - 14	15m 13 - 17	17.5m 15 - 20	25.5m 22 - 29	38m 33 - 43	47.5m 41 - 54	55.5m 51 - 60*	60 - 60*	60 - 60*

- ✓ For gang-related felonies where the court found the offender involved a minor (RCW 9.94A.833) see page 186 for standard range adjustment.
- ✓ For deadly weapon enhancement, see page 190.
- ✓ For sentencing alternatives, see page 177.
- ✓ For community custody eligibility, see page 187.
- ✓ For any applicable enhancements other than deadly weapon enhancement, see page 183.
- ✓ If the offender is not a persistent offender and has a prior conviction for an offense listed in RCW 9.94A.030(38)(b), then the sentence is subject to the requirements of RCW 9.94A.507.

The Caseload Forecast Council is not liable for errors or omissions in the manual, for sentences that may be inappropriately calculated as a result of a practitioner's or court's reliance on the manual, or for any other written or verbal information related to adult or juvenile sentencing. The scoring sheets are intended to provide assistance in most cases but do not cover all permutations of the scoring rules. If you find any errors or omissions, we encourage you to report them to the Caseload Forecast Council.

Deliver Or Possess With Intent To Deliver Methamphetamine

RCW 69.50.401(2)(b)
CLASS B – NONVIOLENT/DRUG

OFFENDER SCORING RCW 9.94A.525(13)

If it was found that this offense was committed with sexual motivation (RCW 9.94A.533(8)) on or after 7/01/2006, use the General Drug Offense with a Sexual Motivation Finding scoring form on page 195.

If the present conviction is for a felony domestic violence offense where domestic violence was plead and proven, use the General Drug Offense Where Domestic Violence Has Been Plead and Proven scoring form on page 194.

ADULT HISTORY:
Does the offender have a prior sex or serious violent offense in history?
  YES Enter number of felony drug convictions .... _____ x 3 = _____
  NO Enter number of felony drug convictions .... _____ x 1 = _____

  Enter number of felony convictions .... _____ x 1 = _____

JUVENILE HISTORY:
Does the offender have a prior sex or serious violent offense in history?
  YES Enter number of felony drug dispositions .... _____ x 2 = _____
  NO Enter number of felony drug dispositions .... _____ x ½ = _____

  Enter number of serious violent and violent felony dispositions .... _____ x 1 = _____

  Enter number of nonviolent felony dispositions .... _____ x ½ = _____

OTHER CURRENT OFFENSES:
(Other current offenses that do not encompass the same conduct count in offender score)
Does the offender have other prior sex or serious violent offense in history?
  YES Enter number of other felony drug convictions .... _____ x 3 = _____
  NO Enter number of other felony drug convictions .... _____ x 1 = _____

  Enter number of other felony convictions .... _____ x 1 = _____

STATUS:
Was the offender on community custody on the date the current offense was committed? (if yes) .... + 1 = _____

Total the last column to get the **Offender Score** (Round down to the nearest whole number) [____]

SENTENCE RANGE – DRUG

	Offender Score		
	0 to 2	3 to 5	6 to 9+
LEVEL II	16m	40m	90m
	12+ - 20	20+ - 60	60+ - 120

- ✓ For attempt, solicitation or conspiracy drug felonies see page 25 or for gang-related felonies where the court found the offender involved a minor (RCW 9.94A.833) see page 186 for standard range adjustments.
- ✓ Per RCW 9.94A.518, any felony offense under chapter 69.50 RCW with a deadly weapon special verdict under RCW 9.94A.602 becomes a level III offense.
- ✓ For deadly weapon enhancement, see page 190.
- ✓ For sentencing alternatives, see page 177.
- ✓ For community custody eligibility, see page 187.
- ✓ For any applicable enhancements other than deadly weapon enhancement, see page 183.
- ✓ Per RCW 69.50.408, the statutory maximum for a **subsequent conviction** under chapter 69.50 RCW is 240 months.
- ✓ Per RCW 69.50.435, if the offense occurred within a **protected zone**, 24 months shall be added to the standard range and the statutory maximum is 240 months.

The Caseload Forecast Council is not liable for errors or omissions in the manual, for sentences that may be inappropriately calculated as a result of a practitioner's or court's reliance on the manual, or for any other written or verbal information related to adult or juvenile sentencing. The scoring sheets are intended to provide assistance in most cases but do not cover all permutations of the scoring rules. If you find any errors or omissions, we encourage you to report them to the Caseload Forecast Council.

Delivery Of Imitation Controlled Substance By Person 18 Or Over To Person Under 18

RCW 69.52.030(2)
CLASS B – NONVIOLENT

OFFENDER SCORING RCW 9.94A.525(7)

If it was found that this offense was committed with sexual motivation (RCW 9.94A.533(8)) on or after 7/01/2006, use the General Nonviolent Offense with a Sexual Motivation Finding scoring form on page 193.

If the present conviction is for a felony domestic violence offense where domestic violence was plead and proven, use the General Nonviolent Offense Where Domestic Violence Has Been Plead and Proven scoring form on page 191.

ADULT HISTORY:
    Enter number of felony convictions .... _____ x 1 = _____

JUVENILE HISTORY:
    Enter number of serious violent and violent felony dispositions .... _____ x 1 = _____
    Enter number of nonviolent felony dispositions .... _____ x ½ = _____

OTHER CURRENT OFFENSES:
(Other current offenses that do not encompass the same conduct count in offender score)
    Enter number of other felony convictions .... _____ x 1 = _____

STATUS:
    Was the offender on community custody on the date the current offense was committed? (if yes) ...... + 1 = _____

Total the last column to get the **Offender Score** (Round down to the nearest whole number)

SENTENCE RANGE – DRUG

	Offender Score		
	0 to 2	3 to 5	6 to 9+
LEVEL III	59.5m 51 - 68	84m 68+ - 100	110m 100+ - 120

- ✓ For attempt, solicitation, conspiracy (RCW 9.94A.595) see page 23 or for gang-related felonies where the court found the offender involved a minor (RCW 9.94A.833) see page 186 for standard range adjustments.
- ✓ For deadly weapon enhancement, see page 190.
- ✓ For sentencing alternatives, see page 177.
- ✓ For community custody eligibility, see page 187.
- ✓ For any applicable enhancements other than deadly weapon enhancement, see page 183.

Delivery Of A Material In Lieu Of A Controlled Substance

RCW 69.50.4012
CLASS C* – NONVIOLENT/DRUG
OFFENDER SCORING RCW 9.94A.525(13)

If it was found that this offense was committed with sexual motivation (RCW 9.94A.533(8)) on or after 7/01/2006, use the General Drug Offense with a Sexual Motivation Finding scoring form on page 195.

If the present conviction is for a felony domestic violence offense where domestic violence was plead and proven, use the General Drug Offense Where Domestic Violence Has Been Plead and Proven scoring form on page 194.

ADULT HISTORY:
   Does the offender have a prior sex or serious violent offense in history?
      YES Enter number of felony drug convictions .... _____ x 3 = _____
      NO Enter number of felony drug convictions .... _____ x 1 = _____
   Enter number of felony convictions .... _____ x 1 = _____

JUVENILE HISTORY:
   Does the offender have a prior sex or serious violent offense in history?
      YES Enter number of felony drug dispositions .... _____ x 2 = _____
      NO Enter number of felony drug dispositions .... _____ x ½ = _____
   Enter number of serious violent and violent felony dispositions .... _____ x 1 = _____
   Enter number of nonviolent felony dispositions .... _____ x ½ = _____

OTHER CURRENT OFFENSES:
(Other current offenses that do not encompass the same conduct count in offender score)
   Does the offender have other prior sex or serious violent offense in history?
      YES Enter number of other felony drug convictions .... _____ x 3 = _____
      NO Enter number of other felony drug convictions .... _____ x 1 = _____
   Enter number of other felony convictions .... _____ x 1 = _____

STATUS:
   Was the offender on community custody on the date the current offense was committed? (if yes) .... + 1 = _____

Total the last column to get the **Offender Score** (Round down to the nearest whole number)

SENTENCE RANGE – DRUG

	Offender Score		
	0 to 2	**3 to 5**	**6 to 9+**
LEVEL II	16m 12+ - 20	40m 20+ - 60	60 - 60*

- ✓ For attempt, solicitation or conspiracy drug felonies see page 25 or for gang-related felonies where the court found the offender involved a minor (RCW 9.94A.833) see page 186 for standard range adjustments.
- ✓ Per RCW 9.94A.518, any felony offense under chapter 69.50 RCW with a deadly weapon special verdict under RCW 9.94A.602 becomes a level III offense.
- ✓ For deadly weapon enhancement, see page 190.
- ✓ For sentencing alternatives, see page 177.
- ✓ For community custody eligibility, see page 187.
- ✓ For any applicable enhancements other than deadly weapon enhancement, see page 183.
- ✓ Per RCW 69.50.408, the statutory maximum for a **subsequent conviction** under chapter 69.50 RCW is 120 months.

The Caseload Forecast Council is not liable for errors or omissions in the manual, for sentences that may be inappropriately calculated as a result of a practitioner's or court's reliance on the manual, or for any other written or verbal information related to adult or juvenile sentencing. The scoring sheets are intended to provide assistance in most cases but do not cover all permutations of the scoring rules. If you find any errors or omissions, we encourage you to report them to the Caseload Forecast Council.

Domestic Violence Court Order Violation

RCW 26.50.110
CLASS C* – NONVIOLENT

OFFENDER SCORING RCW 9.94A.525(21)

If it was found that this offense was committed with sexual motivation (RCW 9.94A.533(8)) on or after 7/01/2006, use the General Nonviolent/Sex Offense where domestic violence has been plead and proven scoring form *on page 192.*

ADULT HISTORY:
Enter number of domestic violence felony convictions as listed below* .... _____ x 2 = _____

Enter number of repetitive domestic violence offense convictions (RCW 9.94A.030(42)) plead and proven after 8/1/11 .... _____ x 1 = _____

Enter number of other felony convictions .... _____ x 1 = _____

JUVENILE HISTORY:
Enter number of subsequent domestic violence felony dispositions as listed below* .... _____ x 1 = _____

Enter number of serious violent and violent felony dispositions .... _____ x 1 = _____

Enter number of nonviolent felony dispositions .... _____ x ½ = _____

OTHER CURRENT OFFENSES:
(Other current offenses that do not encompass the same conduct count in offender score)
Enter number of other domestic violence felony convictions as listed below* .... _____ x 2 = _____

Enter number of other repetitive domestic violence offense convictions plead and proven after 8/1/11............................... _____ x 1 = _____

Enter number of other felony convictions .... _____ x 1 = _____

STATUS:
Was the offender on community custody on the date the current offense was committed? (if yes) ...... + 1 = _____

*If domestic violence was plead and proven after 8/1/2011 for the following felony offenses:
Violation of a No-Contact Order, Violation of a Protection Order, Domestic Violence Harassment, Domestic Violence Stalking, Domestic Violence Burglary 1, Domestic Violence Kidnapping 1, Domestic Violence Kidnapping 2, Domestic Violence Unlawful Imprisonment, Domestic Violence Robbery 1, Domestic Violence Robbery 2, Domestic Violence Assault 1, Domestic Violence Assault 2, Domestic Violence Assault 3, Domestic Violence Arson 1, Domestic Violence Arson 2.

Total the last column to get the **Offender Score** (Round down to the nearest whole number)

SENTENCE RANGE

Offender Score	0	1	2	3	4	5	6	7	8	9+
LEVEL V	9m 6 - 12	13m 12+ - 14	15m 13 - 17	17.5m 15 - 20	25.5m 22 - 29	38m 33 - 43	47.5m 41 - 54	55.5m 51 - 60*	60 - 60*	60 - 60*

- ✓ For gang-related felonies where the court found the offender involved a minor (RCW 9.94A.833) see page 186 for standard range adjustment.
- ✓ For deadly weapon enhancement, see page 190.
- ✓ For sentencing alternatives, see page 177.
- ✓ For community custody eligibility, see page 187.
- ✓ For any applicable enhancements other than deadly weapon enhancement, see page 183.

The Caseload Forecast Council is not liable for errors or omissions in the manual, for sentences that may be inappropriately calculated as a result of a practitioner's or court's reliance on the manual, or for any other written or verbal information related to adult or juvenile sentencing. The scoring sheets are intended to provide assistance in most cases but do not cover all permutations of the scoring rules. If you find any errors or omissions, we encourage you to report them to the Caseload Forecast Council.

Drive-By Shooting

RCW 9A.36.045
CLASS B – VIOLENT

OFFENDER SCORING RCW 9.94A.525(8)

If it was found that this offense was committed with sexual motivation (RCW 9.94A.533(8)) on or after 7/01/2006, use the General Violent Offense with a Sexual Motivation Finding scoring form on page 201.

If the present conviction is for a felony domestic violence offense where domestic violence was plead and proven, use the General Violent Offense Where Domestic Violence Has Been Plead and Proven scoring form on page 199.

ADULT HISTORY:
    Enter number of serious violent and violent felony convictions .... _____ x 2 = _____

    Enter number of nonviolent felony convictions .... _____ x 1 = _____

JUVENILE HISTORY:
    Enter number of serious violent and violent felony dispositions .... _____ x 2 = _____

    Enter number of nonviolent felony dispositions .... _____ x ½ = _____

OTHER CURRENT OFFENSES:
(Other current offenses that do not encompass the same conduct count in offender score)
    Enter number of other serious violent and violent felony convictions .... _____ x 2 = _____

    Enter number of other nonviolent felony convictions .... _____ x 1 = _____

STATUS:
    Was the offender on community custody on the date the current offense was committed? (if yes)....... + 1 = _____

Total the last column to get the **Offender Score** (Round down to the nearest whole number)

SENTENCE RANGE

	Offender Score									
	0	1	2	3	4	5	6	7	8	9+
LEVEL VII	17.5m	24m	30m	36m	42m	47.5m	66m	78m	89.5m	101.5m
	15 - 20	21 - 27	26 - 34	31 - 41	36 - 48	41 - 54	57 - 75	67 - 89	77 - 102	87 - 116

- ✓ For attempt, solicitation, conspiracy (RCW 9.94A.595) see page 23 or for gang-related felonies where the court found the offender involved a minor (RCW 9.94A.833) see page 186 for standard range adjustments.
- ✓ For deadly weapon enhancement, see page 190.
- ✓ For sentencing alternatives, see page 177.
- ✓ For community custody eligibility, see page 187.
- ✓ For any applicable enhancements other than deadly weapon enhancement, see page 183.

The Caseload Forecast Council is not liable for errors or omissions in the manual, for sentences that may be inappropriately calculated as a result of a practitioner's or court's reliance on the manual, or for any other written or verbal information related to adult or juvenile sentencing. The scoring sheets are intended to provide assistance in most cases but do not cover all permutations of the scoring rules. If you find any errors or omissions, we encourage you to report them to the Caseload Forecast Council.

Driving While Under The Influence Of Intoxicating Liquor Or Any Drug

RCW 46.61.502(6)
CLASS B – NONVIOLENT/TRAFFIC OFFENSE
OFFENDER SCORING RCW 9.94A.525(11)

ADULT HISTORY:
Enter number of Vehicular Homicide and Vehicular Assault felony convictions .... _____   x 2 = _____
Enter number of Operation of a Vessel While Under the Influence of Intoxicating Liquor or Any Drug felony convictions .... _____   x 1 = _____
Enter number of felony convictions .... _____   x 1 = _____
Enter number of Driving While Under the Influence of Intoxicating Liquor or Any Drug and Actual Physical Control While Under the Influence of Intoxicating Liquor or Any Drug and Reckless Driving and Hit-And-Run Attended Vehicle <u>non-felony</u> convictions .... _____   x 1 = _____

JUVENILE HISTORY:
Enter number of Vehicular Homicide and Vehicular Assault dispositions .... _____   x 2 = _____
Enter number of Operation of a Vessel While Under the Influence of Intoxicating Liquor or Any Drug felony dispositions .... _____   x ½ = _____
Enter number of felony dispositions .... _____   x ½ = _____
Enter number of Driving While Under the Influence of Intoxicating Liquor or Any Drug and Actual Physical Control While Under the Influence of Intoxicating Liquor or Any Drug and Reckless Driving and Hit-And-Run Attended Vehicle <u>non-felony</u> convictions .... _____   x ½ = _____

OTHER CURRENT OFFENSES:
(Other current offenses that do not encompass the same conduct count in offender score)
Enter number of Vehicular Homicide and Vehicular Assault convictions .... _____   x 2 = _____
Enter number of other Operation of a Vessel While Under the Influence of Intoxicating Liquor or Any Drug felony convictions .... _____   x 1 = _____
Enter number of other felony convictions .... _____   x 1 = _____
Enter number of Driving While Under the Influence of Intoxicating Liquor or Any Drug and Actual Physical Control While Under the Influence of Intoxicating Liquor or Any Drug and Reckless Driving and Hit-And-Run Attended Vehicle <u>non-felony</u> convictions .... _____   x 1 = _____

STATUS:
Was the offender on community custody on the date the current offense was committed? (if yes) ......   + 1 = _____

Total the last column to get the **Offender Score** (Round down to the nearest whole number)

SENTENCE RANGE

	\multicolumn{10}{c}{Offender Score}

	0	1	2	3	4	5	6	7	8	9+
LEVEL V	9m	13m	15m	17.5m	25.5m	38m	47.5m	59.5m	72m	84m
	6 - 12	12+ - 14	13 - 17	15 - 20	22 - 29	33 - 43	41 - 54	51 - 68	62 - 82	72 - 96

- ✓ For attempt, solicitation, conspiracy (RCW 9.94A.595) see page 23 or for gang-related felonies where the court found the offender involved a minor (RCW 9.94A.833) see page 186 for standard range adjustments.
- ✓ For deadly weapon enhancement, see page 190.
- ✓ For sentencing alternatives, see page 177.
- ✓ For community custody eligibility, see page 187.
- ✓ For any applicable enhancements other than deadly weapon enhancement, see page 183.
- ✓ **For consecutive/concurrent provisions, see page 31.**

The Caseload Forecast Council is not liable for errors or omissions in the manual, for sentences that may be inappropriately calculated as a result of a practitioner's or court's reliance on the manual, or for any other written or verbal information related to adult or juvenile sentencing. The scoring sheets are intended to provide assistance in most cases but do not cover all permutations of the scoring rules. If you find any errors or omissions, we encourage you to report them to the Caseload Forecast Council.

Endangerment With A Controlled Substance

RCW 9A.42.100
CLASS B – NONVIOLENT

OFFENDER SCORING RCW 9.94A.525(7)

If it was found that this offense was committed with sexual motivation (RCW 9.94A.533(8)) on or after 7/01/2006, use the General Nonviolent Offense with a Sexual Motivation Finding scoring form on page 193.

If the present conviction is for a felony domestic violence offense where domestic violence was plead and proven, use the General Nonviolent Offense Where Domestic Violence Has Been Plead and Proven scoring form on page 191.

ADULT HISTORY:
    Enter number of felony convictions .... _____ x 1 = _____

JUVENILE HISTORY:
    Enter number of serious violent and violent felony dispositions .... _____ x 1 = _____

    Enter number of nonviolent felony dispositions .... _____ x ½ = _____

OTHER CURRENT OFFENSES:
(Other current offenses that do not encompass the same conduct count in offender score)
    Enter number of other felony convictions .... _____ x 1 = _____

STATUS:
    Was the offender on community custody on the date the current offense was committed? (if yes)....... + 1 = _____

Total the last column to get the **Offender Score** (Round down to the nearest whole number)

SENTENCE RANGE

	\multicolumn{10}{c}{Offender Score}
	0	1	2	3	4	5	6	7	8	9+
LEVEL IV	6m	9m	13m	15m	17.5m	25.5m	38m	50m	61.5m	73.5m
	3 - 9	6 - 12	12+ - 14	13 - 17	15 - 20	22 - 29	33 - 43	43 - 57	53 - 70	63 - 84

- ✓ For attempt, solicitation, conspiracy (RCW 9.94A.595) see page 23 or for gang-related felonies where the court found the offender involved a minor (RCW 9.94A.833) see page 186 for standard range adjustments.
- ✓ For deadly weapon enhancement, see page 190.
- ✓ For sentencing alternatives, see page 177.
- ✓ For community custody eligibility, see page 187.
- ✓ For any applicable enhancements other than deadly weapon enhancement, see page 183.

The Caseload Forecast Council is not liable for errors or omissions in the manual, for sentences that may be inappropriately calculated as a result of a practitioner's or court's reliance on the manual, or for any other written or verbal information related to adult or juvenile sentencing. The scoring sheets are intended to provide assistance in most cases but do not cover all permutations of the scoring rules. If you find any errors or omissions, we encourage you to report them to the Caseload Forecast Council.

Escape First Degree

RCW 9A.76.110
CLASS B – NONVIOLENT
OFFENDER SCORING RCW 9.94A.525(15)

If it was found that this offense was committed with sexual motivation (RCW 9.94A.533(8)) on or after 7/01/2006, use the General Nonviolent Offense with a Sexual Motivation Finding scoring form on page 193.

If the present conviction is for a felony domestic violence offense where domestic violence was plead and proven, use the General Nonviolent Offense Where Domestic Violence Has Been Plead and Proven scoring form on page 191.

ADULT HISTORY:
    Enter number of felony convictions .... _____ x 1 = _____

JUVENILE HISTORY:
    Enter number of felony dispositions .... _____ x ½ = _____

OTHER CURRENT OFFENSES:
(Other current offenses that do not encompass the same conduct count in offender score)
    Enter number of other felony convictions .... _____ x 1 = _____

STATUS:
    Was the offender on community custody on the date the current offense was committed? (if yes) ...... + 1 = _____

Total the last column to get the **Offender Score** (Round down to the nearest whole number)

SENTENCE RANGE

	\multicolumn{10}{c}{Offender Score}
	0	1	2	3	4	5	6	7	8	9+
LEVEL IV	6m 3 - 9	9m 6 - 12	13m 12+ - 14	15m 13 - 17	17.5m 15 - 20	25.5m 22 - 29	38m 33 - 43	50m 43 - 57	61.5m 53 - 70	73.5m 63 - 84

- ✓ For attempt, solicitation, conspiracy (RCW 9.94A.595) see page 23 or for gang-related felonies where the court found the offender involved a minor (RCW 9.94A.833) see page 186 for standard range adjustments.
- ✓ For deadly weapon enhancement, see page 190.
- ✓ For sentencing alternatives, see page 177.
- ✓ For community custody eligibility, see page 187.
- ✓ For any applicable enhancements other than deadly weapon enhancement, see page 183.

The Caseload Forecast Council is not liable for errors or omissions in the manual, for sentences that may be inappropriately calculated as a result of a practitioner's or court's reliance on the manual, or for any other written or verbal information related to adult or juvenile sentencing. The scoring sheets are intended to provide assistance in most cases but do not cover all permutations of the scoring rules. If you find any errors or omissions, we encourage you to report them to the Caseload Forecast Council.

Escape Second Degree

RCW 9A.76.120
CLASS C* – NONVIOLENT
OFFENDER SCORING RCW 9.94A.525(15)

If it was found that this offense was committed with sexual motivation (RCW 9.94A.533(8)) on or after 7/01/2006, use the General Nonviolent Offense with a Sexual Motivation Finding scoring form on page 193.

If the present conviction is for a felony domestic violence offense where domestic violence was plead and proven, use the General Nonviolent Offense Where Domestic Violence Has Been Plead and Proven scoring form on page 191.

ADULT HISTORY:
    Enter number of felony convictions .... _____   x 1 = _____

JUVENILE HISTORY:
    Enter number of felony dispositions .... _____   x ½ = _____

OTHER CURRENT OFFENSES:
(Other current offenses that do not encompass the same conduct count in offender score)
    Enter number of other felony convictions .... _____   x 1 = _____

STATUS:
    Was the offender on community custody on the date the current offense was committed? (if yes).......   + 1 = _____

Total the last column to get the **Offender Score** (Round down to the nearest whole number)

SENTENCE RANGE

	\ Offender Score									
	0	**1**	**2**	**3**	**4**	**5**	**6**	**7**	**8**	**9+**
LEVEL III	2m 1 - 3	5m 3 - 8	8m 4 - 12	11m 9 - 12	14m 12+ - 16	19.5m 17 - 22	25.5m 22 - 29	38m 33 - 43	50m 43 - 57	55.5m 51 - 60*

- ✓ For gang-related felonies where the court found the offender involved a minor (RCW 9.94A.833) see page 186 for standard range adjustment.
- ✓ For deadly weapon enhancement, see page 190.
- ✓ For sentencing alternatives, see page 177.
- ✓ For community custody eligibility, see page 187.
- ✓ For any applicable enhancements other than deadly weapon enhancement, see page 183.

The Caseload Forecast Council is not liable for errors or omissions in the manual, for sentences that may be inappropriately calculated as a result of a practitioner's or court's reliance on the manual, or for any other written or verbal information related to adult or juvenile sentencing. The scoring sheets are intended to provide assistance in most cases but do not cover all permutations of the scoring rules. If you find any errors or omissions, we encourage you to report them to the Caseload Forecast Council.

Escape From Community Custody

RCW 72.09.310
CLASS C – NONVIOLENT

OFFENDER SCORING RCW 9.94A.525(14)

If it was found that this offense was committed with sexual motivation (RCW 9.94A.533(8)) on or after 7/01/2006, use the General Nonviolent Offense with a Sexual Motivation Finding scoring form on page 193.

If the present conviction is for a felony domestic violence offense where domestic violence was plead and proven, use the General Nonviolent Offense Where Domestic Violence Has Been Plead and Proven scoring form on page 191.

ADULT HISTORY:
    Enter number of Escape 1, Escape 2, Willful Failure to Return from Furlough,
    Willful Failure to Return from Work Release and Escape from Community Custody convictions ...... _____ x 1 = _____

JUVENILE HISTORY:
    Enter number of Escape 1, Escape 2, Willful Failure to Return from Furlough,
    Willful Failure to Return from Work Release dispositions .... _____ x ½ = _____

OTHER CURRENT OFFENSES:
(Other current offenses that do not encompass the same conduct count in offender score)
    Enter number of Escape 1, Escape 2, Willful Failure to Return from Furlough,
    Willful Failure to Return from Work Release and Escape from Community Custody convictions ...... _____ x 1 = _____

Total the last column to get the **Offender Score** (Round down to the nearest whole number)

SENTENCE RANGE

	Offender Score									
	0	1	2	3	4	5	6	7	8	9+
LEVEL II	0-90 days	4m 2 - 6	6m 3 - 9	8m 4 - 12	13m 12+ - 14	16m 14 - 18	19.5m 17 - 22	25.5m 22 - 29	38m 33 - 43	50m 43 - 57

- ✓ For gang-related felonies where the court found the offender involved a minor (RCW 9.94A.833) see page 186 for standard range adjustment.
- ✓ For deadly weapon enhancement, see page 190.
- ✓ For sentencing alternatives, see page 177.
- ✓ For community custody eligibility, see page 187.
- ✓ For any applicable enhancements other than deadly weapon enhancement, see page 183.

Explosive Devices Prohibited

RCW 70.74.180
CLASS A – VIOLENT

OFFENDER SCORING RCW 9.94A.525(8)

If it was found that this offense was committed with sexual motivation (RCW 9.94A.533(8)) on or after 7/01/2006, use the General Violent Offense with a Sexual Motivation Finding scoring form on page 201.

If the present conviction is for a felony domestic violence offense where domestic violence was plead and proven, use the General Violent Offense Where Domestic Violence Has Been Plead and Proven scoring form on page 199.

ADULT HISTORY:
    Enter number of serious violent and violent felony convictions .... _____ x 2 = _____
    Enter number of nonviolent felony convictions .... _____ x 1 = _____

JUVENILE HISTORY:
    Enter number of serious violent and violent felony dispositions .... _____ x 2 = _____
    Enter number of nonviolent felony dispositions .... _____ x ½ = _____

OTHER CURRENT OFFENSES:
(Other current offenses that do not encompass the same conduct count in offender score)
    Enter number of other serious violent and violent felony convictions .... _____ x 2 = _____
    Enter number of other felony convictions .... _____ x 1 = _____

STATUS:
    Was the offender on community custody on the date the current offense was committed? (if yes) .... + 1 = _____

Total the last column to get the **Offender Score** (Round down to the nearest whole number)

SENTENCE RANGE

	\multicolumn{10}{c}{Offender Score}
	0	1	2	3	4	5	6	7	8	9+
LEVEL IX	36m 31 - 41	42m 36 - 48	47.5m 41 - 54	53.5m 46 - 61	59.5m 51 - 68	66m 57 - 75	89.5m 77 - 102	101.5m 87 - 116	126m 108 - 144	150m 129 - 171

- ✓ For attempt, solicitation, conspiracy (RCW 9.94A.595) see page 23 or for gang-related felonies where the court found the offender involved a minor (RCW 9.94A.833) see page 186 for standard range adjustments.
- ✓ For deadly weapon enhancement, see page 190.
- ✓ For sentencing alternatives, see page 177.
- ✓ For community custody eligibility, see page 187.
- ✓ For any applicable enhancements other than deadly weapon enhancement, see page 183.

The Caseload Forecast Council is not liable for errors or omissions in the manual, for sentences that may be inappropriately calculated as a result of a practitioner's or court's reliance on the manual, or for any other written or verbal information related to adult or juvenile sentencing. The scoring sheets are intended to provide assistance in most cases but do not cover all permutations of the scoring rules. If you find any errors or omissions, we encourage you to report them to the Caseload Forecast Council.

Extortion First Degree

RCW 9A.56.120
CLASS B – VIOLENT

OFFENDER SCORING RCW 9.94A.525(8)

If it was found that this offense was committed with sexual motivation (RCW 9.94A.533(8)) on or after 7/01/2006, use the General Violent Offense with a Sexual Motivation Finding scoring form on page 201.

If the present conviction is for a felony domestic violence offense where domestic violence was plead and proven, use the General Violent Offense Where Domestic Violence Has Been Plead and Proven scoring form on page 199.

ADULT HISTORY:
    Enter number of serious violent and violent felony convictions .... _____ x 2 = _____
    Enter number of nonviolent felony convictions .... _____ x 1 = _____

JUVENILE HISTORY:
    Enter number of serious violent and violent felony dispositions .... _____ x 2 = _____
    Enter number of nonviolent felony dispositions .... _____ x ½ = _____

OTHER CURRENT OFFENSES:
(Other current offenses that do not encompass the same conduct count in offender score)
    Enter number of other serious violent and violent felony convictions .... _____ x 2 = _____
    Enter number of other felony convictions .... _____ x 1 = _____

STATUS:
    Was the offender on community custody on the date the current offense was committed? (if yes) ...... + 1 = _____

Total the last column to get the **Offender Score** (Round down to the nearest whole number)

SENTENCE RANGE

Offender Score	0	1	2	3	4	5	6	7	8	9+
LEVEL V	9m 6 - 12	13m 12+ - 14	15m 13 - 17	17.5m 15 - 20	25.5m 22 - 29	38m 33 - 43	47.5m 41 - 54	59.5m 51 - 68	72m 62 - 82	84m 72 - 96

✓ For attempt, solicitation, conspiracy (RCW 9.94A.595) see page 23 or for gang-related felonies where the court found the offender involved a minor (RCW 9.94A.833) see page 186 for standard range adjustments.

✓ For deadly weapon enhancement, see page 190.

✓ For sentencing alternatives, see page 177.

✓ For community custody eligibility, see page 187.

✓ For any applicable enhancements other than deadly weapon enhancement, see page 183.

Extortion Second Degree

RCW 9A.56.130
CLASS C* – NONVIOLENT

OFFENDER SCORING RCW 9.94A.525(7)

If it was found that this offense was committed with sexual motivation (RCW 9.94A.533(8)) on or after 7/01/2006, use the General Nonviolent Offense with a Sexual Motivation Finding scoring form on page 193.

If the present conviction is for a felony domestic violence offense where domestic violence was plead and proven, use the General Nonviolent Offense Where Domestic Violence Has Been Plead and Proven scoring form on page 191.

ADULT HISTORY:
  Enter number of felony convictions .... _____ x 1 = _____

JUVENILE HISTORY:
  Enter number of serious violent and violent felony dispositions .... _____ x 1 = _____
  Enter number of nonviolent felony dispositions .... _____ x ½ = _____

OTHER CURRENT OFFENSES:
(Other current offenses that do not encompass the same conduct count in offender score)
  Enter number of other felony convictions .... _____ x 1 = _____

STATUS:
  Was the offender on community custody on the date the current offense was committed? (if yes) .... + 1 = _____

Total the last column to get the **Offender Score** (Round down to the nearest whole number)   [____]

SENTENCE RANGE

	\multicolumn{10}{c	}{Offender Score}
	0	1	2	3	4	5	6	7	8	9+
LEVEL III	2m	5m	8m	11m	14m	19.5m	25.5m	38m	50m	55.5m
	1 - 3	3 - 8	4 - 12	9 - 12	12+ - 16	17 - 22	22 - 29	33 - 43	43 - 57	51 - 60*

- ✓ For gang-related felonies where the court found the offender involved a minor (RCW 9.94A.833) see page 186 for standard range adjustment.
- ✓ For deadly weapon enhancement, see page 190.
- ✓ For sentencing alternatives, see page 177.
- ✓ For community custody eligibility, see page 187.
- ✓ For any applicable enhancements other than deadly weapon enhancement, see page 183.

Extortionate Extension Of Credit/Use of Extortionate Means To Collect Extensions Of Credit

RCW 9A.82.020 & RCW 9A.82.040
CLASS B – NONVIOLENT

OFFENDER SCORING RCW 9.94A.525(7)

If it was found that this offense was committed with sexual motivation (RCW 9.94A.533(8)) on or after 7/01/2006, use the General Nonviolent Offense with a Sexual Motivation Finding scoring form on page 193.

If the present conviction is for a felony domestic violence offense where domestic violence was plead and proven, use the General Nonviolent Offense Where Domestic Violence Has Been Plead and Proven scoring form on page 191.

ADULT HISTORY:
    Enter number of felony convictions .... _____ x 1 = _____

JUVENILE HISTORY:
    Enter number of serious violent and violent felony dispositions .... _____ x 1 = _____
    Enter number of nonviolent felony dispositions .... _____ x ½ = _____

OTHER CURRENT OFFENSES:
(Other current offenses that do not encompass the same conduct count in offender score)
    Enter number of other felony convictions .... _____ x 1 = _____

STATUS:
    Was the offender on community custody on the date the current offense was committed? (if yes) ...... + 1 = _____

Total the last column to get the **Offender Score** (Round down to the nearest whole number)

SENTENCE RANGE

	Offender Score									
	0	1	2	3	4	5	6	7	8	9+
LEVEL V	9m 6 - 12	13m 12+ - 14	15m 13 - 17	17.5m 15 - 20	25.5m 22 - 29	38m 33 - 43	47.5m 41 - 54	59.5m 51 - 68	72m 62 - 82	84m 72 - 96

- ✓ For attempt, solicitation, conspiracy (RCW 9.94A.595) see page 23 or for gang-related felonies where the court found the offender involved a minor (RCW 9.94A.833) see page 186 for standard range adjustments.
- ✓ For deadly weapon enhancement, see page 190.
- ✓ For sentencing alternatives, see page 177.
- ✓ For community custody eligibility, see page 187.
- ✓ For any applicable enhancements other than deadly weapon enhancement, see page 183.

The Caseload Forecast Council is not liable for errors or omissions in the manual, for sentences that may be inappropriately calculated as a result of a practitioner's or court's reliance on the manual, or for any other written or verbal information related to adult or juvenile sentencing. The scoring sheets are intended to provide assistance in most cases but do not cover all permutations of the scoring rules. If you find any errors or omissions, we encourage you to report them to the Caseload Forecast Council.

Failure To Register As A Sex Offender Second Or Subsequent Violation Committed On Or After 6/7/2006 But Before 6/10/2010

RCW 9A.44.132(1)(a)
CLASS C – NONVIOLENT/SEX
OFFENDER SCORING RCW 9.94A.525(18)

If the present conviction is for a felony domestic violence offense where domestic violence was plead and proven, use the General Nonviolent/Sex Offense Where Domestic Violence Has Been Plead and Proven scoring form on page 192.

ADULT HISTORY:
Enter number of sex offense felony convictions .... _____ x 3 = _____
Enter number of Failure to Register as a Sex Offender* felony convictions .... _____ x 1 = _____
Enter number of felony convictions .... _____ x 1 = _____

JUVENILE HISTORY:
Enter number of sex offense felony dispositions .... _____ x 3 = _____
Enter number of Failure to Register as a Sex Offender* felony dispositions .... _____ x 1 = _____
Enter number of serious violent and violent felony dispositions .... _____ x 1 = _____
Enter number of nonviolent felony dispositions .... _____ x ½ = _____

OTHER CURRENT OFFENSES:
(Other current offenses that do not encompass the same conduct count in offender score)
Enter number of other sex offense felony convictions .... _____ x 3 = _____
Enter number of other Failure to Register as a Sex Offender* felony dispositions .... _____ x 1 = _____
Enter number of other felony convictions .... _____ x 1 = _____

STATUS:
Was the offender on community custody on the date the current offense was committed? .... + 1 = _____

Total the last column to get the **Offender Score** (Round down to the nearest whole number)

SENTENCE RANGE

	Offender Score									
	0	1	2	3	4	5	6	7	8	9+
LEVEL II	0-90 days	4m 2 - 6	6m 3 - 9	8m 4 - 12	13m 12+ - 14	16m 14 - 18	19.5m 17 - 22	25.5m 22 - 29	38m 33 - 43	50m 43 - 57

- ✓ For attempt, solicitation, conspiracy (RCW 9.94A.595) see page 23 or for gang-related felonies where the court found the offender involved a minor (RCW 9.94A.833) see page 186 for standard range adjustments.
- ✓ For deadly weapon enhancement, see page 190.
- ✓ For sentencing alternatives, see page 177.
- ✓ For community custody eligibility, see page 187.
- ✓ For any applicable enhancements other than deadly weapon enhancement, see page 183.

* The first violation of Failure to Register as a Sex Offender (unranked level and class C felony) is **NOT** a sex offense per RCW 9.94A.030(47)(v).

NOTE: In 2008 it was noted that Failure to Register as a Sex Offender would become a class B offense as of ninety days sine die 2010 Legislative Session. The statute was changed before this could take effect.

The Caseload Forecast Council is not liable for errors or omissions in the manual, for sentences that may be inappropriately calculated as a result of a practitioner's or court's reliance on the manual, or for any other written or verbal information related to adult or juvenile sentencing. The scoring sheets are intended to provide assistance in most cases but do not cover all permutations of the scoring rules. If you find any errors or omissions, we encourage you to report them to the Caseload Forecast Council.

Failure To Register As A Sex Offender Second Violation Committed On Or After 6/10/2010

RCW 9A.44.132(1)(a)
CLASS C – NONVIOLENT/SEX

OFFENDER SCORING RCW 9.94A.525(18)

If the present conviction is for a felony domestic violence offense where domestic violence was plead and proven, use the General Nonviolent/Sex Offense Where Domestic Violence Has Been Plead and Proven scoring form on page 192.

ADULT HISTORY:
Enter number of sex offense felony convictions .... _____ x 3 = _____
Enter number of Failure to Register as a Sex Offender* felony convictions .... _____ x 1 = _____
Enter number of felony convictions .... _____ x 1 = _____

JUVENILE HISTORY:
Enter number of sex offense felony dispositions .... _____ x 3 = _____
Enter number of Failure to Register as a Sex Offender* felony dispositions .... _____ x 1 = _____
Enter number of serious violent and violent felony dispositions .... _____ x 1 = _____
Enter number of nonviolent felony dispositions .... _____ x ½ = _____

OTHER CURRENT OFFENSES:
(Other current offenses that do not encompass the same conduct count in offender score)
Enter number of other sex offense felony convictions .... _____ x 3 = _____
Enter number of other Failure to Register as a Sex Offender* felony dispositions . _____ x 1 = _____
Enter number of other felony convictions .... _____ x 1 = _____

STATUS:
Was the offender on community custody on the date the current offense was committed?......... + 1 = _____

Total the last column to get the **Offender Score** (Round down to the nearest whole number)

SENTENCE RANGE

	Offender Score									
	0	1	2	3	4	5	6	7	8	9+
LEVEL II		4m	6m	8m	13m	16m	19.5m	25.5m	38m	50m
	0-90 days	2 - 6	3 - 9	4 - 12	12+ - 14	14 - 18	17 - 22	22 - 29	33 - 43	43 - 57

- ✓ For attempt, solicitation, conspiracy (RCW 9.94A.595) see page 23 or for gang-related felonies where the court found the offender involved a minor (RCW 9.94A.833) see page 186 for standard range adjustments.
- ✓ For deadly weapon enhancement, see page 190.
- ✓ For sentencing alternatives, see page 177.
- ✓ For community custody eligibility, see page 187.
- ✓ For any applicable enhancements other than deadly weapon enhancement, see page 183.

* **The first violation of Failure to Register as a Sex Offender (unranked level and class C felony) is NOT a sex offense per RCW 9.94A.030(47)(v).**

NOTE: In 2008 it was noted that Failure to Register as a Sex Offender would become a class B offense as of ninety days sine die 2010 Legislative Session. The statute was changed before this could take effect.

The Caseload Forecast Council is not liable for errors or omissions in the manual, for sentences that may be inappropriately calculated as a result of a practitioner's or court's reliance on the manual, or for any other written or verbal information related to adult or juvenile sentencing. The scoring sheets are intended to provide assistance in most cases but do not cover all permutations of the scoring rules. If you find any errors or omissions, we encourage you to report them to the Caseload Forecast Council.

Failure To Register As A Sex Offender Third Or Subsequent Violation Committed On Or After 6/10/2010

RCW 9A.44.132(1)(b)
CLASS B – NONVIOLENT/SEX

OFFENDER SCORING RCW 9.94A.525(18)

If the present conviction is for a felony domestic violence offense where domestic violence was plead and proven, use the General Nonviolent/Sex Offense Where Domestic Violence Has Been Plead and Proven scoring form on page 192.

ADULT HISTORY:
    Enter number of sex offense felony convictions .... _____ x 3 = _____
    Enter number of Failure to Register as a Sex Offender* felony convictions .... _____ x 1 = _____
    Enter number of felony convictions .... _____ x 1 = _____

JUVENILE HISTORY:
    Enter number of sex offense felony dispositions .... _____ x 3 = _____
    Enter number of Failure to Register as a Sex Offender* felony dispositions .... _____ x 1 = _____
    Enter number of serious violent and violent felony dispositions .... _____ x 1 = _____
    Enter number of nonviolent felony dispositions .... _____ x ½ = _____

OTHER CURRENT OFFENSES:
(Other current offenses that do not encompass the same conduct count in offender score)
    Enter number of other sex offense felony convictions .... _____ x 3 = _____
    Enter number of other Failure to Register as a Sex Offender* felony dispositions .... _____ x 1 = _____
    Enter number of other felony convictions .... _____ x 1 = _____

STATUS:
    Was the offender on community custody on the date the current offense was committed? .... + 1 = _____

Total the last column to get the **Offender Score** (Round down to the nearest whole number)

SENTENCE RANGE

	Offender Score									
	0	1	2	3	4	5	6	7	8	9+
LEVEL II	0-90 days	4m 2 - 6	6m 3 - 9	8m 4 - 12	13m 12+ - 14	16m 14 - 18	19.5m 17 - 22	25.5m 22 - 29	38m 33 - 43	50m 43 - 57

- ✓ For attempt, solicitation, conspiracy (RCW 9.94A.595) see page 23 or for gang-related felonies where the court found the offender involved a minor (RCW 9.94A.833) see page 186 for standard range adjustments.
- ✓ For deadly weapon enhancement, see page 190.
- ✓ For sentencing alternatives, see page 177.
- ✓ For community custody eligibility, see page 187.
- ✓ For any applicable enhancements other than deadly weapon enhancement, see page 183.

* The first violation of Failure to Register as a Sex Offender (unranked level and class C felony) is **NOT** a sex offense per RCW 9.94A.030(47)(v).

NOTE: In 2008 it was noted that Failure to Register as a Sex Offender would become a class B offense as of ninety days sine die 2010 Legislative Session. The statute was changed before this could take effect.

The Caseload Forecast Council is not liable for errors or omissions in the manual, for sentences that may be inappropriately calculated as a result of a practitioner's or court's reliance on the manual, or for any other written or verbal information related to adult or juvenile sentencing. The scoring sheets are intended to provide assistance in most cases but do not cover all permutations of the scoring rules. If you find any errors or omissions, we encourage you to report them to the Caseload Forecast Council.

False Verification For Welfare

RCW 74.08.055(2)
CLASS B – NONVIOLENT
OFFENDER SCORING RCW 9.94A.525(7)

If it was found that this offense was committed with sexual motivation (RCW 9.94A.533(8)) on or after 7/01/2006, use the General Nonviolent Offense with a Sexual Motivation Finding scoring form on page 193.

If the present conviction is for a felony domestic violence offense where domestic violence was plead and proven, use the General Nonviolent Offense Where Domestic Violence Has Been Plead and Proven scoring form on page 191.

ADULT HISTORY:
　Enter number of felony convictions .... _____ x 1 = _____

JUVENILE HISTORY:
　Enter number of serious violent and violent felony dispositions .... _____ x 1 = _____
　Enter number of nonviolent felony dispositions .... _____ x ½ = _____

OTHER CURRENT OFFENSES:
(Other current offenses that do not encompass the same conduct count in offender score)
　Enter number of other felony convictions .... _____ x 1 = _____

STATUS:
　Was the offender on community custody on the date the current offense was committed? (if yes) ...... + 1 = _____

Total the last column to get the **Offender Score** (Round down to the nearest whole number)

SENTENCE RANGE

	\ 0	\ 1	\ 2	\ 3	\ 4	\ 5	\ 6	\ 7	\ 8	\ 9+
LEVEL I	0-60 days	0-90 days	3m 2 - 5	4m 2 - 6	5.5m 3 - 8	8m 4 - 12	13m 12+ - 14	16m 14 - 18	19.5m 17 - 22	25.5m 22 - 29

- ✓ For attempt, solicitation, conspiracy (RCW 9.94A.595) see page 23 or for gang-related felonies where the court found the offender involved a minor (RCW 9.94A.833) see page 186 for standard range adjustments.
- ✓ For deadly weapon enhancement, see page 190.
- ✓ For sentencing alternatives, see page 177.
- ✓ For community custody eligibility, see page 187.
- ✓ For any applicable enhancements other than deadly weapon enhancement, see page 183.

The Caseload Forecast Council is not liable for errors or omissions in the manual, for sentences that may be inappropriately calculated as a result of a practitioner's or court's reliance on the manual, or for any other written or verbal information related to adult or juvenile sentencing. The scoring sheets are intended to provide assistance in most cases but do not cover all permutations of the scoring rules. If you find any errors or omissions, we encourage you to report them to the Caseload Forecast Council.

Forged Prescription Legend Drug

RCW 69.41.020
CLASS B – NONVIOLENT
OFFENDER SCORING RCW 9.94A.525(7)

If it was found that this offense was committed with sexual motivation (RCW 9.94A.533(8)) on or after 7/01/2006, use the General Nonviolent Offense with a Sexual Motivation Finding scoring form on page 193.

If the present conviction is for a felony domestic violence offense where domestic violence was plead and proven, use the General Nonviolent Offense Where Domestic Violence Has Been Plead and Proven scoring form on page 191.

ADULT HISTORY:
　Enter number of felony convictions .... _____ x 1 = _____

JUVENILE HISTORY:
　Enter number of serious violent and violent felony dispositions .... _____ x 1 = _____

　Enter number of nonviolent felony dispositions .... _____ x ½ = _____

OTHER CURRENT OFFENSES:
(Other current offenses that do not encompass the same conduct count in offender score)
　Enter number of other felony convictions .... _____ x 1 = _____

STATUS:
　Was the offender on community custody on the date the current offense was committed? (if yes) .... + 1 = _____

Total the last column to get the **Offender Score** (Round down to the nearest whole number)

SENTENCE RANGE – DRUG

	Offender Score		
	0 to 2	3 to 5	6 to 9+
LEVEL I	3m	9m	18m
	0 - 6	6+ - 12	12+ - 24

- ✓ For attempt, solicitation, conspiracy (RCW 9.94A.595) see page 23 or for gang-related felonies where the court found the offender involved a minor (RCW 9.94A.833) see page 186 for standard range adjustments.
- ✓ For deadly weapon enhancement, see page 190.
- ✓ For sentencing alternatives, see page 177.
- ✓ For community custody eligibility, see page 187.
- ✓ For any applicable enhancements other than deadly weapon enhancement, see page 183.

The Caseload Forecast Council is not liable for errors or omissions in the manual, for sentences that may be inappropriately calculated as a result of a practitioner's or court's reliance on the manual, or for any other written or verbal information related to adult or juvenile sentencing. The scoring sheets are intended to provide assistance in most cases but do not cover all permutations of the scoring rules. If you find any errors or omissions, we encourage you to report them to the Caseload Forecast Council.

Forged Prescription For A Controlled Substance

RCW 69.50.403
CLASS C – NONVIOLENT

OFFENDER SCORING RCW 9.94A.525(7)

If it was found that this offense was committed with sexual motivation (RCW 9.94A.533(8)) on or after 7/01/2006, use the General Nonviolent Offense with a Sexual Motivation Finding scoring form on page 193.

If the present conviction is for a felony domestic violence offense where domestic violence was plead and proven, use the General Nonviolent Offense Where Domestic Violence Has Been Plead and Proven scoring form on page 191.

ADULT HISTORY:
    Enter number of felony convictions .... _____ x 1 = _____

JUVENILE HISTORY:
    Enter number of serious violent and violent felony dispositions .... _____ x 1 = _____

    Enter number of nonviolent felony dispositions .... _____ x ½ = _____

OTHER CURRENT OFFENSES:
(Other current offenses that do not encompass the same conduct count in offender score)
    Enter number of other felony convictions .... _____ x 1 = _____

STATUS:
    Was the offender on community custody on the date the current offense was committed? (if yes) ...... + 1 = _____

Total the last column to get the **Offender Score** (Round down to the nearest whole number)

SENTENCE RANGE - DRUG

	Offender Score		
	0 to 2	3 to 5	6 to 9+
LEVEL I	3m 0 - 6	9m 6+ - 12	18m 12+ - 24

✓ For attempt, solicitation, conspiracy (RCW 9.94A.595) see page 23 or for gang-related felonies where the court found the offender involved a minor (RCW 9.94A.833) see page 186 for standard range adjustments.

✓ Per RCW 9.94A.518, any felony offense under chapter 69.50 RCW with a deadly weapon special verdict under RCW 9.94A.602 becomes a level III offense.

✓ For deadly weapon enhancement, see page 190.

✓ For sentencing alternatives, see page 177.

✓ For community custody eligibility, see page 187.

✓ For any applicable enhancements other than deadly weapon enhancement, see page 183.

✓ Per RCW 69.50.408, the statutory maximum for a **subsequent conviction** under Chapter 69.50 RCW is 48 months.

The Caseload Forecast Council is not liable for errors or omissions in the manual, for sentences that may be inappropriately calculated as a result of a practitioner's or court's reliance on the manual, or for any other written or verbal information related to adult or juvenile sentencing. The scoring sheets are intended to provide assistance in most cases but do not cover all permutations of the scoring rules. If you find any errors or omissions, we encourage you to report them to the Caseload Forecast Council.

Forgery

RCW 9A.60.020
CLASS C – NONVIOLENT
OFFENDER SCORING RCW 9.94A.525(7)

If it was found that this offense was committed with sexual motivation (RCW 9.94A.533(8)) on or after 7/01/2006, use the General Nonviolent Offense with a Sexual Motivation Finding scoring form on page 193.

If the present conviction is for a felony domestic violence offense where domestic violence was plead and proven, use the General Nonviolent Offense Where Domestic Violence Has Been Plead and Proven scoring form on page 191.

ADULT HISTORY:
Enter number of felony convictions .... _____ x 1 = _____

JUVENILE HISTORY:
Enter number of serious violent and violent felony dispositions .... _____ x 1 = _____

Enter number of nonviolent felony dispositions .... _____ x ½ = _____

OTHER CURRENT OFFENSES:
(Other current offenses that do not encompass the same conduct count in offender score)
Enter number of other felony convictions .... _____ x 1 = _____

STATUS:
Was the offender on community custody on the date the current offense was committed? (if yes) .... + 1 = _____

Total the last column to get the **Offender Score** (Round down to the nearest whole number) _____

SENTENCE RANGE

	\multicolumn{10}{c}{Offender Score}
	0	1	2	3	4	5	6	7	8	9+
LEVEL I	0-60 days	0-90 days	3m 2 - 5	4m 2 - 6	5.5m 3 - 8	8m 4 - 12	13m 12+ - 14	16m 14 - 18	19.5m 17 - 22	25.5m 22 - 29

- ✓ For gang-related felonies where the court found the offender involved a minor (RCW 9.94A.833) see page 186 for standard range adjustment.
- ✓ For deadly weapon enhancement, see page 190.
- ✓ For sentencing alternatives, see page 177.
- ✓ For community custody eligibility, see page 187.
- ✓ For any applicable enhancements other than deadly weapon enhancement, see page 183.

Harassment Subsequent Conviction Or Threat Of Death

RCW 9A.46.020(2)(b)
CLASS C* – NONVIOLENT

OFFENDER SCORING RCW 9.94A.525(7)

If it was found that this offense was committed with sexual motivation (RCW 9.94A.533(8)) on or after 7/01/2006, use the General Nonviolent Offense with a Sexual Motivation Finding scoring form on page 193.

If the present conviction is for a felony domestic violence offense where domestic violence was plead and proven, use the General Nonviolent Offense Where Domestic Violence Has Been Plead and Proven scoring form on page 191.

ADULT HISTORY:
    Enter number of felony convictions .... _____ x 1 = _____

JUVENILE HISTORY:
    Enter number of serious violent and violent felony dispositions .... _____ x 1 = _____

    Enter number of nonviolent felony dispositions .... _____ x ½ = _____

OTHER CURRENT OFFENSES:
(Other current offenses that do not encompass the same conduct count in offender score)
    Enter number of other felony convictions .... _____ x 1 = _____

STATUS:
    Was the offender on community custody on the date the current offense was committed? (if yes) ...... + 1 = _____

Total the last column to get the **Offender Score** (Round down to the nearest whole number)

SENTENCE RANGE

	Offender Score									
	0	1	2	3	4	5	6	7	8	9+
LEVEL III	2m 1 - 3	5m 3 - 8	8m 4 - 12	11m 9 - 12	14m 12+ - 16	19.5m 17 - 22	25.5m 22 - 29	38m 33 - 43	50m 43 - 57	55.5m 51 - 60*

✓ For gang-related felonies where the court found the offender involved a minor (RCW 9.94A.833) see page 186 for standard range adjustment.

✓ For deadly weapon enhancement, see page 190.

✓ For sentencing alternatives, see page 177.

✓ For community custody eligibility, see page 187.

✓ For any applicable enhancements other than deadly weapon enhancement, see page 183.

The Caseload Forecast Council is not liable for errors or omissions in the manual, for sentences that may be inappropriately calculated as a result of a practitioner's or court's reliance on the manual, or for any other written or verbal information related to adult or juvenile sentencing. The scoring sheets are intended to provide assistance in most cases but do not cover all permutations of the scoring rules. If you find any errors or omissions, we encourage you to report them to the Caseload Forecast Council.

Health Care False Claims

RCW 48.80.030
CLASS C – NONVIOLENT
OFFENDER SCORING RCW 9.94A.525(7)

If it was found that this offense was committed with sexual motivation (RCW 9.94A.533(8)) on or after 7/01/2006, use the General Nonviolent Offense with a Sexual Motivation Finding scoring form on page 193.

If the present conviction is for a felony domestic violence offense where domestic violence was plead and proven, use the General Nonviolent Offense Where Domestic Violence Has Been Plead and Proven scoring form on page 191.

ADULT HISTORY:
　Enter number of felony convictions .... _____ x 1 = _____

JUVENILE HISTORY:
　Enter number of serious violent and violent felony dispositions .... _____ x 1 = _____
　Enter number of nonviolent felony dispositions .... _____ x ½ = _____

OTHER CURRENT OFFENSES:
(Other current offenses that do not encompass the same conduct count in offender score)
　Enter number of other felony convictions .... _____ x 1 = _____

STATUS:
　Was the offender on community custody on the date the current offense was committed? (if yes) .... + 1 = _____

Total the last column to get the **Offender Score** (Round down to the nearest whole number)

SENTENCE RANGE

	\multicolumn{10}{c}{Offender Score}
	0	1	2	3	4	5	6	7	8	9+
LEVEL II	0-90 days	4m 2 - 6	6m 3 - 9	8m 4 - 12	13m 12+ - 14	16m 14 - 18	19.5m 17 - 22	25.5m 22 - 29	38m 33 - 43	50m 43 - 57

- ✓ For gang-related felonies where the court found the offender involved a minor (RCW 9.94A.833) see page 186 for standard range adjustment.
- ✓ For deadly weapon enhancement, see page 190.
- ✓ For sentencing alternatives, see page 177.
- ✓ For community custody eligibility, see page 187.
- ✓ For any applicable enhancements other than deadly weapon enhancement, see page 183.

Hit And Run - Death

RCW 46.52.020(4)(a)
CLASS B* – NONVIOLENT/TRAFFIC OFFENSE
OFFENDER SCORING RCW 9.94A.525(11)

ADULT HISTORY:

Enter number of Vehicular Homicide and Vehicular Assault felony convictions .... _____ x 2 = _____

Enter number of Operation of a Vessel While Under the Influence of Intoxicating Liquor or Any Drug felony convictions .... _____ x 1 = _____

Enter number of felony convictions .... _____ x 1 = _____

Enter number of Driving While Under the Influence of Intoxicating Liquor or Any Drug and Actual Physical Control While Under the Influence of Intoxicating Liquor or Any Drug and Reckless Driving and Hit-And-Run Attended Vehicle <u>non-felony</u> convictions .... _____ x 1 = _____

JUVENILE HISTORY:

Enter number of Vehicular Homicide and Vehicular Assault dispositions .... _____ x 2 = _____

Enter number of Operation of a Vessel While Under the Influence of Intoxicating Liquor or Any Drug felony dispositions .... _____ x ½ = _____

Enter number of felony dispositions .... _____ x ½ = _____

Enter number of Driving While Under the Influence of Intoxicating Liquor or Any Drug and Actual Physical Control While Under the Influence of Intoxicating Liquor or Any Drug and Reckless Driving and Hit-And-Run Attended Vehicle <u>non-felony</u> convictions .... _____ x ½ = _____

OTHER CURRENT OFFENSES:
(Other current offenses that do not encompass the same conduct count in offender score)

Enter number of Vehicular Homicide and Vehicular Assault convictions .... _____ x 2 = _____

Enter number of other Operation of a Vessel While Under the Influence of Intoxicating Liquor or Any Drug felony convictions .... _____ x 1 = _____

Enter number of other felony convictions .... _____ x 1 = _____

Enter number of Driving While Under the Influence of Intoxicating Liquor or Any Drug and Actual Physical Control While Under the Influence of Intoxicating Liquor or Any Drug and Reckless Driving and Hit-And-Run Attended Vehicle <u>non-felony</u> convictions .... _____ x 1 = _____

STATUS:

Was the offender on community custody on the date the current offense was committed? (if yes) ...... + 1 = _____

Total the last column to get the **Offender Score** (Round down to the nearest whole number)

SENTENCE RANGE

	\multicolumn{11}{c	}{Offender Score}
	0	1	2	3	4	5	6	7	8	9+
LEVEL IX	36m 31 - 41	42m 36 - 48	47.5m 41 - 54	53.5m 46 - 61	59.5m 51 - 68	66m 57 - 75	89.5m 77 - 102	101.5m 87 - 116	114m 108 - 120*	120 - 120*

- ✓ For attempt, solicitation, conspiracy (RCW 9.94A.595) see page 23 or for gang-related felonies where the court found the offender involved a minor (RCW 9.94A.833) see page 186 for standard range adjustments.
- ✓ For deadly weapon enhancement, see page 190.
- ✓ For sentencing alternatives, see page 177.
- ✓ For community custody eligibility, see page 187.
- ✓ For any applicable enhancements other than deadly weapon enhancement, see page 183.

The Caseload Forecast Council is not liable for errors or omissions in the manual, for sentences that may be inappropriately calculated as a result of a practitioner's or court's reliance on the manual, or for any other written or verbal information related to adult or juvenile sentencing. The scoring sheets are intended to provide assistance in most cases but do not cover all permutations of the scoring rules. If you find any errors or omissions, we encourage you to report them to the Caseload Forecast Council.

Hit And Run - Injury

RCW 46.52.020(4)(b)
CLASS C* – NONVIOLENT/TRAFFIC OFFENSE

OFFENDER SCORING RCW 9.94A.525(11)

ADULT HISTORY:
   Enter number of Vehicular Homicide and Vehicular Assault felony convictions .... _____ x 2 = _____
   Enter number of Operation of a Vessel While Under the Influence of Intoxicating Liquor or Any Drug felony convictions .... _____ x 1 = _____
   Enter number of felony convictions .... _____ x 1 = _____
   Enter number of Driving While Under the Influence of Intoxicating Liquor or Any Drug and Actual Physical Control While Under the Influence of Intoxicating Liquor or Any Drug and Reckless Driving and Hit-And-Run Attended Vehicle <u>non-felony</u> convictions .... _____ x 1 = _____

JUVENILE HISTORY:
   Enter number of Vehicular Homicide and Vehicular Assault dispositions .... _____ x 2 = _____
   Enter number of Operation of a Vessel While Under the Influence of Intoxicating Liquor or Any Drug felony dispositions .... _____ x 1 = _____
   Enter number of felony dispositions .... _____ x ½ = _____
   Enter number of Driving While Under the Influence of Intoxicating Liquor or Any Drug and Actual Physical Control While Under the Influence of Intoxicating Liquor or Any Drug and Reckless Driving and Hit-And-Run Attended Vehicle <u>non-felony</u> convictions .... _____ x ½ = _____

OTHER CURRENT OFFENSES:
(Other current offenses that do not encompass the same conduct count in offender score)
   Enter number of Vehicular Homicide and Vehicular Assault convictions .... _____ x 2 = _____
   Enter number of other Operation of a Vessel While Under the Influence of Intoxicating Liquor or Any Drug felony convictions .... _____ x 1 = _____
   Enter number of other felony convictions .... _____ x 1 = _____
   Enter number of Driving While Under the Influence of Intoxicating Liquor or Any Drug and Actual Physical Control While Under the Influence of Intoxicating Liquor or Any Drug and Reckless Driving and Hit-And-Run Attended Vehicle <u>non-felony</u> convictions .... _____ x 1 = _____

STATUS:
   Was the offender on community custody on the date the current offense was committed? (if yes)....... + 1 = _____

Total the last column to get the **Offender Score** (Round down to the nearest whole number) [ ]

SENTENCE RANGE

	Offender Score									
	0	**1**	**2**	**3**	**4**	**5**	**6**	**7**	**8**	**9+**
LEVEL IV	6m 3 - 9	9m 6 - 12	13m 12+ - 14	15m 13 - 17	17.5m 15 - 20	25.5m 22 - 29	38m 33 - 43	50m 43 - 57	56.5m 53 - 60*	60 - 60*

- ✓ For gang-related felonies where the court found the offender involved a minor (RCW 9.94A.833) see page 186 for standard range adjustment.
- ✓ For deadly weapon enhancement, see page 190.
- ✓ For sentencing alternatives, see page 177.
- ✓ For community custody eligibility, see page 187.
- ✓ For any applicable enhancements other than deadly weapon enhancement, see page 183.

The Caseload Forecast Council is not liable for errors or omissions in the manual, for sentences that may be inappropriately calculated as a result of a practitioner's or court's reliance on the manual, or for any other written or verbal information related to adult or juvenile sentencing. The scoring sheets are intended to provide assistance in most cases but do not cover all permutations of the scoring rules. If you find any errors or omissions, we encourage you to report them to the Caseload Forecast Council.

Hit And Run With A Vessel – Injury Accident

RCW 79A.60.200(3)
CLASS C* – NONVIOLENT

OFFENDER SCORING RCW 9.94A.525(7)

If it was found that this offense was committed with sexual motivation (RCW 9.94A.533(8)) on or after 7/01/2006, use the General Nonviolent Offense with a Sexual Motivation Finding scoring form on page 193.

If the present conviction is for a felony domestic violence offense where domestic violence was plead and proven, use the General Nonviolent Offense Where Domestic Violence Has Been Plead and Proven scoring form on page 191.

ADULT HISTORY:
Enter number of felony convictions .... _____ x 1 = _____

JUVENILE HISTORY:
Enter number of serious violent and violent felony dispositions .... _____ x 1 = _____

Enter number of nonviolent felony dispositions .... _____ x ½ = _____

OTHER CURRENT OFFENSES:
(Other current offenses that do not encompass the same conduct count in offender score)
Enter number of other felony convictions .... _____ x 1 = _____

STATUS:
Was the offender on community custody on the date the current offense was committed? (if yes) ...... + 1 = _____

Total the last column to get the **Offender Score** (Round down to the nearest whole number)

SENTENCE RANGE

	Offender Score									
	0	1	2	3	4	5	6	7	8	9+
LEVEL IV	6m	9m	13m	15m	17.5m	25.5m	38m	50m	56.5m	
	3 - 9	6 - 12	12+ - 14	13 - 17	15 - 20	22 - 29	33 - 43	43 - 57	53 - 60*	60 - 60*

- ✓ For gang-related felonies where the court found the offender involved a minor (RCW 9.94A.833) see page 186 for standard range adjustment.
- ✓ For deadly weapon enhancement, see page 190.
- ✓ For sentencing alternatives, see page 177.
- ✓ For community custody eligibility, see page 187.
- ✓ For any applicable enhancements other than deadly weapon enhancement, see page 183.

Homicide By Abuse

RCW 9A.32.055
CLASS A – SERIOUS VIOLENT

OFFENDER SCORING RCW 9.94A.525(9)

If the present conviction is for a felony domestic violence offense where domestic violence was plead and proven, use the General Serious Violent Offense Where Domestic Violence Has Been Plead and Proven scoring form on page 196.

ADULT HISTORY:
    Enter number of serious violent felony convictions .... _____ x 3 = _____
    Enter number of violent felony convictions .... _____ x 2 = _____
    Enter number of nonviolent felony convictions .... _____ x 1 = _____

JUVENILE HISTORY:
    Enter number of serious violent felony dispositions .... _____ x 3 = _____
    Enter number of violent felony dispositions .... _____ x 2 = _____
    Enter number of nonviolent felony dispositions .... _____ x ½ = _____

OTHER CURRENT OFFENSES:
(Other current offenses that do not encompass the same conduct count in offender score)
    Enter number of other violent felony convictions .... _____ x 2 = _____
    Enter number of other nonviolent felony convictions .... _____ x 1 = _____

STATUS:
    Was the offender on community custody on the date the current offense was committed? .... + 1 = _____

Total the last column to get the **Offender Score** (Round down to the nearest whole number)

SENTENCE RANGE

	\multicolumn{10}{c}{Offender Score}
	0	**1**	**2**	**3**	**4**	**5**	**6**	**7**	**8**	**9+**
LEVEL XV	280m 240 - 320	291.5m 250 - 333	304m 261 - 347	316m 271 - 361	327.5m 281 - 374	339.5m 291 - 388	364m 312 - 416	394m 338 - 450	431.5m 370 - 493	479.5m 411 - 548

- ✓ For attempt, solicitation, conspiracy (RCW 9.94A.595) see page 23 or for gang-related felonies where the court found the offender involved a minor (RCW 9.94A.833) see page 186 for standard range adjustments.
- ✓ For deadly weapon enhancement, see page 190.
- ✓ For sentencing alternatives, see page 177.
- ✓ For community custody eligibility, see page 187.
- ✓ For any applicable enhancements other than deadly weapon enhancement, see page 183.
- ✓ Multiple current serious violent offenses shall have consecutive sentences imposed per the rules of RCW 9.94A.589(1)(b).

The Caseload Forecast Council is not liable for errors or omissions in the manual, for sentences that may be inappropriately calculated as a result of a practitioner's or court's reliance on the manual, or for any other written or verbal information related to adult or juvenile sentencing. The scoring sheets are intended to provide assistance in most cases but do not cover all permutations of the scoring rules. If you find any errors or omissions, we encourage you to report them to the Caseload Forecast Council.

Homicide By Abuse With A Finding Of Sexual Motivation

RCW 9A.32.055
CLASS A – SERIOUS VIOLENT/SEX

OFFENDER SCORING RCW 9.94A.525(17)

ADULT HISTORY:
- Enter number of sex offense felony convictions .... _____ x 3 = _____
- Enter number of serious violent felony convictions .... _____ x 3 = _____
- Enter number of violent felony convictions .... _____ x 2 = _____
- Enter number of nonviolent felony convictions .... _____ x 1 = _____

JUVENILE HISTORY:
- Enter number of sex offense felony dispositions .... _____ x 3 = _____
- Enter number of serious violent felony dispositions .... _____ x 3 = _____
- Enter number of violent felony dispositions .... _____ x 2 = _____
- Enter number of nonviolent felony dispositions .... _____ x ½ = _____

OTHER CURRENT OFFENSES:
(Other current offenses that do not encompass the same conduct count in offender score)
- Enter number of other sex offense felony convictions .... _____ x 3 = _____
- Enter number of other violent felony convictions .... _____ x 2 = _____
- Enter number of other nonviolent felony convictions .... _____ x 1 = _____

STATUS:
- Was the offender on community custody on the date the current offense was committed? .... + 1 = _____

Total the last column to get the **Offender Score** (Round down to the nearest whole number)

SENTENCE RANGE

Offender Score	0	1	2	3	4	5	6	7	8	9+
LEVEL XV	280m 240 - 320	291.5m 250 - 333	304m 261 - 347	316m 271 - 361	327.5m 281 - 374	339.5m 291 - 388	364m 312 - 416	394m 338 - 450	431.5m 370 - 493	479.5m 411 - 548

Add Sexual Motivation Enhancement (see page 185) [____] to Standard Range = [Low] to [High]

- ✓ For attempt, solicitation, conspiracy (RCW 9.94A.595) see page 23 or for gang-related felonies where the court found the offender involved a minor (RCW 9.94A.833) see page 186 for standard range adjustments.
- ✓ For deadly weapon enhancement, see page 190.
- ✓ For sentencing alternatives, see page 177.
- ✓ For community custody eligibility, see page 187.
- ✓ For any applicable enhancements other than deadly weapon enhancement, see page 183.
- ✓ If the offender is not a persistent offender and the current offense was committed on or after 9/1/2001, then the offender is subject to the requirements under RCW 9.94A.507.
- ✓ Multiple current serious violent offenses shall have consecutive sentences imposed per the rules of RCW 9.94A.589(1)(b).

The Caseload Forecast Council is not liable for errors or omissions in the manual, for sentences that may be inappropriately calculated as a result of a practitioner's or court's reliance on the manual, or for any other written or verbal information related to adult or juvenile sentencing. The scoring sheets are intended to provide assistance in most cases but do not cover all permutations of the scoring rules. If you find any errors or omissions, we encourage you to report them to the Caseload Forecast Council.

Homicide By Watercraft While Under The Influence Of Intoxicating Liquor Or Any Drug

RCW 79A.60.050(1)(a)
CLASS A – VIOLENT

OFFENDER SCORING RCW 9.94A.525(12)

If it was found that this offense was committed with sexual motivation (RCW 9.94A.533(8)) on or after 7/01/2006, use the General Violent Offense with a Sexual Motivation Finding scoring form on page 201.

If the present conviction is for a felony domestic violence offense where domestic violence was plead and proven, use the General Violent Offense Where Domestic Violence Has Been Plead and Proven scoring form on page 199.

ADULT HISTORY:
Enter number of Homicide by Watercraft and Assault by Watercraft felony convictions .... _____ x 2 = _____

Enter number of Driving Under the Influence of Intoxicating Liquor or Any Drug and Actual Physical Control of a Vehicle While Under the Influence of Intoxicating Liquor or Any Drug and Operation of a Vessel While Under the Influence of Intoxicating Liquor or Any Drug felony convictions .... _____ x 1 = _____

Enter number of felony convictions .... _____ x 1 = _____

JUVENILE HISTORY:
Enter number of Homicide by Watercraft and Assault by Watercraft felony dispositions .... _____ x 2 = _____

Enter number of Driving Under the Influence of Intoxicating Liquor or Any Drug and Actual Physical Control of a Vehicle While Under the Influence of Intoxicating Liquor or Any Drug and Operation of a Vessel While Under the Influence of Intoxicating Liquor or Any Drug felony dispositions .... _____ x ½ = _____

Enter number of felony dispositions .... _____ x ½ = _____

OTHER CURRENT OFFENSES:
(Other current offenses that do not encompass the same conduct count in offender score)
Enter number of other Homicide by Watercraft and Assault by Watercraft felony convictions .... _____ x 2 = _____

Enter number of Driving Under the Influence of Intoxicating Liquor or Any Drug and Actual Physical Control of a Vehicle While Under the Influence of Intoxicating Liquor or Any Drug and Operation of a Vessel While Under the Influence of Intoxicating Liquor or Any Drug felony convictions .... _____ x 1 = _____

Enter number of other felony convictions .... _____ x 1 = _____

STATUS:
Was the offender on community custody on the date the current offense was committed? (if yes) .... + 1 = _____

Total the last column to get the **Offender Score** (Round down to the nearest whole number)

SENTENCE RANGE

	_				Offender Score					
	0	**1**	**2**	**3**	**4**	**5**	**6**	**7**	**8**	**9+**
LEVEL IX	36m	42m	47.5m	53.5m	59.5m	66m	89.5m	101.5m	126m	150m
	31 - 41	36 - 48	41 - 54	46 - 61	51 - 68	57 - 75	77 - 102	87 - 116	108 - 144	129 - 171

- ✓ For attempt, solicitation, conspiracy (RCW 9.94A.595) see page 23 or for gang-related felonies where the court found the offender involved a minor (RCW 9.94A.833) see page 186 for standard range adjustments.
- ✓ For deadly weapon enhancement, see page 190.
- ✓ For sentencing alternatives, see page 177.
- ✓ For community custody eligibility, see page 187.
- ✓ For any applicable enhancements other than deadly weapon enhancement, see page 183.

The Caseload Forecast Council is not liable for errors or omissions in the manual, for sentences that may be inappropriately calculated as a result of a practitioner's or court's reliance on the manual, or for any other written or verbal information related to adult or juvenile sentencing. The scoring sheets are intended to provide assistance in most cases but do not cover all permutations of the scoring rules. If you find any errors or omissions, we encourage you to report them to the Caseload Forecast Council.

Homicide By Watercraft Disregard For The Safety Of Others

RCW 79A.60.050(1)(c)
CLASS A – VIOLENT

OFFENDER SCORING RCW 9.94A.525(12)

If it was found that this offense was committed with sexual motivation (RCW 9.94A.533(8)) on or after 7/01/2006, use the General Violent Offense with a Sexual Motivation Finding scoring form on page 201.

If the present conviction is for a felony domestic violence offense where domestic violence was plead and proven, use the General Violent Offense Where Domestic Violence Has Been Plead and Proven scoring form on page 199.

ADULT HISTORY:
Enter number of Homicide by Watercraft and Assault by Watercraft felony convictions .... _____   x 2 = _____

Enter number of Driving Under the Influence of Intoxicating Liquor or Any Drug and Actual Physical Control of a Vehicle While Under the Influence of Intoxicating Liquor or Any Drug and Operation of a Vessel While Under the Influence of Intoxicating Liquor or Any Drug felony convictions .... _____   x 1 = _____

Enter number of felony convictions .... _____   x 1 = _____

JUVENILE HISTORY:
Enter number of Homicide by Watercraft and Assault by Watercraft felony dispositions .... _____   x 2 = _____

Enter number of Driving Under the Influence of Intoxicating Liquor or Any Drug and Actual Physical Control of a Vehicle While Under the Influence of Intoxicating Liquor or Any Drug and Operation of a Vessel While Under the Influence of Intoxicating Liquor or Any Drug felony dispositions .... _____   x ½ = _____

Enter number of felony dispositions .... _____   x ½ = _____

OTHER CURRENT OFFENSES:
(Other current offenses that do not encompass the same conduct count in offender score)
Enter number of other Homicide by Watercraft and Assault by Watercraft felony convictions .... _____   x 2 = _____

Enter number of Driving Under the Influence of Intoxicating Liquor or Any Drug and Actual Physical Control of a Vehicle While Under the Influence of Intoxicating Liquor or Any Drug and Operation of a Vessel While Under the Influence of Intoxicating Liquor or Any Drug felony convictions .... _____   x 1 = _____

Enter number of other felony convictions .... _____   x 1 = _____

STATUS:
Was the offender on community custody on the date the current offense was committed? (if yes) ...... + 1 = _____

Total the last column to get the **Offender Score** (Round down to the nearest whole number)

SENTENCE RANGE

Offender Score	0	1	2	3	4	5	6	7	8	9+
LEVEL VII	17.5m	24m	30m	36m	42m	47.5m	66m	78m	89.5m	101.5m
	15 - 20	21 - 27	26 - 34	31 - 41	36 - 48	41 - 54	57 - 75	67 - 89	77 - 102	87 - 116

- ✓ For attempt, solicitation, conspiracy (RCW 9.94A.595) see page 23 or for gang-related felonies where the court found the offender involved a minor (RCW 9.94A.833) see page 186 for standard range adjustments.
- ✓ For deadly weapon enhancement, see page 190.
- ✓ For sentencing alternatives, see page 177.
- ✓ For community custody eligibility, see page 187.
- ✓ For any applicable enhancements other than deadly weapon enhancement, see page 183.

The Caseload Forecast Council is not liable for errors or omissions in the manual, for sentences that may be inappropriately calculated as a result of a practitioner's or court's reliance on the manual, or for any other written or verbal information related to adult or juvenile sentencing. The scoring sheets are intended to provide assistance in most cases but do not cover all permutations of the scoring rules. If you find any errors or omissions, we encourage you to report them to the Caseload Forecast Council.

Homicide By Watercraft In A Reckless Manner

RCW 79A.60.050(1)(b)
CLASS A – VIOLENT

OFFENDER SCORING RCW 9.94A.525(12)

If it was found that this offense was committed with sexual motivation (RCW 9.94A.533(8)) on or after 7/01/2006, use the General Violent Offense with a Sexual Motivation Finding scoring form on page 201.

If the present conviction is for a felony domestic violence offense where domestic violence was plead and proven, use the General Violent Offense Where Domestic Violence Has Been Plead and Proven scoring form on page 199.

ADULT HISTORY:
   Enter number of Homicide by Watercraft and Assault by Watercraft felony convictions .... _____   x 2 = _____

   Enter number of Driving Under the Influence of Intoxicating Liquor or Any Drug and
   Actual Physical Control of a Vehicle While Under the Influence of Intoxicating Liquor or Any Drug and
   Operation of a Vessel While Under the Influence of Intoxicating Liquor or Any Drug
   felony convictions .... _____   x 1 = _____

   Enter number of felony convictions .... _____   x 1 = _____

JUVENILE HISTORY:
   Enter number of Homicide by Watercraft and Assault by Watercraft felony dispositions .... _____   x 2 = _____

   Enter number of Driving Under the Influence of Intoxicating Liquor or Any Drug and
   Actual Physical Control of a Vehicle While Under the Influence of Intoxicating Liquor or Any Drug and
   Operation of a Vessel While Under the Influence of Intoxicating Liquor or Any Drug
   felony dispositions .... _____   x ½ = _____

   Enter number of felony dispositions .... _____   x ½ = _____

OTHER CURRENT OFFENSES:
(Other current offenses that do not encompass the same conduct count in offender score)
   Enter number of other Homicide by Watercraft and Assault by Watercraft felony convictions .... _____   x 2 = _____

   Enter number of Driving Under the Influence of Intoxicating Liquor or Any Drug and
   Actual Physical Control of a Vehicle While Under the Influence of Intoxicating Liquor or Any Drug and
   Operation of a Vessel While Under the Influence of Intoxicating Liquor or Any Drug
   felony convictions .... _____   x 1 = _____

   Enter number of other felony convictions .... _____   x 1 = _____

STATUS:
   Was the offender on community custody on the date the current offense was committed? (if yes) .... + 1 = _____

Total the last column to get the **Offender Score** (Round down to the nearest whole number)

SENTENCE RANGE

	Offender Score									
	0	1	2	3	4	5	6	7	8	9+
LEVEL VIII	24m	30m	36m	42m	47.5m	53.5m	78m	89.5m	101.5m	126m
	21 - 27	26 - 34	31 - 41	36 - 48	41 - 54	46 - 61	67 - 89	77 - 102	87 - 116	108 - 144

- ✓ For attempt, solicitation, conspiracy (RCW 9.94A.595) see page 23 or for gang-related felonies where the court found the offender involved a minor (RCW 9.94A.833) see page 186 for standard range adjustments.
- ✓ For deadly weapon enhancement, see page 190.
- ✓ For sentencing alternatives, see page 177.
- ✓ For community custody eligibility, see page 187.
- ✓ For any applicable enhancements other than deadly weapon enhancement, see page 183.

The Caseload Forecast Council is not liable for errors or omissions in the manual, for sentences that may be inappropriately calculated as a result of a practitioner's or court's reliance on the manual, or for any other written or verbal information related to adult or juvenile sentencing. The scoring sheets are intended to provide assistance in most cases but do not cover all permutations of the scoring rules. If you find any errors or omissions, we encourage you to report them to the Caseload Forecast Council.

Identity Theft First Degree

RCW 9.35.020(2)
CLASS B – NONVIOLENT
OFFENDER SCORING RCW 9.94A.525(7)

If it was found that this offense was committed with sexual motivation (RCW 9.94A.533(8)) on or after 7/01/2006, use the General Nonviolent Offense with a Sexual Motivation Finding scoring form on page 193.

If the present conviction is for a felony domestic violence offense where domestic violence was plead and proven, use the General Nonviolent Offense Where Domestic Violence Has Been Plead and Proven scoring form on page 191.

ADULT HISTORY:
    Enter number of felony convictions .... _____ x 1 = _____

JUVENILE HISTORY:
    Enter number of serious violent and violent felony dispositions .... _____ x 1 = _____
    Enter number of nonviolent felony dispositions .... _____ x ½ = _____

OTHER CURRENT OFFENSES:
(Other current offenses that do not encompass the same conduct count in offender score)
    Enter number of other felony convictions .... _____ x 1 = _____

STATUS:
    Was the offender on community custody on the date the current offense was committed? (if yes) ...... + 1 = _____

Total the last column to get the **Offender Score** (Round down to the nearest whole number)

SENTENCE RANGE

	\multicolumn{11}{c}{Offender Score}
	0	1	2	3	4	5	6	7	8	9+
LEVEL IV	6m	9m	13m	15m	17.5m	25.5m	38m	50m	61.5m	73.5m
	3 - 9	6 - 12	12+ - 14	13 - 17	15 - 20	22 - 29	33 - 43	43 - 57	53 - 70	63 - 84

- ✓ For attempt, solicitation, conspiracy (RCW 9.94A.595) see page 23 or for gang-related felonies where the court found the offender involved a minor (RCW 9.94A.833) see page 186 for standard range adjustments.
- ✓ For deadly weapon enhancement, see page 190.
- ✓ For sentencing alternatives, see page 177.
- ✓ For community custody eligibility, see page 187.
- ✓ For any applicable enhancements other than deadly weapon enhancement, see page 183.

The Caseload Forecast Council is not liable for errors or omissions in the manual, for sentences that may be inappropriately calculated as a result of a practitioner's or court's reliance on the manual, or for any other written or verbal information related to adult or juvenile sentencing. The scoring sheets are intended to provide assistance in most cases but do not cover all permutations of the scoring rules. If you find any errors or omissions, we encourage you to report them to the Caseload Forecast Council.

Identity Theft Second Degree

RCW 9.35.020(3)

CLASS C – NONVIOLENT

OFFENDER SCORING RCW 9.94A.525(7)

If it was found that this offense was committed with sexual motivation (RCW 9.94A.533(8)) on or after 7/01/2006, use the General Nonviolent Offense with a Sexual Motivation Finding scoring form on page 193.

If the present conviction is for a felony domestic violence offense where domestic violence was plead and proven, use the General Nonviolent Offense Where Domestic Violence Has Been Plead and Proven scoring form on page 191.

ADULT HISTORY:
  Enter number of felony convictions .... _____ x 1 = _____

JUVENILE HISTORY:
  Enter number of serious violent and violent felony dispositions .... _____ x 1 = _____
  Enter number of nonviolent felony dispositions .... _____ x ½ = _____

OTHER CURRENT OFFENSES:
(Other current offenses that do not encompass the same conduct count in offender score)
  Enter number of other felony convictions .... _____ x 1 = _____

STATUS:
  Was the offender on community custody on the date the current offense was committed? (if yes) .... + 1 = _____

Total the last column to get the **Offender Score** (Round down to the nearest whole number)

SENTENCE RANGE

					Offender Score					
	0	**1**	**2**	**3**	**4**	**5**	**6**	**7**	**8**	**9+**
LEVEL II	0-90 days	4m 2 - 6	6m 3 - 9	8m 4 - 12	13m 12+ - 14	16m 14 - 18	19.5m 17 - 22	25.5m 22 - 29	38m 33 - 43	50m 43 - 57

- ✓ For gang-related felonies where the court found the offender involved a minor (RCW 9.94A.833) see page 186 for standard range adjustment.
- ✓ For deadly weapon enhancement, see page 190.
- ✓ For sentencing alternatives, see page 177.
- ✓ For community custody eligibility, see page 187.
- ✓ For any applicable enhancements other than deadly weapon enhancement, see page 183.

Improperly Obtaining Financial Information

RCW 9.35.010
CLASS C – NONVIOLENT
OFFENDER SCORING RCW 9.94A.525(7)

If it was found that this offense was committed with sexual motivation (RCW 9.94A.533(8)) on or after 7/01/2006, use the General Nonviolent Offense with a Sexual Motivation Finding scoring form on page 193.

If the present conviction is for a felony domestic violence offense where domestic violence was plead and proven, use the General Nonviolent Offense Where Domestic Violence Has Been Plead and Proven scoring form on page 191.

ADULT HISTORY:
    Enter number of felony convictions .... _____ x 1 = _____

JUVENILE HISTORY:
    Enter number of serious violent and violent felony dispositions .... _____ x 1 = _____
    Enter number of nonviolent felony dispositions .... _____ x ½ = _____

OTHER CURRENT OFFENSES:
(Other current offenses that do not encompass the same conduct count in offender score)
    Enter number of other felony convictions .... _____ x 1 = _____

STATUS:
    Was the offender on community custody on the date the current offense was committed? (if yes) ...... + 1 = _____

Total the last column to get the **Offender Score** (Round down to the nearest whole number)

SENTENCE RANGE

	Offender Score									
	0	1	2	3	4	5	6	7	8	9+
LEVEL II	0-90 days	4m 2 - 6	6m 3 - 9	8m 4 - 12	13m 12+ - 14	16m 14 - 18	19.5m 17 - 22	25.5m 22 - 29	38m 33 - 43	50m 43 - 57

- ✓ For gang-related felonies where the court found the offender involved a minor (RCW 9.94A.833) see page 186 for standard range adjustment.
- ✓ For deadly weapon enhancement, see page 190.
- ✓ For sentencing alternatives, see page 177.
- ✓ For community custody eligibility, see page 187.
- ✓ For any applicable enhancements other than deadly weapon enhancement, see page 183.

The Caseload Forecast Council is not liable for errors or omissions in the manual, for sentences that may be inappropriately calculated as a result of a practitioner's or court's reliance on the manual, or for any other written or verbal information related to adult or juvenile sentencing. The scoring sheets are intended to provide assistance in most cases but do not cover all permutations of the scoring rules. If you find any errors or omissions, we encourage you to report them to the Caseload Forecast Council.

Incest First Degree

RCW 9A.64.020(1)
CLASS B – NONVIOLENT/SEX
OFFENDER SCORING RCW 9.94A.525(17)

If the present conviction is for a felony domestic violence offense where domestic violence was plead and proven, use the General Nonviolent/Sex Offense Where Domestic Violence Has Been Plead and Proven scoring form on page 192.

ADULT HISTORY:
- Enter number of sex offense felony convictions .... _____ x 3 = _____
- Enter number of felony convictions .... _____ x 1 = _____

JUVENILE HISTORY:
- Enter number of sex offense felony dispositions .... _____ x 3 = _____
- Enter number of serious violent and violent felony dispositions .... _____ x 1 = _____
- Enter number of nonviolent felony dispositions .... _____ x ½ = _____

OTHER CURRENT OFFENSES:
(Other current offenses that do not encompass the same conduct count in offender score)
- Enter number of other sex offense felony convictions .... _____ x 3 = _____
- Enter number of other felony convictions .... _____ x 1 = _____

STATUS:
- Was the offender on community custody on the date the current offense was committed? (if yes) .... + 1 = _____

Total the last column to get the **Offender Score** (Round down to the nearest whole number) ☐

SENTENCE RANGE

	\	Offender Score								
	0	**1**	**2**	**3**	**4**	**5**	**6**	**7**	**8**	**9+**
LEVEL VI	13m	17.5m	24m	30m	36m	42m	53.5m	66m	78m	89.5m
	12+ - 14	15 - 20	21 - 27	26 - 34	31 - 41	36 - 48	46 - 61	57 - 75	67 - 89	77 - 102

- ✓ For attempt, solicitation, conspiracy (RCW 9.94A.595) see page 23 or for gang-related felonies where the court found the offender involved a minor (RCW 9.94A.833) see page 186 for standard range adjustments.
- ✓ For deadly weapon enhancement, see page 190.
- ✓ For sentencing alternatives, see page 177.
- ✓ For community custody eligibility, see page 187.
- ✓ For any applicable enhancements other than deadly weapon enhancement, see page 183.
- ✓ If the offender is not a persistent offender and has a prior conviction for an offense listed in RCW 9.94A.030(38)(b), then the sentence is subject to the requirements of RCW 9.94A.507.

The Caseload Forecast Council is not liable for errors or omissions in the manual, for sentences that may be inappropriately calculated as a result of a practitioner's or court's reliance on the manual, or for any other written or verbal information related to adult or juvenile sentencing. The scoring sheets are intended to provide assistance in most cases but do not cover all permutations of the scoring rules. If you find any errors or omissions, we encourage you to report them to the Caseload Forecast Council.

Incest Second Degree

RCW 9A.64.020(2)

CLASS C* – NONVIOLENT/SEX

OFFENDER SCORING RCW 9.94A.525(17)

If the present conviction is for a felony domestic violence offense where domestic violence was plead and proven, use the General Nonviolent/Sex Offense Where Domestic Violence Has Been Plead and Proven scoring form on page 192.

ADULT HISTORY:
    Enter number of sex offense felony convictions .... _____ x 3 = _____
    Enter number of felony convictions .... _____ x 1 = _____

JUVENILE HISTORY:
    Enter number of sex offense felony dispositions .... _____ x 3 = _____
    Enter number of serious violent and violent felony dispositions .... _____ x 1 = _____
    Enter number of nonviolent felony dispositions .... _____ x ½ = _____

OTHER CURRENT OFFENSES:
(Other current offenses that do not encompass the same conduct count in offender score)
    Enter number of other sex offense felony convictions .... _____ x 3 = _____
    Enter number of other felony convictions .... _____ x 1 = _____

STATUS:
    Was the offender on community custody on the date the current offense was committed? (if yes) ...... + 1 = _____

Total the last column to get the **Offender Score** (Round down to the nearest whole number)

SENTENCE RANGE

	\multicolumn{10}{c}{Offender Score}									
	0	**1**	**2**	**3**	**4**	**5**	**6**	**7**	**8**	**9+**
LEVEL V	9m	13m	15m	17.5m	25.5m	38m	47.5m	55.5m		
	6 - 12	12+ - 14	13 - 17	15 - 20	22 - 29	33 - 43	41 - 54	51 - 60*	60 - 60*	60 - 60*

- ✓ For gang-related felonies where the court found the offender involved a minor (RCW 9.94A.833) see page 186 for standard range adjustment.
- ✓ For deadly weapon enhancement, see page 190.
- ✓ For sentencing alternatives, see page 177.
- ✓ For community custody eligibility, see page 187.
- ✓ For any applicable enhancements other than deadly weapon enhancement, see page 183.
- ✓ If the offender is not a persistent offender and has a prior conviction for an offense listed in RCW 9.94A.030(38)(b), then the sentence is subject to the requirements of RCW 9.94A.507.

The Caseload Forecast Council is not liable for errors or omissions in the manual, for sentences that may be inappropriately calculated as a result of a practitioner's or court's reliance on the manual, or for any other written or verbal information related to adult or juvenile sentencing. The scoring sheets are intended to provide assistance in most cases but do not cover all permutations of the scoring rules. If you find any errors or omissions, we encourage you to report them to the Caseload Forecast Council.

Indecent Exposure To A Person Under Age 14 Subsequent Conviction Or Has Prior Sex Offense Conviction

RCW 9A.88.010(2)(c)
CLASS C* – NONVIOLENT

OFFENDER SCORING RCW 9.94A.525(7)

If it was found that this offense was committed with sexual motivation (RCW 9.94A.533(8)) on or after 7/01/2006, use the General Nonviolent Offense with a Sexual Motivation Finding scoring form on page 193.

ADULT HISTORY:
   Enter number of felony convictions .... _____ x 1 = _____

JUVENILE HISTORY:
   Enter number of serious violent and violent felony dispositions .... _____ x 1 = _____

   Enter number of nonviolent felony dispositions .... _____ x ½ = _____

OTHER CURRENT OFFENSES:
(Other current offenses that do not encompass the same conduct count in offender score)
   Enter number of other felony convictions .... _____ x 1 = _____

STATUS:
   Was the offender on community custody on the date the current offense was committed? (if yes) .... + 1 = _____

Total the last column to get the **Offender Score** (Round down to the nearest whole number)

SENTENCE RANGE

Offender Score	0	1	2	3	4	5	6	7	8	9+
LEVEL IV	6m 3 - 9	9m 6 - 12	13m 12+ - 14	15m 13 - 17	17.5m 15 - 20	25.5m 22 - 29	38m 33 - 43	50m 43 - 57	56.5m 53 - 60*	60 - 60*

- ✓ For gang-related felonies where the court found the offender involved a minor (RCW 9.94A.833) see page 186 for standard range adjustment.
- ✓ For deadly weapon enhancement, see page 190.
- ✓ For sentencing alternatives, see page 177.
- ✓ For community custody eligibility, see page 187.
- ✓ For any applicable enhancements other than deadly weapon enhancement, see page 183.

The Caseload Forecast Council is not liable for errors or omissions in the manual, for sentences that may be inappropriately calculated as a result of a practitioner's or court's reliance on the manual, or for any other written or verbal information related to adult or juvenile sentencing. The scoring sheets are intended to provide assistance in most cases but do not cover all permutations of the scoring rules. If you find any errors or omissions, we encourage you to report them to the Caseload Forecast Council.

Indecent Liberties With Forcible Compulsion

RCW 9A.44.100(1)(a)
CLASS A – VIOLENT/SEX
ATTEMPT = CLASS A

OFFENDER SCORING RCW 9.94A.525(17)

If the present conviction is for a felony domestic violence offense where domestic violence was plead and proven, use the General Violent/Sex Offense Where Domestic Violence Has Been Plead and Proven scoring form on page 200.

ADULT HISTORY:
- Enter number of sex offense felony convictions .... _____ x 3 = _____
- Enter number of serious violent and violent felony convictions .... _____ x 2 = _____
- Enter number of nonviolent felony convictions .... _____ x 1 = _____

JUVENILE HISTORY:
- Enter number of sex offense felony dispositions .... _____ x 3 = _____
- Enter number of serious violent and violent felony dispositions .... _____ x 2 = _____
- Enter number of nonviolent felony dispositions .... _____ x ½ = _____

OTHER CURRENT OFFENSES:
(Other current offenses that do not encompass the same conduct count in offender score)
- Enter number of other sex offense felony convictions .... _____ x 3 = _____
- Enter number of other serious violent and violent felony convictions .... _____ x 2 = _____
- Enter number of other nonviolent felony convictions .... _____ x 1 = _____

STATUS:
- Was the offender on community custody on the date the current offense was committed? (if yes) ...... + 1 = _____

Total the last column to get the **Offender Score** (Round down to the nearest whole number)

SENTENCE RANGE

	\multicolumn{10}{c}{Offender Score}
	0	1	2	3	4	5	6	7	8	9+
LEVEL X	59.5m	66m	72m	78m	84m	89.5m	114m	126m	150m	230.5m
	51 - 68	57 - 75	62 - 82	67 - 89	72 - 96	77 - 102	98 - 130	108 - 144	129 - 171	149 - 198

- ✓ For attempt, (RCW 9.94A.595) see page 23 or for gang-related felonies where the court found the offender involved a minor (RCW 9.94A.833) see page 186 for standard range adjustments.
- ✓ For deadly weapon enhancement, see page 190.
- ✓ For sentencing alternatives, see page 177.
- ✓ For community custody eligibility, see page 187.
- ✓ For any applicable enhancements other than deadly weapon enhancement, see page 183.
- ✓ If the offender is not a persistent offender and the <u>current offense</u> was committed on or after 9/1/2001, then the offender is subject to the requirements under RCW 9.94A.507.
- ✓ Per RCW 9.94A.507(3)(c)(ii), <u>excluding convictions for an attempt</u>, the <u>minimum</u> term shall be either the maximum of the standard sentence range for the offense or 25 years, whichever is greater, for a finding that the victim was **under the age of 15** at the time of the offense under RCW 9.94A.837 or found to be **developmentally disabled, mentally disordered, a frail elder or vulnerable adult** at the time of the offense under RCW 9.94A.838.

The Caseload Forecast Council is not liable for errors or omissions in the manual, for sentences that may be inappropriately calculated as a result of a practitioner's or court's reliance on the manual, or for any other written or verbal information related to adult or juvenile sentencing. The scoring sheets are intended to provide assistance in most cases but do not cover all permutations of the scoring rules. If you find any errors or omissions, we encourage you to report them to the Caseload Forecast Council.

Indecent Liberties With Forcible Compulsion

RCW 9A.44.100(1)(a)
VIOLENT/SEX
SOLICITATION = CLASS A
CONSPIRACY = CLASS B

OFFENDER SCORING RCW 9.94A.525(17)

If the present conviction is for a felony domestic violence offense where domestic violence was plead and proven, use the General Violent/Sex Offense Where Domestic Violence Has Been Plead and Proven scoring form on page 200.

ADULT HISTORY:
Enter number of sex offense felony convictions .... _____ x 3 = _____
Enter number of serious violent and violent felony convictions .... _____ x 2 = _____
Enter number of nonviolent felony convictions .... _____ x 1 = _____

JUVENILE HISTORY:
Enter number of sex offense felony dispositions .... _____ x 3 = _____
Enter number of serious violent and violent felony dispositions .... _____ x 2 = _____
Enter number of nonviolent felony dispositions .... _____ x ½ = _____

OTHER CURRENT OFFENSES:
(Other current offenses that do not encompass the same conduct count in offender score)
Enter number of other sex offense felony convictions .... _____ x 3 = _____
Enter number of other serious violent and violent felony convictions .... _____ x 2 = _____
Enter number of other nonviolent felony convictions .... _____ x 1 = _____

STATUS:
Was the offender on community custody on the date the current offense was committed? (if yes) .... + 1 = _____

Total the last column to get the **Offender Score** (Round down to the nearest whole number)

SENTENCE RANGE

	\multicolumn{10}{c	}{Offender Score}
	0	1	2	3	4	5	6	7	8	9+
LEVEL X	59.5m	66m	72m	78m	84m	89.5m	114m	126m	150m	230.5m
	51 - 68	57 - 75	62 - 82	67 - 89	72 - 96	77 - 102	98 - 130	108 - 144	129 - 171	149 - 198

- For solicitation, conspiracy (RCW 9.94A.595) see page 23 or for gang-related felonies where the court found the offender involved a minor (RCW 9.94A.833) see page 186 for standard range adjustments.
- For deadly weapon enhancement, see page 190.
- For sentencing alternatives, see page 177.
- For community custody eligibility, see page 187.
- For any applicable enhancements other than deadly weapon enhancement, see page 183.
- If the offender is not a persistent offender and has a prior conviction for an offense listed in RCW 9.94A.030(38)(b), then the sentence is subject to the requirements of RCW 9.94A.507.

The Caseload Forecast Council is not liable for errors or omissions in the manual, for sentences that may be inappropriately calculated as a result of a practitioner's or court's reliance on the manual, or for any other written or verbal information related to adult or juvenile sentencing. The scoring sheets are intended to provide assistance in most cases but do not cover all permutations of the scoring rules. If you find any errors or omissions, we encourage you to report them to the Caseload Forecast Council.

Indecent Liberties Without Forcible Compulsion

RCW 9A.44.100(1)(b) and (c)
CLASS B – NONVIOLENT/SEX

OFFENDER SCORING RCW 9.94A.525(17)

If the present conviction is for a felony domestic violence offense where domestic violence was plead and proven, use the General Nonviolent/Sex Offense Where Domestic Violence Has Been Plead and Proven scoring form on page 192.

ADULT HISTORY:
    Enter number of sex offense felony convictions .... _____ x 3 = _____
    Enter number of nonviolent felony convictions .... _____ x 1 = _____

JUVENILE HISTORY:
    Enter number of sex offense felony dispositions .... _____ x 3 = _____
    Enter number of serious violent and violent felony dispositions .... _____ x 1 = _____
    Enter number of nonviolent felony dispositions .... _____ x ½ = _____

OTHER CURRENT OFFENSES:
(Other current offenses that do not encompass the same conduct count in offender score)
    Enter number of other sex offense felony convictions .... _____ x 3 = _____
    Enter number of other nonviolent felony convictions .... _____ x 1 = _____

STATUS:
    Was the offender on community custody on the date the current offense was committed? (if yes) ...... + 1 = _____

Total the last column to get the **Offender Score** (Round down to the nearest whole number)

SENTENCE RANGE

	\tOffender Score									
	0	**1**	**2**	**3**	**4**	**5**	**6**	**7**	**8**	**9+**
LEVEL VII	17.5m	24m	30m	36m	42m	47.5m	66m	78m	89.5m	101.5m
	15 - 20	21 - 27	26 - 34	31 - 41	36 - 48	41 - 54	57 - 75	67 - 89	77 - 102	87 - 116

✓ For attempt, solicitation, conspiracy (RCW 9.94A.595) see page 23 or for gang-related felonies where the court found the offender involved a minor (RCW 9.94A.833) see page 186 for standard range adjustments.

✓ For deadly weapon enhancement, see page 190.

✓ For sentencing alternatives, see page 177.

✓ For community custody eligibility, see page 187.

✓ For any applicable enhancements other than deadly weapon enhancement, see page 183.

✓ If the offender is not a persistent offender and has a prior conviction for an offense listed in RCW 9.94A.030(38)(b), then the sentence is subject to the requirements of RCW 9.94A.507.

Influencing Outcome Of Sporting Event

RCW 9A.82.070
CLASS C* – NONVIOLENT

OFFENDER SCORING RCW 9.94A.525(7)

If it was found that this offense was committed with sexual motivation (RCW 9.94A.533(8)) on or after 7/01/2006, use the General Nonviolent Offense with a Sexual Motivation Finding scoring form on page 193.

If the present conviction is for a felony domestic violence offense where domestic violence was plead and proven, use the General Nonviolent Offense Where Domestic Violence Has Been Plead and Proven scoring form on page 191.

ADULT HISTORY:
  Enter number of felony convictions .... _____ x 1 = _____

JUVENILE HISTORY:
  Enter number of serious violent and violent felony dispositions .... _____ x 1 = _____

  Enter number of nonviolent felony dispositions .... _____ x ½ = _____

OTHER CURRENT OFFENSES:
(Other current offenses that do not encompass the same conduct count in offender score)
  Enter number of other felony convictions .... _____ x 1 = _____

STATUS:
  Was the offender on community custody on the date the current offense was committed? (if yes) .... + 1 = _____

Total the last column to get the **Offender Score** (Round down to the nearest whole number)

SENTENCE RANGE

	Offender Score									
	0	1	2	3	4	5	6	7	8	9+
LEVEL IV	6m	9m	13m	15m	17.5m	25.5m	38m	50m	56.5m	
	3 - 9	6 - 12	12+ - 14	13 - 17	15 - 20	22 - 29	33 - 43	43 - 57	53 - 60*	60 - 60*

- ✓ For gang-related felonies where the court found the offender involved a minor (RCW 9.94A.833) see page 186 for standard range adjustment.
- ✓ For deadly weapon enhancement, see page 190.
- ✓ For sentencing alternatives, see page 177.
- ✓ For community custody eligibility, see page 187.
- ✓ For any applicable enhancements other than deadly weapon enhancement, see page 183.

The Caseload Forecast Council is not liable for errors or omissions in the manual, for sentences that may be inappropriately calculated as a result of a practitioner's or court's reliance on the manual, or for any other written or verbal information related to adult or juvenile sentencing. The scoring sheets are intended to provide assistance in most cases but do not cover all permutations of the scoring rules. If you find any errors or omissions, we encourage you to report them to the Caseload Forecast Council.

Intimidating A Judge, Intimidating A Juror, Intimidating A Witness

RCW 9A.72.160 & RCW 9A.72.130 & RCW 9A.72.110
CLASS B – NONVIOLENT
OFFENDER SCORING RCW 9.94A.525(7)

If it was found that this offense was committed with sexual motivation (RCW 9.94A.533(8)) on or after 7/01/2006, use the General Nonviolent Offense with a Sexual Motivation Finding scoring form on page 193.

If the present conviction is for a felony domestic violence offense where domestic violence was plead and proven, use the General Nonviolent Offense Where Domestic Violence Has Been Plead and Proven scoring form on page 191.

ADULT HISTORY:
  Enter number of felony convictions .... _____ x 1 = _____

JUVENILE HISTORY:
  Enter number of serious violent and violent felony dispositions .... _____ x 1 = _____
  Enter number of nonviolent felony dispositions .... _____ x ½ = _____

OTHER CURRENT OFFENSES:
(Other current offenses that do not encompass the same conduct count in offender score)
  Enter number of other felony convictions .... _____ x 1 = _____

STATUS:
  Was the offender on community custody on the date the current offense was committed? (if yes) ...... + 1 = _____

Total the last column to get the **Offender Score** (Round down to the nearest whole number)

SENTENCE RANGE

	Offender Score									
	0	1	2	3	4	5	6	7	8	9+
LEVEL VI	13m	17.5m	24m	30m	36m	42m	53.5m	66m	78m	89.5m
	12+ - 14	15 - 20	21 - 27	26 - 34	31 - 41	36 - 48	46 - 61	57 - 75	67 - 89	77 - 102

✓ For attempt, solicitation, conspiracy (RCW 9.94A.595) see page 23 or for gang-related felonies where the court found the offender involved a minor (RCW 9.94A.833) see page 186 for standard range adjustments.

✓ For deadly weapon enhancement, see page 190.

✓ For sentencing alternatives, see page 177.

✓ For community custody eligibility, see page 187.

✓ For any applicable enhancements other than deadly weapon enhancement, see page 183.

The Caseload Forecast Council is not liable for errors or omissions in the manual, for sentences that may be inappropriately calculated as a result of a practitioner's or court's reliance on the manual, or for any other written or verbal information related to adult or juvenile sentencing. The scoring sheets are intended to provide assistance in most cases but do not cover all permutations of the scoring rules. If you find any errors or omissions, we encourage you to report them to the Caseload Forecast Council.

Intimidating A Public Servant

RCW 9A.76.180
CLASS B – NONVIOLENT
OFFENDER SCORING RCW 9.94A.525(7)

If it was found that this offense was committed with sexual motivation (RCW 9.94A.533(8)) on or after 7/01/2006, use the General Nonviolent Offense with a Sexual Motivation Finding scoring form on page 193.

If the present conviction is for a felony domestic violence offense where domestic violence was plead and proven, use the General Nonviolent Offense Where Domestic Violence Has Been Plead and Proven scoring form on page 191.

ADULT HISTORY:
Enter number of felony convictions .... _____ x 1 = _____

JUVENILE HISTORY:
Enter number of serious violent and violent felony dispositions .... _____ x 1 = _____
Enter number of nonviolent felony dispositions .... _____ x ½ = _____

OTHER CURRENT OFFENSES:
(Other current offenses that do not encompass the same conduct count in offender score)
Enter number of other felony convictions .... _____ x 1 = _____

STATUS:
Was the offender on community custody on the date the current offense was committed? (if yes) .... + 1 = _____

Total the last column to get the **Offender Score** (Round down to the nearest whole number) [ ]

SENTENCE RANGE

	\multicolumn{10}{c	}{Offender Score}
	0	1	2	3	4	5	6	7	8	9+
LEVEL III	2m 1 - 3	5m 3 - 8	8m 4 - 12	11m 9 - 12	14m 12+ - 16	19.5m 17 - 22	25.5m 22 - 29	38m 33 - 43	50m 43 - 57	59.5m 51 - 68

- ✓ For attempt, solicitation, conspiracy (RCW 9.94A.595) see page 23 or for gang-related felonies where the court found the offender involved a minor (RCW 9.94A.833) see page 186 for standard range adjustments.
- ✓ For deadly weapon enhancement, see page 190.
- ✓ For sentencing alternatives, see page 177.
- ✓ For community custody eligibility, see page 187.
- ✓ For any applicable enhancements other than deadly weapon enhancement, see page 183.

The Caseload Forecast Council is not liable for errors or omissions in the manual, for sentences that may be inappropriately calculated as a result of a practitioner's or court's reliance on the manual, or for any other written or verbal information related to adult or juvenile sentencing. The scoring sheets are intended to provide assistance in most cases but do not cover all permutations of the scoring rules. If you find any errors or omissions, we encourage you to report them to the Caseload Forecast Council.

Introducing Contraband First Degree

RCW 9A.76.140
CLASS B – NONVIOLENT

OFFENDER SCORING RCW 9.94A.525(7)

If it was found that this offense was committed with sexual motivation (RCW 9.94A.533(8)) on or after 7/01/2006, use the General Nonviolent Offense with a Sexual Motivation Finding scoring form on page 193.

If the present conviction is for a felony domestic violence offense where domestic violence was plead and proven, use the General Nonviolent Offense Where Domestic Violence Has Been Plead and Proven scoring form on page 191.

ADULT HISTORY:
  Enter number of felony convictions .... _____ x 1 = _____

JUVENILE HISTORY:
  Enter number of serious violent and violent felony dispositions .... _____ x 1 = _____
  Enter number of nonviolent felony dispositions .... _____ x ½ = _____

OTHER CURRENT OFFENSES:
(Other current offenses that do not encompass the same conduct count in offender score)
  Enter number of other felony convictions .... _____ x 1 = _____

STATUS:
  Was the offender on community custody on the date the current offense was committed? (if yes) ...... + 1 = _____

Total the last column to get the **Offender Score** (Round down to the nearest whole number)

SENTENCE RANGE

	\multicolumn{10}{c}{Offender Score}									
	0	1	2	3	4	5	6	7	8	9+
LEVEL VII	17.5m	24m	30m	36m	42m	47.5m	66m	78m	89.5m	101.5m
	15 - 20	21 - 27	26 - 34	31 - 41	36 - 48	41 - 54	57 - 75	67 - 89	77 - 102	87 - 116

- ✓ For attempt, solicitation, conspiracy (RCW 9.94A.595) see page 23 or for gang-related felonies where the court found the offender involved a minor (RCW 9.94A.833) see page 186 for standard range adjustments.
- ✓ For deadly weapon enhancement, see page 190.
- ✓ For sentencing alternatives, see page 177.
- ✓ For community custody eligibility, see page 187.
- ✓ For any applicable enhancements other than deadly weapon enhancement, see page 183.

The Caseload Forecast Council is not liable for errors or omissions in the manual, for sentences that may be inappropriately calculated as a result of a practitioner's or court's reliance on the manual, or for any other written or verbal information related to adult or juvenile sentencing. The scoring sheets are intended to provide assistance in most cases but do not cover all permutations of the scoring rules. If you find any errors or omissions, we encourage you to report them to the Caseload Forecast Council.

Introducing Contraband Second Degree

RCW 9A.76.150
CLASS C* – NONVIOLENT

OFFENDER SCORING RCW 9.94A.525(7)

If it was found that this offense was committed with sexual motivation (RCW 9.94A.533(8)) on or after 7/01/2006, use the General Nonviolent Offense with a Sexual Motivation Finding scoring form on page 193.

If the present conviction is for a felony domestic violence offense where domestic violence was plead and proven, use the General Nonviolent Offense Where Domestic Violence Has Been Plead and Proven scoring form on page 191.

ADULT HISTORY:
   Enter number of felony convictions .... _____ x 1 = _____

JUVENILE HISTORY:
   Enter number of serious violent and violent felony dispositions .... _____ x 1 = _____

   Enter number of nonviolent felony dispositions .... _____ x ½ = _____

OTHER CURRENT OFFENSES:
(Other current offenses that do not encompass the same conduct count in offender score)
   Enter number of other felony convictions .... _____ x 1 = _____

STATUS:
   Was the offender on community custody on the date the current offense was committed? (if yes)....... + 1 = _____

Total the last column to get the **Offender Score** (Round down to the nearest whole number)

SENTENCE RANGE

	Offender Score									
	0	1	2	3	4	5	6	7	8	9+
LEVEL III	2m	5m	8m	11m	14m	19.5m	25.5m	38m	50m	55.5m
	1 - 3	3 - 8	4 - 12	9 - 12	12+ - 16	17 - 22	22 - 29	33 - 43	43 - 57	51 - 60*

- ✓ For gang-related felonies where the court found the offender involved a minor (RCW 9.94A.833) see page 186 for standard range adjustment.
- ✓ For deadly weapon enhancement, see page 190.
- ✓ For sentencing alternatives, see page 177.
- ✓ For community custody eligibility, see page 187.
- ✓ For any applicable enhancements other than deadly weapon enhancement, see page 183.

The Caseload Forecast Council is not liable for errors or omissions in the manual, for sentences that may be inappropriately calculated as a result of a practitioner's or court's reliance on the manual, or for any other written or verbal information related to adult or juvenile sentencing. The scoring sheets are intended to provide assistance in most cases but do not cover all permutations of the scoring rules. If you find any errors or omissions, we encourage you to report them to the Caseload Forecast Council.

Involving A Minor In Drug Dealing

RCW 69.50.4015
CLASS C* – NONVIOLENT/DRUG
OFFENDER SCORING RCW 9.94A.525(13)

If it was found that this offense was committed with sexual motivation (RCW 9.94A.533(8)) on or after 7/01/2006, use the General Drug Offense with a Sexual Motivation Finding scoring form on page 195.

If the present conviction is for a felony domestic violence offense where domestic violence was plead and proven, use the General Drug Offense Where Domestic Violence Has Been Plead and Proven scoring form on page 194.

ADULT HISTORY:
    Does the offender have a prior sex or serious violent offense in history?
        YES Enter number of felony drug convictions... _____ x 3 = _____
        NO Enter number of felony drug convictions... _____ x 1 = _____
    Enter number of felony convictions .... _____ x 1 = _____

JUVENILE HISTORY:
    Does the offender have a prior sex or serious violent offense in history?
        YES Enter number of felony drug dispositions... _____ x 2 = _____
        NO Enter number of felony drug dispositions... _____ x ½ = _____
    Enter number of serious violent and violent felony dispositions .... _____ x 1 = _____
    Enter number of nonviolent felony dispositions .... _____ x ½ = _____

OTHER CURRENT OFFENSES:
(Other current offenses that do not encompass the same conduct count in offender score)
    Does the offender have other prior sex or serious violent offense in history?
        YES Enter number of other felony drug convictions... _____ x 3 = _____
        NO Enter number of other felony drug convictions... _____ x 1 = _____
    Enter number of other felony convictions .... _____ x 1 = _____

STATUS:
    Was the offender on community custody on the date the current offense was committed? (if yes) ...... + 1 = _____

Total the last column to get the **Offender Score** (Round down to the nearest whole number)

SENTENCE RANGE – DRUG

	Offender Score		
	0 to 2	3 to 5	6 to 9+
LEVEL III	55.5m 51 - 60*	60 - 60*	60 - 60*

- ✓ For attempt, solicitation or conspiracy drug felonies see page 25 or for gang-related felonies where the court found the offender involved a minor (RCW 9.94A.833) see page 186 for standard range adjustments.
- ✓ Per RCW 9.94A.518, any felony offense under chapter 69.50 RCW with a deadly weapon special verdict under RCW 9.94A.602 becomes a level III offense.
- ✓ For deadly weapon enhancement, see page 190.
- ✓ For sentencing alternatives, see page 177.
- ✓ For community custody eligibility, see page 187.
- ✓ For any applicable enhancements other than deadly weapon enhancement, see page 183.
- ✓ Per RCW 69.50.408, the statutory maximum for a **subsequent conviction** under chapter 69.50 RCW is 120 months.

The Caseload Forecast Council is not liable for errors or omissions in the manual, for sentences that may be inappropriately calculated as a result of a practitioner's or court's reliance on the manual, or for any other written or verbal information related to adult or juvenile sentencing. The scoring sheets are intended to provide assistance in most cases but do not cover all permutations of the scoring rules. If you find any errors or omissions, we encourage you to report them to the Caseload Forecast Council.

Kidnapping First Degree

RCW 9A.40.020
CLASS A – SERIOUS VIOLENT
OFFENDER SCORING RCW 9.94A.525(9)

If the present conviction is for a felony domestic violence offense where domestic violence was plead and proven, use the General Serious Violent Offense Where Domestic Violence Has Been Plead and Proven scoring form on page 196.

ADULT HISTORY:
    Enter number of serious violent felony convictions .... _____ x 3 = _____
    Enter number of violent felony convictions .... _____ x 2 = _____
    Enter number of nonviolent felony convictions .... _____ x 1 = _____

JUVENILE HISTORY:
    Enter number of serious violent felony dispositions .... _____ x 3 = _____
    Enter number of violent felony dispositions .... _____ x 2 = _____
    Enter number of nonviolent felony dispositions .... _____ x ½ = _____

OTHER CURRENT OFFENSES:
(Other current offenses that do not encompass the same conduct count in offender score)
    Enter number of other violent felony convictions .... _____ x 2 = _____
    Enter number of other nonviolent felony convictions .... _____ x 1 = _____

STATUS:
    Was the offender on community custody on the date the current offense was committed? .... + 1 = _____

Total the last column to get the **Offender Score** (Round down to the nearest whole number)

SENTENCE RANGE

	\multicolumn{10}{c}{Offender Score}
	0	**1**	**2**	**3**	**4**	**5**	**6**	**7**	**8**	**9+**
LEVEL X	59.5m	66m	72m	78m	84m	89.5m	114m	126m	150m	230.5m
	51 - 68	57 - 75	62 - 82	67 - 89	72 - 96	77 - 102	98 - 130	108 - 144	129 - 171	149 - 198

- ✓ For attempt, solicitation, conspiracy (RCW 9.94A.595) see page 23 or for gang-related felonies where the court found the offender involved a minor (RCW 9.94A.833) see page 186 for standard range adjustments.
- ✓ For deadly weapon enhancement, see page 190.
- ✓ For sentencing alternatives, see page 177.
- ✓ For community custody eligibility, see page 187.
- ✓ For any applicable enhancements other than deadly weapon enhancement, see page 183.
- ✓ Multiple current serious violent offenses shall have consecutive sentences imposed per the rules of RCW 9.94A.589(1)(b).

The Caseload Forecast Council is not liable for errors or omissions in the manual, for sentences that may be inappropriately calculated as a result of a practitioner's or court's reliance on the manual, or for any other written or verbal information related to adult or juvenile sentencing. The scoring sheets are intended to provide assistance in most cases but do not cover all permutations of the scoring rules. If you find any errors or omissions, we encourage you to report them to the Caseload Forecast Council.

Kidnapping First Degree With A Finding Of Sexual Motivation

RCW 9A.40.020
CLASS A – SERIOUS VIOLENT/SEX
ATTEMPT = CLASS B

OFFENDER SCORING RCW 9.94A.525(17)

ADULT HISTORY:
Enter number of sex offense felony convictions .... _____ x 3 = _____
Enter number of serious violent felony convictions .... _____ x 3 = _____
Enter number of violent felony convictions .... _____ x 2 = _____
Enter number of nonviolent felony convictions .... _____ x 1 = _____

JUVENILE HISTORY:
Enter number of sex offense felony dispositions .... _____ x 3 = _____
Enter number of serious violent felony dispositions .... _____ x 3 = _____
Enter number of violent felony dispositions .... _____ x 2 = _____
Enter number of nonviolent felony dispositions .... _____ x ½ = _____

OTHER CURRENT OFFENSES:
(Other current offenses that do not encompass the same conduct count in offender score)
Enter number of other sex offense felony convictions .... _____ x 3 = _____
Enter number of other violent felony convictions .... _____ x 2 = _____
Enter number of other nonviolent felony convictions .... _____ x 1 = _____

STATUS:
Was the offender on community custody on the date the current offense was committed?.......... + 1 = _____

Total the last column to get the **Offender Score** (Round down to the nearest whole number) _____

SENTENCE RANGE

	Offender Score									
	0	1	2	3	4	5	6	7	8	9+
LEVEL X	59.5m	66m	72m	78m	84m	89.5m	114m	126m	150m	230.5m
	51 - 68	57 - 75	62 - 82	67 - 89	72 - 96	77 - 102	98 - 130	108 - 144	129 - 171	149 - 198

Add Sexual Motivation Enhancement (see page 185) _____ to Standard Range = Low _____ to High _____

- ✓ For attempt, (RCW 9.94A.595) see page 23 or for gang-related felonies where the court found the offender involved a minor (RCW 9.94A.833) see page 186 for standard range adjustments.
- ✓ For deadly weapon enhancement, see page 190.
- ✓ For sentencing alternatives, see page 177.
- ✓ For community custody eligibility, see page 187.
- ✓ For any applicable enhancements other than deadly weapon enhancement, see page 183.
- ✓ Multiple current serious violent offenses shall have consecutive sentences imposed per the rules of RCW 9.94A.589(1)(b).
- ✓ If the offender is not a persistent offender and the current offense was committed on or after 9/1/2001, then the offender is subject to the requirements under RCW 9.94A.507.
- ✓ Per RCW 9.94A.507(3)(c)(ii), excluding convictions for an attempt, the minimum term shall be either the maximum of the standard sentence range for the offense or 25 years, whichever is greater, for a finding that the victim was **under the age of 15** at the time of the offense under RCW 9.94A.837 or found to be **developmentally disabled, mentally disordered, a frail elder or vulnerable adult** at the time of the offense under RCW 9.94A.838.

The Caseload Forecast Council is not liable for errors or omissions in the manual, for sentences that may be inappropriately calculated as a result of a practitioner's or court's reliance on the manual, or for any other written or verbal information related to adult or juvenile sentencing. The scoring sheets are intended to provide assistance in most cases but do not cover all permutations of the scoring rules. If you find any errors or omissions, we encourage you to report them to the Caseload Forecast Council.

Kidnapping First Degree With A Finding Of Sexual Motivation

RCW 9A.40.020
SERIOUS VIOLENT/SEX
SOLICIATION/CONSPIRACY = CLASS B*

OFFENDER SCORING RCW 9.94A.525(17)

ADULT HISTORY:
Enter number of sex offense felony convictions .... _____ x 3 = _____
Enter number of serious violent felony convictions .... _____ x 3 = _____
Enter number of violent felony convictions .... _____ x 2 = _____
Enter number of nonviolent felony convictions .... _____ x 1 = _____

JUVENILE HISTORY:
Enter number of sex offense felony dispositions .... _____ x 3 = _____
Enter number of serious violent felony dispositions .... _____ x 3 = _____
Enter number of violent felony dispositions .... _____ x 2 = _____
Enter number of nonviolent felony dispositions .... _____ x ½ = _____

OTHER CURRENT OFFENSES:
(Other current offenses that do not encompass the same conduct count in offender score)
Enter number of other sex offense felony convictions .... _____ x 3 = _____
Enter number of other violent felony convictions .... _____ x 2 = _____
Enter number of other nonviolent felony convictions .... _____ x 1 = _____

STATUS:
Was the offender on community custody on the date the current offense was committed? .... + 1 = _____

Total the last column to get the **Offender Score** (Round down to the nearest whole number)

SENTENCE RANGE

	\multicolumn{10}{c	}{Offender Score}
	0	1	2	3	4	5	6	7	8	9+
LEVEL X	59.5m 51 - 68	66m 57 - 75	72m 62 - 82	78m 67 - 89	84m 72 - 96	89.5m 77 - 102	114m 98 - 130	114m 108 - 120*	120 - 120*	120 - 120*

Add Sexual Motivation Enhancement (see page 185) [ ] to Standard Range = [Low] to [High]

- ✓ For solicitation, conspiracy (RCW 9.94A.595) see page 23 or for gang-related felonies where the court found the offender involved a minor (RCW 9.94A.833) see page 186 for standard range adjustments.
- ✓ For deadly weapon enhancement, see page 190.
- ✓ For sentencing alternatives, see page 177.
- ✓ For community custody eligibility, see page 187.
- ✓ For any applicable enhancements other than deadly weapon enhancement, see page 183.
- ✓ Multiple current serious violent offenses shall have consecutive sentences imposed per the rules of RCW 9.94A.589(1)(b).
- ✓ If the offender is not a persistent offender and has a prior conviction for an offense listed in RCW 9.94A.030(38)(b), then the sentence is subject to the requirements of RCW 9.94A.507.

The Caseload Forecast Council is not liable for errors or omissions in the manual, for sentences that may be inappropriately calculated as a result of a practitioner's or court's reliance on the manual, or for any other written or verbal information related to adult or juvenile sentencing. The scoring sheets are intended to provide assistance in most cases but do not cover all permutations of the scoring rules. If you find any errors or omissions, we encourage you to report them to the Caseload Forecast Council.

Kidnapping Second Degree

RCW 9A.40.030(3)(a)
CLASS B – VIOLENT
OFFENDER SCORING RCW 9.94A.525(8)

If the present conviction is for a felony domestic violence offense where domestic violence was plead and proven, use the General Violent Offense Where Domestic Violence Has Been Plead and Proven scoring form on page 199.

ADULT HISTORY:
- Enter number of serious violent and violent felony convictions .... _____ x 2 = _____
- Enter number of nonviolent felony convictions .... _____ x 1 = _____

JUVENILE HISTORY:
- Enter number of serious violent and violent felony dispositions .... _____ x 2 = _____
- Enter number of nonviolent felony dispositions .... _____ x ½ = _____

OTHER CURRENT OFFENSES:
(Other current offenses that do not encompass the same conduct count in offender score)
- Enter number of other serious violent and violent felony convictions .... _____ x 2 = _____
- Enter number of other nonviolent felony convictions .... _____ x 1 = _____

STATUS:
- Was the offender on community custody on the date the current offense was committed? (if yes) ...... + 1 = _____

Total the last column to get the **Offender Score** (Round down to the nearest whole number)

SENTENCE RANGE

	\multicolumn{10}{c}{Offender Score}
	0	**1**	**2**	**3**	**4**	**5**	**6**	**7**	**8**	**9+**
LEVEL V	9m 6 - 12	13m 12+ - 14	15m 13 - 17	17.5m 15 - 20	25.5m 22 - 29	38m 33 - 43	47.5m 41 - 54	59.5m 51 - 68	72m 62 - 82	84m 72 - 96

- ✓ For attempt, solicitation, conspiracy (RCW 9.94A.595) see page 23 or for gang-related felonies where the court found the offender involved a minor (RCW 9.94A.833) see page 186 for standard range adjustments.
- ✓ For deadly weapon enhancement, see page 190.
- ✓ For sentencing alternatives, see page 177.
- ✓ For community custody eligibility, see page 187.
- ✓ For any applicable enhancements other than deadly weapon enhancement, see page 183.

The Caseload Forecast Council is not liable for errors or omissions in the manual, for sentences that may be inappropriately calculated as a result of a practitioner's or court's reliance on the manual, or for any other written or verbal information related to adult or juvenile sentencing. The scoring sheets are intended to provide assistance in most cases but do not cover all permutations of the scoring rules. If you find any errors or omissions, we encourage you to report them to the Caseload Forecast Council.

Kidnapping Second Degree With A Finding Of Sexual Motivation

RCW 9A.40.030(3)(b)
CLASS A – VIOLENT/SEX
ATTEMPT = CLASS B

OFFENDER SCORING RCW 9.94A.525(17)

ADULT HISTORY:
Enter number of sex offense felony convictions .... _____ x 3 = _____
Enter number of serious violent and violent felony convictions .... _____ x 2 = _____
Enter number of nonviolent felony convictions .... _____ x 1 = _____

JUVENILE HISTORY:
Enter number of sex offense felony dispositions .... _____ x 3 = _____
Enter number of serious violent and violent felony dispositions .... _____ x 2 = _____
Enter number of nonviolent felony dispositions .... _____ x ½ = _____

OTHER CURRENT OFFENSES:
(Other current offenses that do not encompass the same conduct count in offender score)
Enter number of other sex offense felony dispositions .... _____ x 3 = _____
Enter number of other serious violent and violent felony convictions .... _____ x 2 = _____
Enter number of other nonviolent felony convictions .... _____ x 1 = _____

STATUS:
Was the offender on community custody on the date the current offense was committed? (if yes)....... + 1 = _____

Total the last column to get the **Offender Score** (Round down to the nearest whole number)

SENTENCE RANGE

	\multicolumn{11}{c}{Offender Score}
	0	**1**	**2**	**3**	**4**	**5**	**6**	**7**	**8**	**9+**
LEVEL V	9m	13m	15m	17.5m	25.5m	38m	47.5m	59.5m	72m	84m
	6 - 12	12+ - 14	13 - 17	15 - 20	22 - 29	33 - 43	41 - 54	51 - 68	62 - 82	72 - 96

Add Sexual Motivation Enhancement (see page 185) _____ to Standard Range = Low _____ to High _____

- ✓ For attempt, (RCW 9.94A.595) see page 23 or for gang-related felonies where the court found the offender involved a minor (RCW 9.94A.833) see page 186 for standard range adjustments.
- ✓ For deadly weapon enhancement, see page 190.
- ✓ For sentencing alternatives, see page 177.
- ✓ For community custody eligibility, see page 187.
- ✓ For any applicable enhancements other than deadly weapon enhancement, see page 183.
- ✓ If the offender is not a persistent offender and the <u>current offense</u> was committed on or after 9/1/2001, then the offender is subject to the requirements under RCW 9.94A.507.

The Caseload Forecast Council is not liable for errors or omissions in the manual, for sentences that may be inappropriately calculated as a result of a practitioner's or court's reliance on the manual, or for any other written or verbal information related to adult or juvenile sentencing. The scoring sheets are intended to provide assistance in most cases but do not cover all permutations of the scoring rules. If you find any errors or omissions, we encourage you to report them to the Caseload Forecast Council.

Kidnapping Second Degree With A Finding Of Sexual Motivation

RCW 9A.40.030(3)(b)
VIOLENT/SEX
SOLICITATION/CONSPIRACY = CLASS B

OFFENDER SCORING RCW 9.94A.525(17)

ADULT HISTORY:
Enter number of sex offense felony convictions .... _____ x 3 = _____
Enter number of serious violent and violent felony convictions .... _____ x 2 = _____
Enter number of nonviolent felony convictions .... _____ x 1 = _____

JUVENILE HISTORY:
Enter number of sex offense felony dispositions .... _____ x 3 = _____
Enter number of serious violent and violent felony dispositions .... _____ x 2 = _____
Enter number of nonviolent felony dispositions .... _____ x ½ = _____

OTHER CURRENT OFFENSES:
(Other current offenses that do not encompass the same conduct count in offender score)
Enter number of other sex offense felony dispositions .... _____ x 3 = _____
Enter number of other serious violent and violent felony convictions .... _____ x 2 = _____
Enter number of other nonviolent felony convictions .... _____ x 1 = _____

STATUS:
Was the offender on community custody on the date the current offense was committed? (if yes) ...... + 1 = _____

Total the last column to get the **Offender Score** (Round down to the nearest whole number) [____]

SENTENCE RANGE

	Offender Score									
	0	1	2	3	4	5	6	7	8	9+
LEVEL V	9m	13m	15m	17.5m	25.5m	38m	47.5m	59.5m	72m	84m
	6 - 12	12+ - 14	13 - 17	15 - 20	22 - 29	33 - 43	41 - 54	51 - 68	62 - 82	72 - 96

Add Sexual Motivation Enhancement (see page 185) [____] to Standard Range = [Low] to [High]

- ✓ For solicitation, conspiracy (RCW 9.94A.595) see page 23 or for gang-related felonies where the court found the offender involved a minor (RCW 9.94A.833) see page 186 for standard range adjustments.
- ✓ For deadly weapon enhancement, see page 190.
- ✓ For sentencing alternatives, see page 177.
- ✓ For community custody eligibility, see page 187.
- ✓ For any applicable enhancements other than deadly weapon enhancement, see page 183.
- ✓ If the offender is not a persistent offender and has a prior conviction for an offense listed in RCW 9.94A.030(38)(b), then the sentence is subject to the requirements of RCW 9.94A.507.

The Caseload Forecast Council is not liable for errors or omissions in the manual, for sentences that may be inappropriately calculated as a result of a practitioner's or court's reliance on the manual, or for any other written or verbal information related to adult or juvenile sentencing. The scoring sheets are intended to provide assistance in most cases but do not cover all permutations of the scoring rules. If you find any errors or omissions, we encourage you to report them to the Caseload Forecast Council.

Leading Organized Crime Inciting Criminal Profiteering

RCW 9A.82.060(1)(b)
CLASS B* – NONVIOLENT
OFFENDER SCORING RCW 9.94A.525(7)

If it was found that this offense was committed with sexual motivation (RCW 9.94A.533(8)) on or after 7/01/2006, use the General Nonviolent Offense with a Sexual Motivation Finding scoring form on page 193.

If the present conviction is for a felony domestic violence offense where domestic violence was plead and proven, use the General Nonviolent Offense Where Domestic Violence Has Been Plead and Proven scoring form on page 191.

ADULT HISTORY:
　Enter number of felony convictions .... _____ x 1 = _____

JUVENILE HISTORY:
　Enter number of serious violent and violent felony dispositions .... _____ x 1 = _____
　Enter number of nonviolent felony dispositions .... _____ x ½ = _____

OTHER CURRENT OFFENSES:
(Other current offenses that do not encompass the same conduct count in offender score)
　Enter number of other felony convictions .... _____ x 1 = _____

STATUS:
　Was the offender on community custody on the date the current offense was committed? (if yes) .... + 1 = _____

Total the last column to get the **Offender Score** (Round down to the nearest whole number)

SENTENCE RANGE

	\multicolumn{10}{c}{Offender Score}
	0	1	2	3	4	5	6	7	8	9+
LEVEL IX	36m 31 - 41	42m 36 - 48	47.5m 41 - 54	53.5m 46 - 61	59.5m 51 - 68	66m 57 - 75	89.5m 77 - 102	101.5m 87 - 116	114m 108 - 120*	120- 120*

- ✓ For attempt, solicitation, conspiracy (RCW 9.94A.595) see page 23 or for gang-related felonies where the court found the offender involved a minor (RCW 9.94A.833) see page 186 for standard range adjustments.
- ✓ For deadly weapon enhancement, see page 190.
- ✓ For sentencing alternatives, see page 177.
- ✓ For community custody eligibility, see page 187.
- ✓ For any applicable enhancements other than deadly weapon enhancement, see page 183.

The Caseload Forecast Council is not liable for errors or omissions in the manual, for sentences that may be inappropriately calculated as a result of a practitioner's or court's reliance on the manual, or for any other written or verbal information related to adult or juvenile sentencing. The scoring sheets are intended to provide assistance in most cases but do not cover all permutations of the scoring rules. If you find any errors or omissions, we encourage you to report them to the Caseload Forecast Council.

Leading Organized Crime Organizing Criminal Profiteering

RCW 9A.82.060(1)(a)
CLASS A – VIOLENT

OFFENDER SCORING RCW 9.94A.525(8)

If it was found that this offense was committed with sexual motivation (RCW 9.94A.533(8)) on or after 7/01/2006, use the General Violent Offense with a Sexual Motivation Finding scoring form on page 201.

If the present conviction is for a felony domestic violence offense where domestic violence was plead and proven, use the General Violent Offense Where Domestic Violence Has Been Plead and Proven scoring form on page 199.

ADULT HISTORY:
    Enter number of serious violent and violent felony convictions .... _____ x 2 = _____
    Enter number of nonviolent felony convictions .... _____ x 1 = _____

JUVENILE HISTORY:
    Enter number of serious violent and violent felony dispositions .... _____ x 2 = _____
    Enter number of nonviolent felony dispositions .... _____ x ½ = _____

OTHER CURRENT OFFENSES:
(Other current offenses that do not encompass the same conduct count in offender score)
    Enter number of other serious violent and violent felony convictions .... _____ x 2 = _____
    Enter number of other nonviolent felony convictions .... _____ x 1 = _____

STATUS:
    Was the offender on community custody on the date the current offense was committed? (if yes) ...... + 1 = _____

Total the last column to get the **Offender Score** (Round down to the nearest whole number)

SENTENCE RANGE

	\multicolumn{10}{c}{Offender Score}
	0	1	2	3	4	5	6	7	8	9+
LEVEL X	59.5m 51 - 68	66m 57 - 75	72m 62 - 82	78m 67 - 89	84m 72 - 96	89.5m 77 - 102	114m 98 - 130	126m 108 - 144	150m 129 - 171	230.5m 149 - 198

- ✓ For attempt, solicitation, conspiracy (RCW 9.94A.595) see page 23 or for gang-related felonies where the court found the offender involved a minor (RCW 9.94A.833) see page 186 for standard range adjustments.
- ✓ For deadly weapon enhancement, see page 190.
- ✓ For sentencing alternatives, see page 177.
- ✓ For community custody eligibility, see page 187.
- ✓ For any applicable enhancements other than deadly weapon enhancement, see page 183.

The Caseload Forecast Council is not liable for errors or omissions in the manual, for sentences that may be inappropriately calculated as a result of a practitioner's or court's reliance on the manual, or for any other written or verbal information related to adult or juvenile sentencing. The scoring sheets are intended to provide assistance in most cases but do not cover all permutations of the scoring rules. If you find any errors or omissions, we encourage you to report them to the Caseload Forecast Council.

Maintaining A Dwelling Or Place For Controlled Substances

RCW 69.50.402
CLASS C* – NONVIOLENT/DRUG
OFFENDER SCORING RCW 9.94A.525(13)

If it was found that this offense was committed with sexual motivation (RCW 9.94A.533(8)) on or after 7/01/2006, use the General Drug Offense with a Sexual Motivation Finding scoring form on page 195.

If the present conviction is for a felony domestic violence offense where domestic violence was plead and proven, use the General Drug Offense Where Domestic Violence Has Been Plead and Proven scoring form on page 194.

ADULT HISTORY:
    Does the offender have a prior sex or serious violent offense in history?
        YES Enter number of felony drug convictions .... _____ x 3 = _____
        NO Enter number of felony drug convictions .... _____ x 1 = _____
    Enter number of felony convictions .... _____ x 1 = _____

JUVENILE HISTORY:
    Does the offender have a prior sex or serious violent offense in history?
        YES Enter number of felony drug dispositions... _____ x 2 = _____
        NO Enter number of felony drug dispositions .... _____ x ½ = _____
    Enter number of serious violent and violent felony dispositions .... _____ x 1 = _____
    Enter number of nonviolent felony dispositions .... _____ x ½ = _____

OTHER CURRENT OFFENSES:
(Other current offenses that do not encompass the same conduct count in offender score)
    Does the offender have other prior sex or serious violent offense in history?
        YES Enter number of other felony drug convictions .... _____ x 3 = _____
        NO Enter number of other felony drug convictions .... _____ x 1 = _____
    Enter number of other felony convictions .... _____ x 1 = _____

STATUS:
    Was the offender on community custody on the date the current offense was committed? (if yes)....... + 1 = _____

Total the last column to get the **Offender Score** (Round down to the nearest whole number)

SENTENCE RANGE – DRUG

	Offender Score		
	0 to 2	3 to 5	6 to 9+
LEVEL II	16m 12+ - 20	22m 20+ - 24*	24*

- ✓ For attempt, solicitation or conspiracy drug felonies see page 25 or for gang-related felonies where the court found the offender involved a minor (RCW 9.94A.833) see page 186 for standard range adjustments.
- ✓ Per RCW 9.94A.518, any felony offense under chapter 69.50 RCW with a deadly weapon special verdict under RCW 9.94A.602 becomes a level III offense.
- ✓ For deadly weapon enhancement, see page 190.
- ✓ For sentencing alternatives, see page 177.
- ✓ For community custody eligibility, see page 187.
- ✓ For any applicable enhancements other than deadly weapon enhancement, see page 183.
- ✓ Per RCW 69.50.402, any person who violates this section may be imprisoned for not more than 24 months.
- ✓ Per RCW 69.50.408, the statutory maximum for a **subsequent conviction** under chapter 69.50 RCW is 48 months.

The Caseload Forecast Council is not liable for errors or omissions in the manual, for sentences that may be inappropriately calculated as a result of a practitioner's or court's reliance on the manual, or for any other written or verbal information related to adult or juvenile sentencing. The scoring sheets are intended to provide assistance in most cases but do not cover all permutations of the scoring rules. If you find any errors or omissions, we encourage you to report them to the Caseload Forecast Council.

Maintaining A Dwelling Or Place For Controlled Substances (Subsequent)

RCW 69.50.402
CLASS C* – NONVIOLENT/DRUG

OFFENDER SCORING RCW 9.94A.525(13)

If it was found that this offense was committed with sexual motivation (RCW 9.94A.533(8)) on or after 7/01/2006, use the General Drug Offense with a Sexual Motivation Finding scoring form on page 195.

If the present conviction is for a felony domestic violence offense where domestic violence was plead and proven, use the General Drug Offense Where Domestic Violence Has Been Plead and Proven scoring form on page 194.

ADULT HISTORY:
    Does the offender have a prior sex or serious violent offense in history?
        YES Enter number of felony drug convictions.. _____   x 3 = _____
        NO Enter number of felony drug convictions.. _____   x 1 = _____
    Enter number of felony convictions .... _____   x 1 = _____

JUVENILE HISTORY:
    Does the offender have a prior sex or serious violent offense in history?
        YES Enter number of felony drug dispositions.. _____   x 2 = _____
        NO Enter number of felony drug dispositions.. _____   x ½ = _____
    Enter number of serious violent and violent felony dispositions .... _____   x 1 = _____
    Enter number of nonviolent felony dispositions .... _____   x ½ = _____

OTHER CURRENT OFFENSES:
(Other current offenses that do not encompass the same conduct count in offender score)
    Does the offender have other prior sex or serious violent offense in history?
        YES Enter number of other felony drug convictions.. _____   x 3 = _____
        NO Enter number of other felony drug convictions .... _____   x 1 = _____
    Enter number of other felony convictions .... _____   x 1 = _____

STATUS:
    Was the offender on community custody on the date the current offense was committed? (if yes) ...... + 1 = _____

Total the last column to get the **Offender Score** (Round down to the nearest whole number)

SENTENCE RANGE – DRUG

	Offender Score		
	0 to 2	**3 to 5**	**6 to 9+**
LEVEL II	16m 12+ - 20	34m 20+ - 48*	48*

- ✓ For attempt, solicitation or conspiracy drug felonies see page 25 or for gang-related felonies where the court found the offender involved a minor (RCW 9.94A.833) see page 186 for standard range adjustments.
- ✓ Per RCW 9.94A.518, any felony offense under chapter 69.50 RCW with a deadly weapon special verdict under RCW 9.94A.602 becomes a level III offense.
- ✓ For deadly weapon enhancement, see page 190.
- ✓ For sentencing alternatives, see page 177.
- ✓ For community custody eligibility, see page 187.
- ✓ For any applicable enhancements other than deadly weapon enhancement, see page 183.
- ✓ Per RCW 69.50.408, the statutory maximum for a **subsequent conviction** under chapter 69.50 RCW is 48 months.

The Caseload Forecast Council is not liable for errors or omissions in the manual, for sentences that may be inappropriately calculated as a result of a practitioner's or court's reliance on the manual, or for any other written or verbal information related to adult or juvenile sentencing. The scoring sheets are intended to provide assistance in most cases but do not cover all permutations of the scoring rules. If you find any errors or omissions, we encourage you to report them to the Caseload Forecast Council.

Malicious Explosion Of A Substance First Degree

RCW 70.74.280(1)
CLASS A – VIOLENT

OFFENDER SCORING RCW 9.94A.525(8)

If it was found that this offense was committed with sexual motivation (RCW 9.94A.533(8)) on or after 7/01/2006, use the General Violent Offense with a Sexual Motivation Finding scoring form on page 201.

If the present conviction is for a felony domestic violence offense where domestic violence was plead and proven, use the General Violent Offense Where Domestic Violence Has Been Plead and Proven scoring form on page 199.

ADULT HISTORY:
Enter number of serious violent and violent felony convictions .... _____ x 2 = _____
Enter number of nonviolent felony convictions .... _____ x 1 = _____

JUVENILE HISTORY:
Enter number of serious violent and violent felony dispositions .... _____ x 2 = _____
Enter number of nonviolent felony dispositions .... _____ x ½ = _____

OTHER CURRENT OFFENSES:
(Other current offenses that do not encompass the same conduct count in offender score)
Enter number of other serious violent and violent felony convictions .... _____ x 2 = _____
Enter number of other nonviolent felony convictions .... _____ x 1 = _____

STATUS:
Was the offender on community custody on the date the current offense was committed? (if yes) .... + 1 = _____

Total the last column to get the **Offender Score** (Round down to the nearest whole number)

SENTENCE RANGE

	\				Offender Score					
	0	**1**	**2**	**3**	**4**	**5**	**6**	**7**	**8**	**9+**
LEVEL XV	280m	291.5m	304m	316m	327.5m	339.5m	364m	394m	431.5m	479.5m
	240 - 320	250 - 333	261 - 347	271 - 361	281 - 374	291 - 388	312 - 416	338 - 450	370 - 493	411 - 548

- ✓ For attempt, solicitation, conspiracy (RCW 9.94A.595) see page 23 or for gang-related felonies where the court found the offender involved a minor (RCW 9.94A.833) see page 186 for standard range adjustments.
- ✓ For deadly weapon enhancement, see page 190.
- ✓ For sentencing alternatives, see page 177.
- ✓ For community custody eligibility, see page 187.
- ✓ For any applicable enhancements other than deadly weapon enhancement, see page 183.

The Caseload Forecast Council is not liable for errors or omissions in the manual, for sentences that may be inappropriately calculated as a result of a practitioner's or court's reliance on the manual, or for any other written or verbal information related to adult or juvenile sentencing. The scoring sheets are intended to provide assistance in most cases but do not cover all permutations of the scoring rules. If you find any errors or omissions, we encourage you to report them to the Caseload Forecast Council.

Malicious Explosion Of A Substance Second Degree

RCW 70.74.280(2)
CLASS A – VIOLENT

OFFENDER SCORING RCW 9.94A.525(8)

If it was found that this offense was committed with sexual motivation (RCW 9.94A.533(8)) on or after 7/01/2006, use the General Violent Offense with a Sexual Motivation Finding scoring form on page 201.

If the present conviction is for a felony domestic violence offense where domestic violence was plead and proven, use the General Violent Offense Where Domestic Violence Has Been Plead and Proven scoring form on page 199.

ADULT HISTORY:
    Enter number of serious violent and violent felony convictions .... _____ x 2 = _____

    Enter number of nonviolent felony convictions .... _____ x 1 = _____

JUVENILE HISTORY:
    Enter number of serious violent and violent felony dispositions .... _____ x 2 = _____

    Enter number of nonviolent felony dispositions .... _____ x ½ = _____

OTHER CURRENT OFFENSES:
(Other current offenses that do not encompass the same conduct count in offender score)
    Enter number of other serious violent and violent felony convictions .... _____ x 2 = _____

    Enter number of other nonviolent felony convictions .... _____ x 1 = _____

STATUS:
    Was the offender on community custody on the date the current offense was committed? (if yes) ...... + 1 = _____

Total the last column to get the **Offender Score** (Round down to the nearest whole number)

SENTENCE RANGE

	\multicolumn{10}{c}{Offender Score}
	0	1	2	3	4	5	6	7	8	9+
LEVEL XIII	143.5m	156m	168m	179.5m	192m	204m	227.5m	252m	299.5m	347.5m
	123 - 164	134 - 178	144 - 192	154 - 205	165 - 219	175 - 233	195 - 260	216 - 288	257 - 342	298 - 397

- ✓ For attempt, solicitation, conspiracy (RCW 9.94A.595) see page 23 or for gang-related felonies where the court found the offender involved a minor (RCW 9.94A.833) see page 186 for standard range adjustments.
- ✓ For deadly weapon enhancement, see page 190.
- ✓ For sentencing alternatives, see page 177.
- ✓ For community custody eligibility, see page 187.
- ✓ For any applicable enhancements other than deadly weapon enhancement, see page 183.

The Caseload Forecast Council is not liable for errors or omissions in the manual, for sentences that may be inappropriately calculated as a result of a practitioner's or court's reliance on the manual, or for any other written or verbal information related to adult or juvenile sentencing. The scoring sheets are intended to provide assistance in most cases but do not cover all permutations of the scoring rules. If you find any errors or omissions, we encourage you to report them to the Caseload Forecast Council.

Malicious Explosion Of A Substance Third Degree

RCW 70.74.280(3)
CLASS B* – NONVIOLENT
OFFENDER SCORING RCW 9.94A.525(7)

If it was found that this offense was committed with sexual motivation (RCW 9.94A.533(8)) on or after 7/01/2006, use the General Nonviolent Offense with a Sexual Motivation Finding scoring form on page 193.

If the present conviction is for a felony domestic violence offense where domestic violence was plead and proven, use the General Nonviolent Offense Where Domestic Violence Has Been Plead and Proven scoring form on page 191.

ADULT HISTORY:
Enter number of felony convictions .... _____ x 1 = _____

JUVENILE HISTORY:
Enter number of serious violent and violent felony dispositions .... _____ x 1 = _____
Enter number of nonviolent felony dispositions .... _____ x ½ = _____

OTHER CURRENT OFFENSES:
(Other current offenses that do not encompass the same conduct count in offender score)
Enter number of other felony convictions .... _____ x 1 = _____

STATUS:
Was the offender on community custody on the date the current offense was committed? (if yes) .... + 1 = _____

Total the last column to get the **Offender Score** (Round down to the nearest whole number)

SENTENCE RANGE

	\multicolumn{10}{c	}{Offender Score}

	0	1	2	3	4	5	6	7	8	9+
LEVEL X	59.5m	66m	72m	78m	84m	89.5m	109m	114m		
	51 - 68	57 - 75	62 - 82	67 - 89	72 - 96	77 - 102	98 - 120*	108 - 120*	120 - 120*	120 - 120*

- ✓ For attempt, solicitation, conspiracy (RCW 9.94A.595) see page 23 or for gang-related felonies where the court found the offender involved a minor (RCW 9.94A.833) see page 186 for standard range adjustments.
- ✓ For deadly weapon enhancement, see page 190.
- ✓ For sentencing alternatives, see page 177.
- ✓ For community custody eligibility, see page 187.
- ✓ For any applicable enhancements other than deadly weapon enhancement, see page 183.

The Caseload Forecast Council is not liable for errors or omissions in the manual, for sentences that may be inappropriately calculated as a result of a practitioner's or court's reliance on the manual, or for any other written or verbal information related to adult or juvenile sentencing. The scoring sheets are intended to provide assistance in most cases but do not cover all permutations of the scoring rules. If you find any errors or omissions, we encourage you to report them to the Caseload Forecast Council.

Malicious Harassment

RCW 9A.36.080
CLASS C* – NONVIOLENT
OFFENDER SCORING RCW 9.94A.525(7)

If it was found that this offense was committed with sexual motivation (RCW 9.94A.533(8)) on or after 7/01/2006, use the General Nonviolent Offense with a Sexual Motivation Finding scoring form on page 193.

If the present conviction is for a felony domestic violence offense where domestic violence was plead and proven, use the General Nonviolent Offense Where Domestic Violence Has Been Plead and Proven scoring form on page 191.

ADULT HISTORY:
    Enter number of felony convictions .... _____ x 1 = _____

JUVENILE HISTORY:
    Enter number of serious violent and violent felony dispositions .... _____ x 1 = _____
    Enter number of nonviolent felony dispositions .... _____ x ½ = _____

OTHER CURRENT OFFENSES:
(Other current offenses that do not encompass the same conduct count in offender score)
    Enter number of other felony convictions .... _____ x 1 = _____

STATUS:
    Was the offender on community custody on the date the current offense was committed? (if yes) ...... + 1 = _____

Total the last column to get the **Offender Score** (Round down to the nearest whole number)

SENTENCE RANGE

	\multicolumn{11}{c}{Offender Score}
	0	1	2	3	4	5	6	7	8	9+
LEVEL IV	6m 3 - 9	9m 6 - 12	13m 12+ - 14	15m 13 - 17	17.5m 15 - 20	25.5m 22 - 29	38m 33 - 43	50m 43 - 57	56.5m 53 - 60*	60 - 60*

- ✓ For or gang-related felonies where the court found the offender involved a minor (RCW 9.94A.833) see page 186 for standard range adjustment.
- ✓ For deadly weapon enhancement, see page 190.
- ✓ For sentencing alternatives, see page 177.
- ✓ For community custody eligibility, see page 187.
- ✓ For any applicable enhancements other than deadly weapon enhancement, see page 183.

The Caseload Forecast Council is not liable for errors or omissions in the manual, for sentences that may be inappropriately calculated as a result of a practitioner's or court's reliance on the manual, or for any other written or verbal information related to adult or juvenile sentencing. The scoring sheets are intended to provide assistance in most cases but do not cover all permutations of the scoring rules. If you find any errors or omissions, we encourage you to report them to the Caseload Forecast Council.

Malicious Injury To Railroad Property

RCW 81.60.070
CLASS B – NONVIOLENT

OFFENDER SCORING RCW 9.94A.525(7)

If it was found that this offense was committed with sexual motivation (RCW 9.94A.533(8)) on or after 7/01/2006, use the General Nonviolent Offense with a Sexual Motivation Finding scoring form on page 193.

If the present conviction is for a felony domestic violence offense where domestic violence was plead and proven, use the General Nonviolent Offense Where Domestic Violence Has Been Plead and Proven scoring form on page 191.

ADULT HISTORY:
    Enter number of felony convictions .... _____ x 1 = _____

JUVENILE HISTORY:
    Enter number of serious violent and violent felony dispositions .... _____ x 1 = _____
    Enter number of nonviolent felony dispositions .... _____ x ½ = _____

OTHER CURRENT OFFENSES:
(Other current offenses that do not encompass the same conduct count in offender score)
    Enter number of other felony convictions .... _____ x 1 = _____

STATUS:
    Was the offender on community custody on the date the current offense was committed? (if yes)....... + 1 = _____

Total the last column to get the **Offender Score** (Round down to the nearest whole number)

SENTENCE RANGE

	\ Offender Score									
	0	1	2	3	4	5	6	7	8	9+
LEVEL III	2m 1 - 3	5m 3 - 8	8m 4 - 12	11m 9 - 12	14m 12+ - 16	19.5m 17 - 22	25.5m 22 - 29	38m 33 - 43	50m 43 - 57	59.5m 51 - 68

- ✓ For attempt, solicitation, conspiracy (RCW 9.94A.595) see page 23 or for gang-related felonies where the court found the offender involved a minor (RCW 9.94A.833) see page 186 for standard range adjustments.
- ✓ For deadly weapon enhancement, see page 190.
- ✓ For sentencing alternatives, see page 177.
- ✓ For community custody eligibility, see page 187.
- ✓ For any applicable enhancements other than deadly weapon enhancement, see page 183.

The Caseload Forecast Council is not liable for errors or omissions in the manual, for sentences that may be inappropriately calculated as a result of a practitioner's or court's reliance on the manual, or for any other written or verbal information related to adult or juvenile sentencing. The scoring sheets are intended to provide assistance in most cases but do not cover all permutations of the scoring rules. If you find any errors or omissions, we encourage you to report them to the Caseload Forecast Council.

Malicious Mischief First Degree

RCW 9A.48.070
CLASS B – NONVIOLENT
OFFENDER SCORING RCW 9.94A.525(7)

If it was found that this offense was committed with sexual motivation (RCW 9.94A.533(8)) on or after 7/01/2006, use the General Nonviolent Offense with a Sexual Motivation Finding scoring form on page 193.

If the present conviction is for a felony domestic violence offense where domestic violence was plead and proven, use the General Nonviolent Offense Where Domestic Violence Has Been Plead and Proven scoring form on page 191.

ADULT HISTORY:
    Enter number of felony convictions .... _____ x 1 = _____

JUVENILE HISTORY:
    Enter number of serious violent and violent felony dispositions .... _____ x 1 = _____
    Enter number of nonviolent felony dispositions .... _____ x ½ = _____

OTHER CURRENT OFFENSES:
(Other current offenses that do not encompass the same conduct count in offender score)
    Enter number of other felony convictions .... _____ x 1 = _____

STATUS:
    Was the offender on community custody on the date the current offense was committed? (if yes) ...... + 1 = _____

Total the last column to get the **Offender Score** (Round down to the nearest whole number)

SENTENCE RANGE

	Offender Score									
	0	1	2	3	4	5	6	7	8	9+
LEVEL II	0-90 days	4m 2 - 6	6m 3 - 9	8m 4 - 12	13m 12+ - 14	16m 14 - 18	19.5m 17 - 22	25.5m 22 - 29	38m 33 - 43	50m 43 - 57

✓ For attempt, solicitation, conspiracy (RCW 9.94A.595) see page 23 or for gang-related felonies where the court found the offender involved a minor (RCW 9.94A.833) see page 186 for standard range adjustments.

✓ For deadly weapon enhancement, see page 190.

✓ For sentencing alternatives, see page 177.

✓ For community custody eligibility, see page 187.

✓ For any applicable enhancements other than deadly weapon enhancement, see page 183.

Malicious Mischief Second Degree

RCW 9A.48.080
CLASS C – NONVIOLENT
OFFENDER SCORING RCW 9.94A.525(7)

If it was found that this offense was committed with sexual motivation (RCW 9.94A.533(8)) on or after 7/01/2006, use the General Nonviolent Offense with a Sexual Motivation Finding scoring form on page 193.

If the present conviction is for a felony domestic violence offense where domestic violence was plead and proven, use the General Nonviolent Offense Where Domestic Violence Has Been Plead and Proven scoring form on page 191.

ADULT HISTORY:
    Enter number of felony convictions .... _____ x 1 = _____

JUVENILE HISTORY:
    Enter number of serious violent and violent felony dispositions .... _____ x 1 = _____
    Enter number of nonviolent felony dispositions .... _____ x ½ = _____

OTHER CURRENT OFFENSES:
(Other current offenses that do not encompass the same conduct count in offender score)
    Enter number of other felony convictions .... _____ x 1 = _____

STATUS:
    Was the offender on community custody on the date the current offense was committed? (if yes) .... + 1 = _____

Total the last column to get the **Offender Score** (Round down to the nearest whole number)

SENTENCE RANGE

	Offender Score									
	0	1	2	3	4	5	6	7	8	9+
LEVEL I	0-60 days	0-90 days	3m 2 - 5	4m 2 - 6	5.5m 3 - 8	8m 4 - 12	13m 12+ - 14	16m 14 - 18	19.5m 17 - 22	25.5m 22 - 29

✓ For gang-related felonies where the court found the offender involved a minor (RCW 9.94A.833) see page 186 for standard range adjustment.

✓ For deadly weapon enhancement, see page 190.

✓ For sentencing alternatives, see page 177.

✓ For community custody eligibility, see page 187.

✓ For any applicable enhancements other than deadly weapon enhancement, see page 183.

The Caseload Forecast Council is not liable for errors or omissions in the manual, for sentences that may be inappropriately calculated as a result of a practitioner's or court's reliance on the manual, or for any other written or verbal information related to adult or juvenile sentencing. The scoring sheets are intended to provide assistance in most cases but do not cover all permutations of the scoring rules. If you find any errors or omissions, we encourage you to report them to the Caseload Forecast Council.

Malicious Placement Of An Explosive First Degree

RCW 70.74.270(1)
CLASS A – VIOLENT

OFFENDER SCORING RCW 9.94A.525(8)

If it was found that this offense was committed with sexual motivation (RCW 9.94A.533(8)) on or after 7/01/2006, use the General Violent Offense with a Sexual Motivation Finding scoring form on page 201.

If the present conviction is for a felony domestic violence offense where domestic violence was plead and proven, use the General Violent Offense Where Domestic Violence Has Been Plead and Proven scoring form on page 199.

ADULT HISTORY:
    Enter number of serious violent and violent felony convictions .... _____ x 2 = _____
    Enter number of nonviolent felony convictions .... _____ x 1 = _____

JUVENILE HISTORY:
    Enter number of serious violent and violent felony dispositions .... _____ x 2 = _____
    Enter number of nonviolent felony dispositions .... _____ x ½ = _____

OTHER CURRENT OFFENSES:
(Other current offenses that do not encompass the same conduct count in offender score)
    Enter number of other serious violent and violent felony convictions .... _____ x 2 = _____
    Enter number of other nonviolent felony convictions .... _____ x 1 = _____

STATUS:
    Was the offender on community custody on the date the current offense was committed? (if yes) ...... + 1 = _____

Total the last column to get the **Offender Score** (Round down to the nearest whole number)

SENTENCE RANGE

Offender Score	0	1	2	3	4	5	6	7	8	9+
LEVEL XIII	143.5m	156m	168m	179.5m	192m	204m	227.5m	252m	299.5m	347.5m
	123 - 164	134 - 178	144 - 192	154 - 205	165 - 219	175 - 233	195 - 260	216 - 288	257 - 342	298 - 397

- ✓ For attempt, solicitation, conspiracy (RCW 9.94A.595) see page 23 or for gang-related felonies where the court found the offender involved a minor (RCW 9.94A.833) see page 186 for standard range adjustments.
- ✓ For deadly weapon enhancement, see page 190.
- ✓ For sentencing alternatives, see page 177.
- ✓ For community custody eligibility, see page 187.
- ✓ For any applicable enhancements other than deadly weapon enhancement, see page 183.

The Caseload Forecast Council is not liable for errors or omissions in the manual, for sentences that may be inappropriately calculated as a result of a practitioner's or court's reliance on the manual, or for any other written or verbal information related to adult or juvenile sentencing. The scoring sheets are intended to provide assistance in most cases but do not cover all permutations of the scoring rules. If you find any errors or omissions, we encourage you to report them to the Caseload Forecast Council.

Malicious Placement Of An Explosive Second Degree

RCW 70.74.270(2)
CLASS B* – NONVIOLENT

OFFENDER SCORING RCW 9.94A.525(7)

If it was found that this offense was committed with sexual motivation (RCW 9.94A.533(8)) on or after 7/01/2006, use the General Nonviolent Offense with a Sexual Motivation Finding scoring form on page 193.

If the present conviction is for a felony domestic violence offense where domestic violence was plead and proven, use the General Nonviolent Offense Where Domestic Violence Has Been Plead and Proven scoring form on page 191.

ADULT HISTORY:
    Enter number of felony convictions .... _____ x 1 = _____

JUVENILE HISTORY:
    Enter number of serious violent and violent felony dispositions .... _____ x 1 = _____
    Enter number of nonviolent felony dispositions .... _____ x ½ = _____

OTHER CURRENT OFFENSES:
(Other current offenses that do not encompass the same conduct count in offender score)
    Enter number of other felony convictions .... _____ x 1 = _____

STATUS:
    Was the offender on community custody on the date the current offense was committed? (if yes)....... + 1 = _____

Total the last column to get the **Offender Score** (Round down to the nearest whole number)

SENTENCE RANGE

	\multicolumn{10}{c}{Offender Score}									
	0	1	2	3	4	5	6	7	8	9+
LEVEL IX	36m 31 - 41	42m 36 - 48	47.5m 41 - 54	53.5m 46 - 61	59.5m 51 - 68	66m 57 - 75	89.5m 77 - 102	101.5m 87 - 116	114m 108 - 120*	120 - 120*

✓ For attempt, solicitation, conspiracy (RCW 9.94A.595) see page 23 or for gang-related felonies where the court found the offender involved a minor (RCW 9.94A.833) see page 186 for standard range adjustments.

✓ For deadly weapon enhancement, see page 190.

✓ For sentencing alternatives, see page 177.

✓ For community custody eligibility, see page 187.

✓ For any applicable enhancements other than deadly weapon enhancement, see page 183.

The Caseload Forecast Council is not liable for errors or omissions in the manual, for sentences that may be inappropriately calculated as a result of a practitioner's or court's reliance on the manual, or for any other written or verbal information related to adult or juvenile sentencing. The scoring sheets are intended to provide assistance in most cases but do not cover all permutations of the scoring rules. If you find any errors or omissions, we encourage you to report them to the Caseload Forecast Council.

Malicious Placement Of An Explosive Third Degree

RCW 70.74.270(3)
CLASS B – NONVIOLENT
OFFENDER SCORING RCW 9.94A.525(7)

If it was found that this offense was committed with sexual motivation (RCW 9.94A.533(8)) on or after 7/01/2006, use the General Nonviolent Offense with a Sexual Motivation Finding scoring form on page 193.

If the present conviction is for a felony domestic violence offense where domestic violence was plead and proven, use the General Nonviolent Offense Where Domestic Violence Has Been Plead and Proven scoring form on page 191.

ADULT HISTORY:
  Enter number of felony convictions .... _____ x 1 = _____

JUVENILE HISTORY:
  Enter number of serious violent and violent felony dispositions .... _____ x 1 = _____
  Enter number of nonviolent felony dispositions .... _____ x ½ = _____

OTHER CURRENT OFFENSES:
(Other current offenses that do not encompass the same conduct count in offender score)
  Enter number of other felony convictions .... _____ x 1 = _____

STATUS:
  Was the offender on community custody on the date the current offense was committed? (if yes) ...... + 1 = _____

Total the last column to get the **Offender Score** (Round down to the nearest whole number)

SENTENCE RANGE

	\multicolumn{10}{c}{Offender Score}
	0	1	2	3	4	5	6	7	8	9+
LEVEL VII	17.5m	24m	30m	36m	42m	47.5m	66m	78m	89.5m	101.5m
	15 - 20	21 - 27	26 - 34	31 - 41	36 - 48	41 - 54	57 - 75	67 - 89	77 - 102	87 - 116

- ✓ For attempt, solicitation, conspiracy (RCW 9.94A.595) see page 23 or for gang-related felonies where the court found the offender involved a minor (RCW 9.94A.833) see page 186 for standard range adjustments.
- ✓ For deadly weapon enhancement, see page 190.
- ✓ For sentencing alternatives, see page 177.
- ✓ For community custody eligibility, see page 187.
- ✓ For any applicable enhancements other than deadly weapon enhancement, see page 183.

Malicious Placement Of An Imitation Device First Degree

RCW 70.74.272(1)(a)
CLASS B* – NONVIOLENT
OFFENDER SCORING RCW 9.94A.525(7)

If it was found that this offense was committed with sexual motivation (RCW 9.94A.533(8)) on or after 7/01/2006, use the General Nonviolent Offense with a Sexual Motivation Finding scoring form on page 193.

If the present conviction is for a felony domestic violence offense where domestic violence was plead and proven, use the General Nonviolent Offense Where Domestic Violence Has Been Plead and Proven scoring form on page 191.

ADULT HISTORY:
    Enter number of felony convictions .... _____ x 1 = _____

JUVENILE HISTORY:
    Enter number of serious violent and violent felony dispositions .... _____ x 1 = _____
    Enter number of nonviolent felony dispositions .... _____ x ½ = _____

OTHER CURRENT OFFENSES:
(Other current offenses that do not encompass the same conduct count in offender score)
    Enter number of other felony convictions .... _____ x 1 = _____

STATUS:
    Was the offender on community custody on the date the current offense was committed? (if yes) .... + 1 = _____

Total the last column to get the **Offender Score** (Round down to the nearest whole number)

SENTENCE RANGE

Offender Score	0	1	2	3	4	5	6	7	8	9+
LEVEL XII	106.5m 93 - 120*	111m 102 - 120*	115.5m 111 - 120*	120 - 120*	120 - 120*	120 - 120*	120 - 120*	120 - 120*	120 - 120*	120 - 120*

- ✓ For attempt, solicitation, conspiracy (RCW 9.94A.595) see page 23 or for gang-related felonies where the court found the offender involved a minor (RCW 9.94A.833) see page 186 for standard range adjustments.
- ✓ For deadly weapon enhancement, see page 190.
- ✓ For sentencing alternatives, see page 177.
- ✓ For community custody eligibility, see page 187.
- ✓ For any applicable enhancements other than deadly weapon enhancement, see page 183..

Malicious Placement Of An Imitation Device Second Degree

RCW 70.74.272(1)(b)
CLASS C* – NONVIOLENT
OFFENDER SCORING RCW 9.94A.525(7)

If it was found that this offense was committed with sexual motivation (RCW 9.94A.533(8)) on or after 7/01/2006, use the General Nonviolent Offense with a Sexual Motivation Finding scoring form on page 193.

If the present conviction is for a felony domestic violence offense where domestic violence was plead and proven, use the General Nonviolent Offense Where Domestic Violence Has Been Plead and Proven scoring form on page 191.

ADULT HISTORY:
  Enter number of felony convictions .... _____ x 1 = _____

JUVENILE HISTORY:
  Enter number of serious violent and violent felony dispositions .... _____ x 1 = _____
  Enter number of nonviolent felony dispositions .... _____ x ½ = _____

OTHER CURRENT OFFENSES:
(Other current offenses that do not encompass the same conduct count in offender score)
  Enter number of other felony convictions .... _____ x 1 = _____

STATUS:
  Was the offender on community custody on the date the current offense was committed? (if yes) ...... + 1 = _____

Total the last column to get the **Offender Score** (Round down to the nearest whole number)

SENTENCE RANGE

	_	_	_	_	Offender Score	_	_	_	_	_
	0	1	2	3	4	5	6	7	8	9+
LEVEL VI	13m	17.5m	24m	30m	36m	42m	53m	58.5m		
	12+ - 14	15 - 20	21 - 27	26 - 34	31 - 41	36 - 48	46 - 60*	57 - 60*	60 - 60*	60 - 60*

- ✓ For gang-related felonies where the court found the offender involved a minor (RCW 9.94A.833) see page 186 for standard range adjustment.
- ✓ For deadly weapon enhancement, see page 190.
- ✓ For sentencing alternatives, see page 177.
- ✓ For community custody eligibility, see page 187.
- ✓ For any applicable enhancements other than deadly weapon enhancement, see page 183.

Manslaughter First Degree

RCW 9A.32.060
CLASS A – SERIOUS VIOLENT

OFFENDER SCORING RCW 9.94A.525(9)

If it was found that this offense was committed with sexual motivation (RCW 9.94A.533(8)) on or after 7/01/2006, use the General Serious Violent Offense with a Sexual Motivation Finding scoring form on page 198.

If the present conviction is for a felony domestic violence offense where domestic violence was plead and proven, use the General Serious Violent Offense Where Domestic Violence Has Been Plead and Proven scoring form on page 196.

ADULT HISTORY:
   Enter number of serious violent felony convictions .... _____ x 3 = _____
   Enter number of violent felony convictions .... _____ x 2 = _____
   Enter number of nonviolent felony convictions .... _____ x 1 = _____

JUVENILE HISTORY:
   Enter number of serious violent felony dispositions .... _____ x 3 = _____
   Enter number of violent felony dispositions .... _____ x 2 = _____
   Enter number of nonviolent felony dispositions .... _____ x ½ = _____

OTHER CURRENT OFFENSES:
(Other current offenses that do not encompass the same conduct count in offender score)
   Enter number of other violent felony convictions .... _____ x 2 = _____
   Enter number of other nonviolent felony convictions .... _____ x 1 = _____

STATUS:
   Was the offender on community custody on the date the current offense was committed? .... + 1 = _____

Total the last column to get the **Offender Score** (Round down to the nearest whole number)

SENTENCE RANGE

	\ Offender Score									
	0	1	2	3	4	5	6	7	8	9+
LEVEL XI	90m 78 - 102	100m 86 - 114	110m 95 - 125	119m 102 - 136	129m 111 - 147	139m 120 - 158	170m 146 - 194	185m 159 - 211	215m 185 - 245	245m 210 - 280

- ✓ For attempt, solicitation, conspiracy (RCW 9.94A.595) see page 23 or for gang-related felonies where the court found the offender involved a minor (RCW 9.94A.833) see page 186 for standard range adjustments.
- ✓ For deadly weapon enhancement, see page 190.
- ✓ For sentencing alternatives, see page 177.
- ✓ For community custody eligibility, see page 187.
- ✓ For any applicable enhancements other than deadly weapon enhancement, see page 183.
- ✓ Multiple current serious violent offenses shall have consecutive sentences imposed per the rules of RCW 9.94A.589(1)(b).

The Caseload Forecast Council is not liable for errors or omissions in the manual, for sentences that may be inappropriately calculated as a result of a practitioner's or court's reliance on the manual, or for any other written or verbal information related to adult or juvenile sentencing. The scoring sheets are intended to provide assistance in most cases but do not cover all permutations of the scoring rules. If you find any errors or omissions, we encourage you to report them to the Caseload Forecast Council.

Manslaughter Second Degree

RCW 9A.32.070
CLASS B* – VIOLENT

OFFENDER SCORING RCW 9.94A.525(8)

If it was found that this offense was committed with sexual motivation (RCW 9.94A.533(8)) on or after 7/01/2006, use the General Violent Offense with a Sexual Motivation Finding scoring form on page 201.

If the present conviction is for a felony domestic violence offense where domestic violence was plead and proven, use the General Violent Offense Where Domestic Violence Has Been Plead and Proven scoring form on page 199.

ADULT HISTORY:
 Enter number of serious violent and violent felony convictions .... _____ x 2 = _____
 Enter number of nonviolent felony convictions .... _____ x 1 = _____

JUVENILE HISTORY:
 Enter number of serious violent and violent felony dispositions .... _____ x 2 = _____
 Enter number of nonviolent felony dispositions .... _____ x ½ = _____

OTHER CURRENT OFFENSES:
(Other current offenses that do not encompass the same conduct count in offender score)
 Enter number of other serious violent and violent felony convictions .... _____ x 2 = _____
 Enter number of other nonviolent felony convictions .... _____ x 1 = _____

STATUS:
 Was the offender on community custody on the date the current offense was committed? .... + 1 = _____

Total the last column to get the **Offender Score** (Round down to the nearest whole number)

SENTENCE RANGE

	\multicolumn{10}{c}{Offender Score}
	0	1	2	3	4	5	6	7	8	9+
LEVEL VIII	24m	30m	36m	42m	47.5m	53.5m	78m	89.5m	101.5m	114m
	21 - 27	26 - 34	31 - 41	36 - 48	41 - 54	46 - 61	67 - 89	77 - 102	87 - 116	108 - 120*

- ✓ For attempt, solicitation, conspiracy (RCW 9.94A.595) see page 23 or for gang-related felonies where the court found the offender involved a minor (RCW 9.94A.833) see page 186 for standard range adjustments.
- ✓ For deadly weapon enhancement, see page 190.
- ✓ For sentencing alternatives, see page 177.
- ✓ For community custody eligibility, see page 187.
- ✓ For any applicable enhancements other than deadly weapon enhancement, see page 183.

The Caseload Forecast Council is not liable for errors or omissions in the manual, for sentences that may be inappropriately calculated as a result of a practitioner's or court's reliance on the manual, or for any other written or verbal information related to adult or juvenile sentencing. The scoring sheets are intended to provide assistance in most cases but do not cover all permutations of the scoring rules. If you find any errors or omissions, we encourage you to report them to the Caseload Forecast Council.

Manufacture, Deliver Or Possess With Intent To Deliver Amphetamine

RCW 69.50.401(2)(b)
CLASS B – NONVIOLENT/DRUG

OFFENDER SCORING RCW 9.94A.525(13)

If it was found that this offense was committed with sexual motivation (RCW 9.94A.533(8)) on or after 7/01/2006, use the General Drug Offense with a Sexual Motivation Finding scoring form on page 195.

If the present conviction is for a felony domestic violence offense where domestic violence was plead and proven, use the General Drug Offense Where Domestic Violence Has Been Plead and Proven scoring form on page 194.

ADULT HISTORY:
Does the offender have a prior sex or serious violent offense in history?
- **YES** Enter number of felony drug convictions .... _____ x 3 = _____
- **NO** Enter number of felony drug convictions .... _____ x 1 = _____

Enter number of felony convictions .... _____ x 1 = _____

JUVENILE HISTORY:
Does the offender have a prior sex or serious violent offense in history?
- **YES** Enter number of felony drug dispositions .... _____ x 2 = _____
- **NO** Enter number of felony drug dispositions .... _____ x ½ = _____

Enter number of serious violent and violent felony dispositions .... _____ x 1 = _____

Enter number of nonviolent felony dispositions .... _____ x ½ = _____

OTHER CURRENT OFFENSES:
(Other current offenses that do not encompass the same conduct count in offender score)
Does the offender have other prior sex or serious violent offense in history?
- **YES** Enter number of other felony drug convictions .... _____ x 3 = _____
- **NO** Enter number of other felony drug convictions .... _____ x 1 = _____

Enter number of other felony convictions .... _____ x 1 = _____

STATUS:
Was the offender on community custody on the date the current offense was committed? (if yes) .... + 1 = _____

Total the last column to get the **Offender Score** (Round down to the nearest whole number)

SENTENCE RANGE – DRUG

	Offender Score		
	0 to 2	3 to 5	6 to 9+
LEVEL II	16m 12+ - 20	40m 20+ - 60	90m 60+ - 120

- ✓ For attempt, solicitation or conspiracy drug felonies see page 25 or for gang-related felonies where the court found the offender involved a minor (RCW 9.94A.833) see page 186 for standard range adjustments.
- ✓ Per RCW 9.94A.518, any felony offense under chapter 69.50 RCW with a deadly weapon special verdict under RCW 9.94A.602 becomes a level III offense.
- ✓ For deadly weapon enhancement, see page 190.
- ✓ For sentencing alternatives, see page 177.
- ✓ For community custody eligibility, see page 187.
- ✓ For any applicable enhancements other than deadly weapon enhancement, see page 183.
- ✓ Per RCW 69.50.408, the statutory maximum for a **subsequent conviction** under chapter 69.50 RCW is 240 months.
- ✓ Per RCW 69.50.435, if the offense occurred within a **protected zone**, 24 months shall be added to the standard range and the statutory maximum will be 240 months.

The Caseload Forecast Council is not liable for errors or omissions in the manual, for sentences that may be inappropriately calculated as a result of a practitioner's or court's reliance on the manual, or for any other written or verbal information related to adult or juvenile sentencing. The scoring sheets are intended to provide assistance in most cases but do not cover all permutations of the scoring rules. If you find any errors or omissions, we encourage you to report them to the Caseload Forecast Council.

Manufacture, Deliver Or Possess With Intent To Deliver Marijuana

RCW 69.50.401(2)(c)
CLASS C – NONVIOLENT/DRUG

OFFENDER SCORING RCW 9.94A.525(13)

If it was found that this offense was committed with sexual motivation (RCW 9.94A.533(8)) on or after 7/01/2006, use the General Drug Offense with a Sexual Motivation Finding scoring form on page 195.

If the present conviction is for a felony domestic violence offense where domestic violence was plead and proven, use the General Drug Offense Where Domestic Violence Has Been Plead and Proven scoring form on page 194.

ADULT HISTORY:
Does the offender have a prior sex or serious violent offense in history?
    YES Enter number of felony drug convictions .... _____ x 3 = _____
    NO Enter number of felony drug convictions .... _____ x 1 = _____

Enter number of felony convictions .... _____ x 1 = _____

JUVENILE HISTORY:
Does the offender have a prior sex or serious violent offense in history?
    YES Enter number of felony drug dispositions .... _____ x 2 = _____
    NO Enter number of felony drug dispositions .... _____ x ½ = _____

Enter number of serious violent and violent felony dispositions .... _____ x 1 = _____

Enter number of nonviolent felony dispositions .... _____ x ½ = _____

OTHER CURRENT OFFENSES:
(Other current offenses that do not encompass the same conduct count in offender score)
Does the offender have other prior sex or serious violent offense in history?
    YES Enter number of other felony drug convictions .... _____ x 3 = _____
    NO Enter number of other felony drug convictions .... _____ x 1 = _____

Enter number of other felony convictions .... _____ x 1 = _____

STATUS:
Was the offender on community custody on the date the current offense was committed? (if yes) .... + 1 = _____

Total the last column to get the **Offender Score** (Round down to the nearest whole number)

SENTENCE RANGE – DRUG

	Offender Score		
	0 to 2	3 to 5	6 to 9+
LEVEL I	3m	9m	18m
	0 - 6	6+ - 12	12+ - 24

- ✓ For attempt, solicitation or conspiracy drug felonies see page 25 or for gang-related felonies where the court found the offender involved a minor (RCW 9.94A.833) see page 186 for standard range adjustments.
- ✓ Per RCW 9.94A.518, any felony offense under chapter 69.50 RCW with a deadly weapon special verdict under RCW 9.94A.602 becomes a level III offense.
- ✓ For deadly weapon enhancement, see page 190.
- ✓ For sentencing alternatives, see page 177.
- ✓ For community custody eligibility, see page 187.
- ✓ For any applicable enhancements other than deadly weapon enhancement, see page 183.
- ✓ Per RCW 69.50.408, the statutory maximum for a **subsequent conviction** under chapter 69.50 RCW is 120 months.
- ✓ Per RCW 69.50.435, if the offense occurred within a **protected zone**, 24 months shall be added to the standard range and the statutory maximum will be 120 months.

The Caseload Forecast Council is not liable for errors or omissions in the manual, for sentences that may be inappropriately calculated as a result of a practitioner's or court's reliance on the manual, or for any other written or verbal information related to adult or juvenile sentencing. The scoring sheets are intended to provide assistance in most cases but do not cover all permutations of the scoring rules. If you find any errors or omissions, we encourage you to report them to the Caseload Forecast Council.

Manufacture, Deliver Or Possess With Intent To Deliver Narcotics From Schedule I Or II Or Flunitrazepam From Schedule IV

RCW 69.50.401(2)(a)
CLASS B – NONVIOLENT/DRUG

OFFENDER SCORING RCW 9.94A.525(13)

If it was found that this offense was committed with sexual motivation (RCW 9.94A.533(8)) on or after 7/01/2006, use the General Drug Offense with a Sexual Motivation Finding scoring form on page 195.

If the present conviction is for a felony domestic violence offense where domestic violence was plead and proven, use the General Drug Offense Where Domestic Violence Has Been Plead and Proven scoring form on page 194.

ADULT HISTORY:
Does the offender have a prior sex or serious violent offense in history?
    YES Enter number of felony drug convictions .... _____ x 3 = _____
    NO Enter number of felony drug convictions .... _____ x 1 = _____

Enter number of felony convictions .... _____ x 1 = _____

JUVENILE HISTORY:
Does the offender have a prior sex or serious violent offense in history?
    YES Enter number of felony drug dispositions .... _____ x 2 = _____
    NO Enter number of felony drug dispositions .... _____ x ½ = _____

Enter number of serious violent and violent felony dispositions .... _____ x 1 = _____

Enter number of nonviolent felony dispositions .... _____ x ½ = _____

OTHER CURRENT OFFENSES:
(Other current offenses that do not encompass the same conduct count in offender score)
Does the offender have other prior sex or serious violent offense in history?
    YES Enter number of other felony drug convictions .... _____ x 3 = _____
    NO Enter number of other felony drug convictions .... _____ x 1 = _____

Enter number of other felony convictions .... _____ x 1 = _____

STATUS:
Was the offender on community custody on the date the current offense was committed? (if yes) .... + 1 = _____

Total the last column to get the **Offender Score** (Round down to the nearest whole number)

SENTENCE RANGE – DRUG

	Offender Score		
	0 to 2	3 to 5	6 to 9+
LEVEL II	16m	40m	90m
	12+ - 20	20+ - 60	60+ - 120

- ✓ For attempt, solicitation or conspiracy drug felonies see page 25 or for gang-related felonies where the court found the offender involved a minor (RCW 9.94A.833) see page 186 for standard range adjustments.
- ✓ Per RCW 9.94A.518, any felony offense under chapter 69.50 RCW with a deadly weapon special verdict under RCW 9.94A.602 becomes a level III offense.
- ✓ For deadly weapon enhancement, see page 190.
- ✓ For sentencing alternatives, see page 177.
- ✓ For community custody eligibility, see page 187.
- ✓ For any applicable enhancements other than deadly weapon enhancement, see page 183.
- ✓ Per RCW 69.50.408, the statutory maximum for a **subsequent conviction** under chapter 69.50 RCW is 240 months.
- ✓ Per RCW 69.50.435, if the offense occurred within a **protected zone**, 24 months shall be added to the standard range and the statutory maximum will be 240 months.

The Caseload Forecast Council is not liable for errors or omissions in the manual, for sentences that may be inappropriately calculated as a result of a practitioner's or court's reliance on the manual, or for any other written or verbal information related to adult or juvenile sentencing. The scoring sheets are intended to provide assistance in most cases but do not cover all permutations of the scoring rules. If you find any errors or omissions, we encourage you to report them to the Caseload Forecast Council.

Manufacture, Deliver Or Possess With Intent To Deliver Narcotics From Schedule III, IV Or V Or Nonnarcotics From Schedule I-V Except Marijuana, Amphetamine, Methamphetamine Or Flunitrazepam

RCW 69.50.401(2)(c-e)
CLASS C* – NONVIOLENT/DRUG

OFFENDER SCORING RCW 9.94A.525(13)

If it was found that this offense was committed with sexual motivation (RCW 9.94A.533(8)) on or after 7/01/2006, use the General Drug Offense with a Sexual Motivation Finding scoring form on page 195.

If the present conviction is for a felony domestic violence offense where domestic violence was plead and proven, use the General Drug Offense Where Domestic Violence Has Been Plead and Proven scoring form on page 194.

ADULT HISTORY:
    Does the offender have a prior sex or serious violent offense in history?
        YES Enter number of felony drug convictions.. _____ x 3 = _____
        NO Enter number of felony drug convictions .... _____ x 1 = _____
    Enter number of felony convictions .... _____ x 1 = _____

JUVENILE HISTORY:
    Does the offender have a prior sex or serious violent offense in history?
        YES Enter number of felony drug dispositions.. _____ x 2 = _____
        NO Enter number of felony drug dispositions.. _____ x ½ = _____
    Enter number of serious violent and violent felony dispositions .... _____ x 1 = _____
    Enter number of nonviolent felony dispositions .... _____ x ½ = _____

OTHER CURRENT OFFENSES:
(Other current offenses that do not encompass the same conduct count in offender score)
    Does the offender have other prior sex or serious violent offense in history?
        YES Enter number of other felony drug convictions .... _____ x 3 = _____
        NO Enter number of other felony drug convictions .... _____ x 1 = _____
    Enter number of other felony convictions .... _____ x 1 = _____

STATUS:
    Was the offender on community custody on the date the current offense was committed? (if yes)......................... + 1 = _____

Total the last column to get the **Offender Score** (Round down to the nearest whole number)

SENTENCE RANGE – DRUG

	Offender Score		
	0 to 2	3 to 5	6 to 9+
LEVEL II	16m	40m	
	12+ - 20	20+ - 60	60 - 60*

- ✓ For attempt, solicitation or conspiracy drug felonies see page 25 or for gang-related felonies where the court found the offender involved a minor (RCW 9.94A.833) see page 186 for standard range adjustments.
- ✓ Per RCW 9.94A.518, any felony offense under chapter 69.50 RCW with a deadly weapon special verdict under RCW 9.94A.602 becomes a level III offense.
- ✓ For deadly weapon enhancement, see page 190.
- ✓ For sentencing alternatives, see page 177.
- ✓ For community custody eligibility, see page 187.
- ✓ For any applicable enhancements other than deadly weapon enhancement, see page 183.
- ✓ Per RCW 69.50.408, the statutory maximum for a **subsequent conviction** under chapter 69.50 RCW is 120 months.
- ✓ Per RCW 69.50.435, if the offense occurred within a **protected zone**, 24 months shall be added to the standard range and the statutory maximum will be 120 months.

The Caseload Forecast Council is not liable for errors or omissions in the manual, for sentences that may be inappropriately calculated as a result of a practitioner's or court's reliance on the manual, or for any other written or verbal information related to adult or juvenile sentencing. The scoring sheets are intended to provide assistance in most cases but do not cover all permutations of the scoring rules. If you find any errors or omissions, we encourage you to report them to the Caseload Forecast Council.

Manufacture, Distribute Or Possess With Intent To Distribute An Imitation Controlled Substance

RCW 69.52.030(1)
CLASS C* – NONVIOLENT

OFFENDER SCORING RCW 9.94A.525(7)

If it was found that this offense was committed with sexual motivation (RCW 9.94A.533(8)) on or after 7/01/2006, use the General Nonviolent Offense with a Sexual Motivation Finding scoring form on page 193.

If the present conviction is for a felony domestic violence offense where domestic violence was plead and proven, use the General Nonviolent Offense Where Domestic Violence Has Been Plead and Proven scoring form on page 191.

ADULT HISTORY:
Enter number of felony convictions .... _____ x 1 = _____

JUVENILE HISTORY:
Enter number of serious violent and violent felony dispositions .... _____ x 1 = _____

Enter number of nonviolent felony dispositions .... _____ x ½ = _____

OTHER CURRENT OFFENSES:
(Other current offenses that do not encompass the same conduct count in offender score)
Enter number of other felony convictions .... _____ x 1 = _____

STATUS:
Was the offender on community custody on the date the current offense was committed? (if yes) .... + 1 = _____

Total the last column to get the **Offender Score** (Round down to the nearest whole number)

SENTENCE RANGE – DRUG

	Offender Score		
	0 to 2	3 to 5	6 to 9+
LEVEL II	16m	40m	90m
	12+ - 20	20+ - 60	60* - 60*

- ✓ For attempt, solicitation, conspiracy (RCW 9.94A.595) see page 23 or for gang-related felonies where the court found the offender involved a minor (RCW 9.94A.833) see page 186 for standard range adjustments.
- ✓ For deadly weapon enhancement, see page 190.
- ✓ For sentencing alternatives, see page 177.
- ✓ For community custody eligibility, see page 187.
- ✓ For any applicable enhancements other than deadly weapon enhancement, see page 183.

The Caseload Forecast Council is not liable for errors or omissions in the manual, for sentences that may be inappropriately calculated as a result of a practitioner's or court's reliance on the manual, or for any other written or verbal information related to adult or juvenile sentencing. The scoring sheets are intended to provide assistance in most cases but do not cover all permutations of the scoring rules. If you find any errors or omissions, we encourage you to report them to the Caseload Forecast Council.

Manufacture, Distribute Or Possess With Intent To Distribute An Imitation Controlled Substance By A Person 18 Or Older To A Person Under 18

RCW 69.52.030(2)
CLASS B – NONVIOLENT

OFFENDER SCORING RCW 9.94A.525(7)

If it was found that this offense was committed with sexual motivation (RCW 9.94A.533(8)) on or after 7/01/2006, use the General Nonviolent Offense with a Sexual Motivation Finding scoring form on page 193.

If the present conviction is for a felony domestic violence offense where domestic violence was plead and proven, use the General Nonviolent Offense Where Domestic Violence Has Been Plead and Proven scoring form on page 191.

ADULT HISTORY:
    Enter number of felony convictions .... _____ x 1 = _____

JUVENILE HISTORY:
    Enter number of serious violent and violent felony dispositions .... _____ x 1 = _____

    Enter number of nonviolent felony dispositions .... _____ x ½ = _____

OTHER CURRENT OFFENSES:
(Other current offenses that do not encompass the same conduct count in offender score)
    Enter number of other felony convictions .... _____ x 1 = _____

STATUS:
    Was the offender on community custody on the date the current offense was committed? (if yes) ...... + 1 = _____

Total the last column to get the **Offender Score** (Round down to the nearest whole number)

SENTENCE RANGE – DRUG

	Offender Score		
	0 to 2	**3 to 5**	**6 to 9+**
LEVEL III	59.5m	84m	110m
	51 - 68	68+ - 100	100+ - 120

✓ For attempt, solicitation, conspiracy (RCW 9.94A.595) see page 23 or for gang-related felonies where the court found the offender involved a minor (RCW 9.94A.833) see page 186 for standard range adjustments.

✓ For deadly weapon enhancement, see page 190.

✓ For sentencing alternatives, see page 177.

✓ For community custody eligibility, see page 187.

✓ For any applicable enhancements other than deadly weapon enhancement, see page 183.

Manufacture Methamphetamine

RCW 69.50.401(2)(b)
CLASS B – NONVIOLENT/DRUG

OFFENDER SCORING RCW 9.94A.525(13)

If it was found that this offense was committed with sexual motivation (RCW 9.94A.533(8)) on or after 7/01/2006, use the General Drug Offense with a Sexual Motivation Finding scoring form on page 195.

If the present conviction is for a felony domestic violence offense where domestic violence was plead and proven, use the General Drug Offense Where Domestic Violence Has Been Plead and Proven scoring form on page 194.

ADULT HISTORY:
    Enter number of Manufacture Methamphetamine felony convictions .... _____ x 3 = _____
    Does the offender have a prior sex or serious violent offense in history?
        YES Enter number of felony drug convictions .... _____ x 3 = _____
        NO Enter number of felony drug convictions .... _____ x 1 = _____
    Enter number of felony convictions .... _____ x 1 = _____

JUVENILE HISTORY:
    Enter number of Manufacture Methamphetamine felony dispositions .... _____ x 2 = _____
    Does the offender have a prior sex or serious violent offense in history?
        YES Enter number of felony drug dispositions .... _____ x 2 = _____
        NO Enter number of felony drug dispositions .... _____ x ½ = _____
    Enter number of serious violent and violent felony dispositions .... _____ x 1 = _____
    Enter number of nonviolent felony dispositions .... _____ x ½ = _____

OTHER CURRENT OFFENSES:
(Other current offenses that do not encompass the same conduct count in offender score)
    Enter number of other Manufacture Methamphetamine felony convictions .... _____ x 3 = _____
    Does the offender have other prior sex or serious violent offense in history?
        YES Enter number of other felony drug convictions .... _____ x 3 = _____
        NO Enter number of other felony drug convictions .... _____ x 1 = _____
    Enter number of other felony convictions .... _____ x 1 = _____

STATUS:
    Was the offender on community custody on the date the current offense was committed? (if yes) .... + 1 = _____

Total the last column to get the **Offender Score** (Round down to the nearest whole number)

SENTENCE RANGE – DRUG

	Offender Score		
	0 to 2	**3 to 5**	**6 to 9+**
LEVEL III	59.5m 51 - 68	84m 68+ - 100	110m 100+ - 120

- ✓ For attempt, solicitation or conspiracy drug felonies see page 25 or for gang-related felonies where the court found the offender involved a minor (RCW 9.94A.833) see page 186 for standard range adjustments.
- ✓ Per RCW 9.94A.518, any felony offense under chapter 69.50 RCW with a deadly weapon special verdict under RCW 9.94A.602 becomes a level III offense.
- ✓ For deadly weapon enhancement, see page 190.
- ✓ For sentencing alternatives, see page 177.
- ✓ For community custody eligibility, see page 187.
- ✓ For any applicable enhancements other than deadly weapon enhancement, see page 183.
- ✓ Per RCW 69.50.408, the statutory maximum for a **subsequent conviction** under chapter 69.50 RCW is 240 months.
- ✓ Per RCW 69.50.435, if the offense occurred within a **protected zone**, 24 months shall be added to the standard range and the statutory maximum will be 240 months.
- ✓ Per RCW 9.94A.827, if the offense is also a violation of **Manufacture of Methamphetamine with a Child on Premise**, 24 months shall be added to the standard range.

The Caseload Forecast Council is not liable for errors or omissions in the manual, for sentences that may be inappropriately calculated as a result of a practitioner's or court's reliance on the manual, or for any other written or verbal information related to adult or juvenile sentencing. The scoring sheets are intended to provide assistance in most cases but do not cover all permutations of the scoring rules. If you find any errors or omissions, we encourage you to report them to the Caseload Forecast Council.

Mortgage Fraud

RCW 19.144.080
CLASS B – NONVIOLENT
OFFENDER SCORING RCW 9.94A.525(7)

If it was found that this offense was committed with sexual motivation (RCW 9.94A.533(8)) on or after 7/01/2006, use the General Nonviolent Offense with a Sexual Motivation Finding scoring form on page 193.

If the present conviction is for a felony domestic violence offense where domestic violence was plead and proven, use the General Nonviolent Offense Where Domestic Violence Has Been Plead and Proven scoring form on page 191.

ADULT HISTORY:
    Enter number of felony convictions .... _____ x 1 = _____

JUVENILE HISTORY:
    Enter number of serious violent and violent felony dispositions .... _____ x 1 = _____
    Enter number of nonviolent felony dispositions .... _____ x ½ = _____

OTHER CURRENT OFFENSES:
(Other current offenses that do not encompass the same conduct count in offender score)
    Enter number of other felony convictions .... _____ x 1 = _____

STATUS:
    Was the offender on community custody on the date the current offense was committed? (if yes) ...... + 1 = _____

Total the last column to get the **Offender Score** (Round down to the nearest whole number)

SENTENCE RANGE

	\multicolumn{10}{c}{Offender Score}
	0	1	2	3	4	5	6	7	8	9+
LEVEL III	2m 1 - 3	5m 3 - 8	8m 4 - 12	11m 9 - 12	14m 12+ - 16	19.5m 17 - 22	25.5m 22 - 29	38m 33 - 43	50m 43 - 57	59.5m 51 - 68

- ✓ For attempt, solicitation, conspiracy (RCW 9.94A.595) see page 23 or for gang-related felonies where the court found the offender involved a minor (RCW 9.94A.833) see page 186 for standard range adjustments.
- ✓ For deadly weapon enhancement, see page 190.
- ✓ For sentencing alternatives, see page 177.
- ✓ For community custody eligibility, see page 187.
- ✓ For any applicable enhancements other than deadly weapon enhancement, see page 183.

The Caseload Forecast Council is not liable for errors or omissions in the manual, for sentences that may be inappropriately calculated as a result of a practitioner's or court's reliance on the manual, or for any other written or verbal information related to adult or juvenile sentencing. The scoring sheets are intended to provide assistance in most cases but do not cover all permutations of the scoring rules. If you find any errors or omissions, we encourage you to report them to the Caseload Forecast Council.

Murder First Degree

RCW 9A.32.030
CLASS A – SERIOUS VIOLENT
ATTEMPT/SOLICIATION/CONSPIRACY = CLASS A
OFFENDER SCORING RCW 9.94A.525(9)

If the present conviction is for a felony domestic violence offense where domestic violence was plead and proven, use the General Serious Violent Offense Where Domestic Violence Has Been Plead and Proven scoring form on page 196.

ADULT HISTORY:
 Enter number of serious violent felony convictions .... _____ x 3 = _____

 Enter number of violent felony convictions .... _____ x 2 = _____

 Enter number of nonviolent felony convictions .... _____ x 1 = _____

JUVENILE HISTORY:
 Enter number of serious violent felony dispositions .... _____ x 3 = _____

 Enter number of violent felony dispositions .... _____ x 2 = _____

 Enter number of nonviolent felony dispositions .... _____ x ½ = _____

OTHER CURRENT OFFENSES:
(Other current offenses that do not encompass the same conduct count in offender score)
 Enter number of other violent felony convictions .... _____ x 2 = _____

 Enter number of other nonviolent felony convictions .... _____ x 1 = _____

STATUS:
 Was the offender on community custody on the date the current offense was committed? .... + 1 = _____

Total the last column to get the **Offender Score** (Round down to the nearest whole number)

SENTENCE RANGE

	\multicolumn{10}{c}{Offender Score}
	0	**1**	**2**	**3**	**4**	**5**	**6**	**7**	**8**	**9+**
LEVEL XV	280m	291.5m	304m	316m	327.5m	339.5m	364m	394m	431.5m	479.5m
	240 - 320	250 - 333	261 - 347	271 - 361	281 - 374	291 - 388	312 - 416	338 - 450	370 - 493	411 - 548

- ✓ For attempt, solicitation, conspiracy (RCW 9.94A.595) see page 23 or for gang-related felonies where the court found the offender involved a minor (RCW 9.94A.833) see page 186 for standard range adjustments.
- ✓ For deadly weapon enhancement, see page 190.
- ✓ For sentencing alternatives, see page 177.
- ✓ For community custody eligibility, see page 187.
- ✓ For any applicable enhancements other than deadly weapon enhancement, see page 183.
- ✓ Multiple current serious violent offenses shall have consecutive sentences imposed per the rules of RCW 9.94A.589(1)(b).
- ✓ <u>Excluding attempt, solicitation and conspiracy convictions,</u> the statutory <u>minimum</u> sentence is 240 months (RCW 9.94A.540). The statutory minimum sentence shall not be varied or modified under RCW 9.94A.535.
- ✓ Per RCW 9A.32.040, an offender convicted of Murder 1 shall be sentenced to life imprisonment.

The Caseload Forecast Council is not liable for errors or omissions in the manual, for sentences that may be inappropriately calculated as a result of a practitioner's or court's reliance on the manual, or for any other written or verbal information related to adult or juvenile sentencing. The scoring sheets are intended to provide assistance in most cases but do not cover all permutations of the scoring rules. If you find any errors or omissions, we encourage you to report them to the Caseload Forecast Council.

Murder First Degree With A Finding Of Sexual Motivation

RCW 9A.32.030
CLASS A – SERIOUS VIOLENT/SEX
ATTEMPT = CLASS A
OFFENDER SCORING RCW 9.94A.525(17)

ADULT HISTORY:
Enter number of sex offense felony convictions .... _____ x 3 = _____
Enter number of serious violent felony convictions .... _____ x 3 = _____
Enter number of violent felony convictions .... _____ x 2 = _____
Enter number of nonviolent felony convictions .... _____ x 1 = _____

JUVENILE HISTORY:
Enter number of sex offense felony dispositions .... _____ x 3 = _____
Enter number of serious violent felony dispositions .... _____ x 3 = _____
Enter number of violent felony dispositions .... _____ x 2 = _____
Enter number of nonviolent felony dispositions .... _____ x ½ = _____

OTHER CURRENT OFFENSES:
(Other current offenses that do not encompass the same conduct count in offender score)
Enter number of other sex offense felony convictions .... _____ x 3 = _____
Enter number of other violent felony convictions .... _____ x 2 = _____
Enter number of other nonviolent felony convictions .... _____ x 1 = _____

STATUS:
Was the offender on community custody on the date the current offense was committed?.................. + 1 = _____

Total the last column to get the **Offender Score** (Round down to the nearest whole number)

SENTENCE RANGE

	Offender Score									
	0	1	2	3	4	5	6	7	8	9+
LEVEL XV	280m	291.5m	304m	316m	327.5m	339.5m	364m	394m	431.5m	479.5m
	240 - 320	250 - 333	261 - 347	271 - 361	281 - 374	291 - 388	312 - 416	338 - 450	370 - 493	411 - 548

Add Sexual Motivation Enhancement (see page 185) [____] to Standard Range = Low [____] to High [____]

- ✓ For attempt, solicitation, conspiracy (RCW 9.94A.595) see page 23 or for gang-related felonies where the court found the offender involved a minor (RCW 9.94A.833) see page 186 for standard range adjustments.
- ✓ For deadly weapon enhancement, see page 190.
- ✓ For sentencing alternatives, see page 177.
- ✓ For community custody eligibility, see page 187.
- ✓ For any applicable enhancements other than deadly weapon enhancement, see page 183.
- ✓ If the offender is not a persistent offender and the current offense was committed on or after 9/1/2001, then the offender is subject to the requirements under RCW 9.94A.507.
- ✓ Multiple current serious violent offenses shall have consecutive sentences imposed per the rules of RCW 9.94A.589(1)(b).
- ✓ Excluding attempt convictions, the statutory minimum sentence is 240 months (RCW 9.94A.540). The statutory minimum sentence shall not be varied or modified under RCW 9.94A.535.
- ✓ Per RCW 9A.32.040, an offender convicted of Murder 1 shall be sentenced to life imprisonment.

The Caseload Forecast Council is not liable for errors or omissions in the manual, for sentences that may be inappropriately calculated as a result of a practitioner's or court's reliance on the manual, or for any other written or verbal information related to adult or juvenile sentencing. The scoring sheets are intended to provide assistance in most cases but do not cover all permutations of the scoring rules. If you find any errors or omissions, we encourage you to report them to the Caseload Forecast Council.

Murder First Degree With A Finding Of Sexual Motivation

RCW 9A.32.030
SERIOUS VIOLENT/SEX
SOLICIATION/CONSPIRACY = CLASS A

OFFENDER SCORING RCW 9.94A.525(17)

ADULT HISTORY:
Enter number of sex offense felony convictions .... _____ x 3 = _____
Enter number of serious violent felony convictions .... _____ x 3 = _____
Enter number of violent felony convictions .... _____ x 2 = _____
Enter number of nonviolent felony convictions .... _____ x 1 = _____

JUVENILE HISTORY:
Enter number of sex offense felony dispositions .... _____ x 3 = _____
Enter number of serious violent felony dispositions .... _____ x 3 = _____
Enter number of violent felony dispositions .... _____ x 2 = _____
Enter number of nonviolent felony dispositions .... _____ x ½ = _____

OTHER CURRENT OFFENSES:
(Other current offenses that do not encompass the same conduct count in offender score)
Enter number of other sex offense felony convictions .... _____ x 3 = _____
Enter number of other violent felony convictions .... _____ x 2 = _____
Enter number of other nonviolent felony convictions .... _____ x 1 = _____

STATUS:
Was the offender on community custody on the date the current offense was committed? .... + 1 = _____

Total the last column to get the **Offender Score** (Round down to the nearest whole number)

SENTENCE RANGE

	\multicolumn{10}{c	}{Offender Score}
	0	1	2	3	4	5	6	7	8	9+
LEVEL XV	280m	291.5m	304m	316m	327.5m	339.5m	364m	394m	431.5m	479.5m
	240 - 320	250 - 333	261 - 347	271 - 361	281 - 374	291 - 388	312 - 416	338 - 450	370 - 493	411 - 548

Add Sexual Motivation Enhancement (see page 185) [_____] to Standard Range = [Low] to [High]

- ✓ For attempt, solicitation, conspiracy (RCW 9.94A.595) see page 23 or for gang-related felonies where the court found the offender involved a minor (RCW 9.94A.833) see page 186 for standard range adjustments.
- ✓ For deadly weapon enhancement, see page 190.
- ✓ For sentencing alternatives, see page 177.
- ✓ For community custody eligibility, see page 187.
- ✓ For any applicable enhancements other than deadly weapon enhancement, see page 183.
- ✓ If the offender is not a persistent offender and has a prior conviction for an offense listed in RCW 9.94A.030(38)(b), then the sentence is subject to the requirements of RCW 9.94A.507.
- ✓ Multiple current serious violent offenses shall have consecutive sentences imposed per the rules of RCW 9.94A.589(1)(b).

The Caseload Forecast Council is not liable for errors or omissions in the manual, for sentences that may be inappropriately calculated as a result of a practitioner's or court's reliance on the manual, or for any other written or verbal information related to adult or juvenile sentencing. The scoring sheets are intended to provide assistance in most cases but do not cover all permutations of the scoring rules. If you find any errors or omissions, we encourage you to report them to the Caseload Forecast Council.

Murder Second Degree

RCW 9A.32.050
CLASS A – SERIOUS VIOLENT
ATTEMPT/SOLICIATION = CLASS A
CONSPIRACY = CLASS B

OFFENDER SCORING RCW 9.94A.525(9)

If the present conviction is for a felony domestic violence offense where domestic violence was plead and proven, use the General Serious Violent Offense Where Domestic Violence Has Been Plead and Proven scoring form on page 196.

ADULT HISTORY:
    Enter number of serious violent felony convictions .... _____ x 3 = _____

    Enter number of violent felony convictions .... _____ x 2 = _____

    Enter number of nonviolent felony convictions .... _____ x 1 = _____

JUVENILE HISTORY:
    Enter number of serious violent felony dispositions .... _____ x 3 = _____

    Enter number of violent felony dispositions .... _____ x 2 = _____

    Enter number of nonviolent felony dispositions .... _____ x ½ = _____

OTHER CURRENT OFFENSES:
(Other current offenses that do not encompass the same conduct count in offender score)
    Enter number of other violent felony convictions .... _____ x 2 = _____

    Enter number of other nonviolent felony convictions .... _____ x 1 = _____

STATUS:
    Was the offender on community custody on the date the current offense was committed?................. + 1 = _____

Total the last column to get the **Offender Score** (Round down to the nearest whole number)

SENTENCE RANGE

	Offender Score									
	0	1	2	3	4	5	6	7	8	9+
LEVEL XIV	171.5m	184m	194m	204m	215m	225m	245m	266m	307m	347.5m
	123 - 220	134 - 234	144 - 244	154 - 254	165 - 265	175 - 275	195 - 295	216 - 316	257 - 357	298 - 397

✓ For attempt, solicitation, conspiracy (RCW 9.94A.595) see page 23 or for gang-related felonies where the court found the offender involved a minor (RCW 9.94A.833) see page 186 for standard range adjustments.

✓ For deadly weapon enhancement, see page 190.

✓ For sentencing alternatives, see page 177.

✓ For community custody eligibility, see page 187.

✓ For any applicable enhancements other than deadly weapon enhancement, see page 183.

✓ Multiple current serious violent offenses shall have consecutive sentences imposed per the rules of RCW 9.94A.589(1)(b).

The Caseload Forecast Council is not liable for errors or omissions in the manual, for sentences that may be inappropriately calculated as a result of a practitioner's or court's reliance on the manual, or for any other written or verbal information related to adult or juvenile sentencing. The scoring sheets are intended to provide assistance in most cases but do not cover all permutations of the scoring rules. If you find any errors or omissions, we encourage you to report them to the Caseload Forecast Council.

Murder Second Degree With A Finding Of Sexual Motivation

RCW 9A.32.050
CLASS A – SERIOUS VIOLENT/SEX
ATTEMPT = CLASS A

OFFENDER SCORING RCW 9.94A.525(17)

ADULT HISTORY:
Enter number of sex offense felony convictions .... _____ x 3 = _____
Enter number of serious violent felony convictions .... _____ x 3 = _____
Enter number of violent felony convictions .... _____ x 2 = _____
Enter number of nonviolent felony convictions .... _____ x 1 = _____

JUVENILE HISTORY:
Enter number of sex offense felony dispositions .... _____ x 3 = _____
Enter number of serious violent felony dispositions .... _____ x 3 = _____
Enter number of violent felony dispositions .... _____ x 2 = _____
Enter number of nonviolent felony dispositions .... _____ x ½ = _____

OTHER CURRENT OFFENSES:
(Other current offenses that do not encompass the same conduct count in offender score)
Enter number of other sex offense felony convictions .... _____ x 3 = _____
Enter number of other violent felony convictions .... _____ x 2 = _____
Enter number of other nonviolent felony convictions .... _____ x 1 = _____

STATUS:
Was the offender on community custody on the date the current offense was committed? .... + 1 = _____

Total the last column to get the **Offender Score** (Round down to the nearest whole number)   [____]

SENTENCE RANGE

	\multicolumn{10}{c}{Offender Score}
	0	**1**	**2**	**3**	**4**	**5**	**6**	**7**	**8**	**9+**
LEVEL XIV	171.5m	184m	194m	204m	215m	225m	245m	266m	307m	347.5m
	123 - 220	134 - 234	144 - 244	154 - 254	165 - 265	175 - 275	195 - 295	216 - 316	257 - 357	298 - 397

Add Sexual Motivation Enhancement (see page 185) [____] to Standard Range = [Low] to [High]

- ✓ For attempt, solicitation, conspiracy (RCW 9.94A.595) see page 23 or for gang-related felonies where the court found the offender involved a minor (RCW 9.94A.833) see page 186 for standard range adjustments.
- ✓ For deadly weapon enhancement, see page 190.
- ✓ For sentencing alternatives, see page 177.
- ✓ For community custody eligibility, see page 187.
- ✓ For any applicable enhancements other than deadly weapon enhancement, see page 183.
- ✓ If the offender is not a persistent offender and the <u>current offense</u> was committed on or after 9/1/2001, then the offender is subject to the requirements under RCW 9.94A.507.
- ✓ Multiple current serious violent offenses shall have consecutive sentences imposed per the rules of RCW 9.94A.589(1)(b).

The Caseload Forecast Council is not liable for errors or omissions in the manual, for sentences that may be inappropriately calculated as a result of a practitioner's or court's reliance on the manual, or for any other written or verbal information related to adult or juvenile sentencing. The scoring sheets are intended to provide assistance in most cases but do not cover all permutations of the scoring rules. If you find any errors or omissions, we encourage you to report them to the Caseload Forecast Council.

Murder Second Degree With A Finding Of Sexual Motivation

RCW 9A.32.050
SERIOUS VIOLENT/SEX
SOLICIATION = CLASS A
CONSPIRACY = CLASS B

OFFENDER SCORING RCW 9.94A.525(17)

ADULT HISTORY:
    Enter number of sex offense felony convictions .... _____ x 3 = _____
    Enter number of serious violent felony convictions .... _____ x 3 = _____
    Enter number of violent felony convictions .... _____ x 2 = _____
    Enter number of nonviolent felony convictions .... _____ x 1 = _____

JUVENILE HISTORY:
    Enter number of sex offense felony dispositions .... _____ x 3 = _____
    Enter number of serious violent felony dispositions .... _____ x 3 = _____
    Enter number of violent felony dispositions .... _____ x 2 = _____
    Enter number of nonviolent felony dispositions .... _____ x ½ = _____

OTHER CURRENT OFFENSES:
(Other current offenses that do not encompass the same conduct count in offender score)
    Enter number of other sex offense felony convictions .... _____ x 3 = _____
    Enter number of other violent felony convictions .... _____ x 2 = _____
    Enter number of other nonviolent felony convictions .... _____ x 1 = _____

STATUS:
    Was the offender on community custody on the date the current offense was committed?.............. + 1 = _____

Total the last column to get the **Offender Score** (Round down to the nearest whole number)

SENTENCE RANGE

	Offender Score									
	0	1	2	3	4	5	6	7	8	9+
LEVEL XIV	171.5m	184m	194m	204m	215m	225m	245m	266m	307m	347.5m
	123 - 220	134 - 234	144 - 244	154 - 254	165 - 265	175 - 275	195 - 295	216 - 316	257 - 357	298 - 397

Add Sexual Motivation Enhancement (see page 185) [___] to Standard Range = [Low] to [High]

- ✓ For attempt, solicitation, conspiracy (RCW 9.94A.595) see page 23 or for gang-related felonies where the court found the offender involved a minor (RCW 9.94A.833) see page 186 for standard range adjustments.
- ✓ For deadly weapon enhancement, see page 190.
- ✓ For sentencing alternatives, see page 177.
- ✓ For community custody eligibility, see page 187.
- ✓ For any applicable enhancements other than deadly weapon enhancement, see page 183.
- ✓ Multiple current serious violent offenses shall have consecutive sentences imposed per the rules of RCW 9.94A.589(1)(b).
- ✓ If the offender is not a persistent offender and has a prior conviction for an offense listed in RCW 9.94A.030(38)(b), then the sentence is subject to the requirements of RCW 9.94A.507.

The Caseload Forecast Council is not liable for errors or omissions in the manual, for sentences that may be inappropriately calculated as a result of a practitioner's or court's reliance on the manual, or for any other written or verbal information related to adult or juvenile sentencing. The scoring sheets are intended to provide assistance in most cases but do not cover all permutations of the scoring rules. If you find any errors or omissions, we encourage you to report them to the Caseload Forecast Council.

Organized Retail Theft First Degree

RCW 9A.56.350(2)
CLASS B – NONVIOLENT

OFFENDER SCORING RCW 9.94A.525(7)

If it was found that this offense was committed with sexual motivation (RCW 9.94A.533(8)) on or after 7/01/2006, use the General Nonviolent Offense with a Sexual Motivation Finding scoring form on page 193.

If the present conviction is for a felony domestic violence offense where domestic violence was plead and proven, use the General Nonviolent Offense Where Domestic Violence Has Been Plead and Proven scoring form on page 191.

ADULT HISTORY:
  Enter number of felony convictions .... _____ x 1 = _____

JUVENILE HISTORY:
  Enter number of serious violent and violent felony dispositions .... _____ x 1 = _____
  Enter number of nonviolent felony dispositions .... _____ x ½ = _____

OTHER CURRENT OFFENSES:
(Other current offenses that do not encompass the same conduct count in offender score)
  Enter number of other felony convictions .... _____ x 1 = _____

STATUS:
  Was the offender on community custody on the date the current offense was committed? (if yes)....... + 1 = _____

Total the last column to get the **Offender Score** (Round down to the nearest whole number)

SENTENCE RANGE

	Offender Score									
	0	1	2	3	4	5	6	7	8	9+
LEVEL III	2m	5m	8m	11m	14m	19.5m	25.5m	38m	50m	59.5m
	1 - 3	3 - 8	4 - 12	9 - 12	12+ - 16	17 - 22	22 - 29	33 - 43	43 - 57	51 - 68

✓ For attempt, solicitation, conspiracy (RCW 9.94A.595) see page 23 or for gang-related felonies where the court found the offender involved a minor (RCW 9.94A.833) see page 186 for standard range adjustments.

✓ For deadly weapon enhancement, see page 190.

✓ For sentencing alternatives, see page 177.

✓ For community custody eligibility, see page 187.

✓ For any applicable enhancements other than deadly weapon enhancement, see page 183.

The Caseload Forecast Council is not liable for errors or omissions in the manual, for sentences that may be inappropriately calculated as a result of a practitioner's or court's reliance on the manual, or for any other written or verbal information related to adult or juvenile sentencing. The scoring sheets are intended to provide assistance in most cases but do not cover all permutations of the scoring rules. If you find any errors or omissions, we encourage you to report them to the Caseload Forecast Council.

Organized Retail Theft Second Degree

RCW 9A.56.350(3)
CLASS C – NONVIOLENT

OFFENDER SCORING RCW 9.94A.525(7)

If it was found that this offense was committed with sexual motivation (RCW 9.94A.533(8)) on or after 7/01/2006, use the General Nonviolent Offense with a Sexual Motivation Finding scoring form on page 193.

If the present conviction is for a felony domestic violence offense where domestic violence was plead and proven, use the General Nonviolent Offense Where Domestic Violence Has Been Plead and Proven scoring form on page 191.

ADULT HISTORY:
    Enter number of felony convictions .... _____ x 1 = _____

JUVENILE HISTORY:
    Enter number of serious violent and violent felony dispositions .... _____ x 1 = _____
    Enter number of nonviolent felony dispositions .... _____ x ½ = _____

OTHER CURRENT OFFENSES:
(Other current offenses that do not encompass the same conduct count in offender score)
    Enter number of other felony convictions .... _____ x 1 = _____

STATUS:
    Was the offender on community custody on the date the current offense was committed? (if yes) ...... + 1 = _____

Total the last column to get the **Offender Score** (Round down to the nearest whole number)

SENTENCE RANGE

	Offender Score									
	0	1	2	3	4	5	6	7	8	9+
LEVEL II	0-90 days	4m 2 - 6	6m 3 - 9	8m 4 - 12	13m 12+ - 14	16m 14 - 18	19.5m 17 - 22	25.5m 22 - 29	38m 33 - 43	50m 43 - 57

- ✓ For or gang-related felonies where the court found the offender involved a minor (RCW 9.94A.833) see page 186 for standard range adjustment.
- ✓ For deadly weapon enhancement, see page 190.
- ✓ For sentencing alternatives, see page 177.
- ✓ For community custody eligibility, see page 187.
- ✓ For any applicable enhancements other than deadly weapon enhancement, see page 183.

The Caseload Forecast Council is not liable for errors or omissions in the manual, for sentences that may be inappropriately calculated as a result of a practitioner's or court's reliance on the manual, or for any other written or verbal information related to adult or juvenile sentencing. The scoring sheets are intended to provide assistance in most cases but do not cover all permutations of the scoring rules. If you find any errors or omissions, we encourage you to report them to the Caseload Forecast Council.

Over 18 And Deliver Heroin, Methamphetamine, A Narcotic From Schedule I Or II Or Flunitrazepam From Schedule IV To Someone Under 18

RCW 69.50.406(1)
CLASS A – VIOLENT/DRUG

OFFENDER SCORING RCW 9.94A.525(13)

If it was found that this offense was committed with sexual motivation (RCW 9.94A.533(8)) on or after 7/01/2006, use the General Drug Offense with a Sexual Motivation Finding scoring form on page 195.

If the present conviction is for a felony domestic violence offense where domestic violence was plead and proven, use the General Drug Offense Where Domestic Violence Has Been Plead and Proven scoring form on page 194.

ADULT HISTORY:
   Does the offender have a prior sex or serious violent offense in history?
      YES Enter number of felony drug convictions .... _____ x 3 = _____
      NO Enter number of felony drug convictions .... _____ x 1 = _____
   Enter number of serious violent and violent felony convictions .... _____ x 2 = _____
   Enter number of nonviolent felony convictions .... _____ x 1 = _____

JUVENILE HISTORY:
   Does the offender have a prior sex or serious violent offense in history?
      YES Enter number of felony drug dispositions .... _____ x 2 = _____
      NO Enter number of felony drug dispositions .... _____ x ½ = _____
   Enter number of serious violent and violent felony dispositions .... _____ x 2 = _____
   Enter number of nonviolent felony dispositions .... _____ x ½ = _____

OTHER CURRENT OFFENSES:
(Other current offenses that do not encompass the same conduct count in offender score)
   Does the offender have other prior sex or serious violent offense in history?
      YES Enter number of other felony drug convictions .... _____ x 3 = _____
      NO Enter number of other felony drug convictions .... _____ x 1 = _____
   Enter number of other serious violent and violent felony convictions .... _____ x 2 = _____
   Enter number of other nonviolent felony convictions .... _____ x 1 = _____

STATUS:
   Was the offender on community custody on the date the current offense was committed? (if yes) .... + 1 = _____

Total the last column to get the **Offender Score** (Round down to the nearest whole number)

SENTENCE RANGE – DRUG

	Offender Score		
	0 to 2	**3 to 5**	**6 to 9+**
LEVEL III	59.5m 51 - 68	84m 68+ - 100	110m 100+ - 120

- ✓ For attempt, solicitation or conspiracy drug felonies see page 25 or for gang-related felonies where the court found the offender involved a minor (RCW 9.94A.833) see page 186 for standard range adjustments.
- ✓ Per RCW 9.94A.518, any felony offense under chapter 69.50 RCW with a deadly weapon special verdict under RCW 9.94A.602 becomes a level III offense.
- ✓ For deadly weapon enhancement, see page 190.
- ✓ For sentencing alternatives, see page 177.
- ✓ For community custody eligibility, see page 187.
- ✓ For any applicable enhancements other than deadly weapon enhancement, see page 183.
- ✓ Per RCW 69.50.408, the statutory maximum for a **subsequent conviction** under chapter 69.50 RCW is 240 months (based on RCW 69.50.406(1)).
- ✓ Per RCW 69.50.406(1), the current offense is punishable by a term of imprisonment up to 480 months, i.e. twice that authorized by RCW 69.50.401(2)(a) or (b).

The Caseload Forecast Council is not liable for errors or omissions in the manual, for sentences that may be inappropriately calculated as a result of a practitioner's or court's reliance on the manual, or for any other written or verbal information related to adult or juvenile sentencing. The scoring sheets are intended to provide assistance in most cases but do not cover all permutations of the scoring rules. If you find any errors or omissions, we encourage you to report them to the Caseload Forecast Council.

Over 18 And Deliver Narcotic From Schedule III, IV, Or V Or A Nonnarcotic, Except Flunitrazepam Or Methamphetamine, From Schedule IV To Someone Under 18 And 3 Years Junior

RCW 69.50.406(2)
CLASS B – NONVIOLENT/DRUG

OFFENDER SCORING RCW 9.94A.525(13)

If it was found that this offense was committed with sexual motivation (RCW 9.94A.533(8)) on or after 7/01/2006, use the General Drug Offense with a Sexual Motivation Finding scoring form on page 195.

If the present conviction is for a felony domestic violence offense where domestic violence was plead and proven, use the General Drug Offense Where Domestic Violence Has Been Plead and Proven scoring form on page 194.

ADULT HISTORY:
Does the offender have a prior sex or serious violent offense in history?
    YES Enter number of felony drug convictions... _____ x 3 = _____
    NO Enter number of felony drug convictions .... _____ x 1 = _____

Enter number of felony convictions .... _____ x 1 = _____

JUVENILE HISTORY:
Does the offender have a prior sex or serious violent offense in history?
    YES Enter number of felony drug dispositions... _____ x 2 = _____
    NO Enter number of felony drug dispositions... _____ x ½ = _____

Enter number of serious violent and violent felony dispositions .... _____ x 1 = _____

Enter number of nonviolent felony dispositions .... _____ x ½ = _____

OTHER CURRENT OFFENSES:
(Other current offenses that do not encompass the same conduct count in offender score)
Does the offender have other prior sex or serious violent offense in history?
    YES Enter number of other felony drug convictions .... _____ x 3 = _____
    NO Enter number of other felony drug convictions .... _____ x 1 = _____

Enter number of other felony convictions .... _____ x 1 = _____

STATUS:
Was the offender on community custody on the date the current offense was committed? (if yes)............ + 1 = _____

Total the last column to get the **Offender Score** (Round down to the nearest whole number)

SENTENCE RANGE – DRUG

	Offender Score		
	0 to 2	3 to 5	6 to 9+
LEVEL III	59.5m	84m	110m
	51 - 68	68+ - 100	100+ - 120

✓ For attempt, solicitation or conspiracy drug felonies see page 25 or for gang-related felonies where the court found the offender involved a minor (RCW 9.94A.833) see page 186 for standard range adjustments.
✓ Per RCW 9.94A.518, any felony offense under chapter 69.50 RCW with a deadly weapon special verdict under RCW 9.94A.602 becomes a level III offense.
✓ For deadly weapon enhancement, see page 190.
✓ For sentencing alternatives, see page 177.
✓ For community custody eligibility, see page 187.
✓ For any applicable enhancements other than deadly weapon enhancement, see page 183.
✓ Per RCW 69.50.408, the statutory maximum for a **subsequent conviction** under chapter 69-50 RCW is 240 months.
✓ Per RCW 69.50.406(1), the current offense is punishable by a term of imprisonment up to 120 months, i.e. twice that authorized by RCW 69.50.401(2)(c),(d) or (e).

The Caseload Forecast Council is not liable for errors or omissions in the manual, for sentences that may be inappropriately calculated as a result of a practitioner's or court's reliance on the manual, or for any other written or verbal information related to adult or juvenile sentencing. The scoring sheets are intended to provide assistance in most cases but do not cover all permutations of the scoring rules. If you find any errors or omissions, we encourage you to report them to the Caseload Forecast Council.

Perjury First Degree

RCW 9A.72.020
CLASS B – NONVIOLENT

OFFENDER SCORING RCW 9.94A.525(7)

If it was found that this offense was committed with sexual motivation (RCW 9.94A.533(8)) on or after 7/01/2006, use the General Nonviolent Offense with a Sexual Motivation Finding scoring form on page 193.

If the present conviction is for a felony domestic violence offense where domestic violence was plead and proven, use the General Nonviolent Offense Where Domestic Violence Has Been Plead and Proven scoring form on page 191.

ADULT HISTORY:
　Enter number of felony convictions .... _____ x 1 = _____

JUVENILE HISTORY:
　Enter number of serious violent and violent felony dispositions .... _____ x 1 = _____
　Enter number of nonviolent felony dispositions .... _____ x ½ = _____

OTHER CURRENT OFFENSES:
(Other current offenses that do not encompass the same conduct count in offender score)
　Enter number of other felony convictions .... _____ x 1 = _____

STATUS:
　Was the offender on community custody on the date the current offense was committed? (if yes)....... + 1 = _____

Total the last column to get the **Offender Score** (Round down to the nearest whole number)

SENTENCE RANGE

	_				Offender Score					
	0	**1**	**2**	**3**	**4**	**5**	**6**	**7**	**8**	**9+**
LEVEL V	9m	13m	15m	17.5m	25.5m	38m	47.5m	59.5m	72m	84m
	6 - 12	12+ - 14	13 - 17	15 - 20	22 - 29	33 - 43	41 - 54	51 - 68	62 - 82	72 - 96

- ✓ For attempt, solicitation, conspiracy (RCW 9.94A.595) see page 23 or for gang-related felonies where the court found the offender involved a minor (RCW 9.94A.833) see page 186 for standard range adjustments.
- ✓ For deadly weapon enhancement, see page 190.
- ✓ For sentencing alternatives, see page 177.
- ✓ For community custody eligibility, see page 187.
- ✓ For any applicable enhancements other than deadly weapon enhancement, see page 183.

The Caseload Forecast Council is not liable for errors or omissions in the manual, for sentences that may be inappropriately calculated as a result of a practitioner's or court's reliance on the manual, or for any other written or verbal information related to adult or juvenile sentencing. The scoring sheets are intended to provide assistance in most cases but do not cover all permutations of the scoring rules. If you find any errors or omissions, we encourage you to report them to the Caseload Forecast Council.

Perjury Second Degree

RCW 9A.72.030
CLASS C* – NONVIOLENT
OFFENDER SCORING RCW 9.94A.525(7)

If it was found that this offense was committed with sexual motivation (RCW 9.94A.533(8)) on or after 7/01/2006, use the General Nonviolent Offense with a Sexual Motivation Finding scoring form on page 193.

If the present conviction is for a felony domestic violence offense where domestic violence was plead and proven, use the General Nonviolent Offense Where Domestic Violence Has Been Plead and Proven scoring form on page 191.

ADULT HISTORY:
  Enter number of felony convictions .... _____ x 1 = _____

JUVENILE HISTORY:
  Enter number of serious violent and violent felony dispositions .... _____ x 1 = _____
  Enter number of nonviolent felony dispositions .... _____ x ½ = _____

OTHER CURRENT OFFENSES:
(Other current offenses that do not encompass the same conduct count in offender score)
  Enter number of other felony convictions .... _____ x 1 = _____

STATUS:
  Was the offender on community custody on the date the current offense was committed? (if yes) ...... + 1 = _____

Total the last column to get the **Offender Score** (Round down to the nearest whole number)

SENTENCE RANGE

	Offender Score									
	0	1	2	3	4	5	6	7	8	9+
LEVEL III	2m	5m	8m	11m	14m	19.5m	25.5m	38m	50m	55.5m
	1 - 3	3 - 8	4 - 12	9 - 12	12+ - 16	17 - 22	22 - 29	33 - 43	43 - 57	51 - 60*

- ✓ For or gang-related felonies where the court found the offender involved a minor (RCW 9.94A.833) see page 186 for standard range adjustment.
- ✓ For deadly weapon enhancement, see page 190.
- ✓ For sentencing alternatives, see page 177.
- ✓ For community custody eligibility, see page 187.
- ✓ For any applicable enhancements other than deadly weapon enhancement, see page 183.

The Caseload Forecast Council is not liable for errors or omissions in the manual, for sentences that may be inappropriately calculated as a result of a practitioner's or court's reliance on the manual, or for any other written or verbal information related to adult or juvenile sentencing. The scoring sheets are intended to provide assistance in most cases but do not cover all permutations of the scoring rules. If you find any errors or omissions, we encourage you to report them to the Caseload Forecast Council.

Persistent Prison Misbehavior

RCW 9.94.070
CLASS C* – NONVIOLENT
OFFENDER SCORING RCW 9.94A.525(7)

If it was found that this offense was committed with sexual motivation (RCW 9.94A.533(8)) on or after 7/01/2006, use the General Nonviolent Offense with a Sexual Motivation Finding scoring form on page 193.

If the present conviction is for a felony domestic violence offense where domestic violence was plead and proven, use the General Nonviolent Offense Where Domestic Violence Has Been Plead and Proven scoring form on page 191.

ADULT HISTORY:
    Enter number of felony convictions .... _____ x 1 = _____

JUVENILE HISTORY:
    Enter number of serious violent and violent felony dispositions .... _____ x 1 = _____

    Enter number of nonviolent felony dispositions .... _____ x ½ = _____

OTHER CURRENT OFFENSES:
(Other current offenses that do not encompass the same conduct count in offender score)
    Enter number of other felony convictions .... _____ x 1 = _____

STATUS:
    Was the offender on community custody on the date the current offense was committed? (if yes) .... + 1 = _____

Total the last column to get the **Offender Score** (Round down to the nearest whole number)

SENTENCE RANGE

	\multicolumn{11}{c}{Offender Score}
	0	1	2	3	4	5	6	7	8	9+
LEVEL V	9m	13m	15m	17.5m	25.5m	38m	47.5m	55.5m		
	6 - 12	12+ - 14	13 - 17	15 - 20	22 - 29	33 - 43	41 - 54	51 - 60*	60 - 60*	60 - 60*

- ✓ For gang-related felonies where the court found the offender involved a minor (RCW 9.94A.833) see page 186 for standard range adjustment.
- ✓ For deadly weapon enhancement, see page 190.
- ✓ For sentencing alternatives, see page 177.
- ✓ For community custody eligibility, see page 187.
- ✓ For any applicable enhancements other than deadly weapon enhancement, see page 183.

Physical Control Of A Vehicle While Under The Influence Of Intoxicating Liquor Or Any Drug

RCW 46.61.504(6)
CLASS C* – NONVIOLENT/TRAFFIC OFFENSE
OFFENDER SCORING RCW 9.94A.525(11)

ADULT HISTORY:
    Enter number of Vehicular Homicide and Vehicular Assault felony convictions .... _____ x 2 = _____
    Enter number of Operation of a Vessel While Under the Influence of Intoxicating Liquor or Any Drug felony convictions .... _____ x 1 = _____
    Enter number of felony convictions .... _____ x 1 = _____
    Enter number of Driving While Under the Influence of Intoxicating Liquor or Any Drug and Actual Physical Control While Under the Influence of Intoxicating Liquor or Any Drug and Reckless Driving and Hit-And-Run Attended Vehicle <u>non-felony</u> convictions .... _____ x 1 = _____

JUVENILE HISTORY:
    Enter number of Vehicular Homicide and Vehicular Assault dispositions........................... _____ x 2 = _____
    Enter number of Operation of a Vessel While Under the Influence of Intoxicating Liquor or Any Drug felony dispositions .... _____ x ½ = _____
    Enter number of felony dispositions .... _____ x ½ = _____
    Enter number of Driving While Under the Influence of Intoxicating Liquor or Any Drug and Actual Physical Control While Under the Influence of Intoxicating Liquor or Any Drug and Reckless Driving and Hit-And-Run Attended Vehicle <u>non-felony</u> convictions .... _____ x ½ = _____

OTHER CURRENT OFFENSES:
(Other current offenses that do not encompass the same conduct count in offender score)
    Enter number of Vehicular Homicide and Vehicular Assault convictions .... _____ x 2 = _____
    Enter number of other Operation of a Vessel While Under the Influence of Intoxicating Liquor or Any Drug felony convictions .... _____ x 1 = _____
    Enter number of other felony convictions .... _____ x 1 = _____
    Enter number of Driving While Under the Influence of Intoxicating Liquor or Any Drug and Actual Physical Control While Under the Influence of Intoxicating Liquor or Any Drug and Reckless Driving and Hit-And-Run Attended Vehicle <u>non-felony</u> convictions .... _____ x 1 = _____

STATUS:
    Was the offender on community custody on the date the current offense was committed? (if yes) ...... + 1 = _____

Total the last column to get the **Offender Score** (Round down to the nearest whole number)

SENTENCE RANGE

	Offender Score									
	0	1	2	3	4	5	6	7	8	9+
LEVEL V	9m 6 - 12	13m 12+ - 14	15m 13 - 17	17.5m 15 - 20	25.5m 22 - 29	38m 33 - 43	47.5m 41 - 54	55.5m 51 - 60*	60 - 60*	60 - 60*

- ✓ For attempt, solicitation, conspiracy (RCW 9.94A.595) see page 23 or for gang-related felonies where the court found the offender involved a minor (RCW 9.94A.833) see page 186 for standard range adjustments.
- ✓ For deadly weapon enhancement, see page 190.
- ✓ For sentencing alternatives, see page 177.
- ✓ For community custody eligibility, see page 187.
- ✓ For any applicable enhancements other than deadly weapon enhancement, see page 183.
- ✓ **For consecutive/concurrent provisions, see page 31.**

The Caseload Forecast Council is not liable for errors or omissions in the manual, for sentences that may be inappropriately calculated as a result of a practitioner's or court's reliance on the manual, or for any other written or verbal information related to adult or juvenile sentencing. The scoring sheets are intended to provide assistance in most cases but do not cover all permutations of the scoring rules. If you find any errors or omissions, we encourage you to report them to the Caseload Forecast Council.

Possession Of Controlled Substance That Is Either Heroin Or Narcotics From Schedule I Or II

RCW 69.50.4013
CLASS C – NONVIOLENT

OFFENDER SCORING RCW 9.94A.525(7)

If it was found that this offense was committed with sexual motivation (RCW 9.94A.533(8)) on or after 7/01/2006, use the General Nonviolent Offense with a Sexual Motivation Finding scoring form on page 193.

If the present conviction is for a felony domestic violence offense where domestic violence was plead and proven, use the General Nonviolent Offense Where Domestic Violence Has Been Plead and Proven scoring form on page 191.

ADULT HISTORY:
Enter number of felony convictions .... _____ x 1 = _____

JUVENILE HISTORY:
Enter number of serious violent and violent felony dispositions .... _____ x 1 = _____
Enter number of nonviolent felony dispositions .... _____ x ½ = _____

OTHER CURRENT OFFENSES:
(Other current offenses that do not encompass the same conduct count in offender score)
Enter number of other felony convictions .... _____ x 1 = _____

STATUS:
Was the offender on community custody on the date the current offense was committed? (if yes)....... + 1 = _____

Total the last column to get the **Offender Score** (Round down to the nearest whole number)

SENTENCE RANGE - DRUG

	Offender Score		
	0 to 2	3 to 5	6 to 9+
LEVEL I	3m 0 - 6	9m 6+ - 12	18m 12+ - 24

- ✓ For attempt, solicitation, conspiracy (RCW 9.94A.595) see page 23 or for gang-related felonies where the court found the offender involved a minor (RCW 9.94A.833) see page 186 for standard range adjustments.
- ✓ Per RCW 9.94A.518, any felony offense under chapter 69.50 RCW with a deadly weapon special verdict under RCW 9.94A.602 becomes a level III offense.
- ✓ For deadly weapon enhancement, see page 190.
- ✓ For sentencing alternatives, see page 177.
- ✓ For community custody eligibility, see page 187.
- ✓ For any applicable enhancements other than deadly weapon enhancement, see page 183.

The Caseload Forecast Council is not liable for errors or omissions in the manual, for sentences that may be inappropriately calculated as a result of a practitioner's or court's reliance on the manual, or for any other written or verbal information related to adult or juvenile sentencing. The scoring sheets are intended to provide assistance in most cases but do not cover all permutations of the scoring rules. If you find any errors or omissions, we encourage you to report them to the Caseload Forecast Council.

Possession Of Controlled Substance That Is A Narcotic From Schedule III, IV Or V Or Nonnarcotic From Schedule I-V

RCW 69.50.4013
CLASS C – NONVIOLENT

OFFENDER SCORING RCW 9.94A.525(7)

If it was found that this offense was committed with sexual motivation (RCW 9.94A.533(8)) on or after 7/01/2006, use the General Nonviolent Offense with a Sexual Motivation Finding scoring form on page 193.

If the present conviction is for a felony domestic violence offense where domestic violence was plead and proven, use the General Nonviolent Offense Where Domestic Violence Has Been Plead and Proven scoring form on page 191.

ADULT HISTORY:
    Enter number of felony convictions .... _____ x 1 = _____

JUVENILE HISTORY:
    Enter number of serious violent and violent felony dispositions .... _____ x 1 = _____
    Enter number of nonviolent felony dispositions .... _____ x ½ = _____

OTHER CURRENT OFFENSES:
(Other current offenses that do not encompass the same conduct count in offender score)
    Enter number of other felony convictions .... _____ x 1 = _____

STATUS:
    Was the offender on community custody on the date the current offense was committed? (if yes) ...... + 1 = _____

Total the last column to get the **Offender Score** (Round down to the nearest whole number)

SENTENCE RANGE - DRUG

	Offender Score		
	0 to 2	3 to 5	6 to 9+
LEVEL I	3m 0 - 6	9m 6+ - 12	18m 12+ - 24

- ✓ For attempt, solicitation, conspiracy (RCW 9.94A.595) see page 23 or for gang-related felonies where the court found the offender involved a minor (RCW 9.94A.833) see page 186 for standard range adjustments.
- ✓ Per RCW 9.94A.518, any felony offense under chapter 69.50 RCW with a deadly weapon special verdict under RCW 9.94A.602 becomes a level III offense.
- ✓ For deadly weapon enhancement, see page 190.
- ✓ For sentencing alternatives, see page 177.
- ✓ For community custody eligibility, see page 187.
- ✓ For any applicable enhancements other than deadly weapon enhancement, see page 183.

2016 Washington State Adult Sentencing Guidelines Manual   Ver. 20161220

Possession Of Depictions Of Minor Engaged In Sexually Explicit Conduct First Degree

RCW 9.68A.070(1)
CLASS B – NONVIOLENT/SEX
OFFENDER SCORING RCW 9.94A.525(17)

If the present conviction is for a felony domestic violence offense where domestic violence was plead and proven, use the General Nonviolent/Sex Offense Where Domestic Violence Has Been Plead and Proven scoring form on page 192.

ADULT HISTORY:
    Enter number of sex offense felony convictions .... _____ x 3 = _____
    Enter number of felony convictions .... _____ x 1 = _____

JUVENILE HISTORY:
    Enter number of sex offense felony dispositions .... _____ x 3 = _____
    Enter number of serious violent and violent felony dispositions .... _____ x 1 = _____
    Enter number of nonviolent felony dispositions .... _____ x ½ = _____

OTHER CURRENT OFFENSES:
(Other current offenses that do not encompass the same conduct count in offender score)
    Enter number of sex offense felony convictions .... _____ x 3 = _____
    Enter number of other felony convictions .... _____ x 1 = _____

STATUS:
    Was the offender on community custody on the date the current offense was committed? (if yes) .... + 1 = _____

Total the last column to get the **Offender Score** (Round down to the nearest whole number)

SENTENCE RANGE

	\multicolumn{10}{c}{Offender Score}
	0	1	2	3	4	5	6	7	8	9+
LEVEL VI	13m	17.5m	24m	30m	36m	42m	53.5m	66m	78m	89.5m
	12+ - 14	15 - 20	21 - 27	26 - 34	31 - 41	36 - 48	46 - 61	57 - 75	67 - 89	77 - 102

- ✓ For attempt, solicitation, conspiracy (RCW 9.94A.595) see page 23 or for gang-related felonies where the court found the offender involved a minor (RCW 9.94A.833) see page 186 for standard range adjustments.
- ✓ For deadly weapon enhancement, see page 190.
- ✓ For sentencing alternatives, see page 177.
- ✓ For community custody eligibility, see page 187.
- ✓ For any applicable enhancements other than deadly weapon enhancement, see page 183.
- ✓ If the offender is not a persistent offender and has a prior conviction for an offense listed in RCW 9.94A.030(38)(b), then the sentence is subject to the requirements of RCW 9.94A.507.

The Caseload Forecast Council is not liable for errors or omissions in the manual, for sentences that may be inappropriately calculated as a result of a practitioner's or court's reliance on the manual, or for any other written or verbal information related to adult or juvenile sentencing. The scoring sheets are intended to provide assistance in most cases but do not cover all permutations of the scoring rules. If you find any errors or omissions, we encourage you to report them to the Caseload Forecast Council.

Possession Of Depictions Of Minor Engaged In Sexually Explicit Conduct Second Degree

RCW 9.68A.070(2)
CLASS C* – NONVIOLENT/SEX

OFFENDER SCORING RCW 9.94A.525(17)

If the present conviction is for a felony domestic violence offense where domestic violence was plead and proven, use the General Nonviolent/Sex Offense Where Domestic Violence Has Been Plead and Proven scoring form on page 192.

ADULT HISTORY:
    Enter number of sex offense felony convictions .... _____ x 3 = _____
    Enter number of felony convictions .... _____ x 1 = _____

JUVENILE HISTORY:
    Enter number of sex offense felony dispositions .... _____ x 3 = _____
    Enter number of serious violent and violent felony dispositions .... _____ x 1 = _____
    Enter number of nonviolent felony dispositions .... _____ x ½ = _____

OTHER CURRENT OFFENSES:
(Other current offenses that do not encompass the same conduct count in offender score)
    Enter number of sex offense felony convictions .... _____ x 3 = _____
    Enter number of other felony convictions .... _____ x 1 = _____

STATUS:
    Was the offender on community custody on the date the current offense was committed? (if yes) ...... + 1 = _____

Total the last column to get the **Offender Score** (Round down to the nearest whole number)

SENTENCE RANGE

	\multicolumn{11}{c}{Offender Score}
	0	1	2	3	4	5	6	7	8	9+
LEVEL IV	6m 3 - 9	9m 6 - 12	13m 12+ - 14	15m 13 - 17	17.5m 15 - 20	25.5m 22 - 29	38m 33 - 43	50m 43 - 57	56.5m 53 - 60*	60 - 60*

✓ For attempt, solicitation, conspiracy (RCW 9.94A.595) see page 23 or for gang-related felonies where the court found the offender involved a minor (RCW 9.94A.833) see page 186 for standard range adjustments.

✓ For deadly weapon enhancement, see page 190.

✓ For sentencing alternatives, see page 177.

✓ For community custody eligibility, see page 187.

✓ For any applicable enhancements other than deadly weapon enhancement, see page 183.

✓ If the offender is not a persistent offender and has a prior conviction for an offense listed in RCW 9.94A.030(38)(b), then the sentence is subject to the requirements of RCW 9.94A.507.

The Caseload Forecast Council is not liable for errors or omissions in the manual, for sentences that may be inappropriately calculated as a result of a practitioner's or court's reliance on the manual, or for any other written or verbal information related to adult or juvenile sentencing. The scoring sheets are intended to provide assistance in most cases but do not cover all permutations of the scoring rules. If you find any errors or omissions, we encourage you to report them to the Caseload Forecast Council.

Possession Of Ephedrine, Pseudoephedrine Or Anhydrous Ammonia With Intent To Manufacture Methamphetamine

RCW 69.50.440
CLASS B – NONVIOLENT/DRUG

OFFENDER SCORING RCW 9.94A.525(13)

If it was found that this offense was committed with sexual motivation (RCW 9.94A.533(8)) on or after 7/01/2006, use the General Drug Offense with a Sexual Motivation Finding scoring form on page 195.

If the present conviction is for a felony domestic violence offense where domestic violence was plead and proven, use the General Drug Offense Where Domestic Violence Has Been Plead and Proven scoring form on page 194.

ADULT HISTORY:
   Does the offender have a prior sex or serious violent offense in history?
      YES Enter number of felony drug convictions .... _____ x 3 = _____
      NO Enter number of felony drug convictions .... _____ x 1 = _____
   Enter number of felony convictions .... _____ x 1 = _____

JUVENILE HISTORY:
   Does the offender have a prior sex or serious violent offense in history?
      YES Enter number of felony drug dispositions .... _____ x 2 = _____
      NO Enter number of felony drug dispositions .... _____ x ½ = _____
   Enter number of serious violent and violent felony dispositions .... _____ x 1 = _____
   Enter number of nonviolent felony dispositions .... _____ x ½ = _____

OTHER CURRENT OFFENSES:
(Other current offenses that do not encompass the same conduct count in offender score)
   Does the offender have other prior sex or serious violent offense in history?
      YES Enter number of other felony drug convictions .... _____ x 3 = _____
      NO Enter number of other felony drug convictions .... _____ x 1 = _____
   Enter number of other felony convictions .... _____ x 1 = _____

STATUS:
   Was the offender on community custody on the date the current offense was committed? (if yes) .... + 1 = _____

Total the last column to get the **Offender Score** (Round down to the nearest whole number)

SENTENCE RANGE – DRUG

	Offender Score		
	0 to 2	3 to 5	6 to 9+
LEVEL III	59.5m	84m	110m
	51 - 68	68+ - 100	100+ - 120

- ✓ For attempt, solicitation or conspiracy drug felonies see page 25 or for gang-related felonies where the court found the offender involved a minor (RCW 9.94A.833) see page 186 for standard range adjustments.
- ✓ Per RCW 9.94A.518, any felony offense under chapter 69.50 RCW with a deadly weapon special verdict under RCW 9.94A.602 becomes a level III offense.
- ✓ For deadly weapon enhancement, see page 190.
- ✓ For sentencing alternatives, see page 177.
- ✓ For community custody eligibility, see page 187.
- ✓ For any applicable enhancements other than deadly weapon enhancement, see page 183.
- ✓ Per RCW 69.50.408, the statutory maximum for a **subsequent conviction** under chapter 69.50 RCW is 240 months.

The Caseload Forecast Council is not liable for errors or omissions in the manual, for sentences that may be inappropriately calculated as a result of a practitioner's or court's reliance on the manual, or for any other written or verbal information related to adult or juvenile sentencing. The scoring sheets are intended to provide assistance in most cases but do not cover all permutations of the scoring rules. If you find any errors or omissions, we encourage you to report them to the Caseload Forecast Council.

Possession Of An Incendiary Device

RCW 9.40.120
CLASS B – NONVIOLENT
OFFENDER SCORING RCW 9.94A.525(7)

If it was found that this offense was committed with sexual motivation (RCW 9.94A.533(8)) on or after 7/01/2006, use the General Nonviolent Offense with a Sexual Motivation Finding scoring form on page 193.

If the present conviction is for a felony domestic violence offense where domestic violence was plead and proven, use the General Nonviolent Offense Where Domestic Violence Has Been Plead and Proven scoring form on page 191.

ADULT HISTORY:
  Enter number of felony convictions .... _____ x 1 = _____

JUVENILE HISTORY:
  Enter number of serious violent and violent felony dispositions .... _____ x 1 = _____
  Enter number of nonviolent felony dispositions .... _____ x ½ = _____

OTHER CURRENT OFFENSES:
(Other current offenses that do not encompass the same conduct count in offender score)
  Enter number of other felony convictions .... _____ x 1 = _____

STATUS:
  Was the offender on community custody on the date the current offense was committed? (if yes) ...... + 1 = _____

Total the last column to get the **Offender Score** (Round down to the nearest whole number)

SENTENCE RANGE

	\multicolumn{10}{c}{Offender Score}
	0	1	2	3	4	5	6	7	8	9+
LEVEL III	2m	5m	8m	11m	14m	19.5m	25.5m	38m	50m	59.5m
	1 - 3	3 - 8	4 - 12	9 - 12	12+ - 16	17 - 22	22 - 29	33 - 43	43 - 57	51 - 68

- ✓ For attempt, solicitation, conspiracy (RCW 9.94A.595) see page 23 or for gang-related felonies where the court found the offender involved a minor (RCW 9.94A.833) see page 186 for standard range adjustments.
- ✓ For deadly weapon enhancement, see page 190.
- ✓ For sentencing alternatives, see page 177.
- ✓ For community custody eligibility, see page 187.
- ✓ For any applicable enhancements other than deadly weapon enhancement, see page 183.

Possession Of A Machine Gun, Short-Barreled Shotgun Or Short-Barreled Rifle

RCW 9.41.190
CLASS C* – NONVIOLENT

OFFENDER SCORING RCW 9.94A.525(7)

If it was found that this offense was committed with sexual motivation (RCW 9.94A.533(8)) on or after 7/01/2006, use the General Nonviolent Offense with a Sexual Motivation Finding scoring form on page 193.

If the present conviction is for a felony domestic violence offense where domestic violence was plead and proven, use the General Nonviolent Offense Where Domestic Violence Has Been Plead and Proven scoring form on page 191.

ADULT HISTORY:
Enter number of felony convictions .... _____ x 1 = _____

JUVENILE HISTORY:
Enter number of serious violent and violent felony dispositions .... _____ x 1 = _____

Enter number of nonviolent felony dispositions .... _____ x ½ = _____

OTHER CURRENT OFFENSES:
(Other current offenses that do not encompass the same conduct count in offender score)
Enter number of other felony convictions .... _____ x 1 = _____

STATUS:
Was the offender on community custody on the date the current offense was committed? (if yes)....... + 1 = _____

Total the last column to get the **Offender Score** (Round down to the nearest whole number)

SENTENCE RANGE

	\multicolumn{11}{c}{Offender Score}
	0	1	2	3	4	5	6	7	8	9+
LEVEL III	2m 1 - 3	5m 3 - 8	8m 4 - 12	11m 9 - 12	14m 12+ - 16	19.5m 17 - 22	25.5m 22 - 29	38m 33 - 43	50m 43 - 57	55.5m 51 - 60*

- ✓ For gang-related felonies where the court found the offender involved a minor (RCW 9.94A.833) see page 186 for standard range adjustment.
- ✓ For sentencing alternatives, see page 177.
- ✓ For community custody eligibility, see page 187.
- ✓ For any applicable enhancements other than deadly weapon enhancement, see page 183.

The Caseload Forecast Council is not liable for errors or omissions in the manual, for sentences that may be inappropriately calculated as a result of a practitioner's or court's reliance on the manual, or for any other written or verbal information related to adult or juvenile sentencing. The scoring sheets are intended to provide assistance in most cases but do not cover all permutations of the scoring rules. If you find any errors or omissions, we encourage you to report them to the Caseload Forecast Council.

Possession Of A Stolen Firearm

RCW 9A.56.310
CLASS B – NONVIOLENT

OFFENDER SCORING RCW 9.94A.525(7)

If it was found that this offense was committed with sexual motivation (RCW 9.94A.533(8)) on or after 7/01/2006, use the General Nonviolent Offense with a Sexual Motivation Finding scoring form on page 193.

If the present conviction is for a felony domestic violence offense where domestic violence was plead and proven, use the General Nonviolent Offense Where Domestic Violence Has Been Plead and Proven scoring form on page 191.

ADULT HISTORY:
  Enter number of felony convictions .... _____ x 1 = _____

JUVENILE HISTORY:
  Enter number of serious violent and violent felony dispositions .... _____ x 1 = _____
  Enter number of nonviolent felony dispositions .... _____ x ½ = _____

OTHER CURRENT OFFENSES:
(Other current offenses that do not encompass the same conduct count in offender score)
  Enter number of other felony convictions .... _____ x 1 = _____

STATUS:
  Was the offender on community custody on the date the current offense was committed? (if yes) ...... + 1 = _____

Total the last column to get the **Offender Score** (Round down to the nearest whole number)

SENTENCE RANGE

	\multicolumn{10}{c}{Offender Score}
	0	**1**	**2**	**3**	**4**	**5**	**6**	**7**	**8**	**9+**
LEVEL V	9m 6 - 12	13m 12+ - 14	15m 13 - 17	17.5m 15 - 20	25.5m 22 - 29	38m 33 - 43	47.5m 41 - 54	59.5m 51 - 68	72m 62 - 82	84m 72 - 96

- ✓ For attempt, solicitation, conspiracy (RCW 9.94A.595) see page 23 or for gang-related felonies where the court found the offender involved a minor (RCW 9.94A.833) see page 186 for standard range adjustments.
- ✓ For sentencing alternatives, see page 177.
- ✓ For community custody eligibility, see page 187.
- ✓ For any applicable enhancements other than deadly weapon enhancement, see page 183.
- ✓ Each firearm possessed under this section is a separate offense.
- ✓ The offender shall be sentenced according to RCW 9.94A.589(1)(c) if the offender is convicted of Unlawful Possession of a Firearm 1 or 2 (RCW 9.41.040) and for felonies Theft of a Firearm or Possession of a Stolen Firearm, or both, as current offenses.
- ✓ If the present conviction is for Unlawful Possession of a Firearm 1 or 2 and felonies Theft of a Firearm or Possession of a Stolen Firearm, or both, charged under RCW 9.41.040, other current convictions for Unlawful Possession of a Firearm 1 or 2, Possession of a Stolen Firearm or Theft of a Firearm may not be included in the computation of the offender score per RCW 9.94A.589(1)(c). The offender will serve consecutive sentences for these particular offenses.

The Caseload Forecast Council is not liable for errors or omissions in the manual, for sentences that may be inappropriately calculated as a result of a practitioner's or court's reliance on the manual, or for any other written or verbal information related to adult or juvenile sentencing. The scoring sheets are intended to provide assistance in most cases but do not cover all permutations of the scoring rules. If you find any errors or omissions, we encourage you to report them to the Caseload Forecast Council.

Possession Of Stolen Property First Degree Other Than A Firearm Or Motor Vehicle

RCW 9A.56.150
CLASS B – NONVIOLENT

OFFENDER SCORING RCW 9.94A.525(7)

If it was found that this offense was committed with sexual motivation (RCW 9.94A.533(8)) on or after 7/01/2006, use the General Nonviolent Offense with a Sexual Motivation Finding scoring form on page 193.

If the present conviction is for a felony domestic violence offense where domestic violence was plead and proven, use the General Nonviolent Offense Where Domestic Violence Has Been Plead and Proven scoring form on page 191.

ADULT HISTORY:
Enter number of felony convictions .... _____ x 1 = _____

JUVENILE HISTORY:
Enter number of serious violent and violent felony dispositions .... _____ x 1 = _____

Enter number of nonviolent felony dispositions .... _____ x ½ = _____

OTHER CURRENT OFFENSES:
(Other current offenses that do not encompass the same conduct count in offender score)
Enter number of other felony convictions .... _____ x 1 = _____

STATUS:
Was the offender on community custody on the date the current offense was committed? (if yes) .... + 1 = _____

Total the last column to get the **Offender Score** (Round down to the nearest whole number)

SENTENCE RANGE

	Offender Score									
	0	1	2	3	4	5	6	7	8	9+
LEVEL II	0-90 days	4m 2 - 6	6m 3 - 9	8m 4 - 12	13m 12+ - 14	16m 14 - 18	19.5m 17 - 22	25.5m 22 - 29	38m 33 - 43	50m 43 - 57

- ✓ For attempt, solicitation, conspiracy (RCW 9.94A.595) see page 23 or for gang-related felonies where the court found the offender involved a minor (RCW 9.94A.833) see page 186 for standard range adjustments.
- ✓ For deadly weapon enhancement, see page 190.
- ✓ For sentencing alternatives, see page 177.
- ✓ For community custody eligibility, see page 187.
- ✓ For any applicable enhancements other than deadly weapon enhancement, see page 183.

The Caseload Forecast Council is not liable for errors or omissions in the manual, for sentences that may be inappropriately calculated as a result of a practitioner's or court's reliance on the manual, or for any other written or verbal information related to adult or juvenile sentencing. The scoring sheets are intended to provide assistance in most cases but do not cover all permutations of the scoring rules. If you find any errors or omissions, we encourage you to report them to the Caseload Forecast Council.

Possession Of Stolen Property Second Degree Other Than A Firearm Or Motor Vehicle

RCW 9A.56.160
CLASS C – NONVIOLENT

OFFENDER SCORING RCW 9.94A.525(7)

If it was found that this offense was committed with sexual motivation (RCW 9.94A.533(8)) on or after 7/01/2006, use the General Nonviolent Offense with a Sexual Motivation Finding scoring form on page 193.

If the present conviction is for a felony domestic violence offense where domestic violence was plead and proven, use the General Nonviolent Offense Where Domestic Violence Has Been Plead and Proven scoring form on page 191.

ADULT HISTORY:
    Enter number of felony convictions .... _____ x 1 = _____

JUVENILE HISTORY:
    Enter number of serious violent and violent felony dispositions .... _____ x 1 = _____
    Enter number of nonviolent felony dispositions .... _____ x ½ = _____

OTHER CURRENT OFFENSES:
(Other current offenses that do not encompass the same conduct count in offender score)
    Enter number of other felony convictions .... _____ x 1 = _____

STATUS:
    Was the offender on community custody on the date the current offense was committed? (if yes) ...... + 1 = _____

Total the last column to get the **Offender Score** (Round down to the nearest whole number)

SENTENCE RANGE

	Offender Score									
	0	1	2	3	4	5	6	7	8	9+
LEVEL I	0-60 days	0-90 days	3m 2 - 5	4m 2 - 6	5.5m 3 - 8	8m 4 - 12	13m 12+ - 14	16m 14 - 18	19.5m 17 - 22	25.5m 22 - 29

- ✓ For gang-related felonies where the court found the offender involved a minor (RCW 9.94A.833) see page 186 for standard range adjustment.
- ✓ For deadly weapon enhancement, see page 190.
- ✓ For sentencing alternatives, see page 177.
- ✓ For community custody eligibility, see page 187.
- ✓ For any applicable enhancements other than deadly weapon enhancement, see page 183.

Possession Of A Stolen Vehicle

RCW 9A.56.068
CLASS B – NONVIOLENT

OFFENDER SCORING RCW 9.94A.525(20)

If it was found that this offense was committed with sexual motivation (RCW 9.94A.533(8)) on or after 7/01/2006, use the General Nonviolent Offense with a Sexual Motivation Finding scoring form on page 193.

If the present conviction is for a felony domestic violence offense where domestic violence was plead and proven, use the General Nonviolent Offense Where Domestic Violence Has Been Plead and Proven scoring form on page 191.

ADULT HISTORY:
Enter number of Theft of a Motor Vehicle, Theft 1 & 2 (of a Motor Vehicle), Possession of Stolen Property 1 & 2 (of a Motor Vehicle), Possession of a Stolen Vehicle and Taking a Motor Vehicle Without Permission 1 & 2 felony convictions .... _____ x 3 = _____

Enter number of Vehicle Prowling 2 convictions .... _____ x 1 = _____

Enter number of felony convictions .... _____ x 1 = _____

JUVENILE HISTORY:
Enter number of Theft of a Motor Vehicle, Theft 1 & 2 (of a Motor Vehicle), Possession of Stolen Property 1 & 2 (of a Motor Vehicle), Possession of a Stolen Vehicle and Taking a Motor Vehicle Without Permission 1 & 2 felony dispositions .... _____ x 3 = _____

Enter number of Vehicle Prowling 2 dispositions .... _____ x 1 = _____

Enter number of serious violent and violent felony dispositions .... _____ x 1 = _____

Enter number of nonviolent felony dispositions .... _____ x ½ = _____

OTHER CURRENT OFFENSES:
(Other current offenses that do not encompass the same conduct count in offender score)
Enter number of other Theft of a Motor Vehicle, Theft 1 & 2 (of a Motor Vehicle), Possession of Stolen Property 1 & 2 (of a Motor Vehicle), Possession of a Stolen Vehicle and Taking a Motor Vehicle Without Permission 1 & 2 felony convictions .... _____ x 3 = _____

Enter number of other Vehicle Prowling 2 convictions .... _____ x 1 = _____

Enter number of other felony convictions .... _____ x 1 = _____

STATUS:
Was the offender on community custody on the date the current offense was committed? (if yes) .... + 1 = _____

Total the last column to get the **Offender Score** (Round down to the nearest whole number)

SENTENCE RANGE

	Offender Score									
	0	1	2	3	4	5	6	7	8	9+
LEVEL II	0-90 days	4m 2 - 6	6m 3 - 9	8m 4 - 12	13m 12+ - 14	16m 14 - 18	19.5m 17 - 22	25.5m 22 - 29	38m 33 - 43	50m 43 - 57

- ✓ For attempt, solicitation, conspiracy (RCW 9.94A.595) see page 23 or for gang-related felonies where the court found the offender involved a minor (RCW 9.94A.833) see page 186 for standard range adjustments.
- ✓ For deadly weapon enhancement, see page 190.
- ✓ For sentencing alternatives, see page 177.
- ✓ For community custody eligibility, see page 187.
- ✓ For any applicable enhancements other than deadly weapon enhancement, see page 183.

The Caseload Forecast Council is not liable for errors or omissions in the manual, for sentences that may be inappropriately calculated as a result of a practitioner's or court's reliance on the manual, or for any other written or verbal information related to adult or juvenile sentencing. The scoring sheets are intended to provide assistance in most cases but do not cover all permutations of the scoring rules. If you find any errors or omissions, we encourage you to report them to the Caseload Forecast Council.

Promoting Commercial Sexual Abuse Of A Minor

RCW 9.68A.101
CLASS A – VIOLENT/SEX

OFFENDER SCORING RCW 9.94A.525(17)

If the present conviction is for a felony domestic violence offense where domestic violence was plead and proven, use the General Violent/Sex Offense Where Domestic Violence Has Been Plead and Proven scoring form on page 200.

ADULT HISTORY:
    Enter number of sex offense convictions .... _____ x 3 = _____
    Enter number of serious violent and violent felony convictions .... _____ x 2 = _____
    Enter number of nonviolent felony convictions .... _____ x 1 = _____

JUVENILE HISTORY:
    Enter number of sex offense dispositions .... _____ x 3 = _____
    Enter number of serious violent and violent felony dispositions .... _____ x 2 = _____
    Enter number of nonviolent felony dispositions .... _____ x ½ = _____

OTHER CURRENT OFFENSES:
(Other current offenses that do not encompass the same conduct count in offender score)
    Enter number of other sex offense convictions .... _____ x 3 = _____
    Enter number of other serious violent and violent felony convictions .... _____ x 2 = _____
    Enter number of other nonviolent felony convictions .... _____ x 1 = _____

STATUS:
    Was the offender on community custody on the date the current offense was committed?................. + 1 = _____

Total the last column to get the **Offender Score** (Round down to the nearest whole number)

SENTENCE RANGE

Offender Score	0	1	2	3	4	5	6	7	8	9+
LEVEL XII	108m 93 - 123	119m 102 - 136	129m 111 - 147	140m 120 - 160	150m 129 - 171	161m 138 - 184	189m 162 - 216	207m 178 - 236	243m 209 - 277	279m 240 - 318

- ✓ For attempt, solicitation, conspiracy (RCW 9.94A.595) see page 23 or for gang-related felonies where the court found the offender involved a minor (RCW 9.94A.833) see page 186 for standard range adjustments.
- ✓ For deadly weapon enhancement, see page 190.
- ✓ For sentencing alternatives, see page 177.
- ✓ For community custody eligibility, see page 187.
- ✓ For any applicable enhancements other than deadly weapon enhancement, see page 183.
- ✓ If the offender is not a persistent offender and has a prior conviction for an offense listed in RCW 9.94A.030(38)(b), then the sentence is subject to the requirements of RCW 9.94A.507.

Promoting Prostitution First Degree

RCW 9A.88.070
CLASS B* – NONVIOLENT
OFFENDER SCORING RCW 9.94A.525(7)

If it was found that this offense was committed with sexual motivation (RCW 9.94A.533(8)) on or after 7/01/2006, use the General Nonviolent Offense with a Sexual Motivation Finding scoring form on page 193.

If the present conviction is for a felony domestic violence offense where domestic violence was plead and proven, use the General Nonviolent Offense Where Domestic Violence Has Been Plead and Proven scoring form on page 191.

ADULT HISTORY:
Enter number of felony convictions .... _____ x 1 = _____

JUVENILE HISTORY:
Enter number of serious violent and violent felony dispositions .... _____ x 1 = _____

Enter number of nonviolent felony dispositions .... _____ x ½ = _____

OTHER CURRENT OFFENSES:
(Other current offenses that do not encompass the same conduct count in offender score)
Enter number of other felony convictions .... _____ x 1 = _____

STATUS:
Was the offender on community custody on the date the current offense was committed? (if yes) .... + 1 = _____

Total the last column to get the **Offender Score** (Round down to the nearest whole number)

SENTENCE RANGE

	\\multicolumn{10}{c}{Offender Score}									
	0	1	2	3	4	5	6	7	8	9+
LEVEL VIII	24m 21 - 27	30m 26 - 34	36m 31 - 41	42m 36 - 48	47.5m 41 - 54	53.5m 46 - 61	78m 67 - 89	89.5m 77 - 102	101.5m 87 - 116	114m 108 - 120*

- ✓ For attempt, solicitation, conspiracy (RCW 9.94A.595) see page 23 or for gang-related felonies where the court found the offender involved a minor (RCW 9.94A.833) see page 186 for standard range adjustments.
- ✓ For deadly weapon enhancement, see page 190.
- ✓ For sentencing alternatives, see page 177.
- ✓ For community custody eligibility, see page 187.
- ✓ For any applicable enhancements other than deadly weapon enhancement, see page 183.

The Caseload Forecast Council is not liable for errors or omissions in the manual, for sentences that may be inappropriately calculated as a result of a practitioner's or court's reliance on the manual, or for any other written or verbal information related to adult or juvenile sentencing. The scoring sheets are intended to provide assistance in most cases but do not cover all permutations of the scoring rules. If you find any errors or omissions, we encourage you to report them to the Caseload Forecast Council.

Promoting Prostitution Second Degree

RCW 9A.88.080
CLASS C* – NONVIOLENT

OFFENDER SCORING RCW 9.94A.525(7)

If it was found that this offense was committed with sexual motivation (RCW 9.94A.533(8)) on or after 7/01/2006, use the General Nonviolent Offense with a Sexual Motivation Finding scoring form on page 193.

If the present conviction is for a felony domestic violence offense where domestic violence was plead and proven, use the General Nonviolent Offense Where Domestic Violence Has Been Plead and Proven scoring form on page 191.

ADULT HISTORY:
    Enter number of felony convictions .... _____ x 1 = _____

JUVENILE HISTORY:
    Enter number of serious violent and violent felony dispositions .... _____ x 1 = _____
    Enter number of nonviolent felony dispositions .... _____ x ½ = _____

OTHER CURRENT OFFENSES:
(Other current offenses that do not encompass the same conduct count in offender score)
    Enter number of other felony convictions .... _____ x 1 = _____

STATUS:
    Was the offender on community custody on the date the current offense was committed? (if yes) ...... + 1 = _____

Total the last column to get the **Offender Score** (Round down to the nearest whole number)

SENTENCE RANGE

	\multicolumn{10}{c}{Offender Score}
	0	1	2	3	4	5	6	7	8	9+
LEVEL III	2m	5m	8m	11m	14m	19.5m	25.5m	38m	50m	55.5m
	1 - 3	3 - 8	4 - 12	9 - 12	12+ - 16	17 - 22	22 - 29	33 - 43	43 - 57	51 - 60*

✓ For gang-related felonies where the court found the offender involved a minor (RCW 9.94A.833) see page 186 for standard range adjustment.

✓ For deadly weapon enhancement, see page 190.

✓ For sentencing alternatives, see page 177.

✓ For community custody eligibility, see page 187.

✓ For any applicable enhancements other than deadly weapon enhancement, see page 183.

Rape First Degree

RCW 9A.44.040
CLASS A – SERIOUS VIOLENT/SEX
ATTEMPT = CLASS A

OFFENDER SCORING RCW 9.94A.525(17)

If the present conviction is for a felony domestic violence offense where domestic violence was plead and proven, use the General Serious Violent/Sex Offense Where Domestic Violence Has Been Plead and Proven scoring form on page 197.

ADULT HISTORY:
- Enter number of sex offense convictions .... x 3 = _____
- Enter number of serious violent felony convictions .... x 3 = _____
- Enter number of violent felony convictions .... x 2 = _____
- Enter number of nonviolent felony convictions .... x 1 = _____

JUVENILE HISTORY:
- Enter number of sex offense dispositions .... x 3 = _____
- Enter number of serious violent felony dispositions .... x 3 = _____
- Enter number of violent felony dispositions .... x 2 = _____
- Enter number of nonviolent felony dispositions .... x ½ = _____

OTHER CURRENT OFFENSES:
(Other current offenses that do not encompass the same conduct count in offender score)
- Enter number of other sex offense convictions .... x 3 = _____
- Enter number of other violent felony convictions .... x 2 = _____
- Enter number of other nonviolent felony convictions .... x 1 = _____

STATUS:
- Was the offender on community custody on the date the current offense was committed? .... + 1 = _____

Total the last column to get the **Offender Score** (Round down to the nearest whole number)

SENTENCE RANGE

					Offender Score					
	0	**1**	**2**	**3**	**4**	**5**	**6**	**7**	**8**	**9+**
LEVEL XII	108m	119m	129m	140m	150m	161m	189m	207m	243m	279m
	93 - 123	102 - 136	111 - 147	120 - 160	129 - 171	138 - 184	162 - 216	178 - 236	209 - 277	240 - 318

- ✓ For attempt (RCW 9.94A.595) see page 23 or for gang-related felonies where the court found the offender involved a minor (RCW 9.94A.833) see page 186 for standard range adjustments.
- ✓ For deadly weapon enhancement, see page 190.
- ✓ For sentencing alternatives, see page 177.
- ✓ For community custody eligibility, see page 187.
- ✓ For any applicable enhancements other than deadly weapon enhancement, see page 183.
- ✓ If the offender is not a persistent offender and the current offense was committed on or after 9/1/2001, then the offender is subject to the requirements under RCW 9.94A.507.
- ✓ Multiple current serious violent offenses shall have consecutive sentences imposed per the rules of RCW 9.94A.589(1)(b).
- ✓ Excluding convictions for attempt, the statutory minimum sentence is 60 months per RCW 9.94A.540 and is imposed under the rules of RCW 9.94A.507
- ✓ Per RCW 9.94A.507(3)(c)(ii), excluding convictions for attempt, the minimum term shall be either the maximum of the standard sentence range for the offense or 25 years, whichever is greater, for a finding that the victim was **under the age of 15** at the time of the offense under RCW 9.94A.837 or found to be **developmentally disabled, mentally disordered, a frail elder or vulnerable adult** at the time of the offense under RCW 9.94A.838.

The Caseload Forecast Council is not liable for errors or omissions in the manual, for sentences that may be inappropriately calculated as a result of a practitioner's or court's reliance on the manual, or for any other written or verbal information related to adult or juvenile sentencing. The scoring sheets are intended to provide assistance in most cases but do not cover all permutations of the scoring rules. If you find any errors or omissions, we encourage you to report them to the Caseload Forecast Council.

Rape First Degree

RCW 9A.44.040
SERIOUS VIOLENT/SEX
SOLICITATION = CLASS A
CONSPIRACY = CLASS B

OFFENDER SCORING RCW 9.94A.525(17)

If the present conviction is for a felony domestic violence offense where domestic violence was plead and proven, use the General Serious Violent/Sex Offense Where Domestic Violence Has Been Plead and Proven scoring form on page 197.

ADULT HISTORY:
  Enter number of sex offense convictions .... _____ x 3 = _____
  Enter number of serious violent felony convictions .... _____ x 3 = _____
  Enter number of violent felony convictions .... _____ x 2 = _____
  Enter number of nonviolent felony convictions .... _____ x 1 = _____

JUVENILE HISTORY:
  Enter number of sex offense dispositions .... _____ x 3 = _____
  Enter number of serious violent felony dispositions .... _____ x 3 = _____
  Enter number of violent felony dispositions .... _____ x 2 = _____
  Enter number of nonviolent felony dispositions .... _____ x ½ = _____

OTHER CURRENT OFFENSES:
(Other current offenses that do not encompass the same conduct count in offender score)
  Enter number of other sex offense convictions .... _____ x 3 = _____
  Enter number of other violent felony convictions .... _____ x 2 = _____
  Enter number of other nonviolent felony convictions .... _____ x 1 = _____

STATUS:
  Was the offender on community custody on the date the current offense was committed?.......... + 1 = _____

Total the last column to get the **Offender Score** (Round down to the nearest whole number)

SENTENCE RANGE

	\multicolumn{10}{c}{Offender Score}
	0	**1**	**2**	**3**	**4**	**5**	**6**	**7**	**8**	**9+**
LEVEL XII	108m	119m	129m	140m	150m	161m	189m	207m	243m	279m
	93 - 123	102 - 136	111 - 147	120 - 160	129 - 171	138 - 184	162 - 216	178 - 236	209 - 277	240 - 318

- ✓ For solicitation, conspiracy (RCW 9.94A.595) see page 23 or for gang-related felonies where the court found the offender involved a minor (RCW 9.94A.833) see page 186 for standard range adjustments.
- ✓ For deadly weapon enhancement, see page 190.
- ✓ For sentencing alternatives, see page 177.
- ✓ For community custody eligibility, see page 187.
- ✓ For any applicable enhancements other than deadly weapon enhancement, see page 183.
- ✓ If the offender is not a persistent offender and has a prior conviction for an offense listed in RCW 9.94A.030(38)(b), then the sentence is subject to the requirements of RCW 9.94A.507.
- ✓ Multiple current serious violent offenses shall have consecutive sentences imposed per the rules of RCW 9.94A.589(1)(b)

The Caseload Forecast Council is not liable for errors or omissions in the manual, for sentences that may be inappropriately calculated as a result of a practitioner's or court's reliance on the manual, or for any other written or verbal information related to adult or juvenile sentencing. The scoring sheets are intended to provide assistance in most cases but do not cover all permutations of the scoring rules. If you find any errors or omissions, we encourage you to report them to the Caseload Forecast Council.

Rape Second Degree

RCW 9A.44.050
CLASS A – VIOLENT/SEX
ATTEMPT = CLASS A

OFFENDER SCORING RCW 9.94A.525(17)

If the present conviction is for a felony domestic violence offense where domestic violence was plead and proven, use the General Violent/Sex Offense Where Domestic Violence Has Been Plead and Proven scoring form on page 200.

ADULT HISTORY:
    Enter number of sex offense convictions .... _____   x 3 = _____
    Enter number of serious violent and violent felony convictions .... _____   x 2 = _____
    Enter number of nonviolent felony convictions .... _____   x 1 = _____

JUVENILE HISTORY:
    Enter number of sex offense dispositions .... _____   x 3 = _____
    Enter number of serious violent and violent felony dispositions .... _____   x 2 = _____
    Enter number of nonviolent felony dispositions .... _____   x ½ = _____

OTHER CURRENT OFFENSES:
(Other current offenses that do not encompass the same conduct count in offender score)
    Enter number of other sex offense convictions .... _____   x 3 = _____
    Enter number of other serious violent and violent felony convictions .... _____   x 2 = _____
    Enter number of other nonviolent felony convictions .... _____   x 1 = _____

STATUS:
    Was the offender on community custody on the date the current offense was committed? ....   + 1 = _____

Total the last column to get the **Offender Score** (Round down to the nearest whole number)

SENTENCE RANGE

	\multicolumn{10}{c}{Offender Score}
	0	**1**	**2**	**3**	**4**	**5**	**6**	**7**	**8**	**9+**
LEVEL XI	90m 78 - 102	100m 86 - 114	110m 95 - 125	119m 102 - 136	129m 111 - 147	139m 120 - 158	170m 146 - 194	185m 159 - 211	215m 185 - 245	245m 210 - 280

- ✓ For attempt (RCW 9.94A.595) see page 23 or for gang-related felonies where the court found the offender involved a minor (RCW 9.94A.833) see page 186 for standard range adjustments.
- ✓ For deadly weapon enhancement, see page 190.
- ✓ For sentencing alternatives, see page 177.
- ✓ For community custody eligibility, see page 187.
- ✓ For any applicable enhancements other than deadly weapon enhancement, see page 183.
- ✓ If the offender is not a persistent offender and the <u>current offense</u> was committed on or after 9/1/2001, then the offender is subject to the requirements under RCW 9.94A.507.
- ✓ Per RCW 9.94A.507(3)(c)(ii), <u>excluding convictions for attempt</u>, the <u>minimum</u> term shall be either the maximum of the standard sentence range for the offense or 25 years, whichever is greater, for a finding that the victim was **under the age of 15** at the time of the offense under RCW 9.94A.837.
- ✓ For Rape 2 With Forcible Compulsion: Per RCW 9.94A.507(3)(c)(ii), <u>excluding convictions for attempt</u>, the <u>minimum</u> term shall be either the maximum of the standard sentence range for the offense or 25 years, whichever is greater, for a finding that the victim found to be **developmentally disabled, mentally disordered, a frail elder or vulnerable adult** at the time of the offense under RCW 9.94A.838.

The Caseload Forecast Council is not liable for errors or omissions in the manual, for sentences that may be inappropriately calculated as a result of a practitioner's or court's reliance on the manual, or for any other written or verbal information related to adult or juvenile sentencing. The scoring sheets are intended to provide assistance in most cases but do not cover all permutations of the scoring rules. If you find any errors or omissions, we encourage you to report them to the Caseload Forecast Council.

Rape Second Degree

RCW 9A.44.050
VIOLENT/SEX
SOLICITATION = CLASS A
CONSPIRACY = CLASS B

OFFENDER SCORING RCW 9.94A.525(17)

If the present conviction is for a felony domestic violence offense where domestic violence was plead and proven, use the General Violent/Sex Offense Where Domestic Violence Has Been Plead and Proven scoring form on page 200.

ADULT HISTORY:
    Enter number of sex offense convictions .... _____ x 3 = _____

    Enter number of serious violent and violent felony convictions .... _____ x 2 = _____

    Enter number of nonviolent felony convictions .... _____ x 1 = _____

JUVENILE HISTORY:
    Enter number of sex offense dispositions .... _____ x 3 = _____

    Enter number of serious violent and violent felony dispositions .... _____ x 2 = _____

    Enter number of nonviolent felony dispositions .... _____ x ½ = _____

OTHER CURRENT OFFENSES:
(Other current offenses that do not encompass the same conduct count in offender score)
    Enter number of other sex offense convictions .... _____ x 3 = _____

    Enter number of other serious violent and violent felony convictions .... _____ x 2 = _____

    Enter number of other nonviolent felony convictions .... _____ x 1 = _____

STATUS:
    Was the offender on community custody on the date the current offense was committed?................. + 1 = _____

Total the last column to get the **Offender Score** (Round down to the nearest whole number)

SENTENCE RANGE

	_	_	_	_	Offender Score	_	_	_	_	_
	0	**1**	**2**	**3**	**4**	**5**	**6**	**7**	**8**	**9+**
LEVEL XI	90m 78 - 102	100m 86 - 114	110m 95 - 125	119m 102 - 136	129m 111 - 147	139m 120 - 158	170m 146 - 194	185m 159 - 211	215m 185 - 245	245m 210 - 280

✓ For solicitation, conspiracy (RCW 9.94A.595) see page 23 or for gang-related felonies where the court found the offender involved a minor (RCW 9.94A.833) see page 186 for standard range adjustments.

✓ For deadly weapon enhancement, see page 190.

✓ For sentencing alternatives, see page 177.

✓ For community custody eligibility, see page 187.

✓ For any applicable enhancements other than deadly weapon enhancement, see page 183.

✓ If the offender is not a persistent offender and has a prior conviction for an offense listed in RCW 9.94A.030(38)(b), then the sentence is subject to the requirements of RCW 9.94A.507.

The Caseload Forecast Council is not liable for errors or omissions in the manual, for sentences that may be inappropriately calculated as a result of a practitioner's or court's reliance on the manual, or for any other written or verbal information related to adult or juvenile sentencing. The scoring sheets are intended to provide assistance in most cases but do not cover all permutations of the scoring rules. If you find any errors or omissions, we encourage you to report them to the Caseload Forecast Council.

Rape Third Degree

RCW 9A.44.060
CLASS C* – NONVIOLENT/SEX
OFFENDER SCORING RCW 9.94A.525(17)

If the present conviction is for a felony domestic violence offense where domestic violence was plead and proven, use the General Nonviolent/Sex Offense Where Domestic Violence Has Been Plead and Proven scoring form on page 192.

ADULT HISTORY:
    Enter number of sex offense felony convictions .... _____ x 3 = _____
    Enter number of felony convictions .... _____ x 1 = _____

JUVENILE HISTORY:
    Enter number of sex offense felony dispositions .... _____ x 3 = _____
    Enter number of serious violent and violent felony dispositions .... _____ x 1 = _____
    Enter number of nonviolent felony dispositions .... _____ x ½ = _____

OTHER CURRENT OFFENSES:
(Other current offenses that do not encompass the same conduct count in offender score)
    Enter number of sex offense felony convictions .... _____ x 3 = _____
    Enter number of other felony convictions .... _____ x 1 = _____

STATUS:
    Was the offender on community custody on the date the current offense was committed? (if yes)........ + 1 = _____

Total the last column to get the **Offender Score** (Round down to the nearest whole number)

SENTENCE RANGE

	Offender Score									
	0	1	2	3	4	5	6	7	8	9+
LEVEL V	9m	13m	15m	17.5m	25.5m	38m	47.5m	55.5m		
	6 - 12	12+ - 14	13 - 17	15 - 20	22 - 29	33 - 43	41 - 54	51 - 60*	60 - 60*	60 - 60*

- ✓ For gang-related felonies where the court found the offender involved a minor (RCW 9.94A.833) see page 186 for standard range adjustment.
- ✓ For deadly weapon enhancement, see page 190.
- ✓ For sentencing alternatives, see page 177.
- ✓ For community custody eligibility, see page 187.
- ✓ For any applicable enhancements other than deadly weapon enhancement, see page 183.
- ✓ If the offender is not a persistent offender and has a prior conviction for an offense listed in RCW 9.94A.030(38)(b), then the sentence is subject to the requirements of RCW 9.94A.507.

The Caseload Forecast Council is not liable for errors or omissions in the manual, for sentences that may be inappropriately calculated as a result of a practitioner's or court's reliance on the manual, or for any other written or verbal information related to adult or juvenile sentencing. The scoring sheets are intended to provide assistance in most cases but do not cover all permutations of the scoring rules. If you find any errors or omissions, we encourage you to report them to the Caseload Forecast Council.

Rape Of A Child First Degree

RCW 9A.44.073
CLASS A – VIOLENT/SEX
ATTEMPT = CLASS A

OFFENDER SCORING RCW 9.94A.525(17)

If the present conviction is for a felony domestic violence offense where domestic violence was plead and proven, use the General Violent/Sex Offense Where Domestic Violence Has Been Plead and Proven scoring form on page 200.

ADULT HISTORY:
    Enter number of sex offense convictions .... _____ x 3 = _____
    Enter number of serious violent and violent felony convictions .... _____ x 2 = _____
    Enter number of nonviolent felony convictions .... _____ x 1 = _____

JUVENILE HISTORY:
    Enter number of sex offense dispositions .... _____ x 3 = _____
    Enter number of serious violent and violent felony dispositions .... _____ x 2 = _____
    Enter number of nonviolent felony dispositions .... _____ x ½ = _____

OTHER CURRENT OFFENSES:
(Other current offenses that do not encompass the same conduct count in offender score)
    Enter number of other sex offense convictions .... _____ x 3 = _____
    Enter number of other serious violent and violent felony convictions .... _____ x 2 = _____
    Enter number of other nonviolent felony convictions .... _____ x 1 = _____

STATUS:
    Was the offender on community custody on the date the current offense was committed?................ + 1 = _____

Total the last column to get the **Offender Score** (Round down to the nearest whole number)

SENTENCE RANGE

					Offender Score					
	0	**1**	**2**	**3**	**4**	**5**	**6**	**7**	**8**	**9+**
LEVEL XII	108m	119m	129m	140m	150m	161m	189m	207m	243m	279m
	93 - 123	102 - 136	111 - 147	120 - 160	129 - 171	138 - 184	162 - 216	178 - 236	209 - 277	240 - 318

- ✓ For attempt (RCW 9.94A.595) see page 23 or for gang-related felonies where the court found the offender involved a minor (RCW 9.94A.833) see page 186 for standard range adjustments.
- ✓ For deadly weapon enhancement, see page 190.
- ✓ For sentencing alternatives, see page 177.
- ✓ For community custody eligibility, see page 187.
- ✓ For any applicable enhancements other than deadly weapon enhancement, see page 183.
- ✓ If the offender is older than 17 years of age and is not a persistent offender and the current offense was committed on or after 9/1/2001, then the offender is subject to the requirements under RCW 9.94A.507.
- ✓ If the offender engaged the victim in sexual conduct in exchange for a fee, an additional 12 months shall be added to the standard sentence range (RCW 9.94A.533(9)).
- ✓ Per RCW 9.94A.507(3)(c)(ii), excluding convictions for attempt, the minimum term shall be either the maximum of the standard sentence range for the offense or 25 years, whichever is greater, for a finding that the offense was **predatory** under RCW 9.94A.836.

The Caseload Forecast Council is not liable for errors or omissions in the manual, for sentences that may be inappropriately calculated as a result of a practitioner's or court's reliance on the manual, or for any other written or verbal information related to adult or juvenile sentencing. The scoring sheets are intended to provide assistance in most cases but do not cover all permutations of the scoring rules. If you find any errors or omissions, we encourage you to report them to the Caseload Forecast Council.

Rape Of A Child First Degree

RCW 9A.44.073
VIOLENT/SEX
SOLICITATION = CLASS A
CONSPIRACY = CLASS B

OFFENDER SCORING RCW 9.94A.525(17)

If the present conviction is for a felony domestic violence offense where domestic violence was plead and proven, use the General Violent/Sex Offense Where Domestic Violence Has Been Plead and Proven scoring form on page 200.

ADULT HISTORY:
Enter number of sex offense convictions .... _____ x 3 = _____
Enter number of serious violent and violent felony convictions .... _____ x 2 = _____
Enter number of nonviolent felony convictions .... _____ x 1 = _____

JUVENILE HISTORY:
Enter number of sex offense dispositions .... _____ x 3 = _____
Enter number of serious violent and violent felony dispositions .... _____ x 2 = _____
Enter number of nonviolent felony dispositions .... _____ x ½ = _____

OTHER CURRENT OFFENSES:
(Other current offenses that do not encompass the same conduct count in offender score)
Enter number of other sex offense convictions .... _____ x 3 = _____
Enter number of other serious violent and violent felony convictions .... _____ x 2 = _____
Enter number of other nonviolent felony convictions .... _____ x 1 = _____

STATUS:
Was the offender on community custody on the date the current offense was committed? .... + 1 = _____

Total the last column to get the **Offender Score** (Round down to the nearest whole number)

SENTENCE RANGE

	\	\	\	\	Offender Score	\	\	\	\	\
	0	**1**	**2**	**3**	**4**	**5**	**6**	**7**	**8**	**9+**
LEVEL XII	108m	119m	129m	140m	150m	161m	189m	207m	243m	279m
	93 - 123	102 - 136	111 - 147	120 - 160	129 - 171	138 - 184	162 - 216	178 - 236	209 - 277	240 - 318

- ✓ For solicitation, conspiracy (RCW 9.94A.595) see page 23 or for gang-related felonies where the court found the offender involved a minor (RCW 9.94A.833) see page 186 for standard range adjustments.
- ✓ For deadly weapon enhancement, see page 190.
- ✓ For sentencing alternatives, see page 177.
- ✓ For community custody eligibility, see page 187.
- ✓ For any applicable enhancements other than deadly weapon enhancement, see page 183.
- ✓ If the offender is not a persistent offender and has a prior conviction for an offense listed in RCW 9.94A.030(38)(b), then the sentence is subject to the requirements of RCW 9.94A.507.
- ✓ If the offender engaged the victim in sexual conduct in exchange for a fee, an additional 12 months shall be added to the standard sentence range (RCW 9.94A.533(9)).

The Caseload Forecast Council is not liable for errors or omissions in the manual, for sentences that may be inappropriately calculated as a result of a practitioner's or court's reliance on the manual, or for any other written or verbal information related to adult or juvenile sentencing. The scoring sheets are intended to provide assistance in most cases but do not cover all permutations of the scoring rules. If you find any errors or omissions, we encourage you to report them to the Caseload Forecast Council.

Rape Of A Child Second Degree

RCW 9A.44.076
CLASS A – VIOLENT/SEX
ATTEMPT = CLASS A

OFFENDER SCORING RCW 9.94A.525(17)

If the present conviction is for a felony domestic violence offense where domestic violence was plead and proven, use the General Violent/Sex Offense Where Domestic Violence Has Been Plead and Proven scoring form on page 200.

ADULT HISTORY:
- Enter number of sex offense convictions .... _____ x 3 = _____
- Enter number of serious violent and violent felony convictions .... _____ x 2 = _____
- Enter number of nonviolent felony convictions .... _____ x 1 = _____

JUVENILE HISTORY:
- Enter number of sex offense dispositions .... _____ x 3 = _____
- Enter number of serious violent and violent felony dispositions .... _____ x 2 = _____
- Enter number of nonviolent felony dispositions .... _____ x ½ = _____

OTHER CURRENT OFFENSES:
(Other current offenses that do not encompass the same conduct count in offender score)
- Enter number of other sex offense convictions .... _____ x 3 = _____
- Enter number of other serious violent and violent felony convictions .... _____ x 2 = _____
- Enter number of other nonviolent felony convictions .... _____ x 1 = _____

STATUS:
- Was the offender on community custody on the date the current offense was committed?........... + 1 = _____

Total the last column to get the **Offender Score** (Round down to the nearest whole number)

SENTENCE RANGE

	Offender Score									
	0	1	2	3	4	5	6	7	8	9+
LEVEL XI	90m	100m	110m	119m	129m	139m	170m	185m	215m	245m
	78 - 102	86 - 114	95 - 125	102 - 136	111 - 147	120 - 158	146 - 194	159 - 211	185 - 245	210 - 280

- ✓ For attempt (RCW 9.94A.595) see page 23 or for gang-related felonies where the court found the offender involved a minor (RCW 9.94A.833) see page 186 for standard range adjustments.
- ✓ For deadly weapon enhancement, see page 190.
- ✓ For sentencing alternatives, see page 177.
- ✓ For community custody eligibility, see page 187.
- ✓ For any applicable enhancements other than deadly weapon enhancement, see page 183.
- ✓ If the offender is older than 17 years of age and is not a persistent offender and the current offense was committed on or after 9/1/2001, then the offender is subject to the requirements under RCW 9.94A.507.
- ✓ If the offender engaged the victim in sexual conduct in exchange for a fee, an additional 12 months shall be added to the standard sentence range (RCW 9.94A.533(9)).
- ✓ Per RCW 9.94A.507(3)(c)(ii), excluding convictions for attempt, the minimum term shall be either the maximum of the standard sentence range for the offense or 25 years, whichever is greater, for a finding that the offense was **predatory** under RCW 9.94A.836.

The Caseload Forecast Council is not liable for errors or omissions in the manual, for sentences that may be inappropriately calculated as a result of a practitioner's or court's reliance on the manual, or for any other written or verbal information related to adult or juvenile sentencing. The scoring sheets are intended to provide assistance in most cases but do not cover all permutations of the scoring rules. If you find any errors or omissions, we encourage you to report them to the Caseload Forecast Council.

Rape Of A Child Second Degree

RCW 9A.44.
VIOLENT/SEX
SOLICITATION = CLASS A
CONSPIRACY = CLASS B

OFFENDER SCORING RCW 9.94A.525(17)

If the present conviction is for a felony domestic violence offense where domestic violence was plead and proven, use the General Violent/Sex Offense Where Domestic Violence Has Been Plead and Proven scoring form on page 200.

ADULT HISTORY:
    Enter number of sex offense convictions .... _____ x 3 = _____
    Enter number of serious violent and violent felony convictions .... _____ x 2 = _____
    Enter number of nonviolent felony convictions .... _____ x 1 = _____

JUVENILE HISTORY:
    Enter number of sex offense dispositions .... _____ x 3 = _____
    Enter number of serious violent and violent felony dispositions .... _____ x 2 = _____
    Enter number of nonviolent felony dispositions .... _____ x ½ = _____

OTHER CURRENT OFFENSES:
(Other current offenses that do not encompass the same conduct count in offender score)
    Enter number of other sex offense convictions .... _____ x 3 = _____
    Enter number of other serious violent and violent felony convictions .... _____ x 2 = _____
    Enter number of other nonviolent felony convictions .... _____ x 1 = _____

STATUS:
    Was the offender on community custody on the date the current offense was committed? .... + 1 = _____

Total the last column to get the **Offender Score** (Round down to the nearest whole number)

SENTENCE RANGE

	\\				Offender Score					
	0	**1**	**2**	**3**	**4**	**5**	**6**	**7**	**8**	**9+**
LEVEL XI	90m 78 - 102	100m 86 - 114	110m 95 - 125	119m 102 - 136	129m 111 - 147	139m 120 - 158	170m 146 - 194	185m 159 - 211	215m 185 - 245	245m 210 - 280

- ✓ For solicitation, conspiracy (RCW 9.94A.595) see page 23 or for gang-related felonies where the court found the offender involved a minor (RCW 9.94A.833) see page 186 for standard range adjustments.
- ✓ For deadly weapon enhancement, see page 190.
- ✓ For sentencing alternatives, see page 177.
- ✓ For community custody eligibility, see page 187.
- ✓ For any applicable enhancements other than deadly weapon enhancement, see page 183.
- ✓ If the offender is not a persistent offender and has a prior conviction for an offense listed in RCW 9.94A.030(38)(b), then the sentence is subject to the requirements of RCW 9.94A.507.
- ✓ If the offender engaged the victim in sexual conduct in exchange for a fee, an additional 12 months shall be added to the standard sentence range (RCW 9.94A.533(9)).

The Caseload Forecast Council is not liable for errors or omissions in the manual, for sentences that may be inappropriately calculated as a result of a practitioner's or court's reliance on the manual, or for any other written or verbal information related to adult or juvenile sentencing. The scoring sheets are intended to provide assistance in most cases but do not cover all permutations of the scoring rules. If you find any errors or omissions, we encourage you to report them to the Caseload Forecast Council.

Rape Of A Child Third Degree

RCW 9A.44.079
CLASS C* – NONVIOLENT/SEX

OFFENDER SCORING RCW 9.94A.525(17)

If the present conviction is for a felony domestic violence offense where domestic violence was plead and proven, use the General Nonviolent/Sex Offense Where Domestic Violence Has Been Plead and Proven scoring form on page 192.

ADULT HISTORY:
    Enter number of sex offense felony convictions .... _____ x 3 = _____
    Enter number of felony convictions .... _____ x 1 = _____

JUVENILE HISTORY:
    Enter number of sex offense felony dispositions .... _____ x 3 = _____
    Enter number of serious violent and violent felony dispositions .... _____ x 1 = _____
    Enter number of nonviolent felony dispositions .... _____ x ½ = _____

OTHER CURRENT OFFENSES:
(Other current offenses that do not encompass the same conduct count in offender score)
    Enter number of sex offense felony convictions .... _____ x 3 = _____
    Enter number of other felony convictions .... _____ x 1 = _____

STATUS:
    Was the offender on community custody on the date the current offense was committed? (if yes) ...... + 1 = _____

Total the last column to get the **Offender Score** (Round down to the nearest whole number) [____]

SENTENCE RANGE

Offender Score	0	1	2	3	4	5	6	7	8	9+
LEVEL VI	13m 12+ - 14	17.5m 15 - 20	24m 21 - 27	30m 26 - 34	36m 31 - 41	42m 36 - 48	53m 46 - 60*	58.5m 57 - 60*	60 - 60*	60 - 60*

- ✓ For gang-related felonies where the court found the offender involved a minor (RCW 9.94A.833) see page 186 for standard range adjustment.
- ✓ For deadly weapon enhancement, see page 190.
- ✓ For sentencing alternatives, see page 177.
- ✓ For community custody eligibility, see page 187.
- ✓ For any applicable enhancements other than deadly weapon enhancement, see page 183.
- ✓ If the offender is not a persistent offender and has a prior conviction for an offense listed in RCW 9.94A.030(38)(b), then the sentence is subject to the requirements of RCW 9.94A.507.
- ✓ If the offender engaged the victim in sexual conduct in exchange for a fee, an additional 12 months shall be added to the standard sentence range (RCW 9.94A.533(9)).

The Caseload Forecast Council is not liable for errors or omissions in the manual, for sentences that may be inappropriately calculated as a result of a practitioner's or court's reliance on the manual, or for any other written or verbal information related to adult or juvenile sentencing. The scoring sheets are intended to provide assistance in most cases but do not cover all permutations of the scoring rules. If you find any errors or omissions, we encourage you to report them to the Caseload Forecast Council.

Reckless Burning First Degree

RCW 9A.48.040
CLASS C – NONVIOLENT

OFFENDER SCORING RCW 9.94A.525(7)

If it was found that this offense was committed with sexual motivation (RCW 9.94A.533(8)) on or after 7/01/2006, use the General Nonviolent Offense with a Sexual Motivation Finding scoring form on page 193.

If the present conviction is for a felony domestic violence offense where domestic violence was plead and proven, use the General Nonviolent Offense Where Domestic Violence Has Been Plead and Proven scoring form on page 191.

ADULT HISTORY:
  Enter number of felony convictions .... _____ x 1 = _____

JUVENILE HISTORY:
  Enter number of serious violent and violent felony dispositions .... _____ x 1 = _____
  Enter number of nonviolent felony dispositions .... _____ x ½ = _____

OTHER CURRENT OFFENSES:
(Other current offenses that do not encompass the same conduct count in offender score)
  Enter number of other felony convictions .... _____ x 1 = _____

STATUS:
  Was the offender on community custody on the date the current offense was committed? (if yes) .... + 1 = _____

Total the last column to get the **Offender Score** (Round down to the nearest whole number)

SENTENCE RANGE

	Offender Score									
	0	1	2	3	4	5	6	7	8	9+
LEVEL I	0-60 days	0-90 days	3m 2 - 5	4m 2 - 6	5.5m 3 - 8	8m 4 - 12	13m 12+ - 14	16m 14 - 18	19.5m 17 - 22	25.5m 22 - 29

- ✓ For gang-related felonies where the court found the offender involved a minor (RCW 9.94A.833) see page 186 for standard range adjustment.
- ✓ For deadly weapon enhancement, see page 190.
- ✓ For sentencing alternatives, see page 177.
- ✓ For community custody eligibility, see page 187.
- ✓ For any applicable enhancements other than deadly weapon enhancement, see page 183.

The Caseload Forecast Council is not liable for errors or omissions in the manual, for sentences that may be inappropriately calculated as a result of a practitioner's or court's reliance on the manual, or for any other written or verbal information related to adult or juvenile sentencing. The scoring sheets are intended to provide assistance in most cases but do not cover all permutations of the scoring rules. If you find any errors or omissions, we encourage you to report them to the Caseload Forecast Council.

Rendering Criminal Assistance First Degree

RCW 9A.76.070(2)(a)
CLASS B – NONVIOLENT

OFFENDER SCORING RCW 9.94A.525(7)

If it was found that this offense was committed with sexual motivation (RCW 9.94A.533(8)) on or after 7/01/2006, use the General Nonviolent Offense with a Sexual Motivation Finding scoring form on page 193.

If the present conviction is for a felony domestic violence offense where domestic violence was plead and proven, use the General Nonviolent Offense Where Domestic Violence Has Been Plead and Proven scoring form on page 191.

ADULT HISTORY:
    Enter number of felony convictions .... _____ x 1 = _____

JUVENILE HISTORY:
    Enter number of serious violent and violent felony dispositions .... _____ x 1 = _____
    Enter number of nonviolent felony dispositions .... _____ x ½ = _____

OTHER CURRENT OFFENSES:
(Other current offenses that do not encompass the same conduct count in offender score)
    Enter number of other felony convictions .... _____ x 1 = _____

STATUS:
    Was the offender on community custody on the date the current offense was committed? (if yes) ...... + 1 = _____

Total the last column to get the **Offender Score** (Round down to the nearest whole number)

SENTENCE RANGE

	Offender Score									
	0	1	2	3	4	5	6	7	8	9+
LEVEL V	9m 6 - 12	13m 12+ - 14	15m 13 - 17	17.5m 15 - 20	25.5m 22 - 29	38m 33 - 43	47.5m 41 - 54	59.5m 51 - 68	72m 62 - 82	84m 72 - 96

✓ For attempt, solicitation, conspiracy (RCW 9.94A.595) see page 23 or for gang-related felonies where the court found the offender involved a minor (RCW 9.94A.833) see page 186 for standard range adjustments.

✓ For deadly weapon enhancement, see page 190.

✓ For sentencing alternatives, see page 177.

✓ For community custody eligibility, see page 187.

✓ For any applicable enhancements other than deadly weapon enhancement, see page 183.

Residential Burglary

RCW 9A.52.025
CLASS B – NONVIOLENT
OFFENDER SCORING RCW 9.94A.525(16)

If the present conviction is for a felony domestic violence offense where domestic violence was plead and proven, use the General Burglary 2/Residential Burglary Offense Where Domestic Violence Has Been Plead and Proven scoring form on page 203.

ADULT HISTORY:
    Enter number of Burglary 1 felony convictions .... _____ x 2 = _____
    Enter number of Burglary 2 and Residential Burglary felony convictions .... _____ x 2 = _____
    Enter number of felony convictions .... _____ x 1 = _____

JUVENILE HISTORY:
    Enter number of Burglary 1 felony dispositions .... _____ x 2 = _____
    Enter number of Burglary 2 and Residential Burglary felony dispositions .... _____ x 1 = _____
    Enter number of serious violent and violent felony dispositions .... _____ x 1 = _____
    Enter number of nonviolent felony dispositions .... _____ x ½ = _____

OTHER CURRENT OFFENSES:
(Other current offenses that do not encompass the same conduct count in offender score)
    Enter number of other Burglary 1 felony convictions .... _____ x 2 = _____
    Enter number of other Burglary 2 and Residential Burglary felony convictions ... _____ x 2 = _____
    Enter number of other felony convictions .... _____ x 1 = _____

STATUS:
    Was the offender on community custody on the date the current offense was committed? .... + 1 = _____

Total the last column to get the **Offender Score** (Round down to the nearest whole number)

SENTENCE RANGE

	Offender Score									
	0	1	2	3	4	5	6	7	8	9+
LEVEL IV	6m 3 - 9	9m 6 - 12	13m 12+ - 14	15m 13 - 17	17.5m 15 - 20	25.5m 22 - 29	38m 33 - 43	50m 43 - 57	61.5m 53 - 70	73.5m 63 - 84

✓ For attempt, solicitation, conspiracy (RCW 9.94A.595) see page 23 or for gang-related felonies where the court found the offender involved a minor (RCW 9.94A.833) see page 186 for standard range adjustments.

✓ For deadly weapon enhancement, see page 190.

✓ For sentencing alternatives, see page 177.

✓ For community custody eligibility, see page 187.

✓ For any applicable enhancements other than deadly weapon enhancement, see page 183.

The Caseload Forecast Council is not liable for errors or omissions in the manual, for sentences that may be inappropriately calculated as a result of a practitioner's or court's reliance on the manual, or for any other written or verbal information related to adult or juvenile sentencing. The scoring sheets are intended to provide assistance in most cases but do not cover all permutations of the scoring rules. If you find any errors or omissions, we encourage you to report them to the Caseload Forecast Council.

Residential Burglary With A Finding Of Sexual Motivation

RCW 9A.52.025
CLASS B – NONVIOLENT/SEX

OFFENDER SCORING RCW 9.94A.525(17)

ADULT HISTORY:
Enter number of sex offense felony convictions .... _____ x 3 = _____
Enter number of Burglary 1 felony convictions .... _____ x 2 = _____
Enter number of Burglary 2 and Residential Burglary felony convictions .... _____ x 2 = _____
Enter number of felony convictions .... _____ x 1 = _____

JUVENILE HISTORY:
Enter number of sex offense felony dispositions .... _____ x 3 = _____
Enter number of Burglary 1 felony dispositions .... _____ x 2 = _____
Enter number of Burglary 2 and Residential Burglary felony dispositions .... _____ x 1 = _____
Enter number of serious violent and violent felony dispositions .... _____ x 1 = _____
Enter number of nonviolent felony dispositions .... _____ x ½ = _____

OTHER CURRENT OFFENSES:
(Other current offenses that do not encompass the same conduct count in offender score)
Enter number of other sex offense felony convictions .... _____ x 3 = _____
Enter number of other Burglary 1 felony convictions .... _____ x 2 = _____
Enter number of other Burglary 2 and Residential Burglary felony convictions .... _____ x 2 = _____
Enter number of other felony convictions .... _____ x 1 = _____

STATUS:
Was the offender on community custody on the date the current offense was committed?.......... + 1 = _____

Total the last column to get the **Offender Score** (Round down to the nearest whole number) _____

SENTENCE RANGE

Offender Score	0	1	2	3	4	5	6	7	8	9+
LEVEL IV	6m 3 - 9	9m 6 - 12	13m 12+ - 14	15m 13 - 17	17.5m 15 - 20	25.5m 22 - 29	38m 33 - 43	50m 43 - 57	61.5m 53 - 70	73.5m 63 - 84

Add Sexual Motivation Enhancement (see page 185) [____] to Standard Range = [Low] to [High]

- ✓ For attempt, solicitation, conspiracy (RCW 9.94A.595) see page 23 or for gang-related felonies where the court found the offender involved a minor (RCW 9.94A.833) see page 186 for standard range adjustments.
- ✓ For deadly weapon enhancement, see page 190.
- ✓ For sentencing alternatives, see page 177.
- ✓ For community custody eligibility, see page 187.
- ✓ For any applicable enhancements other than deadly weapon enhancement, see page 183.
- ✓ If the offender is not a persistent offender and has a prior conviction for an offense listed in RCW 9.94A.030(38)(b), then the sentence is subject to the requirements of RCW 9.94A.507.

The Caseload Forecast Council is not liable for errors or omissions in the manual, for sentences that may be inappropriately calculated as a result of a practitioner's or court's reliance on the manual, or for any other written or verbal information related to adult or juvenile sentencing. The scoring sheets are intended to provide assistance in most cases but do not cover all permutations of the scoring rules. If you find any errors or omissions, we encourage you to report them to the Caseload Forecast Council.

Retail Theft With Special Circumstances First Degree

RCW 9A.56.360(2)
CLASS B – NONVIOLENT
OFFENDER SCORING RCW 9.94A.525(7)

If it was found that this offense was committed with sexual motivation (RCW 9.94A.533(8)) on or after 7/01/2006, use the General Nonviolent Offense with a Sexual Motivation Finding scoring form on page 193.

If the present conviction is for a felony domestic violence offense where domestic violence was plead and proven, use the General Nonviolent Offense Where Domestic Violence Has Been Plead and Proven scoring form on page 191.

ADULT HISTORY:
　Enter number of felony convictions .... _____ x 1 = _____

JUVENILE HISTORY:
　Enter number of serious violent and violent felony dispositions .... _____ x 1 = _____
　Enter number of nonviolent felony dispositions .... _____ x ½ = _____

OTHER CURRENT OFFENSES:
(Other current offenses that do not encompass the same conduct count in offender score)
　Enter number of other felony convictions .... _____ x 1 = _____

STATUS:
　Was the offender on community custody on the date the current offense was committed? (if yes) .... + 1 = _____

Total the last column to get the **Offender Score** (Round down to the nearest whole number)　[ ]

SENTENCE RANGE

	Offender Score									
	0	1	2	3	4	5	6	7	8	9+
LEVEL III	2m	5m	8m	11m	14m	19.5m	25.5m	38m	50m	59.5m
	1 - 3	3 - 8	4 - 12	9 - 12	12+ - 16	17 - 22	22 - 29	33 - 43	43 - 57	51 - 68

- ✓ For attempt, solicitation, conspiracy (RCW 9.94A.595) see page 23 or for gang-related felonies where the court found the offender involved a minor (RCW 9.94A.833) see page 186 for standard range adjustments.
- ✓ For deadly weapon enhancement, see page 190.
- ✓ For sentencing alternatives, see page 177.
- ✓ For community custody eligibility, see page 187.
- ✓ For any applicable enhancements other than deadly weapon enhancement, see page 183.

The Caseload Forecast Council is not liable for errors or omissions in the manual, for sentences that may be inappropriately calculated as a result of a practitioner's or court's reliance on the manual, or for any other written or verbal information related to adult or juvenile sentencing. The scoring sheets are intended to provide assistance in most cases but do not cover all permutations of the scoring rules. If you find any errors or omissions, we encourage you to report them to the Caseload Forecast Council.

Retail Theft With Special Circumstances Second Degree

RCW 9A.56.360(3)
CLASS C – NONVIOLENT

OFFENDER SCORING RCW 9.94A.525(7)

If it was found that this offense was committed with sexual motivation (RCW 9.94A.533(8)) on or after 7/01/2006, use the General Nonviolent Offense with a Sexual Motivation Finding scoring form on page 193.

If the present conviction is for a felony domestic violence offense where domestic violence was plead and proven, use the General Nonviolent Offense Where Domestic Violence Has Been Plead and Proven scoring form on page 191.

ADULT HISTORY:
    Enter number of felony convictions .... _____ x 1 = _____

JUVENILE HISTORY:
    Enter number of serious violent and violent felony dispositions .... _____ x 1 = _____
    Enter number of nonviolent felony dispositions .... _____ x ½ = _____

OTHER CURRENT OFFENSES:
(Other current offenses that do not encompass the same conduct count in offender score)
    Enter number of other felony convictions .... _____ x 1 = _____

STATUS:
    Was the offender on community custody on the date the current offense was committed? (if yes) ...... + 1 = _____

Total the last column to get the **Offender Score** (Round down to the nearest whole number)

SENTENCE RANGE

	Offender Score									
	0	1	2	3	4	5	6	7	8	9+
LEVEL II	0-90 days	4m 2 - 6	6m 3 - 9	8m 4 - 12	13m 12+ - 14	16m 14 - 18	19.5m 17 - 22	25.5m 22 - 29	38m 33 - 43	50m 43 - 57

- ✓ For gang-related felonies where the court found the offender involved a minor (RCW 9.94A.833) see page 186 for standard range adjustment.
- ✓ For deadly weapon enhancement, see page 190.
- ✓ For sentencing alternatives, see page 177.
- ✓ For community custody eligibility, see page 187.
- ✓ For any applicable enhancements other than deadly weapon enhancement, see page 183.

Robbery First Degree

RCW 9A.56.200
CLASS A – VIOLENT

OFFENDER SCORING RCW 9.94A.525(8)

If it was found that this offense was committed with sexual motivation (RCW 9.94A.533(8)) on or after 7/01/2006, use the General Violent Offense with a Sexual Motivation Finding scoring form on page 201.

If the present conviction is for a felony domestic violence offense where domestic violence was plead and proven, use the General Violent Offense Where Domestic Violence Has Been Plead and Proven scoring form on page 199.

ADULT HISTORY:
    Enter number of serious violent and violent felony convictions .... _____ x 2 = _____
    Enter number of nonviolent felony convictions .... _____ x 1 = _____

JUVENILE HISTORY:
    Enter number of serious violent and violent felony dispositions .... _____ x 2 = _____
    Enter number of nonviolent felony dispositions .... _____ x ½ = _____

OTHER CURRENT OFFENSES:
(Other current offenses that do not encompass the same conduct count in offender score)
    Enter number of other serious violent and violent felony convictions .... _____ x 2 = _____
    Enter number of other nonviolent felony convictions .... _____ x 1 = _____

STATUS:
    Was the offender on community custody on the date the current offense was committed? .... + 1 = _____

Total the last column to get the **Offender Score** (Round down to the nearest whole number)

SENTENCE RANGE

	Offender Score									
	0	1	2	3	4	5	6	7	8	9+
LEVEL IX	36m 31 - 41	42m 36 - 48	47.5m 41 - 54	53.5m 46 - 61	59.5m 51 - 68	66m 57 - 75	89.5m 77 - 102	101.5m 87 - 116	126m 108 - 144	150m 129 - 171

- ✓ For attempt, solicitation, conspiracy (RCW 9.94A.595) see page 23 or for gang-related felonies where the court found the offender involved a minor (RCW 9.94A.833) see page 186 for standard range adjustments.
- ✓ For deadly weapon enhancement, see page 190.
- ✓ For sentencing alternatives, see page 177.
- ✓ For community custody eligibility, see page 187.
- ✓ For any applicable enhancements other than deadly weapon enhancement, see page 183.

The Caseload Forecast Council is not liable for errors or omissions in the manual, for sentences that may be inappropriately calculated as a result of a practitioner's or court's reliance on the manual, or for any other written or verbal information related to adult or juvenile sentencing. The scoring sheets are intended to provide assistance in most cases but do not cover all permutations of the scoring rules. If you find any errors or omissions, we encourage you to report them to the Caseload Forecast Council.

Robbery Second Degree

RCW 9A.56.210
CLASS B – VIOLENT

OFFENDER SCORING RCW 9.94A.525(8)

If it was found that this offense was committed with sexual motivation (RCW 9.94A.533(8)) on or after 7/01/2006, use the General Violent Offense with a Sexual Motivation Finding scoring form on page 201.

If the present conviction is for a felony domestic violence offense where domestic violence was plead and proven, use the General Violent Offense Where Domestic Violence Has Been Plead and Proven scoring form on page 199.

ADULT HISTORY:
    Enter number of serious violent and violent felony convictions .... _____   x 2 = _____
    Enter number of nonviolent felony convictions .... _____   x 1 = _____

JUVENILE HISTORY:
    Enter number of serious violent and violent felony dispositions .... _____   x 2 = _____
    Enter number of nonviolent felony dispositions .... _____   x ½ = _____

OTHER CURRENT OFFENSES:
(Other current offenses that do not encompass the same conduct count in offender score)
    Enter number of other serious violent and violent felony convictions .... _____   x 2 = _____
    Enter number of other nonviolent felony convictions .... _____   x 1 = _____

STATUS:
    Was the offender on community custody on the date the current offense was committed?.............. + 1 = _____

Total the last column to get the **Offender Score** (Round down to the nearest whole number)

SENTENCE RANGE

	Offender Score									
	0	1	2	3	4	5	6	7	8	9+
LEVEL IV	6m	9m	13m	15m	17.5m	25.5m	38m	50m	61.5m	73.5m
	3 - 9	6 - 12	12+ - 14	13 - 17	15 - 20	22 - 29	33 - 43	43 - 57	53 - 70	63 - 84

✓ For attempt, solicitation, conspiracy (RCW 9.94A.595) see page 23 or for gang-related felonies where the court found the offender involved a minor (RCW 9.94A.833) see page 186 for standard range adjustments.

✓ For deadly weapon enhancement, see page 190.

✓ For sentencing alternatives, see page 177.

✓ For community custody eligibility, see page 187.

✓ For any applicable enhancements other than deadly weapon enhancement, see page 183.

The Caseload Forecast Council is not liable for errors or omissions in the manual, for sentences that may be inappropriately calculated as a result of a practitioner's or court's reliance on the manual, or for any other written or verbal information related to adult or juvenile sentencing. The scoring sheets are intended to provide assistance in most cases but do not cover all permutations of the scoring rules. If you find any errors or omissions, we encourage you to report them to the Caseload Forecast Council.

Securities Act Violation

RCW 21.20.400
CLASS B – NONVIOLENT

OFFENDER SCORING RCW 9.94A.525(7)

If it was found that this offense was committed with sexual motivation (RCW 9.94A.533(8)) on or after 7/01/2006, use the General Nonviolent Offense with a Sexual Motivation Finding scoring form on page 193.

If the present conviction is for a felony domestic violence offense where domestic violence was plead and proven, use the General Nonviolent Offense Where Domestic Violence Has Been Plead and Proven scoring form on page 191.

ADULT HISTORY:
　Enter number of felony convictions .... _____ x 1 = _____

JUVENILE HISTORY:
　Enter number of serious violent and violent felony dispositions .... _____ x 1 = _____
　Enter number of nonviolent felony dispositions .... _____ x ½ = _____

OTHER CURRENT OFFENSES:
(Other current offenses that do not encompass the same conduct count in offender score)
　Enter number of other felony convictions .... _____ x 1 = _____

STATUS:
　Was the offender on community custody on the date the current offense was committed? (if yes) .... + 1 = _____

Total the last column to get the **Offender Score** (Round down to the nearest whole number)

SENTENCE RANGE

	\multicolumn{10}{c}{Offender Score}
	0	1	2	3	4	5	6	7	8	9+
LEVEL III	2m 1 - 3	5m 3 - 8	8m 4 - 12	11m 9 - 12	14m 12+ - 16	19.5m 17 - 22	25.5m 22 - 29	38m 33 - 43	50m 43 - 57	59.5m 51 - 68

- ✓ For attempt, solicitation, conspiracy (RCW 9.94A.595) see page 23 or for gang-related felonies where the court found the offender involved a minor (RCW 9.94A.833) see page 186 for standard range adjustments.
- ✓ For deadly weapon enhancement, see page 190.
- ✓ For sentencing alternatives, see page 177.
- ✓ For community custody eligibility, see page 187.
- ✓ For any applicable enhancements other than deadly weapon enhancement, see page 183.

The Caseload Forecast Council is not liable for errors or omissions in the manual, for sentences that may be inappropriately calculated as a result of a practitioner's or court's reliance on the manual, or for any other written or verbal information related to adult or juvenile sentencing. The scoring sheets are intended to provide assistance in most cases but do not cover all permutations of the scoring rules. If you find any errors or omissions, we encourage you to report them to the Caseload Forecast Council.

Selling For Profit (Controlled Or Counterfeit) Any Controlled Substance In Schedule I

RCW 69.50.410
CLASS C* – NONVIOLENT/DRUG
OFFENDER SCORING RCW 9.94A.525(13)

If it was found that this offense was committed with sexual motivation (RCW 9.94A.533(8)) on or after 7/01/2006, use the General Drug Offense with a Sexual Motivation Finding scoring form on page 195.

If the present conviction is for a felony domestic violence offense where domestic violence was plead and proven, use the General Drug Offense Where Domestic Violence Has Been Plead and Proven scoring form on page 194.

ADULT HISTORY:
   Does the offender have a prior sex or serious violent offense in history?
      YES Enter number of felony drug convictions .... _____ x 3 = _____
      NO Enter number of felony drug convictions .... _____ x 1 = _____

   Enter number of felony convictions .... _____ x 1 = _____

JUVENILE HISTORY:
   Does the offender have a prior sex or serious violent offense in history?
      YES Enter number of felony drug dispositions .... _____ x 2 = _____
      NO Enter number of felony drug dispositions .... _____ x ½ = _____

   Enter number of serious violent and violent felony dispositions .... _____ x 1 = _____

   Enter number of nonviolent felony dispositions .... _____ x ½ = _____

OTHER CURRENT OFFENSES:
(Other current offenses that do not encompass the same conduct count in offender score)
   Does the offender have other prior sex or serious violent offense in history?
      YES Enter number of other felony drug convictions .... _____ x 3 = _____
      NO Enter number of other felony drug convictions .... _____ x 1 = _____

   Enter number of other felony convictions .... _____ x 1 = _____

STATUS:
   Was the offender on community custody on the date the current offense was committed? (if yes) .... + 1 = _____

Total the last column to get the **Offender Score** (Round down to the nearest whole number)

SENTENCE RANGE – DRUG

	Offender Score		
	0 to 2	**3 to 5**	**6 to 9+**
LEVEL III	55.5m 51 - 60*	60 - 60*	60 - 60*

- ✓ For attempt, solicitation or conspiracy drug felonies see page 25 or for gang-related felonies where the court found the offender involved a minor (RCW 9.94A.833) see page 186 for standard range adjustments.
- ✓ Per RCW 9.94A.518, any felony offense under chapter 69.50 RCW with a deadly weapon special verdict under RCW 9.94A.602 becomes a level III offense.
- ✓ For deadly weapon enhancement, see page 190.
- ✓ For sentencing alternatives, see page 177.
- ✓ For community custody eligibility, see page 187.
- ✓ For any applicable enhancements other than deadly weapon enhancement, see page 183.
- ✓ Per RCW 69.50.408, the statutory maximum for a **subsequent conviction** under chapter 69.50 RCW is 120 months.
- ✓ Per RCW 69.50.435, if the offense occurred within a **protected zone**, 24 months shall be added to the standard range and the statutory maximum will be 120 months.
- ✓ Per RCW 69.50.410, **subsequent convictions** under RCW 69.50.410(1) shall receive a mandatory sentence of 5 years which shall not be suspended or deferred.
- ✓ Per RCW 69.50.410, if the violation involved **selling heroin**, a mandatory sentence of 2 years shall be imposed and shall not be suspended or deferred. A **subsequent conviction of selling heroin** shall receive a mandatory sentence of 10 years which shall not be suspended or deferred.

The Caseload Forecast Council is not liable for errors or omissions in the manual, for sentences that may be inappropriately calculated as a result of a practitioner's or court's reliance on the manual, or for any other written or verbal information related to adult or juvenile sentencing. The scoring sheets are intended to provide assistance in most cases but do not cover all permutations of the scoring rules. If you find any errors or omissions, we encourage you to report them to the Caseload Forecast Council.

Sending, Bringing Into The State Depictions Of Minor Engaged In Sexually Explicit Conduct First Degree

RCW 9.68A.060(1)
CLASS B – NONVIOLENT/SEX

OFFENDER SCORING RCW 9.94A.525(17)

If the present conviction is for a felony domestic violence offense where domestic violence was plead and proven, use the General Nonviolent/Sex Offense Where Domestic Violence Has Been Plead and Proven scoring form on page 192.

ADULT HISTORY:
    Enter number of sex offense felony convictions .... _____ x 3 = _____

    Enter number of felony convictions .... _____ x 1 = _____

JUVENILE HISTORY:
    Enter number of sex offense felony dispositions .... _____ x 3 = _____

    Enter number of serious violent and violent felony dispositions .... _____ x 1 = _____

    Enter number of nonviolent felony dispositions .... _____ x ½ = _____

OTHER CURRENT OFFENSES:
(Other current offenses that do not encompass the same conduct count in offender score)
    Enter number of sex offense felony convictions .... _____ x 3 = _____

    Enter number of other felony convictions .... _____ x 1 = _____

STATUS:
    Was the offender on community custody on the date the current offense was committed? (if yes)....... + 1 = _____

Total the last column to get the **Offender Score** (Round down to the nearest whole number)

SENTENCE RANGE

Offender Score	0	1	2	3	4	5	6	7	8	9+
LEVEL VII	17.5m	24m	30m	36m	42m	47.5m	66m	78m	89.5m	101.5m
	15 - 20	21 - 27	26 - 34	31 - 41	36 - 48	41 - 54	57 - 75	67 - 89	77 - 102	87 - 116

- ✓ For attempt, solicitation, conspiracy (RCW 9.94A.595) see page 23 or for gang-related felonies where the court found the offender involved a minor (RCW 9.94A.833) see page 186 for standard range adjustments.
- ✓ For deadly weapon enhancement, see page 190.
- ✓ For sentencing alternatives, see page 177.
- ✓ For community custody eligibility, see page 187.
- ✓ For any applicable enhancements other than deadly weapon enhancement, see page 183.
- ✓ If the offender is not a persistent offender and has a prior conviction for an offense listed in RCW 9.94A.030(38)(b), then the sentence is subject to the requirements of RCW 9.94A.507.

The Caseload Forecast Council is not liable for errors or omissions in the manual, for sentences that may be inappropriately calculated as a result of a practitioner's or court's reliance on the manual, or for any other written or verbal information related to adult or juvenile sentencing. The scoring sheets are intended to provide assistance in most cases but do not cover all permutations of the scoring rules. If you find any errors or omissions, we encourage you to report them to the Caseload Forecast Council.

Sending, Bringing Into The State Depictions Of Minor Engaged In Sexually Explicit Conduct Second Degree

RCW 9.68A.060(2)
CLASS C* – NONVIOLENT/SEX

OFFENDER SCORING RCW 9.94A.525(17)

If the present conviction is for a felony domestic violence offense where domestic violence was plead and proven, use the General Nonviolent/Sex Offense Where Domestic Violence Has Been Plead and Proven scoring form on page 192.

ADULT HISTORY:
    Enter number of sex offense felony convictions .... _____ x 3 = _____
    Enter number of felony convictions .... _____ x 1 = _____

JUVENILE HISTORY:
    Enter number of sex offense felony dispositions .... _____ x 3 = _____
    Enter number of serious violent and violent felony dispositions .... _____ x 1 = _____
    Enter number of nonviolent felony dispositions .... _____ x ½ = _____

OTHER CURRENT OFFENSES:
(Other current offenses that do not encompass the same conduct count in offender score)
    Enter number of sex offense felony convictions .... _____ x 3 = _____
    Enter number of other felony convictions .... _____ x 1 = _____

STATUS:
    Was the offender on community custody on the date the current offense was committed? (if yes) ...... + 1 = _____

Total the last column to get the **Offender Score** (Round down to the nearest whole number)

SENTENCE RANGE

	\multicolumn{10}{c}{Offender Score}									
	0	1	2	3	4	5	6	7	8	9+
LEVEL V	9m 6 - 12	13m 12+ - 14	15m 13 - 17	17.5m 15 - 20	25.5m 22 - 29	38m 33 - 43	47.5m 41 - 54	55.5m 51 - 60*	60 - 60*	60 - 60*

- ✓ For gang-related felonies where the court found the offender involved a minor (RCW 9.94A.833) see page 186 for standard range adjustments.
- ✓ For deadly weapon enhancement, see page 190.
- ✓ For sentencing alternatives, see page 177.
- ✓ For community custody eligibility, see page 187.
- ✓ For any applicable enhancements other than deadly weapon enhancement, see page 183.
- ✓ If the offender is not a persistent offender and has a prior conviction for an offense listed in RCW 9.94A.030(38)(b), then the sentence is subject to the requirements of RCW 9.94A.507.

The Caseload Forecast Council is not liable for errors or omissions in the manual, for sentences that may be inappropriately calculated as a result of a practitioner's or court's reliance on the manual, or for any other written or verbal information related to adult or juvenile sentencing. The scoring sheets are intended to provide assistance in most cases but do not cover all permutations of the scoring rules. If you find any errors or omissions, we encourage you to report them to the Caseload Forecast Council.

Sexual Exploitation Of A Minor

RCW 9.68A.040
CLASS B* – NONVIOLENT/SEX
OFFENDER SCORING RCW 9.94A.525(17)

If the present conviction is for a felony domestic violence offense where domestic violence was plead and proven, use the General Nonviolent/Sex Offense Where Domestic Violence Has Been Plead and Proven scoring form on page 192.

ADULT HISTORY:
    Enter number of sex offense felony convictions .... _____   x 3 = _____
    Enter number of felony convictions .... _____   x 1 = _____

JUVENILE HISTORY:
    Enter number of sex offense felony dispositions .... _____   x 3 = _____
    Enter number of serious violent and violent felony dispositions .... _____   x 1 = _____
    Enter number of nonviolent felony dispositions .... _____   x ½ = _____

OTHER CURRENT OFFENSES:
(Other current offenses that do not encompass the same conduct count in offender score)
    Enter number of sex offense felony convictions .... _____   x 3 = _____
    Enter number of other felony convictions .... _____   x 1 = _____

STATUS:
    Was the offender on community custody on the date the current offense was committed? (if yes) ....   + 1 = _____

Total the last column to get the **Offender Score** (Round down to the nearest whole number)

SENTENCE RANGE

	Offender Score									
	0	1	2	3	4	5	6	7	8	9+
LEVEL IX	36m 31 - 41	42m 36 - 48	47.5m 41 - 54	53.5m 46 - 61	59.5m 51 - 68	66m 57 - 75	89.5m 77 - 102	101.5m 87 - 116	114m 108 - 120*	120 - 120*

- ✓ For attempt, solicitation, conspiracy (RCW 9.94A.595) see page 23 or for gang-related felonies where the court found the offender involved a minor (RCW 9.94A.833) see page 186 for standard range adjustments.
- ✓ For deadly weapon enhancement, see page 190.
- ✓ For sentencing alternatives, see page 177.
- ✓ For community custody eligibility, see page 187.
- ✓ For any applicable enhancements other than deadly weapon enhancement, see page 183.
- ✓ If the offender is not a persistent offender and has a prior conviction for an offense listed in RCW 9.94A.030(38)(b), then the sentence is subject to the requirements of RCW 9.94A.507.

The Caseload Forecast Council is not liable for errors or omissions in the manual, for sentences that may be inappropriately calculated as a result of a practitioner's or court's reliance on the manual, or for any other written or verbal information related to adult or juvenile sentencing. The scoring sheets are intended to provide assistance in most cases but do not cover all permutations of the scoring rules. If you find any errors or omissions, we encourage you to report them to the Caseload Forecast Council.

Sexual Misconduct With A Minor First Degree

RCW 9A.44.093

CLASS C* – NONVIOLENT/SEX

OFFENDER SCORING RCW 9.94A.525(17)

If the present conviction is for a felony domestic violence offense where domestic violence was plead and proven, use the General Nonviolent/Sex Offense Where Domestic Violence Has Been Plead and Proven scoring form on page 192.

ADULT HISTORY:
    Enter number of sex offense felony convictions .... _____ x 3 = _____
    Enter number of felony convictions .... _____ x 1 = _____

JUVENILE HISTORY:
    Enter number of sex offense felony dispositions .... _____ x 3 = _____
    Enter number of serious violent and violent felony dispositions .... _____ x 1 = _____
    Enter number of nonviolent felony dispositions .... _____ x ½ = _____

OTHER CURRENT OFFENSES:
(Other current offenses that do not encompass the same conduct count in offender score)
    Enter number of sex offense felony convictions .... _____ x 3 = _____
    Enter number of other felony convictions .... _____ x 1 = _____

STATUS:
    Was the offender on community custody on the date the current offense was committed? (if yes) ...... + 1 = _____

Total the last column to get the **Offender Score** (Round down to the nearest whole number)

SENTENCE RANGE

	\multicolumn{10}{c	}{Offender Score}

	0	1	2	3	4	5	6	7	8	9+
LEVEL V	9m 6 - 12	13m 12+ - 14	15m 13 - 17	17.5m 15 - 20	25.5m 22 - 29	38m 33 - 43	47.5m 41 - 54	55.5m 51 - 60*	60 - 60*	60 - 60*

✓ For gang-related felonies where the court found the offender involved a minor (RCW 9.94A.833) see page 186 for standard range adjustment.

✓ For deadly weapon enhancement, see page 190.

✓ For sentencing alternatives, see page 177.

✓ For community custody eligibility, see page 187.

✓ For any applicable enhancements other than deadly weapon enhancement, see page 183.

✓ If the offender is not a persistent offender and has a prior conviction for an offense listed in RCW 9.94A.030(38)(b), then the sentence is subject to the requirements of RCW 9.94A.507.

Sexually Violating Human Remains

RCW 9A.44.105
CLASS C* – NONVIOLENT/SEX
OFFENDER SCORING RCW 9.94A.525(17)

If the present conviction is for a felony domestic violence offense where domestic violence was plead and proven, use the General Nonviolent/Sex Offense Where Domestic Violence Has Been Plead and Proven scoring form on page 192.

ADULT HISTORY:
    Enter number of sex offense felony convictions .... _____ x 3 = _____
    Enter number of felony convictions .... _____ x 1 = _____

JUVENILE HISTORY:
    Enter number of sex offense felony dispositions .... _____ x 3 = _____
    Enter number of serious violent and violent felony dispositions .... _____ x 1 = _____
    Enter number of nonviolent felony dispositions .... _____ x ½ = _____

OTHER CURRENT OFFENSES:
(Other current offenses that do not encompass the same conduct count in offender score)
    Enter number of sex offense felony convictions .... _____ x 3 = _____
    Enter number of other felony convictions .... _____ x 1 = _____

STATUS:
    Was the offender on community custody on the date the current offense was committed? (if yes)....... + 1 = _____

Total the last column to get the **Offender Score** (Round down to the nearest whole number)

SENTENCE RANGE

	Offender Score									
	0	1	2	3	4	5	6	7	8	9+
LEVEL V	9m	13m	15m	17.5m	25.5m	38m	47.5m	55.5m		
	6 - 12	12+ - 14	13 - 17	15 - 20	22 - 29	33 - 43	41 - 54	51 - 60*	60 - 60*	60 - 60*

- ✓ For gang-related felonies where the court found the offender involved a minor (RCW 9.94A.833) see page 186 for standard range adjustment.
- ✓ For deadly weapon enhancement, see page 190.
- ✓ For sentencing alternatives, see page 177.
- ✓ For community custody eligibility, see page 187.
- ✓ For any applicable enhancements other than deadly weapon enhancement, see page 183.
- ✓ If the offender is not a persistent offender and has a prior conviction for an offense listed in RCW 9.94A.030(38)(b), then the sentence is subject to the requirements of RCW 9.94A.507.

The Caseload Forecast Council is not liable for errors or omissions in the manual, for sentences that may be inappropriately calculated as a result of a practitioner's or court's reliance on the manual, or for any other written or verbal information related to adult or juvenile sentencing. The scoring sheets are intended to provide assistance in most cases but do not cover all permutations of the scoring rules. If you find any errors or omissions, we encourage you to report them to the Caseload Forecast Council.

Sexually Violent Predator Escape

RCW 9A.76.115
CLASS A – VIOLENT

OFFENDER SCORING RCW 9.94A.525(8)

If it was found that this offense was committed with sexual motivation (RCW 9.94A.533(8)) on or after 7/01/2006, use the General Violent Offense with a Sexual Motivation Finding scoring form on page 201.

If the present conviction is for a felony domestic violence offense where domestic violence was plead and proven, use the General Violent Offense Where Domestic Violence Has Been Plead and Proven scoring form on page 199.

ADULT HISTORY:
    Enter number of serious violent and violent felony convictions .... _____ x 2 = _____
    Enter number of nonviolent felony convictions .... _____ x 1 = _____

JUVENILE HISTORY:
    Enter number of serious violent and violent felony dispositions .... _____ x 2 = _____
    Enter number of nonviolent felony dispositions .... _____ x ½ = _____

OTHER CURRENT OFFENSES:
(Other current offenses that do not encompass the same conduct count in offender score)
    Enter number of other serious violent and violent felony convictions .... _____ x 2 = _____
    Enter number of other nonviolent felony convictions .... _____ x 1 = _____

STATUS:
    Was the offender on community custody on the date the current offense was committed? .... + 1 = _____

Total the last column to get the **Offender Score** (Round down to the nearest whole number)

SENTENCE RANGE

	\	\	\	\	Offender Score	\	\	\	\	\
	0	1	2	3	4	5	6	7	8	9+
LEVEL X	59.5m	66m	72m	78m	84m	89.5m	114m	126m	150m	230.5m
	51 - 68	57 - 75	62 - 82	67 - 89	72 - 96	77 - 102	98 - 130	108 - 144	129 - 171	149 - 198

- ✓ For attempt, solicitation, conspiracy (RCW 9.94A.595) see page 23 or for gang-related felonies where the court found the offender involved a minor (RCW 9.94A.833) see page 186 for standard range adjustments.
- ✓ For deadly weapon enhancement, see page 190.
- ✓ For sentencing alternatives, see page 177.
- ✓ For community custody eligibility, see page 187.
- ✓ For any applicable enhancements other than deadly weapon enhancement, see page 183.
- ✓ Statutory <u>minimum</u> sentence is 60 months per RCW 9.94A.540 and is imposed under the rules of RCW 9.94A.507

The Caseload Forecast Council is not liable for errors or omissions in the manual, for sentences that may be inappropriately calculated as a result of a practitioner's or court's reliance on the manual, or for any other written or verbal information related to adult or juvenile sentencing. The scoring sheets are intended to provide assistance in most cases but do not cover all permutations of the scoring rules. If you find any errors or omissions, we encourage you to report them to the Caseload Forecast Council.

Stalking

RCW 9A.46.110
CLASS B – NONVIOLENT

OFFENDER SCORING RCW 9.94A.525(7)

If it was found that this offense was committed with sexual motivation (RCW 9.94A.533(8)) on or after 7/01/2006, use the General Nonviolent Offense with a Sexual Motivation Finding scoring form on page 193.

If the present conviction is for a felony domestic violence offense where domestic violence was plead and proven, use the General Nonviolent Offense Where Domestic Violence Has Been Plead and Proven scoring form on page 191.

ADULT HISTORY:
    Enter number of felony convictions .... _____ x 1 = _____

JUVENILE HISTORY:
    Enter number of serious violent and violent felony dispositions .... _____ x 1 = _____

    Enter number of nonviolent felony dispositions .... _____ x ½ = _____

OTHER CURRENT OFFENSES:
(Other current offenses that do not encompass the same conduct count in offender score)
    Enter number of other felony convictions .... _____ x 1 = _____

STATUS:
    Was the offender on community custody on the date the current offense was committed? (if yes)....... + 1 = _____

Total the last column to get the **Offender Score** (Round down to the nearest whole number)

SENTENCE RANGE

	\multicolumn{11}{c}{Offender Score}
	0	**1**	**2**	**3**	**4**	**5**	**6**	**7**	**8**	**9+**
LEVEL V	9m 6 - 12	13m 12+ - 14	15m 13 - 17	17.5m 15 - 20	25.5m 22 - 29	38m 33 - 43	47.5m 41 - 54	59.5m 51 - 68	72m 62 - 82	84m 72 - 96

- ✓ For gang-related felonies where the court found the offender involved a minor (RCW 9.94A.833) see page 186 for standard range adjustment.
- ✓ For deadly weapon enhancement, see page 190.
- ✓ For sentencing alternatives, see page 177.
- ✓ For community custody eligibility, see page 187.
- ✓ For any applicable enhancements other than deadly weapon enhancement, see page 183.

The Caseload Forecast Council is not liable for errors or omissions in the manual, for sentences that may be inappropriately calculated as a result of a practitioner's or court's reliance on the manual, or for any other written or verbal information related to adult or juvenile sentencing. The scoring sheets are intended to provide assistance in most cases but do not cover all permutations of the scoring rules. If you find any errors or omissions, we encourage you to report them to the Caseload Forecast Council.

Taking Motor Vehicle Without Permission First Degree

RCW 9A.56.070
CLASS B – NONVIOLENT
OFFENDER SCORING RCW 9.94A.525(20)

If it was found that this offense was committed with sexual motivation (RCW 9.94A.533(8)) on or after 7/01/2006, use the General Nonviolent Offense with a Sexual Motivation Finding scoring form on page 193.

If the present conviction is for a felony domestic violence offense where domestic violence was plead and proven, use the General Nonviolent Offense Where Domestic Violence Has Been Plead and Proven scoring form on page 191.

ADULT HISTORY:
   Enter number of Theft of a Motor Vehicle, Theft 1 & 2 (of a Motor Vehicle),
   Possession of Stolen Property 1 & 2 (of a Motor Vehicle), Possession of a Stolen Vehicle and
   Taking a Motor Vehicle Without Permission 1 & 2 felony convictions .... _____ x 3 = _____
   Enter number of Vehicle Prowling 2 convictions .... _____ x 1 = _____
   Enter number of felony convictions .... _____ x 1 = _____

JUVENILE HISTORY:
   Enter number of Theft of a Motor Vehicle, Theft 1 & 2 (of a Motor Vehicle),
   Possession of Stolen Property 1 & 2 (of a Motor Vehicle), Possession of a Stolen Vehicle and
   Taking a Motor Vehicle Without Permission 1 & 2 felony dispositions .... _____ x 3 = _____
   Enter number of Vehicle Prowling 2 dispositions .... _____ x 1 = _____
   Enter number of serious violent and violent felony dispositions .... _____ x 1 = _____
   Enter number of nonviolent felony dispositions .... _____ x ½ = _____

OTHER CURRENT OFFENSES:
(Other current offenses that do not encompass the same conduct count in offender score)
   Enter number of other Theft of a Motor Vehicle, Theft 1 & 2 (of a Motor Vehicle),
   Possession of Stolen Property 1 & 2 (of a Motor Vehicle), Possession of a Stolen Vehicle and
   Taking a Motor Vehicle Without Permission 1 & 2 felony convictions .... _____ x 3 = _____
   Enter number of other Vehicle Prowling 2 convictions .... _____ x 1 = _____
   Enter number of other felony convictions .... _____ x 1 = _____

STATUS:
   Was the offender on community custody on the date the current offense was committed? (if yes) ...... + 1 = _____

Total the last column to get the **Offender Score** (Round down to the nearest whole number)

SENTENCE RANGE

	Offender Score									
	0	1	2	3	4	5	6	7	8	9+
LEVEL V	9m	13m	15m	17.5m	25.5m	38m	47.5m	59.5m	72m	84m
	6 - 12	12+ - 14	13 - 17	15 - 20	22 - 29	33 - 43	41 - 54	51 - 68	62 - 82	72 - 96

- ✓ For attempt, solicitation, conspiracy (RCW 9.94A.595) see page 23 or for gang-related felonies where the court found the offender involved a minor (RCW 9.94A.833) see page 186 for standard range adjustments.
- ✓ For deadly weapon enhancement, see page 190.
- ✓ For sentencing alternatives, see page 177.
- ✓ For community custody eligibility, see page 187.
- ✓ For any applicable enhancements other than deadly weapon enhancement, see page 183.

The Caseload Forecast Council is not liable for errors or omissions in the manual, for sentences that may be inappropriately calculated as a result of a practitioner's or court's reliance on the manual, or for any other written or verbal information related to adult or juvenile sentencing. The scoring sheets are intended to provide assistance in most cases but do not cover all permutations of the scoring rules. If you find any errors or omissions, we encourage you to report them to the Caseload Forecast Council.

Taking Motor Vehicle Without Permission Second Degree

RCW 9A.56.075
CLASS C – NONVIOLENT
OFFENDER SCORING RCW 9.94A.525(20)

If it was found that this offense was committed with sexual motivation (RCW 9.94A.533(8)) on or after 7/01/2006, use the General Nonviolent Offense with a Sexual Motivation Finding scoring form on page 193.

If the present conviction is for a felony domestic violence offense where domestic violence was plead and proven, use the General Nonviolent Offense Where Domestic Violence Has Been Plead and Proven scoring form on page 191.

ADULT HISTORY:
Enter number of Theft of a Motor Vehicle, Theft 1 & 2 (of a Motor Vehicle), Possession of Stolen Property 1 & 2 (of a Motor Vehicle), Possession of a Stolen Vehicle and Taking a Motor Vehicle Without Permission 1 & 2 felony convictions .... _____ x 3 = _____

Enter number of Vehicle Prowling 2 convictions .... _____ x 1 = _____

Enter number of felony convictions .... _____ x 1 = _____

JUVENILE HISTORY:
Enter number of Theft of a Motor Vehicle, Theft 1 & 2 (of a Motor Vehicle), Possession of Stolen Property 1 & 2 (of a Motor Vehicle), Possession of a Stolen Vehicle and Taking a Motor Vehicle Without Permission 1 & 2 felony dispositions .... _____ x 3 = _____

Enter number of Vehicle Prowling 2 dispositions .... _____ x 1 = _____

Enter number of serious violent and violent felony dispositions .... _____ x 1 = _____

Enter number of nonviolent felony dispositions .... _____ x ½ = _____

OTHER CURRENT OFFENSES:
(Other current offenses that do not encompass the same conduct count in offender score)
Enter number of other Theft of a Motor Vehicle, Theft 1 & 2 (of a Motor Vehicle), Possession of Stolen Property 1 & 2 (of a Motor Vehicle), Possession of a Stolen Vehicle and Taking a Motor Vehicle Without Permission 1 & 2 felony convictions .... _____ x 3 = _____

Enter number of other Vehicle Prowling 2 convictions .... _____ x 1 = _____

Enter number of other felony convictions .... _____ x 1 = _____

STATUS:
Was the offender on community custody on the date the current offense was committed? (if yes) .... + 1 = _____

Total the last column to get the **Offender Score** (Round down to the nearest whole number)

SENTENCE RANGE

	Offender Score									
	0	1	2	3	4	5	6	7	8	9+
LEVEL I	0-60 days	0-90 days	3m 2 - 5	4m 2 - 6	5.5m 3 - 8	8m 4 - 12	13m 12+ - 14	16m 14 - 18	19.5m 17 - 22	25.5m 22 - 29

- ✓ For gang-related felonies where the court found the offender involved a minor (RCW 9.94A.833) see page 186 for standard range adjustment.
- ✓ For deadly weapon enhancement, see page 190.
- ✓ For sentencing alternatives, see page 177.
- ✓ For community custody eligibility, see page 187.
- ✓ For any applicable enhancements other than deadly weapon enhancement, see page 183.

The Caseload Forecast Council is not liable for errors or omissions in the manual, for sentences that may be inappropriately calculated as a result of a practitioner's or court's reliance on the manual, or for any other written or verbal information related to adult or juvenile sentencing. The scoring sheets are intended to provide assistance in most cases but do not cover all permutations of the scoring rules. If you find any errors or omissions, we encourage you to report them to the Caseload Forecast Council.

Tampering With A Witness

RCW 9A.72.120

CLASS C* – NONVIOLENT

OFFENDER SCORING RCW 9.94A.525(7)

If it was found that this offense was committed with sexual motivation (RCW 9.94A.533(8)) on or after 7/01/2006, use the General Nonviolent Offense with a Sexual Motivation Finding scoring form on page 193.

If the present conviction is for a felony domestic violence offense where domestic violence was plead and proven, use the General Nonviolent Offense Where Domestic Violence Has Been Plead and Proven scoring form on page 191.

ADULT HISTORY:
    Enter number of felony convictions .... _____ x 1 = _____

JUVENILE HISTORY:
    Enter number of serious violent and violent felony dispositions .... _____ x 1 = _____
    Enter number of nonviolent felony dispositions .... _____ x ½ = _____

OTHER CURRENT OFFENSES:
(Other current offenses that do not encompass the same conduct count in offender score)
    Enter number of other felony convictions .... _____ x 1 = _____

STATUS:
    Was the offender on community custody on the date the current offense was committed? (if yes) ...... + 1 = _____

Total the last column to get the **Offender Score** (Round down to the nearest whole number)

SENTENCE RANGE

	_				Offender Score					
	0	**1**	**2**	**3**	**4**	**5**	**6**	**7**	**8**	**9+**
LEVEL III	2m	5m	8m	11m	14m	19.5m	25.5m	38m	50m	55.5m
	1 - 3	3 - 8	4 - 12	9 - 12	12+ - 16	17 - 22	22 - 29	33 - 43	43 - 57	51 - 60*

✓ For gang-related felonies where the court found the offender involved a minor (RCW 9.94A.833) see page 186 for standard range adjustment.

✓ For deadly weapon enhancement, see page 190.

✓ For sentencing alternatives, see page 177.

✓ For community custody eligibility, see page 187.

✓ For any applicable enhancements other than deadly weapon enhancement, see page 183.

The Caseload Forecast Council is not liable for errors or omissions in the manual, for sentences that may be inappropriately calculated as a result of a practitioner's or court's reliance on the manual, or for any other written or verbal information related to adult or juvenile sentencing. The scoring sheets are intended to provide assistance in most cases but do not cover all permutations of the scoring rules. If you find any errors or omissions, we encourage you to report them to the Caseload Forecast Council.

Telephone Harassment With Prior Harassment Conviction Or Threat Of Death

RCW 9.61.230(2)
CLASS C*– NONVIOLENT

OFFENDER SCORING RCW 9.94A.525(7)

If it was found that this offense was committed with sexual motivation (RCW 9.94A.533(8)) on or after 7/01/2006, use the General Nonviolent Offense with a Sexual Motivation Finding scoring form on page 193.

If the present conviction is for a felony domestic violence offense where domestic violence was plead and proven, use the General Nonviolent Offense Where Domestic Violence Has Been Plead and Proven scoring form on page 191.

ADULT HISTORY:
Enter number of felony convictions .... _____ x 1 = _____

JUVENILE HISTORY:
Enter number of serious violent and violent felony dispositions .... _____ x 1 = _____

Enter number of nonviolent felony dispositions .... _____ x ½ = _____

OTHER CURRENT OFFENSES:
(Other current offenses that do not encompass the same conduct count in offender score)
Enter number of other felony convictions .... _____ x 1 = _____

STATUS:
Was the offender on community custody on the date the current offense was committed? (if yes)....... + 1 = _____

Total the last column to get the **Offender Score** (Round down to the nearest whole number)

SENTENCE RANGE

	\multicolumn{10}{c	}{Offender Score}
	0	1	2	3	4	5	6	7	8	9+
LEVEL III	2m	5m	8m	11m	14m	19.5m	25.5m	38m	50m	55.5m
	1 - 3	3 - 8	4 - 12	9 - 12	12+ - 16	17 - 22	22 - 29	33 - 43	43 - 57	51 - 60*

- ✓ For gang-related felonies where the court found the offender involved a minor (RCW 9.94A.833) see page 186 for standard range adjustment.
- ✓ For deadly weapon enhancement, see page 190.
- ✓ For sentencing alternatives, see page 177.
- ✓ For community custody eligibility, see page 187.
- ✓ For any applicable enhancements other than deadly weapon enhancement, see page 183.

Theft First Degree Excluding Firearm And Motor Vehicle

RCW 9A.56.030
CLASS B – NONVIOLENT

OFFENDER SCORING RCW 9.94A.525(7)

If it was found that this offense was committed with sexual motivation (RCW 9.94A.533(8)) on or after 7/01/2006, use the General Nonviolent Offense with a Sexual Motivation Finding scoring form on page 193.

If the present conviction is for a felony domestic violence offense where domestic violence was plead and proven, use the General Nonviolent Offense Where Domestic Violence Has Been Plead and Proven scoring form on page 191.

ADULT HISTORY:
 Enter number of felony convictions .... _____ x 1 = _____

JUVENILE HISTORY:
 Enter number of serious violent and violent felony dispositions .... _____ x 1 = _____
 Enter number of nonviolent felony dispositions .... _____ x ½ = _____

OTHER CURRENT OFFENSES:
(Other current offenses that do not encompass the same conduct count in offender score)
 Enter number of other felony convictions .... _____ x 1 = _____

STATUS:
 Was the offender on community custody on the date the current offense was committed? (if yes) ...... + 1 = _____

Total the last column to get the **Offender Score** (Round down to the nearest whole number)

SENTENCE RANGE

	Offender Score									
	0	1	2	3	4	5	6	7	8	9+
LEVEL II	0-90 days	4m 2 - 6	6m 3 - 9	8m 4 - 12	13m 12+ - 14	16m 14 - 18	19.5m 17 - 22	25.5m 22 - 29	38m 33 - 43	50m 43 - 57

✓ For attempt, solicitation, conspiracy (RCW 9.94A.595) see page 23 or for gang-related felonies where the court found the offender involved a minor (RCW 9.94A.833) see page 186 for standard range adjustments.

✓ For deadly weapon enhancement, see page 190.

✓ For sentencing alternatives, see page 177.

✓ For community custody eligibility, see page 187.

✓ For any applicable enhancements other than deadly weapon enhancement, see page 183.

Theft Second Degree Excluding Firearm And Motor Vehicle

RCW 9A.56.040
CLASS C – NONVIOLENT
OFFENDER SCORING RCW 9.94A.525(7)

If it was found that this offense was committed with sexual motivation (RCW 9.94A.533(8)) on or after 7/01/2006, use the General Nonviolent Offense with a Sexual Motivation Finding scoring form on page 193.

If the present conviction is for a felony domestic violence offense where domestic violence was plead and proven, use the General Nonviolent Offense Where Domestic Violence Has Been Plead and Proven scoring form on page 191.

ADULT HISTORY:
    Enter number of felony convictions .... _____ x 1 = _____

JUVENILE HISTORY:
    Enter number of serious violent and violent felony dispositions .... _____ x 1 = _____
    Enter number of nonviolent felony dispositions .... _____ x ½ = _____

OTHER CURRENT OFFENSES:
(Other current offenses that do not encompass the same conduct count in offender score)
    Enter number of other felony convictions .... _____ x 1 = _____

STATUS:
    Was the offender on community custody on the date the current offense was committed? (if yes) .... + 1 = _____

Total the last column to get the **Offender Score** (Round down to the nearest whole number)

SENTENCE RANGE

	Offender Score									
	0	**1**	**2**	**3**	**4**	**5**	**6**	**7**	**8**	**9+**
LEVEL I	0-60 days	0-90 days	3m 2 - 5	4m 2 - 6	5.5m 3 - 8	8m 4 - 12	13m 12+ - 14	16m 14 - 18	19.5m 17 - 22	25.5m 22 - 29

✓ For gang-related felonies where the court found the offender involved a minor (RCW 9.94A.833) see page 186 for standard range adjustment.

✓ For deadly weapon enhancement, see page 190.

✓ For sentencing alternatives, see page 177.

✓ For community custody eligibility, see page 187.

✓ For any applicable enhancements other than deadly weapon enhancement, see page 183.

Theft Of Ammonia

RCW 69.55.010
CLASS C* – NONVIOLENT

OFFENDER SCORING RCW 9.94A.525(7)

If it was found that this offense was committed with sexual motivation (RCW 9.94A.533(8)) on or after 7/01/2006, use the General Nonviolent Offense with a Sexual Motivation Finding scoring form on page 193.

If the present conviction is for a felony domestic violence offense where domestic violence was plead and proven, use the General Nonviolent Offense Where Domestic Violence Has Been Plead and Proven scoring form on page 191.

ADULT HISTORY:
    Enter number of felony convictions .... _____ x 1 = _____

JUVENILE HISTORY:
    Enter number of serious violent and violent felony dispositions .... _____ x 1 = _____

    Enter number of nonviolent felony dispositions .... _____ x ½ = _____

OTHER CURRENT OFFENSES:
(Other current offenses that do not encompass the same conduct count in offender score)
    Enter number of other felony convictions .... _____ x 1 = _____

STATUS:
    Was the offender on community custody on the date the current offense was committed? (if yes) ...... + 1 = _____

Total the last column to get the **Offender Score** (Round down to the nearest whole number)

SENTENCE RANGE

	\multicolumn{11}{c}{Offender Score}
	0	1	2	3	4	5	6	7	8	9+
LEVEL VIII	24m 21 - 27	30m 26 - 34	36m 31 - 41	42m 36 - 48	47.5m 41 - 54	53.m 46 - 60*	60 - 60*	60 - 60*	60 - 60*	60 - 60*

✓ For gang-related felonies where the court found the offender involved a minor (RCW 9.94A.833) see page 186 for standard range adjustment.

✓ For deadly weapon enhancement, see page 190.

✓ For sentencing alternatives, see page 177.

✓ For community custody eligibility, see page 187.

✓ For any applicable enhancements other than deadly weapon enhancement, see page 183.

The Caseload Forecast Council is not liable for errors or omissions in the manual, for sentences that may be inappropriately calculated as a result of a practitioner's or court's reliance on the manual, or for any other written or verbal information related to adult or juvenile sentencing. The scoring sheets are intended to provide assistance in most cases but do not cover all permutations of the scoring rules. If you find any errors or omissions, we encourage you to report them to the Caseload Forecast Council.

Theft Of A Firearm

RCW 9A.56.300
CLASS B – NONVIOLENT

OFFENDER SCORING RCW 9.94A.525(7)

If it was found that this offense was committed with sexual motivation (RCW 9.94A.533(8)) on or after 7/01/2006, use the General Nonviolent Offense with a Sexual Motivation Finding scoring form on page 193.

If the present conviction is for a felony domestic violence offense where domestic violence was plead and proven, use the General Nonviolent Offense Where Domestic Violence Has Been Plead and Proven scoring form on page 191.

ADULT HISTORY:
    Enter number of felony convictions .... _____ x 1 = _____

JUVENILE HISTORY:
    Enter number of serious violent and violent felony dispositions .... _____ x 1 = _____
    Enter number of nonviolent felony dispositions .... _____ x ½ = _____

OTHER CURRENT OFFENSES:
(Other current offenses that do not encompass the same conduct count in offender score)
    Enter number of other felony convictions .... _____ x 1 = _____

STATUS:
    Was the offender on community custody on the date the current offense was committed? (if yes) .... + 1 = _____

Total the last column to get the **Offender Score** (Round down to the nearest whole number)

SENTENCE RANGE

	\multicolumn{10}{c}{Offender Score}									
	0	**1**	**2**	**3**	**4**	**5**	**6**	**7**	**8**	**9+**
LEVEL VI	13m	17.5m	24m	30m	36m	42m	53.5m	66m	78m	89.5m
	12+ - 14	15 - 20	21 - 27	26 - 34	31 - 41	36 - 48	46 - 61	57 - 75	67 - 89	77 - 102

- ✓ For attempt, solicitation, conspiracy (RCW 9.94A.595) see page 23 or for gang-related felonies where the court found the offender involved a minor (RCW 9.94A.833) see page 186 for standard range adjustments.
- ✓ For deadly weapon enhancement, see page 190.
- ✓ For sentencing alternatives, see page 177.
- ✓ For community custody eligibility, see page 187.
- ✓ For any applicable enhancements other than deadly weapon enhancement, see page 183.
- ✓ Each firearm possessed under this section is a separate offense.
- ✓ The offender shall be sentenced according to RCW 9.94A.589(1)(c) if the offender is convicted of Unlawful Possession of a Firearm 1 or 2 (RCW 9.41.040) <u>and</u> for felonies Theft of a Firearm or Possession of a Stolen Firearm, or both, as current offenses.
- ✓ If the present conviction is for Unlawful Possession of a Firearm 1 or 2 <u>and</u> felonies Theft of a Firearm or Possession of a Stolen Firearm, or both, charged under RCW 9.41.040, other current convictions for Unlawful Possession of a Firearm 1 or 2, Possession of a Stolen Firearm or Theft of a Firearm may not be included in the computation of the offender score per RCW 9.94A.589(1)(c). The offender will serve consecutive sentences for these particular offenses.

The Caseload Forecast Council is not liable for errors or omissions in the manual, for sentences that may be inappropriately calculated as a result of a practitioner's or court's reliance on the manual, or for any other written or verbal information related to adult or juvenile sentencing. The scoring sheets are intended to provide assistance in most cases but do not cover all permutations of the scoring rules. If you find any errors or omissions, we encourage you to report them to the Caseload Forecast Council.

Theft Of Livestock First Degree

RCW 9A.56.080
CLASS B – NONVIOLENT

OFFENDER SCORING RCW 9.94A.525(7)

If it was found that this offense was committed with sexual motivation (RCW 9.94A.533(8)) on or after 7/01/2006, use the General Nonviolent Offense with a Sexual Motivation Finding scoring form on page 193.

If the present conviction is for a felony domestic violence offense where domestic violence was plead and proven, use the General Nonviolent Offense Where Domestic Violence Has Been Plead and Proven scoring form on page 191.

ADULT HISTORY:
  Enter number of felony convictions .... _____ x 1 = _____

JUVENILE HISTORY:
  Enter number of serious violent and violent felony dispositions .... _____ x 1 = _____
  Enter number of nonviolent felony dispositions .... _____ x ½ = _____

OTHER CURRENT OFFENSES:
(Other current offenses that do not encompass the same conduct count in offender score)
  Enter number of other felony convictions .... _____ x 1 = _____

STATUS:
  Was the offender on community custody on the date the current offense was committed? (if yes) ...... + 1 = _____

Total the last column to get the **Offender Score** (Round down to the nearest whole number)

SENTENCE RANGE

	Offender Score									
	0	1	2	3	4	5	6	7	8	9+
LEVEL IV	6m	9m	13m	15m	17.5m	25.5m	38m	50m	61.5m	73.5m
	3 - 9	6 - 12	12+ - 14	13 - 17	15 - 20	22 - 29	33 - 43	43 - 57	53 - 70	63 - 84

✓ For attempt, solicitation, conspiracy (RCW 9.94A.595) see page 23 or for gang-related felonies where the court found the offender involved a minor (RCW 9.94A.833) see page 186 for standard range adjustments.

✓ For deadly weapon enhancement, see page 190.

✓ For sentencing alternatives, see page 177.

✓ For community custody eligibility, see page 187.

✓ For any applicable enhancements other than deadly weapon enhancement, see page 183.

✓ Per RCW 9A.56.085, the convicting court shall order the person to pay the amount of $2,000 for each animal killed or possessed.

The Caseload Forecast Council is not liable for errors or omissions in the manual, for sentences that may be inappropriately calculated as a result of a practitioner's or court's reliance on the manual, or for any other written or verbal information related to adult or juvenile sentencing. The scoring sheets are intended to provide assistance in most cases but do not cover all permutations of the scoring rules. If you find any errors or omissions, we encourage you to report them to the Caseload Forecast Council.

Theft Of Livestock Second Degree

RCW 9A.56.083
CLASS C* – NONVIOLENT
OFFENDER SCORING RCW 9.94A.525(7)

If it was found that this offense was committed with sexual motivation (RCW 9.94A.533(8)) on or after 7/01/2006, use the General Nonviolent Offense with a Sexual Motivation Finding scoring form on page 193.

If the present conviction is for a felony domestic violence offense where domestic violence was plead and proven, use the General Nonviolent Offense Where Domestic Violence Has Been Plead and Proven scoring form on page 191.

ADULT HISTORY:
    Enter number of felony convictions .... _____ x 1 = _____

JUVENILE HISTORY:
    Enter number of serious violent and violent felony dispositions .... _____ x 1 = _____
    Enter number of nonviolent felony dispositions .... _____ x ½ = _____

OTHER CURRENT OFFENSES:
(Other current offenses that do not encompass the same conduct count in offender score)
    Enter number of other felony convictions .... _____ x 1 = _____

STATUS:
    Was the offender on community custody on the date the current offense was committed? (if yes) .... + 1 = _____

Total the last column to get the **Offender Score** (Round down to the nearest whole number)

SENTENCE RANGE

	\multicolumn{10}{c}{Offender Score}
	0	1	2	3	4	5	6	7	8	9+
LEVEL III	2m 1 - 3	5m 3 - 8	8m 4 - 12	11m 9 - 12	14m 12+ - 16	19.5m 17 - 22	25.5m 22 - 29	38m 33 - 43	50m 43 - 57	55.5m 51 - 60*

- ✓ For gang-related felonies where the court found the offender involved a minor (RCW 9.94A.833) see page 186 for standard range adjustment.
- ✓ For deadly weapon enhancement, see page 190.
- ✓ For sentencing alternatives, see page 177.
- ✓ For community custody eligibility, see page 187.
- ✓ For any applicable enhancements other than deadly weapon enhancement, see page 183.
- ✓ Per RCW 9A.56.085, the convicting court shall order the person to pay the amount of $2,000 for each animal killed or possessed.

The Caseload Forecast Council is not liable for errors or omissions in the manual, for sentences that may be inappropriately calculated as a result of a practitioner's or court's reliance on the manual, or for any other written or verbal information related to adult or juvenile sentencing. The scoring sheets are intended to provide assistance in most cases but do not cover all permutations of the scoring rules. If you find any errors or omissions, we encourage you to report them to the Caseload Forecast Council.

Theft Of A Motor Vehicle

RCW 9A.56.065
CLASS B – NONVIOLENT

OFFENDER SCORING RCW 9.94A.525(20)

If it was found that this offense was committed with sexual motivation (RCW 9.94A.533(8)) on or after 7/01/2006, use the General Nonviolent Offense with a Sexual Motivation Finding scoring form on page 193.

If the present conviction is for a felony domestic violence offense where domestic violence was plead and proven, use the General Nonviolent Offense Where Domestic Violence Has Been Plead and Proven scoring form on page 191.

ADULT HISTORY:
    Enter number of Theft of a Motor Vehicle, Theft 1 & 2 (of a Motor Vehicle), Possession of Stolen Property 1 & 2 (of a Motor Vehicle), Possession of a Stolen Vehicle and Taking a Motor Vehicle Without Permission 1 & 2 felony convictions .... _____ x 3 = _____

    Enter number of Vehicle Prowling 2 convictions .... _____ x 1 = _____

    Enter number of felony convictions .... _____ x 1 = _____

JUVENILE HISTORY:
    Enter number of Theft of a Motor Vehicle, Theft 1 & 2 (of a Motor Vehicle), Possession of Stolen Property 1 & 2 (of a Motor Vehicle), Possession of a Stolen Vehicle and Taking a Motor Vehicle Without Permission 1 & 2 felony dispositions .... _____ x 3 = _____

    Enter number of Vehicle Prowling 2 dispositions .... _____ x 1 = _____

    Enter number of serious violent and violent felony dispositions .... _____ x 1 = _____

    Enter number of nonviolent felony dispositions .... _____ x ½ = _____

OTHER CURRENT OFFENSES:
(Other current offenses that do not encompass the same conduct count in offender score)
    Enter number of other Theft of a Motor Vehicle, Theft 1 & 2 (of a Motor Vehicle), Possession of Stolen Property 1 & 2 (of a Motor Vehicle), Possession of a Stolen Vehicle and Taking a Motor Vehicle Without Permission 1 & 2 felony convictions .... _____ x 3 = _____

    Enter number of other Vehicle Prowling 2 convictions .... _____ x 1 = _____

    Enter number of other felony convictions .... _____ x 1 = _____

STATUS:
    Was the offender on community custody on the date the current offense was committed? (if yes) ...... + 1 = _____

Total the last column to get the **Offender Score** (Round down to the nearest whole number)

SENTENCE RANGE

	Offender Score									
	0	1	2	3	4	5	6	7	8	9+
LEVEL II		4m	6m	8m	13m	16m	19.5m	25.5m	38m	50m
	0-90 days	2 - 6	3 - 9	4 - 12	12+ - 14	14 - 18	17 - 22	22 - 29	33 - 43	43 - 57

- ✓ For attempt, solicitation, conspiracy (RCW 9.94A.595) see page 23 or for gang-related felonies where the court found the offender involved a minor (RCW 9.94A.833) see page 186 for standard range adjustments.
- ✓ For deadly weapon enhancement, see page 190.
- ✓ For sentencing alternatives, see page 177.
- ✓ For community custody eligibility, see page 187.
- ✓ For any applicable enhancements other than deadly weapon enhancement, see page 183.

Theft Of Rental, Leased, Lease-Purchased Or Loaned Property Valued At $5,000 Or More

RCW 9A.56.096(5)(a)
CLASS B – NONVIOLENT

OFFENDER SCORING RCW 9.94A.525(7)

If it was found that this offense was committed with sexual motivation (RCW 9.94A.533(8)) on or after 7/01/2006, use the General Nonviolent Offense with a Sexual Motivation Finding scoring form on page 193.

If the present conviction is for a felony domestic violence offense where domestic violence was plead and proven, use the General Nonviolent Offense Where Domestic Violence Has Been Plead and Proven scoring form on page 191.

ADULT HISTORY:
  Enter number of felony convictions .... _____ x 1 = _____

JUVENILE HISTORY:
  Enter number of serious violent and violent felony dispositions .... _____ x 1 = _____
  Enter number of nonviolent felony dispositions .... _____ x ½ = _____

OTHER CURRENT OFFENSES:
(Other current offenses that do not encompass the same conduct count in offender score)
  Enter number of other felony convictions .... _____ x 1 = _____

STATUS:
  Was the offender on community custody on the date the current offense was committed? (if yes)....... + 1 = _____

Total the last column to get the **Offender Score** (Round down to the nearest whole number)

SENTENCE RANGE

	Offender Score									
	0	1	2	3	4	5	6	7	8	9+
LEVEL II	0-90 days	4m 2 - 6	6m 3 - 9	8m 4 - 12	13m 12+ - 14	16m 14 - 18	19.5m 17 - 22	25.5m 22 - 29	38m 33 - 43	50m 43 - 57

- ✓ For attempt, solicitation, conspiracy (RCW 9.94A.595) see page 23 or for gang-related felonies where the court found the offender involved a minor (RCW 9.94A.833) see page 186 for standard range adjustments.
- ✓ For deadly weapon enhancement, see page 190.
- ✓ For sentencing alternatives, see page 177.
- ✓ For community custody eligibility, see page 187.
- ✓ For any applicable enhancements other than deadly weapon enhancement, see page 183.

Theft Of Rental, Leased, Lease-Purchased Or Loaned Property Valued At $750 Or More But Less Than $5,000

RCW 9A.56.096(5)(b)
CLASS C – NONVIOLENT

OFFENDER SCORING RCW 9.94A.525(7)

If it was found that this offense was committed with sexual motivation (RCW 9.94A.533(8)) on or after 7/01/2006, use the General Nonviolent Offense with a Sexual Motivation Finding scoring form on page 193.

If the present conviction is for a felony domestic violence offense where domestic violence was plead and proven, use the General Nonviolent Offense Where Domestic Violence Has Been Plead and Proven scoring form on page 191.

ADULT HISTORY:
 Enter number of felony convictions .... _____ x 1 = _____

JUVENILE HISTORY:
 Enter number of serious violent and violent felony dispositions .... _____ x 1 = _____
 Enter number of nonviolent felony dispositions .... _____ x ½ = _____

OTHER CURRENT OFFENSES:
(Other current offenses that do not encompass the same conduct count in offender score)
 Enter number of other felony convictions .... _____ x 1 = _____

STATUS:
 Was the offender on community custody on the date the current offense was committed? (if yes) ...... + 1 = _____

Total the last column to get the **Offender Score** (Round down to the nearest whole number)

SENTENCE RANGE

	Offender Score									
	0	1	2	3	4	5	6	7	8	9+
LEVEL I	0-60 days	0-90 days	3m 2 - 5	4m 2 - 6	5.5m 3 - 8	8m 4 - 12	13m 12+ - 14	16m 14 - 18	19.5m 17 - 22	25.5m 22 - 29

✓ For gang-related felonies where the court found the offender involved a minor (RCW 9.94A.833) see page 186 for standard range adjustment.

✓ For deadly weapon enhancement, see page 190.

✓ For sentencing alternatives, see page 177.

✓ For community custody eligibility, see page 187.

✓ For any applicable enhancements other than deadly weapon enhancement, see page 183.

The Caseload Forecast Council is not liable for errors or omissions in the manual, for sentences that may be inappropriately calculated as a result of a practitioner's or court's reliance on the manual, or for any other written or verbal information related to adult or juvenile sentencing. The scoring sheets are intended to provide assistance in most cases but do not cover all permutations of the scoring rules. If you find any errors or omissions, we encourage you to report them to the Caseload Forecast Council.

Theft With Intent To Resell First Degree

RCW 9A.56.340(2)
CLASS B – NONVIOLENT

OFFENDER SCORING RCW 9.94A.525(7)

If it was found that this offense was committed with sexual motivation (RCW 9.94A.533(8)) on or after 7/01/2006, use the General Nonviolent Offense with a Sexual Motivation Finding scoring form on page 193.

If the present conviction is for a felony domestic violence offense where domestic violence was plead and proven, use the General Nonviolent Offense Where Domestic Violence Has Been Plead and Proven scoring form on page 191.

ADULT HISTORY:
　Enter number of felony convictions .... _____ x 1 = _____

JUVENILE HISTORY:
　Enter number of serious violent and violent felony dispositions .... _____ x 1 = _____
　Enter number of nonviolent felony dispositions .... _____ x ½ = _____

OTHER CURRENT OFFENSES:
(Other current offenses that do not encompass the same conduct count in offender score)
　Enter number of other felony convictions .... _____ x 1 = _____

STATUS:
　Was the offender on community custody on the date the current offense was committed? (if yes) .... + 1 = _____

Total the last column to get the **Offender Score** (Round down to the nearest whole number)　　　☐

SENTENCE RANGE

	Offender Score									
	0	1	2	3	4	5	6	7	8	9+
LEVEL III	2m 1 - 3	5m 3 - 8	8m 4 - 12	11m 9 - 12	14m 12+ - 16	19.5m 17 - 22	25.5m 22 - 29	38m 33 - 43	50m 43 - 57	59.5m 51 - 68

- ✓ For attempt, solicitation, conspiracy (RCW 9.94A.595) see page 23 or for gang-related felonies where the court found the offender involved a minor (RCW 9.94A.833) see page 186 for standard range adjustments.
- ✓ For deadly weapon enhancement, see page 190.
- ✓ For sentencing alternatives, see page 177.
- ✓ For community custody eligibility, see page 187.
- ✓ For any applicable enhancements other than deadly weapon enhancement, see page 183.

The Caseload Forecast Council is not liable for errors or omissions in the manual, for sentences that may be inappropriately calculated as a result of a practitioner's or court's reliance on the manual, or for any other written or verbal information related to adult or juvenile sentencing. The scoring sheets are intended to provide assistance in most cases but do not cover all permutations of the scoring rules. If you find any errors or omissions, we encourage you to report them to the Caseload Forecast Council.

Theft With Intent To Resell Second Degree

RCW 9A.56.340(3)
CLASS C – NONVIOLENT
OFFENDER SCORING RCW 9.94A.525(7)

If it was found that this offense was committed with sexual motivation (RCW 9.94A.533(8)) on or after 7/01/2006, use the General Nonviolent Offense with a Sexual Motivation Finding scoring form on page 193.

If the present conviction is for a felony domestic violence offense where domestic violence was plead and proven, use the General Nonviolent Offense Where Domestic Violence Has Been Plead and Proven scoring form on page 191.

ADULT HISTORY:
    Enter number of felony convictions .... _____ x 1 = _____

JUVENILE HISTORY:
    Enter number of serious violent and violent felony dispositions .... _____ x 1 = _____
    Enter number of nonviolent felony dispositions .... _____ x ½ = _____

OTHER CURRENT OFFENSES:
(Other current offenses that do not encompass the same conduct count in offender score)
    Enter number of other felony convictions .... _____ x 1 = _____

STATUS:
    Was the offender on community custody on the date the current offense was committed? (if yes) ...... + 1 = _____

Total the last column to get the **Offender Score** (Round down to the nearest whole number)

SENTENCE RANGE

	_				Offender Score					
	0	**1**	**2**	**3**	**4**	**5**	**6**	**7**	**8**	**9+**
LEVEL II		4m	6m	8m	13m	16m	19.5m	25.5m	38m	50m
	0-90 days	2 - 6	3 - 9	4 - 12	12+ - 14	14 - 18	17 - 22	22 - 29	33 - 43	43 - 57

- ✓ For gang-related felonies where the court found the offender involved a minor (RCW 9.94A.833) see page 186 for standard range adjustments.
- ✓ For deadly weapon enhancement, see page 190.
- ✓ For sentencing alternatives, see page 177.
- ✓ For community custody eligibility, see page 187.
- ✓ For any applicable enhancements other than deadly weapon enhancement, see page 183.

The Caseload Forecast Council is not liable for errors or omissions in the manual, for sentences that may be inappropriately calculated as a result of a practitioner's or court's reliance on the manual, or for any other written or verbal information related to adult or juvenile sentencing. The scoring sheets are intended to provide assistance in most cases but do not cover all permutations of the scoring rules. If you find any errors or omissions, we encourage you to report them to the Caseload Forecast Council.

Threats To Bomb

RCW 9.61.160
CLASS B – NONVIOLENT

OFFENDER SCORING RCW 9.94A.525(7)

If it was found that this offense was committed with sexual motivation (RCW 9.94A.533(8)) on or after 7/01/2006, use the General Nonviolent Offense with a Sexual Motivation Finding scoring form on page 193.

If the present conviction is for a felony domestic violence offense where domestic violence was plead and proven, use the General Nonviolent Offense Where Domestic Violence Has Been Plead and Proven scoring form on page 191.

ADULT HISTORY:
    Enter number of felony convictions .... _____ x 1 = _____

JUVENILE HISTORY:
    Enter number of serious violent and violent felony dispositions .... _____ x 1 = _____
    Enter number of nonviolent felony dispositions .... _____ x ½ = _____

OTHER CURRENT OFFENSES:
(Other current offenses that do not encompass the same conduct count in offender score)
    Enter number of other felony convictions .... _____ x 1 = _____

STATUS:
    Was the offender on community custody on the date the current offense was committed? (if yes) .... + 1 = _____

Total the last column to get the **Offender Score** (Round down to the nearest whole number)

SENTENCE RANGE

Offender Score	0	1	2	3	4	5	6	7	8	9+
LEVEL IV	6m 3 - 9	9m 6 - 12	13m 12+ - 14	15m 13 - 17	17.5m 15 - 20	25.5m 22 - 29	38m 33 - 43	50m 43 - 57	61.5m 53 - 70	73.5m 63 - 84

- ✓ For attempt, solicitation, conspiracy (RCW 9.94A.595) see page 23 or for gang-related felonies where the court found the offender involved a minor (RCW 9.94A.833) see page 186 for standard range adjustments.
- ✓ For deadly weapon enhancement, see page 190.
- ✓ For sentencing alternatives, see page 177.
- ✓ For community custody eligibility, see page 187.
- ✓ For any applicable enhancements other than deadly weapon enhancement, see page 183.

The Caseload Forecast Council is not liable for errors or omissions in the manual, for sentences that may be inappropriately calculated as a result of a practitioner's or court's reliance on the manual, or for any other written or verbal information related to adult or juvenile sentencing. The scoring sheets are intended to provide assistance in most cases but do not cover all permutations of the scoring rules. If you find any errors or omissions, we encourage you to report them to the Caseload Forecast Council.

Trafficking In Insurance Claims Subsequent Violation

RCW 48.30A.015
CLASS C – NONVIOLENT
OFFENDER SCORING RCW 9.94A.525(7)

If it was found that this offense was committed with sexual motivation (RCW 9.94A.533(8)) on or after 7/01/2006, use the General Nonviolent Offense with a Sexual Motivation Finding scoring form on page 193.

If the present conviction is for a felony domestic violence offense where domestic violence was plead and proven, use the General Nonviolent Offense Where Domestic Violence Has Been Plead and Proven scoring form on page 191.

ADULT HISTORY:
    Enter number of felony convictions .... _____ x 1 = _____

JUVENILE HISTORY:
    Enter number of serious violent and violent felony dispositions .... _____ x 1 = _____
    Enter number of nonviolent felony dispositions .... _____ x ½ = _____

OTHER CURRENT OFFENSES:
(Other current offenses that do not encompass the same conduct count in offender score)
    Enter number of other felony convictions .... _____ x 1 = _____

STATUS:
    Was the offender on community custody on the date the current offense was committed? (if yes) ...... + 1 = _____

Total the last column to get the **Offender Score** (Round down to the nearest whole number)

SENTENCE RANGE

	\multicolumn{10}{c}{Offender Score}									
	0	1	2	3	4	5	6	7	8	9+
LEVEL II	0-90 days	4m 2 - 6	6m 3 - 9	8m 4 - 12	13m 12+ - 14	16m 14 - 18	19.5m 17 - 22	25.5m 22 - 29	38m 33 - 43	50m 43 - 57

- ✓ For gang-related felonies where the court found the offender involved a minor (RCW 9.94A.833) see page 186 for standard range adjustment.
- ✓ For deadly weapon enhancement, see page 190.
- ✓ For sentencing alternatives, see page 177.
- ✓ For community custody eligibility, see page 187.
- ✓ For any applicable enhancements other than deadly weapon enhancement, see page 183.

The Caseload Forecast Council is not liable for errors or omissions in the manual, for sentences that may be inappropriately calculated as a result of a practitioner's or court's reliance on the manual, or for any other written or verbal information related to adult or juvenile sentencing. The scoring sheets are intended to provide assistance in most cases but do not cover all permutations of the scoring rules. If you find any errors or omissions, we encourage you to report them to the Caseload Forecast Council.

Trafficking In Stolen Property First Degree

RCW 9A.82.050
CLASS B – NONVIOLENT
OFFENDER SCORING RCW 9.94A.525(7)

If it was found that this offense was committed with sexual motivation (RCW 9.94A.533(8)) on or after 7/01/2006, use the General Nonviolent Offense with a Sexual Motivation Finding scoring form on page 193.

If the present conviction is for a felony domestic violence offense where domestic violence was plead and proven, use the General Nonviolent Offense Where Domestic Violence Has Been Plead and Proven scoring form on page 191.

ADULT HISTORY:
　Enter number of felony convictions .... _____　　x 1 = _____

JUVENILE HISTORY:
　Enter number of serious violent and violent felony dispositions .... _____　　x 1 = _____

　Enter number of nonviolent felony dispositions .... _____　　x ½ = _____

OTHER CURRENT OFFENSES:
(Other current offenses that do not encompass the same conduct count in offender score)
　Enter number of other felony convictions .... _____　　x 1 = _____

STATUS:
　Was the offender on community custody on the date the current offense was committed? (if yes) .... + 1 = _____

Total the last column to get the **Offender Score** (Round down to the nearest whole number)

SENTENCE RANGE

	\multicolumn{10}{c}{Offender Score}									
	0	**1**	**2**	**3**	**4**	**5**	**6**	**7**	**8**	**9+**
LEVEL IV	6m 3 - 9	9m 6 - 12	13m 12+ - 14	15m 13 - 17	17.5m 15 - 20	25.5m 22 - 29	38m 33 - 43	50m 43 - 57	61.5m 53 - 70	73.5m 63 - 84

- ✓ For attempt, solicitation, conspiracy (RCW 9.94A.595) see page 23 or for gang-related felonies where the court found the offender involved a minor (RCW 9.94A.833) see page 186 for standard range adjustments.
- ✓ For deadly weapon enhancement, see page 190.
- ✓ For sentencing alternatives, see page 177.
- ✓ For community custody eligibility, see page 187.
- ✓ For any applicable enhancements other than deadly weapon enhancement, see page 183.

The Caseload Forecast Council is not liable for errors or omissions in the manual, for sentences that may be inappropriately calculated as a result of a practitioner's or court's reliance on the manual, or for any other written or verbal information related to adult or juvenile sentencing. The scoring sheets are intended to provide assistance in most cases but do not cover all permutations of the scoring rules. If you find any errors or omissions, we encourage you to report them to the Caseload Forecast Council.

Trafficking In Stolen Property Second Degree

RCW 9A.82.055
CLASS C* – NONVIOLENT

OFFENDER SCORING RCW 9.94A.525(7)

If it was found that this offense was committed with sexual motivation (RCW 9.94A.533(8)) on or after 7/01/2006, use the General Nonviolent Offense with a Sexual Motivation Finding scoring form on page 193.

If the present conviction is for a felony domestic violence offense where domestic violence was plead and proven, use the General Nonviolent Offense Where Domestic Violence Has Been Plead and Proven scoring form on page 191.

ADULT HISTORY:
    Enter number of felony convictions .... _____ x 1 = _____

JUVENILE HISTORY:
    Enter number of serious violent and violent felony dispositions .... _____ x 1 = _____
    Enter number of nonviolent felony dispositions .... _____ x ½ = _____

OTHER CURRENT OFFENSES:
(Other current offenses that do not encompass the same conduct count in offender score)
    Enter number of other felony convictions .... _____ x 1 = _____

STATUS:
    Was the offender on community custody on the date the current offense was committed? (if yes) ...... + 1 = _____

Total the last column to get the **Offender Score** (Round down to the nearest whole number)

SENTENCE RANGE

	\multicolumn{11}{c	}{Offender Score}
	0	1	2	3	4	5	6	7	8	9+
LEVEL III	2m	5m	8m	11m	14m	19.5m	25.5m	38m	50m	55.5m
	1 - 3	3 - 8	4 - 12	9 - 12	12+ - 16	17 - 22	22 - 29	33 - 43	43 - 57	51 - 60*

✓ For gang-related felonies where the court found the offender involved a minor (RCW 9.94A.833) see page 186 for standard range adjustment.

✓ For deadly weapon enhancement, see page 190.

✓ For sentencing alternatives, see page 177.

✓ For community custody eligibility, see page 187.

✓ For any applicable enhancements other than deadly weapon enhancement, see page 183.

The Caseload Forecast Council is not liable for errors or omissions in the manual, for sentences that may be inappropriately calculated as a result of a practitioner's or court's reliance on the manual, or for any other written or verbal information related to adult or juvenile sentencing. The scoring sheets are intended to provide assistance in most cases but do not cover all permutations of the scoring rules. If you find any errors or omissions, we encourage you to report them to the Caseload Forecast Council.

Unlawful Factoring Of A Credit Or Payment Card Transaction

RCW 9A.56.290(4)(a)
CLASS C – NONVIOLENT

OFFENDER SCORING RCW 9.94A.525(7)

If it was found that this offense was committed with sexual motivation (RCW 9.94A.533(8)) on or after 7/01/2006, use the General Nonviolent Offense with a Sexual Motivation Finding scoring form on page 193.

If the present conviction is for a felony domestic violence offense where domestic violence was plead and proven, use the General Nonviolent Offense Where Domestic Violence Has Been Plead and Proven scoring form on page 191.

ADULT HISTORY:
    Enter number of felony convictions .... _____ x 1 = _____

JUVENILE HISTORY:
    Enter number of serious violent and violent felony dispositions .... _____ x 1 = _____

    Enter number of nonviolent felony dispositions .... _____ x ½ = _____

OTHER CURRENT OFFENSES:
(Other current offenses that do not encompass the same conduct count in offender score)
    Enter number of other felony convictions .... _____ x 1 = _____

STATUS:
    Was the offender on community custody on the date the current offense was committed? (if yes) .... + 1 = _____

Total the last column to get the **Offender Score** (Round down to the nearest whole number)

SENTENCE RANGE

Offender Score	0	1	2	3	4	5	6	7	8	9+
LEVEL II	0-90 days	4m 2 - 6	6m 3 - 9	8m 4 - 12	13m 12+ - 14	16m 14 - 18	19.5m 17 - 22	25.5m 22 - 29	38m 33 - 43	50m 43 - 57

- ✓ For gang-related felonies where the court found the offender involved a minor (RCW 9.94A.833) see page 186 for standard range adjustment.
- ✓ For deadly weapon enhancement, see page 190.
- ✓ For sentencing alternatives, see page 177.
- ✓ For community custody eligibility, see page 187.
- ✓ For any applicable enhancements other than deadly weapon enhancement, see page 183.

The Caseload Forecast Council is not liable for errors or omissions in the manual, for sentences that may be inappropriately calculated as a result of a practitioner's or court's reliance on the manual, or for any other written or verbal information related to adult or juvenile sentencing. The scoring sheets are intended to provide assistance in most cases but do not cover all permutations of the scoring rules. If you find any errors or omissions, we encourage you to report them to the Caseload Forecast Council.

Unlawful Factoring Of A Credit Or Payment Card Transaction Subsequent Violation

RCW 9A.56.290(4)(b)
CLASS B – NONVIOLENT

OFFENDER SCORING RCW 9.94A.525(7)

If it was found that this offense was committed with sexual motivation (RCW 9.94A.533(8)) on or after 7/01/2006, use the General Nonviolent Offense with a Sexual Motivation Finding scoring form on page 193.

If the present conviction is for a felony domestic violence offense where domestic violence was plead and proven, use the General Nonviolent Offense Where Domestic Violence Has Been Plead and Proven scoring form on page 191.

ADULT HISTORY:
  Enter number of felony convictions .... _____ x 1 = _____

JUVENILE HISTORY:
  Enter number of serious violent and violent felony dispositions .... _____ x 1 = _____
  Enter number of nonviolent felony dispositions .... _____ x ½ = _____

OTHER CURRENT OFFENSES:
(Other current offenses that do not encompass the same conduct count in offender score)
  Enter number of other felony convictions .... _____ x 1 = _____

STATUS:
  Was the offender on community custody on the date the current offense was committed? (if yes) ...... + 1 = _____

Total the last column to get the **Offender Score** (Round down to the nearest whole number)

SENTENCE RANGE

Offender Score	0	1	2	3	4	5	6	7	8	9+
LEVEL IV	6m 3 - 9	9m 6 - 12	13m 12+ - 14	15m 13 - 17	17.5m 15 - 20	25.5m 22 - 29	38m 33 - 43	50m 43 - 57	61.5m 53 - 70	73.5m 63 - 84

- ✓ For attempt, solicitation, conspiracy (RCW 9.94A.595) see page 23 or for gang-related felonies where the court found the offender involved a minor (RCW 9.94A.833) see page 186 for standard range adjustments.
- ✓ For deadly weapon enhancement, see page 190.
- ✓ For sentencing alternatives, see page 177.
- ✓ For community custody eligibility, see page 187.
- ✓ For any applicable enhancements other than deadly weapon enhancement, see page 183.

The Caseload Forecast Council is not liable for errors or omissions in the manual, for sentences that may be inappropriately calculated as a result of a practitioner's or court's reliance on the manual, or for any other written or verbal information related to adult or juvenile sentencing. The scoring sheets are intended to provide assistance in most cases but do not cover all permutations of the scoring rules. If you find any errors or omissions, we encourage you to report them to the Caseload Forecast Council.

Unlawful Imprisonment

RCW 9A.40.040
CLASS C* – NONVIOLENT
OFFENDER SCORING RCW 9.94A.525(7)

If it was found that this offense was committed with sexual motivation (RCW 9.94A.533(8)) on or after 7/01/2006, use the General Nonviolent Offense with a Sexual Motivation Finding scoring form on page 193.

If the present conviction is for a felony domestic violence offense where domestic violence was plead and proven, use the General Nonviolent Offense Where Domestic Violence Has Been Plead and Proven scoring form on page 191.

ADULT HISTORY:
    Enter number of felony convictions .... _____ x 1 = _____

JUVENILE HISTORY:
    Enter number of serious violent and violent felony dispositions .... _____ x 1 = _____

    Enter number of nonviolent felony dispositions .... _____ x ½ = _____

OTHER CURRENT OFFENSES:
(Other current offenses that do not encompass the same conduct count in offender score)
    Enter number of other felony convictions .... _____ x 1 = _____

STATUS:
    Was the offender on community custody on the date the current offense was committed? (if yes) .... + 1 = _____

Total the last column to get the **Offender Score** (Round down to the nearest whole number)

SENTENCE RANGE

	\multicolumn{10}{c}{Offender Score}									
	0	**1**	**2**	**3**	**4**	**5**	**6**	**7**	**8**	**9+**
LEVEL III	2m	5m	8m	11m	14m	19.5m	25.5m	38m	50m	55.5m
	1 - 3	3 - 8	4 - 12	9 - 12	12+ - 16	17 - 22	22 - 29	33 - 43	43 - 57	51 - 60*

- ✓ For gang-related felonies where the court found the offender involved a minor (RCW 9.94A.833) see page 186 for standard range adjustment.
- ✓ For deadly weapon enhancement, see page 190.
- ✓ For sentencing alternatives, see page 177.
- ✓ For community custody eligibility, see page 187.
- ✓ For any applicable enhancements other than deadly weapon enhancement, see page 183.

The Caseload Forecast Council is not liable for errors or omissions in the manual, for sentences that may be inappropriately calculated as a result of a practitioner's or court's reliance on the manual, or for any other written or verbal information related to adult or juvenile sentencing. The scoring sheets are intended to provide assistance in most cases but do not cover all permutations of the scoring rules. If you find any errors or omissions, we encourage you to report them to the Caseload Forecast Council.

Unlawful Issuance Of Checks Or Drafts Value Greater Than $750

RCW 9A.56.060(4)
CLASS C – NONVIOLENT

OFFENDER SCORING RCW 9.94A.525(7)

If it was found that this offense was committed with sexual motivation (RCW 9.94A.533(8)) on or after 7/01/2006, use the General Nonviolent Offense with a Sexual Motivation Finding scoring form on page 193.

If the present conviction is for a felony domestic violence offense where domestic violence was plead and proven, use the General Nonviolent Offense Where Domestic Violence Has Been Plead and Proven scoring form on page 191.

ADULT HISTORY:
    Enter number of felony convictions .... _____ x 1 = _____

JUVENILE HISTORY:
    Enter number of serious violent and violent felony dispositions .... _____ x 1 = _____

    Enter number of nonviolent felony dispositions .... _____ x ½ = _____

OTHER CURRENT OFFENSES:
(Other current offenses that do not encompass the same conduct count in offender score)
    Enter number of other felony convictions .... _____ x 1 = _____

STATUS:
    Was the offender on community custody on the date the current offense was committed? (if yes) ...... + 1 = _____

Total the last column to get the **Offender Score** (Round down to the nearest whole number)

SENTENCE RANGE

	Offender Score									
	0	1	2	3	4	5	6	7	8	9+
LEVEL I	0-60 days	0-90 days	3m 2 - 5	4m 2 - 6	5.5m 3 - 8	8m 4 - 12	13m 12+ - 14	16m 14 - 18	19.5m 17 - 22	25.5m 22 - 29

✓ For gang-related felonies where the court found the offender involved a minor (RCW 9.94A.833) see page 186 for standard range adjustment.

✓ For deadly weapon enhancement, see page 190.

✓ For sentencing alternatives, see page 177.

✓ For community custody eligibility, see page 187.

✓ For any applicable enhancements other than deadly weapon enhancement, see page 183.

The Caseload Forecast Council is not liable for errors or omissions in the manual, for sentences that may be inappropriately calculated as a result of a practitioner's or court's reliance on the manual, or for any other written or verbal information related to adult or juvenile sentencing. The scoring sheets are intended to provide assistance in most cases but do not cover all permutations of the scoring rules. If you find any errors or omissions, we encourage you to report them to the Caseload Forecast Council.

Unlawful Possession Of Fictitious Identification
Unlawful Possession Of Instruments Of Financial Fraud
Unlawful Possession Of Payment Instruments
Unlawful Possession Of A Personal Identification Device
Unlawful Production Of Payment Instruments

RCW 9A.56.320
CLASS C – NONVIOLENT

OFFENDER SCORING RCW 9.94A.525(7)

If it was found that this offense was committed with sexual motivation (RCW 9.94A.533(8)) on or after 7/01/2006, use the General Nonviolent Offense with a Sexual Motivation Finding scoring form on page 193.

If the present conviction is for a felony domestic violence offense where domestic violence was plead and proven, use the General Nonviolent Offense Where Domestic Violence Has Been Plead and Proven scoring form on page 191.

ADULT HISTORY:
  Enter number of felony convictions .... _____ x 1 = _____

JUVENILE HISTORY:
  Enter number of serious violent and violent felony dispositions .... _____ x 1 = _____

  Enter number of nonviolent felony dispositions .... _____ x ½ = _____

OTHER CURRENT OFFENSES:
(Other current offenses that do not encompass the same conduct count in offender score)
  Enter number of other felony convictions .... _____ x 1 = _____

STATUS:
  Was the offender on community custody on the date the current offense was committed? (if yes)....... + 1 = _____

Total the last column to get the **Offender Score** (Round down to the nearest whole number)

SENTENCE RANGE

	\multicolumn{10}{c}{Offender Score}									
	0	1	2	3	4	5	6	7	8	9+
LEVEL I	0-60 days	0-90 days	3m 2 - 5	4m 2 - 6	5.5m 3 - 8	8m 4 - 12	13m 12+ - 14	16m 14 - 18	19.5m 17 - 22	25.5m 22 - 29

- ✓ For gang-related felonies where the court found the offender involved a minor (RCW 9.94A.833) see page 186 for standard range adjustment.
- ✓ For deadly weapon enhancement, see page 190.
- ✓ For sentencing alternatives, see page 177.
- ✓ For community custody eligibility, see page 187.
- ✓ For any applicable enhancements other than deadly weapon enhancement, see page 183.

Unlawful Possession Of A Firearm First Degree

RCW 9.41.040(1)
CLASS B – NONVIOLENT

OFFENDER SCORING RCW 9.94A.525(7)

If it was found that this offense was committed with sexual motivation (RCW 9.94A.533(8)) on or after 7/01/2006, use the General Nonviolent Offense with a Sexual Motivation Finding scoring form on page 193.

If the present conviction is for a felony domestic violence offense where domestic violence was plead and proven, use the General Nonviolent Offense Where Domestic Violence Has Been Plead and Proven scoring form on page 191.

ADULT HISTORY:
    Enter number of felony convictions .... _____ x 1 = _____

JUVENILE HISTORY:
    Enter number of serious violent and violent felony dispositions .... _____ x 1 = _____
    Enter number of nonviolent felony dispositions .... _____ x ½ = _____

OTHER CURRENT OFFENSES:
(Other current offenses that do not encompass the same conduct count in offender score)
    Enter number of other felony convictions .... _____ x 1 = _____

STATUS:
    Was the offender on community custody on the date the current offense was committed? (if yes) ...... + 1 = _____

Total the last column to get the **Offender Score** (Round down to the nearest whole number)

SENTENCE RANGE

	Offender Score									
	0	**1**	**2**	**3**	**4**	**5**	**6**	**7**	**8**	**9+**
LEVEL VII	17.5m	24m	30m	36m	42m	47.5m	66m	78m	89.5m	101.5m
	15 - 20	21 - 27	26 - 34	31 - 41	36 - 48	41 - 54	57 - 75	67 - 89	77 - 102	87 - 116

- ✓ For attempt, solicitation, conspiracy (RCW 9.94A.595) see page 23 or for gang-related felonies where the court found the offender involved a minor (RCW 9.94A.833) see page 186 for standard range adjustments.
- ✓ For sentencing alternatives, see page 177.
- ✓ For community custody eligibility, see page 187.
- ✓ For any applicable enhancements other than deadly weapon enhancement, see page 183.
- ✓ Each firearm possessed under this section is a separate offense.
- ✓ The offender shall be sentenced according to RCW 9.94A.589(1)(c) if the offender is convicted of Unlawful Possession of a Firearm 1 or 2 (RCW 9.41.040) and for felonies Theft of a Firearm or Possession of a Stolen Firearm, or both, as current offenses.
- ✓ If the present conviction is for Unlawful Possession of a Firearm 1 or 2 and felonies Theft of a Firearm or Possession of a Stolen Firearm, or both, charged under RCW 9.41.040, other current convictions for Unlawful Possession of a Firearm 1 or 2, Possession of a Stolen Firearm or Theft of a Firearm may not be included in the computation of the offender score per RCW 9.94A.589(1)(c). The offender will serve consecutive sentences for these particular offenses.

Unlawful Possession Of A Firearm Second Degree

RCW 9.41.040(2)
CLASS C* – NONVIOLENT
OFFENDER SCORING RCW 9.94A.525(7)

If it was found that this offense was committed with sexual motivation (RCW 9.94A.533(8)) on or after 7/01/2006, use the General Nonviolent Offense with a Sexual Motivation Finding scoring form on page 193.

ADULT HISTORY:
    Enter number of felony convictions .... _____ x 1 = _____

JUVENILE HISTORY:
    Enter number of serious violent and violent felony dispositions .... _____ x 1 = _____
    Enter number of nonviolent felony dispositions .... _____ x ½ = _____

OTHER CURRENT OFFENSES:
(Other current offenses that do not encompass the same conduct count in offender score)
    Enter number of other felony convictions .... _____ x 1 = _____

STATUS:
    Was the offender on community custody on the date the current offense was committed? (if yes) .... + 1 = _____

Total the last column to get the **Offender Score** (Round down to the nearest whole number)

SENTENCE RANGE

	Offender Score									
	0	1	2	3	4	5	6	7	8	9+
LEVEL III	2m	5m	8m	11m	14m	19.5m	25.5m	38m	50m	55.5m
	1 - 3	3 - 8	4 - 12	9 - 12	12+ - 16	17 - 22	22 - 29	33 - 43	43 - 57	51 - 60*

- ✓ For gang-related felonies where the court found the offender involved a minor (RCW 9.94A.833) see page 186 for standard range adjustment.
- ✓ For sentencing alternatives, see page 177.
- ✓ For community custody eligibility, see page 187.
- ✓ For any applicable enhancements other than deadly weapon enhancement, see page 183.
- ✓ Each firearm possessed under this section is a separate offense.
- ✓ The offender shall be sentenced according to RCW 9.94A.589(1)(c) if the offender is convicted of Unlawful Possession of a Firearm 1 or 2 (RCW 9.41.040) and for felonies Theft of a Firearm or Possession of a Stolen Firearm, or both, as current offenses.
- ✓ If the present conviction is for Unlawful Possession of a Firearm 1 or 2 and felonies Theft of a Firearm or Possession of a Stolen Firearm, or both, charged under RCW 9.41.040, other current convictions for Unlawful Possession of a Firearm 1 or 2, Possession of a Stolen Firearm or Theft of a Firearm may not be included in the computation of the offender score per RCW 9.94A.589(1)(c). The offender will serve consecutive sentences for these particular offenses.

The Caseload Forecast Council is not liable for errors or omissions in the manual, for sentences that may be inappropriately calculated as a result of a practitioner's or court's reliance on the manual, or for any other written or verbal information related to adult or juvenile sentencing. The scoring sheets are intended to provide assistance in most cases but do not cover all permutations of the scoring rules. If you find any errors or omissions, we encourage you to report them to the Caseload Forecast Council.

Unlawful Practice Of Law Subsequent Violation

RCW 2.48.180
CLASS C – NONVIOLENT

OFFENDER SCORING RCW 9.94A.525(7)

If it was found that this offense was committed with sexual motivation (RCW 9.94A.533(8)) on or after 7/01/2006, use the General Nonviolent Offense with a Sexual Motivation Finding scoring form on page 193.

If the present conviction is for a felony domestic violence offense where domestic violence was plead and proven, use the General Nonviolent Offense Where Domestic Violence Has Been Plead and Proven scoring form on page 191.

ADULT HISTORY:
    Enter number of felony convictions .... _____ x 1 = _____

JUVENILE HISTORY:
    Enter number of serious violent and violent felony dispositions .... _____ x 1 = _____
    Enter number of nonviolent felony dispositions .... _____ x ½ = _____

OTHER CURRENT OFFENSES:
(Other current offenses that do not encompass the same conduct count in offender score)
    Enter number of other felony convictions .... _____ x 1 = _____

STATUS:
    Was the offender on community custody on the date the current offense was committed? (if yes) ...... + 1 = _____

Total the last column to get the **Offender Score** (Round down to the nearest whole number)

SENTENCE RANGE

	\multicolumn{10}{c}{Offender Score}
	0	**1**	**2**	**3**	**4**	**5**	**6**	**7**	**8**	**9+**
LEVEL II	0-90 days	4m / 2 - 6	6m / 3 - 9	8m / 4 - 12	13m / 12+ - 14	16m / 14 - 18	19.5m / 17 - 22	25.5m / 22 - 29	38m / 33 - 43	50m / 43 - 57

✓ For gang-related felonies where the court found the offender involved a minor (RCW 9.94A.833) see page 186 for standard range adjustments.

✓ For deadly weapon enhancement, see page 190.

✓ For sentencing alternatives, see page 177.

Unlawful Storage Of Ammonia

RCW 69.55.020
CLASS C* – NONVIOLENT
OFFENDER SCORING RCW 9.94A.525(7)

If it was found that this offense was committed with sexual motivation (RCW 9.94A.533(8)) on or after 7/01/2006, use the General Nonviolent Offense with a Sexual Motivation Finding scoring form on page 193.

If the present conviction is for a felony domestic violence offense where domestic violence was plead and proven, use the General Nonviolent Offense Where Domestic Violence Has Been Plead and Proven scoring form on page 191.

ADULT HISTORY:
    Enter number of felony convictions .... _____ x 1 = _____

JUVENILE HISTORY:
    Enter number of serious violent and violent felony dispositions .... _____ x 1 = _____
    Enter number of nonviolent felony dispositions .... _____ x ½ = _____

OTHER CURRENT OFFENSES:
(Other current offenses that do not encompass the same conduct count in offender score)
    Enter number of other felony convictions .... _____ x 1 = _____

STATUS:
    Was the offender on community custody on the date the current offense was committed? (if yes)....... + 1 = _____

Total the last column to get the **Offender Score** (Round down to the nearest whole number)

SENTENCE RANGE

	\-	\-	\-	\-	\-	\-	\-	\-	\-	\-
Offender Score	0	1	2	3	4	5	6	7	8	9+
LEVEL VI	13m	17.5m	24m	30m	36m	42m	53m	58.5m		
	12+ - 14	15 - 20	21 - 27	26 - 34	31 - 41	36 - 48	46 - 60*	57 - 60*	60 - 60*	60 - 60*

- ✓ For gang-related felonies where the court found the offender involved a minor (RCW 9.94A.833) see page 186 for standard range adjustment.
- ✓ For deadly weapon enhancement, see page 190.
- ✓ For sentencing alternatives, see page 177.
- ✓ For community custody eligibility, see page 187.
- ✓ For any applicable enhancements other than deadly weapon enhancement, see page 183.

Unlawful Use Of Building For Drug Purposes

RCW 69.53.010
CLASS C – NONVIOLENT
OFFENDER SCORING RCW 9.94A.525(7)

If it was found that this offense was committed with sexual motivation (RCW 9.94A.533(8)) on or after 7/01/2006, use the General Nonviolent Offense with a Sexual Motivation Finding scoring form on page 193.

If the present conviction is for a felony domestic violence offense where domestic violence was plead and proven, use the General Nonviolent Offense Where Domestic Violence Has Been Plead and Proven scoring form on page 191.

ADULT HISTORY:
    Enter number of felony convictions .... _____ x 1 = _____

JUVENILE HISTORY:
    Enter number of serious violent and violent felony dispositions .... _____ x 1 = _____
    Enter number of nonviolent felony dispositions .... _____ x ½ = _____

OTHER CURRENT OFFENSES:
(Other current offenses that do not encompass the same conduct count in offender score)
    Enter number of other felony convictions .... _____ x 1 = _____

STATUS:
    Was the offender on community custody on the date the current offense was committed? (if yes) ...... + 1 = _____

Total the last column to get the **Offender Score** (Round down to the nearest whole number)

SENTENCE RANGE - DRUG

	Offender Score		
	0 to 2	3 to 5	6 to 9+
LEVEL I	3m 0 - 6	9m 6+ - 12	18m 12+ - 24

- ✓ For attempt, solicitation, conspiracy (RCW 9.94A.595) see page 23 or for gang-related felonies where the court found the offender involved a minor (RCW 9.94A.833) see page 186 for standard range adjustments.
- ✓ For deadly weapon enhancement, see page 190.
- ✓ For sentencing alternatives, see page 177.
- ✓ For community custody eligibility, see page 187.
- ✓ For any applicable enhancements other than deadly weapon enhancement, see page 183.

Unlawful Trafficking Of Food Stamps
Unlawful Redemption Of Food Stamps

RCW 9.91.142(1) & RCW 9.9A.144
CLASS C – NONVIOLENT

OFFENDER SCORING RCW 9.94A.525(7)

If it was found that this offense was committed with sexual motivation (RCW 9.94A.533(8)) on or after 7/01/2006, use the General Nonviolent Offense with a Sexual Motivation Finding scoring form on page 193.

If the present conviction is for a felony domestic violence offense where domestic violence was plead and proven, use the General Nonviolent Offense Where Domestic Violence Has Been Plead and Proven scoring form on page 191.

ADULT HISTORY:
Enter number of felony convictions .... _____ x 1 = _____

JUVENILE HISTORY:
Enter number of serious violent and violent felony dispositions .... _____ x 1 = _____

Enter number of nonviolent felony dispositions .... _____ x ½ = _____

OTHER CURRENT OFFENSES:
(Other current offenses that do not encompass the same conduct count in offender score)
Enter number of other felony convictions .... _____ x 1 = _____

STATUS:
Was the offender on community custody on the date the current offense was committed? (if yes) .... + 1 = _____

Total the last column to get the **Offender Score** (Round down to the nearest whole number)

SENTENCE RANGE

	Offender Score									
	0	1	2	3	4	5	6	7	8	9+
LEVEL I	0-60 days	0-90 days	3m 2 - 5	4m 2 - 6	5.5m 3 - 8	8m 4 - 12	13m 12+ - 14	16m 14 - 18	19.5m 17 - 22	25.5m 22 - 29

- ✓ For gang-related felonies where the court found the offender involved a minor (RCW 9.94A.833) see page 186 for standard range adjustment.
- ✓ For deadly weapon enhancement, see page 190.
- ✓ For sentencing alternatives, see page 177.
- ✓ For community custody eligibility, see page 187.
- ✓ For any applicable enhancements other than deadly weapon enhancement, see page 183.

The Caseload Forecast Council is not liable for errors or omissions in the manual, for sentences that may be inappropriately calculated as a result of a practitioner's or court's reliance on the manual, or for any other written or verbal information related to adult or juvenile sentencing. The scoring sheets are intended to provide assistance in most cases but do not cover all permutations of the scoring rules. If you find any errors or omissions, we encourage you to report them to the Caseload Forecast Council.

Unlicensed Practice Of A Profession Or Business Subsequent Violation

RCW 18.130.190(7)(b)
CLASS C – NONVIOLENT

OFFENDER SCORING RCW 9.94A.525(7)

If it was found that this offense was committed with sexual motivation (RCW 9.94A.533(8)) on or after 7/01/2006, use the General Nonviolent Offense with a Sexual Motivation Finding scoring form on page 193.

If the present conviction is for a felony domestic violence offense where domestic violence was plead and proven, use the General Nonviolent Offense Where Domestic Violence Has Been Plead and Proven scoring form on page 191.

ADULT HISTORY:
    Enter number of felony convictions .... _____ x 1 = _____

JUVENILE HISTORY:
    Enter number of serious violent and violent felony dispositions .... _____ x 1 = _____

    Enter number of nonviolent felony dispositions .... _____ x ½ = _____

OTHER CURRENT OFFENSES:
(Other current offenses that do not encompass the same conduct count in offender score)
    Enter number of other felony convictions .... _____ x 1 = _____

STATUS:
    Was the offender on community custody on the date the current offense was committed? (if yes) ...... + 1 = _____

Total the last column to get the **Offender Score** (Round down to the nearest whole number)

SENTENCE RANGE

	\multicolumn{10}{c	}{Offender Score}
	0	1	2	3	4	5	6	7	8	9+
LEVEL II		4m	6m	8m	13m	16m	19.5m	25.5m	38m	50m
	0-90 days	2 - 6	3 - 9	4 - 12	12+ - 14	14 - 18	17 - 22	22 - 29	33 - 43	43 - 57

- ✓ For gang-related felonies where the court found the offender involved a minor (RCW 9.94A.833) see page 186 for standard range adjustment.
- ✓ For deadly weapon enhancement, see page 190.
- ✓ For sentencing alternatives, see page 177.
- ✓ For community custody eligibility, see page 187.
- ✓ For any applicable enhancements other than deadly weapon enhancement, see page 183.

Use Of Proceeds Of Criminal Profiteering

RCW 9A.82.080(1) & (2)
CLASS B– NONVIOLENT

OFFENDER SCORING RCW 9.94A.525(7)

If it was found that this offense was committed with sexual motivation (RCW 9.94A.533(8)) on or after 7/01/2006, use the General Nonviolent Offense with a Sexual Motivation Finding scoring form on page 193.

If the present conviction is for a felony domestic violence offense where domestic violence was plead and proven, use the General Nonviolent Offense Where Domestic Violence Has Been Plead and Proven scoring form on page 191.

ADULT HISTORY:
    Enter number of felony convictions .... _____ x 1 = _____

JUVENILE HISTORY:
    Enter number of serious violent and violent felony dispositions .... _____ x 1 = _____

    Enter number of nonviolent felony dispositions .... _____ x ½ = _____

OTHER CURRENT OFFENSES:
(Other current offenses that do not encompass the same conduct count in offender score)
    Enter number of other felony convictions .... _____ x 1 = _____

STATUS:
    Was the offender on community custody on the date the current offense was committed? (if yes) .... + 1 = _____

Total the last column to get the **Offender Score** (Round down to the nearest whole number)

SENTENCE RANGE

	\multicolumn{10}{c}{Offender Score}									
	0	**1**	**2**	**3**	**4**	**5**	**6**	**7**	**8**	**9+**
LEVEL IV	6m 3 - 9	9m 6 - 12	13m 12+ - 14	15m 13 - 17	17.5m 15 - 20	25.5m 22 - 29	38m 33 - 43	50m 43 - 57	61.5m 53 - 70	73.5m 63 - 84

✓ For attempt, solicitation, conspiracy (RCW 9.94A.595) see page 23 or for gang-related felonies where the court found the offender involved a minor (RCW 9.94A.833) see page 186 for standard range adjustments.

✓ For deadly weapon enhancement, see page 190.

✓ For sentencing alternatives, see page 177.

✓ For community custody eligibility, see page 187.

✓ For any applicable enhancements other than deadly weapon enhancement, see page 183.

The Caseload Forecast Council is not liable for errors or omissions in the manual, for sentences that may be inappropriately calculated as a result of a practitioner's or court's reliance on the manual, or for any other written or verbal information related to adult or juvenile sentencing. The scoring sheets are intended to provide assistance in most cases but do not cover all permutations of the scoring rules. If you find any errors or omissions, we encourage you to report them to the Caseload Forecast Council.

Use Of Machine Gun In Commission Of A Felony

RCW 9.41.225
CLASS A – VIOLENT

OFFENDER SCORING RCW 9.94A.525(8)

If it was found that this offense was committed with sexual motivation (RCW 9.94A.533(8)) on or after 7/01/2006, use the General Violent Offense with a Sexual Motivation Finding scoring form on page 201.

If the present conviction is for a felony domestic violence offense where domestic violence was plead and proven, use the General Violent Offense Where Domestic Violence Has Been Plead and Proven scoring form on page 199.

ADULT HISTORY:
　　Enter number of serious violent and violent felony convictions .... _____　　x 2 = _____
　　Enter number of nonviolent felony convictions .... _____　　x 1 = _____

JUVENILE HISTORY:
　　Enter number of serious violent and violent felony dispositions .... _____　　x 2 = _____
　　Enter number of nonviolent felony dispositions .... _____　　x ½ = _____

OTHER CURRENT OFFENSES:
(Other current offenses that do not encompass the same conduct count in offender score)
　　Enter number of other serious violent and violent felony convictions .... _____　　x 2 = _____
　　Enter number of other nonviolent felony convictions .... _____　　x 1 = _____

STATUS:
　　Was the offender on community custody on the date the current offense was committed? (if yes) ...... + 1 = _____

Total the last column to get the **Offender Score** (Round down to the nearest whole number)

SENTENCE RANGE

	Offender Score									
	0	1	2	3	4	5	6	7	8	9+
LEVEL VII	17.5m	24m	30m	36m	42m	47.5m	66m	78m	89.5m	101.5m
	15 - 20	21 - 27	26 - 34	31 - 41	36 - 48	41 - 54	57 - 75	67 - 89	77 - 102	87 - 116

✓ For attempt, solicitation, conspiracy (RCW 9.94A.595) see page 23 or for gang-related felonies where the court found the offender involved a minor (RCW 9.94A.833) see page 186 for standard range adjustments.

✓ For sentencing alternatives, see page 177.

✓ For community custody eligibility, see page 187.

✓ For any applicable enhancements other than deadly weapon enhancement, see page 183.

The Caseload Forecast Council is not liable for errors or omissions in the manual, for sentences that may be inappropriately calculated as a result of a practitioner's or court's reliance on the manual, or for any other written or verbal information related to adult or juvenile sentencing. The scoring sheets are intended to provide assistance in most cases but do not cover all permutations of the scoring rules. If you find any errors or omissions, we encourage you to report them to the Caseload Forecast Council.

Vehicle Prowl First Degree

RCW 9A.52.095
CLASS C – NONVIOLENT
OFFENDER SCORING RCW 9.94A.525(7)

If it was found that this offense was committed with sexual motivation (RCW 9.94A.533(8)) on or after 7/01/2006, use the General Nonviolent Offense with a Sexual Motivation Finding scoring form on page 193.

If the present conviction is for a felony domestic violence offense where domestic violence was plead and proven, use the General Nonviolent Offense Where Domestic Violence Has Been Plead and Proven scoring form on page 191.

ADULT HISTORY:
　Enter number of felony convictions .... _____ x 1 = _____

JUVENILE HISTORY:
　Enter number of serious violent and violent felony dispositions .... _____ x 1 = _____
　Enter number of nonviolent felony dispositions .... _____ x ½ = _____

OTHER CURRENT OFFENSES:
(Other current offenses that do not encompass the same conduct count in offender score)
　Enter number of other felony convictions .... _____ x 1 = _____

STATUS:
　Was the offender on community custody on the date the current offense was committed? (if yes) .... + 1 = _____

Total the last column to get the **Offender Score** (Round down to the nearest whole number)

SENTENCE RANGE

	Offender Score									
	0	1	2	3	4	5	6	7	8	9+
LEVEL I	0-60 days	0-90 days	3m 2 - 5	4m 2 - 6	5.5m 3 - 8	8m 4 - 12	13m 12+ - 14	16m 14 - 18	19.5m 17 - 22	25.5m 22 - 29

- ✓ For gang-related felonies where the court found the offender involved a minor (RCW 9.94A.833) see page 186 for standard range adjustment.
- ✓ For deadly weapon enhancement, see page 190.
- ✓ For sentencing alternatives, see page 177.
- ✓ For community custody eligibility, see page 187.
- ✓ For any applicable enhancements other than deadly weapon enhancement, see page 183.

Vehicle Prowling Second Degree (Third or Subsequent Offense)

RCW 9A.52.100(3)
CLASS C* – NONVIOLENT
OFFENDER SCORING RCW 9.94A.525(7)

If it was found that this offense was committed with sexual motivation (RCW 9.94A.533(8)) on or after 7/01/2006, use the General Nonviolent Offense with a Sexual Motivation Finding scoring form on page 193.

If the present conviction is for a felony domestic violence offense where domestic violence was plead and proven, use the General Nonviolent Offense Where Domestic Violence Has Been Plead and Proven scoring form on page 191.

ADULT HISTORY:
    Enter number of felony convictions .... _____ x 1 = _____

JUVENILE HISTORY:
    Enter number of serious violent and violent felony dispositions .... _____ x 1 = _____
    Enter number of nonviolent felony dispositions .... _____ x ½ = _____

OTHER CURRENT OFFENSES:
(Other current offenses that do not encompass the same conduct count in offender score)
    Enter number of other felony convictions .... _____ x 1 = _____

STATUS:
    Was the offender on community custody on the date the current offense was committed? (if yes) ...... + 1 = _____

Total the last column to get the **Offender Score** (Round down to the nearest whole number)

SENTENCE RANGE

	\multicolumn{10}{c}{Offender Score}

	0	1	2	3	4	5	6	7	8	9+
LEVEL IV	6m 3 - 9	9m 6 - 12	13m 12+ - 14	15m 13 - 17	17.5m 15 - 20	25.5m 22 - 29	38m 33 - 43	50m 43 - 57	56.5m 53 - 60*	60 - 60*

- ✓ For gang-related felonies where the court found the offender involved a minor (RCW 9.94A.833) see page 186 for standard range adjustment.
- ✓ For deadly weapon enhancement, see page 190.
- ✓ For sentencing alternatives, see page 177.
- ✓ For community custody eligibility, see page 187.
- ✓ For any applicable enhancements other than deadly weapon enhancement, see page 183.

The Caseload Forecast Council is not liable for errors or omissions in the manual, for sentences that may be inappropriately calculated as a result of a practitioner's or court's reliance on the manual, or for any other written or verbal information related to adult or juvenile sentencing. The scoring sheets are intended to provide assistance in most cases but do not cover all permutations of the scoring rules. If you find any errors or omissions, we encourage you to report them to the Caseload Forecast Council.

Vehicular Assault Disregard For The Safety Of Others

RCW 46.61.522(1)(c)
CLASS B – NONVIOLENT/TRAFFIC OFFENSE
OFFENDER SCORING RCW 9.94A.525(11)

ADULT HISTORY:

Enter number of Vehicular Homicide and Vehicular Assault felony convictions .... _____ x 2 = _____

Enter number of Operation of a Vessel While Under the Influence of Intoxicating Liquor or Any Drug felony convictions .... _____ x 1 = _____

Enter number of felony convictions .... _____ x 1 = _____

Enter number of Driving While Under the Influence of Intoxicating Liquor or Any Drug and Actual Physical Control While Under the Influence of Intoxicating Liquor or Any Drug and Reckless Driving and Hit-And-Run Attended Vehicle <u>non-felony</u> convictions .... _____ x 1 = _____

JUVENILE HISTORY:

Enter number of Vehicular Homicide and Vehicular Assault dispositions .... _____ x 2 = _____

Enter number of Operation of a Vessel While Under the Influence of Intoxicating Liquor or Any Drug felony dispositions .... _____ x ½ = _____

Enter number of felony dispositions .... _____ x ½ = _____

Enter number of Driving While Under the Influence of Intoxicating Liquor or Any Drug and Actual Physical Control While Under the Influence of Intoxicating Liquor or Any Drug and Reckless Driving and Hit-And-Run Attended Vehicle <u>non-felony</u> convictions .... _____ x ½ = _____

OTHER CURRENT OFFENSES:
(Other current offenses that do not encompass the same conduct count in offender score)

Enter number of Vehicular Homicide and Vehicular Assault convictions .... _____ x 2 = _____

Enter number of Operation of a Vessel While Under the Influence of Intoxicating Liquor or Any Drug felony convictions .... _____ x 1 = _____

Enter number of other felony convictions .... _____ x 1 = _____

Enter number of Driving While Under the Influence of Intoxicating Liquor or Any Drug and Actual Physical Control While Under the Influence of Intoxicating Liquor or Any Drug and Reckless Driving and Hit-And-Run Attended Vehicle <u>non-felony</u> convictions .... _____ x 1 = _____

STATUS:

Was the offender on community custody on the date the current offense was committed? (if yes) .... + 1 = _____

Total the last column to get the **Offender Score** (Round down to the nearest whole number)

SENTENCE RANGE

	Offender Score									
	0	1	2	3	4	5	6	7	8	9+
LEVEL III	2m	5m	8m	11m	14m	19.5m	25.5m	38m	50m	59.5m
	1 - 3	3 - 8	4 - 12	9 - 12	12+ - 16	17 - 22	22 - 29	33 - 43	43 - 57	51 - 68

- ✓ For attempt, solicitation, conspiracy (RCW 9.94A.595) see page 23 or for gang-related felonies where the court found the offender involved a minor (RCW 9.94A.833) see page 186 for standard range adjustments.
- ✓ For deadly weapon enhancement, see page 190.
- ✓ For sentencing alternatives, see page 177.
- ✓ For community custody eligibility, see page 187.
- ✓ For any applicable enhancements other than deadly weapon enhancement, see page 183.

The Caseload Forecast Council is not liable for errors or omissions in the manual, for sentences that may be inappropriately calculated as a result of a practitioner's or court's reliance on the manual, or for any other written or verbal information related to adult or juvenile sentencing. The scoring sheets are intended to provide assistance in most cases but do not cover all permutations of the scoring rules. If you find any errors or omissions, we encourage you to report them to the Caseload Forecast Council.

Vehicular Assault In A Reckless Manner Or While Under The Influence Of Intoxicating Liquor Or Any Drug

RCW 46.61.522(1)(a) & (b)
CLASS B – VIOLENT/TRAFFIC OFFENSE

OFFENDER SCORING RCW 9.94A.525(11)

ADULT HISTORY:
Enter number of Vehicular Homicide and Vehicular Assault felony convictions .... _____   x 2 = _____
Enter number of Operation of a Vessel While Under the Influence of Intoxicating Liquor or Any Drug felony convictions .... _____   x 1 = _____
Enter number of felony convictions .... _____   x 1 = _____
Enter number of Driving While Under the Influence of Intoxicating Liquor or Any Drug and Actual Physical Control While Under the Influence of Intoxicating Liquor or Any Drug and Reckless Driving and Hit-And-Run Attended Vehicle <u>non-felony</u> convictions .... _____   x 1 = _____

JUVENILE HISTORY:
Enter number of Vehicular Homicide and Vehicular Assault dispositions............................... _____   x 2 = _____
Enter number of Operation of a Vessel While Under the Influence of Intoxicating Liquor or Any Drug felony dispositions .... _____   x ½ = _____
Enter number of felony dispositions .... _____   x ½ = _____
Enter number of Driving While Under the Influence of Intoxicating Liquor or Any Drug and Actual Physical Control While Under the Influence of Intoxicating Liquor or Any Drug and Reckless Driving and Hit-And-Run Attended Vehicle <u>non-felony</u> convictions .... _____   x ½ = _____

OTHER CURRENT OFFENSES:
(Other current offenses that do not encompass the same conduct count in offender score)
Enter number of Vehicular Homicide and Vehicular Assault convictions .... _____   x 2 = _____
Enter number of Operation of a Vessel While Under the Influence of Intoxicating Liquor or Any Drug felony convictions .... _____   x 1 = _____
Enter number of other felony convictions .... _____   x 1 = _____
Enter number of Driving While Under the Influence of Intoxicating Liquor or Any Drug and Actual Physical Control While Under the Influence of Intoxicating Liquor or Any Drug and Reckless Driving and Hit-And-Run Attended Vehicle <u>non-felony</u> convictions .... _____   x 1 = _____

STATUS:
Was the offender on community custody on the date the current offense was committed? (if yes) ...... + 1 = _____

Total the last column to get the **Offender Score** (Round down to the nearest whole number)

SENTENCE RANGE

	Offender Score									
	0	1	2	3	4	5	6	7	8	9+
LEVEL IV	6m	9m	13m	15m	17.5m	25.5m	38m	50m	61.5m	73.5m
	3 - 9	6 - 12	12+ - 14	13 - 17	15 - 20	22 - 29	33 - 43	43 - 57	53 - 70	63 - 84

✓ For attempt, solicitation, conspiracy (RCW 9.94A.595) see page 23 or for gang-related felonies where the court found the offender involved a minor (RCW 9.94A.833) see page 186 for standard range adjustments.

✓ For deadly weapon enhancement, see page 190.

✓ For sentencing alternatives, see page 177.

✓ For community custody eligibility, see page 187.

✓ For any applicable enhancements other than deadly weapon enhancement, see page 183.

✓ **For consecutive/concurrent provisions, see page 31.**

The Caseload Forecast Council is not liable for errors or omissions in the manual, for sentences that may be inappropriately calculated as a result of a practitioner's or court's reliance on the manual, or for any other written or verbal information related to adult or juvenile sentencing. The scoring sheets are intended to provide assistance in most cases but do not cover all permutations of the scoring rules. If you find any errors or omissions, we encourage you to report them to the Caseload Forecast Council.

Vehicular Homicide Disregard For The Safety Of Others

RCW 46.61.520(1)(c)
CLASS A – VIOLENT/TRAFFIC OFFENSE
OFFENDER SCORING RCW 9.94A.525(11)

ADULT HISTORY:
    Enter number of Vehicular Homicide and Vehicular Assault felony convictions .... _____ x 2 = _____

    Enter number of Operation of a Vessel While Under the Influence of Intoxicating Liquor or Any Drug felony convictions .... _____ x 1 = _____

    Enter number of felony convictions .... _____ x 1 = _____

    Enter number of Driving While Under the Influence of Intoxicating Liquor or Any Drug and Actual Physical Control While Under the Influence of Intoxicating Liquor or Any Drug and Reckless Driving and Hit-And-Run Attended Vehicle <u>non-felony</u> convictions .... _____ x 1 = _____

JUVENILE HISTORY:
    Enter number of Vehicular Homicide and Vehicular Assault dispositions .... _____ x 2 = _____

    Enter number of Operation of a Vessel While Under the Influence of Intoxicating Liquor or Any Drug felony dispositions .... _____ x ½ = _____

    Enter number of felony dispositions .... _____ x ½ = _____

    Enter number of Driving While Under the Influence of Intoxicating Liquor or Any Drug and Actual Physical Control While Under the Influence of Intoxicating Liquor or Any Drug and Reckless Driving and Hit-And-Run Attended Vehicle <u>non-felony</u> convictions .... _____ x ½ = _____

OTHER CURRENT OFFENSES:
(Other current offenses that do not encompass the same conduct count in offender score)
    Enter number of Vehicular Homicide and Vehicular Assault convictions .... _____ x 2 = _____

    Enter number of Operation of a Vessel While Under the Influence of Intoxicating Liquor or Any Drug felony convictions .... _____ x 1 = _____

    Enter number of other felony convictions .... _____ x 1 = _____

    Enter number of Driving While Under the Influence of Intoxicating Liquor or Any Drug and Actual Physical Control While Under the Influence of Intoxicating Liquor or Any Drug and Reckless Driving and Hit-And-Run Attended Vehicle <u>non-felony</u> convictions .... _____ x 1 = _____

STATUS:
    Was the offender on community custody on the date the current offense was committed? (if yes)....... + 1 = _____

Total the last column to get the **Offender Score** (Round down to the nearest whole number)

SENTENCE RANGE

	\multicolumn{10}{c}{Offender Score}
	0	1	2	3	4	5	6	7	8	9+
LEVEL VII	17.5m	24m	30m	36m	42m	47.5m	66m	78m	89.5m	101.5m
	15 - 20	21 - 27	26 - 34	31 - 41	36 - 48	41 - 54	57 - 75	67 - 89	77 - 102	87 - 116

- ✓ For attempt, solicitation, conspiracy (RCW 9.94A.595) see page 23 or for gang-related felonies where the court found the offender involved a minor (RCW 9.94A.833) see page 186 for standard range adjustments.
- ✓ For deadly weapon enhancement, see page 190.
- ✓ For sentencing alternatives, see page 177.
- ✓ For community custody eligibility, see page 187.
- ✓ For any applicable enhancements other than deadly weapon enhancement, see page 183.

The Caseload Forecast Council is not liable for errors or omissions in the manual, for sentences that may be inappropriately calculated as a result of a practitioner's or court's reliance on the manual, or for any other written or verbal information related to adult or juvenile sentencing. The scoring sheets are intended to provide assistance in most cases but do not cover all permutations of the scoring rules. If you find any errors or omissions, we encourage you to report them to the Caseload Forecast Council.

Vehicular Homicide In A Reckless Manner

RCW 46.61.520(1)(b)
CLASS A – VIOLENT/TRAFFIC OFFENSE

OFFENDER SCORING RCW 9.94A.525(11)

ADULT HISTORY:

Enter number of Vehicular Homicide and Vehicular Assault felony convictions .... _____ x 2 = _____

Enter number of Operation of a Vessel While Under the Influence of Intoxicating Liquor or Any Drug felony convictions .... _____ x 1 = _____

Enter number of felony convictions .... _____ x 1 = _____

Enter number of Driving While Under the Influence of Intoxicating Liquor or Any Drug and Actual Physical Control While Under the Influence of Intoxicating Liquor or Any Drug and Reckless Driving and Hit-And-Run Attended Vehicle <u>non-felony</u> convictions .... _____ x 1 = _____

JUVENILE HISTORY:

Enter number of Vehicular Homicide and Vehicular Assault dispositions .... _____ x 2 = _____

Enter number of Operation of a Vessel While Under the Influence of Intoxicating Liquor or Any Drug felony dispositions .... _____ x ½ = _____

Enter number of felony dispositions .... _____ x ½ = _____

Enter number of Driving While Under the Influence of Intoxicating Liquor or Any Drug and Actual Physical Control While Under the Influence of Intoxicating Liquor or Any Drug and Reckless Driving and Hit-And-Run Attended Vehicle <u>non-felony</u> convictions .... _____ x ½ = _____

OTHER CURRENT OFFENSES:
(Other current offenses that do not encompass the same conduct count in offender score)

Enter number of Vehicular Homicide and Vehicular Assault convictions .... _____ x 2 = _____

Enter number of Operation of a Vessel While Under the Influence of Intoxicating Liquor or Any Drug felony convictions .... _____ x 1 = _____

Enter number of other felony convictions .... _____ x 1 = _____

Enter number of Driving While Under the Influence of Intoxicating Liquor or Any Drug and Actual Physical Control While Under the Influence of Intoxicating Liquor or Any Drug and Reckless Driving and Hit-And-Run Attended Vehicle <u>non-felony</u> convictions .... _____ x 1 = _____

STATUS:

Was the offender on community custody on the date the current offense was committed? (if yes) ...... + 1 = _____

Total the last column to get the **Offender Score** (Round down to the nearest whole number)

SENTENCE RANGE

	\multicolumn{10}{c}{Offender Score}
	0	1	2	3	4	5	6	7	8	9+
LEVEL XI	90m 78 - 102	100m 86 - 114	110m 95 - 125	119m 102 - 136	129m 111 - 147	139m 120 - 158	170m 146 - 194	185m 159 - 211	215m 185 - 245	245m 210 - 280

- ✓ For attempt, solicitation, conspiracy (RCW 9.94A.595) see page 23 or for gang-related felonies where the court found the offender involved a minor (RCW 9.94A.833) see page 186 for standard range adjustments.
- ✓ For deadly weapon enhancement, see page 190.
- ✓ For sentencing alternatives, see page 177.
- ✓ For community custody eligibility, see page 187.
- ✓ For any applicable enhancements other than deadly weapon enhancement, see page 183.

The Caseload Forecast Council is not liable for errors or omissions in the manual, for sentences that may be inappropriately calculated as a result of a practitioner's or court's reliance on the manual, or for any other written or verbal information related to adult or juvenile sentencing. The scoring sheets are intended to provide assistance in most cases but do not cover all permutations of the scoring rules. If you find any errors or omissions, we encourage you to report them to the Caseload Forecast Council.

Vehicular Homicide While Under The Influence Of Intoxicating Liquor Or Any Drug

RCW 46.61.520(1)(a)
CLASS A – VIOLENT/TRAFFIC OFFENSE

OFFENDER SCORING RCW 9.94A.525(11)

ADULT HISTORY:
Enter number of Vehicular Homicide and Vehicular Assault felony convictions .... _____   x 2 = _____

Enter number of Operation of a Vessel While Under the Influence of Intoxicating Liquor or Any Drug felony convictions .... _____   x 1 = _____

Enter number of felony convictions .... _____   x 1 = _____

Enter number of Driving While Under the Influence of Intoxicating Liquor or Any Drug and Actual Physical Control While Under the Influence of Intoxicating Liquor or Any Drug and Reckless Driving and Hit-And-Run Attended Vehicle <u>non-felony</u> convictions, except those which form the basis for an enhancement pursuant to RCW 46.61.520(2). .... _____   x 1 = _____

JUVENILE HISTORY:
Enter number of Vehicular Homicide and Vehicular Assault dispositions .... _____   x 2 = _____

Enter number of Operation of a Vessel While Under the Influence of Intoxicating Liquor or Any Drug felony dispositions .... _____   x ½ = _____

Enter number of felony dispositions .... _____   x ½ = _____

Enter number of Driving While Under the Influence of Intoxicating Liquor or Any Drug and Actual Physical Control While Under the Influence of Intoxicating Liquor or Any Drug and Reckless Driving and Hit-And-Run Attended Vehicle <u>non-felony</u> convictions, except those which form the basis for an enhancement pursuant to RCW 46.61.520(2). .... _____   x ½ = _____

OTHER CURRENT OFFENSES:
(Other current offenses that do not encompass the same conduct count in offender score)
Enter number of Vehicular Homicide and Vehicular Assault convictions .... _____   x 2 = _____

Enter number of Operation of a Vessel While Under the Influence of Intoxicating Liquor or Any Drug felony convictions .... _____   x 1 = _____

Enter number of other felony convictions .... _____   x 1 = _____

Enter number of Driving While Under the Influence of Intoxicating Liquor or Any Drug and Actual Physical Control While Under the Influence of Intoxicating Liquor or Any Drug and Reckless Driving and Hit-And-Run Attended Vehicle <u>non-felony</u> convictions, except those which form the basis for an enhancement pursuant to RCW 46.61.520(2). .... _____   x 1 = _____

STATUS:
Was the offender on community custody on the date the current offense was committed? (if yes) .... + 1 = _____

Total the last column to get the **Offender Score** (Round down to the nearest whole number)

SENTENCE RANGE

	\multicolumn{10}{c}{Offender Score}
	0	1	2	3	4	5	6	7	8	9+
LEVEL XI	90m 78 - 102	100m 86 - 114	110m 95 - 125	119m 102 - 136	129m 111 - 147	139m 120 - 158	170m 146 - 194	185m 159 - 211	215m 185 - 245	245m 210 - 280

- ✓ For attempt, solicitation, conspiracy (RCW 9.94A.595) see page 23 or for gang-related felonies where the court found the offender involved a minor (RCW 9.94A.833) see page 186 for standard range adjustments.
- ✓ For deadly weapon enhancement, see page 190.
- ✓ For sentencing alternatives, see page 177.
- ✓ For community custody eligibility, see page 187.
- ✓ For any applicable enhancements other than deadly weapon enhancement, see page 183.
- ✓ An additional 24 months shall be added to the sentence for each prior offense as defined in RCW 46.61.5055.
- ✓ **For consecutive/concurrent provisions, see page 31.**

The Caseload Forecast Council is not liable for errors or omissions in the manual, for sentences that may be inappropriately calculated as a result of a practitioner's or court's reliance on the manual, or for any other written or verbal information related to adult or juvenile sentencing. The scoring sheets are intended to provide assistance in most cases but do not cover all permutations of the scoring rules. If you find any errors or omissions, we encourage you to report them to the Caseload Forecast Council.

Viewing Depictions Of Minor Engaged In Sexually Explicit Conduct First Degree

RCW 9.68A.075(1)
CLASS B – NONVIOLENT/SEX

OFFENDER SCORING RCW 9.94A.525(17)

If the present conviction is for a felony domestic violence offense where domestic violence was plead and proven, use the General Nonviolent Offense Where Domestic Violence Has Been Plead and Proven scoring form on page 191.

ADULT HISTORY:
    Enter number of sex offense felony convictions .... _____ x 3 = _____

    Enter number of felony convictions .... _____ x 1 = _____

JUVENILE HISTORY:
    Enter number of sex offense felony dispositions .... _____ x 3 = _____

    Enter number of serious violent and violent felony dispositions .... _____ x 1 = _____

    Enter number of nonviolent felony dispositions .... _____ x ½ = _____

OTHER CURRENT OFFENSES:
(Other current offenses that do not encompass the same conduct count in offender score)
    Enter number of other sex offense felony convictions .... _____ x 3 = _____

    Enter number of other felony convictions .... _____ x 1 = _____

STATUS:
    Was the offender on community custody on the date the current offense was committed?............. + 1 = _____

Total the last column to get the **Offender Score** (Round down to the nearest whole number)

SENTENCE RANGE

	Offender Score									
	0	1	2	3	4	5	6	7	8	9+
LEVEL IV	6m	9m	13m	15m	17.5m	25.5m	38m	50m	61.5m	73.5m
	3 - 9	6 - 12	12+ - 14	13 - 17	15 - 20	22 - 29	33 - 43	43 - 57	53 - 70	63 - 84

- ✓ For attempt, solicitation, conspiracy (RCW 9.94A.595) see page 23 or for gang-related felonies where the court found the offender involved a minor (RCW 9.94A.833) see page 186 for standard range adjustments.

- ✓ For deadly weapon enhancement, see page 190.

- ✓ For sentencing alternatives, see page 177.

- ✓ For community custody eligibility, see page 187.

- ✓ For any applicable enhancements other than deadly weapon enhancement, see page 183.

- ✓ If the offender is not a persistent offender and has a prior conviction for an offense listed in RCW 9.94A.030(38)(b), then the sentence is subject to the requirements of RCW 9.94A.507.

The Caseload Forecast Council is not liable for errors or omissions in the manual, for sentences that may be inappropriately calculated as a result of a practitioner's or court's reliance on the manual, or for any other written or verbal information related to adult or juvenile sentencing. The scoring sheets are intended to provide assistance in most cases but do not cover all permutations of the scoring rules. If you find any errors or omissions, we encourage you to report them to the Caseload Forecast Council.

Voyeurism

RCW 9A.44.115
CLASS C – NONVIOLENT/SEX
OFFENDER SCORING RCW 9.94A.525(17)

If the present conviction is for a felony domestic violence offense where domestic violence was plead and proven, use the General Nonviolent/Sex Offense Where Domestic Violence Has Been Plead and Proven scoring form on page 191.

ADULT HISTORY:
    Enter number of sex offense felony convictions .... _____ x 3 = _____
    Enter number of felony convictions .... _____ x 1 = _____

JUVENILE HISTORY:
    Enter number of sex offense felony dispositions .... _____ x 3 = _____
    Enter number of serious violent and violent felony dispositions .... _____ x 1 = _____
    Enter number of nonviolent felony dispositions .... _____ x ½ = _____

OTHER CURRENT OFFENSES:
(Other current offenses that do not encompass the same conduct count in offender score)
    Enter number of other sex offense felony convictions .... _____ x 3 = _____
    Enter number of other felony convictions .... _____ x 1 = _____

STATUS:
    Was the offender on community custody on the date the current offense was committed? .... + 1 = _____

Total the last column to get the **Offender Score** (Round down to the nearest whole number)

SENTENCE RANGE

	\multicolumn{10}{c}{Offender Score}
	0	1	2	3	4	5	6	7	8	9+
LEVEL II	0-90 days	4m 2 - 6	6m 3 - 9	8m 4 - 12	13m 12+ - 14	16m 14 - 18	19.5m 17 - 22	25.5m 22 - 29	38m 33 - 43	50m 43 - 57

- ✓ For gang-related felonies where the court found the offender involved a minor (RCW 9.94A.833) see page 186 for standard range adjustment.
- ✓ For deadly weapon enhancement, see page 190.
- ✓ For sentencing alternatives, see page 177.
- ✓ For community custody eligibility, see page 187.
- ✓ For any applicable enhancements other than deadly weapon enhancement, see page 183.
- ✓ If the offender is not a persistent offender and has a prior conviction for an offense listed in RCW 9.94A.030(38)(b), then the sentence is subject to the requirements of RCW 9.94A.507.

The Caseload Forecast Council is not liable for errors or omissions in the manual, for sentences that may be inappropriately calculated as a result of a practitioner's or court's reliance on the manual, or for any other written or verbal information related to adult or juvenile sentencing. The scoring sheets are intended to provide assistance in most cases but do not cover all permutations of the scoring rules. If you find any errors or omissions, we encourage you to report them to the Caseload Forecast Council.